DATE			
	JAN 1 4 1991		

DEVELOPMENTAL PSYCHOLOGY
Cognitive, Perceptuo-Motor and
Neuropsychological Perspectives

ADVANCES IN PSYCHOLOGY

64

Editors:

G.E. STELMACH

P.A. VROON

NORTH-HOLLAND
AMSTERDAM • NEW YORK • OXFORD • TOKYO

DEVELOPMENTAL PSYCHOLOGY
Cognitive, Perceptuo-Motor and Neuropsychological Perspectives

Edited by

Claude-Alain HAUERT

Faculty of Psychology and Educational Sciences
University of Geneva, Geneva, Switzerland

1990

NORTH-HOLLAND
AMSTERDAM • NEW YORK • OXFORD • TOKYO

NORTH-HOLLAND

ELSEVIER SCIENCE PUBLISHERS B.V.

Sara Burgerhartstraat 25

P.O. Box 211, 1000 AE Amsterdam, The Netherlands

Distributors for the United States and Canada:

ELSEVIER SCIENCE PUBLISHING COMPANY, INC.

655 Avenue of the Americas

New York, N.Y. 10010, U.S.A.

ISBN: 0 444 88427 0

Printed in The Netherlands

v

FOREWORD

*This volume is the first one devoted to developmental psychology
in the Advances in Psychology series. When G. Stelmach and P.A.
Vroon proposed this edition, we decided to focus on three
perspectives --cognitive, perceptual-motor and neuropsychological
development-- instead of preparing a detailed handbook.*

*The reasons for this choice are largely arbitrary: We believe
that developmental psychology today lacks a general theory and
that it is better to concentrate on a few topics and try to build
theoretical bridges between them, than to continue to accumulate
empirical data.*

*Good illustrations of these theoretical connections can be found
in the different chapters of the volume ... but there also
remains a persistent isolation of the three domains. The reader
will easily come to realize for himself that these bridges are
difficult to establish and remain fragile. However, we still
believe that the efforts of developmental psychology must
continue in the direction of domain interaction, for theoretical
concepts as well as methodological tools.*

*We must inform the reader that an initial project was rejected by
the Editors because they considered, doubtlessly for some good
reasons, that too much emphasis was given to Frensh-speaking
contributors. Although we are completely satisfied with the
whole chapters in this volume, we regret this decision. It can
only contribute to an increase in the communication difficulties
between the scientific communities on both sides of Atlantic
Ocean.*

*Finally we would like to thank Nelly Braure and Karen Olson for
their decisive help in translating and correcting several
chapters of the book, and Françoise Schmitt and Christian Ducret
who have assumed many thankless secretarial tasks.*

LIST OF CONTRIBUTORS

G. BUTTERWORTH
Department of Psychology
University of Stirling
STIRLING FK9 4LA - Scotland

R. CASE
Centre for Applied Cognitive Science
The Ontario Institute for Studies in Education
TORONTO, Ontario M5S 1V6 - Canada

J. CREPAULT
Université de Paris 8
U.F.R. de Psychologie P.C.S.
2, rue de la Liberté
93526 SAINT-DENIS Cédex 02 - France

S. GRIFFIN
Centre for Applied Cognitive Science
The Ontario Institute for Studies in Education
TORONTO, Ontario M5S 1V6 - Canada

C.-A. HAUERT
F.P.S.E.
Université de Genève
24, rue Général-Dufour
1211 GENEVE 4 - Switzerland

F. JOUEN
Laboratoire de Psycho-biologie de l'enfant
41, rue Gay-Lussac
75005 - PARIS - France

O. KOENIG
F.P.S.E.
Université de Genève
24, rue Général-Dufour
1211 GENEVE 4 - Switzerland

J. LANGER
University of California
Department of Psychology
BERKELEY, California 94720 - U.S.A.

J.I. LASZLO
University of Western Australia
Nedlands
WESTERN AUSTRALIA, 6009 - Australia

J.-C. LEPECQ
Laboratoire de Psycho-biologie de l'enfant
41, rue Gay-Lussac
75005 - PARIS - France

J.J. LOCKMAN
Department of Psychology
Tulane University
NEW ORLEANS, LA 70118 - U.S.A.

B. McKENZIE
La Trobe University
Department of Psychology
BUNDOORA, Victoria 3083 - Australia

P. MOUNOUD
F.P.S.E.
Université de Genève
24, rue Général-Dufour
1211 GENEVE 4 - Switzerland

A. NGUYEN-XUAN
Université de Paris 8
U.F.R. de Psychologie P.C.S.
2, rue de la Liberté
93526 SAINT-DENIS Cédex 02 - France

D. O'LEARY
University of Health Sciences
The Chicago Medical School
Building 51
3333 Green Bay Avenue
NORTH CHICAGO, Illinois 60064 - U.S.A.

G. YOUNG
Psychology Department
Glendon College
York University
2275 Bayview Avenue
TORONTO, Ontario, M4N 3N6 - Canada

P.-G. ZANONE
Florida Atlantic University
Center for Complex System
POBOX 3091
BOCA RATON, Floride 33431.0991 - U.S.A.

LIST OF CONTENTS

PART I

INTRODUCTION

DEVELOPMENTAL PSYCHOLOGY
Cognitive, Perceptuo-Motor, and Neuropsychological Perspectives
C-A. Hauert (Editor)
© Elsevier Science Publishers B.V. (North-Holland), 1990

INTRODUCTION: BACK TO SIXTIES. SOME QUESTIONS FOR
DEVELOPMENTALISTS IN THE LATE EIGHTIES

Claude A. HAUERT

Faculty of Psychology and Educational Sciences
University of Geneva, Switzerland

"Yesterday the future was brighter."
G. Béart

*The volume is modelled after a developmental process,
where a period of apparent disorganization often follows a
level of organization and preceeds a new level of integration. At the end of the 60's, Piagetian constructivist
theory offered psychologists a strong general model of
development. Since then, this theory has been progressively challenged, modified, and more or less rejected by
several authors. As a consequence, Piagetian theory today
has lost its power of unification and there is no longer a
general model of development. However, there are several
specific models dealing with some aspects of cognitive,
perceptuo-motor, or neuro-psychological development.
Therefore, the present time can be considered a necessary
stage for the development of a new general theory of child
development. In that sense, this book must be conceived
of as a modest contribution towards the re-unification of
developmental psychology, which attempts to go beyond an
early focus on terminology and extreme specialization.*

1. INTRODUCTION

As a specialist in child psychological development, suppose you have
been asked the following elementary question: Could you briefly
outline the way in which development from birth to adulthood is conceived today ? Answering this question is much more difficult now
than it was even twenty years ago. The reason for this is not
simply the result of a dramatic increase in empirical data on child
development. The actual reason is undoubtedly related to theory.
At the end of the 60's, Piaget's theory of cognitive development
provided a very strong framework in which a general and consistent
answer to this question was possible. Therefore, part two of this
introductory chapter will briefly review such an answer with a con-
cise survey of some basic elements of Piagetian theory.

In recent years, the scene has changed dramatically. There are now
almost as many theories in developmental psychology as there are

authors in this field ! In fact, developmental psychology has ex-
ploded. Moreover, this situation is additionally stressed by the
numerous and often trenchant positions on development proposed by
the educators i.e., parents, teachers, politicians, journalists,
etc. It will be useful, in the third part of this introduction to
attempt to identify, from the 60's, some relevant contributions in
the field of developmental psychology that could be considered as
possible detonators of this explosion.

Finally, the fourth part of the chapter will pose the basic questions --in our opinion-- facing the developmentalists today. These
questions are more or less explicitly confronted throughout the
book by all the contributors.

Our understanding of the latest contributions to developmental psychology, as well as our analysis of some theoretical Piagetian
themes, led us to bring together in one publication several current
studies on cognitive, perceptuo-motor and neuropsychological development. When it was dominant, Piagetian theory focussed almost
exclusively on cognitive aspects of behavior. However, perhaps the
theory declined because of its inability to incorporate increasing
knowledge in the fields of perceptuo-motor and neuropsychological
development. In our opinion, cognitive developmental psychology
cannot progress if it continues to largely ignore studies dealing
with the basic perceptuo-motor processes of gathering information
and using it to prepare, execute and control behavior. The reciprocal should apply to current studies of perceptuo-motor and neuropsychological aspects of behavior. These aspects tend to be mostly
considered as purely physical and biological processes. However, in
order to try to understand the almost infinite variability of the
adapted behavior in human being, the intervention of cognitive dimensions must doubtlessly be postulated besides physical and biological factors.

Consequently, these different approaches need to be brought together
and that is the very aim of the present volume. The structure is
simple. In each of the two main parts --infancy, and childhood and
adolescence-- two chapters deal with cognitive development, two with
perceptuo-motor development and two with the neuropsychological
perspective on development (1). The authors of these chapters have
been asked to address a number of questions --see later, section 4--
with the aim of formulating a synthesis of the different perspectives. Some authors have really tried to answer the questions,
others have more or less avoided them. Furthermore, both parts of
the book end with a chapter of synthesis. Finally, a general concluding chapter will comment on several items we consider as particularly important for developmentalists in the late eighties.

---

(1)   Unfortunately, due to an accident of the chosen author, one
chapter on neuropsychological development during infancy had to be
cancelled.

2. TWENTY YEARS AGO: A BRIEF REVIEW OF PIAGETIAN THEORY

At the end of the 60's, Piaget's theory clearly dominated developmental psychology. Both the publication in French (1966) of a
collective book on "Psychologie et épistémologie génétiques"
subtitled "Thèmes piagétiens - Hommage à Jean Piaget avec une
bibliographie complète de ses oeuvres" (Genetic psychology and
epistemology - Piagetian themes - Homage to Jean Piaget with a
complete bibliography of his works), and the publication in English,
three years later, of "Studies in cognitive development - Essays in
honor of Jean Piaget" (Elkind and Flavell, 1969) are clear evidence
of this position. Obviously, the time of honor was just beginning.

Therefore, some of the main propositions of Piagetian theory must be
reviewed now because they have deeply carved the landscape of modern
developmental psychology.

2.1. Stages and structures in development

Stages, structures and an internal trend towards equilibration are
key terms in the Piagetian conceptualization of development. In several places in the literature, these concepts have been cleverly
summarized. Among them, one can profitably consult Pinard and
Laurendeau (1969) and Case (1985).

In Piagetian theory, post natal cognitive development consists of a
series of three stages: Sensori-motor (6 substages), concrete operations (2 substages) and formal operations. According to Pinard
and Laurendeau (1969), the main criteria that allow us to speak of
stages in psychological development are the following: Structuration, hierarchical organization, integration, and equilibration.

'Structuration' means that *all* the behaviors of a given stage are
not simply juxtaposed in an additive fashion, but are organized into
a whole system or structure. Therefore, a general organization of
actions characterizes the acme of each developmental level. The
important point here is that this criterion allows us to predict a
large developmental synchrony in the mastering of the various dimensions of reality by means of the intellectual tools (operations) the
child progressively builds.

Today, a great deal of empirical data challenge this prediction.
Actually, Piaget was the first author to provide well documented
data about the existence of a "chronological difference between the
ages of acquisition of operations that bear on different concepts
(or contents), but obey identical structural laws" (Pinard and
Laurendeau, 1969) i.e., the so-called 'horizontal decalages'.

A strong assertion of Piagetian model is that the course of the
development proceeds in a fixed order of stages and substages
('hierarchical organization') for the entire population of children.
A considerable amount of empirical data has been collected to assess
this hierarchical trend. It seems today possible to provisory conclude that, beyond the important interindividual variability, the
assertion of a hierarchical organization through the age remains
valid (for detailed review and discussion, see Dasen, 1982, and de
Ribaupierre, Rieben and Lautrey, 1985).

'Integration' means that new stage or substages do not simply replace or add to the previous ones, but integrate and transform them
into a broader entity. Thus, the integration process, often called
re-structuration, is responsible for vertical decalage i.e., "the
development of a given conceptual content (e.g. causality, space)
(...) accomplished on several successive levels (sensorimotor,
concrete-operational, and formal-operational)." (Pinard and
Laurendeau, ibid). Inside each ontogenetic stage, a coordinative
process characterizes the developmental trends.

Finally, according to Piaget, developmental stages consist of a
series of levels of equilibrium under the control of a strictly
internal mechanism: The 'equilibration' mechanism. Piaget claimed
that: "Three disparate factors [maturation, experience, social
interaction] do not add up to oriented development as simple and
regular as that of the three great successive stages described. In
view of the role of the subject and of the general coordination of
action in this development, one might be led to imagine a pre-
established plan in the sense of apriority of internal finality."
(Piaget and Inhelder, 1966, p.124, 1969, p.156). Piaget rejects
both the idea of innateness and finalism because development is seen
as an active construction, and he attributes a decision part to the
internal mechanism of equilibration.

This mechanism consists of pro-active and retro-active capacities
regulating external and internal disturbances. Following Case
(1985), equilibrium is a "cognitive state in which the greatest
number of external events can be explained with the most parsimonious and least contradictory set of internal structures. If cognitive structures were relatively specific entities, or if their construction were dependent on external events only, then the process of
equilibration might proceed relatively rapidly. However, because
cognitive structures have great generality, and because they must be
abstracted from patterns in children's own operations on the world
(i.e., reflexively) rather than by direct apprehension of the world
itself (i.e., "empirically"), Piaget saw the pace of development as
being necessarily a slow one." (p.22)

All of the experimental work carried out by Piaget and his collaborators has been driven by these very strong theoretical hypotheses.
As a result, the abstract figure of an 'epistemic subject' emerged
i.e., a theoretical subject characterized as universal.

2.2. Two types of regulatory mechanisms

In addition to these general points, Piagetian developmental theory
cannot be really understood without also reviewing some of its basic
epistemological principles.

Following Janet, Piaget (1967) defines the object of psychology as
behavior, including interiorized actions and diverse and concomitant
grasps of consciousness. However, he also states that psychologists
must clearly differentiate between consciousness and the organic or
material processes with the body as theater. The question of the
relationship between consciousness and organic or material processes
mainly concerns the nature of the relationship between consciousness
and the underlying neural and neuro-muscular mechanisms. "Is cons-

ciousness the cause of behavior or does the subject simply become
aware of nervous activity ?" asks Piaget (ibid). In other words, is
there a real interaction or a simple parallelism between these two
levels ?

Piaget makes the following interesting preliminary remark according
to this question: "One can, of course, extend these hypotheses into
metaphysical theses, like the idealism according to which all is
conscience or representation, but the problem then reappears in an
unduly enlarged field since the relations between these particular
representations, which are the body and its nervous system, and the
other representations constituting conscience itself have to be determined." (ibid, p.149). This will be considered again later in
relation to the solutions proposed by Bruner and Zaporojets, which
seem particularly relevant for the present time: Their positions
have the merit that material action became a real object for psychological studies of development.

A real *interactionist* solution to the question of the relationship
between consciousness and organic processes is to be rejected for
Piaget. His arguments are simple: If we posit that consciousness
interacts with the neuro-physiological level (as examples of such
possible interactions Piaget mentions the decision to move one limb,
or the slight euphoria following tasting a good glass of wine), this
would mean that consciousness converses with the physiological
level. Now it is well known that the "language" of the latter is
one of energy. Therefore, consciousness should be a source of
energy i.e., it should have a mass (in the meaning of physics) !
This is obviously not the case and consciousness appears to Piaget
only as the concomitant aspect of a broader phenomenon.

Hence, Piaget's question: What is the use of consciousness ?
According to him, the answer must "be sought between two series of
complementary events, but described in essentially different terms.
(...) In brief, the body acts causally, independent of consciousness (...) whereas consciousness expresses its representations and
feelings according to its own means." (ibid, p.153). Its means are
the relations of implication. "Thus laid out, the activity of
conscience can no longer be neglected. For example, all deductive
sciences (logic and mathematics), arts, morality, and law stem from
the different forms of conscious implication and although the
nervous system is perfectly able to make them possible, since it
produces causally their material substratum, consciousness is still
needed to judge truths and real values." (ibid, p.157).

Piaget thus argues for the *parallelist* solution: There is a parallelism and some correspondance between consciousness and the neurophysiological levels, but no causal interaction exists between them.
From this perspective, Piagetian theory assumes the existence of two
basic types of behavioral regulatory mechanisms: An automatic-
biological one at the neuro-physiological level, and a psychological
one at the level of consciousness. The logical consequences of this
solution are numerous and dramatic as far as the links between
perceptuo-motor and cognitive aspects of behaviors are envisioned.

This epistemological position clearly characterizes all Piagetian
work, except for the sensori-motor period, as we will discuss. In

particular, in his 1974 books on the grasp of consciousness and on
success and understanding during childhood, Piaget (1974a, 1974b)
hypothesized the existence of a clear gap between sensori-motor and
active regulation. The setting of the latter is strictly assimilated by the development of operative reversibility i.e., the child's
conceptual anticipatory and retroactive conscious abilities: "Thus,
there is a basic difference between motor coordination and conceptual coordination. On one side, there is an unconscious selection
of possibilities with polarized approximations of the favourable
result. On the other side, there is a generalization with increasing comprehension of all the possibilities specific to a given
device." (1974b, p.41, our translation).

Therefore, as another consequence of this epistemological position
is that the object of Piagetian psychology is the so-defined conceptual coordination or, in other words, conscious coordination.
Cognition cannot be conceived in any way besides being conscious.
Strictly speaking, for psychology, neither the infant nor the internal mechanisms underlying material action can be considered the
object in the Piagetian framework.

These presuppositions have dramatically influenced developmental
cognitive psychology. Kessen (1966), for example, wrote that: "As
for studies of the development of thinking, it is no exaggeration to
say that the turn toward Piaget over the last decade has transformed
developmental psychology. (...) Even without a formal definition,
one may say that a psychology of cognition must include (at least)
perception, thinking, play, aesthetics, dreams, and language." In
other words, relationships (triggering, control, modulation, etc...)
between perception and, for example, play or language, are not
potential topics for a 'psychology of cognition'.

The picture is thus the following: The subject is characterized by
two co-existing levels of behavior. The first one is the biological
level with its automatic coordinations and its automatic control
networks, ensuring the material conditions for behavior. This level
is outside the field of study for psychology. The second level is
the conceptual level where the construction of conscious cognition
is realized: The work of Piaget was devoted mainly to the study of
this level, by means of an ad-hoc methodology.

However, Piaget does not conceive conceptual coordination as totally
independent of the motor coordination from which it stems through
the reflexive abstraction process. The relation is 'one-way':
Automatic motor coordination supplies the material for reflexive
abstraction. Therefore, the biological level also merits attention.
But curiously this level was studied in some detail by Piaget only
for infancy i.e., only during the sensori-motor period. To discuss
the early development, Piaget has used the theoretical concept of
"schema", as introduced by Baldwin (see Case's historical review,
1985). Could the concept of a schema join the two levels previously
described ? It appears as a central theoretical unit and Piaget has
authoritatively described all of development during infancy according to the progressive organization and coordination of schemata.
However, these schemata have been described as sensori-motor, rather
than being representational schemata which characterize the representational stage of intellectual development. Then, speaking of

representational intelligence, Piaget definitely took no further interest in sensori-motor schemata. They were simply thought to become automatic components of behavior after the emergence of semiotic functions i.e., 'real' representational capacities.

A final remark. As mentioned above, the epistemological positions at the basis of Piagetian psychology have determined the choice of a peculiar methodology for the study of behavior. This methodology resorts quasi exclusively to socially coded aspects of behavior (i.e., essentially language and drawing) as soon as children master them. Again the sensori-motor period is an exception. However, between the ages of 2 and 5 years, a period during which these socially coded behaviors are acquired but too poor to authorize an unambiguous dialogue with the observer, children have not been studied by Piaget (Hauert, 1980).

3. TWENTY YEARS AGO: SOME DISAGREEMENTS WITH PIAGETIAN THEORY

Although it largely dominated theoretical developmental psychology at the end of the 60s, Piaget's theory was nevertheless criticized by some authors. We must recognize, however, that at that time, these authors could hardly make themselves heard. Maybe because, as Pinard and Laurendeau wrote in 1969: "Piaget's difficult system has become enveloped in an aura of prestige irreconcilable with the critical spirit necessary to avoid confusion between hypotheses, opinions, and facts."

As mentioned above, Elkind and Flavell edited, in 1969, some 'Essays in honor of Jean Piaget`, largely written by North-American authors. Although this volume was clear evidence of the importance of Piagetian concepts, it was not completely accommodating and contained some criticisms and disagreements.

Disagreements dealt first with the importance Piaget attributed to both environmentalist and maturationalist factors in development. Hunt (1969), for example, compares Piaget with Gesell, one one hand, and with Thorndike, Watson, etc... on the other. This debate has been revived today --in other terms by other authors-- but it is still active (see for example de Ribaupierre, Rieben and Mounoud, 1986; Scarr and Carter-Saltzman, 1982; or Young, this volume). Criticisms were also formulated concerning methodological dimensions. In particular, the cross-sectional method was criticized as inferior to a longitudinal design to investigate the issue of horizontal decalage.

Moreover, particularly important disagreements between Piaget and certain authors focused on the topics of horizontal decalage and representation.

3.1. The question of horizontal decalages

The term horizontal decalage refers to developmental asynchronisms that can be observed within one stage. Even though a child may master operative tools for certain contents (e.g. conservation of liquid), this mastery may not be observed when he/she is confronted with different contents (e.g. conservation of volume). Piaget speaks of relations of *analogy* to explain operations bearing on different concepts (same rules applied to different contents). The progressive mastery of these relations is thus principally asynchronous and depends on the particular situation. Its complete development generally takes several years. In fact, recent findings suggest that only at around the age of ... 13 does the child master conservation of gas (Séré and Weil-Barais, 1988).

We also recall that Piaget opposed the horizontal intra-stage decalages to the vertical inter-stage decalages. The latter are chronological differences in development between the elaboration of comparable contents at different stages i.e., by means of different operative resources (e.g. the sensori-motor or conceptual elaboration of causal relations).

The existence of horizontal decalages in development is generally not considered as compatible with the Piagetian position (except by some authors, see for example Gilliéron's (1980) comments on Montangero, 1980): "... There was little basis, on either empirical or theoretical grounds, for the assumption made by Piaget that all of the component operations comprising [a] stage *develop* in unison." (Flavell and Wohlwill, 1969, p.103).

This assumption was the result of the strong Piagetian postulate of a general organization of action at each developmental level. It allows the prediction of a clear synchrony in the appearance of operations on various contents. Pinard and Laurendeau (1969) suggested that these operations apply to three kinds of relations: *Identity* (intra-object relations, for example the operation of deformation in the conservation tasks), *vicariance* (homogeneous inter-object relations) and *correspondance* (heterogeneous inter-object relations). According to Piaget, these operations appear at the same time in development. He acknowledges only that 'slight' decalages may exist for correspondance relations because of possible perceptual problems.

Today a lot of empirical data challenge Piaget's predictions. We have already mentioned that he was the first author to provide well documented data about the existence of chronological differences in the acquisition of operations according to the different contents on which they apply. The explanation he proposed is based on simple logical arguments (for example, a child is unable to master conservation of weight before having acquired conservation of quantity). These arguments can be summarized in the proposition that horizontal decalages stem from velocity differences between vertical decalages for different contents (Piaget and Inhelder, 1941).

The last item leads to another criticism of Piaget, namely, that horizontal decalages exist for several years (approximately between 7 and 13 years of age). It is unlikely that these chronological differences are only linked to logical causes such as those suggested by Piaget. They are more likely an expression of a complex developmental process where a child's representation of the world must play a decisive role.

Therefore, it is not surprising that the topic of representation appears as another conflict for Piagetian theory.

3.2. The question of representation

For Piaget (1946), the criterion of representation lies in the
subject's capacity to evoke actual events or persons or objects when
they are absent. Representation appears during development when
sensori-motor events in any kind of situation can be assimilated by
an infant to include elements which are not present at that moment
i.e., not perceived.

Particular attention must be paid to Piaget's assertation that at
the sensori-motor level of development, assimilation always consists
of linking the characteristics of a present situation with previous
elements. Why then affirm that at this level, such an assimilation
does not include the capacity for representation ? His answer seems
arbitrary. Sensori-motor assimilation --as opposed to representative assimilation-- is an assimilation to a scheme i.e., an internal
reality constructed by the subject by abstraction in the course of
past experience and due to repeated contact with objects.

Strictly speaking, assimilation in its sensori-motor form does not
include capacities for evocation but only for identification and
recognition. Consequently, since the criterion for representation
is evocation and since nothing indicates that such a mechanism is
necessary for sensori-motor functioning, Piaget's conclusion is that
representative capacities are absent during the sensori-motor stage.
On many occasions in this book, reference will be made to the early
capacities of newborns to identify objects and persons, and to the
difficulty of explaining these behaviors without acknowledging the
newborn's representational competence.

One particularly problematic topic for Piaget's representation
theory is the status of cues, as opposed to symbols and signs. The
criterion of distinction used by Piaget refers to the relationship
of these elements with the objects to which they refer. Cues are
considered to be undifferentiated from objects; however, this is not
the case for symbols and signs. Yet, cues should not be confounded
with parts of objects. On the contrary, they produce internal
translations and are thus also differentiated from objects.

Besides negating the existence of a capacity for representation in
infants, it seems to us that Piaget also dramatically underestimated
the role of this capacity in older children for the organization and
realization of action. The most important reserve we have regarding
Piaget's theory of psychological development is that there is a
missing link between the subject's operative structures and his/her
schemes for action. The capacity for representation could provide
this link, from very early in development.

Around the end of the 60's, and even before, some important authors
developed interesting ideas about psychological development and the
role of representation. Their contribution merit to be briefly
examined.

Let us first mention Zaporojets. This Russian author was interested
in the study of material action and the psychological conditions
necessary for its adapted realization. Galifret-Granjon (1981) has
translated a Russian paper written by Zaporojets in 1948 in which he

is astonished that motor development is "studied much less than the
development of cognitive processes, particularly in foreign coun-
tries." According to Zaporojets, the human subject has at one's
disposal "capacities of orientation dependent on fully interiorized
processes" i.e., representations. It is very important that the
psychologists "analyze the genesis, as well as the function and
structure of subjective images by which the regulation of human
behavior is possible." (...) Indeed, "as the internal image of
objects evolves, action can take advantage of it." Piaget took the
opposing view --although clearly without being conscious of that--
when he formulated his parallelist hypothesis. This virtual debate
remains active today.

Let us mention other authors. Flavell and Wohlwill (1969) considered child development as a progressive modification of *action
programs*. These programs process stored information, which is
accumulated through experience, and deals with both the subject
himself and his/her surroundings. This information consists of
internal representations. Finally, the programs for action contain
"innate and acquired procedures for extracting, processing, and
utilizing information of both the permanently-stored and the
presently-inputted variety. The outcome of a cognitive encounter
with the environment is never more than partly a function of what
the subject knows and of how that knowledge is represented and
organized. It also depends upon his ability to deploy and maintain selective attention, to organize perceptual elements into
intellectually suitable form, to transport information (and just the
right information) to and from memory storage in an efficient
fashion, and so on." (p.74-75). It is obvious that this functiona-
list view differs from the Piagetian perspective. Here, the concept
of representation occupies a central place. However, we must try to
specify the type(s) of representations upon which these programs
operate.

In this perspective, Bruner's work (for a review see Bruner, 1973),
carried out when Piaget's theory was at its apogee, provides an
important contribution towards our understanding of child development. Bruner very clearly expressed his disatisfaction with current
developmental theories, particularly those focusing on early development. Approximately thirty-five years after Piaget completed his
major work on sensori-motor development, Bruner wrote that "There is
simply no adequate literature on skill development in infancy"
(1973, p.245).

As a basis for his conception of behavior, Bruner attributes to the
subject information coding capacities which allow him, as stated in
his now famous expression, to go beyond the information given. "We
propose that when one goes beyond the information given, one does so
by virtue of being able to place the present given in a more generic
coding system and that one essentially reads off from the coding
system additional information either on the basis of learned contingent probabilities or learned principles of relating material. Much
of what has been called transfer or training can be fruitfully considered a case of applying learned coding system to new events.
Positive transfer represents a case where an appropriate coding
system is applied to a new array of events, negative transfer being
a case either of misapplication of a coding system to new events or

of the absence of a coding system that may be applied." (ibid, p.224).

To what coding system does Bruner refer ? His position was quite new at time, especially if we compare it to the traditional Piagetian one: "Growth involves not a series of stages, but rather a successive mastering of three forms of representation along with their partial translation each into the others." (...) "There are three kinds of representational system that are operative during the growth of human intellect and whose interaction is central to growth. (...) They are (...) enactive representation, iconic representation, and symbolic representation-- knowing something through doing it, through a picture or image of it, and through some such symbolic means as language."

The crucial point, no doubt, relates to enactive representation, around which Bruner articulates the concept of action program. An action program is one means, among others, of "representing events" (ibib, p.318). From this perspective, any skill assumes the existence of an intention (which he considers as ontogenetically very precocious, prior to the vision-prehension coordination, for instance), an action program, and control loops. "Skilled activity is a program specifying an objective or terminal state to be achieved, and requiring the serial ordering of a set of constituent, modular subroutines. (...) A developed skill has rules that include appropriate variant orders and exclude inappropriate ones." (ibid, p.248). Moreover, Bruner states that the components of skills do not spring from the reflex repertoire, but from the dissolution of this repertoire. "It is when modularization is achieved and the act becomes smoothly organized, that it then goes through a process of being incorporated into new, more inclusive, and more complex serial pattern."

As pointed out by Anglin (1973) in his introduction to a chapter of Bruner's work: "When skill is viewed in this way, its formal similarity to certain types of cognitive processes becomes evident. In his writing, Bruner has specifically stressed that skilled behavior has much in common with language on the one hand and problem solving on the other. (...) Like language, skilled behavior is productive or generative in that acquired constituent acts can be combined in new ways to achieve different goals, just as familiar words can be combined in new ways to produce novel sentence." The analogy with problem solving behavior is also clear: In both cases, means are elaborated to achieve a certain goal. Thus, such behaviors involve an internal representation of the goal. Finally, growth consists of an increasing ability to coordinate basic components of skills into programs of action.

These ideas have had --and still have-- great heuristic value for developmental psychology. It seems to us that their importance was growing as Piagetian predominance was decreasing.

Bruner's ideas have, of course, also been the object of criticism. The most important relate to his hypothesis of enactive representation and its 'idealistic' connotation (see 2.2). Galifret-Granjon (1981), for example, reminds us of Piaget's objection to the notion of enactive representation: Why speak of representation in this

case, when action is represented only by itself ? However, Bruner
does not consider action to be so limited. Rather, it always
depends on a superior reality, which he calls a motor program. An
action does not exist unless it is generated by a motor program
which potentially generates an infinite number of actions.

Galifret-Granjon raises another criticism in her interesting work of
1981: "In our view, due to a misuse of terms Bruner speaks of representation 'in the course of action'; or else, to be coherent,
representation should be attributed to all animal species which can
be conditioned i.e., which learn to anticipate subsequent events."
(p.291). As a reply, the following question comes up: Why not
attribute this type of representation to animals ? It is clear that
in human ontogenesis, there are other coding possibilities, in
particular, those of a symbolic and semiotic nature. As Galifret-
Granjon remarks herself, the existence of several systems of representation in man is "at present one of the main preoccupations among
developmental psychologists" (p.261). Mounoud's developmental
conceptualizaton (1983, 1985), from which we shall borrow large
parts in our conclusion, is a good illustration of this declaration.

4. CURRENT QUESTIONS REGARDING DEVELOPEMENT

The basic epistemological position adopted by Piaget (c.f. this
chapter, part 2) is clearly responsible for the lack of interest in
material action, perceptuo-motor coordination, and the neuropsychological approach towards child development. However, the main goal
of this volume is to present and discuss these topics, as well as
merely cognitive development, in order to escape from the Piagetian
view of the child as a disincarnate subject.

In addition to the above mentioned authors, many new works have also
challenged the classical Piagetian ideas about development during
the last 20 years. Some of these works will be presented in the
following chapters. Fundamental questions dealing with child development enlightened by these recent works, need to be raised and
discussed. We have therefore asked the authors of this volume to
consider the following questions: 1) Modern experimental studies
describe linear as well as complex age-related trends. How can we
understand these trends ? Are methodological artifacts responsible
for complex trends ? If not, are they clearly task-specific ?
2) Given these trends, is the notion of general developmental
stages, as formulated by Piaget, still relevant ? If not, are there
nevertheless clear criteria allowing the description of "stages" in
development ? 3) What does the concept of information really mean
from a psychological point of view ? Always from the subject's
point of view, what are the links between sensation and perception
and what are the links between information and representation ?
4) What is the relationship between structural and functional
aspects of behavior ? How does the child actually plan and control
his behavior ? Do planning and control of actions evolve through
the age ?

We are convinced that confronting these questions with data from
different domains (cognitive studies, perceptual-motor studies and
neuropsychological studies) should be particularly relevant and may

eventually allow us to partially reconciliate a priori apparently
divergent or foreign concepts of development.

REFERENCES

Anglin, J.M. (1973). Introduction to chapter 14, in: Bruner, J.
  (1973). *Beyond the information given*. New York: W.W. Norton &
  Company.
Bruner, J. (1973). *Beyond the information given*. New York:
  W.W. Norton & Company.
Dasen, P.R. (1982). Cross-cultural aspects of Piaget's theory: The
  competence/performance model. In: L.L. Adler (Ed.), *Cross-
  cultural research at issue*. New York: Academic Press.
Case, R. (1985). *Intellectual development: Birth to adulthood*.
  New York: Academic Press.
Elkind, D., & Flavell, J.H. (1969). *Studies in cognitive develop-
  ment - Essays in honor of Jean Piaget*. New York, London:
  Oxford University Press.
Flavell, J.H., & Wohlwill, J.F. (1969). Formal and functional
  aspects of cognitive development. In: D. Elkind & J.H. Flavell
  (Eds.), *Studies in cognitive development - Essays in honor of
  Jean Piaget*. New York, London: Oxford University Press.
Galifret-Granjon, N. (1981). *Naissance et évolution de la
  représentation chez l'enfant*. Paris: Les Presses Universitaires
  de France.
Gilliéron, C. (1980). Réflexions sur le problème des décalages: A
  propos de l'article de Montangero. *Archives de Psychologie, 48*,
  283-302.
Hauert, C.A. (1980). Propriétés des objets et propriétés des
  actions chez l'enfant de 2 à 5 ans. *Archives de Psychologie, 48*,
  95-168.
Hunt, D.L. (1969). The impact and limitations of the giant of
  developmental psychology. In: D. Elkind & J.H. Flavell (Eds.),
  *Studies in cognitive development - Essays in honor of
  Jean Piaget*. New York, London: Oxford University Press.
Kessen, W. (1966). Questions for a theory of cognitive development.
  Monography of the Society for Research in Child Development, 107,
  31, 5, 55-70.
Montangero, J. (1980). The various aspects of horizontal decalage.
  Archives de Psychologie, 48, 259-282.
Mounoud, P. (1983). L'évolution des conduites de préhension comme
  illustration d'un modèle du développement. In: S. de Schonen
  (Ed.), *Le développement dans la première année*. Paris: Les
  Presses Universitaires de France.
Mounoud, P. (1985). Similarities between developmental sequences at
  different age periods. In: I. Levin (Ed.), *Stage and structure*.
  Norwood: Ablex.
Piaget, J. (1946). *La formation du symbole chez l'enfant*.
  Neuchâtel: Delachaux et Niestlé. (Translation: Piaget, J. (1951),
  Play, dreams and imitation in childhood. London: Routledge
  & Kegan Paul.)
Piaget, J. (1967). L'explication en psychologie et le
  parallélisme psycho-physiologique. In: P. Fraisse & J. Piaget
  (Eds.), *Traité de psychologie expérimentale, Volume 1*. Paris:
  Les Presses Universitaires de France. (Translation: Fraisse, P.,
  & Piaget, J. (1968). *Experimental psychology: Its scope and*

method. Vol. 1. London: Routledge & Kegan Paul.)
Piaget, J. (1974a). *La prise de conscience.* Paris: Les Presses
    Universitaires de France. (Translation: Piaget, J. (1976). *The
    grasp of consciousness: Action and concept in the young child.*
    Cambridge, Ma: Harvard University Press.)
Piaget, J. (1974b). *Réussir et comprendre.* Paris: Les Presses
    Universitaires de France. (Translation: Piaget, J. (1978).
    Success and understanding. Cambridge, Ma: Harvard University
    Press.)
Piaget, J., & Inhelder, B. (1941). *Le développement des quantités
    chez l'enfant. Conservation et atomisme.* Neuchâtel: Delachaux
    et Niestlé.
Piaget, J., & Inhelder, B. (1966). *La psychologie de l'enfant.*
    Paris: Les Presses Universitaires de France. (Translation:
    Piaget, J., & Inhelder, B. (1969). *The psychology of the
    child.* London: Routledge & Kegan Paul.)
Pinard, A., & Laurendeau, M. (1969). "Stage" in Piaget's cognitive-
    developmental theory: Exegesis of a concept. In: D. Elkind &
    J.H. Flavell (Eds.), *Studies in cognitive development - Essays
    in honor of Jean Piaget.* New York, London: Oxford University
    Press.
Psychologie et épistémologie génétiques. Thèmes piagétiens.
    (Collective work) (1966). Paris: Dunod.
Ribaupierre, A. de, Rieben, L., & Lautrey, J. (1985). Horizontal
    decalages and individual differences in the development of con-
    crete operations. In: V. Shulman, L. Restaino-Baumann & L. Butler
    (Eds.), *The future of Piagetian theory: The neo-Piagetians.*
    New York: Plenum Press.
Ribaupierre, A. de, Rieben, L., & Mounoud, P. (1986). Régulations
    épigénétiques et développement cognitif de l'enfant.
    Confrontations Psychiatriques, 27, 121-151.
Scarr, S., & Carter-Saltzman, L. (1982). Genetics and intelligence.
    In: R.J. Sternberg (Ed.), *Handbook of human intelligence.*
    Cambridge: Cambridge University Press.
Séré, M.-G., & Weil-Barais, A. (1988). Conservation des grandeurs
    physiques, *Enfance, 1,* 21-38.
Young, G. (1989). Early neuropsychological development:
    Lateralization of functions - Hemispheric specialization. This
    volume.

PART II

INFANCY (0–2 YEARS)

RECENT APPROACHES

DEVELOPMENTAL PSYCHOLOGY
Cognitive, Perceptuo-Motor, and Neuropsychological Perspectives
C-A. Hauert (Editor)
© Elsevier Science Publishers B.V. (North-Holland), 1990

EARLY COGNITIVE DEVELOPMENT: BASIC FUNCTIONS

Jonas LANGER

Department of Psychology
University of California at Berkeley
Berkeley, USA

*Representative findings are outlined in support of the
hypothesis that infants' sensorimotor activity constructs
elementary logico-mathematical cognition (e.g., classes)
as well as elementary physical cognition (e.g., causality). Comparisons with linguistic and perceptual development in infancy suggest that sensorimotor activity is a
sufficient condition for the origins of logico-
mathematical and physical cognition. We conclude with
findings on comparative cognitive development of different
species and their implications for the evolution of
intelligence.*

1. INTRODUCTION

To know is to act. But to act is not necessarily to know. Agnostic
acting is nothing but moving. Mere moving does not concern us here.
Minimally, gnostic acting is receptively perceiving information.
Maximally, gnostic acting is constructing knowledge.

Newborns are endowed with the functional structures necessary to
act, and thereby potentially to know. In this we follow, with elaborations (Langer, 1969a, 1974, 1986), Piaget's (1936/1952) original
formulation of the biological bases of the origins, transformation,
and development of cognition. The functions of gnostic acting comprise assimilating, accommodating, and organizing knowledge. These
adaptive biopsychological functions are continuous in the phylogeny,
ontogeny, and history of ideas. They span biology and knowledge
(Piaget, 1971). This necessarily includes continuity between ontogenetically and phylogenetically adapted functioning by genetic
transmission to newborns.

The structures of gnostic acting are discontinuous in the phylogeny,
ontogeny, and history of ideas. Structural discontinuity necessarily excludes genetic transmission of so-called phylogenetically
adapted ideas to newborns. Instead, initial gnostic structuring is
inherent in newborns' biopsychological functioning. It is in this
sense that we interpret Piaget's proposal that infants' intellectual
structures are transformational derivatives of their biological
functions.

Newborns' gnostic functional structures, then, are biopsychological.
At their origins they already comprise coordinated sensorimotor
schemes of action (i.e., repeatable and generalizable patterns of
interaction), such as sucking and looking, that begin to generate
practical if transient knowledge about objects, space, time, and
causality, such as permanence-by-searching (Piaget, 1937/1954).
Minimally, permanence-by-searching is manifest in newborn's receptive behavior by, for example, the beginnings of visual following
behavior. Maximally, it is manifest in newborn's constructive behavior by, for example, the beginnings of rooting after nourishment.
Werner (1948) aptly captured this primitive cognitive state of
affairs when he characterized it as "thing-of-action" knowledge. It
has generally been acknowledged by classical theories of cognitive
development (including the range of Bruner, Gibson, Koffka, Piaget,
Vygotsky, and Werner) that prerepresentational forms of physical
cognition by infants is possible.

Traditionally it has usually also been assumed that even the most
elementary ontogenetic instantiation of logico-mathematical, if not
physical cognition is representational; and that the *sine qua non*
of representation is language. Rudiments of language development
(e.g., the 1- and 2-word stages) are phenomena of children's second
year (e.g., Brown, 1973; Maratsos, 1983), while more generally reco-
gnizable grammatical development only begins during children's third
year (e.g., Bickerton, 1988; Bowerman, 1978). It follows, in this
traditional view, that the onset of logico-mathematical cognition is
a post-infancy development that must await at least early childhood.
On this view, a variety of different roles have been ascribed to
linguistic representation in the development of logico-mathematical
cognition. The minimalist supposition is that language is a necessary but not sufficient notational instrument without which logico-
mathematical operations are not possible (e.g., Werner and Kaplan,
1963). The maximalist supposition is that logic is nothing but a
set of syntactic linguistic conventions (e.g., Carnap, 1934/1960).
Minimalists and maximalists agree about the central assumption that
logic is symbolic logic (Cassirer, 1923/1953, 1929/1957). It is an
assumption shared by artificial intelligence perspectives on information processing, including those focusing on cognitive development
(e.g., Klahr, 1989).

Another traditional claim, proposed by the Gestaltists, is that physical, if not logico-mathematical cognition is initially perceptual;
and that the *sine qua non* of perception is spatial perception.
Here too, a variety of different roles have been ascribed to perception in the development of logico-mathematical cognition. The minimalist supposition is that perception is a necessary but not sufficient condition for the development of logical operations. To emerge, logical operations require the re-representation of perceptual
knowledge in culturally transformed and communicable forms (Koffka,
1928). As such, this minimalist outlook sometimes merges with the
symbolic logic perspective. The maximalist supposition is that
logico-mathematical knowledge is nothing but the cultural explication by productive thinking of implicit configurational principles
prefigured in perception (Wertheimer, 1920/1945). Thus, both traditional minimalist and maximalist views, the symbolist and the perceptual, assume that logico-mathematical cognition is a derivative
(secondary) development, not an original (primary) development.

Both (the symbolist and the perceptual) derivationalist hypotheses remain plausible as long as there is no contrary data on the cognitive development of infants. Thus, even Piaget's (1945/1951, 1936/ 1952, 1937/1954) pioneering research only found the origins of physical (i.e., objects, space, causality, and time), not logico-mathematical cognition in infants' sensorimotor actions. Our research (Langer, 1980, 1986), however, is advancing the possibility of a third alternative in which logico-mathematical cognition is no longer viewed as a derivative ontogenetic development, but as an original development during infancy. Our originalist hypothesis takes its cue from the discovery of sensorimotor seriating in infancy by Hetzer (1931) and of sensorimotor classifying in infancy by Riccuiti (1965). Classes and relations, it should not be forgotten, are the generative structures of cognitive development according to Piaget (1972).

Our originalist hypothesis is that infants' gnostic actions generate elementary logico-mathematical cognition as well as elementary physical cognition. This originalist hypothesis clearly includes the corollary hypothesis that the origins of both logico-mathematical and physical cognition are prelinguistic developments and, therefore, that language is not even necessary for, let alone constitutive of, logico-mathematical cognition. The originalist hypothesis does not rule out the possibility that information is contributed by receptive forms of gnostic acting, particularly perception, to the origins of logico-mathematical and physical cognition.

The next four sections will flesh out central aspects of the originalist hypothesis. The first two sections outline some representative findings on infants' developing logico-mathematical and physical cognition that provide empirical support for the originalist hypothesis. The third section briefly elaborates on the corollary hypothesis that logico-mathematical as well as physical cognitive development is possible without language. A fourth section takes up the possible role that infants' perception plays in their cognitive development. We close with some findings on comparative cognitive development and their implications for the evolution of intelligence.

2. DEVELOPING LOGICO-MATHEMATICAL COGNITION

A set of cognitions is structureless unless (a) one or more operations and/or relations on the set are defined, and (b) the elements comprising the set are constant. We have proposed three types of operations that provide foundational structures which are sufficient to generate the fundamentals of logico-mathematical cognition (Langer, 1980, 1986): (1) Combinativity structures of pragmatic composing, decomposing, and deforming; (2) relational structures of pragmatic adding, subtracting, multiplying, and dividing; and (3) conditional structures of pragmatic correspondence, exchange (including commuting and associativity), and negating. The foundational elements of infants' cognition are objects, collections, and series.

These foundational operations (e.g., composing) and elements (e.g., collections) of cognition are inherent in infants' constructive sensorimotor activity (e.g., touching one object to another). The

reason is that constructive activity maps part-whole transformations
onto objects and events (e.g., constructs compositions of objects
where there were none). These foundational operations and elements
are therefore sufficient to produce the structural development of
logico-mathematical cognition. Most importantly, this includes progressively coming to know about necessary: (a) Equivalence, both
quantitative (equality) and qualitative (identity); (b) ordered non-
equivalence, both quantitative (inequality) and qualitative (difference); and (c) reversibility by inversion and reciprocity. If this
structural model of logico-mathematical cognition is valid, then the
most direct avenue for investigating its ontogenetic origins is to
study the construction of their constitutive operations, elements,
and products (e.g., equivalence) by infants.

The *elements* of infants' cognition are initially constructed by
infants themselves. Infants' combinativity operations are fundamental to constructing the elements of cognition (i.e., objects,
collections, series, and eventually mappings). For instance, at
least as early as age 6 months, infants consistently compose discrete objects by uniting them into collections (Hetzer, 1931;
Langer, 1980; Vereeken, 1961). At first the elements are minimal
and unstable, and should probably be called proto-elements. Progressively, they become ever more extensive and stable such that
they increasingly approximate, but never achieve, the status of
fully formed constant givens for logico-mathematical operations.

The difference between minimal and robust elements is not a matter
of sheer rate of productivity. Consider one type of element infants
construct, collections of objects. Their rate of production is high
throughout infancy (see Table 1). By age 6 months infants already
spontaneously generate about 4 to 5 compositions per minute. The
rate of composing increases a bit by age 12 months and then (with
some fluctuations) remains fundamentally unchanged up to age 24
months. Over the entire age period from 6 bo 24 months, then, infants are very productive. They consistently compose objects into
collections.

Table 1. *Range of Mean Compositions Per Minute Produced in
          Four 4-Object and Three 8-Object Conditions*

Age (Months)	4-Object Conditions	8-Object Conditions*
6	4.43-5.41	
8	2.14-4.48	
10	3.53-6.09	
12	4.86-8.29	10.40-11.95
15	4.41-5.74	5.42-7.68
18	6.17-9.60	5.34-9.30
21	3.44-7.19	4.78-6.28
24	5.71-9.97	5.43-7.94

*8-object conditions were not administered to subjects at ages
6, 8, and 10 months (Langer, 1980).*

The difference between minimal and robust elements is to be found in other features such as the size of collections (i.e., the number of objects united) and the temporal relations between collections. At first, collections usually include the minimum of two objects (see Table 2).

Table 2. Percent of 2- to 4-Object Compositions Constructed in the 4-Object Conditions and 2- to 8-Object Compositions Constructed in The 8-Object Conditions

Age (Months)	4-Object Conditions			8-Object Conditions*						
	2	3	4	2	3	4	5	6	7	8
6	85	12	3							
8	82	15	3							
10	90	9	1							
12	83	14	3	68	21	6	2	1	0	1
15	72	20	8	55	24	15	5	1	0	0
18	60	13	27	46	18	18	8	2	2	5
21	75	8	17	58	17	18	4	3	0	1
24	62	14	24	45	20	22	5	2	1	5

*8-object conditions were not administered to subjects at ages 6, 8, and 10 months (Langer, 1980).

Infants construct ever larger collections during their second year (e.g., more than half of their collections exceed the minimum of two objects in the 8-object conditions). Nevertheless, we should not lose sight of a basic datum that runs throughout our findings. Infants combine only very small numbers of objects (e.g., even small collections of 5 to 8 objects are still generated infrequently by age 24 months).

Two significant developments stand out in the temporal relations between the collections that infants construct over their first two years (see Table 3). Single-set composing characterizes infants' constructions during their first year. But even during the first year there is a shift away from individual collections that are constructed in temporal isolation from any other collection to single consecutive collections. A very small but not unimportant percentage of infants' constructions begin to comprise two contemporaneous collections generated and preserved in partial or total temporal overlap. Isolated single collections (i.e., compositions that are neither preceded nor followed immediately by other compositions) become virtually extinct during infants' second year. Concurrently, single collections are almost always constructed consecutively in time. And, contemporaneous compositions are produced ever more frequently.

Cognitive operations, like the elements onto which they are mapped, are initially constructed by infants themselves. As the elements progressively approximate constant givens, they open up new and ever-growing possibilities for infants' operations. These opera-

tions map qualitative or intensive (e.g., classifying objects
within a collection) and quantitative or extensive (e.g., commuting
objects within a collection) part-whole transformations onto the
elements of infants' cognition. At first infants' operations are
elementary and weak, and should probably be called proto-operations.
Progressively they become ever more complex and powerful mappings
that increasingly approximate but never achieve, the status of
fully-formed logico-mathematical operations during infancy. We
refer to the former as first-order operations since they comprise
direct elementary mappings, and to the latter as second-order
operations since they comprise mappings upon mappings.

Table 3.   Percent of Temporal Relations Between Compositions
            (Isol.: Isolate; Consec.: Consecutive)

Ages (Months)	4-Object Conditions			8-Object Conditions*		
	Isol.	Consec.	Overlap	Isol.	Consec.	Overlap
6	34	64	1			
8	37	62	1			
10	18	79	3			
12	25	70	5	12	78	10
15	17	78	5	10	73	17
18	7	88	6	5	71	24
21	9	68	23	10	63	26
24	2	79	20	5	62	33

*8-object conditions were not administered to subjects at age 6, 8,
and 10 months (Langer, 1980).

Composing single collections of objects, we have seen, originates,
develops, and dominates infants' constructions during their first
year. While they begin to lose their primacy during infants' second
year, single collections continue to progress (e.g., in size). As
long as they are limited to constructing single collections, infants
are also limited to mapping elementary operations onto them. So
first-order operations are expected to mark logico-mathematical
cognition exclusively during most of infants' first year. With progress in constructing single collections comes progress in the development of first-order operations so that they are expected to become increasingly powerful even during infants' second year, when they
no longer exclusively mark logico-mathematical cognition. The
guiding hypothesis is that progress in constructing single collections provides progressive elements for increasingly powerful first-
order operations.

A set of operations with which infants can begin to map quantitative
or extensive transformations onto collections are exchange operations of substituting, replacing, and commuting. Parallel development marks all three in human infancy (but not all primates, we
shall see in the final section), so I will illustrate with findings
on substituting only (see Table 4). Only one-third of infants at
age 6 months produce quantitative equivalence within single collec-

tions by substituting objects; and these are limited to the minimum
of substituting objects within 2-object collections without any
inversion. While still limited to single collections, by age 12
months all infants substitute and invert objects within 2-object
collections, and 50% of infants extend substituting objects to 3-
object collections. Progress in first-order substituting continues
during infants' second year. Most notably, some infants begin substituting within single 4-to-8-object collections.

Table 4. Percent Subjects Substituting in Single Compositions
          Comprising 2 to 8 objects and in 2 Contemporaneous
          Compositions Comprising 2 to 4 Objects

| | Single Compositions | | | | 2 Compositions |
Age (Months)	2*	3	4	5-8	2-4
6	33	0	0	0	0
8	83	0	0	0	0
10	100	0	0	0	0
12	100	50	0	0	0
15	---	17	0	0	17
18	---	50	33	17	42
21	---	8	0	0	50
24	---	58	8	25	58

*Single compositions comprising 2 objects were not scored for
substituting in infants' second year because they already
achieve the 100% ceiling by age 10 months.

Exchanges comprise fundamental operations with which infants as well
as adults construct quantitative relations of equivalence and non-
equivalence. Another set of fundamental operations that infants
begin to share with us, albeit in rudimentary forms, are classificatory. These operations map qualitative or intensive transformations
onto collections to produce similarity, identity, and difference
relations. An unexpected finding emerged on the class properties of
the single collections constructed by infants (Langer, 1980). At
age 6 months, infants consistently couple objects from different
classes with each other when presented with two contrasting classes
of two objects (e.g., 2 identical crosses and 2 identical triangles). For example, 6-month-olds consistently pair crosses with
triangles, rather than crosses with crosses or triangles with triangles. At age 8 months, infants no longer consistently couple
objects from different classes with each other. Instead, their
couplings are random. Thus, for example, 8-month-olds are equally
likely to pair crosses with triangles as they are to pair crosses
with crosses and triangles with triangles. By age 12 months, infants begin to couple identical objects with each other (e.g., red
crosses with red crosses), but only infrequently. Somewhat varying
procedures and analyses by Nelson (1973), Riccuiti (1965), Starkey
(1981), and Sugarman (1983) yield comparable results on classifying
by identities at age 12 months. By age 15 months, infants begin to
couple consistently similar (e.g., red with blue crosses) as well as

identical (e.g., red with red crosses) objects with each other
(Langer, 1986). As in other studies, we have found that infants
extend first-order composing by similarities and identities to larger single collections during their second year. But we have also
found that the upper limit is 3- and 4-object collections; random
classifying still marks the 5- to 8-object collections that infants
compose.

While elementary operations, such as substituting and classifying,
completely dominate infants' cognitive development during their
first year, they no longer do so during their second year. The
rudiments of more advanced operations originate towards the end of
their first year and develop rapidly during their second year.
These more advanced second-order operations are the developmental
products of infants' integrating their elementary operations.

Fundamental to infants constructing second-order operations is their
forming elements comprising minimal compositions of compositions.
This advance is manifest by the initiation of composing two collections of objects in temporal overlap at age 12 months; and by the
increase in constructing such contemporaneous collections during
infants' second year (see Table 3). These are still minimal compositions of compositions (i.e., second-order elements) because the
collections usually include no more than the minimum of two objects
per collection and because they rarely include more than two collections, even by age 24 months.

The major new feature marking the development of second-order substituting consists of exchanges involving two contemporaneous collections. At age 18 months these are still transitional forms of
substituting, since infants only exchange objects within, not
between, contemporaneous collections and since they are generated by
less than 50% of infants (see Table 4). Typically, these infants
construct two very small collections of objects near each other in
temporal overlap. After this they substitute one object in one collection and then one object in the other collection. Thereby, they
transform the membership of the two collections while preserving the
initial quantitative relation they had constructed between the two
collections, whether of equality or inequality.

In about half of these constructions, infants first map 1-to-1
correspondence onto two collections by, for example, composing two
parallel stacks of two blocks or two sets of 1-spoon-in-1-cup. Then
they use these equivalent collections as the elements for mapping
equivalence by substituting within the two collections (e.g., by
substituting one block in each stack, or by substituting one spoon
in each cup). The quantitative product of mapping substituting onto
correspondences is equivalences upon equivalences.

By age 24 months, a majority of infants generate second-order substituting (see Table 4). The major advance is that the exchanges
begin to be extended to substituting between, as well as within,
contemporaneous collections. Some of these exchanges include mapping substituting onto correspondences to produce equivalences upon
equivalences.

An important consequence of developing second-order operations is
that infants try them out in situations for which they were not initially constructed. This opens up myriad possibilities for constructing new and more powerful cognitions. For example, infants
begin to apply second-order substituting to classifying objects.
This includes beginning to correct nonverbal counterconditions posed
to them. To illustrate, in one countercondition we presented infants with two alignments of 4 ring shapes each in which one alignment comprised 3 circular rings and 1 square ring and the other
alignment comprised 3 square rings and 1 circular ring. At age 24
months, some infants correct the classificatory errors by substituting the singular square and circular rings for each other.

Classifying by substituting is one way by which infants begin to
construct second-order classification during their second year.
Another more direct way is to construct contemporaneous collections
in which the membership of each collection is identical or similar
objects, while the membership of the two collections is different
objects. Infants only begin to occasionally construct two contrasting classes at age 18 months (Langer, 1982, 1986; Nelson, 1973;
Riccuiti, 1965; Roberts and Fischer, 1979; Sinclair, Stambak,
Lézine, Rayna and Verba, 1982; Starkey, 1981; Sugarman, 1983; and
Woodward and Hunt, 1972). Even as late as age 24 months, infants
only construct class-consistent contemporaneous collections in 1 of
6 class conditions tested, and it is one of the simplest possible
(Langer, 1986).

3. DEVELOPING PHYSICAL COGNITION

The development of physical cognition of objects, space, time and
causality by human infants parallels their development of logico-
mathematical cognition. Nevertheless, physical constructions take
different generative forms (Langer, 1980, 1986). These are mappings
of means-ends transformations that vary by physical category (cf.,
Piaget, Grize, Szeminska and Vinh Bang, 1977, for the related notion
of physical dependency). For instance, spatial means-ends transformations construct placement and displacement relations between
objects; while causal means-ends transformations construct energy
relations between objects, such as when one object is pushed against
another. We have therefore proposed that infants' mapping of means-
ends transformations constitute basic functions that construct contingent dependency relations (i.e., physical possibility and impos-
sibility).

Since causality is central to the development of physical cognition,
it will be the focus of our discussion. Two causal primitives are
hypothesized by Piaget (1937/1954) to mark newborns' sensorimotor
actions. These are efficacy (i.e., that effects are dependent upon
or a function of subjects' efforts or actions upon objects) and
phenomenalism (i.e., that effects are dependent on or a function of
the spatio-temporal contact and movement relations between objects).
While still difficult to verify in the behavior of newborns, both
causal primitives become increasingly evident (albeit in inter-
mingled forms) in the behavior of neonates. For example, neonates
begin to coordinate their hand with their mouth movements to suck on
their hand (Butterworth, Henshall, Johnston, Abd-Fattah and Hopkins,

1985).

At first, the causal relations neonates construct are probably accidental; but they rapidly notice and reproduce them. For instance,
by age 3 months neonates already elaborate (a) accidental kicking of
their crib, which shakes the crib, which swings a mobile hanging
from the crib above them, into (b) well-directed and repeated
kicking of their crib in order to see the mobile swing (Piaget,
1937/1954; see also Rovee and Rovee, 1969; and Watson, 1985). This
does not mean that neonates comprehend the necessary role of spatial
contact or intermediaries in the production of causal relations.
The proof is that after repeatedly pulling on a string tied to a
rattle above them so that it shakes, they continue pulling on the
string even when the string has been visibly detached from the
rattle (Piaget, 1937/1954).

This type of causal behavior (labeled magicophenomenalistic by
Piaget, 1937/1954, because it intermingles efficacy with phenomenalism) progresses markedly during the second half of infants' first
year. By ages 5 to 6 months infants begin to take observable physical contact into account in constructing causality. In some situations this means that they are correct (e.g., they do not pull at a
string that is no longer attached to a rattle). But in other situations they are still wrong (e.g., they do not pull at the string
when part of it is covered so that they cannot see that it is attached to the rattle).

A substantial proportion of the compositions of objects that infants
construct in early infancy are featured by causal properties (e.g.,
propulsion by pushing a block into a cylinder which, as a consequence, rolls away). The proportion increases with age from 6 until 10
months, when almost half of infants' compositions are featured by
causality (see Table 5). Infants' production of causal compositions
declines steeply in their second year so that by age 21 months only
1 in 10 compositions is featured by causality.

Table 5. Percent of Compositions that are Causal

Age (Months)	4-Object Conditions	8-Object Conditions*
6	35	
8	38	
10	47	
12	34	25
15	22	19
18	23	19
21	10	9
24	10	9

*8-object conditions were not administered to subjects at ages 6,
8, and 10 months (see Langer, 1980).

Causal compositions already include constructing two elementary ty-

pes of causal relations or functions by age 6 months. One type begins with infants constructing, replicating, and observing minimal
effects that are directly dependent upon rudimentary causes. To
illustrate, infants use one object as a means to repeatedly push or
bang on another object while observing their construction (Langer,
1980; Piaget, 1937/1954). The second type of causal function begins
when infants anticipate and observe minimal effects that directly
influence their subsequent rudimentary causal constructions. To
illustrate, infants use one object as a means to block and stop
another object that is rolling in front of them while observing the
effects of their causal constructions (Langer, 1980; see von
Hofsten, 1983, on infants' catching skills). Their causal blocking
is directly dependent on the prediction of their targets' trajectories; otherwise they would miss their targets, which would then continue rolling away.

There is marked progress in constructing such direct causal functions during the second year. This includes generating effects
which are direct functions of causes (e.g., objects are pushed
harder and harder). The direct functional dependency may be formalized as one-way ratio-like relations, such as "Moving Further is a
dependent function of Pushing Harder". This is what differentiates
first-order from second-order causal functions that originate during
the second year of infancy.

Second-order functions are integrative means-ends transformation.
They coordinate elementary first-order means-ends mappings to each
other. This produces a second structural level of more powerful
functions. Our structural hypothesis is that the effects are
directly dependent upon the causes in first-order functions. In
contrast, the effects begin to be proportional to the causes in
second-order functions. So, the expected structural developmental
difference is that first-order functions are featured by direct
ratio-like relations, while second-order functions are marked by
more indirect analogical or proportional-like relations.

Older, like younger, infants use one object as an instrument with
which to push a second dependent object. But beginning at age 18
months, when the effect is that the dependent object rolls away,
then infants may also transform the instrument into a means with
which to block the dependent object (Langer, 1986). Correlatively,
infants thereby transform the end or goal from rolling to stopping.
As soon as the dependent object stops rolling infants transform the
same instrumental object back into a means with which to make the
dependent object roll away again. And so on.

Thus, older infants begin to covary their transformations of both
means and ends. These covariations form coordinate proportional-
like dependencies between causes and effects. These protopropor-
tions map previously constructed first-order dependencies onto each
other. The products are second-order causal functions, such as
"Moving is a function of Pushing, as Stopping is a function of
Blocking".

4. COMPARATIVE LINGUISTIC AND SENSORIMOTOR DEVELOPMENT

The findings reviewed in the previous two sections support our
structural developmental hypothesis that second-order operations and
functions are transforms of first-order operations and functions.
While early infancy is dominated by first-order cognition, the developmental trend is toward constructing second-order cognition during
late infancy. Even though the latter is a novel development, it is
still a transformational derivative of the former. Accordingly, we
have proposed that infants' cognitive development is recursive
(Langer, 1969a, 1986). Recursive cognitive development is multi-
leveled (e.g., first- and second-order cognition co-exist in late
infancy), multilinear (e.g., while developing out of first-order
cognition, second-order cognition branches off so that both orders
of cognition diverge in their subsequent development), and multistructural (e.g., comprises both logico-mathematical operations and
physical functions).

We can be very brief about the hypothesis that both first- and
second-order cognition, including logico-mathematical as well as
physical cognition, is possible without language, since the evidence
is so clear-cut. The development of first- and second-order cognition antedate the development of language during infancy. So linguistic development cannot be a cause (not even a necessary, let
alone a sufficient condition) of infants' cognitive development.
Further corroboration is provided by findings of at least first-
order cognition in monkeys (to be discussed in the final section).

The interesting question that remains is the role that infants' more
precocious cognitive development may play in their linguistic development. Elsewhere (see Langer, 1982, 1983, 1986, for extended discussions) we have proposed and presented data to support the hypothesis that while not a derivative of cognitive development, language development begins by "piggybacking" on cognitive development
during infancy. Recent findings, such as on naming and sensorimotor
classifying (Gopnik and Meltzoff, 1987), provide further support for
the hypothesis. Eventually, linguistic development may outstrip
aspects of cognitive development and, indeed, open up new possibilities for cognitive development.

5. COMPARATIVE PERCEPTUAL AND SENSORIMOTOR DEVELOPMENT

Perceiving is undoubtedly a rich source of acquiring and processing
information by infants about logico-mathematical and physical phenomena. The empirical case for this claim is growing rapidly. As
yet, however, the relationship between receptive perceptual acting
and constructive sensorimotor acting in the development of infants'
cognition remains undetermined. To begin to analyze this problem
requires examining logico-mathematical and physical phenomena that
have apparent counterparts in infants' receptive and constructive
activity. Infants' developing cognition of classes and causes serve
as especially good exemplars of the logico-mathematical and physical
domains because they are fundamental categories of knowledge and
because they come with relatively well-documented data bases.

Perceptual categorizing is an apparent receptive counterpart during infancy of the constructive sensorimotor classifying outlined in the first section. Infants' perceptual categorizing has been extensively reviewed recently (e.g., Bornstein, 1981, 1984; Cohen and Younger, 1983; Quinn and Eimas, 1986; and Reznick and Kagan, 1983), so it is possible to succinctly point to the developments that are directly relevant to the present analysis. A growing body of research using perceptual habituation procedures is finding that infants can be familiarized with a variety of single categories of similar stimuli, such as orientations, forms and schematic faces (e.g., McGurk, 1972; Ross, 1980; Sherman, 1985; Younger, 1985). Moreover, evidence is beginning to accumulate that indicates that infants as young as ages 3 and 4 months also habituate to two categories of contrasting stimuli (i.e., squares and triangles) at the same time (Quinn, 1987). While using a different experimental procedure, Husaim and Cohen (1981) provide corroborating evidence of two-category acquisition at age 10 months.

Two objections may be raised to attributing the perception of categories to infants. One objection is methodological and has many technical facets to it (e.g., the inevitable loss of a significant proportion of the sample of subjects tested). The other objection is interpretative. It questions interpreting habituation to similar stimuli as perceptual categorizing when it can be more parsimoniously and traditionally interpreted as nothing more than stimulus discrimination and generalization.

While recognizing a measure of legitimacy in both objections, for purposes of our analysis we will nevertheless treat the reports of perceptual categorizing by infants at face value. Then, the comparative developmental picture that emerges is that perceptual categorizing antedates sensorimotor classifying. Infants habituate to a single category of similar stimuli. They may also already habituate to as many as two contrasting categories as young as ages 3 to 4 months. In comparison, as outlined in the first section, infants' sensorimotor constructions are still limited to single classes of objects during their first year. Moreover, infants do not begin to construct single classes of identical objects until age 12 months, and then only infrequently. At younger ages infants construct single couplings of different objects (at age 6 months); then they shift to random couplings of objects (at age 8 months). Infants do not begin to construct two contrasting classes until age 18 months, and then infrequently.

These findings on receptive perceptual categorizing and constructive sensorimotor classifying during infancy raise fundamental questions about their foundational cognitive and developmental relations. First, does perceptual categorizing merely antedate sensorimotor classifying chronologically, without the former influencing the latter's development ? A positive answer to this question would imply that perceptual categorizing and sensorimotor classifying are segregated, separate, and noninteractive cognitive modules. It would also imply that they follow independent developmental trajectories during infancy without any flow of information from perceptual categorizing to sensorimotor classifying. Second, does earlier developing perceptual categorizing play a facilitating role in the subsequent development of sensorimotor classifying ? A positive answer to this question would imply that perceptual categorizing and

sensorimotor classifying are differentiated but related and interactive cognitive processes. It would also imply that they follow
interdependent developmental trajectories during infancy with information flow from perceptual categorizing to sensorimotor classifying.

If there is information flow from categorizing to classifying, then
we are faced with many additional thorny questions. For instance,
why is perceptual categorizing by *similarity* at ages 3 and 4 month
first followed by sensorimotor classifying by *differences* (rather
than by similarities) at age 6 months ? Why does sensorimotor classifying pass through a phase of randomness or inconsistency at age 8
months when consistent perceptual categorizing by similarities has
already been well established at a much younger age ? And why is
there a longer ontogenetic lag between the sensorimotor and perceptual acquisition of two classes (more than a year) than one class
(much less than a year) ? Are these temporal delays vertical
(stage) or horizontal (domain) decalages from the Piagetian perspective ?

The answers to these questions are not likely to be found in infants' motor development. Identical motor skills and behaviors are
used by infants when they construct single sets of different objects
at age 6 months, single random couplings of objects at age 8 months,
occasional single classes of identical objects at age 12 months, and
single couplings of identical and similar objects at age 15 months.
Again, the same motor skills are used by infants during their second
year, when they begin to construct two contrasting classes. The
essential difference between the sensorimotor construction of one
and two contrasting classes is that when constructing two classes,
infants no longer uncouple their first pairing of identical (or
similar) objects before forming a second coupling of identical (or
similar) objects from a contrasting class. Thus, the acquisition of
motor skills cannot account for the development of sensorimotor
classifying in infancy. This leaves open the questions about the
contribution that infants' perceptual categorizing makes to their
developing sensorimotor classifying.

In order to extend our analysis to the domain of physical as well as
logico-mathematical cognition, we turn to infants' cognition of causality. Perceiving causality is an apparent receptive counterpart
to the sensorimotor construction of causality outlined in the second
section. Like the research on perceptual categorizing, the main
procedure used to study causal perception by infants is habituation.
Unlike the research on perceptual categorizing, which is plentiful,
relatively little research has been done so far on young infants'
perception of causality. There has really been only one kind of
finding so far. Sometime between ages 3 months (Ball, 1973; Borton,
1979) and 6 months (Leslie and Keeble, 1987), infants discriminate
stimulus displays that are causal (e.g., the collision or billiard
ball phenomenon characterized by Michotte, 1946/1963, as the launching effect) from displays that are not causal.

Three objections may be raised to attributing the perception of
causality to young infants. The first two objections are similar in
kind to those raised about the perception of categories by infants.
One objection is methodological, such as significant subject attri-

tion during testing. Another objection is to interpreting infants'
habituation in these tests as causal perception, since the stimuli
are not fully controlled for spatiotemporal differences as well as
for causal differences between the displays. A third, additional
objection is that the stimuli displayed may not be perceived as
causal by adults without the use of higher order cognitive processes. The findings on adults' perception of these stimulus displays as causal were first made by Michotte (1946/1963), whose
research methods have been severely criticized (Boyle, 1972;
Joynson, 1971). If it is doubtful that adults perceive these displays as causal without the input of cognitive processes not available to infants, such as verbal suggestion, then there is no way so
far of knowing what preverbal infants perceive when faced with these
stimuli.

As we did with category perception by infants, we will suspend judgment on these criticisms and treat the perhaps premature reports of
causal perception by infants at face value. Then, the comparative
developmental picture that emerges is that sensorimotor causality
antedates perceptual causality. By age 3 months at the oldest,
infants repeatedly, if sometimes incorrectly, construct causal phenomena. And if Piaget (1954) is correct, then the sensorimotor
actions by neonates construct two primitives of causal cognition
(i.e., efficacy and phenomenalism) at or shortly after birth. The
youngest reported age for perceiving causal phenomena is sometime
between 3 and 6 months. So far, then, the comparative developmental
picture in the physical domain of causal cognition is the antithesis
of that in the logico-mathematical domain of classification:
Sensorimotor causality seems to antedate perceptual causality, while
perceptual categorizing seems to antedate sensorimotor classifying.

Taken together, the findings on the comparative development of sensorimotor and perceptual classification (categorization) and causality raise at least one set of empirical questions and lead to several proposals. First, the questions: Are the reviewed findings
representative of the comparative development of all logico-
mathematical and physical cognition ? Does the perception of all
logico-mathematical phenomena by infants antedate their sensorimotor
construction ? At least one piece of research suggests that we cannot rule out a positive answer (although it suffers from many serious methodological problems of the kind already mentioned in
regard to the perception of categories). Antell and Keating (1983)
report that newborns discriminate between minimal numerosities
(i.e., up to 3 elements). No comparable numerical sensorimotor
constructions are reported until at least age 6 months (Langer,
1980). Conversely, does the sensorimotor construction of all physical phenomena by infants (i.e., objects, space, and time, as well
as causality) antedate their perception ?

These questions are empirical and must therefore await empirical
answers. Meanwhile, if we are correct in a comparative developmental proposal made elsewhere (Langer, 1986, 1988, 1989), then we
can anticipate that the most likely answers to these questions will
be negative. The proposal, in brief, is that precocity in rate of
development is not tied to particular cognitive domains (or sub-
domains) in ontogeny, and for that matter in phylogeny and in history as well. If this proposal is correct, then the likelihood of a

consistent inverse comparative developmental interaction between
processes (i.e., perceptual vs. sensorimotor) and domains (i.e.,
logico-mathematical vs. physical) of cognition becomes remote.
Without a consistent inverse interaction the answers to these
questions are likely to be negative (unless other, so far unknown,
variables intervene).

Perception, as we have tried to show, sometimes develops more precociously and sometimes less precociously than sensorimotor activity. Regardless of which turns out to be the case for particular
domains of knowledge, the comparative extent of perceptual development is extremely limited. The extent of its development is extremely limited for a variety of reasons such as that perception has a
very restricted spatiotemporal span of attention. Perception can
only encompass minimal stimuli within any given fixation. While
this holds true for all domains, it is simplest to illustrate for
numerical phenomena. Throughout ontogeny, including adulthood,
there is little further development in the perception of numerosity
beyond the minimal detection and discrimination of up to 3 or 4 elements by infants (see Klein and Starkey, 1987, for a recent review
of the subitizing data).

In comparison, the extent of sensorimotor development is fairly far-
reaching. To appreciate the more extended development of sensorimotor cognition it is only necessary to recall one findings (Langer,
1986) already described in the first section. By age 24 months infants begin to construct quantitative equivalence upon equivalence
by substituting elements between numerically corresponding sets.
This is not to deny many limitations to the numerical cognition that
can be constructed by sensorimotor activity, for example, it is limited to operating on pragmatic (i.e., concrete, present, and fini-
te) elements (see Langer, 1980, for other limitations).

The phylogenetic evidence on numerosity perception is sufficient to
suggest that the level attained by humans is matched and even excee-
ded by some other species (see Klein and Starkey, 1987, for a recent
review). Most striking in this regard is Koehler's (1951) finding
of discriminating numerosities up to 5 or 6 elements by pigeons, 6
elements by jackdaws, and 7 elements by ravens and parrots. Even
though their capacity for numerosity perception exceeds that of humans, these avian species never develop a number system comparable
to that developed by humans which at a minimum comprises a closed
system of arithmetic operations and necessary products (Klein and
Langer, 1987). Clearly, then, numerosity perception is far from a
sufficient condition for developing advanced logico-mathematical
cognition.

Is numerosity perception even one of several necessary conditions ?
For instance, does it partially prefigure and/or help get the development of advanced logico-mathematical cognition going ? The evidence is not yet in on this question. We do know, however, that
individuals born with multiple perceptual handicaps (such as Helen
Keller) nevertheless develop advanced logico-mathematical cognition.
So we cannot rule out the possibility that numerosity perception is
an inessential peripheral process or encapsulated module that is not
even a necessary condition for the development of advanced logico-
mathematical cognition.

If numerosity perception is neither a necessary nor a sufficient condition for developing advanced logico-mathematical cognition, then we may plausibly wonder what its role is in the evolution of intelligence. The presence of numerosity perception in avian species that do not develop logico-mathematical cognition as well as in humans who do suggests that numerosity perception may play a very limited evolutionary role. Two options stand out. One possibility is that it serves a transitory function. In human ontogeny it enables infants to make minimal receptive judgments about quantitative equality and inequality. As such it complements infants' sensorimotor abilities to construct minimal quantitative equality and inequality. Numerosity perception is rapidly outstripped by children's developing logico-mathematical operations as they grow older (e.g., even older infants already construct equivalences upon equivalences by mapping substitution operations upon correspondence mappings). Then numerosity perception basically ceases to develop in power and play any further evolutionary or developmental role. This would account for the lack of difference in humans between infant and adult subitizing.

The other outstanding possibility is that numerosity perception is a cognitive analogue to an evolutionary appendix. Like an appendix, it may have served an as yet unknown function in the prehistoric evolution of intelligence; but it no longer does so in human cognitive development. Unlike an appendix, it retains its function of discriminating between minimal numerosities. Accordingly, numerosity perception does not develop beyond its primitive infantile stage while logico-mathematical cognition continues to develop far beyond its primitive beginnings in human ontogeny. Numerosity perception may well be an evolutionary dead-end as far as cognitive development is concerned. To gain further leverage on the evolution of intelligence, we turn to the comparative developmental findings that are emerging on sensorimotor cognition in nonhuman and human primates.

6. COMPARATIVE COGNITIVE DEVELOPMENT

There are significant parallels (that is, formal and material, differences as well as similarities) between the cognitive development of nonhuman primates and of human infants, outlined in the first two sections. While of major importance, if considered by themselves the formal similarities would mislead us into adopting a recapitulationist theory of the evolution of intelligence (see Langer, 1988, for further discussion; but see Parker and Gibson, 1979, for a contrary view). We will therefore pay attention to both findings of similarities and differences.

The fundamental formal similarities found in the two monkey species, *Cebus apella* and *Macaca fascicularis*, that have been studied so far (Antinucci, 1989) on their comparative development of logico-mathematical as well as physical cognition are complex in detail. Nevertheless, the overall picture is pretty straightforward. All the basic cognitive structures found in human infants are also found in these two species of monkeys. This includes all first-order intensive (e.g., classifying) and extensive (e.g., substituting) logico-mathematical operations. It includes all first-order physi-

cal cognition, such as ratio-like causal dependency. And it includes other basic categories of physical cognition, particularly of
space and objects such as permanence. Thus, all the basic elements
of cognitive development are in place in cebus and macaques, as well
as in human infants.

This order of shared elementary structures makes the lack of comparable progress toward more advanced cognitive development all the
more striking. Neither cebus nor macaques develops the second-order
cognition that infants develop during their second year, let alone
more advanced (concrete and formal operational) cognition that develops in late childhood and adolescence (e g., Inhelder and Piaget,
1958, 1964). Rare instances of rudimentary second-order logico-
mathematical but not physical cognition are found in cebus, but not
macaques (Poti and Antinucci, 1989). Two alternative explanations
can plausibly account for why this does not lead to any further
cognitive development by cebus. One alternative is that the rare
findings may be false positives due to imprecisions in the methods.
The other possibility is that rare second-order logico-mathematical
cognition is a necessary but not sufficient condition for further
intellectual development. In particular, the crucial missing ingre-
dients for further development may include the lack of concomitantly
producing rudiments of the full range of (a) second-order logico-
mathematical operations and/or (b) second-order physical cognitions.

To begin to understand why the cognitive development of these monkeys is so arrested, so minimal as compared to even human infants,
we must therefore look to the formal differences between the cognition of these primate species. The fundamental differences discovered so far are also complex in detail. Three overall differences,
however, stand out. The organization, sequence, and direction of
cognitive development are formally different in these three species.

The *organization* of elementary (first-order) cognitive structures
differs among the three species throughout their development. Part
of the cognitive organization of cebus at one point in their development should suffice as an illustration (Poti and Antinucci,
1989). At age 48 months (roughly maturity), cebus barely generate
the most rudimentary first-order substituting (comparable to those
6-month-old humans begin to construct), at the same time that they
produce fairly advanced first-order commuting (comparable to those
constructed by 12-to-15-month-old humans). In comparison, parallel
development characterizes the organization of human infants' first-
order (and, in fact, second-order) cognitions (Langer, 1980, 1986).
All structures are fairly well aligned with each other to form a
differentiated and integrated organization. For example, when infants are at the stage of generating rudimentary first-order operations, then all their first-order operations are rudimentary (including substituting and commuting). Their cognitive structures are
coherently organized. In human infants one does not find extreme
mixtures of rudimentary and advanced first-order cognitions comparable to those found throughout the development of cebus and macaques. In comparison, then, cebus' and macaques' cognitive structures are differentiated but unintegrated; they are comparatively
disorganized.

Differentiated and integrated organization means predominant, not

perfect, correlation between cognitive structures in human infants.
The contrast is with the disorganized (i.e., unintegrated mixture of
unaligned) cognitive structures found throughout cebus and macaques
development. Further, the distinction is meant to capture the comparative developmental organization of cognitive competence, not
performance. For instance, the idea is that cebus who can generate
advanced first-order commuting are incapable of producing advanced
first-order substituting. Conversely, the idea is that human infants who can only generate rudimentary first-order substituting are
incapable of also producing advanced first-order commuting.

In an early investigation, Inhelder (1943/1968) found extreme structural disparity between the logico-mathematical and physical cognition of mentally retarded children. Inhelder hypothesized that
extreme disparity produces structural "friction" which impedes cognitive development. Our claim is not that cognitive mixture and
decalage are not found in human infants. Rather, the claim is that
disparities between sensorimotor operations (for example, between
commuting, substituting, and classifying) are typical but comparatively narrow-gauged. The developmental consequence is relatively rapid resolution, with gains made by the lagging operations and, sometimes, by the more advanced operations as well. Indeed, we have
proposed that narrow-gauged disparities are a major source of optimal structural disequilibrium that, together with structural equilibrium, generates progressive development (Langer, 1969b, 1974,
1980, 1986).

In passing, we should not overlook that this formulation also applies to the relations between perceptual and sensorimotor development considered in the previous section. The ever-widening
disparity between perceptual and sensorimotor functioning during
infancy leads to nonoptimal disequilibrium between their structures.
To put it more precisely: The probability of inducing mutual progress decreases as structural disparity increases with age. Structure and development are reciprocal: Extreme (structural) modularity enhances (developmental) disparity and extreme disparity enhances modularity.

The temporal *sequence* in which elementary (first-order) cognitive
structures develop also differs among the three species. One fundamental difference is in the temporal sequencing *between* cognitive
domains. Logico-mathematical and physical cognition develop simultaneously in human infants. They form independent but contemporaneous developmental trajectories. Synchronic developmental trajectories facilitate direct interaction or information flow between
cognitive domains. For example, physical cognition of objects (such
as their permanence) develops at the same time as logico-
mathematical cognition of collections (such as their identity by
class and their equivalence by substitution). In contrast, central
physical conditions (such as object permanence) develop before
logico-mathematical cognition (such as identity by class and equivalence by substitution) in cebus and macaques (Antinucci, 1989).
They form independent and consecutive developmental trajectories.
Asynchronous developmental trajectories do not readily permit direct
interaction or information flow between cognitive domains since they
are out of phase with each other. At most, then, the interactions
between cognitive domains in cebus and macaques may be indirect,

with the main potential lines of influence from relatively developed physical cognition to undeveloped logico-mathematical cognition. By comparison, in human infants mutual and reciprocal influence between logico-mathematical and physical cognition is readily achievable since they develop contemporaneously and in parallel. Similarly, this further suggests that the asynchronies between the perceptual and sensorimotor development of human infants (considered in the previous section) are unlikely to be causes of each other's progressive development. Thus, their development is relatively independent of each other (i.e., they are modular), with sensorimotor development continuing to develop while perception does not.

Another fundamental difference is in the temporal sequencing *within* cognitive domains. One that has been discovered so far is in classifying. Again, for the sake of brevity and simplicity we will paint the picture in broad strokes, leaving aside detailed differences. Recall (from the first section) that the sequence of first-order classificatory development in human infants (Langer, 1980, 1986) is from (a) classifying by differences (at age 6 months), to (b) random classifying (at age 8), to (c) classifying by identities/similarities (at ages 12 to 15 months). In cebus (Spinozzi and Natale, 1989) the sequence is from (a) mostly random classifying and partially classifying by identities/similarities (at age 16 months), to (b) mostly classifying by differences and partially classifying by identities/similarities (at age 36 months), to (c) classifying by identities/similarities (at age 48 months). Only a 2-step sequence is reported for macaques (Spinozzi and Natale, 1989): (a) Mostly classifying by identities/similarities and partially classifying by differences (at age 22 months), to (b) classifying by identities/ similarities (at age 34 months). Thus the sequences differ, but the cognitive developmental end-points are formally similar. The three species take divergent developmental paths towards eventually classifying by identities and similarities. It seems to me that this is the strongest disproof yet of the recapitulation theory of the evolution of intelligence.

Divergent development trajectories do not always meet at common cognitive end-points. Divergent end-points are produced when the *direction* of cognitive development differs among species. Consider causality. As already indicated in section 2 (see Table 5), the production of causal compositions by human infants first increases and then decreases with age. In cebus (Natale, 1989), the rate of production ranges between one-fourth and one-third of their set constructions (from 30% at age 16 months to 25% at age 36 months, to 32% at age 48 months). The data picture for macaques is still incomplete since data at only two age-points are reported (Natale, ibid): 4% at age 22 months and 0% at age 34 months. Thus, the end-points of causal cognition diverge in these species, as well as the direction of their development.

The precise parameters of the organization, sequence, and direction of elementary structural development that constitute optimal conditions for continuing and progressive evolution and development are still to be determined. Nevertheless, it is becoming increasingly apparent that "partially" out-of-phase (disequilibrated) structures are sources of cognitive gaps, conflicts, questions, problems, etc. At the same time, "sufficiently" in-phase (equilibrated) structures

facilitate informational flow between them so that it is possible
for intellectual gaps to be filled, conflicts resolved, questions
answered, problems solved, etc. Possibilities for generating new
knowledge arise under these (yet to be precisely determined) conditions of both structural equilibrium and disequilibrium. A good
illustration, already noted in section 2, is the alignment between
second-order composing and substituting (and perhaps correspondence)
that opens up the possibility of more advanced problems in and new
solutions for classification. Thus, the increasing and permanent
possibilities for self-generated cognitive development are constructed by infants themselves.

Foundational formal differences in organization, sequence, and
direction of cognitive development, then, are at the heart of the
minimal intellectual evolution of cebus and macaques as compared
with humans. As already noted, we have proposed that human cognitive development is the synthetic product of both equilibrated and
disequilibrated structures. In comparison, the relatively disorganized and asynchronic structures of cebus and macaques indicate a
predominance of disequilibrated over equilibrated structures (see
Langer, 1989, for detailed discussions). The synthetic opportunities for opening up new cognitive developments are therefore missing
in cebus and macaques. Our thesis is that it is the equilibrium and
disequilibrium conditions of the organization, sequencing, and
direction of human infants' recursive (i.e., multistructural, multi-
level, and multilinear) cognition that determines their continuing
intellectual progress.

REFERENCES

Antinucci, F. (Ed.) (1989). *Cognitive structure and development of
nonhuman primates*. Hillsdale, NJ.: Erlbaum.
Antell, S.E., & Keating, D.P. (1983). Perception of numerical
invariance in infants. *Child Development, 54*, 695-701.
Ball, W.A. (1973). The perception of causality in the infant.
Presented at the Society for Research in Child Development
meetings, Philadelphia.
Bickerton, D. (1988). Evidence for a two-stage model of language
evolution from ontogeny and phylogeny. In: S. Strauss (Ed.),
Ontogeny, phylogeny, and history. Norwood, NJ: Ablex.
Bornstein, M. (1981). Two kinds of perceptual organization near the
beginning of life. In: A. Collins (Ed.), *Minnesota Symposium on
Child Psychology* (Vol. 14). Hillsdale, N.J.: Erlbaum.
Bornstein, M. (1984). A descriptive taxonomy of psychological
categories used by infants. In: C. Sophian (Ed.), *Origins of
Cognitive Skills*. Hillsdale, N.J.: Erlbaum.
Borton, R.W. (1979). The perception of causality in infants.
Presented at the Society for Research in Child Development
meetings, Denver.
Bowerman, M. (1978). Structural relationships in children's
utterances: Syntactic or semantic ? In: L. Bloom (Ed.),
Readings in language development. New York: Wiley.
Boyle, D.G. (1972). Michotte's ideas. *Bulletin of the British
Psychological Society, 25*, 89-91.
Brown, R.A. (1973). *A first language: The early stages*. Cambridge:
Harvard University Press.

Butterworth, G., Henshall, C., Johnston, S., Abd-Fattah, N., &
    Hopkins, B. (1985). Hand to mouth activity in the newborn baby:
    Evidence for innate sensory-motor coordination. Presented at the
    British Psychological Society meetings, Belfast.
Carnap, R. (1934/1960). *The logical syntax of language.* Paterson,
    N.J.: Littlefield & Adams.
Cassirer, E. (1923/1953). *Philosophy of symbolic forms. Vol. 1:
    Language.* New Haven: Yale University Press.
Cassirer, E. (1929/1957). *Philosophy of symbolic forms. Vol. 3:
    Phenomenology of knowledge.* New Haven: Yale University Press.
Cohen, L.B., & Younger, B.A. (1983). Perceptual categorization in
    infants. In: E.K. Scholnick (Ed.), *New trends in conceptual
    representation.* Hillsdale, N.J.: Erlbaum.
Gopnik, A., & Meltzoff, A. (1987). The development of categori-
    zation in the second year and its relation to other cognitive
    and linguistic developments. *Child Development, 58,* 1523-1531.
Hetzer, H. (1931). *Kind und Schaffen.* Jena: Gustav Fildner.
Husaim, J.S., & Cohen, L.B. (1981). Infant learning of ill-defined
    categories. *Merrill-Palmer Quarterly, 27,* 443-456.
Inhelder, B. (1943/1968). *The diagnosis of reasoning in the
    mentally retarded.* New York: John Day.
Inhelder, B., & Piaget, J. (1958). *The growth of logical thinking
    from childhood to adolescence.* New York: Basic Books.
Inhelder, B., & Piaget, J. (1964). *Early growth of logic in the
    child: Classification and seriation.* New York: Harper & Row.
Joynson, R.B. (1971). Michotte's experimental methods. *British
    Journal of Psychology, 62,* 293-302.
Klahr, D. (1989). Information processing approaches to cognitive
    development. In: R. Vasta (Ed.), *Annals of child development,*
    (Vol.6).
Klein, A., & Langer, J. (1987). Elementary numerical constructions
    by toddlers. Presented at the Society for Research in Child
    Development meetings, Baltimore.
Klein, A., & Starkey, P. (1987). The origins and development of
    numerical cognition: A comparative analysis. In: J. Sloboda &
    D. Rogers (Eds.), *Cognitive processes in mathematics.* Oxford:
    Oxford University Press.
Koehler, O. (1951). The ability of birds to count. *Bulletin of
    Animal Behavior, 9,* 41-45.
Koffka, K. (1928). *The growth of the mind.* London: Routledge &
    Kegan Paul.
Langer, J. (1969a). *Theories of development.* New York: Holt,
    Rinehart & Winston.
Langer, J. (1969b). Disequilibrium as a source of development. In:
    P.H. Mussen, J. Langer & M. Covington (Eds.), *Trends and issues
    in developmental psychology.* New York: Holt, Rinehart & Winston.
Langer, J. (1974). Interactional aspects of mental structures.
    Cognition, 3, 9-28.
Langer, J. (1980). *The origin of logic: Six to twelve months.* New
    York: Academic Press.
Langer, J. (1982). From prerepresentational to representational
    cognition. In: G. Forman (Ed.), *Action and thought.* New York:
    Academic Press.
Langer, J. (1983). Concept and symbol formation by infants. In:
    S. Wapner & B. Kaplan (Eds.), *Toward a holistic developmental
    psychology.* Hillsdale N.J.: Erlbaum.
Langer, J. (1986). *The origins of logic: One to two years.* New

York: Academic Press.
Langer, J. (1988). A note on the comparative psychology of mental development. In: S. Strauss (Ed.), *Ontogeny, phylogeny, and history.* Norwood, N.J.: Ablex.
Langer, J. (1989). Comparison with the human child. In: F. Antinucci (Ed.), *Cognitive structure and development of nonhuman primates.* Hillsdale, N.J.: Erlbaum.
Leslie, A.M., & Keeble, S. (1987). Do six-month-old infants perceive causality ? *Cognition, 25,* 265-288.
Maratsos, M. (1983). Some current issues in the study of the acquisition of grammar. In: P.H. Mussen (Ed.), *Handbook of child Psychology.* New York: Wiley.
McGurk, H. (1972). Infant discrimination of orientation. *Journal of Experimental Child Psychology, 14,* 151-164.
Michotte, A. (1946/1963). *The perception of causality.* New York: Basic Books.
Natale, F. (1989). Patterns of object manipulation. In: F. Antinucci (Ed.), *Cognitive structure and development of nonhuman primates.* Hillsdale, NJ: Erlbaum.
Nelson, K. (1973). Some evidence for the primacy of categorization and its functional basis. *Merrill-Palmer Quarterly, 19,* 21-39.
Parker, S.T., & Gibson, K.R. (1979). A developmental model for the evolution of language and intelligence in early hominids. *Behavioral and Brain Sciences, 2,* 367-408.
Piaget, J. (1945/1951). *Play, dreams and imitation in childhood.* New York: Norton.
Piaget, J. (1936/1952). *The origin of intelligence in children.* New York: International Universities Press.
Piaget, J. (1937/1954). *The construction of reality in the child.* New York: Basic Books.
Piaget, J. (1971). *Biology and knowledge.* Chicago: University of Chicago Press.
Piaget, J. (1972). *Essai de logique opératoire.* Paris: Dunod.
Piaget, J., Grize, J.B., Szeminska, A., & Vinh Bang (1977). *Epistemology and psychology of functions.* Dordrecht: Reidel.
Poti, P., & Antinucci, F. (1989). Logical operations. In: F. Antinucci (Ed.), *Cognitive structure and development of nonhuman primates.* Hillsdale, N.J.: Erlbaum.
Quinn, P.C. (1987). The categorized representation of visual pattern information by very young infants. *Cognition, 27,* 145-179.
Quinn, P.C., & Eimas, P.D. (1986). On categorization in early infancy. *Merrill-Palmer Quarterly, 32,* 331-363.
Reznick, J.S., & Kagan, J. (1983). *Category detection in infancy.* In: L.P. Lipsitt (Ed.), *Advances in infancy research (vol. 2).* Norwood, N.J.: Ablex.
Riccuiti, H.N. (1965). Object grouping and selective ordering behavior in infants 12 to 24 months old. *Merril-Palmer Quarterly, 11,* 129-148.
Roberts, R.J., & Fischer, K.W. (1979. A developmental sequence of classification skills. Paper presented at the Society for Research in Child Development meetings.
Ross, G.S. (1980). Categorization in 1-2-year-olds. *Developmental Psychology, 16,* 391-396.
Rovee, C.K., & Rovee, D.T. (1969). Conjugate reinforcement of infant exploratory behavior. *Journal of Experimental Child*

Psychology, 8, 33-39.
Sherman, T. (1985).   Categorization skills in infants. *Child
    Development, 56,* 1561-1573.
Sinclair, M., Stambak, M., Lézine, I., Rayna, S., & Verba, M.
    (1982).   *Les bébés et les choses.* Paris: P.U.F.
Spinozzi, G., & Natale, F. (1989).   Classification. In: F.
    Antinucci (Ed.), *Cognitive structure and development of nonhuman
    primates.* Hillsdale, N.J.: Erlbaum.
Starkey, D. (1981).   The origins of concept formation: Object
    sorting and object preference in early infancy. *Child
    Development, 52,* 489-497.
Sugarman, S. (1983).   *Children's early thought: Developments in
    classification.* New York: Cambridge University Press.
Vereeken, P. (1961).   *Spatial development: Constructive praxia from
    birth to the age of seven.* Gronigen: Walters.
von Hofsten, C. (1983).   Catching skills in infants. *Journal of
    Experimental Psychology: Human Perception and Performance, 9(1),*
    75-85.
Watson, J.S. (1985).   Bases of causal inference in infancy: Time,
    space, and sensory relations. In: L. Lipsitt & C. Rovee-Collier
    (Eds.), *Advances in infant behavior and development.* Norwood,
    N.J.: Ablex.
Werner, H. (1948).   *Comparative psychology of mental development.*
    New York: International Universities Press.
Werner, H., & Kaplan, B. (1963).   *Symbol formation.* New York: Wiley.
Wertheimer, M. (1920/1945).   *Productive thinking.* New York: Harper.
Woodward, W.M., & Hunt, M.R. (1972).   Exploratory studies of early
    cognitive development. *British Journal of Educational Psychology,
    42,* 248-259.
Younger, B.A. (1985).   The segregation of items into categories by
    10-month-old infants. *Child Development, 56,* 1574-1585.

DEVELOPMENTAL PSYCHOLOGY
Cognitive, Perceptuo-Motor, and Neuropsychological Perspectives
C-A. Hauert (Editor)
© Elsevier Science Publishers B.V. (North-Holland), 1990

EARLY COGNITIVE DEVELOPMENT: NOTIONS OF OBJECTS, SPACE,
AND CAUSALITY IN INFANCY

Beryl E. MCKENZIE*

Department of Psychology
La Trobe University
Bundoora, Australia

*Some studies concerned with infants' understanding of the
nature of objects, spatial relationships and causality are
evaluated. In each of these domains abilities that are
inconsistent with earlier descriptions are suggested. It
is argued that revision of the time table of development
entails a rethinking of the processes that are involved.
Our understanding of these processes is likely to remain
incomplete until we have more longitudinal studies with
several independent and dependent variables.*

1. INTRODUCTION

Because of the quantity of research findings, the task of organizing
a review is a challenging one. The strategy adopted in this chapter
is to discuss some examples of studies concerning infant notions of
objects, space, and causality. The studies have been selected to
illustrate what I consider to be significant findings and, in the
case of space, to describe in more detail my own program of research. Attention will be drawn to some of the ingenious techniques
that are used to answer questions about perceptual and cognitive
abilities of infants less than two years of age. It is the aim of
this chapter to emphasize the assumptions and limitations of these
techniques, to describe the processes that may be involved in each
of the three areas, and to discuss what is known about the interdependence of the sequence of abilities that emerge in development.

Many theorists have argued that there is a marked change in representation at about 18 to 24 months. The first two years have been
characterized as non-symbolic in that infants respond directly to
stimulus objects and events rather than to internal representations
of them. Thus they are thought to have an immature conceptualization of the nature of objects, to have little productive language,
to be unable to use tools or understand the causal interactions

* This work was supported in part by funding from the Australian
Research Committee to B.E. McKenzie and to B.E. McKenzie and R.H.
Day.

between objects, and to be incapable of deferred imitation or symbolic play. In sum, they lack those features described by Piaget
(1954) as typical of the final achievements of the sensori-motor
stage.

The results of recent research challenge many of these beliefs and
lead us to question the ways in which the "under-twos" differ from
older children. A wide range of findings indicate the need for radical revision of our description of the starting points for later
development. This revision may not be just a matter of readjusting
the time table, but may require reinterpretation of the nature of
the processes that are involved. The understanding by young infants
of the nature of objects and events, of spatial relationships, and
causality are a few of the areas where this revision has begun.

2. OBJECT PERCEPTION

Recent findings concerning visual perceptual constancies in newborn
infants will be evaluated. This will be followed by a discussion of
research dealing with early notions of the nature and physical properties of objects such as their continued existence, unity and
substantiality. Finally the question of the distinction between
object perception and conception will be raised.

2.1. Perceptual constancy in the newborn ?

Evidence is beginning to accumulate to support the assertion that at
least some of the objective features of objects, their size and
shape for example, are perceived by neonatal infants. Perceptual
constancy refers to the perceived stability of object features over
changes in their representation at the sense organs. Visual size
constancy is evident when an observer perceives the apparent size of
an object as unchanged over variation in its distance from the observer. Similarly, visual shape constancy is evident when the apparent shape of an object is unchanged over variation in its slant
relative to the observer. There are, of course, degrees of perceived constancy and we refer to underconstancy or overconstancy according to whether there is under or over compensation for the proximal
retinal changes.

Whether newborn infants perceive the actual size or shape of objects
over changes in viewing distance and orientation is of importance
since it has been argued that a process of learning to correct the
proximal stimulation has to occur. For example, the projected retinal size has to be corrected in terms of distance information. If
newborn infants do not respond to proximal stimulation, that is in
terms of retinal size, the proposed mechanism of learning to correct
for distance would need to be revised.

Granrud (1988) attempted to assess the existence of visual size
constancy in two groups of infants aged from one to three days. One
group, called the constant size group, viewed three identical spheres presented one at a time at three different distances. The
other, called the variable size group, saw three different-sized
spheres at the same three distances as the first group. There were
two 20-sec trials for each sphere during which the total duration of

looking at each sphere was recorded. Granrud predicted that, if infants perceive constancy of size, there should be a greater decline in looking time over trials for the constant size group. This prediction was confirmed. It should be noted that the sizes of the retinal images projected by the spheres were the same for the two groups. The spheres were presented against an untextured background and there were no differences in information from binocular disparity, accommodation and convergence between the groups. Thus differential performance could not be attributed to any of these factors. However, the spheres were moved horizontally back and forth through the same distance to attract infants' attention. This meant that the ratio of the retinal projection of distance of movement to object size was constant at all distances for the constant size group but not for the variable size group. To control for this and other factors, a second experiment was conducted. The results of this study were less clear cut than those of the first. Although Granrud interpreted them as consistent with the conclusion of the first experiment in indicating that infants were responding to perceived constant size, it is possible that one or more of the other variables was involved. Nevertheless, the results do suggest that some rudimentary degree of perceived size constancy may be present in newborns.

Slater and Morison (1985) also argue that perceived visual constancy is an organizing feature of perception that is present from birth. Perception of the objective shape of an object despite changes in its slant relative to the observer was studied in infants whose mean age was 1 day 23 hours. Having shown discrimination of small changes in slant, Slater and Morison familiarized infants with either a square or a trapezium, changing the slant of each from trial to trial. Infants then received a paired presentation of the two shapes in a slant different from any that had been shown earlier. They showed a strong preference to look longer at the shape they had not seen before. It was therefore argued that they had abstracted the familiarized shape despite its retinal variation consequent upon the changes in slant.

The results from these two studies suggest that newborn infants do perceive the actual size and shape of objects despite changes in their distance and slant relative to the observer. This implies that the proposed mechanism of learning to correct the proximal information concerning size and shape is incorrect since infants from birth do not respond to the retinal projection of the object alone. These findings may not be all that surprising if one accepts that the retinal projection includes information concerning the layout as well as the stimulus object itself.

Regardless of the earliest age at which any of the perceptual constancies can be demonstrated, it is clear that at least some of them occur long before protracted experience in manipulating objects (see Day, 1987; Cook, 1987). What is not so clear is the mechanisms that are involved and how these may or may not change with development. Most studies so far have been concerned with whether or not a perceptual constancy exists at a particular age. The degree of perceived constancy and its variation with the well-documented improvements in sensory functioning are not yet known.

Yonas and Granrud (1985) have begun to address this question. By
means of cross-sectional studies they have shown a sequence in the
development of sensitivity to depth cues. The early detection of
kinetic information is followed by binocular cues at about 4 months,
and by pictorial depth cues such as interposition, shading, linear
perspective, and texture gradients at about 5 to 7 months. How does
the perceived constancy of object features vary with this sequence
in sensitivity ? Granrud (1986) found evidence for size constancy
in 4- to 5-month-old infants who were sensitive to binocular disparity but not in those who were insensitive. Such dependencies need
to be explored longitudinally and over a range of variables. It
will then be possible to establish for each subject that the proposed sequence obtains. Having shown that one outcome precedes another we can then explore whether the relationship is one of functional dependence or independence. Does perceived size constancy,
for instance, depend on the development of stereopsis ? One possible interpretation of the outcome of Granrud's study with 4- to 5-
month-old infants is that the development of stereopsis is necessary
for perceived constancy of size. In this regard it is of interest
to note that there is an apparent inconsistency in Granrud's later
assertion (1988) of the presence of perceived size constancy in
newborns (who certainly lack stereopsis) and its absence in older
infants who also lack stereopsis. Of course there were many differences between the two studies (see Aslin and Smith, 1988).
Nevertheless the seeming inconsistency serves to underline the
merits of testing the same subject at different ages on abilities
that are likely precursors of later ones.

Until we have multiple tests with several independent and dependent
variables our understanding of the mechanisms of change is incomplete. We need to test contrasting interpretations so that rejection
of an hypothesis does not rest on a single finding. Programs of
research that systematically investigate the relationship between
different domains are rare in infancy research. The studies of
Yonas and Granrud (1985) are a significant contribution in this
respect. The extension of such studies using a longitudinal design
has hardly begun*.

2.2. Notions of the nature and physical properties of objects

Piaget (1954) described how infants come to apprehend the permanent
existence of an object despite its occlusion by another, and how
they recognize that an object retains its physical properties from
one time to another and when it is moved from one spatial position
to another. The sequence of approximations to the mature object
concept that he delineated is well known and does not require repetition here. This account has not gone unchallenged. The amount of
research devoted to the A-not-B error alone is daunting. This error
refers to the observation that if an object is hidden at location A
and then at location B, infants tend to search at location A where
they first found the object. It is disconcerting to realize that a
satisfying comprehensive account of just this aspect of the object
concept has not yet been achieved (see Wellman, Cross and Bartsch,

* I wish to acknowledge the contribution of Professor Ray Over to
the argument presented in the latter portion of this section.

1987). There is now a body of data that does not fit easily with a
Piagetian time frame of when infants come to understand object permanence. Baillargeon (1987), for example, describes studies indicating that long before 9 months of age infants represent the existence and the physical properties of objects that are hidden from view.
Using a method that depends not on manual skills but simply on duration of looking, she examined infants' reactions to events that
would be surprising if they understood that a moving object should
stop when another object lies in its path. Having demonstrated that
infants as young as 3 months were 'surprised' by such an occurrence,
she then went on to assess whether 7-month-old infants recognize
that the moving object should stop at different points depending on
the location, dimensions, and compressibility of another object that
is in its path. On the basis of the degree of recovery of an habituated looking response she found that: "Infants expect that (a) a
sliding screen will stop sooner when an object is placed 10, as
opposed to 25-cm, behind it; (b) a rotating screen will stop sooner
when a 20-cm, as opposed to a 4-cm, object is placed behind it; and
(c) a rotating screen will stop sooner when a 15-cm incompressible,
as opposed to compressible, object is placed behind it." (p.197-
198). These findings indicate either that Piaget's time table of
development is wrong or that at least some notion of the existence
of an occluded object obtains at about 4 months and that, by 7
months, its dimensions and the substance of which it is composed are
retained during occlusion. Furthermore, these properties are not
only encoded and remembered, they are also used to reason about the
physical consequences of these features in relation to another
object.

This precocity for object permanence, representation of object characteristics, and physical reasoning makes it surprising that the
stage IV error that typically occurs around 9 months is exhibited.
Although others have used prolonged manual search or other behavioural indices of surprise such as smiling, looks of puzzlement and so
on, Baillargeon's index is one of duration of looking. To equate
longer looking at one display rather than another with surprise may
not be entirely justified. Nevertheless, the longer looking in the
one case when seemingly impossible events occur needs to be explained. Confirmation of these findings with alternative procedures
would strengthen the conclusions. In this area also longitudinal
studies with several independent and dependent variables would enhance our understanding of the functional relationships in development.

Halford (1982) defines the object concept as follows: "A person has
the object concept if they have stored information about the way an
object behaves with respect to transformations in physical space"
(p.104). He points out that it is not possible to discuss Piaget's
account of the object concept without considering at the same time
the child's understanding of space. If an object disappears it must
either have ceased to exist (a change of state) or exist somewhere
else (a change of position). Baillargeon's studies certainly have
implications for the understanding of space in so far as an object
is thought to maintain its position and physical features when hidden. They also imply that infants understand that two objects cannot occupy the one place at the same time. However they do not
address the issue of maintenance of the identity of an object over

its own spatial transformations. As Halford notes, moving an object
changes its position but not its colour or its shape. A mature
object concept takes account of the effect of movement transformations on an object's position; a change in position must be distinguished from a change in state. The difficulties that infants experience with these kinds of transformations is well attested to by
the A-not-B error of Stage IV.

It is not my intention here to review the evidence concerning the
Stage IV error. However it is appropriate to point out that many
explanations of it draw attention to the key role played by infants'
understanding of spatial transformations. Butterworth (1977) for
instance, attributes the Stage IV error to conflict between two ways
of defining object position: An "egocentric" way in terms of position relative to oneself, and an "allocentric" way in terms of position relative to an environmental cue. Infants at Stage IV make
errors because they do not coordinate the egocentric and allocentric
codes. They do not update the egocentric code to bring it into line
with the allocentric one. In Section 3.1 I shall show that, at
least with respect to a visual index, infants at this stage are not
restricted to a definition of position relative to themselves that
is fixed or unchanging over their own movements. That is, they are
able to revise the spatial relationship of a fixed stationary object
relative to themselves. Yet in manual search they reach to position
A even though they have seen the object being moved to position B.

There are many differences between studies in these two areas.
First, there is the difference in response index, one manual, the
other visual. Second, in one instance the object is moved and the
infant is stationary, and in the other the reverse is the case,
i.e., the infant is moved and the object is stationary. Third, there are differences in training procedure (see Section 3.1). It is
not possible as yet to specify the reason for this apparent discre-
pancy in assessment of spatial competence in the two domains. The
work of Diamond and her colleagues (e.g. Diamond and Goldman-Rakic,
1985) is promising in this regard. On the basis of comparative studies with human infants and rhesus monkeys she suggests that maturation of the prefrontal cortex underlies the behavioural changes that
occur in reaching for hidden objects.

2.3. Perception or conception of objects ?

It is not clear whether we should speak about object perception or
conception in these studies of the object concept. For Piaget,
cognitive development involves the ability to go beyond what is perceptually given and to resist what he calls perceptual seduction.
With his emphasis on symbolic representation and the internally stored information relating to a group of spatial transformations, it
seems that the term object concept is no accident.

Aslin and Smith (1988) postulate a system of representations whose
most elementary level is that of perception. Like Gibson (1979),
they argue that infants from the beginning perceive distal stimulation (relating to objects and events in the real world) rather than
proximal stimulation (stimulation at the receptor level) and that
the meanings of objects and events are perceived immediately. Perceptual representation refers to transformation over time of proxi-

mal stimulation into a neural code. This perceptual representation
depends on sensory primitives but can be influenced by cognition.
In talking about the debate between direct perception theorists and
constructivists Aslin and Smith comment that "this debate is largely
semantic and likely to be essentially unresolvable" (p.443).

Spelke (1987) on the other hand, argues that objects are conceived,
not perceived. Infants apprehend objects by analysing properties of
the perceived surface layout. This she argues is a cognitive act.
Infants are endowed with an object concept that goes beyond that
which is perceptually available. They conceive of objects as cohesive, bounded, substantial and spatio-temporally continuous. This
view is in marked contrast to that of Piaget. Infants do not have
to construct their conception of objects; rather they are born with
the understanding that objects "move as cohesive and bounded bodies
on continuous paths through unoccupied space" (Spelke, 1987 p.227).
Spelke's theory is complex and in opposition to many that are well
established. Whether it provides us with guidelines for a closer
understanding of perceptual and cognitive development in infancy is
not yet resolved.

3. THE PERCEPTION OF SPACE

As mobile creatures in a world of stable and moveable objects we
have continually to face the problem of determining where things
are. Adults have a variety of strategies for coping with such problems. They may, for instance, remember that a target has a specific spatial relationship to one or more other objects. Alternatively the target may be located within a more general frame of
reference, such as a system of geographical coordinates. If there
are no available visual cues, however, they are forced to rely on
proprioceptive stimulation arising from their own spatial displacement. In this case the original spatial relationship between the
target and themselves has to be reinterpreted in accordance with
their subsequent displacements.

In a series of studies we have been concerned with the development
of such strategies in infants, making use of a method first described by Acredolo (1978). This involves training infants to expect an
event to happen at one particular place and then testing whether
they can find that same place from a physically different starting
point. It is of interest to examine the effects of visual landmarks, of more general frames of reference such as the shape of the
room, and of different kinds of subject movements.

3.1. Localization of an event after rotational shifts

Keating, McKenzie and Day (1986) tested the ability of 8-month-old
infants to find the site of an event in a square and a round room
both with and without a distinctive visual landmark at the event
site. The procedure differed from that used earlier by Acredolo
(1978) in several respects. Infants were first trained to expect
the event --an experimenter playing peek-a-boo-- from two directions
of facing before being rotated into another. We argued that training from facing directions on opposite sides of the event site was
necessary to distinguish response learning from place learning. In

Acredolo's study infants had been reinforced after only right (or
left) head turns. It was likely that generalization of this response could occur after rotation. If infants had received reinforcement for both kinds of turns before they were rotated on the test
trial they should not have been biased to turn in either direction.
The second difference from Acredolo's procedure was that only rotational shifts were used. In her original study the test shift involved both rotation of the infant about the vertical body axis and
translation from one point in space to another. Landau and Spelke
(in press) have pointed out that difficulty of spatial orientation
may vary according to type of displacement. We therefore chose to
study each kind of shift separately before studying more complex
combinations.

In our study localization was indicated by where infants looked
first after they had been turned to the new orientation, and how
long they looked at particular places in a 5-sec period after their
first change in direction of looking. If infants remembered the
place where the event had occurred earlier, we predicted that they
would look there first and look more frequently and persistently at
it than at other places. The results showed that they could find
this place when they were tested in the square room both when the
visual landmark was present and when it was not. However in the
round room they only succeeded when the landmark was available.
These outcomes seemed to suggest that localization at this age was
dependent on visual support. This could be in the form of information provided by the room frame --its corners and parallel walls--
or a distinctive visual cue at the site itself. In the round featureless room there was little possibility of encoding the spatial
relationship between the site and other visual cues. Infants would
therefore have had to attend to information concerning the direction
and extent of their reorientation. Our results implied that they
were able to use strategies based on visual information but were not
yet able to use strategies based on proprioception. Although this
conclusion is in accord with that of other studies (Acredolo and
Evans, 1980; Bremner, 1978; Cornell and Heth, 1979; Rieser, 1979;
Rieser and Heiman, 1982), later work suggests that this conclusion
may be incorrect.

The purpose of the procedure used by Keating et al. (1986) was to
avoid the difficulties of interpretation associated with earlier
methods in which only one response was reinforced. We sought to
discourage the acquisition of a response strategy of turning in one
particular direction. However in the situation of reduced visual
cues --the round featureless room-- it seemed possible that infants
may still have acquired a response strategy, albeit a more complex
one than that which we had sought to avoid. This propensity to use
a non spatial strategy was enhanced in the absence of visual support; it was hardly evident in the square room and in the round room
with the landmark.

To examine this question Tyler and McKenzie (in preparation) developed a new procedure that would further discourage response learning.
We tested 8-month-old infants in the round room with and without a
landmark at the event site. Our aim was to compare localization
after two types of training. The first was the procedure already
described (Keating et al., 1986) in which reinforcement was contin-

Figure 1. A schematic outline of the demonstration
trials in expectancy training.

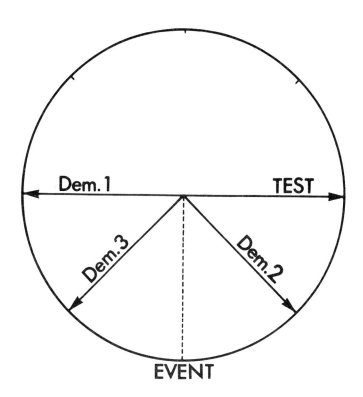

gent on the infant's anticipatory response and a criterion of learning was imposed. We called this instrumental training. The second, called expectancy training, was designed as before to inform
the infant that an event would occur in the one fixed place, but
reinforcement was independent of any response by the infant. The
experimenter appeared at the selected site to play peek-a-boo
immediately after the signal stimulus (a flashing light), without
waiting for any response by the infant. Both procedures involved
exposure to the event occurrence from multiple facing directions.
In expectancy training there was no learning criterion. There were
six "demonstration" trials, two from each of three facing directions. An instance of one such sequence is given in Figure 1.

The results were very clear. The number of infants looking first at
the event site is shown in Table 1. Markedly fewer infants looked
first to the site in the instrumental training - no landmark condition. The data relating to persistence of looking at the site are
given in Table 2.

Table 1. The Number of Infants Looking First at the Event Site
          (n=12)

	Expectancy Training	Instrumental Training
Landmark	11	8
No Landmark	11	2

Table 2. The Mean Duration of Looking at the Event Site
          (Maximum = 5 sec)

	Expectancy Training	Instrumental Training
Landmark	2.69	2.53
No Landmark	2.84	0.60

Infants in the instrumental training - no landmark group looked at
the site for far less time than did those in any of the other conditions. Thus it is clear that localization after instrumental
training was dependent on visual support. This finding reproduces
the outcome of the earlier study for these conditions (Keating et
al., 1986). The novel finding is that there was no such dependency
after expectancy training. That is to say after expectancy but not
after instrumental training infants in the no landmark group were
successful.

In further studies with the expectancy procedure we tested groups of
12 4- and 6-month-olds in the no landmark condition. Seven of the
older and two of the younger group looked first at the event site.

In summary, from at least 8 months of age infants detect several
sources of information that can be used to locate a target after rotational shifts. These include visual cues such as a distinctive
stimulus at the target site. Subsidiary observations showed that it
was not the landmark by itself that controlled looking behaviour.
Without association with the site of the experimenter's appearance,
it elicited few looks, was rarely looked at first, and was looked at
overall for only brief periods. It is therefore its spatial relationship with the site that attracts attention. These results are
in accord with the many studies examining the role of landmarks in
spatial orientation (Acredolo, 1978, 1985, 1987; Acredolo and Evans,
1980; Bremner, 1978, 1982; Cornell and Heth, 1979; McKenzie, 1987;
Meuwissen and McKenzie, 1987; Rieser, 1979). Visual cues are also
provided by features of the room that are not coincident with the
target (Keating et al., 1986).

The most surprising result of these studies is the finding concerning a successful updating strategy based on proprioception. In order to determine target location relative to a new orientation in a visually-impoverished setting, infants must have encoded the original egocentric relationship of the target and the direction and extent of their subsequent rotation. Our results show that this was accomplished by almost all of the 8-month olds and over half of the 6-month olds. This is considerably earlier than has been suggested by others. Rieser and Heiman (1982), for instance, found that such a strategy did not emerge until well into the second year. Our studies suggest that instrumental training in an impoverished visual setting emphasizes response learning. Exposure to the target from multiple facing directions without response-contingent reinforcement however leads readily to an encoding of place. The dependence of instrumental training on visual support and the independence of expectancy training from such support warrants further investigation. In addition, it might be expected that the resolution of visual space would be far better than the resolution of proprioceptive space. If the two sources were placed in conflict, the more informative source could well have the greatest influence on perceptual outcome.

3.2. Localization of an event after translational shifts

The egocentric spatial relationship of a target may be changed in many different ways. Studies of the effect of change in direction of facing without change in position have already been discussed in the preceding section. Here I will discuss the effect of change brought about by moving from one position to another without changing the direction of facing i.e., translational shifts, and the effects of various combinations of shifts during training and testing. McKenzie, Day, Colussa and Connell (1988), using the expectancy training procedure described earlier, studied the efficiency of visual localization of an event by 8-month-old infants when the type of shift during training and testing was the same and when it was different. In these studies testing took place in a rectangular room and the event always occurred in the one place marked by a distinctive visual stimulus. Infants saw the event occur from two vantage points before being shifted to a third for testing. There were only four training trials preceding the test shift, two from each vantage point. In the first study, the effect of rotational and translational shifts was compared. The same kind of shift, either rotational or translational, occurred in training and testing. There was little difference in where infants looked after reorientation but greater persistence in looking at the site after a change in direction of facing than after a change in position. In the second study we asked whether localization would occur independently of the similarity of the type of shift during training and testing. Half the infants received rotational shifts in training followed by a translational shift to the test position, and the other half received translational shifts in training followed by a rotational shift. There was no difference in outcome between the two training-test sequences. In both, infants located the event site after reorientation. It was concluded that a mental representation of the space and the event had been formed and used as the basis of localization.

Devine (1987) argued that this conclusion may not be justified when
the landmark is coincident with the event site. In the case of
rotational shifts the spatial relationship between the landmark and
the site is not noticeably changed by subject orientation. From
different facing directions the two remain coincident. A more
stringent test of using the landmark as a reference for the site
would be provided by translational shifts when the arrangement ensures that, from the subject's test position, the landmark is no longer in alignment with the event site but with an alternative one.
If localization occurs in this instance it would serve as stronger
evidence that infants have formed a mental representation of the
space and are able to revise the landmark-target relationship in
terms of their own movement. Devine found that 8-month-old infants
looked longer at the event site than at the alternative site on test
trials. This finding lends support to the suggestion that at least
by 8 months of age infants are able to form a mental representation
of space that includes object-object relationships as well as self-
object relationships.

3.3. Localization on the basis of auditory and visual information

Most research so far has been concerned with the strategies that infants use to encode space on the basis of visual information. There
is very little research addressing this same problem using information from other sensory modalities. In a recent program of research
Garino (1988) compared localization of a target on the basis of
auditory and visual information. Using an adaptation of the 8-arm
radial maze that has been commonly employed in studies of spatial
memory in rats (Olton and Collinson, 1979), he showed superior performance in both two- and three-year olds when they were provided
with visual as compared with auditory information concerning the
whereabouts of their mother. Children were placed in the centre of
the maze and either saw or heard where the mother was. The child
was rotated into one of several facing directions before being released to find the mother who was out of view in one of the arms of
the maze. Their search was more efficient after they had seen
rather than heard where she was located. Further studies attempted
to establish the basis for this differential performance, whether in
terms of the precision of registering the initial location of the
mother, in memory of where she was, or in the intersensory processing involved in testing in the light and in the dark. Garino concluded that the inferior performance for auditory relative to visual
targets was a result of differences in encoding and memory of the
location of the targets, and in the integration of this information
with that arising from rotation. The relative efficiency of spatial
orientation of auditory and visual sources in younger infants has
not been studied. It is an area of some significance since it is
only by such investigations that we can determine whether similar
processes are involved in the different sensory modalities. These
findings have obvious implications for the development of programs
for children with sensory handicap.

3.4. Conclusions

In considering the development of spatial orientation Acredolo
(1978) concluded that there was a gradual change in infancy from a
subjective basis of reference (based on an unmodified egocentric

relationship) to an objective one. Although this conclusion was supported by others, Acredolo's was the only longitudinal study. It now appears that this conclusion should be revised in several ways.

First, perception of the constancy of an object's position despite changes in the egocentric spatial relationship between it and the observer can be demonstrated early in life. Kellman, Gleitman and Spelke (1987) found that 16-week-old infants are capable of position constancy since they clearly distinguished optical displacements produced by motion of the self from those produced by moving objects even when the proximal retinal stimulation was the same. The findings of McKenzie, Ihsen and Day (1984) and Rieser (1979) also show that at six months infants are able to orient objectively and not solely in terms of an assumed unchanging relationship between object and observer. Because of the age of infants in these studies it is clear that self produced locomotion cannot have been responsible.

Second, a mental representation of space that includes the self, the target, and other visual objects or features is constructed and used to determine where things are by at least eight months of age (Devine, 1987; Keating et al., 1986; McKenzie et al., 1988). Infants are capable of more than a specific "cue-directed" search. They can learn to use this cue as a reference for a specific place even when, from their point of view, the two appear not to be coincident (Devine, 1987).

Third, an updating strategy based on stimulation associated with body movement is available from at least eight months and probably even earlier (Tyler and McKenzie, in preparation).

Finally, the dependence of findings on the method used to assess spatial ability is noteworthy. This observation is not new in research on spatial perception (see Liben, 1981). The lessons associated with the debate on place versus response learning in the rat (Restle, 1957) were not readily transferred to research with infants perhaps because we have underestimated the active exploratory nature of infants' perceptual activities. The major difference between outcomes based on instrumental and expectancy training procedures may be a consequence of the greater provision in the latter of opportunities for infants to exercise their natural exploratory responses.

4. CAUSALITY

How a mature understanding of causal relationships arises has long been a topic of philosophical debate. Several types of causal relationships may be distinguished. The first concerns mechanical interaction of objects. The collision events studied by Michotte (1963) are instances of this type as, for example, when one billiard ball is made to collide with another. Michotte termed this the launching effect. He demonstrated that adult observers report a compelling impression of a causal interaction of the two objects even when they know that the effect is created by artifice. A systematic series of studies on this effect has been carried out by Leslie (1982, 1984a, 1984b, 1986) and a discussion of his findings and their interpretation will constitute the major portion of this

section. The others types of causal relationships will not be considered here. These involve the use of tools, the perception of
others as agents, and self-controlled events. These types are
discussed in Gibson and Spelke (1983) and in Golinkoff, Uzgiris,
Gibson, Harding, Carlson, Sexton and Watson (1984).

4.1. Mechanical interaction of objects

The possibility that infants, like adults, might perceive a launching effect has recently been explored (Leslie and Keeble, 1987).
Six-month-old infants saw a film of an object colliding with another
in one of two different ways. For the launching group, the event
consisted of a red brick moving toward a green brick, making contact
with it, and the green brick being immediately displaced or launched
while the red brick remained stationary. For the delayed group, the
same sequence was shown but a brief delay was imposed when the two
bricks made contact. Only the former sequence is perceived as a
causal interaction by adults. Leslie and Keeble reasoned that if
infants also perceive a causal interaction, those in the launching
group should be more surprised by a reversal of the sequence (produced by reversing the cinematic record) than those in the delayed
group. This is because there would be a perceived change in the
causal agent (red brick launching green brick versus green brick
launching red brick) in the former but not in the latter. Note that
there is a similar change in the order of movement of the bricks and
in the direction of movement in the two conditions. Greater recovery of an habituated looking response was therefore predicted for
the launching group. The results were consistent with this prediction.

Leslie and Keeble suggest that the same mechanism that produces the
illusion of launching in Michotte's studies operates in 6-month-old
infants. This does not imply that infants understand causality in
the same way as adults. The authors posit that the low level visual
mechanism that feeds input to higher levels operates early in life
and is one of the initial descriptions "produced by perception and
inherited by thought" (1987, p.286).

The question arises as to why the difference in looking time after
reversal should be attributed to a perception of causal interaction
between two objects. In my understanding of this work, the reason
for this attribution is by analogy with what adults report. The
logic of the argument is as follows. When two objects are seen to
collide and one of them moves off, adults perceive a causal sequence. A reversal of the portrayed event would also be perceived as a
causal sequence but one in which the causal agency is altered. The
results of the study with infants are consistent with an hypothesis
that they perceive the events in the same way as do adults. It
would be elegant if this were so. But are there other feasible
interpretations of these data ? Is it not equally possible that infants perceive a red figure hitting (perhaps punching or threate-
ning) a green figure and then a green figure hitting a red figure ?
A reversal in who is the aggressor may be more interesting than a
reversal in a more peaceful interchange between two actors. Of
course this account is not very plausible but it illustrates the
difficulty of interpreting a difference in duration of looking. It
is challenging to devise other ways to assess the preverbal infant's

perception of the mechanical interaction of objects. Until this is done, the interpretation that has so far been offered is one of several possibilities.

On the basis of his studies using an habituation-recovery procedure, Leslie (1986) hypothesizes that there is a perceptual module that has as its input representations as coded by the visual system. These representations of motion, amplitude, phase, and orientation are then transformed into a more abstract representation, such as a causal or non-causal sequence. The perceptual module is impenetrable by knowledge. Leslie's proposals concerning modularity are in the Fodor (1984) tradition (for an opposing view, see Massaro, 1987).

Over a series of studies with duration of looking as the dependent variable, the pattern of looking behaviour is thought by Leslie to show the characteristics of infants' representation of the events they have seen. It is important to specify the assumptions involved. There is an eye-mind assumption that the eye remains fixed on the stimulus for as long as that stimulus is being processed. A novel stimulus is looked at longer than a familiar one because it requires more processing. There is also the assumption that there is a direct relationship between duration of looking and the degree of perceived contrast between stimuli. The greater the contrast the longer the looking. If a particular change leads to longer fixation than another it therefore involved more processing. It is also assumed that only information from the immediate fixation is being analysed. These assumptions are involved in all studies that use the habituation-recovery method. Duration of looking carries a heavy interpretative burden in studies of this kind. A series of convergent operations with different methods and other variables is urgently required to distinguish one possible interpretation from another.

5. CONCLUSIONS

In this chapter some thought provoking studies on infants' notions of objects, space, and causality have been reviewed. These studies illustrate the advances that have been made. The field of infancy research is clearly active, dynamic and exciting. The ways now available for assessing the abilities of subjects who are verbally uncommunicative and often uncooperative constitute an impressive armoury. The temptation to demonstrate unexpected functioning at earlier and earlier ages is being replaced with a greater concern with the nature and limitations of that functioning.

Nevertheless there is a strong tendency in many programs of research to rely exclusively on the habituation-recovery paradigm (for examples see the special issue of *Journal of Experimental Psychology: Human Perception and Performance, 1987, 13,* No.4, and for a similar critical comment on reliance on this method see Rovee-Collier, 1988). The need for convergent operations with several methods applied to the same problem is obvious. Equally obvious is our inability to specify what are the necessary and sufficient conditions for developmental changes in cognition and perception. As we have already noted, longitudinal studies with the same infant tested repea-

tedly over time on several related abilities are rare but necessary
for determining the sequential dependencies that may exist in
development.

With the revision of the time table of infant abilities has come increasing attention to not only the output of behaviour but to information about the mechanisms and processing that lead to that output.
We have the beginnings of descriptions of the origins of object,
spatial, and causal concepts in infancy. The challenge is to extend
these descriptions so that we may specify how inherent characteristics of human thought interact with those that are constructed by
an active, exploratory, and inquiring mind.

REFERENCES

Acredolo, L.P. (1978). Development of spatial orientation in
    infancy. *Developmental Psychology*, *14*, 224-234.
Acredolo, L.P. (1985). Coordinating perspectives on infant spatial
    orientation. In: R. Cohen (Ed.), *The development of spatial
    cognition*. New York: Lawrence Erlbaum.
Acredolo, L.P. (1987). Early development of spatial orientation in
    humans. In: P. Ellen & C. Thinus Blanc (Eds.), *Cognitive
    processes and spatial orientation in animal and man*. Dordrecht,
    Holland: Martinus Nijhoff.
Acredolo, L.P., & Evans, D. (1980). Developmental changes in the
    effects of landmarks on infant spatial behaviour. *Developmental
    Psychology*, *16*, 312-318.
Aslin, R.N., & Smith, L.B. (1988). Perceptual development. *Annual
    Review of Psychology*, *39*, 435-473.
Baillargeon, R. (1987). Young infants' reasoning about the physical
    and spatial properties of a hidden object. *Cognitive Development*,
    2, 179-200.
Bremner, J.G. (1978). Egocentric versus allocentric spatial coding
    in 9 month old infants: Factors influencing the choice of code.
    Developmental Psychology, *14*, 346-355.
Bremner, J.G. (1982). Object localization in infancy. In:
    M. Potegal (Ed.), *Spatial abilities: Developmental and
    physiological foundations*. New York: Academic Press.
Cook, M. (1987). The origins of form perception. In:
    B.E. McKenzie & R.H. Day (Eds.), *Perceptual development in early
    infancy: Problems and issues*. Hillsdale, New Jersey: Lawrence
    Erlbaum Associates, pp.93-123.
Cornell, E.H., & Heth, C.D. (1979). Response versus place learning
    by human infants. *Journal of Experimental Psychology: Human
    Learning and Memory*, *5*, 188-196.
Day, R.H. (1987). Visual size constancy in infancy. In:
    B.E. McKenzie & R.H. Day (Eds.), *Perceptual development in early
    infancy: Problems and issues*. Hillsdale, New Jersey: Lawrence
    Erlbaum Associates, pp.67-91.
Devine, C. (1987). Infant spatial orientation: The ability to
    relocate an event following lateral translation to a new
    position. Unpublished honours thesis, Australian National
    University.
Diamond, A., & Goldman-Rakic, P.S. (1985). Evidence that
    maturation of the frontal cortex underlies behavioral changes
    during the first year of life: 1. The AB task. 2. Object

retrieval. *Society for Research in Child Development Abstracts*, 5, 85.
Fodor, J.A. (1984). *The modularity of mind*. Cambridge, Massachusetts: MIT Press.
Garino, E. (1988). A comparison of auditory and visual localization in two- and three-year old children. Unpublished PhD thesis, La Trobe University.
Gibson, J.J. (1979). *The ecological approach to visual perception*. Boston: Houghton Mifflin.
Gibson, E., & Spelke, E.S. (1983). The development of perception. In: J.H. Flavell & E.M. Markman (Eds.), *Handbook of child psychology, Vol. III*. New York: Wiley, pp.1-76.
Golinkoff, R., Uzgiris, I.C., Gibson, E.J., Harding, C.G., Carlson, V., Sexton, M.E., & Watson, J.S. (1984). The development of causality in infancy: A symposium. In: L.P. Lipsitt & C. Rovee-Collier (Eds.), *Advances in Infancy Research, Vol. 3*. Norwood, New Jersey: Ablex, pp.127-161.
Granrud, C.E. (1986). Binocular vision and spatial perception in 4- and 5-month-old infants. *Journal of Experimental Psychology: Human Perception and Performance, 12*, 36-49.
Granrud, C.E. (1988). Perceptual constancy in newborn infants. Paper presented at the XXIV International Congress of Psychology, Sydney, Australia, August 28 - September 2.
Keating, M.B., McKenzie, B.E., & Day, R.H. (1986). Spatial localization in infancy: Position constancy in a square and circular room with and without a landmark. *Child Development, 57*, 115-124.
Kellman, P.J., Gleitman, H., & Spelke, E.S. (1987). Object and observer motion in the perception of objects by infants. *Journal of Experimental Psychology: Human Perception and Performance, 13*, 586-593.
Landau, B., & Spelke, E.S. (in press). Geometric complexity and object search in infancy. *Developmental Psychology*.
Leslie, A. (1982). The perception of causality in infants. *Perception, 11*, 173-186.
Leslie, A. (1984a). Infant perception of a manual pick-up event. *British Journal of Developmental Psychology, 2*, 19-32.
Leslie, A. (1984b). Spatiotemporal continuity and the perception of causality in infants. *Perception, 13*, 287-305.
Leslie, A.M. (1986). Getting development off the ground: Modularity and the infant's perception of causality. In: P. van Geert (Ed.), *Theory building in development*. Amsterdam: Elsevier North-Holland, pp.405-437.
Leslie, A.M., & Keeble, S. (1987). Do six-month-old infants perceive causality ? *Cognition, 25*, 265-288.
Liben, L.S. (1981). Spatial representation and behaviour: Multiple perspectives. In: L.S. Liben, A.H. Patterson & N. Newcombe (Eds.), *Spatial representation and behaviour across the life span: Theory and application*. New York: Academic Press, pp.3-32.
Massaro, D.W. (1987). *Speech perception by ear and eye: A paradigm for psychological inquiry*. Hillsdale, New Jersey: Lawrence Erlbaum Associates.
McKenzie, B.E. (1987). The development of spatial orientation in human infancy: What changes ? In: B.E. McKenzie & R.H. Day (Eds.), *Perceptual development in early infancy: Problems and issues*. Hillsdale, New Jersey: Lawrence Erlbaum

Associates, pp.125-141.
McKenzie, B.E., Day, R.H., & Ihsen, E. (1984). Localization of events in space: Young infants are not always egocentric. *British Journal of Developmental Psychology, 2,* 1-9.
McKenzie, B.E., Day, R.H., Colussa, S., & Connell, S. (1988). Spatial localization by infants after rotational and translational shifts. *Australian Journal of Psychology, 40,* 165-178.
Meuwissen, I., & McKenzie, B.E. (1987). Localization of an event by young infants: The effects of visual and body movement information. *British Journal of Developmental Psychology, 5,* 1-8.
Olton, D.S., & Collinson, C. (1977). Spatial memory and radial arm performance of rats. *Learning and Motivation, 8,* 289-314.
Piaget, J. (1954). *The construction of reality in the child.* New York: Basic Books.
Restle, F. (1957). Discrimination of cues in mazes: A resolution of the "Place-vs-Response" question. *Psychological Review, 64,* 217-228.
Rieser, J.J. (1979). Spatial orientation of six-month-old infants. *Child Development, 50,* 1078-1087.
Rieser, J.J., & Heiman, M.L. (1982). Spatial self-reference systems and shortest-route behavior in toddlers. *Child Development, 53,* 524-533.
Rovee-Collier, C. (1987). Learning and memory in infancy. In: J.D. Osofsky (Ed.), *Handbook of infant development. 2nd edition.* New York: Wiley, pp.98-148.
Slater, A., & Morison, V. (1985). Shape constancy and slant perception at birth. *Perception, 14,* 337-344.
Spelke, E.S. (1987). Where perceiving ends and thinking begins: The apprehension of objects in infancy. In: A. Yonas (Ed.), *Minnesota Symposia on Child Psychology, Vol. 20.* Hillsdale: Lawrence Erlbaum Associates.
Tyler, D., & McKenzie, B.E. (in preparation). The development of spatial updating in infants aged from 4 to 8 months.
Yonas, A., & Granrud, C.E. (1985). The development of sensitivity to kinetic, binocular, and pictorial depth information in human infants. In: D. Ingle, D. Lee & M. Jeannerod (Eds.), *Brain mechanisms and spatial vision.* Dordrecht, Netherlands: Martinus Nijoff, pp.113-145.

DEVELOPMENTAL PSYCHOLOGY
Cognitive, Perceptuo-Motor, and Neuropsychological Perspectives
C-A. Hauert (Editor)
© Elsevier Science Publishers B.V. (North-Holland), 1990

EARLY PERCEPTUO-MOTOR DEVELOPMENT:
POSTURE AND LOCOMOTION

François JOUEN and Jean-Claude LEPECQ

Laboratoire de Psycho-biologie de l'Enfant
EPHE/CNRS
Paris, France

*After a brief review of the neuronal organization involved
in postural control, this chapter looks at the neonatal
postural repertoire and its development during the first
two years of life. Then classical maturationist approaches are challenged by recent research on the effects of
biomechanical constraints and intersensory integration on
posturo-locomotor development. Finally, a wider framework
than a purely maturationist one is proposed.*

1. INTRODUCTION

The early development of posture and locomotor control systems has
interested not only developmental psychologists but also researchers
from other domains. However, until recently, this field has been
dominated by an essentially maturationist approach, and has not extended much beyond an accurate description of observed postural
behavior and accounting for all aspects of postural and locomotor
development simply in terms of the general maturation of the central
nervous system. As will be discussed, recent research on infants'
exteroceptive sensory systems, particularly vision, has revealed a
complexity overlooked by the maturationist point of view. Thus, it
is necessary to reconsider early posturo-locomotor development in a
wider framework, integrating all the different inputs involved from
proprio- to exproprioceptive signals.

2. THE POSTURAL CONTROL SYSTEM

Posture is classically defined as the positions adopted by different
parts of the body or by the body as a whole. In each posture, the
body holds a definite position in which each part has a specific relationship with the others. Maintaining a stable overall posture
requires muscle tone in all the segments of the body. This muscle
tone is regulated by various structures and nervous system pathways
(Roberts, 1967; Gribenski and Caston, 1973).

2.1. Muscle tone regulation

One of the basic mechanisms involved in the regulation of muscle

tone consists of the *myotatic reflex* (Paillard, 1963). Muscle
stretch (mainly by gravity) induces this reflex by stimulating the
receptors in the muscles, *spindles and Golgi bodies*. This stimulation activates the alpha motor neurons located in the spinal cord
and provokes a tonic muscle contraction against gravity. The Golgi
bodies have the opposite effect; an inhibitory interneuron decreases
alpha motor neuron activity and hence, muscle contraction. These
motor neurons are also inhibited by *Renshaw cells* which receive direct innervation from the alpha motor neurons. Supplementary control of muscle tone is achieved by the *reciprocal inhibitory* innervation between the motor meurons of an agonist and an antagonist
muscle. This regulatory mechanism seems to have the function of
preventing a muscle contraction from being too abrupt or non-
adaptive during a movement or a change of posture.

Gamma activity constitutes another important factor, originating at
the medullary gamma motor neurons which innervate muscle fibers.
This activity in fibers is permanent and muscle tone can be maintained by gamma activity alone (Hermann and Cier, 1975). Muscle tone
regulation is also influenced by signals from various other systems.
Proprioceptive joint receptors are involved, activated by changes in
joint positions which are mediated by the gamma motor neurons. The
vestibular system also sends impulses down the vestibulo-spinal
tracts to end at the motor neurons of the cervical cord, thereby
assisting the local myotatic reflex and reinforcing the tonus of the
extensor muscles of the head, neck, and limbs. This produces an
extra force to support the body against gravity and to maintain
posture. *Exteroceptive information* is the final factor involved in
the regulation of muscle tone. For example, a *support reflex* is
triggered by plantar receptor stimulation from the pressure of body
weight, and this increases extensor muscle tone in the leg and
thigh. As will be discussed visual signals modify muscle tone to
achieve postures involved in picking up information from the
environment.

2.2. Neuronal pathways and structures

The purpose of this section is to briefly summarize the different
parts of the central nervous system (CNS) involved in the control of
muscle tone. As described above, the spinal cord is essential in
the regulation of muscle activity.

The *vestibular nuclei* have an important role in the maintenance of
tone and postural control through the vestibulo-spinal tracts and
the central connections with the reticular formation, basal ganglia,
and temporal cortex. Integration of vestibular and motor responses
seems to occur in the *red nucleus* which exerts an inhibitory action
on muscle tone (Eviatar and Eviatar, 1978).

The *reticular formation* has a complex effect on muscle tone because
of the presence of two different --and antagonistic-- pathways: The
inhibitory descending and the facilitatory descending reticular
tracts. The signals originating from these two pathways are similar, with impulses being sent to the cranial and medullary motor
neurons. However, their afferent pathways are different. While the
facilitatory tract is connected to the whole brain, the inhibitory
system receives inputs originating essentially from the cerebellum

and cortical areas.

The anatomical origin of the fibers innervating the motor cortex indicates that the activity of cortical neurons depends to a large extent on impulses from the *cerebellum and basal ganglia* which reach the cortex via the thalamus. Axons of neurons from the cerebellum and basal ganglia do not have direct access to the spinal cord and their inputs must be relayed via either cortical pathways or the brain stem (Evarts, 1975). In fact, these structures receive information from the whole brain, and then seem to process this information and send a new signal back to the cortex. Rather than being considered a lower level of postural control (i.e., close to the spinal motor neurons) which corrects motor cortex discharge, both cerebellum and basal ganglia are now seen as structures which send commands to the cortex. From there, signals pass down to the spinal cord via an action on brain stem neurons involved in the control of muscle tone.

In primates and humans, different zones of the cerebral cortex are involved in motor and postural control. Area 4 (primary motor cortex) generates the *efferent pyramidal tract* which consists of two separate pathways, cortico-spinal and cortico-nuclear. This tract directly drives the brain stem and spinal motor neurons. Its function is essential in generating accurate motor control. The more sophisticated *extra-pyramidal* tract originates from various cortical zones: Frontal motor area 6, parietal zones 5 and 7, and temporal area 21. This pathway involves many structures along the CNS and is mainly concerned with the control of automatic and semi-voluntary movements of the whole body. To conclude, it is important to note that both pyramidal and extra-pyramidal tracts are involved in a postural control system which depends on their reciprocal coordination.

3. THE DEVELOPMENT OF THE POSTURAL CONTROL SYSTEM

The development of postural control is generally described in terms of spinal reflex modifications, the development of primitive reflexes, and the maturation of postural reactions.

3.1. The development of spinal reflex activity

Changes in the excitability of the monosynaptic pathway in normal development have been reported and may be correlated with the acquisition of motor skills (Bawa, 1981; Forssberg and Nashner, 1981). In an electromyographic study of awake newborns, Mortier and Prechtl (1971) found no evidence of *reciprocal activity* in flexor and extensor muscles of the limbs during spontaneous body movements. They did note an important synergistic activity between the antagonist muscles studied. Hopkins and Prechtl (1984) present data that suggest this synergistic activity persists until 6 weeks of age.

Myklebust, Gottlieb and Agarwal (1986) have studied stretch reflexes in the normal infant by an EMG measure of the T-reflex (Achilles tendon stimulation). In adults, the normal stretch reflex is produced by an activation of soleus motor neurons through monosynaptic pathways (Burke, Gandevia and McKeon, 1984). This activation is ac-

companied by an inhibition of the antagonist muscle (reciprocal inhibition in tibialis anterior) through a disynaptic path.
T-reflexes are a measure of the *sum of alpha and gamma activities*.
In the neonate, tapping the Achilles tendon consistently evokes
simultaneous EMG burst in the soleus and tibialis anterior. This
stimulation induces *more activity from the antagonist* muscle than
from the stretched muscle. These results suggest that *excitatory
connections* from primary afferent neurons to both agonist and
antagonist motor neuron pools exist.

The H-reflex (Hoffmann reflex), by which one can measure the activity of alpha motor neurons only, has been studied in normal infants
to evaluate the excitability of the monosynaptic reflex pathways
(Thomas and Lambert, 1960; Mayer and Mosser, 1969, 1973; Veccherini-
Blineau and Guihennec, 1981). In spite of slight differences in the
stability, amplitude, and latency of this reflex, it is similar in
newborn and adults. Antonova and Vakhrameeva (1973) have been able
to record an H-reflex in newborn infants during vestibular stimulation. Muscle responses were recorded by EMG with the following results: 1) The H-reflex is less stable in the newborn than in the
adult; 2) on the first day of life, only inhibitory vestibulo-spinal
influences on the monosynaptic reflex can be recorded; 3) by the second day, facilitatory as well inhibitory vestibulo-spinal influences are seen.

To summarize, changes in spinal reflex activity during early childhood have been attributed to differences in the myelination of descending pathways (Mayer and Mosser, 1973) and alterations in the level of supraspinal inhibition (Veccherini-Blineau and Guihennec,
1981). Myklebust et al. (1986) suggest an interesting hypothesis of
reciprocal excitation: A functional and reciprocal excitatory spinal-cord pathway may exist at birth which is eliminated during development, leaving only disynaptic reciprocal inhibition functional.
This hypothesis could explain the observations reported by Gatev
(1972) and Thelen (1985) who have shown that, in infants between
birth and 2 months of age, movements usually begin *without the antagonist inhibition* that appears during the second month of life.

3.2. The development of primitive reflexes

As stressed by many developmentalists, the repartition of muscle tone during the first 3 months of life can be characterized by a general hypertonicity of flexor muscles and a general weakness of axial
tone (Saint-Anne Dargassies, 1982). Most newborns prefer to lie supine with the head turned to the right (for a review, see Michel,
1983). According to Casaer (1979) this head postural preference
seems to be a part of a general body posture which includes limb
flexion.

Several mechanisms have been proposed to explain the flexed posture
of infants' limbs. Based on observations of a limb flexed posture
in adults with cortical lesions, Peiper (1963) suggested that limb
flexion might occur because the globus pallidus achieves a supraspinal influence on spinal reflexes before other cortical inhibitory
processes are present. Beintema (1968), and Maekawa and Ochiai
(1975) claimed that this initial limb flexion posture results from
the properties of reflexes and muscles rather than from higher order

central mechanisms because the alpha motor neurons controlling the
flexor muscles seem to receive direct excitatory signals from primary and secondary spindle afferents. However, motor neurons of extensor muscles might receive only indirect inputs from spindles via
the secondary innervation of interneurons (Schulte, 1974).
Gribenski and Caston (1973) suggested that neonatal hypotonicity
could be explained by prevailing gamma activity. Schloon, O'Brien,
Scholten, and Prechtl (1976) have demonstrated state-dependent changes in postural behavior and electromyographic activity in the
newborn. Tonic activity of different muscles was recorded during
maintained anti-gravity postures in state 1 (eyes closed, regular
respiration and no gross body movements) (Prechtl and Beintema,
1964). In state 2 (eyes closed, irregular respiration), posture was
described as flaccid and no tonic activity was recorded in the
muscles. Therefore, the flexed posture observed in state 2 appears
to be the result of purely mechanical properties and the influence
of gravity.

This specific early postural organization has also been related to
the *primitive reflexes*. These reflexes are one of the priviledged
tools used to assess CNS integrity in newborns (see Saint-Clair,
1978, for a historical review of neonatal assessment procedures).
They are brain-stem mediated, complex, automatic movement patterns
that are present at birth, and with CNS maturation, become more difficult to elicit later on in the first year when voluntary motor
activity becomes predominant (Capute, Accardo, Vining, Rubenstein,
Walcher, Harryman and Rose, 1978). They are assumed to have a prenatal origin, unlike postural righting reactions that develop post-
natally. Although some have argued that these responses are neither
primitive nor reflexive (Touwen, 1984), their developmental course
is considered fundamental for an assessment of neurological development. It must be noted that observers using ultrasound techniques
have found fetal movements but have failed to record primitive reflexes in utero (Birnholz, Stephens and Faira, 1978; De Vries,
Visser and Prechtl, 1982), except for a response similar to the Moro
reflex (Wyke, 1975).

Tonic neck reflexes belong to the category of primitive reflexes.
Both the *symmetrical* (STNR) and the *asymmetrical* (ATNR) tonic neck
reflex originate from proprioceptive receptors in the neck extensors
(Peiper, 1962). With extension of the head in the midline, arms extend and legs flex. The flexion of the head has the opposite effect: Arms flex and legs extend (STNR). Considerable controversy
exists over the presence of STNR in normal development and its significance when elicited (Capute et al., 1978). The STNR is elicited in less than 30% of normal infants with a peak frequency between
4 and 6 months of age (Capute, Watchel, Palmer, Shapiro and Accardo,
1982). These observations are not consistent with a prenatal origin
for the STNR. Generally, a predominent STNR is noticed only in
motor-impaired children (Capute et al., 1982).

Turning the infant's head affects the position of his/her arms and
legs (Gesell, 1938; Peiper, 1962, 1963; Turkewitz, Gordon and Birch,
1965): The limbs on the side toward which the face is turned will
extend and the limbs on the opposite side will be in flexion (ATNR).
This pattern seems relatively rare in premature and newborn infants
(Mellier and Jouen, 1985; Allen and Caput, 1986) but reaches a peak

frequency around 6-8 weeks after birth (Coryell and Michel, 1978;
Coryell and Cardinalli, 1979). This reflex is supposed to disappear
around the third month. The majority of infants exhibit a preference for the right in ATNR. From this right predominance, Gesell and
Ames (1950) suggested that the direction of ATNR is predictive of
the infant's handedness.

The origin of the head orientation preference in the asymmetrical
tonic neck reflexes is not really understood. Baker and Prechtl
(1979) observed that in state 1 (eyes closed, regular respiration
and no gross body movements), maintenance of the asymmetrical head
position would be passive, based on the constant influence of the
force of gravity which is counteracted by tonic activity in the neck
muscles. In state 2 (eyes closed and irregular respiration) and in
awake states, the head would be actively maintained in an asymmetrical position as revealed by an asymmetry in the EMG activity of the
sternocleidomastoid muscle.

Liederman (1983) proposes a general asymmetry of the CNS relative to
the hemispheric specialization and the heterochrony of maturation of
each hemisphere. These postures possibly result from asymmetrically
lateralized tonic activation of neuromotor mechanisms at the level
of brain stem nuclei, cerebellum, basal ganglia, and cortex. At
present, there is no evidence which directly supports this hypothesis. Michel (1983) suggests that asymmetrical postures involve a-
symmetries in segmental patterns rather than supraspinal mechanisms.
This hypothesis is consistent with data concerning the development
of spinal reflexes and muscle tone.

The tonic labyrinthine reflexes are closely connected to the tonic
neck reflexes and also have an action on the limbs. They are
thought to be mediated by the medial and lateral vestibulo-spinal
tracts and the reticulo-spinal pathway with primary afferents in the
otoliths and perhaps the neck extensors. Little is known about
their appearance, strength, and disappearance in normal children.
In cerebral palsied children, these reflexes have strong effects on
the regulation of muscle tone (Illingworth, 1978). These reflexes
are involved in basic postural activities such as the change of body
position (by body rolling) or the extension of the head when prone.
The tonic labyrinthine reflex in prone position (TLP) has been systematically studied in 149 infants followed from birth to 2 years by
Capute et al. (1982). For a child held in prone suspension, the position of the limbs changes with respect to the position of the head
in space and the orientation of the labyrinths. With the neck extended 45 degrees, the limbs extend, with the neck flexed 45 degrees, the limbs flex. The TLP is present in 80% of infants at 2
weeks of age and persists throughout the first 18 months of life,
with a maximum prevalence between 4 and 6 months. This decreases to
30% at 24 months of age.

Since the princeps description of the Moro reflex (Moro, 1918), the
origin, prevalence, and timing of this reaction has been widely de-
bated (Mc Graw, 1963; Mitchell, 1960). In this reflex, the baby
lies supine with the head ventroflexed and supported by the exami-
ner's hands. The reflex is elicited by a sudden drop of the head
about 30 degrees in relation to the trunk. The normal response is
characterized by an extension and abduction of the arms followed by

an embrace. In fetuses, this reflex seems to mature around the 32nd week (Schulte, Linke, Michaelis and Nolte, 1969; Wyke, 1975). Hooker (1952) has found this reaction in premature infants as early as 25 weeks. The reflex is consistently present during the first 3 months of life and progressively disappears by 6 months (Peiper, 1962). Eviatar and Eviatar (1978) have described a reaction to a rapid downward vertical acceleration which is comparable to the Moro reflex. However, the absence of head dorsiflexion in this case eliminates proprioceptive inputs from the cervical vertebrae, while vertical body motion provides vestibular impulses to the utriculus and sacculus.

3.3. The development of early postural reactions

With the progressive decrease of primitive reflexes, the onset of *righting responses* can be observed in infants. These basic reactions are considered as forming the beginning of body equilibrium development. An integration of visual, proprioceptive, and vestibular stimuli seems necessary to elaborate these motor reactions. Eviatar and Eviatar (1978) suggest that the red nucleus could ensure the integration of the various inputs involved in righting responses.

One of the most essential reactions is the *head righting reflex* which appears at about 3 months and is obtained by rapidly changing the infant's position from upright to prone or supine (Eviatar and Eviatar, 1978) or by tilting him sideways (Peiper, 1962, 1963). In each testing situation, this change of position of the body in space elicits vestibular responses which induce a vestibulo-ocular reaction (Doll's eye phenomenon) and a vertical positionning of the head. Jouen (1984) has demonstrated that these reactions, which develop between birth and 6 months, are conjointly determined by vestibular and visual inputs.

The *Landau reflex* consists of two distinct phases: A voluntary extension of the head and neck in prone infants followed by trunk extension (Landau, 1923). Additional components have been reported, such as leg extension (Peiper, 1963) and leg kicking (Cupps, Plescia and Houser, 1976). Landau observed this reaction in infants between 6 and 8 months of age but failed to find it before 7 weeks. The reflex disappears or is difficult to elicit by 15 months. Mc Grew, Catlin and Bridgford (1985) have compared fullterm and preterm infants at 4 months of age, and although they may not show differences when assessed on the motor developmental level, variations in the Landau reactions and muscle tone may be present at this age. Differences in muscle tone and primitive reflexes between fullterm and preterm infants have also been described (Saint-Anne Dargassies, 1966; Kurtzberg, Vaughan, Daum, Grellong, Albin and Rotkin, 1979).

The mechanism of the Landau response has been systematically studied in normal infants. Between 3 and 12 months of age, the reaction is not altered by the elimination of optical righting reactions (Mitchell, 1962). Cupps et al. (1976) reported that EMG recordings demonstrated the role of the vestibular system in inducing strong contractions of the neck extensor muscles. The Landau reaction is present in most babies between 4 months and 2 years of age. It enables the infant to maintain his posture against gravity in prone

suspension *only if the head is voluntarily righted.* According to
Capute et al. (1982) the Landau response can be considered an early
body righting reaction which emerges after head control acquisition,
after and separately from the tonic labyrinthine reflex in prone position, and before the symmetrical tonic neck reflex.

Another example of the righting response is the *propping reaction*
which is tested when the infant controls his/her sitting position at
about 6 months of age. When the baby is tilted sideways and forward, a propping reaction of the upper extremities with righting of
the head is observed. Acquisition of this reflex enables the child
to maintain his/her equilibrium while sitting (Peiper, 1963;
Illingworth, 1978; Eviatar and Eviatar, 1978). The *body righting
over head* is similar to the primitive neck reflexes in which head
turning induces turning of the body. In older babies (at 8 months),
rolling occurs in a segmental fashion involving the shoulder girdle,
trunk, and limbs. These responses are the basic mechanisms by which
the child acquires crawling and sitting.

Some body equilibrium reactions have been described in infants who
have just acquired standing balance between 9 and 12 months of age.
The *hopping reaction* is characterized by the initiation of a few
steps in the direction of the body tilt followed by righting of the
head and trunk. The *parachute reaction* (Peiper, 1962, 1963) is an
immediate extension of arms with abduction and extension of fingers
which occurs in response to a vertical downward acceleration applied
to the baby. These reactions constitue a basis for the acquisition
of walking balance (Peiper, 1962; Eviatar and Eviatar, 1978).

4. MATURATIONIST APPROACHES TO EARLY POSTURO-LOCOMOTOR DEVELOPMENT

Early research on posturo-locomotor development has its origins in
the physiological studies of reflexes by Sherrington (1906). This
work was based on specific transections or ablations of brain structures in adult animals. As pointed out by Peiper (1963) and Touwen
(1984), findings about the organization of reflexes are thus drawn
from artificial and pathological cases in mature organisms of various species.

Magnus (1924) found a number of these reflexes and postural reactions in newborn animals born in his laboratory. Schaltenbrand
(1925) observed comparable reactions in small groups of human infants and suggested that the primitive postural reactions, recorded
in damaged animals (midbrain), might be present in human newborns.
The reflexes were thought to be the basis of early brain functionning, implying that the infant is a *reflex organism* controlled at
the midbrain level. Wallon (1949) suggested that before 3 months of
age, postural reactions are just invariable postural control systems. These responses are uniquely related to gravity and do not
take into consideration any external environmental information.
This sensitivity is simply postural and self-contained. The concept
of the infant as a reflex organism with a hierarchical construction
of functional levels is still suggested in recent works on postural
development (Fiorentino, 1973; Wyke, 1975; Capute et al., 1978;
Ajuriaguerra, 1978; Amiel-Tison and Grenier, 1980).

Similarly, Gesell and his colleagues have studied the development of posture to accurately describe its milestones (Gesell and Ames, 1950; Gesell and Amatruda, 1947). The French pediatric school dealing with neurological development (André-Thomas, Chesni and Saint-Anne Dargassies, 1960; Saint-Anne Dargassies, 1954, 1982), has also tried to find psychological milestones in early postural development. According to Illingworth (1978), general principles of postural development can be summarized as follows:

1) Postural development proceeds continuously from conception up to postural maturity i.e., up to the acquisition of upright control and walking. This idea supposes a relationship between the different reactions to explain the successive onset of levels of postural control (e.g., Prechtl, 1984). Changes in postural control are thought to be directly related to neurological maturation.

2) The sequence of postural development is similar in all infants, but the rate of development varies. Many researchers present data about the variability of postural development within the same culture or between different cultures during the 2 first years of life (for a review of cross-cultural studies, see Bril and Lehalle, 1988). The importance of intra- and inter-individual differences (suggested as early as 1947 by Gesell and Amatruda) is now considered as fundamental (Mc Graw, 1963; Bloch, 1977, 1983; Touwen, 1976).

3) Early postural and locomotor development depends on the maturation of the central nervous system. The infant is described as an organism which functions mainly on the basis of subcortically controlled reflexes or reflex-like reactions (Paine, 1960; Zelazo, 1976; Gallahue, 1982). Development is conceived as a gradual increase in cortical influences which must suppress subcortical reflexive behaviors.

4) The primitive reflexes (e.g., stepping or grasping reflexes) will progressively disappear, and be replaced by voluntary activities corresponding to the early forms of these postural reactions (Twitchell, 1965).

5) Postures develop according to the general physiological principle that neurological development proceeds in a cephalo-caudal direction. From this perspective, head postural control represents the basis for the acquisition of walking.

To summarize, early postural and locomotor development can be characterized by a succession of stages (head control, sitting, standing, and walking) all directly related to the maturation of the CNS. The change from one stage to another depends upon the intervention of increasingly high levels of control.

The maturationist approach to early posturo-locomotor development has been criticized (see Touwen, 1984, for review). As noted in previous sections, reflexes do exist in newborns and infants. Also, the phasic myotatic reflexes can be elicited in babies as well as in adults. However, it appears that the term "reflex" has often been used to describe any functional response organization in the infant. The relationship between infant reflexes or reflex-like re-

actions, the results of neurophysiological experiments, and the disappearance of these reactions during the first year have led to a
conception of development as a progressive domination and/or inhibition of reflexes by the maturing cortical structures. However, there are considerable differences between infant reflexes and posturo-
motor responses observed in damaged adults or lesioned animals
(Hopkins and Prechtl, 1984). Infant postural behavior is characterized by high intra- and inter-individual variability (Bloch, 1988)
quite unlike the stereotyped nature of either pathological responses
observed in adults with cerebral lesions or reactions recorded in
neurophysiological experiments on lesions (Touwen, 1978). This variability and the complexity of infant performances suggest that
large parts of the CNS are involved in postural behavior even though
the performances may seem rather simple compared to adult performance. The infant brain is now described as a predominantly active
system with a capacity to react to various stimuli (Touwen, 1984).
It is no longer considered as a collection of separate structures
located one above the other wich gradually become interconnected,
but rather, is seen as a whole system which matures early in prenatal development (Nowakowski, 1987). At a behavioral level, an
analogous point of view has been proposed in global involvement
approaches (see for example Vurpillot and Bullinger, 1983; or
Touwen, 1984).

In the maturationist approach primitive reflexes such as those observed in newborns and young infants, must disappear and be replaced
by higher voluntarily controlled behaviors. Thus, there is a strong
relationship between primitive reactions and voluntary behavior.
For example, walking in babies is thought to originate from the
stepping reflex, and manual capture from the grasping reflex. Such
a conception is inconsistent with observations that some primitive
reflexes persist throughout the development of more controlled
behaviors. Therefore, to account for early postural and locomotor
development, new approaches have recently been put forward that are
based on considerations of bio-mechanical factors and/or the infant
brain's capacity to react to various stimuli.

5. ANATOMICAL AND MUSCULAR CONSTRAINTS ON POSTURE AND LOCOMOTION

Infancy is a period of rapid somatic growth and the infant's bodily
proportion and composition are dramatically different from those of
the older child. It is surprising that this important fact concerning posturo-locomotor development has often been overlooked. However, during the past decade, the consideration of anatomical and
muscular factors has led to a revival of classical maturationist approaches to the study of posturo-locomotor development. Two areas
are particularly representative of this revival. The first concerns
the *free motricity* obtained before 2 months of age by manual holding
of the infant's head, the second, the *disappearance of the stepping*
reflex.

5.1. Free motricity in the newborn

Newborn muscle tone distribution is opposite to that the older infant's and is characterized by axial hypotony (absence of righting
response of the vertebral axis) and distal hypertony (limbs flexed

and grasping reflex). This distribution could result from a natural
lack of head control (Amiel-Tison and Grenier 1980; Grenier, 1981).
Manually lining up the nape of the neck with the vertebral axis enables the infant to remain seated and elicits a particular state
characterized by a high level of alertness (comparable to the
Prechtl state IV) and a different muscle tone distribution. The
vertebral axis straightens, the distal flexion and the grasping reflex disappear. Furthermore, the infant is capable of reaching gestures resembling those occurring spontaneously later on in development (Fontaine, 1985). Thus, when the infant's head is supported, a
new free motricity occurs. Freed from the work load of head control, newborn behavior appears developmentally advanced by several
weeks. This suggests that newborns have some neurological predispositions which cannot be behaviorally expressed because of strong
anatomical and muscular constraints. If Grenier's observations are
confirmed, then traditional maturationist explanations concerning
both neonatal muscle tone distribution and the emergence of the
reaching gesture need to be revised.

5.2. The disappearance of the stepping reflex

The ontogeny of walking raises questions about the relationship between neonatal stepping and the subsequent development of walking.
When newborns are held in an upright posture with their feet on a
surface, they perform alternating leg movements resembling walking.
This stepping reflex normally disappears by 3 to 4 months of age.
Within the maturationist approach, the traditional explanation for
this disappearance is that maturing cortical centers inhibit subcortically controlled primitive reflexes (André-Thomas and Autgaerden,
1966; Mc Graw, 1932; Peiper, 1963; Touwen, 1976).

This traditional explanation has recently been challenged from two
opposite points of view (Fisher-Thompson, Patti and Pilliteri,
1988; Maciaszczyk and Bloch, 1988). Zelazo and his colleagues showed that when infants were given daily stepping training, the number
of steps per time unit increased. Additionally, these trained infants walked earlier than untrained control subjects (Zelazo, Zelazo
and Kolb, 1972). Zelazo hypothesized that the stepping reflex usually disappears because of non-use. With training, the reflex con-
verted into an instrumental behavior, a necessary transition before
walking (Zelazo, 1976).

However, Thelen and her colleagues argue that stepping is not a reflex at all, but instead is the manifestation of a spontaneous pattern generator like other rhythmical activities such as kicking
(Thelen, 1979; Thelen, 1981; Thelen, Bradshaw and Ward, 1981). Based on kinematic and electromyographic analyses, Thelen and Fisher
(1982) conclude that stepping and kicking are isomorphic and suggest
that kicking is a developmental continuity of stepping. So why does
neonatal stepping disappear while kicking does not ? Thelen (1984)
invokes biomechanical factors as potentially responsible for this
disappearance. The first explanation lies in the upright posture
used to test stepping. Upright infants have to work harder than
supine infants to lift their legs. However, as long as the upright
infant is capable of lifting his/her legs (during the first weeks of
life), this biodynamic difference has no influence on the behavioral
expression of the pattern generator in either stepping or kicking

modes. But the 2 first months of life are known to involve a dramatic change in body proportion and composition. At a segmental
level, the mass of the infant's legs increases disproportionately
with respect to length (Bayley and Davis, 1935). Additionally, this
increase in mass involves more subcutaneous fat deposition than
muscle tissue gain (Fomon, 1966). This fat deposition, which probably has a thermoregulatory function, exerts constraints on limb
movements. In fact, the development of this fat/muscle ratio implies that at some stage in development, the infant's contractile
power will be insufficient to lift his/her legs while in an upright
posture.

Such a biomechanical hypothesis would be able to explain not only
the disappearance of stepping and the maintaining of kicking, but
also to explain the inter-individual or inter-cultural variability
of this stepping disappearance simply in terms of physical training
(Zelazo et al., 1972; Korner, 1979; Super, 1980; Bril and Lehalle,
1988). This hypothesis has recently received confirmation. Different characteristics of the stepping response (e.g., stepping rate,
joint angles) clearly depend on the mass of the legs and on the muscle strength (Thelen, Fisher, Ridley-Johnson and Griffin, 1982;
Thelen, Fisher and Ridley-Johnson, 1984). Thus there is now evidence according to which the early physical characteristics of the
body have important behavioral consequences.

These two examples indicate how important non-neurological factors
are in posturo-locomotor development. Surprisingly, these factors,
particularly the biomechanical ones, have been widely ignored until
recently, within with classical maturationist perspectives, the
capacities and limitations of infant behavior are attributed solely
to the maturation of the nervous system. This unifactorial causal
attribution may have led to erroneous inferences about posturo-
locomotor development. The traditional explanation for the disappearance of stepping is that this reflex is suppressed by the maturation of inhibitory tracts from the cortex. However, evidence
supporting this cortical inhibition hypothesis is circuitous and
mainly depends on the reappearance of infantile motor patterns in
aged or brain damaged patients (Paulson and Gottlieb, 1968; Prechtl,
1981). Also, the neurological explanation of the onset of erect
locomotion relies on a hypothetical reorganization of the relationships between cortical and subcortical centers. In these approaches, the ontogeny of walking is seen as being U-shaped. However,
when seen from a different point of view, the ontogeny of walking
appears to be a linear, continuous process whose behavioral expressions change according to the biomechanical obstacles encountered
during the first year of life.

This "continuity" hypothesis is not incompatible with recent data
(Forssberg, 1985). In spite of the various and important differences observed between newborn stepping (0-2 months), supported locomotion (6-12 months), independent locomotion (10-18 months) and a-
dult walking, Forssberg suggests that innate pattern generators in
the spinal cord produce infant stepping as well as adult locomotor
rhythm. These pattern generators, initially programmed for non-
plantigrade gate, create an original pattern (stepping) which is
gradually transformed into a plantigrad pattern by ontogenetically
late developping neural circuits that are specifically human.

6. INTER-SENSORY COORDINATION IN THE POSTURAL CONTROL SYSTEM

As emphasized in the previous sections, the development of posture
and stability is critical to the acquisition of many motor skills.
This requires the development of at least two separate and coordinated processes those enabling the coordination of muscles into an
appropriate postural pattern, and those responsible for the consistent adaptation of postural reactions to the environment. Until the
last decade, only the development of responses against gravity had
been systematically studied in infants. However, some recent neurophysiological (e.g., Paillard, 1982) and psychological (e.g., Lee,
1977) studies have begun to recently focus on systems that ensure
that postural responses remain context-dependent (Shumway-Cook and
Woollacott, 1985). Like proprioceptive information, exteroceptive
input, such as visual or auditory information, also participates in
the control of posture. As suggested by Lee (1977) *exproprioceptive*
information, related to the position and orientation of the body in
the spatial environment, must be considered. This conception of the
postural control system implies that one continuously acts upon
redundant visual, auditory, proprioceptive, and vestibular inputs.

6.1. The development of visual-proprioceptive control of posture

Studies by Lishman and Lee (1973) and Lee and Aronson (1974) have
shown that misleading visual information can induce postural reactions in adults and in infants who have just learnt to stand. The
initial technique involved using a back-and-forth moving room that
brought proprioceptive-vestibular information into conflict with the
visual information. This visual information causes them to sway
and/or fall in the direction of the visual motion despite the presence of accurate proprioceptive and vestibular signals. This proprioceptive effect of vision has been confirmed for both standing
and sitting postures by Butterworth and Hicks (1977) and Butterworth
and Cicchetti (1978). Stoffregen, Schmuckler and Gibson, (1987) have also observed that in 12-24 month-old infants, variations of optical flow induce loss of stability while the subjects are walking.
This loss is probably induced by the baby's attempt to compensate
for a non-existent loss of balance signalled by vision. A series of
experiments by Berthental and Bay (1988) has also shown that by 9
months of age, stimulation of the retinal periphery alone is sufficient to produce a postural compensation as observed in adults.
These studies raise a number of questions about the origins of the
visual-proprioceptive control of posture in infancy. Does vision
acquire its proprioceptive function as a consequence of motor activities observed during each stage of postural development such as
sitting or standing ? It has recently been demonstrated that postures acquired earlier in development, such as control of the head,
are also influenced by visual inputs (Butterworth and Pope, 1983;
Jouen, 1984, 1986). Finally, a series of recent experiments have
shown the presence of visual-proprioceptive control of head posture
in newborn infants (Jouen, 1988; Jouen and Lepecq, 1988).

From these results, it is evident that the infant uses visual proprioception in maintaining his/her posture. In the case of conflict
between mechanical and visual proprioception, the infant's postural
reaction appears to be dominated by vision in most cases. As stressed in the previous sections, mechano-receptors and ankle joints are

sensitive to the growth changes in length and weight of the body.
Therefore, during postural development, a calibration of the mechanical postural control system is performed continously. However,
there seems to be no reason why the calibration of the visual-
proprioceptive system should be affected by skeletal growth since
the eye is quite near to its final form and ocular motor control is
well developped at birth. Lee and Aronson (1974) suggest that visual proprioception may calibrate or finely tune mechanical proprioception and/or vestibular functions so that infants gain autonomous
motor control. This hypothesis is congruent with data reported by
Butterworth and Cicchetti (1978) and Butterworth and Pope (1983)
about the effect of postural motor experience on the proprioceptive
influence of vision in infancy. By comparing babies with different
levels of postural development, it was shown that whatever the studied posture (control of the head, sitting or standing), a similar
modulation of posture by vision was observed. During the few first
months following the acquisition of each posture, infants are almost
completely dependent upon visual proprioception. The effect of visual input gradually decreases thereafter. These results imply that
the use of vision predominates in the postural control system during
the phases of transition between each level of postural development
as the infant acquires the control of new postures.

6.2. Inter-sensory conflict resolution in infancy

Recent findings by Forssberg and Nashner (1981) suggest that in
children aged 7 years, the temporal and spatial structures of automatic postural adjustments are mediated by mechanical proprioceptive
receptors as observed in adults. These results indicate that in
children under 7 and in infants, postural reactions induced by vision could be explained by the subject's inability to resolve intersensory conflict, rather than by a primary visual dependence in postural control.

Riach and Hayes (1987) have followed the maturation of *spontaneous
postural sway* between 2 and 14 years of age. Two major results e-
merge from this research. The first is related to the large amount
of inter-subject variability in postural sway which is seen in the
youngest subjects. This fact is not readily statistically explained
by differences in physical stature. Spectral analysis reveals that
the variable postural instability in young children is related to
the appearance of high frequency sways in the .8 to 1 Hz bandwidth.
This may indicate impoverished proprioceptive inputs, but also a
lack in processing capacities, as has been demonstrated in peripheral neuropathology in adults (Mauritz and Dietz, 1980). The second
point concerns the effect of eye closure on postural stability in
children. In contrast to adults, eye closure had remarkably little
effect on chidren's stability. These results are consistent with
Odendrick and Sandstedt's data (1984) and indicate that the youngest
children are able to use mechanical information for controlling the
posture with and without stable vision. This also suggests that the
postural reactions induced by misleading vision are probably explained by qualitative differences in the child's integrative processing. Pertinent to this point is the observation that young chidren
fixate stationary objects less effectively when maintaining balance,
compared to adults (Zernicke, Gregor and Cratty, 1982).

Other lines of evidence give some support to the hypothesis of age-dependency in children's ability to produce appropriate postural adjustements. Shumway-Cook and Woollacott (1985) have used a moveable platform to unexpectedly disturb the child's balance in the saggital direction. Surface EMG was used to quantify latency and amplitude of the gastrocnemius, hamstrings, tibialis anterior and quadriceps muscle responses. The results of this experiment can be summarized as follows:

1) Postural synergies underlying stance balance appear to be present in young children (15 months) though not in an adult-like form.

2) Transition from immature to mature response patterns is not linear, but stage-like, with greatest variability in 4 to 6 year-old children.

3) Results of balance tests under altered sensory conditions suggest a shift in controlling posture from visual dependence to a co-ordinate proprioceptive and visual dependence which occurs between 4 and 6 years of age.

4) The ability to resolve inter-sensory conflict seems to be absent at 15 months and emerges between 4 and 6 years of age.

Similar experiments with a moveable platform (Woollacott, Debu and Mowatt, 1987) confirmed the presence of stage-like transitions from immature to mature response patterns in younger infants. In infants between 4 and 6 months of age, appropriate neck muscle responses were recorded in 60% of the cases under normal visual conditions. Responses recorded in trunk and leg muscles were inappropriate to the direction of platform motion. However, when the eyes were covered with opaque goggles, neck muscles were correctly and consistently activated in 100% of the cases with the same latency range as those seen in adults. In older subjects (8 months of age), consistent responses were observed in neck and trunk muscles with and without vision. These results suggest that by 8 months of age, visual and mechanical proprioception are co-ordinated in the control of body balance when sitting.

7. DISCUSSION

Several important points emerge from the data presented in this chapter. As emphasized in the second section, there is an early onset of the postural control system in human infants. The fundamental spinal-cord mechanisms are present even though there are differences in nerve conduction velocity (Miller and Kuntz, 1988), excitability of monosynaptic reflex pathways, and the functional organization of spinal reflexes (Myklebust et al., 1986). However, this postural control system is not only devoted to antigravity activity, but also enables the newborn to perform different motor activities involved in exteroceptive information processing (e.g., visual pursuit, Bullinger, 1977, 1981). Additionally the amount of intra-and inter-subject variability in postural repertoires is hardly compatible with a description relying simply on reflexes or reflex-like responses.

Postural development in infancy clearly reveals at least three major
milestones: Acquisition of head control (at 3 months), sitting posture (at 6 months), and upright standing and walking (at 12 months).
This development probably begins in utero and continues after the
acquisition of walking as demonstrated in studies on young children's control of balance. Maturationist approaches do not explain
overall postural changes in the first two years of life (section 4).
The development of adult-like postural synergies appears to be a
complex process which cannot be summarized simply as a linear decline in the variability of response parameters with age or as an increase in cortical inhibitory influences on spinal and brain stem
structures. The emergence of synergies seems to occur in a stage-
like manner. Kugler, Kelso and Turvey (1982) have suggested that
stage-like development of the postural control system or motor
skills may be the result of bio-mechanical changes in body mass and
composition (section 5). The interactions between these body changes and posture and motor control systems can be seen as twofold.
On the one hand, previously adapted programs have to change to keep
place with the emergence of new body characteristics. On the other
hand, the behavioral expression of basically identical and permanent
programs changes with respect to bio-mechanical obstacles. Integration of non-neurological factors into developmental studies leads
one to treat inferences drawn exclusively from naturally expressed
behavior with caution.

The presence of periods of transition during posturo-locomotor development should be systematically studied. There are clear cut-off
and transitional periods (section 6) that perhaps could be better
explained in terms of inter-sensory factors rather than by the development of specific modalities. This is particularly true for the
role of visual inputs in postural control. The shift from a purely
visual to a vestibulo-proprioceptive dominance in postural control
has now been established. Thus, the most important question which
remains to be considered is that of the nature of this hierarchical
organization of the sensory systems involved in postural control and
the successive dominance of each system during early postural and
locomotor development.

ACKNOWLEDGEMENTS

The authors are greatly indebted to Rosalind Pears for her constant
help in translating and correcting this chapter.

REFERENCES

Ajuriaguerra J. (1978). Ontogenèse de la motricité. In: H. Hécaen
    & M. Jeannerod (Eds.), Du contrôle moteur à l'organisation du
    geste. Paris: Masson.
Allen M.C., & Capute, A.J. (1986). The evolution of primitive
    reflexes in extremely premature infants. Pediatric Research, 20,
    1284-1289.
Amiel-Tison, C., & Grenier, A. (1980). Evaluation neurologique du
    nouveau-né et du nourrisson. Paris: Masson.
André-Thomas, A.S., & Autgaerden, S. (1966). Locomotion from pre-
    to post-natal life. London: Spastics Society and William

Heineman.
André-Thomas, A.S., Chesni, Y., & Saint-Anne Dargassies, S. (1960). *The neurological examination of the infant*. London: National Spastics Society.
Antonova, T., & Vakhrameeva, I. (1973). Vestibulospinal influences in early postnatal development. *Neurosciences and Behavioral Physiology, 6*, 151-156.
Baker, H.H., & Prechtl, H.F.R. (1979). EMG activity in neck muscles related to head and body position in the human newborn. In: S. Trojan (Ed.), *Ontogenesis of brain*. Praga: Carolina University Press.
Bayley, N., & Davis, F.C. (1935). Growth changes in bodily size and proportions in the first three years: A developmental study of sixty-one children by repeated measurements. *Biometrika, 27*, 26-87.
Bawa, P. (1981). Neural development in children: A neurophysiological study. *Electroencephalography and Clinical Neurophysiology, 52*, 249-256.
Beintema, D. (1968). *A neurological study of the newborn infants*. London: Spastics Society and William Heineman.
Berthental, B.I., & Bay, D.L. (1988). Visual-vestibular integration in early infancy. In: C. Butler and K. Jaffe (Eds.), *Childhood powered mobility: Developmental, technical and clinical perspective*. In press.
Birnholz, J.C., Stephens, J.C., & Faira, M. (1978). Foetal movements patterns: A possible means of defining neurologic developmental milestones in utero. *American Journal of Roentgenology, 130*, 537-540.
Bloch, H. (1977). Quelques données sur les possibilités de structuration spatiale chez le nourrisson. In: G. Oléron (Ed.), *Psychologie expérimentale et comparée*. Paris: Les Presses Universitaires de France.
Bloch, H. (1983). Les relations entre les paliers de maturation biologique et les organisations comportementales. In: S. de Schonen (Ed.), *Le développement dans la première année*. Paris: Les Presses Universitaires de France.
Bloch, H. (1988). On early coordinations and their future. In: A. de Ribaupierre (Ed.), *Transition mechanisms in child development*. Oxford: Cambridge University Press.
Bril, B., & Lehalle, H. (1988). *Le développement psychologique est-il universel ?* Paris: Les Presses Universitaires de France.
Burke, D., & Gandevia, S.C., McKeon, B. (1984). Monosynaptic and oligosynaptic contributions to human ankle jerk and H-reflex. *Journal of Neurophysiology, 165*, 403-420.
Bullinger, A. (1977). Orientation de la tête du nouveau-né en présence d'un stimulus visuel. *Année Psychologique, 2*, 357-364.
Bullinger, A. (1981). Cognitive elaboration of sensori-motor behavior. In: G. Butterworth (Ed.), *Infancy and epistemology*. London: Harvester Press.
Butterworth, G., & Hicks, L. (1977). Visual calibration and postural stability in infancy. A developmental study. *Perception, 6*, 255-263.
Butterworth, G., & Cicchetti, D. (1978). Visual calibration of posture in normal and retarded Down's syndrome infants. *Perception, 7*, 513-525.
Butterworth, G., & Pope, M. (1983). Origine et fonction de la

proprioception visuelle chez l'enfant. In: S. de Schonen (Ed.),
Le développement dans la première année. Paris: Les Presses
Universitaires de France.
Capute, A.J., Accardo, P.J., Vining, E.P., Rubenstein, J.E.,
Walcher, J.R., Harryman, S., & Rose, A. (1978). Primitive
reflexes profile. A pilot study. *Physiological Therapy, 50*,
1061-1065.
Capute, A.J, Watchel, R.C., Palmer, F.B., Shapiro, B.K., & Accardo,
P.J. (1982). A prospective study of three postural reactions.
Developmental Medicine and Child Neurology, 24, 314-320.
Casaer, P. (1979). *Postural behavior in newborn infants. Clinics in
developmental medicine*. Philadelphia: J.B. Lippincott.
Coryell, J.F, & Michel, G. (1978). How supine preferences of
infants can contribute toward the development of handedness.
Infant Behavior and Development, 1, 245-257.
Coryell, J.F, & Cardinalli, N. (1979). The asymmetrical tonic neck
reflex in normal fullterm infants. *American Journal of
Occupational Therapy*, 225-260.
Cupps, C., Plescia, M.G., & Houser, C. (1976). The Landau reaction:
A clinical and electromyographic analysis. *Developmental Medicine
and Child Neurology, 18*, 41-53.
De Vries, J., Visser, G., & Prechtl, H.F.R. (1982). The emergence
of fetal behavior. *Early Human Development, 7*, 301-322.
Evarts, E.V. (1975). Brain mechanisms in motor control. *Life
Sciences, 15*, 1393-1399.
Eviatar, L., & Eviatar, A. (1978). Neurovestibular examination of
infants and children. *Advances in Otorhinolaryngology, 23*,
169-191.
Fiorentino, M.R. (1973). *Reflex testing methods for evaluating CNS
development*. Springfield: C.C. Thomas.
Fisher-Thompson, D., Patti, M.E., Pilliteri, D.M., & Lesswing-
Pellnat, E. (1988). *Newborn stepping: Leg strength and
practice effects*. Poster presented at the Sixth International
Conference on Infants Studies. Washington D.C., April 1988.
Fomon, S.J. (1966). Body composition of the infant. In: F. Falkner
(Ed.), *Human development*. Philadelphia: W.B. Saunders.
Fontaine, R. (1985). Fixation manuelle de la nuque et organisation
du geste d'atteinte chez le nouveau-né. *Comportements, 1*,
119-121.
Forssberg, H. (1985). Ontogeny of human locomotor control.
I. Infant stepping, supported locomotion and transition to
independent locomotion. *Experimental Brain Research, 57*,
480-493.
Forssberg, H., & Nashner, L.M. (1981). Ontogenetic development of
postural control in man: Adaptation to altered support and
visual conditions. *Journal of Neuroscience, 2*, 545-552.
Gallahue, D.L. (1982). *Understanding motor development in children*.
New York: Wiley.
Gatev, U. (1972). Role of inhibition in the development of motor
co-ordination in early childhood. *Developmental Medicine and
Child Neurology, 14*, 336-341.
Gesell, A. (1938). The tonic neck reflex in human infants. *Journal
of Pediatrics, 13*, 455-464.
Gesell, A., & Amatruda, C. (1947). *Developmental diagnose*. New
York: Harper.
Gesell, A., & Ames, L.B. (1950). Tonic neck reflex and
symmetrotonic behavior. *Journal of Pediatrics, 36*, 165-176.

symmetrotonic behavior. *Journal of Pediatrics, 36*, 165-176.
Grenier, A. (1981). La "motricité libérée" par fixation manuelle de la nuque au cours des premières semaines de la vie. *Archives Françaises de Pédiatrie, 38*, 557-561.
Gribenski, A., & Caston, J.(1973). *La posture et l'équilibration*. Paris: Les Presses Universitaires de France.
Hermann, H., & Cier, J.F. (1975). *Précis de physiologie*. Paris: Masson.
Hooker, D. (1952). *The prenatal origin of behavior*. Lawrence: Kansas University Press.
Hopkins, B., & Prechtl, H.F.R. (1984). A qualitative approach to the development of movements during early infancy. In: H.F.R. Prechtl (Ed.), *Continuity of neural functions from prenatal to postnatal life*. London: Spastics Society and William Heineman.
Illingworth, R.S. (1978). *Le développement psycho-moteur de l'enfant*. Paris: Masson.
Jouen, F. (1984). Visual-vestibular interactions in infancy. *Infant Behavior and Development, 7*, 135-145.
Jouen, F. (1986). La contribution des détecteurs visuels et labyrinthiques à la détection des mouvements du corps propre chez le nourrisson. *Année Psychologique, 86*, 169-192.
Jouen, F. (1988). Visual-proprioceptive control of posture in newborn infants. In: B. Amblard, A. Berthoz & F. Clarac (Eds.), *The development of posture and locomotion*. Amsterdam: Elsevier.
Jouen, F., & Lepecq, J.C. (1988, in press). La sensibilité au flux optique chez le nouveau-né. *Psychologie Française*.
Korner, A.F. (1979). Conceptual issues in infancy research. In: J.D. Osofsky (Ed.), *Handbook of infant development*. New York: Wiley.
Kugler, P.N., Kelso, J.A.S., & Turvey, M.T. (1982). On the control and coordination of naturally developing systems. In: J.A.S. Kelso & T.E. Clark (Eds.), *The development of movement control and coordination*. New York: Wiley.
Kurtzberg, D., Vaughan, H.G., Daum, C., Grellong, B.A., Albin, S., & Rotkin, L. (1979). Neurobehavioural performances of low-birthweight infants at 40 weeks conceptual age: Comparaison with normal full term infants. *Developmental Medicine and Child Neurology, 21*, 590-607.
Landau, A. (1923). Ueber einen tonischen Lagereflex beim älteren Saügling. *Klinische Wochenschrift, 2*, 1253-1255.
Lee, D.N. (1977). The functions of vision. In: H.L. Pick and E. Salzman (Eds.), *Mode of perceiving and processing information*. Hillsdale: Erlbaum Press.
Lee, D.N., & Aronson, E. (1974). Visual proprioceptive control of standing in human infants. *Perception and Pschophysics, 15*, 529-532.
Lishman, J.R., & Lee, D.N. (1973). The autonomy of visual kinaesthesis. *Perception, 2*, 287-294.
Liederman, J. (1983). Mechanisms underlying instability in the development of hand preference. In: G. Young, C. Corter, S. Segalowitz and S. Trehub (Eds.), *Manual specialization and the developing brain*. New York: Academic Press.
Maciaszczyk, S., & Bloch, H. (1988). Effects of training in automatic walking on posture and movement organization. Poster presented at the Sixth International Conference on Infant Studies. Washington, April 21-24.
Maekawa, K., & Ochiai, Y. (1975). Electromyographic studies on

Developmental Medicine and Child Neurology, 17, 440-446.
Magnus, R. (1924). Körperstellung. Berlin: Springer Verlag.
Mauritz, K.H., & Dietz, V. (1980). Characteristics of postural instability induced by ischemic blocking of leg afferents. Experimental Brain Research, 38, 117-119.
Mayer, R.F., & Mosser, R.S. (1969). Excitability of motoneurons in infants. Neurology, 19, 932-945.
Mayer, R.F., & Mosser, R.S. (1973). Maturation of human reflexes. In: J.E. Desmedt (Ed.), New developments in electromyography and clinical neurophysiology. Basel: Karger.
Mc Graw, M.B. (1932). From reflex to muscular control in the assumption of an erect posture and ambulation in the human infant. Child Development, 3, 291-297.
Mc Graw, M.B. (1963). The neuromuscular maturation of the human infant. New York: Hafner.
Mc Grew, L., Catlin, P.A, & Bridgford, J. (1985). The Landau reaction in fullterm and preterm infants at four months of age. Developmental Medicine and Child Neurology, 27, 161-169.
Mellier, D., & Jouen, F. (1985). Postural activities as behavioral organization cues in pre-term infants. Communication presented at the 8th Congress of ISSBD, Tours, France, 1985.
Michel, G. (1983). Development of hand-use preference during infancy. In: G. Young, C. Corter, S. Segalowitz and S. Trehub (Eds.), Manual specialization and the developing brain. New York: Academic Press.
Mitchell, R.G. (1960). The Moro reflex. Cerebral Palsy Bulletin, 4, 135-140.
Mitchell, R.G. (1962). The Landau reaction. Developmental Medicine and Child Neurology, 4, 65-70.
Miller, R.G., & Kuntz, N.L. (1988). Nerve conduction studies in infants and children. Journal of Child Neurology, 1, 19-26.
Moro, E. (1918). Das erste Tremenon. Münchener Medizinische Wochenschrift, 65, 1147-1150.
Mortier, W., & Prechtl, H.F.R. (1971). Spontaneous motor activity in newborn infants. Polymyographic sudies. Proceedings of XIIth International Congress of Pediatrics. Vienna: Wiener Medizinischen Akademie.
Myklebust, B.M., Gottlieb, G.L., & Agarwal, G.C. (1986). Stretch reflexes of the normal infant. Developmental Medicine and Child Neurology, 28, 440-449.
Nowakowski, R.S. (1987). Basic concepts of CNS development. Child Development, 58, 568-595.
Odendrick, P., & Sandstedt, P. (1984). Development of postural sway in normal child. Human Neurobiology, 3, 241-244.
Paillard, J. (1963). Tonus, posture et motricité téléocinétique. In: C. Kayser (Ed.), Traité de physiologie, tome II, p.403-512. Paris: Flammarion.
Paillard, J. (1982). Le corps et ses langages d'espace. Nouvelles contributions psychophysiologiques à l'étude du schéma corporel. In: E. Jeddi (Ed.), Le corps en psychiatrie. Paris: Masson.
Paine, R.S. (1960). Neurological examination of infants and children. Pediatric Clin. North Am., 7, 471-510.
Paulson, G., & Gottlieb, G. (1968). Developmental reflexes: The reappearance of foetal and neonatal reflexes in aged patients. Brain, 91, 37-52.
Peiper, A. (1962). Réflexes de posture et de mouvements chez le nourrisson. Revue de Neuropsychiatrie Infantile, 10, 411-530.

nourrisson. *Revue de Neuropsychiatrie Infantile, 10*, 411-530.
Peiper, A. (1963). *Cerebral function in infancy and childhood*. New
    York: Consultants' Bureau.
Prechtl, H.F.R. (1981). The study of neural development as a
    perspective of clinical problems. In: K.J. Connolly & H.F.R
    Prechtl (Eds.), *Maturation and development: Biological and
    psychological perspectives*. London: Spastics International &
    Heinemann.
Prechtl, H.F.R. (1984). Continuity and change in early neural
    development. In: H.F.R. Prechtl (Ed.), *Continuity of neural
    functions from prenatal to postnatal life*. London: Spastics
    Society and William Heineman, 1984.
Prechtl, H.F.R., & Beintema, D. (1964). *The neurological
    examination of the fullterm newborn infant*. London: Spastics
    Society and William Heineman.
Riach, C.L., & Hayes, K.C. (1987). Maturation of postural sway in
    young children. *Developmental Medicine and Child Neurology, 29*,
    650-658.
Roberts, T. (1967). *The neurophysiology of postural mechanisms*.
    London: Butterworths.
Saint-Anne Dargassies, S. (1954). Méthode d'examen neurologique
    du nouveau-né. *Etudes Néonatales, 3*, 101.
Saint-Anne Dargassies, S. (1966). The neurological maturation of
    the premature infant of 28-41 weeks gestational age. In: F.
    Falkner (Ed.), *Human development*. Philadelphia: W.B. Saunders.
Saint-Anne Dargassies, S. (1982). *Le développement neuro-moteur et
    psycho-affectif du nourrisson*. Paris: Masson.
Saint-Clair, K.L. (1978). Neonatal assessment procedures: A
    historical review. *Child Development, 49*, 280-292.
Schaltenbrand, G. (1925). Normale Bewegungs und Lagereacktionen bei
    Kindern. *Deutsche Zeitschrift für Nervenheilkunde, 87*, 23-59.
Schloon, H., O'Brien. M.J., Scholten, C.A., & Prechtl, H.F.R.
    (1976). Muscle activity and postural behavior in newborn
    infants. A polymyographic study. *Neuropaediatrie, 7*, 384-415.
Schulte, F.J. (1974). The neurological development of the neonate.
    In: J.A. Davis and J. Dobbing (Eds.), *Scientific foundations of
    pediatrics*. Philadelphia: Saunders.
Schulte, F.K., Linke, I., Michaelis, E., & Nolte, M. (1969). Exci-
    tation, inhibition and impulse conduction in spinal motoneurones
    of pre-term, term and small-for-date ingants. In: G. Robinson
    (Ed.), *Brain and early behavior development in the fetus and the
    infant*. New York: Academic Press.
Sherrington, C. (1906). *The integrative action of the nervous
    system*. New York: Scribners (Reprinted 1961, New Haven: Yale
    University Press).
Shumway-Cook, A., & Woollacott, M. (1985). The growth of stability:
    Postural control from a developmental perspective. *Journal of
    Motor Behavior, 17*, 131-147.
Stoffregen, T.A., Schmuckler, M.A., & Gibson, E.J. (1987). Use of
    central and peripheral optic flow in stance and locomotion in
    young walkers. *Perception, 16(1)*, 121-133.
Super, C.M. (1980). Behavioral development in infancy. In: R.H.
    Monroe, R.L. Monroe & B.B. Whiting (Eds.), *Handbook of cross-
    cultural human development*. New-York: Garland STPM.
Thelen, E. (1979). Rhythmical stereotypies in normal human infants.
    Animal Behavior, 27, 699-715.
Thelen, E. (1981). Rhythmical behavior in infancy: An ethological

perspective. *Developmental Psychology, 17(3),* 237-257.
Thelen, E. (1984). Learning to walk: Ecological demands and
  phylogenetic constraints. In: L.P. Lipsitt & C. Rovee-Collier
  (Eds.), *Advances in infancy research.* Norwood, N.J.: Ablex.
Thelen, E. (1985). Developmental origin of motor co-ordination:
  Leg movements in human infants. *Developmental Psychobiology, 18,*
  1-22.
Thelen, E., & Fisher, D.M. (1982). Newborn stepping: An
  explanation for a "disappearing reflex". *Developmental
  Psychology, 18,* 760-775.
Thelen, E., Bradshaw, G., & Ward, J.A. (1981). Spontaneous kicking
  in month-old infant: Manifestation of a human central locomotor
  program. *Behavioral and Neural Biology, 32,* 45-53.
Thelen, E., Fisher, D.M., & Ridley-Johnson, R. (1984). The
  relationship between physical growth and a newborn reflex.
  Infant Behavior and Development, 7, 479-493.
Thelen, E., Fisher, D.M., Ridley-Johnson, R., & Griffin, N. (1982).
  The effects of body build and arousal on newborn infant stepping.
  Developmental Psychobiology, 15, 447-453.
Thomas, J.E, & Lambert, E.H. (1960). Ulnar nerve conduction
  velocity and H-reflexes in infants and children. *Journal of
  Applied Physiology, 15,* 1-9.
Touwen, B. (1976). *Neurological development in infancy.* London:
  Spastics International and Heinemann.
Touwen, B. (1978). Variability and stereotypy in normal and deviant
  infants. In: J. Appley (Ed.), *Care of the handicapped child.*
  London: SIMP with Heinemann.
Touwen, B. (1984). Primitive reflexes: Conceptional or semantic
  problems ? In: H.F.R. Prechtl (Ed.), *Continuity of neural
  functions from prenatal to postnatal life.* London: Spastics
  Society and William Heineman.
Turkewitz, G., Gordon, E., & Birch, H. (1965). Head turning in the
  human neonate: Spontaneous patterns. *Journal of Genetic
  Psychology, 107,* 143-158.
Twitchell, T.E. (1965). Normal motor development. *Journal of
  Physical Therapy Association, 45,* 419-443.
Veccherini-Blineau, M.F, Guihennec, P. (1981). Excitability of the
  monosynaptic reflex pathway in child from birth to four years of
  age. *Journal of Neurology, Neurosurgery and Psychiatry, 44,*
  309-314.
Vurpillot, E., & Bullinger, A. (1983). Y a-t-il des âges clés dans
  la première année ? In: S. de Schonen (Ed.), *Le développement
  dans la première année.* Paris: Les Presses Universitaires de
  France.
Wallon, H. (1949). *L'évolution psychologique de l'enfant.* Paris:
  Armand Colin.
Woollacott, M., Debu, B., & Mowatt, M. (1987). Neuromuscular
  control of posture in the infant and the child: Is vision
  dominant ? *Journal of Motor Behavior, 19,* 167-186.
Wyke, B. (1975). The neurological basis of movement. A
  developmental review. In: K. Holt (Ed.), *Movement and child
  development.* London: SIMP.
Zelazo, P.R. (1976). From reflexive to instrumental behavior. In:
  L.P. Lipsitt (Ed.), *Developmental psychobiology: The
  significance of infancy.* Hillsdale, N.J.: Lawrence Erlbaum
  Associates.
Zelazo, P.R., Zelazo, N.A., & Kolb, S. (1972). Walking in the

newborn. *Science*, *176(4032)*, 314-315.
Zernicke, R.F., Gregor, R.J., & Cratty, B.J. (1982). Balance and visual proprioception in children. *Journal of Human Movement Studies*, *8*, 1-13.

DEVELOPMENTAL PSYCHOLOGY
Cognitive, Perceptuo-Motor, and Neuropsychological Perspectives
C-A. Hauert (Editor)
© Elsevier Science Publishers B.V. (North-Holland), 1990

PERCEPTUOMOTOR COORDINATION IN INFANCY

Jeffrey J. LOCKMAN

Department of Psychology
Tulane University
New Orleans, USA

This chapter reviews and discusses recent research and thinking about infant perceptuo-motor coordination, according to the Piagetian and Gibsonian theoretical positions. Coordination within as well as across perceptuomotor systems are considered. Developmental changes are examined in the following perceptuomotor systems: Oculomotor, vision and posture, auditory-motor, audition and prehension, and vision and prehension. In conclusion, future directions for research are suggested.

1. INTRODUCTION

As adults, we perform many skills that require coordinating perception and action. This coordination is evident when we make quick movements with our eyes or slower movements with our arms and legs. Indeed, the coordination between perception and action that is found in most skilled activities involves more than one mode of perception and action, more than one perceptuomotor system. In actuality, individual perceptuomotor systems do not function in total isolation from each other. Rather, they often operate in an integrated fashion, in service of some goal beyond the immediate one of each individual system. For investigators of development, this raises an important issue. It means that there are really two levels at which the origins of perceptuomotor coordination must be addressed. At the level of individual perceptuomotor abilities, we must ask how does a particular system come to function in a coordinated manner. And at the level of the perceiving acting organism, we need to consider how the many perceptuomotor systems available to the individual become linked together to function as an integrated unit.

The goal of the present chapter is to consider the development of perceptuomotor coordination at these two levels of analysis. I will review the theoretical questions that have guided recent research and thinking about infant perceptuomotor coordination. Although the writings of Piaget (1952, 1954) have been very influential in this area, theoretical contributions from the Gibsons (E.J. Gibson, 1969, 1982; J.J. Gibson, 1966, 1979), and the field of motor behavior (Bernstein, 1967; Thelen and Fogel, 1989) have suggested new ways of conceptualizing the development of perceptuomotor coordination. These new ways represent challenges to Piaget's theory and center on

issues regarding the roles and types of experience involved in the
development of perceptuomotor coordination, the degree to which such
coordination is innate and more generally, the relationship between
perception and action in development.

I will also review representative empirical studies on a variety of
infant perceptuomotor systems and examine their theoretical implications. Most studies have been concerned with the problem of coordination within a perceptuomotor system: Whether young infants
coordinate a specific mode of perception with a specific mode of
action. Far less empirical attention, however, has been devoted to
the problem of coordination across perceptuomotor systems (Gibson,
1966), despite the fact that the functioning of one system is usually embedded in the functioning of another, all geared toward some
informational or instrumental goal. The chapter concludes with a
discussion of how a joint consideration of these two levels of perceptuomotor functioning can enhance our understanding of perceptuo-
motor development in general.

2. THEORETICAL PERSPECTIVES ON PERCEPTUOMOTOR DEVELOPMENT

Piaget's (1952, 1954) theory of sensorimotor development has long
been the dominant framework for conceptualizing the development of
perceptuomotor coordination in infancy. But with the intense scrutiny accorded to infant development in the last 2 decades, many of
Piaget's empirical and theoretical proposals have been challenged.
The present section is devoted to a consideration of Piaget's proposals and to the alternate theoretical frameworks that also attempt
to account for the development of coordinated perceptuomotor activity.

2.1. Piaget

Piaget's (1952, 1954) proposals about the development of perceptuo-
motor coordination cannot really be separated from his general proposals about how infants come to know and differentiate themselves
from their surrounding environments. Although many of Piaget's specific claims about perceptuomotor activities pertain to the early
parts of the sensorimotor period, these achievements represent the
initial steps in a broader coordination process which will eventually enable infants to combine schemes in flexible, intelligent and
novel ways. Piaget also argued that infants begin to appreciate the
organization and structure of the world by observing and interpreting the results of their coordinated activities. Thus the initial
coordination between perceptual and motor schemes are but first
steps in a more complex constructive process that is geared toward
understanding the properties of objective reality.

At this juncture, it is important to recognize that Piaget actually
addressed the problem of perceptuomotor coordination at two levels
of functioning. At a more basic level and at a point earlier in
development, he was concerned with how individual pairs of schemes
become coordinated or reciprocally assimilated such that one can
evoke the other. It is here where researchers have focused most of
their attention, looking at the extent to which young infants relate
particular perceptual and motor activities. Research on the deve-

lopment of eye-hand coordination is just one example of this within-
system focus (von Hofsten, 1982; White, Castle and Held, 1964). At
a more general level, however, Piaget was also concerned with the
problem of integration across various perceptuomotor systems. According to Piaget, it is only when objects or events evoke various
sensorimotor coordinations simultaneously --not just one scheme or
sensorimotor coordination in isolation, that we can speak of objects
becoming external to and differentiated from the self.

As noted, Piaget's proposals about the extent to which young infants
relate *particular* perceptual and motor schemes have attracted the
most attention from contemporary researchers of perceptuomotor development. Piaget maintained that infants achieve this coordination
gradually by registering the results of their own activity. During
the first weeks of life infants may exercise individual schemes,
simply for the sake of doing so (reproductive or functional assimilation). Soon they apply each scheme to a wider variety of situations (generalizing assimilation) and they may even indicate some
motor recognition of these situations through appropriate or selective adjustments of certain schemes (recognitory assimilation).

Up to this point, sometime between the first and fourth month or
Stage 2 of sensorimotor development, Piaget contended that individual schemes have not become intercoordinated with one another.
Nevertheless, certain pairs of schemes are sometimes used simultaneously or contiguously. For example, infants may turn their heads
in the direction of a sound and in doing also look toward the source
of the sound. Similarly, infants may move their arms and by chance
bring their hands into view and begin looking at them. Piaget was
careful to point out that these are not true coordinations. In the
former case, infants are simply looking while hearing, not trying to
look at what they are hearing. In the latter case, infants are
simply moving their hands and looking, not initially trying to look
at what their hands are doing. Yet in these juxtapositions lie the
seeds of true coordination. Piaget argued that infants relate the
activity of each scheme to that of the other from these non-
intentional or accidental combinations. Eventually, by the end of
Stage 2 of sensorimotor development, previously independent schemes
have become so completely assimilated to certain other ones that the
activity of one can evoke the activity of the other.

Moreover, by the end of Stage 2, there is also evidence of coordination across pairs of schemes or of integrated functioning
across several perceptuomotor systems. Objects have now become
things to be looked at, grasped and mouthed; they no longer evoke
only individual schemes or separate pairs of schemes. In addition,
this type of coordinated functioning marks an important step toward
objectification of the world: Infants have begun to differentiate
objects from elementary associations with actions. Of course, this
process will continue throughout the remainder sensorimotor period.
Nevertheless, according to Piaget, the first evidence for coordination within and across perceptuomotor systems can be found by
the end of Stage 2 of sensorimotor development, around the fourth
month.

More generally, Piaget's proposals about the development of perceptuomotor coordination contain important claims about the role of

experience and the relationship between perception and action in
development. In this regard, it is obvious that Piaget stressed the
importance of self-generated experience in the development of perceptuomotor coordination. To a lesser degree, Piaget also emphasized the primacy of action over perception in the development of
such coordination. This emphasis is perhaps clearest in his account
of prehensile development, where Piaget observed an asymmetry in the
initial steps of this coordinative process: The hand controls
vision or where infants look but not the reverse. More broadly, the
emphasis of action over perception is also apparent in Piaget's proposals about the construction of reality. According to Piaget,
infants intuit the structure and properties of the world by observing and interpreting the results of their own actions.

In other instances, however, the distinction between perception and
action and hence their relationship are not entirely clear. The
individual sensorimotor schemes discussed by Piaget involve both
perceptual and motor components. The scheme of looking, for example, contains elements perceptual and motor in nature. In fact, in
trying to glean conclusions about the early development of perceptuomotor coordination from Piaget's writings, it is often difficult
to determine exactly what type of coordination is occurring:
Intersensory, perceptuomotor or some combination of both. Despite
these problems, Piaget's proposals have remained a dominant framework for conceptualizing perceptuomotor development in infancy.

2.2. Alternative theoretical views

An alternative to this view of perceptuomotor coordination can be
found in the work of the Gibsons on perception and its development
(E.J. Gibson, 1969, 1982; J.J. Gibson, 1966, 1979). The Gibsons'
approach is anchored in the ecology of organisms, in the fit between
organisms and their environments. According to the Gibsons, organisms do not simply perceive the physical properties of their environments; rather they perceive the properties of their environments
in relation to their action capabilities. J.J. Gibson coined the
term "affordances" to express this concept. What is perceived, according to Gibson, are the affordances of the environment --"what it
offers the animal, what it provides or furnishes, either for good or
ill" (1979, p.127). The Gibsons maintain that organisms actively
seek this information through perceptual systems that have evolved
for this purpose. Additionally, this information is perceived directly: It is completely specified in the environment and not pie-
ced together from separate sensory inputs.

The affordance notion reflects a different way of conceptualizing
the relationship between perception and action in development, especially when considered in relation to Piaget's theory. According to
the Gibsonian formulation, neither action nor perception is "prior"
to the other (E.J. Gibson, 1984, 1985). Perception involves picking
up affordances, but at the same time perception is viewed as an
active process, employing available action systems. In effect, perception and action are seen as complementary processes, mutually
guiding one another. Additionally, the Gibsons suggest that even
very young infants have some preadapted perceptuomotor systems that
are used to register affordances (E.J. Gibson, 1984; Gibson and

Spelke, 1983). With age, these systems not only become more refined; new perceptuomotor systems also become available to register
affordances as new modes of action develop.

It is clear that the Gibsonian perspective on perceptuomotor development differs in crucial respects from that of Piaget's. First,
the Gibsons, unlike Piaget, allow for the possibility that perceptuomotor systems, either individually or together, may be coordinated to some extent early in development. This view contrasts
sharply with that of Piaget who argued that individual schemes,
including perceptual and motor ones, are not related early in development and require self-generated experience to become coordinated.

Second, the Gibsons maintain that in both ontogenetic and behavioral
time frames, action and perception are fundamentally linked, with
one almost always implicating the other. As noted, this view also
differs sharply from the Piagetian position that motor activity precedes perception, in that perceptual knowledge is constructed from
action.

Third, the questions asked regarding perceptuomotor development are
quite different in Gibsonian theory. Since perceptuomotor systems
have evolved to detect affordances, developmental questions center
on the extent to which these systems are functional at or soon after
birth and how these systems become increasingly refined for differentiating information for affordances in the environment. Newly
emerging modes of action are studied to examine how they become used
to detect affordances, how new affordances are learned and how new
modes of action influence which affordances are registered (Gibson,
Riccio, Schmuckler, Stoffregen, Rosenberg and Taormina, 1987).

Finally, the goals or purposes of perceptuomotor functioning in
early development are very different according to the Gibsonian and
Piagetian views. The Gibsonian position holds that perceptuomotor
systems are geared toward picking up affordances in the environment.
Although affordances depend upon the action capabilities of the
organism and by implication, whether such capabilities have developed, the information for affordances is potentially available in
the environment and need not be constructed or inferred from incomplete inputs, sensory or otherwise. In contrast, Piaget maintained
that actions and coordinated perceptuomotor activity enable infants
to construct basic notions about the physical world and its properties. Infants use the results of their perceptuomotor activities to
infer these properties; the properties are not directly specified to
the functioning perceptuomotor systems.

In spite of these differences, both positions are linked in an important way. The Gibsonian view like the Piagetian one both stress
the systemic nature of perceptuomotor activity. Both views emphasize that individual perceptuomotor systems function in a coordinated manner, geared to or activated by some common goal. For
Piaget, this goal centers on constructing knowledge (at a motor or
practical level) about the physical world. For the Gibsons, the
goal centers on differentiating invariant information in the environment that directly specifies affordances, an ability that may be
evident even in the first month of life (Gibson and Walker, 1984).
Obviously, the two positions differ as to how and when such systemic

coordination is achieved and the goals associated with this achievement. Nevertheless both positions hold that coordinated perceptuo-
motor functioning across various systems is a basic feature of human
exploratory and instrumental activity.

Despite this shared emphasis, research on the development of perceptuomotor coordination, has not typically been concerned with the
systemic nature of perceptuomotor activity or how such systemicity
is achieved. In fact most research on the development of perceptuo-
motor coordination has focused on the development of coordination
within rather than across systems of perceptuomotor functioning. In
the review of empirical studies that follows, findings are considered with reference to these two levels of functioning and with reference to the Piagetian and Gibsonian views of perceptuomotor development.

3. EMPIRICAL WORK

In examining recent empirical work on the development of early perceptuomotor coordination, it is important to keep several considerations in mind. First, a key question has been whether young infants
display any evidence of perceptuomotor coordination. Such a finding
would be of theoretical interest, for many of the reasons just discussed. However, the fact that coordination may be present at or
soon after birth, does not rule out the possibility of experience
playing a role in the further development of perceptuomotor functioning. Experience may serve to maintain any coordination that is
present and/or promote the development of even finer coordinated
abilities (cf. Gottlieb, 1976). Second, experience may be important, indeed mandatory, in another respect. Physical and anatomical
growth may necessitate adjustments in any coordination that initially might be present. Aslin (1988) and Banks (1988) have pointed out
that simple nativist views of visuomotor development (and by implication perceptuomotor development in general) fail to take into
account growth-related changes in the body, especially in the relevant sensory apparatus. Adjustment to these changes requires some
type of recalibration based on experience. Thus viewing the problem
of perceptuomotor development just in nature/nurture terms may be
overly simplistic. It may be more fruitful to ask how does the biological endowment of the organism determine the kinds of experience
that perceptuomotor systems are responsive to and the ways in which
these experiences are used. Determining whether specific perceptuo-
motor systems are at all coordinated at or near birth --the focus of
a good deal of empirical work, is but a first step in addressing
these larger issues.

The study of perceptuomotor development is also complicated by
another factor. The development of perceptuomotor coordination is
closely aligned with the development of intermodal coordination. In
many instances, it is difficult to say where one of these abilities
ends and the other begins. For example, the problem of eye-hand
coordination, which is often treated as a perceptuomotor ability,
can also be viewed as a problem of intermodal coordination: In
reaching the individual relates the felt location of the hand to the
visual location of a target. More generally, although perceptuo-
motor and intermodal abilities are in principle separable, one often

entails the other. Perhaps this is not surprising given recent formulations about the complementary relationship between perception
and action (Gibson, 1979). It is also consistent with recent
accounts of cross-modal perception that emphasize how exploratory
activity in one modality may influence or direct exploratory
activity in another modality (Bushnell and Weinberger, 1987). For
present purposes, the important point is that in many cases, the
development of perceptuomotor and intersensory coordination are very
much linked; problems in one domain may constrain functioning in the
other.

With these considerations in mind, I now turn to recent empirical
work on the development of perceptuomotor coordination. The review
is selective but designed to illustrate recent thinking and progress
in the area. Developmental changes are examined in the following
perceptuomotor systems: Oculomotor, vision and posture, auditory-
motor, audition and prehension and vision and prehension. In recent
years, these systems have been the subject of numerous empirical
studies. Results from these efforts have important theoretical implications for understanding the extent to which such coordination
is present at birth and what roles experience play in the subsequent
development of these systems.

3.1. Oculomotor coordinations

Eye movement or oculomotor systems are especially good candidates in
which to seek evidence of early perceptuomotor coordination. There
are virtually no other voluntary perceptuomotor systems available so
early in development that are as functional or are as well-practiced
(Haith, Hazan and Goodman, 1988). In the following section, the
development of several types of coordinated oculomotor activity will
be considered (for a more detailed review of oculomotor development,
see Aslin, 1987).

Accommodation

Accommodation, which nearly all individuals exhibit, refers to adjustments in the shape of the lens of the eye so that the image
refracted onto the retina remains in focus. Accommodation can be
thought of as a sensory-motor system in that adjustment of the lens'
shape is dependent on sensory information --the blur or focus of the
perceived visual stimulus. From a developmental standpoint, investigators have been interested in when infants first exhibit accommodation in response to such sensory information. Evidence of such
responding would indicate a form of coordinated sensory-motor functioning.

Previous findings had indicated that infants of 1 month and under
showed little evidence of accommodation and that this ability improved substantially by the third or fourth month (Haynes, White and
Held, 1965). Banks (1980), however, has recently provided new
details about the development of accommodation during the first few
months of life. He has shown that even 1-month-olds display accommodation as a function of stimulus distance, a finding which suggests that infants appear capable of some coordinated sensory-motor
functioning very soon after birth. Nevertheless, this ability improves considerably by the third month.

The subsequent improvement in accommodative ability that does occur
during the first 3 months of life may be due to improvements in the
motor or sensory aspects of the system or in the coordinated functioning of the two. Banks (1980), however, has argued that most of
the improvements are due to changes in the sensory component of the
accommodation system: Very young infants exhibit limited accommodative ability because the effective stimulus for accommodation --a
change in the sharpness of the retinal image-- is not being detected. Banks (1980) has shown that very young infants have a large
depth of focus, meaning that across a wide range of stimulus distances, they do not detect a change in blurring of the retinal image.
Of course, this large depth of focus is related to limits in visual
acuity at these young ages. In contrast, the motor elements of the
system seem functional very soon after birth. Even very young
infants have the capacity to effect a change in lens shape. However, at these young ages, the wide range of refractive states that
are exhibited are not strongly correlated with stimulus distance
(Banks, 1980).

The fact that accommodative ability improves rapidly in the first
few months as depth of focus and visual acuity change also suggests
that infants have little difficulty in coordinating the motor and
sensory elements of the system once the sensory limits have been
overcome. In other words, deficiencies in sensory processing appear
to constrain the functioning of a system which to a large degree is
already coordinated.

Accommodation-convergence

In most individuals changes in accommodation also induce changes in
convergence. Individuals employ convergent eye movements --rotating
the two eyes or lines of sight toward each other-- to keep the
visual stimulus on the fovea of each eye. Because accommodation and
convergence are normally linked, individuals are able to maintain
vision that is neither blurred nor double.

From the standpoint of perceptuomotor development, the relationship
between accommodation and convergence is of particular interest. It
represents an instance where two *individual* sensory-motor systems,
each with different sensory and motor components, are coordinated
(Aslin and Jackson, 1979). Investigating the origins of this linkage
might provide some evidence for a type of coordination that exists
across sensory-motor systems early in development.

The relationship between accommodation and convergence in young
infants has been examined by Aslin and Jackson (1979). They found
that these two systems are already linked by 8 weeks of age, the
youngest age group that they studied. Eight-week-olds as well as
older infants evidenced convergence under monocular viewing conditions, suggesting that a change in accommodation induced a change in
convergence even when the stimulus for convergence (double vision)
was not present.

Although accommodation and convergence are linked by 8 weeks of age,
experience may still play a role in the subsequent development of
this linkage. As Aslin and Jackson (1979) have pointed out, physical growth virtually necessitates changes in whatever relationship

originally existed between the two systems. For example, the same accommodative stimulus requires a larger convergence change in adults than in infants due to the increase in interocular separation that occurs with age. Developmental plasticity (within of course certain constraints) may be the norm as far as the ontogenesis of the accommodative-convergence system is concerned.

3.2. Saccadic eye-movements

Saccadic eye-movements are one of several eye-movement systems that individuals use to direct the eyes to specific parts of the visual array. Specifically, saccadic eye-movements refer to very rapid movements of the eye, typically to shift the position of a portion of the visual field on the peripheral retina onto the fovea.

The development of saccadic eye-movements raises a number of interesting issues regarding perceptuomotor coordination. If very young infants can execute a saccade to a target, it might indicate an early form of perceptuomotor sensitivity to the spatial features of direction and displacement. Aslin and Salapatek (1975) found that infants at 1 month of age were capable of making *directionally* appropriate saccades to a visual target that appeared suddenly in their periphery. Furthermore, they found that 1- and 2-month-old infants were able to localize the target thus showing some sensitivity to the targets *displacement*. In fact, infants in both age groups made a series of multiple saccades to the target, with individual saccadic movements of approximately equal magnitude. In addition there was some evidence that within such a series, infants appropriately adjusted the *magnitude* of the individual saccadic steps. For example, infants made longer individual saccades to 20° targets than to 10° ones. Adults, of course, typically make a single saccade to these target displacements. Despite these differences from adult patterns of responding, the infant findings suggest that early in development, sensory information and motor output are coordinated with reference to direction, displacement and magnitude. It should be noted, however, that in saccadic localization studies with young infants, only a limited range of target displacements have been used (e.g., up to 40° along the horizontal axis in the Aslin and Salapatek (1975) experiment). It is not clear whether such coordination is present when targets with greater retinal eccentricities are employed.

The fact that sensory and motor components of the saccadic system are coordinated with respect to location, including magnitude, early in life does not preclude a role for experience in the subsequent development of this system. As noted, physical and anatomical changes associated with development virtually necessitate changes in early sensory-motor linkages. Aslin (1987, 1988) has discussed this problem in detail with reference to the saccadic system. One of the known anatomical changes that occurs early in visual development is the migration of photoreceptors in the retina toward the fovea. A consequence of this migration is that the relationship between a given photoreceptor and its corresponding locus in the visual field changes during ontogenesis (Aslin, 1987, 1988). If a photoreceptor or stimulation of it is linked to a given saccadic response early in development, there must be some recalibration process that occurs to compensate for the photoreceptor's migration (also see Banks, 1988).

The capacity for recalibration, and by implication a role for *sensorimotor* experience, appears to be a normative feature of developing oculomotor systems. Related arguments concerning photoreceptor migration and recalibration have also been made to describe the development of smooth pursuit eye movements (Aslin, 1987, 1988).

3.3. Optic flow and action

J.J. Gibson (1966) has argued that the pattern of optic flow information across the retina specifies a great deal about the environment and the relationship between the self and surrounding environment. Among other things, patterns of optic flow can specify environmental layout (e.g. the relative distance between objects in the environment) as well as the direction of self-movement through the environment. While sensitivity to optic flow information has usually been studied as an aspect of space perception (Yonas, Pettersen, Lockman and Eisenberg, 1980) and motion perception (Warren, 1976), it may also be viewed as a problem of perceptuomotor coordination: Optic flow patterns typically reflect something about an individual's actions and at the same time have direct implications for action.

In recent years, investigators have been studying how infants relate their actions to optic flow information. One type of optic flow pattern that has been the subject of considerable research has been information for impending collision. When an individual directly approaches an upright environmental surface such as a wall or obstacle, the projection of this surface symmetrically expands across the retina and rapidly fills the field of view (Gibson and Spelke, 1983). Because this type of explosive pattern specifies imminent collision, an observer will normally engage in some type action to void the impending impact. Developmentalists have asked when do infants first evidence sensitivity to such displays by exhibiting appropriate avoidant behavior.

Although there have been conflicting reports regarding the ability of 1-month-old infants to respond to information for impending collision (Bower, Broughton and Moore, 1971; Yonas, Bechtold, Frankel, Gordon, McRoberts, Norcia and Sternfels, 1977), by 3 months of age, infants appear very sensitive to it. Yonas et al. (1980) found that 3-month-old infants would reliably withdraw their heads in response to optical transformations whose expansion patterns were explosive: The expansion pattern accelerated geometrically as it rapidly filled a large portion (100°) of the visual field. In contrast, optical displays that expanded linearly (non-explosively) and/or filled only a small portion of the visual field (30°) evoked less avoidant behavior. In short, 3-month-olds withdraw their heads in response to optical transformations associated with imminent collision, not simply to any approaching display.

Parametric studies like these are important because they imply that infants possess more than a crude form of perceptuomotor coordination. To examine whether an even more refined form of perceptuomotor coordination exists, it would be necessary to show that different patterns of perceptual information influence the form of the motor response, not simply the magnitude of it. For example, in looking at the relationship between optic flow and head withdrawal, it would be important to know whether particular trajectories of object or surface approach influence the direction in which infants withdraw or move their heads: Straight back or to the left or right and back. It is conceivable that although a mapping of sorts exists between optic flow and head movement by 3 months of age, infants may require additional experience to finely calibrate head withdrawal with different directional patterns of optic flow.

3.4. Visual proprioception

Individuals also relate optical flow information and action when they use visual information for feedback about self-movement. In fact, individuals rely on the patterns of optic flow from environmental surfaces to inform them about the orientation of their bodies in relation to the surrounding environment. Under normal circumstances, vestibular and optical flow information regarding postural orientation are consistent. However, it is possible to put these two sources of information into conflict and study how individuals react to this situation. Lee and Aronson (1974) presented such a conflict situation to 12-month-old standing infants by placing them in a room whose walls could be moved either forward or backward. To an observer in the room, forward motion of the room (away from the observer) would specify that the observer was falling backward and might lead to a compensatory forward movement. The reverse would be true for a movement of the room's walls toward the observer. Lee and Aronson (1974) found that 12-month-olds executed appropriate compensatory movements in response to the visual change, suggesting a form of coordination between perception and action.

The Lee and Aronson (1974) findings do not tell us what role experience plays in the development of this perception-action relationship. Infants may need some experience standing to appreciate the significance of these optic flow transformations for upright posture. However, Butterworth and Hicks (1977) found that 10-month-old infants who were seated and not yet standing on their own also reacted appropriately to the directional movement of the room. And Butterworth (1981) has reported that even 2-month-old infants will make appropriate adjustments of the head in relation to the visually specified movement of the room. Collectively, these findings indicate that a basic unlearned coordination may exist between optical motion and posture (Gibson and Spelke, 1983).

As has been the case with other early emerging perceptuomotor competencies, experience may still play an important role in the subsequent development of visual postural control. During visual development, changes in the projective geometry of the eye and migration of retinal photoreceptors lead to significant changes in the mapping between environmental points and their underlying neural representations (Banks, 1988). Because these neural-environmental mappings are altered, any information registered from optical flow fields, such as depth or self-movement, will be affected as well. Indeed, Banks (1988) has argued that some type of recalibration process must occur during development to ensure that optical flow information continues to be accurately used.

In recent work, Banks (1988) has shown, via computer simulation, how the infant visual system could in principle use available visual

information to recalibrate optic flow perception by deducing the
changes associated with optical and neural growth. Banks' (1988)
model is significant because it accomplishes the recalibration by
relying on perceptual information and discrepancies *within* the system being recalibrated. Although this work is largely concerned
with the perception of optic flow, it has important implications for
understanding age-related changes in perceptuomotor coordination,
especially changes associated with physical growth.

3.5. Visual expectations and action

Recently, psychologists have also turned their attention to study
the origins of the ability to form expectations and to act on them.
In past work, the development of expectations has often been viewed
as a problem involving cognition about time or causality (Piaget,
1954). However, to the extent that expectations are derived from
perceptual information, the ability to relate actions appropriately
to expectations can be viewed as a form of perceptuomotor coordination.

Haith (1988) and his colleagues have been investigating this problem
by studying the acquisition of visual expectations by young infants.
In one experiment, 3 1/2-month-olds were presented a series of
slides in a regular or irregular spatiotemporal pattern and their
eye-movements were recorded (Haith, Hazan and Goodman, 1988). When
infants witnessed the regular series, they exhibited shorter reaction times and reliably anticipated the next event in the sequence,
suggesting that they had formed expectations and had acted on them.
The role of experience in the development of this early appearing
ability, however, is by no means clear. Haith (1988) has estimated
that by 3 1/2 months of age, infants have already made 3 to 6 mil-
lion eye movements. It is certainly possible that all this practice
enables infants to form visual expectations so early in life.

More generally, these early visual expectation-action sequences may
also tell us something about the properties or principles underlying
the development of other perception-action or expectation-action
systems. As Haith (1988) has pointed out, the elements in the
visual expectation-action sequence --detecting an environmental
regularity, controlling an action, relating an action to the detected regularity-- are similar to those in other, later-developing
expectation-action systems involving reaching or locomotion. In
reality, of course, the problem is even more complex since expectations are being acted upon by several action systems simultaneously.
How young children achieve this overall coordination is a problem
that has barely been addressed.

3.6. Auditory-motor coordination

Researchers have devoted far less attention to the development of
perceptuomotor abilities involving auditory information. In fact,
much of our knowledge about the development of perceptuomotor coordination is based on investigations of visuomotor abilities.
Studies of perceptuomotor systems involving modalities other than
vision, however, can broaden our understanding of perceptuomotor
development and highlight any general principles or properties that
are associated with this process.

Most studies of early auditory-motor coordination concern the ability to localize an object or event specified by sound. In these
studies, the most common localization responses that have been investigated are eye and head movements and to a lesser extent, arm
movements. It is important to note, however, that any changes evidenced by infants in auditory-localization may entail developments
not just in a given auditory-motor ability but in other capacities
as well. For example, when infants move their eyes and head in the
direction of a sound, an intermodal component may also be involved:
A sound's location may be specifying where an object or event can be
seen. Similarly, the auditory-motor task may require infants to
relate more than one motor response to the relevant auditory information. In the above example, infants are coordinating both eye and
head movements in relation to a sound source. Researchers of auditory localization have recognized these problems (cf. Ashmead,
Clifton and Perris, 1987) although it is often difficult to control
for them experimentally.

3.7. Auditory localization: Eye and/or head movements

Research on the ability of young infants to turn their eyes and/or
heads in the direction of a sound has indicated that this capacity
is present very soon after birth. The theoretical implications of
this finding, are less clear, however. First, the evidence. After
an earlier demonstration that newborns will look in the direction of
a sound (Wertheimer, 1961) and some subsequent difficulty in replicating this result (McGurk, Turnure and Creighton, 1977), there have
now been several convincing reports that newborns will turn their
heads (Clifton, Morrongiello, Kulig and Dowd, 1981; Muir and Field,
1979) as well as move their eyes (Turner and Macfarlane, 1978) in
the direction of a sound source. Surprisingly, though, during the
second and third months, this behavior declines. Upon presentation
of a sound off to one side, 2- and 3-month-olds keep their heads
stationary or turn very little, sometimes in the wrong direction
(Muir, Abraham, Forbes and Harris, 1979). But after the end of the
third month, infants begin again to turn their heads consistently to
a sound source. Additionally, the response now appears to be organized in a different fashion. Infants initiate the response relatively quickly, and importantly --especially for theoretical reasons,
they appear to be using the response to search for the visual source
of the sound (Muir and Clifton, 1985).

Interestingly, around this time as well, infants begin to react to
precedence effect stimuli. In the precedence effect, two identical
sounds are fed into two loci with one sound arriving before the
other by several milliseconds. Individuals who exhibit the precedence effect will report hearing only one sound in the direction of
the leading one. Clifton et al. (1981) have shown that 5-month-olds
turn their heads in the direction of the leading sound but newborns
do not. Based on the auditory localization and precedence effect
findings, Clifton et al. (1981) and Muir and Clifton (1985) have
suggested that newborns' early localization of sound may be subcortically based. Cortical control of auditory localization abilities may not emerge until the fourth or fifth month.

Besides the significance of these findings for understanding early
brain-behavior relationships, these results also have important

theoretical implications for understanding the development of early
perceptuomotor coordination. The findings on early auditory localization suggest several possibilities. One is that newborns' orientation to sound may reflect some type of reflexive or tropistic tendency (Field, 1987; Spelke, 1987) or relatedly, some type of strategy to minimize binaural sound differences (Clifton et al., 1981;
Muir and Clifton, 1985) rather than an underlying auditory-motor
representation of space. Such a reflexive or tropistic tendency,
however, could be the basis from which infants form an auditory-
motor map of space (Butterworth, 1981; Spelke, 1987). This possibility would not be entirely inconsistent with Piaget's proposals,
although it does suggest that auditory and motor abilities are already related, albeit crudely, at birth. Another possibility is
that the auditory-motor system is coordinated in a spatial sense to
some degree at birth. In this view, subsequent developments in
auditory-motor functioning would also reflect changes in auditory,
motor and/or auditory-motor coordination.

It is difficult to confirm any of these possibilities because developmental changes in the precision of infant auditory-motor abilities have not been fully charted (Ashmead et al., 1987). In most
auditory-localization studies, directional sensitivity has been
assessed by noting whether infants turn either to the right or left,
rather than the extent of such a turn. However, some recent data
indicate that in the first months of life infants become more precise when they turn their heads to a sound source. Muir and Clifton
(1985), summarizing work by Muir and Forbes, report that when newborns attempt to localize a sound in the dark, they show more rotation to a sound source 90° off midline than to one 45° off midline.
By 4 1/2 months of age, infants are even more accurate, rotating
their heads almost exactly to sounds located 30° off midline and to
within less than 12° degrees of sounds located 60° off midline.

In contrast to the head rotation data, there is less work that has
carefully looked at how well infants relate the magnitude of their
eye movements to an off midline sound source. Bechtold, Bushnell
and Salapatek (1979) found that although 2-month-olds looked in the
appropriate direction of a sound source, the extent of their eye
movements was not related to the location of the auditory stimulus.
Bechtold et al. (1979) suggest that infants may require additional
experience to calibrate their eye movements with the perceived location of a sound. However the infants in the Bechtold et al. (1979)
study were in the age range where head rotation to a sound source
has been found to decline, a problem which complicates any developmental comparisons.

In sum, it appears that auditory and motor abilities are related in
some way at birth but the theoretical significance of this early
relationship is ambiguous. Whether subsequent improvements in
auditory-motor coordination are due to improvements in auditory,
motor and/or the calibration of eye/head movements with perceived
auditory location is not presently known. Similarly it is not clear
what role experience plays in the development of auditory-motor coordination, although animal work suggests that accurate sound localization may be dependent upon normal binaural experience (Aslin,
Pisoni and Jucsyzk, 1983). Perhaps relevant auditory-motor experience is required as well.

3.8. Auditory localization: Manual movements

Researchers have also examined how infants localize auditory targets by reaching. There are several important reasons for investigating this mode of auditory localization. First, reaching may provide more direct evidence for the existence of an auditory representation of space and hence for a form of perceptuomotor coordination based not simply on proximal binaural cues but on the spatial meaning of the auditory information (Perris and Clifton, 1988). Additionally, from an applied standpoint, it is important to understand how reaching to sounds develops in order to design age-appropriate assessments and interventions for visually-impaired infants.

The most direct evidence concerning the early presence of auditory-manual coordination comes from studies in which infants have to reach for sounding objects in the dark. Wishart, Bower and Dunkeld (1978) found that at 5 months of age, infants reached frequently to such objects, although reaching occurred infrequently throughout the 6 to 9 month age period. Wishart et al. (1978) suggested that this temporary decline may have stemmed from motivational factors rather than from any changes in auditory sensitivity or perceptuomotor coordination. However, the findings of Wishart et al. (1978) have been questioned because of the small number of subjects tested and trials presented at a given age and because reaching accuracy as a function of stimulus location was not reported (Perris and Clifton, 1988).

More recently, Perris and Clifton (1988) have shown that 7-month-old infants will reach in the dark to sounding objects, positioned within a 120° radius of the infants. Their work suggests that by 7 months of age, auditory and manual space are coordinated to a considerable degree, at least in terms of radial direction. Additional work is needed to determine what role experience plays in the ontogenesis of this ability and whether developments in eye-hand and auditory-hand coordination are at all related.

Up to this point, auditory-manual coordination has been considered as an individual perceptuomotor skill as if it were unrelated to other forms of auditory localization or other perceptuomotor activities. Perris and Clifton (1988), however, also reported some intriguing observations on how 7-month-old infants orient their heads when reaching to sounding objects in the light and dark. In the light, the 7-month-olds virtually always turned their heads to the sounding object while reaching but did not always do so while initially reaching to the object in the dark. A complementary dissociation was found when 7-month-olds reached *incorrectly* to the sounding object in the dark. On roughly 70% of these trials, infants oriented their heads correctly to the sounding object. In short, reaching to a sounding object and orienting the head to it do not necessarily co-occur in the dark but almost always do so in the light.

This pattern of results may be interpreted in several ways. One possibility is that when 7-month-old infants attempt to localize a sound in the dark, they have not yet interrelated all of their auditory localization abilities. Of course, 7-month-olds may not be always turning their heads to the sound in the dark because this

action would not enable them to see the object. Still, this cannot
be the full explanation since infants are orienting their heads to
the sound on a majority of the trials in the dark, regardless of the
accuracy of the reach. Longitudinal studies are clearly needed to
understand how infants come to intercoordinate various modes of
action to localize a sound. Such work might help us better understand how individual perceptuomotor skills become progressively
interrelated during development.

Research on blind infants' use of sonar aids to localize silent
objects has also been conducted to understand the development of
auditory-manual coordination. Aitken and Bower (1982a, 1982b) have
reported that a 5-month-old infant reached almost immediately to a
signaled object when fitted with a sonar device. However, the problem of auditory-manual coordination in sighted and blind infants
may involve different processes. During development, sighted
infants may use visual information about object location to relate
auditory and manual space. Additionally, sonar aid studies with
blind infants may not be directly relevant for understanding how
auditory-manual coordination develops in sighted infants because the
information specifying location by many sonar devices is different
from the information obtained naturally from sounding objects. For
instance, in the case study reported by Harris, Humphrey, Muir and
Dodwell (1985), the blind infant used a sonar device which compres-
sed the directional cue into a field of about 45 degrees to the
right and left of midline from the naturally occurring 90 degree
fields. Harris et al. (1985) suggest that the less than exact correspondence between signal and target may explain why the infant
reached more frequently and accurately at an earlier age to sounding
objects than to silent ones signaled by the aid.

There are other limitations associated with blind infants' use of
sonar aids. Bullinger (1987) observed that blind infants tend to
rely on sonar aids during times of motor transitions --for example,
when new postures (i.e., standing) or action modes (locomotion) are
emerging. Once these transitions are negotiated, however, these
infants often reject the device. Obviously more research is needed
to understand how blind infants come to use sonar aids and the relationship of this achievement to the natural auditory-manual coordination that blind as well as sighted infants display.

In sum, developmentalists are on the threshold of understanding how
auditory-manual coordination emerges during the infancy period.
Although the available evidence indicates that 7-month-olds can
reach to a sounding target in the dark, it is not clear what role
experience plays in the development of this ability or to what
extent auditory, motor and/or auditory-motor factors account for
developmental changes in auditory-motor coordination. Even less is
known about how infants come to intercoordinate the functioning of
different auditory-motor localization systems in the dark. The
current evidence suggests that at 7 months, turning the head and
reaching to a sound in the dark do not always co-occur. It is not
clear, however, whether this pattern stems from a problem in coordinating several auditory-motor systems simultaneously or more
simply, from a lack of motivation since head turning will not put
the object into view. More generally, work is needed on the broader
problem of how infants integrate the functioning of the individual

perceptuomotor systems that are available to them.

3.9. Eye-hand coordination

The development of eye-hand coordination is a classic problem for students of perceptuomotor coordination. As noted, constructionist accounts like Piaget's posit that eye and hand are not related at birth and only become coordinated through experience. According to Piaget, young infants attempt to visually follow movements of the hand and thereby relate visual and manual activity. By the fourth or fifth month, the two activities are so coordinated that infants can relate the felt position of the hand to the visual location of the target, now reaching immediately to a target without having to look at the hand. In contrast, other accounts, including the Gibsons', allow for the possibility that eye and hand are already coordinated at birth. Experience, however, may serve to improve such coordination or other aspects of manual skill including the temporal sequencing of the component motor acts (Bruner, 1970).

Investigators interested in testing these competing views on the development of eye-hand coordination have focused most of their attention on early reaching: Whether young infants will either reach to a target or extend their arms in the target's direction. However, in an earlier review, Dan Ashmead and I argued that focusing on only one or two object features such as location or direction may lead to potentially misleading impressions about the overall development of eye-hand coordination (Lockman and Ashmead, 1983). In fact, broad conclusions about the extent of early eye-hand competence have been made with evidence from investigations that collectively only employ a limited range of object features. A more integrated view on the development of eye-hand coordination may be attainable by examining how infants relate their manual behaviors to a wider range of object features. Additionally, with such an approach it may be possible to infer some organizing principles that characterize the developmental patterns in eye-hand coordination which do emerge. In the subsequent review of research, the development of eye-hand coordination is considered with reference to several object features, not just those involving location. The organization of the review largely follows that used by Lockman and Ashmead (1983) in a recent examination of this literature. Since that time there has been additional work on the development of eye-hand coordination, but the theoretical implications of this work are still open to several differing interpretations.

Location: Direction and distance

A key question in the literature on eye-hand coordination has been whether young infants can extend their hands to the location of a visually perceived target. Location, however, may be broken down into two components --direction and distance. Visuomanual sensitivity to either of these components soon after birth would imply that eye and hand are initially coordinated to some degree and that this initial coordination is not dependent on experience.

The actual literature on the development of reaching and especially eye-hand coordination in the first weeks of life has been full of controversy. For a long time Piaget's (1952) experiential account

describing the development of eye-hand coordination had been accepted within developmental circles. White, Castle and Held's (1964)
longitudinal observations of infants in an institutional setting
seemed to corroborate Piaget's own observations. Furthermore,
White's (1967) work on how the development of reaching could be
accelerated through appropriate enrichment of the physical environment were consistent with Piaget's discussions about the crucial
role of experience in the development of eye-hand coordination.
However, by 1970, Bower and his colleagues (Bower, Broughton and
Moore, 1970) had begun to publish a number of papers that challenged
many of Piagets conclusions. Most of the challenges centered on the
assertion that very young infants could not relate the arm's or
hand's movement to the visually perceived direction of a target.
Bower et al. (1970) reported that infants around 1 week of age were
able to reach to within 5° of a target that had been placed at 1 of
5 varying positions within a 120° radius of the infants; contact of
the target occurred less frequently. Given the Piagetian sway at
the time, this report was greeted with a good deal of surprise.
Moreover, some crucial information about the procedure and the data
analyses was missing from the report. Additionally, only a single
camera view was used which prevented an accurate assessment of the
actual position of the hand.

Because of the important theoretical implications of the Bower et
al. (1970) study, it was not surprising that several investigators
attempted to replicate it as well as introduce some additional controls. Ruff and Halton (1978), for instance, used a baseline condition in which no near objects were present. Their results indicated
that the direction of arm extensions did not differ between this
period and a period when a visible object was present. Rader and
Stern (1982), however, obtained somewhat different results when they
used a control condition that more closely approximated a true
"blank field". They found that 1 to 2-week-olds extended their arms
more frequently when an object or picture of an object was presented
than in the blank field condition. This finding suggests that very
young infants display at least a gross form of visuomanual coordination in that they are more likely to reach in the presence of
an object or a picture of it. However, since only one radical position was used, it is not possible to draw any conclusions about
visuomanual sensitivity to direction at those young ages.

By far, the most impressive evidence for the existence of early directionally appropriate reaching comes from the work of von Hofsten
(1982). He found that infants about a week of age were more likely
to extend their arms in the direction of a target when they were
actively attending to the target; during less alert or attentive
states arm movements were not as systematically related to target
direction. Still, even when infants were attentive, their directional reaching was not completely accurate. On average, they were off
by more than 30° (von Hofsten 1982; in press), a figure much higher
than the analogous one reported by Bower et al. (1970). Although
the von Hofsten work suggests that there is more than a rudimentary
coordination between eye and hand with reference to direction at
birth, the reason(s) for the subsequent improvement in this ability
is not entirely clear. Von Hofsten (in press) has argued that the
improvement primarily reflects developmental advances in perception
and motor control rather than in increased visuomotor coordination.

However, this latter possibility should not be ruled out entirely. Additional *visuomanual* experience may be required to sharpen or more finely tune whatever type or degree of eye-hand coordination that infants initially possess.

The above considerations are based on findings for reaching in the direction of a target --one aspect of location. However, another aspect of location is distance or extent. When do infants first relate their arm movements to the visually perceived distance or displacement of a target ? It is obvious that this question cannot be answered without also reference to the literature on depth perception in infancy. In fact, measures of reaching have figured prominently in efforts to study infant space perception (Yonas and Granrud, 1985). But it should also be clear that the development of visuomanual coordination regarding information for distance may not be entirely separable from the development of depth perception. Any problems that infants may have in accurately extending their arms to a target may reflect difficulty in depth perception as well as visuomotor coordination and/or motor control.

Despite these potential interpretive problems, researchers have investigated infants' visuomanual sensitivity to distance informa- tion by measuring both the *frequency* and *extent* of infants' arm movements to targets placed just within or clearly out of reach. For frequency, even infants as young as 2 months seem to reach less when an object is clearly beyond reach. Field (1976a, 1976b) found that 2-month-olds made fewer reaching movements for objects that were well out of reach whereas infants 5 months and older showed even greater sensitivity, making fewer reaching movements to objects that were also *just* beyond reach. The basis for this improvement, however, is not entirely clear. As noted, it may reflect develop- ments in depth perception, manual control and/or visuomotor co- ordination.

As for distance or extent, the available evidence suggests that infants can appropriately adjust the extent of their arm movements to object distance by 4 or 5 months (von Hofsten, 1979; White, Castle and Held, 1964) although some studies have not found clear evidence for this before 6 months (Field, 1976a, 1976b, 1977; Gordon and Yonas, 1976). Moreover, infants as young as 18 weeks can anti- cipate the position of a laterally moving object and extend their arms appropriately and catch the object (von Hofsten and Lindhagen, 1979). At an even younger age --15 weeks, infants may contact the moving object but have difficulty grasping it. Taken together these findings suggest that around 4 months of age, infants are beginning to adjust the extent of their arm movements in relation to the vi- sually perceived or anticipated position of a target.

Von Hofsten (in press) has argued that this achievement primarily reflects advances in depth perception and motor or neuromotor matu- ration. The neuromotor advances result in increasing postural sta- bility and the decoupling of arm and neck movements stemming from a weakening asymmetric tonic neck reflex. Although von Hofsten (in press) does not emphasize the contribution of visuomotor experience in the development of reaching, it may be premature to rule out such an experiential role. Careful studies that investigate how diffe- rent histories of early visuomotor experience affect the ability of

infants to extend the arm accurately to a visually perceived target
have not been conducted.

Moreover, relevant visuomotor experience may be important for another reason. The boundary between what is in and out of reach
changes with age due to physical growth of the arm. Nevertheless,
children past 4 or 5 months apparently have little difficulty in
making judgments about what is within reach and can accurately
extend their arms to targets. The task for developmentalists may
not be to debate whether visuomotor experience plays a role in the
ontogenesis of reaching, but rather to elucidate the processes by
which such experience is used early in reaching development and
whether similar processes occur throughout development as the relationship between eye and hand is recalibrated because of physical
growth. The two processes may be very much related. Even infants
in the second half year will exhibit adaptation of reaching after
being exposed to a displacing prism under conditions of active movement (McDonell and Abraham, 1979).

Other object features: Size, orientation, concavity/convexity

Although infants can extend their hands appropriately to a target's
location by 4 or 5 months and even show some eye-hand coordination
for radial direction very soon after birth, it seems that eye-hand
coordination for other spatial features of objects such as size or
orientation becomes evident sometime within the second half year.
Research on infants' visuomanual adjustments to object size, for
example, indicates that 5-6-month-olds do not systematically relate
the amount of opening of their hands to the size of a target during
the approach phase of the reach whereas 9-month-olds do (von Hofsten
and Ronnquist, in press). Likewise, 5-month-olds do not often relate the orientation of their hands to that of a target during the approach phase of the reach whereas 9-month-olds do (Lockman, Ashmead
and Bushnell, 1984). By 6 months infants begin to evidence manual
adjustments for orientation (von Hofsten and Fazel-Zandy, 1984).
And finally, infants 8 months and younger do not appropriately modify the shape of their hands when reaching to a concave or convex
object; appropriate modifications occur only after the object has
been touched (Piérault-le-Bonniec, 1985).

How can the eye-hand results for features like direction and distance indicating early coordination be related to the results just
discussed for other object features indicating a later developing
type of coordination ? It seems that visuomotor sensitivity to
spatial features that primarily require adjustments of the whole
arm, as is the case with location, emerges earlier than visuomotor
sensitivity to spatial features requiring adjustments of the hands
or fingers, as is the case with other object features like orientation or size (Lockman and Ashmead, 1983). This progression is undoubtedly tied to motor maturation, especially the proximal and
distal components of reaching (Lockman and Ashmead, 1983; von
Hofsten, in press): Infants gain control of their arms before
gaining control of their hands and fingers. But in addition to the
maturation of the requisite motor abilities, the development of eye-
hand coordination with reference to various object features may also
depend upon *relevant* visuomotor experience. Thus even though
infants may possess the necessary motor abilities as well as be

capable of registering the appropriate perceptual information, they
still may have difficulty in coordinating the two. This idea is
consistent with some of the findings from the previously mentioned
studies. Lockman et al. (1984) reported that 5-month-olds demonstrated the full range of hand orientations during the approach phase
of the reach but did not systematically relate these rotations to
the visually perceived orientation of the target. Similarly,
Piérault-le-Bonniec (1985) noted that even though 8-month-olds sha-
ped their hands appropriately after they contacted concave or convex
objects, they did not do so during the approach phase of the reach,
when concavity or convexity was only specified visually. It appears
then that at least with respect to eye-hand coordination for some
object features, infants may possess the constituent perceptual and
motor skills before they fully coordinate them. The development of
such coordination may depend in part upon relevant visuomanual experience.

In the preceding discussion, eye-hand coordination was considered
with respect to single objects or individual object features. These
can be considered instances of object-body relations (Pick and
Lockman, 1981). However, a good deal of eye-hand activity is directed toward establishing relationships between objects, such as fitting one object in or placing one object on another. These may be
considered examples of object-object relations. More generally,
object-body relations differ from object-object relations in that
different frames of reference need to be coordinated in each type of
problem. In the case of object-body relations, the arm or hand is
related to a single object or stimulus. In establishing object-
object relations, however, more than one frame of reference needs to
be taken into account: In addition to relating the hand to an object, an object is also being related to another object. Developmentally, children may evidence eye-hand coordination for object-
body relations before they do so for analogous object-object relations.

We have recently obtained some evidence that is consistent with this
proposal (Lockman and Staff, in preparation). Toddlers were observed as they placed a rod, initially positioned in either a horizontal, vertical or diagonal orientation, into a vertical or horizontal
slot. The problem is conceptually similar to the one used by
Lockman et al. (1984) on how infants adjust their hands when they
reach for rods in different orientations. However, in the latter
case, only a body-object relation was involved; in the present case,
an object-object relation is also implicated. The results from this
more recent work indicated that 24-month-olds but not 18-month-olds
rotated their hands and aligned the rod with the orientation of the
slot during the approach phase of the reach --that is, on the basis
of purely visual information. In contrast, the 18-month-olds did
not show much anticipatory alignment of the rod even though many
were eventually able to fit it into the slot after contacting the
slot. Taken together, the present results and the Lockman et al.
(1984) findings suggest that the development of eye-hand coordination is not completed by the end of the infancy period. As
toddlers, children apparently are only beginning to evidence eye-
hand coordination in problems that require them to establish relations between objects. This may reflect a more general difficulty
in coordinating several frames of reference simultaneously, espe-

cially in manual tasks.

In summary, the recent work on the development of eye-hand coordination raises questions about the validity of Piaget's proposals. Almost immediately after birth, infants can move their arms
in the direction of a visually perceived target (von Hofsten, 1982).
The fact that eye and hand are coordinated in this respect so early
in life clearly runs counter to Piagetian theory. Still, other
forms of eye-hand coordination are not plainly evident until the
second half year, particularly coordinations that require adjustments of the hand or fingers. The reason(s) why these types of coordination are not immediately evident is a matter of some debate.
Some investigators have suggested that once the relevant motor and
perceptual limitations are overcome, infants will demonstrate the
visuomanual coordinations in question. The implication here is that
coordination between eye and hand is largely innate; little visuo-
manual experience is required for this type of coordination to develop (von Hofsten, in press). Others have suggested that even though
there may be some prespecified linkages between eye and hand, visuomotor experience may still be important either for sharpening or
facilitating the development of these linkages (cf. Lockman and
Ashmead, 1983). Additionally, although recent empirical work has
focused on infants, it appears that important developments in eye-
hand coordination occur beyond the infancy period, particularly in
problems where relations need to be established between objects.
Finally, most of the work on the development of eye-hand coordination has been concerned with how this system functions individually rather than in conjunction with other perceptuomotor systems
that are functioning and developing at the same time. Future work
should be concerned with how the activity of the eye-hand system
becomes integrated with the activity of the other perceptuomotor
systems also available to the infant. With the exception of some
preliminary work by Rochat (1985) on how young infants coordinate
visual, oral and manual modes of exploration, this question has
received little empirical attention.

4. CONCLUSIONS AND FUTURE DIRECTIONS

The idea that very young infants are incapable of coordinating perception and action has clearly been challenged by recent research.
Across a variety of perception-action systems, the evidence has
typically shown that at or very soon after birth, infants exhibit
some rudimentary forms of perceptuomotor coordination. These results are consistent with those theoretical positions, like that of
the Gibsons, which maintain that some forms of perceptuomotor activity are innately coordinated and functional at birth. Nevertheless, the presence of these early forms of coordinated perceptuo-
motor activity should not be seen as justification for de-emphasi-
zing the role of experience in this aspect of development. Indeed,
there are several good reasons to suppose that active perceptuomotor
experience plays some type of role in the development of coordinated
perceptuomotor activity. First, physical growth may mandate changes
in whatever kind of coordination that is initially present. This
issue has been most clearly treated in the literature on oculomotor
development (Aslin, 1988; Banks, 1988), but it has received little
attention in discussions about the development of other forms of

perceptuomotor coordination, especially eye-hand coordination.
Second, although many studies have been concerned with establishing
the earliest age at which infants are capable of a specific form of
coordinated perceptuomotor activity, less attention has been focused
on the subsequent development of the particular activity. Yet without such developmental information, it is virtually impossible to
form any hypotheses about the role of experience, much less know
which aspects of a given perceptuomotor ability should be affected
or *when* to expect such effects. The charge then for investigators
of perceptuomotor development is to adopt a more explicit developmental focus. Rather than continue debating the nature-nurture
controversy, researchers need to describe the processes by which
changes occur in the perceptuomotor systems available to infants and
whether these processes and the susceptibility to change vary by
age.

Another problem that was identified in the literature on perceptuo-
motor development concerns the level at which such coordination is
routinely investigated. In most instances, investigators have focused on the development of coordination within rather than across
systems of perceptuomotor functioning. Yet children as well as
adults do not typically use perceptuomotor systems individually, in
isolation from the other systems available to them. Rather the
functioning of one system is usually integrated with the functioning
of other systems, all in the service of some informational or instrumental goal. A rich problem for future investigation concerns
the way in which infants come to coordinate the functioning of the
various perceptuomotor systems available to them.

In conceptualizing this problem, it may be important to consider
approaches that integrate work on the control of movement
(Bernstein, 1967) and dynamical systems in development (Thelen and
Fogel, 1989). According to this perspective, behavioral and developmental organization emerge from properties inherent in the "peripheral" organs of action and their physical relationship to the
surrounding environment, not just from central commands or top-down
instructions "issued" by the brain. For example, the idea suggested
by von Hofsten (in press) that postural instability may limit the
infant's ability to demonstrate eye-hand coordination is consistent
with such a formulation.

More generally, it may be possible to apply this framework to the
study of perceptuomotor development, especially to the problem of
understanding how the perceptuomotor systems available to the individual come to function in an integrated fashion. Just as the control of the many possible degrees of freedom in movement is posited
to reside largely in the functional characteristics and interactions
of the peripheral organs (Bernstein, 1967; Thelen and Fogel, 1989),
the coordinated activity of the many perceptuomotor systems available to the individual may largely be a product of related peripheral
factors. In fact, it is difficult to conceive how an adult much
less an infant would be able to control all the potential sources of
variation associated with the simultaneous functioning of several
perceptuomotor systems by continually programming a series of motor
commands. Examining the sources of order present in actual movements holds promise for understanding how perceptuomotor systems
develop and function individually and together.

In conclusion, a great deal of progress has been made in describing the early perceptuomotor capabilities of infants. Less progress has been made in describing the development of individual perceptuomotor systems and how these systems come to function in an integrated manner. Although the findings with very young infants may cause some problems for theories of development that posit few if any ties between perceptual and motor abilities early in life (Piaget, 1952) more data are needed to describe developmental changes in perceptuomotor abilities and to address critical questions about the mechanisms underlying these changes. With such developmental data, we will be in a much better position to evaluate and possibly formulate new theories on the development of perceptuomotor coordination.

REFERENCES

Aitken, S., & Bower, T.G.R. (1982a). Intersensory substitution in the blind. *Journal of Experimental Child Psychology, 33,* 309-323.
Aitken, S., & Bower, T.G.R. (1982b). The use of the sonicguide in infancy. *Journal of Visual Impairment and Blindness, 76,* 91-100.
Ashmead, D. H., Clifton, R.K., & Perris, E.E. (1987). Precision of auditory localization in human infants. *Developmental Psychology, 23,* 641-647.
Aslin, R.N. (1987). Motor aspects of visual development in infancy. In: P. Salapatek & L.B. Cohen (Eds.), *Handbook of infant percep-; tion: Vol. 1. From sensation to perception* (pp. 43-113). Orlando, FL: Academic Press.
Aslin, R.N. (1988). Anatomical constraints on oculomotor development: Implications for infant perception. In: A. Yonas (Ed.), *Perceptual development in infancy: The Minnesota Symposium on Child Development* (Vol. 20, pp. 67-104). Hillsdale, NJ: Lawrence Erlbaum Associates.
Aslin, R.N., & Jackson R.W. (1979). Accommodative-convergence in young infants: Development of a synergistic sensory-motor system. *Canadian Journal of Psychology, 33,* 222-231.
Aslin, R.N., Pisoni, D.B., & Jusczyk, P.W. (1983). Auditory development and speech perception in infancy. In: M.M. Haith & J.W. Campos (Eds.), P.H. Mussen (Series Ed.), *Handbook of child psychology: Vol. 2. Infancy and developmental psychobiology* (pp. 583-687). New York: Wiley.
Aslin, R.N., & Salapatek, P. (1975). Saccadic localization of visual targets by the very young human infant. *Perception & Psychophysics, 17,* 293-302.
Banks, M.S. (1980). The development of visual accommodation during early infancy. *Child Development, 51,* 646-666.
Banks, M.S. (1988). Visual recalibration and the development of contrast and optical flow perception. In: A. Yonas (Ed.), *Perceptual development in infancy: The Minnesota Symposium on Child Psychology* (Vol. 20, pp. 145-196). Hillsdale, NJ: Lawrence Erlbaum Associates.
Bechtold, A.G., Bushnell, E.W., & Salapatek, P. (March, 1979). Infants' visual localization of visual and auditory targets. Paper presented at the biennial meetings of the Society for Research in Child Development, San Francisco.
Bernstein, N. (1967). *The coordination and regulation of movement.* New York: Pergamon Press.
Bower, T.G.R., Broughton, J.M., & Moore, M.K. (1970). Demonstration

of intention in the reaching behavior of neonate humans. *Nature,* 228, 679-681.

Bower, T.G.R., Broughton, J.M., & Moore, M.K. (1971). Infant responses to approaching objects: An indicator of response to distal variables. *Perception and Psychophysics, 9,* 193-196.

Bruner, J.S. (1970). The growth and structure of skill. In: K. Connolly (Ed.), *Mechanisms of motor skill development,* (pp. 63-92). New York: Academic Press.

Bullinger, A. (1987). Space, organism and objects, a Piagetian approach. In: P. Ellen & C. Thinus-Blanc (Eds.), *Cognitive processes and spatial orientation in animal and man* (Vol. 2, pp. 220-232). Dordrecht, The Netherlands: Martinus Nijhoff.

Bushnell, E.W., & Weinberger, N. (1987). Infants detection of visual-tactual discrepancies: Asymmetries that indicate a directive role of visual information. *Journal of Experimental Psychology: Human Perception and Performance, 13,* 601-608.

Butterworth, G. (1981). Structure of the mind in human infancy. Paper presented at the meeting of the International Society for the Study of Behavioral Development, Toronto, Canada.

Butterworth, G., & Hicks, L. (1977). Visual proprioception and postural stability in infancy: A developmental study. *Perception, 6,* 255-262.

Clifton, R.K., Morrongiello, B.A., Kulig, J.W., & Dowd, J.M. (1981). Newborns' orientation toward sound: Possible implications for cortical development. *Child Development, 52,* 833-838.

Field, J. (1976a). The adjustment of reaching behavior to object distance in early infancy. *Child Development, 47,* 304-308.

Field, J. (1976b). Relation of young infants' reaching behavior to stimulus distance and solidity. *Developmental Psychology, 12,* 444-448.

Field, J. (1987). The development of auditory-visual localization in infancy. In: B.E. McKenzie & R.H. Day (Eds.), *Perceptual development in early infancy* (pp. 175-197). Hillsdale, NJ: Lawrence Erlbaum Associates.

Gibson, E.J. (1969). *Principles of perceptual learning and development.* New York: Appleton-Century Crofts.

Gibson, E.J. (1982). The concept of affordances in development: The renascence of functionalism. In: W.A. Collins (Ed.), *The Minnesota Symposia on Child Psychology: The concept of development* (Vol. 15, pp. 55-81). Hillsdale, NJ: Erlbaum.

Gibson, E.J. (1984, April). Perception and affordances for action. Paper presented at the International Conference on Infant Studies, New York.

Gibson, E.J., Riccio, G., Schmuckler, M.A., Stoffregen, T.A., Rosenberg, D., & Taormina, J. (1987). Detection of the traversability of surfaces by crawling and walking infants. *Journal of Experimental Psychology: Human Perception and Performance, 13,* 533-544.

Gibson, E.J., & Spelke, E.S. (1983). The development of perception. In: J.H. Flavell & E.M. Markman (Eds.), P.H. Mussen (Series Ed.), *Handbook of child psychology: Vol 3, Cognitive development* (pp. 1-76). New York: Wiley.

Gibson, E.J., & Walker, A.S. (1984). Development of knowledge of visual-tactual affordances of substances. *Child Development, 55,* 453-460.

Gibson, J.J. (1966). *The senses considered as perceptual systems.* Boston: Houghton Mifflin.

Gibson, J.J. (1979). *The ecological approach to visual perception.* Boston: Houghton-Mifflin.

Gordon, F.R., & Yonas, A. (1976). Sensitivity to binocular depth information in infants. *Journal of Experimental Child Psychology, 22,* 413-422.

Gottlieb, G. (1976). Conceptions of prenatal development: Behavioral embryology. *Psychological Review, 83,* 215-234.

Haith, M.M. (March, 1988). Visual expectations in early infancy. Paper presented at the meetings of the Southwestern Society for Research in Human Development, New Orleans, LA.

Haith, M.M., Hazan, C., & Goodman, G.S. (1988). Expectation and anticipation of dynamic visual events by 3.5-month-old babies. *Child Development, 59,* 467-479.

Haynes, H., White, B.L., & Held, R. (1965). Visual accommodation in human infants. *Science, 148,* 528-530.

Hofsten, C. von (1982). Eye-hand coordination in the newborn. *Developmental Psychology, 18,* 450-461.

Hofsten, C. von (in press). Mastering reaching and grasping: The development of manual skills in infancy. In: S.A. Wallace (Ed.), *Perspectives on the coordination of movement.*

Hofsten, C. von, & Fazel-Zandy, S. (1984). Development of visually guided hand orientation in reaching. *Journal of Experimental Child Psychology, 38,* 208-219.

Hofsten, C. von, & Lindhagen, K. (1979). Observations on the development of reaching for moving objects. *Journal of Experimental Child Psychology, 28,* 158-173.

Hofsten, C. von, & Ronnquist, L. (in press). Preparation for grasping an object: A developmental study. *Journal of Experimental Psychology: Human Perception and Performance.*

Lee, D.N., & Aronson, E. (1974). Visual proprioceptive control of standing in human infants. *Perception and Psychophysics, 15,* 529-532.

Lockman, J.J., & Ashmead, D.H. (1983). Asynchronies in the development of manual behavior. In: L.P. Lipsitt (Ed.), *Advances in infancy research* (Vol. 2, pp. 113-136). Norwood, NJ: Ablex.

Lockman, J.J., Ashmead, D.H., & Bushnell, E.W. (1984). The development of anticipatory hand orientation during infancy. *Journal of Experimental Child Psychology, 37,* 176-186.

Lockman, J.J., & Staff, B. (in preparation). Orienting objects in relation to each other.

McDonnell, P., & Abraham, W.C. (1979). Adaptation to displacing prisms in human infants. *Perception, 8,* 175-185.

McGurk, H., Turnure, C., & Creighton, S. (1977). Auditory visual coordination in neonates. *Child Development, 48,* 138-143.

Muir, D., Abraham, W., Forbes, B., & Harris, L. (1979). The ontogenesis of an auditory localization response from birth to four months of age. *Canadian Journal of Psychology, 33,* 320-333.

Muir, D., & Clifton, R.K. (1985). Infants' orientation to the location of sound sources. In: G. Gottlieb & N.A. Krasnegor (Eds.), *Measurement of audition and vision in the first year of postnatal life* (pp. 171-194). Norwood, NJ: Ablex.

Muir, D., & Field, J. (1979). Newborn infants orient to sounds. *Child Development, 50,* 431-436.

Perris, E.E., & Clifton, R.K. (1988). Reaching in the dark toward sound as a measure of auditory localization in infants. *Infant Behavior and Development, 11,* 473-491.

Piaget, J. (1952). *The origins of intelligence in children*. New York: International Universities Press.
Piaget, J. (1954). *The construction of reality in the child*. New York: Basic Books.
Pick, H.L., Jr., & Lockman, J.J. (1981). From frames of reference to spatial representations. In: L.S. Liben, A.H. Patterson, & N. Newcombe (Eds.), *Spatial representation and behavior across the life span* (pp. 39-61). New York: Academic Press.
Piéraut-le-Bonniec, G. (1985). Hand-eye coordination and infants' construction of convexity and concavity properties. *British Journal of Developmental Psychology, 3,* 273-280.
Rader, N., & Stern, J.D. (1982). Visually elicited reaching in neonates. *Child Development, 53,* 1004-1007.
Rochat, P. (1985, July). From hand to mouth and eye: Development of intermodal exploration by young infants. Paper presented at the biennial meeting of the International Society for the Study of Behavioural Development, Tours, France.
Ruff, H.A., & Halton, A. (1978). Is there directed reaching in the human neonate ? *Developmental Psychology, 14,* 425-426.
Spelke, E.S. (1987). The development of intermodal perception. In: L.B. Cohen & P. Salapatek (Eds.), *Handbook of infant perception* (Vol. 2, 233-273). Orlando, FL: Academic Press.
Thelen, E., & Fogel, A. (1989). Toward an action-based theory of infant development. In: J.J. Lockman & N.L. Hazen (Eds.), *Action in social context: Perspectives on early development* (pp. 23-63). New York: Plenum.
Turner, S., & MacFarlane, A. (1978). Localization of human speech by the newborn baby and the effects of pethidine ('meperidine'). *Developmental Medicine and Child Neurology, 20,* 727-734.
Warren, R. (1976). The perception of egomotion. *Journal of Experimental Psychology: Human Perception and Performance, 2,* 448-456.
Wertheimer, M. (1961). Psychomotor coordination of auditory and visual space at birth. *Science, 134,* 1692.
White, B. (1967). An experimental approach to the effects of experience on early human behavior. In: J.P. Hill (Ed.), *The Minnesota Symposia on Child Psychology* (Vol. 1). Minneapolis: University of Minnesota.
White, B.L., Castle, P., & Held, R. (1964). Observations on the development of visually directed reaching. *Child Development, 35,* 349-364.
Wishart, J.G., Bower, T.G.R., & Dunkeld, J. (1978). Reaching in the dark. *Perception, 7,* 507-512.
Yonas, A., Bechtold, A.G., Frankel, D., Gordon, F.R., McRoberts, G., Norcia, A., & Sternfels, S. (1977). Development of sensitivity to information for impending collision. *Perception and Psychophysics, 21,* 97-104.
Yonas, A., & Granrud, C.E. (1985). Reaching as a measure of infants' spatial perception. In: G. Gottlieb & N.A. Krasnegor (Eds.), *Measurement of audition and vision in the first year of postnatal life* (pp. 301-322). Norwood, NJ: Ablex.
Yonas, A., Pettersen, L., Lockman, J.J., & Eisenberg, P. (1980). The perception of impending collision in 3-month-old infants. Paper presented at the International Conference on Infant Studies, New Haven, CT.

DEVELOPMENTAL PSYCHOLOGY
Cognitive, Perceptuo-Motor, and Neuropsychological Perspectives
C-A. Hauert (Editor)
© Elsevier Science Publishers B.V. (North-Holland), 1990

EARLY NEUROPSYCHOLOGICAL DEVELOPMENT:
LATERALIZATION OF FUNCTIONS - HEMISPHERIC SPECIALIZATION

Gerald YOUNG

Department of Psychology
Glendon College, York University
Toronto, Canada

*A progressive inhibition theory of developmental stages in
left hemisphere specialization is described. The theory
is built on a new model of neo-Piagetian cognitive development. Comparisons are made with a novel multidimensional model of general development and with current
developmental research and theory. In particular, the
former especially deals with early lateralized behavior
and longitudinal relations involving such behavior. The
latter concerns the points of view of invariant lateralization and additions, stages, and transfers in progressive lateralization. Implications for socioemotional
development are discussed in conclusion.*

1. A MULTIDIMENSIONAL MODEL OF DEVELOPMENT

1.1. Introduction

Hemispheric specialization does not develop. Early reaching is
left-handed. The right hemisphere is specialized for inhibition.
Piagetians need not study the brain. These are some of the assumptions found currently in the study of the development of hemispheric
specialization and cognition that will be shown to be untenable.
The chapter begins with a discussion of what processes underlie
development. Simplistic accounts of how genetics, the environment,
and their interaction contribute to ontogenesis are dismissed in
favor of a multidimensional model. The next three sections are
concerned with a review of the nature of hemispheric specialization
and its development. First, a view of hemispheric specialization is
presented which emphasizes that the hemispheres possess different
inhibitory skills, with the left hemisphere being dominant for the
more complex of these skills. This position is examined both in
terms of theory and supporting evidence. Then, the development of
laterality in the first few years of normal human growth is analyzed. An emphasis is placed on manual and other behavior in the
first months of life and on various longitudinal relations. Next,
current theories about the development of hemispheric specialization
are summarized. An attempt is made to relate them to the empirical
evidence in the preceding section and to the multidimensional model
of general development presented at the chapter's outset. In the

last sections of the chapter the focus is on cognitive development and its potential role in the development of hemispheric speciali- zation. First, I present a neo-Piagetian stage theory which seems to integrate various aspects of different current theorists. Next, a progressive inhibition theory is introduced, and it is shown how this novel neo-Piagetian theory can be expanded to include manual and hemispheric specialization, especially in terms of underlying left hemisphere inhibition skills. Concluding comments suggest that structured developmental stages and the mechanisms of their trans- formation should be reconsidered in terms of an interdependence with a developing hemispheric specialization. Also, questions and impli- cations, especially in terms of socioemotional development, are dis- cussed.

Before delving into the developing lateralized cortex, it would be wise to inform those unfamiliar with this field about some axiomatic caveats. (a) The concept of hemispheric specialization refers to a relative difference in ability between the cerebral hemispheres and not an absolute one. A similar proviso applies to manual speciali- zation. (b) Handedness differs from manual specialization in seve- ral ways (Young, Corter, Segalowitz and Trehub, 1983a). It concerns performance on more common, simpler tasks usually involving one hand, most often the right one. In contrast, manual specialization can involve more complex, unpractised tasks. Thus, depending on task demands, it can involve either hand, and consequently either hemisphere. For example, Ingram (1975) found that right-handed preschoolers performed certain spatial tasks better with the left hand. This took place presumably because of the right hemisphere's superiority in spatial skills (and because of the contralateral con- nections between the hemispheres and the hands). Fagot and Vauclair (1988; in press) have emphasized a similar distinction between handedness and manual specialization in their discussion of nonhuman primate manual behavior. (c) For purposes of simplicity, the terms lateralization, specialization, and dominance are used interchan- geably. Each can apply to the various levels treated in the chap- ter, e.g., cortical, subcortical, manual, behavioral, and functio- nal.

1.2. The classic dichotomy

Study of the ontogenesis of lateralization development may offer an illuminating window on development, in general. Development is a process that covers the lifespan beginning from conception; it in- volves brain-behavior relationships; and it reveals biological, environmental, and combined influences. Reciprocally, the general debate on what is development should interest investigators of late- ralization development. Developing behavior is being construed as a dynamic interrelation between networked influences, processes, and subsystems. Discontinuous stages may manifest in growth, but these may be limited in scope and individual in nature. A discussion of this emerging view of development is now offered in order to provide a general guide for a review of the development of lateralization.

The classic dichotomies, such as those between nature and nurture or genes and experience, which are used in explaining the ontogenesis of behavior can no longer be replaced by a simplistic call for a respect for their interrelation (Bateson, 1987). We must desist from referring to these dichotomies, and elaborate our understanding of their interaction; for example, the latter concept of interaction is more than a statistical term or a combination (Johnston, 1987). Genes are biochemical blueprints which do not interact with the environment, per se. Rather, they lead to structural and behavioral consequences called phenotypes. Phenotypes interact with the environment, and they are complex systems. That is, development is conceived of cascades flowing from the interaction of aspects of phenotypes with each other and from the interaction of phenotype and environment. Moreover, environmental effects are not always obvious.

But is the concept of a nature-nurture interaction sufficient to understand development, even if refined as in Johnston's account ? In Table 1, a model of determinants of behavioral development is offered in response to this query. It highlights a dynamic interaction among multiple ontogenetic influences on the growing organism. It reminds us that although some behavior may be constant across a species, others may concern individual differences. Thus, in three of the four parts of Table 1, there is a 2 x 2 grid involving the intersection of the biological-environmental distinction and the behavioral constant-variability distinction. However, the model does not adhere to the traditional distinction between biology and environment.

Table 1. *Multiple Inherited and Experiential Influences on Phenotypic Development.*

	Individual			Experience	
	Constant	*Variable*		*Constant*	*Variable*
Genotype			External		
Biol.(a)	One genetic program only	alternate genetic programs	Biol.	constrained learning, imprinting	differential match, scaffold in env.
Env.	cytoplasmic inheritance	inherited ontogenetic niche	Env.	environmental communalities	parent, home differences, etc.
Phenotype(b)			Organismic		
Related	part of structure, stage	different links therein	Biol.	e.g., CNS embryogenesis	e.g., induced insults therein
Not Related	isolated species adaptation	isolated conditional variation	Env.	self-generated experience	accidental variation therein

(a) Biol. = biological influence; Env. = environmental one.
(b) Is emergent developing behavior related to others ? Constant or variable across individuals ?

1.3. Multiple influences on behavior

Current conceptualizations of ontogenesis lead us to question as to
whether inherited influences are purely biological and whether experiential ones are purely environmental. There seem to be environmental influences on what is inherited and biological ones on what
is experienced. In terms of inherited influences (upper left portion of Table 1), the simplistic idea of a genetic program leading
to a determined outcome is being complemented by more subtle notions. (a) There may be an inherited environment or ontogenetic
niche to complicate the classic nature-nurture dichotomy (West and
King, 1987). Ontogenetic niche refers to the familial and ecological links that accompany genes (e.g., parents, peers, nest).
Clearly, these can differ from one individual to another. (b) Genes
may regulate more than one outcome, as they can guide alternate programs which different environments may help activate (Bateson,
1987). Individuals in the same species will manifest different
options among the alternatives, depending on the environmental niche
in which they are found. (c) Inherited influences may be extra-
genetic, lying in the surround environment of the maternal cytoplasm
(Corballis and Morgan, 1978).

As for experiential determinants of development, not all are independent of biology. Experience can be classified (a) as due to the
external environment or (b) as organismic, relating to personal or
corporal structure (the right side of Table 1). In each case one
can provide examples showing biological influence. First, we examine the external environment in this regard. Granted, the external
milieu may directly influence development through either its com-
munalities or its differential learning opportunities (conditioning,
shaping, allowing modelling) and its social and physical parameters
(variability in parents, toys, etc.). But the milieu may also be
canalized or filtered by specific, biologically determined mechanisms of perception or information processing so that it does not
really act directly on development. Such effects may be quite
constant. For example, there are instances of biologically constrained learning where one learned outcome is inevitable given the
normal universal environment with which it is associated (e.g., the
imprinting of young altricial birds on their parents shortly after
hatching). Or constraints partly related to biological factors may
channel environmental reactivity to structured options. The child
may seek out or elicit environmental reactions conducive to the
individual differences in its biological or congenital make-up. For
example, there are individual differences in parental scaffolding,
filtering, etc., in response to the givens of the young child's language development (Hoff-Ginsburg, 1986; Seidman, Allen and
Wasserman, 1986). Also, a particular infant temperament may or may
not engage the appropriate parental match in the transactional exchange which characterizes development (e.g., Kagan, Reznick and
Snidman, 1988).

In terms of organismic experience, one usually refers to self-
generated environmental experiences. These are considered to be
more or less constant across individuals, but accidental variations
can occur producing some differential effects (Michel, 1987). As a
case in point, watching the right hand when it is active in the
first months of life may follow from the neonate's natural right

side head turning preference, and this sequence may ultimately
determine why the majority of us are right-handed. Nevertheless,
there are some neonatal left head-turners who end up reaching with
the left hand. Room for such accidental variations seems built into
the system because of their biological advantage. Yet they are not
fully deterministic, but are probabilistic, for the chain of subsequent experiences are relevant. One can qualify this conception
of organismic experience by introducing examples with a decided biological bent. Central nervous system embryogenesis is much concerned with neuronal proliferation, migration, loss, and related processes such as synaptic stabilization (Aboitiz, 1988; Geschwind and
Galaburda, 1985a). Linked effects are found during this growth, as
each step may serve as a catalyst for another. Thus, abnormalities
at one point in a universal progression may have longterm delete-
rious consequences which may only become obvious at points beyond.
These accidents may be a) biologically or b) environmentally induced
(e.g., malnutrition, acquired brain lesion). In the latter case,
environmental intrusions alter the developing biological substrate,
bringing permanent effects on ontogenesis.

1.4. The developing phenotype

The developing phenotype is being constantly buffeted by the myriad
multiple influences just documented. But it is not a passive agent,
for the filter of its own construction can modulate the deterministic effects of these influences. Thus, structures interrelating
behaviors and channelling environmental effects are found, and new
stages involving them are seen to develop. However, these stages
are no longer seen as all encompassing, and they are now perceived
as permitting important individual differences (lower left of Table
1). For example, Thelen, Kelso and Fogel (1987) perceive the growing phenotype as a cooperative interaction of many subsystems and
systems. Moreover, each component normally develops in small incre-
ments or continuously, but with qualitative discontinuous shifts or
stages in the whole possible. This process usually involves amplification of a critical change in a crucial component. The examples
Thelen et al. provide especially refer to early motor development,
showing that stages in ontogenesis may not only refer to higher-
order functions.

Beyond this, the general conception of stages in development is
changing. Neo-Piagetians are debating to what extent cognitive
developmental stages are rigidly organized or are open to situational and anterior personal experience (T. Brown, 1988; Gratch and
Schatz, 1988). The nature of cognitive stage proposed by these
investigators somewhat resembles Thelen et al.'s (1987) model derived from early motor behavior. Mind is conceived in the plural,
i.e., as a loose coupling of schemes and agencies. These may initially emerge as autonomous units, but they come to form interconnected hierarchies potentially in different ways across individuals according to experience. Fischer's (1980; Fischer and
Lamborn, in press) skill theory approach to neo-Piagetian cognitive
development also emphasizes this perspective.

One simpler way of summarizing the above concerns in contemporary
developmental psychology is to focus on newly emergent behavior in
ontogenesis. The above points of view seem to emphasize that such

behavior can vary in two ways: (a) Whether it relates to other
behavior as it emerges, and (b) whether there are individual differences as it emerges. There are four cells formed by the intersection of these two issues, as shown in the lower left portion of
Table 1. Each of the four cells is now briefly discussed. When
emergent behavior in development is related to others in a constant
way, the most likely possibility is that it is part of an encompassing or global structure or stage. However, simpler kinds of relations are possible. If the relationship of an emergent behavior and
others can vary across individuals, a good possibility is that the
structure is more loosely organized and less ecompassing. This permits different precursors and contexts to bring different behavioral
linkages. In contrast to these last two possibilities, newly emergent behavior in development need not necessarily be related to
other behavior as it emerges. When this occurs and the behavior
does not vary across individuals, a species-wide adaptation for the
age period concerned seems likely. When behavior can emerge unrelated to others, yet in different ways across individuals, contextual
and precursor-induced variation seems likely.

Theories often are flagrantly extreme in their polar oppositions in
a young science. Development is not as extreme in the young human.
The growing individual must show a mixture of the above four developmental patterns in behavior, especially given the myriad genetic
and experiential influences that can come into play. In section
4.6, the development of lateralization will be examined from this
perspective. But first the general nature of hemispheric specialization will be analyzed.

2. HEMISPHERIC SPECIALIZATION AND INHIBITION

2.1. Left hemisphere inhibition

Contemporary and past (L. Harris, 1983) approaches to understanding
the functional differences between the hemispheres often emphasize
the left hemisphere's dominance for language, fine motor behavior,
and sequential skills, in particular. In contrast, the right hemisphere's superiority in spatial and related skills is underscored.
For example, Bradshaw and Nettleton (1981) suggested that the left
hemisphere specializes in relating individual components of dynamic
movement sequences to corporal and target schemes. The right hemisphere was thought to perform simpler activities requiring no monitoring, such as realizing configurations between features. Other
theorists have been less traditional. For example, Goldberg and
Costa (1981) characterized the left hemisphere as a locus of routi-
nized descriptive coding (e.g., language) systems, perhaps because
of its better interregional connections. In contrast, the right
hemisphere was perceived as being adapted for novel demands where
there is no pre-existing code, and for assembling new coding systems.

In 1983, I inverted the question by wondering what the hemispheres
prevent from doing rather than help to do as they function. In
consequence, I proposed that the left hemisphere is specialized for
multiple inhibitory processes especially of the intrahemispheric
variety (Young, Bowman, Methot, Finlayson, Quintal and

Boissonneault, 1983b). It was argued that a facility with inhibitory skills may underlie the left hemisphere's ability to dynami-
cally sequence language, fine motor behavior, etc.

> "The left hemisphere seems to excel in at least two kinds
> of inhibition - (a) coordination with activation to pro-
> duce smooth sequential, goal-appropriate behavior; and (b)
> control of [i] gross, secondary, competing behavior dis-
> tinct in nature from the appropriate behavior, and [ii]
> fine-tuned, interfering, parallel behavior similar in na-
> ture to the appropriate behavior". (p.122)

In support of the theory, Young et al. found that when one-month-old
infants reached unilaterally, the unused hand was closed more if it
was the left one. They attributed the results to a better ipsilateral inhibition of irrelevant opening movements of the unused
hand by the left compared to the right hemisphere. They also noted
that this pattern may be founded in a better bilateral manual control in the left hemisphere (Geschwind, 1975). Other evidence in
support of the theory pertained to a superior ability of the right
hand of one-month-old infants not only to reach but also to coordinate reaching and hand opening. The left hemisphere seems to
inhibit premature, interfering hand opening during young infant
reaching better than its mate.

A corollary postulate of the left hemisphere inhibition theory is
that the more the left hemisphere's inhibitory skills are fostered
by parents (or the environment, in general) early in life, the
better it will develop.

> "Could it not be that the more the parent manifests social
> behavior relevant to the infant's developing left, compa-
> red to right hemisphere, whether the behavior be of an
> activation and/or inhibition variety, the more the in-
> fant's left hemisphere will be differentially developed
> and affect behavior in turn ?" (Young et al., 1983,
> p.126).

In support of this hypothesis, Young et al. found that the more parents mouthed in a face-to-face interaction situation, the less
their one-month-old infants opened the left unused hand during the
unilateral reaching situation. Also, the more parents vocalized-
verbalized, the more the infants used the right hand in target
directed activity. Left hemisphere oriented social stimulation
seemed to augment left hemisphere's specialization for its skills,
thus increasing right hand manual behavior and parallel left hand
inhibition during young infant reaching.

The aesthetic simplicity of the inhibition hypothesis of hemispheric
specialization should not escape our attention. The concept of inhibition applies fluidly across many levels of psychological analysis concerning lateralization. There are biochemical mediators of
inhibition. Inhibition is a central characteristic of neuronal network and central nervous system function. Importance is attached to
inhibition in overt behavior at multiple levels: Motoric, cognitive, social, personality, etc. Even environmental influences such
as parents' behavior can be conceived in these terms. We will now

examine to what extent the evidence supports the concept that inhibitory skills are lateralized in the left hemisphere.

2.2. Alternative views

In 1983, the same year that Young et al. proposed their left hemisphere inhibition hypothesis, Levy (1983; Levy, Heller, Banich and Burton, 1983) argued that the right hemisphere is the seat of inhibition specialization. In Levy et al. (1983) she stated that Luria (1962/1966) and Penfield and Jasper (1954) showed that right prefrontal regions are specialized to modulate and inhibit cerebral arousal. In Levy (1983) she argued that the evidence indicating right frontal desynchronization in sadness suggests that the right hemisphere controls the inhibitory suppression of arousal (see Flor-Henry, 1985, p.160). Also in 1983, Swartzburg stated that the right hemisphere has a "general inhibitory function" as it suppresses behavioral activity and positive affect.

Since these pronunciations, a series of studies with left and right brain-damaged patients have shown that the right hemisphere is specialized for the inhibition of automatisms (De Renzi, Gentilini and Bazolli, 1986; Mori and Yamadori, 1985; Verfaellie and Heilman, 1987). For example, De Renzi et al. (1986) showed that patients with right but not left hemisphere damage could not follow the request to maintain the eyes closed for 10 seconds. Verfaellie and Heilman (1987) examined two patients with a chronic medial frontal lobe lesion. The right-sided patient had problems in inhibiting the unnecessary raising of the left arm when required to raise the right one.

There may even be an underlying neuronal substrate conducive to inhibitory functioning which is more prevalent in the right hemisphere. Scheibel (1984) found that the dendritic patterns of pyramidal neurons in and around Broca's area differed between the hemispheres. Right side neurons had more inhibitory and less excitory synapses since they had more first-order dendritic branching with fewer dendritic spines, a larger diameter, and lower resistance. However, Liederman (in press) points out that Scheibel's results should be considered preliminary because of the few cells and patients analyzed.

On the surface, it seems that the left hemisphere inhibition hypothesis must be invalid. However, consider the following alternative. Each of the hemispheres has its own inhibition specializations, and those of the right compared to the left hemisphere are less complex, refined, and dynamic. The right hemisphere seems to inhibit either in the sense of a general dampening of (positive) activity or a suppression of simple automatisms when no other dynamic activity is required. It is even possible to relate this apparent right hemisphere inhibition skill to that hemisphere's specialization for spatial and gestalt processing. Perhaps the right hemisphere is adept in such skills since they occur rapidly and do not need subtle, sequential inhibitions for their successful completion. Rather, it could be that such processing depends on a global inhibition of all other potentially concurrent processes in the short time period necessary for it to be performed. In short, spatial and gestalt processing may be more examples of a right hemi-

sphere specialization for general, instantaneous/time-limited inhibition. That is, it seems that right hemisphere inhibition can be
deployed either (a) by itself (without activation) over a limited
time, as in general positive affect dampening, or (b) in coordination with activation but not over time, as in instantaneous spatial
processing. In contrast, the left hemisphere seems specialized for
more intricate, serial inhibition functions, as it can especially
coordinate activation with inhibition more than momentarily, combining in one sophisticated skill aspects of both (a) and (b) above.
As Young et al. (1983b) emphasized, it seems especially involved in
sequential, goal-appropriate behavior, inhibiting potentially interfering activities before goal oriented behavior begins and as it
proceeds. In this sense, the left hemisphere seems to possess superior inhibitory skills, although those of the right may be equally
important to normal behavior. The abundant evidence in support of
the hypothesis of left hemisphere inhibition will now be presented.

2.3. Similar views

Although Young et al. (1983b) were the first to speculate that there
are multiple left hemisphere inhibition skills and that these skills
may underlie much of the functions involved in left hemisphere specialization, others have considered these issues, as well. Flor-
Henry (1985), in particular, has developed a somewhat similar idea,
as he wrote that "overall, the left brain is inhibitory" (p.172).
However, there are differences with the present model. In his model, the left hemisphere is seen as adept in the contralateral inhibition of right hemisphere specializations for emotionality and
sexual arousal (an idea first ventured in Flor-Henry, 1983a, 1983b).
An intrahemispheric posterior to anterior inhibition is also hypothesized, e.g., temporal-parietal inhibition of frontal euphoria.

It should be noted that stating that one hemisphere contralaterally
inhibits the other needs not imply that the inhibiting hemisphere is
specialized for inhibition. Usually, such contralateral inhibition
is viewed as part of a bihemispheric model of inhibition. That is,
the hemispheres are seen to work in tandem, with each reciprocally
inhibiting some of the other's specializations, and with no one
hemisphere more adept in the process of inhibition, per se. Even if
the lists of left and right side contralateral inhibitory influences
differ quantitatively, a qualitative difference is not implied. In
this vein, the first of Flor-Henry's (1985) two types of left hemisphere inhibition specialization is not a qualitative difference in
inhibitory skill, per se. The same can be said of Cook's (1984)
elegant model of mirror image homotopic contralateral inhibition
during a hemisphere's activation. In Cook's model, with a hemisphere's activation, ipsilateral surround and contralateral homotopic regions are inhibited, while contralateral extrahomotopic
regions are activated. But no special importance is given to left
hemisphere inhibition, per se. This is true even if left hemisphere
language activity and consequent right hemisphere inhibition provide
Cook's main example. Similarly, Corballis and Morgan (1978) argued
that there is a contralateral left hemisphere inhibition from early
in life. They posit an earlier or more rapid maturational gradient
development on the left compared to the right side of the body.

That is, the left hemisphere, and consequently the contralaterally
controlled right hand, mature earlier than the right hemisphere (and
left hand). The left hemisphere not only continues to lead in maturation, but it also generally exercises an inhibitory influence on
the right one for whatever skills that hemisphere has in parallel to
the left one. However, just as in Cook (1984), no differential importance is given to left hemisphere inhibition itself.

Others have dealt with left hemisphere inhibition prior to 1983, but
not from the perspective of attributing a general multiple inhibitory function to that hemisphere. The history of this work is now
described. The concept of a left hemisphere specialization for inhibition begins with eminent names in neuropsychology. Jasper and
Luria (Jasper and Raney, 1937; Penfield and Jasper, 1954; Luria,
1962/1966; Luria, Homskaya, Blinkov and Critchley, 1967) were the
first to suggest such specialization (see Levy, 1983, in section 2.2
for another reading of these sources). Jasper and Raney (1937) referred to longer dominant hand reaction times in simultaneous release movements, and thus suggested a "greater" "inhibition" of movement on the "dominant" side. Penfield and Jasper (1954) described
how direct electrical stimulation of the left supplementary motor
area in 20 patients produced an arrest, slowing, or hesitation in
voluntary speech movements. They argued that in this region there
is "a separate mechanism for the production or inhibition of movement" (p.99). Luria (1962/1966) found that lesions in the premotor
region of the dominant hemisphere, in particular, produced a "disturbance in the automatic inhibition of a movement already in process" (p.197). Luria et al. (1967) studied perseverations in cases
of lesions deep within the mesial parts of the frontal lobe. The
left side patient showed perseverations in word series, inertia in
choice, and contaminating associations. The results were seen as
due to a "low potential of cortical excitation which equalizes the
intensity of different traces" (p.116).

2.4. Contemporary neuropsychological evidence

Hudson (1968) linked the increase in problems with perseveration
following left hemisphere damage to that hemisphere's skill in inhibition. In such cases, Hudson (1968) suggested that there is an
"impairment of an inhibitory system influencing memory" (p.581).
Recent research has confirmed that left more than right hemisphere
patients has also various perseveration problems (Albert and
Sandson, 1986; Milner and Petrides, 1984; Pietro and Rigrodsky,
1986), and have also evoked inhibition impairment as an explanation
(Pietro and Rigrodsky, 1986).

Unilaterally brain-damaged patients have been studied more directly
with respect to the question of inhibition. Bruyer and Guerit
(1983) studied left- and right-damaged patients on a voluntary inhibition battery. The subjects had to maintain in place a body part
positioned by the experimenter for as long as possible. Left side
patients had difficulty, especially with the limbs. Haaland (1984)
found that when left hemisphere damage is severe enough to include
motor apraxia, response inhibition as measured by static steadiness
was affected. Mintz and Myslobodsky (1983) studied electrodermal
amplitude asymmetries to orienting stimuli in hemi-parkinsonism
patients. They found results suggesting that left hemisphere cir-

cuits modulate right hemisphere pathways by facilitation and inhibition. Finally, Buck and Duffy (1980) examined unilaterally
damaged patients for spontaneous nonverbal expressiveness while
watching slides. Left side patients were more expressive, implying
that left hemisphere contralateral inhibition of their expressivity
was impaired. In all this research, more than a simple kind of inhibition was required. The task length was extreme (Bruyer and
Guerit), or the behavior was demanding (and over time, Haaland), or
a balance with activation was evident (Mintz and Myslobodsky), or
continual control of spontaneous expressions was required (Buck and
Duffy).

Neuropsychological research with other kinds of patients also implicate a left hemisphere control for inhibition. In 1985, Yeudall
suggested that the left prefrontal regions normally inhibit the
right side of the brain during language functioning, but stutterers
may have an overactive right hemisphere interfering with this process. He described EEG data during expressive speech consistent
with this hypothesis. Griener, Fitzgerald and Cooke (1986) elaborated on this work by arguing that in stutterers the right hemisphere interferes with the normal balancing of activation and inhibition that occurs in the left hemisphere. They found that on a
dual control task, involving concurrent spontaneous speech and
tapping, stutterers were especially interfered with, as they both
tapped and spoke more slowly than controls. Stutterers were also
more dysfluent, except when left-handed ones concurrently tapped
with the left hand. According to the authors, both intrahemispheric
and interhemispheric activation-inhibition balancing by the left
hemisphere are implicated in the results. For example, right-
handers showed more of the former and left-handers more of the latter on the dual tasks. Griener et al. referred to Young et al.'s
(1983b) theory of left hemisphere inhibition when explaining their
results, and also mention three other articles written in 1980
(Denenberg, 1980; Lomas, 1980; Wolff and Cohen, 1980; however, a
left hemisphere inhibition can be inferred only indirectly). Recently, problems in left hemisphere inhibition have been suggested
as a possible basis for infantile autism (Dawson, in press) and for
dyslexia (Kinsbourne, in press). The specific problem suggested by
Dawson for autism resembles Yeudall's for stuttering, underscoring
the need for more differentiated hypotheses about how left hemisphere inhibition problems may vary across certain disturbances in
behavior.

Since 1979, Gruzelier has discussed left hemisphere inhibition in
relation to schizophrenia. Gruzelier and Hammond (1979) studied ear
differences in absolute threshold in these patients, and found more
right ear threshold deterioration. According to the authors, the
left hemisphere thus seemed more susceptible to inhibitory influences such as fatigue and adaptation. However, these processes do not
seem comparable to the ones under discussion here. Gruzelier and
Hammond (1980) found that more aroused schizophrenics taking chlor-
promazine showed deficient left brain side inhibitory processes compared to controls. In particular, unlike controls, they had difficulty suppressing loud right ear digits when these stimuli had to be
reported after quieter left ones. Finally, Gruzelier (1983) mentioned a possible role for left hemisphere inhibition in subtypes of
schizophrenia (his Table 2). The acute, reactive type seems to show

an increase in left hemisphere activation and thus a decrease in
inhibition, unlike the case for the chronic, nonreactive patient who
seems to show right hemisphere activation. Gruzelier's interesting
speculations should be followed up with research.

2.5. Other nondevelopmental evidence

Research with normal populations has also supported the left hemisphere inhibition hypothesis. Bruno and Auerbach (1983) found that
the left hemisphere was more active in acquiring voluntary inhibitory control over skin resistance levels in right-handers receiving
auditory click feedback. Liederman and Foley (1987) asked right-
handers to lift the middle or ring finger once a weight was placed
on it. Involuntary contralateral activity was recorded. Weights
were adjusted relative to body weight or finger strength, depending
on the study in the series performed, thus controlling for these
contaminants. The subjects displayed more right hand involuntary
movement. Similar results are consistently found in children, although the studies do not use comparable weight and strength controls (e.g., Wolff, Gunnoe and Cohen, 1983, p.420). Moreover,
Liederman and Foley (1987) noted that these findings are comparable
to Young et al'.s (1983b) data where one-month-old infants opened
the unused right hand more than the left one during unilateral reaching by the contralateral hand. Liederman and Foley concluded that
a superior left hemisphere inhibition may in part help to account
for the results.

Surprisingly, experiments with animals also implicate a left hemisphere inhibition specialization. Rogers (1980) listed three activities activated in the right hemisphere in chicks which are normally inhibited contralaterally by the left hemisphere (e.g., detection
and response to novelty). In contrast, no relationship involving a
right hemisphere inhibition was listed. Also, he listed four other
activities which seem to have an inhibitory component, and which are
normally activated by the left hemisphere, for example, peck-no-peck
decisions and visual discrimination learning. For the latter, he
mentioned that the left hemisphere seems "more able to inhabit [sic]
pecking when the stimulus is non-rewarding" (p.4). Similarly,
Denenberg (1981) listed various behavioral laterality effects in the
rat where one hemisphere activates a behavior and the other one
contralaterally inhibits it. This list clearly shows more cases
involving left hemisphere inhibition (e.g., taste aversion, spatial
choice behavior). It is worthwhile noting that Denenberg also
showed that early experience can act to increase pre-existing lateralities in rats, and can even induce them. These data suggest that
Young et al.'s (1983b) corollary hypothesis on the role of early
social experience in hemispheric specialization development should
be investigated further (see section 2.1).

Although underlying structural and biochemical differences between
the hemispheres may not relate to behavioral and functional differences, they may be meaningful. Rossor, Garrett and Iversen (1980)
analyzed nine areas of post-mortem human brains for GABA, which has
an inhibition function, and other neurotransmitters. The only
significant left-right difference concerned more GABA in the left
substantia nigra. However, this difference was considered a chance
occurrence. Moreover, Glick, Ross and Hough (1982) re-analyzed the

data, and did not replicate this result. However, Glick et al. did find across all areas a positive correlation between left-right asymmetries in GABA and GAD, a related neurotransmitter. They concluded that the GABA-GAD system may function to maintain overall asymmetries. These findings have been cited in support of the left hemisphere inhibition hypothesis (e.g., Flor-Henry, 1985). Goldberg and Costa (1981) suggested that the left hemisphere manifests better intraregional connections. Such focal, dense networking may underlie that hemisphere's suggested superior inhibition skills.

2.6. Developmental evidence

To this point, the left hemisphere inhibition hypothesis has been scrutinized using all but human developmental research. We now turn to these latter studies for a rich source of relevant data. Liederman (1983, 1987) has clearly enunciated a developmental theory of left hemisphere inhibition specialization. She reviewed some research showing that after one month of life, several reflexes become inhibited more on the right vs. the left side of the body. First, she cites Subirana (1964). He reported that Tournay (1924) observed that a baby who would eventually become right-handed evidenced disappearance of the Babinski reflex earlier on the right. McGraw (1943, 1969 edition cited) found a similar result after 6 weeks of life for unilateral reflex grasping to support the body (Darwinian reflex). Liederman and Coryell (1981) found that left compared to right head turns better elicited the asymmetric tonic neck reflex in this age period. After considering all this evidence, Liederman (1983, 1987) suggests that there is a left brain side inhibition center which either develops earlier than the one on the right, or else imposes itself with greater strength on contralateral activity. Reference to a similar hypothesis is made in Liederman and Coryell (1981), but a competing interactionist explanation seems to have been preferred. It should be noted that the clearest data here are Liederman and Coryell's. First, Subirana's summary of Tournay was erroneous. Rather than finding that the Babinski reflex disappeared earlier on the right, Tournay showed that it changed to the adult form earlier on the right, probably due to pyramidal tract maturation. Also, McGraw's data concerning the Darwinian reflex were presented in a figure which was not amenable to statistical analysis.

N. Kamptner, Cornwell, Fitzgerald and L. Harris (1985) have found results which support Liederman. They studied stepping movements in familial right- and left-handed infants five times from birth to 3 months. According to the authors, the familial right-handers, in particular, shifted from the right to the left in stepping laterality after the first session, in support of Liederman's hypothesis. However, inspection of the data show that on the average the left- and not the right-handed familial group showed the indicated trend after the first session. Moreover, Liederman's relevant age period does not concern neonates but begins at 6 weeks. Nevertheless, one group did show the appropriate shift at about the required age period - the right-handed familial males at 1 month, fitting the Liederman hypothesis. However, it should be noted that such shifts were not analyzed statistically.

Ramsay has performed a series of studies where changes in manual
preference were shown to be linked to onsets of various vocal and
verbal behaviors, as shall be shown in section 4.4. In a longitudinal investigation, he studied how right hand toy manipulation and
duplicate syllable babbling were interrelated (Ramsay, 1984). The
latter behavior emerged between 5 and 8 months, varying across infants, and the former only at the week of babbling onset. Moreover, right hand manipulation temporarily disappeared 3 to 4 weeks
after its emergence due to an increase in left hand activity.
Ramsay concluded that a temporary "release of [contralateral] inhibition by the left hemisphere" (p.69) may have taken place, perhaps due to an emergence of new nondominant hemisphere skills for
perception and emotion. Goldfield and Michel (1986) also researched
lateralized manual behavior at around the middle of the first year.
A barrier was placed in the way as 7- to 12-month-olds reached bima-
nually, with one hand often leading, to a toy box requiring bimanual
activity to open it. A separate situation examined initial contacts
of simple toys. The 8-month-olds were the most right-handed age
group in the latter situation and also one of the groups least affected by a barrier blocking the advancing right hand in the former
situation. A plausible interpretation of these results could be the
following. Perhaps the more a group is left hemisphere lateralized
for a task in the age period concerned, the more its inhibition
skills can be deployed to work around environmental intrusions on
the hand it controls contralaterally.

Fox and Davidson (1984) have studied the lateralization of emotions.
They argued that in the second year the toddler better attenuates
negative emotions because the left hemisphere comes to acquire inhibitory control over the right hemisphere, which is specialized for
negative emotions. In this age period, Fox and Davidson note that
left hemisphere activities (e.g., language) increase disproportionately and transcallosal fibers mature rapidly. In support of their
hypothesis, they cite Weinraub and Smolak's (1983) study which
showed that 18-month-olds with better verbal facility could better
inhibit distress during maternal separation.

2.7. Conclusions

In summary, the evidence clearly suggests that from early in life
the left side of the brain possesses superior inhibitory skills.
Early reflexes disappear earlier on the side of the body controlled
by this hemisphere (Liederman, 1983). The left hemisphere can balance activation and inhibition intrahemispherically to better coordinate reaching and hand opening on that side, and to better
inhibit irrelevant activity on the other side (Young et al., 1983b).
The left hemisphere also evidences contralateral inhibition of right
hemisphere emotional specialization as early as the first year (Fox
and Davidson, 1984; Ramsay, 1984). Both hemispheres possess various
contralateral interhemispheric inhibitions, but the left hemisphere
seems to perform more such activities (Denenberg, 1981). The range
of behavior controlled by left hemisphere inhibitory mechanisms include perseverations (Pietro and Rigrodsky, 1986), steadiness
(Bruyer and Guerit, 1983), and manual involuntary movements
(Liederman and Foley, 1987). Neuropsychological studies are revea-
ling variations in this control (stutterers: Griener et al., 1986;
schizophrenics: Gruzelier, 1983) and possible structural localiza-

tions (Yeudall, 1985). There may be a biochemical basis involving
GABA underlying this lateralization (Glick et al., 1982). In contrast, right hemisphere inhibition specializations seem less complex, as they involve contralateral suppression of (positive) left
hemisphere activity (Levy, 1983), or inhibition of simple automatisms (Verfaellie and Hailman, 1987).

Despite all this evidence, Best and Queen (1989) recently argued for
a right hemisphere inhibition superiority. They found that infants
seemed to express emotions more intensely on the right side of the
mouth region. They suggested that this may reflect a greater
reflexive/nonvoluntary (subcortical) inhibition by the right brain,
which is also seen as involved in activation. However, Fox and
Davidson (1986, 1988) found left hemisphere EEG activation in
certain positive expressions in infancy. Moreover, a key for Best
and Queen rested in McDonnell, Anderson and Abraham's (1983) result
that young infants extend to a target better with the left than the
right hand. However, one can question this view (see below).

3. RESEARCH ON BEHAVIORAL LATERALIZATION IN INFANCY

3.1. Early reaching, grasping, turning

The 1 1/2- to 2-year-old seems adultlike on handedness batteries
(Archer, Campbell and Segalowitz, 1988a; Kaufman, Zalman and
Kaufman, 1978), left hemisphere oriented tasks (dichotic word listening; Lokker and Morais, 1985), and right hemisphere oriented tasks
(tactual processing; Rose, 1984). However, a recurrent theme is
that early reaching in very young infants is not adultlike in lateralization. Careful scrutiny shows otherwise. Some data showing a
left hand reaching preference in the early months (e.g., Gesell and
Ames, 1947) are not statistically significant (Young, 1977a).
Others do not concern reaching, per se. For example, Young,
Segalowitz, Misek, Alp and Boulet (1983c) showed that McDonnell et
al. (1983) confounded midline and forward movement. In fact,
research with significant results concerning early reaching mostly
reveals a right hand preference (e.g., Bigsby, 1983; von Hofsten,
1982, 1984; Young et al., 1983c).

However, de Schonen and Bresson (1984; Bresson and de Schonen, 1983;
Brésard and Bresson, 1987) reported that 5-day-olds prefer the left
hand in ballistic reaching without visual guidance for objects placed to a side. They inferred a left hemisphere dominance for the
movement via ipsilateral pathways. However, another possible explanation of their results stems from Young et al. (1983c). As seen
above, their literature review shows an early right hand reaching
preference. Moreover, this preference fits into a general pattern
of manual specialization. Already early in life infants manifest a
right hand specialization for all target directed behaviors (e.g.,
reaching, precision grasping) and a left hand specialization for
complementary functions (e.g., nondirected activation, passive holding). In this context, de Schonen and Bresson's early ballistic
left hand reaching may perform a complementary spatial or marker
function and thus be controlled by the right hemisphere. Note that
since Young et al.'s (1983c) review, a group has reported a left
preference in unilateral grasping of an object by 12-week-olds (Yu-

Yan, Cun-Ren and Over, 1983). However, this task is difficult to
interpret since an infant may drop an object out of disinterest in
it or interest in something else. Moreover, past research generally
indicates that the right hand is preferred in this activity and in
related grasping behavior (Young et al., 1983c).

The voluminous remaining studies published since 1983 all show a
right side preference in infant behavior. For example, Hopkins,
Lems, Janssen and Butterworth (1987) found that awake newborns only
26 minutes old were right-sided in head turning and in hand-to-mouth
behavior. The preference for early right head turning is a general
phenomenon in fullterm (Liederman, 1987) and preterm (Konishi,
Kuriyama, Mikawa and Suzuki, 1987) newborns, but it varies with age,
state, sex, familial handedness, and supine-prone position (Barnes,
Cornwell, Fitzgerald and L. Harris, 1985; Cornwell, Fitzgerald and
L. Harris, 1985; Konishi et al., 1987). Moreover, it seems to reflect an innate motor rather than a sensory bias to the right side,
and thus may be indicative of an early left subcortical specialization (Cornwell, Barnes, Fitzgerald and L. Harris, 1985; Liederman,
1987). The neonatal stepping reflex does not give results as clear
as those for the hand and head. N. Kamptner et al. (1985) and
Trehub, Corter and Shosenberg (1983) have not replicated the work of
Peters and Petrie (1979) and Melekian (1981) who found an early
right-side lead in the stepping reflex (Peters, 1988).

3.2. Other research up to 6 months

There are many studies on early brain damage relevant to the question of neonatal lateralization (see Liederman, in press; Witelson,
1987). For example, Kiessling, Denkla and Carlton (1983) tested
children with right or left infantile hemiplegia. Onset of their
motor problems was diagnosed as prenatal or perinatal and none was
evaluated as retarded. Siblings were used as normal controls.
"High level" language functions (repetition test, syntactic test),
in particular, were significantly affected in the right hemiplegic
children. In fact, the more these children's manual dexterity was
impaired, the lower were their scores on these language measures.
The authors concluded that "the neuronal substrate of language
ability is present at birth and shows clear laterality" (p.731).

Research with normal neonates also reveals a congenital lateralization of language function somewhat along adult lines. The
Molfeses (D. Molfese and V. Molfese, 1979, 1980, 1983), in particular, have shown that preterm and term neonates manifest a differential hemispheric contribution to the analysis of speech sounds
varying in place of articulation. Computer synthesized consonant-
vowel pairs were presented. Statistical factors derived from evoked
potentials in the temporal region showed mostly bilateral but some
hemisphere specific activity. For term neonates, an early component
of the waveform reflected left hemisphere discrimination of consonants presented in normal formant structure. As for prematures,
left hemisphere components differentiated phonetic from nonphonetic
transitions in normal formant structure, in particular. Similarly,
Bertoncini, Lokker, Morais and Mehler (in press, in Mehler, 1985)
found a right ear (left hemisphere) advantage for speech stimuli in
4-day-olds by using a behavioral methodology appropriate to this
age.

Best (in press) showed that structural asymmetries exist even in the foetus, and that their nature are consonant with functional properties with which the hemispheres are associated. For example, the planum temporale, which includes Wernicke's area, important for language, is already larger on the left in the foetus (Wada, Clarke and Hamm, 1975). Other foetal cerebral asymmetries involve the left occipital and right frontal regions (Weinberger, Luchins, Morihisa and Wyatt, 1982). However, catch-up, inversion, and three dimensional torque twisting of the foetal brain complicates these asymmetries (Best, in press). It should be noted that there may also be structural asymmetries in the limbs which are already evident foetally (Peters, 1988).

The last finding in this section brings us back to behavior. The young infant has been found to use the right more than the left hand when with the mother. Trevarthen (1986) noticed more right hand positive expressive but not self-touching movements in young infants with their mothers. Fogel and Hannan (1985) observed more right hand opening in face-to-face mother interaction at 9 weeks. Hannan (1987) found more right hand pointing when with the mother and a toy beginning at 3 months. However, pointing was left-handed when the infant was alone with the mother. This suggests that different contexts involving the mother at different ages may evoke different functional demands. Thus, to suggest either a left (e.g., Trevarthen) or right (e.g., Segalowitz, 1986) hemispheric specialization in positive expressive manual behavior when with the mother may be simplistic. This conclusion speaks to the issue of manual specialization raised at the outset. Each hand will be specialized for the skills lateralized in the hemisphere contralateral to it on tasks of a relatively demanding or nonautomatic nature. Such specialization seems to begin early in life, even for situations which are more social in nature.

3.3. Lateralized behavior after 6 months

After 5 to 6 months, there is little doubt that the infant becomes clearly right lateralized for reaching and related behavior (McCormick and Mauer, 1988; Michel, Ovrut and Harkins, 1986; A. Young, Lock and Service, 1985). Also, the stability of these behaviors increases. McCormick and Mauer (1988) and Michel et al. (1986) have found that at around 6 months reaching is reliable, i.e., not very variable in direction within any one session (using split-half calculations). In terms of a consistency over a longer time period, the results begin to show more shifts in hand preference. For example, McCormick and Mauer examined the reach, grasp, then move sequence three times in three weeks using both correlational and classification consistency techniques. A small, modest stability was evident even though there was large shifting (per contra, Carlson and Harris, 1985, for reaching, and Michel et al., 1986, for manipulation). It should be noted that in both McCormick and Mauer's and Michel et al.'s research, a laterality index equivalent to a z score transformation is employed to determine overall right or left hand preference. The use of this index as a z score to determine significant individual preferences in Michel et al. may not be acceptable. The repeated trials upon which the z score calculation is based are not independent for any one individual, unlike what is required for significance testing involving the z score.

Even though reaching and manipulation are right lateralized at about
6 months, there are some uncertainties concerning their developmental course. (a) The percentage of lateralized infants is not always
very high, and (b) its stability varies with familial handedness
(McCormick and Mauer, 1988). (c) There is not a steady increase
with age in the number of right-lateralized reachers. Goldfield and
Michel (1986) found a peak of right lateralization in reaching at
8-10 months in the period between 7 and 12 months. (d) Behavior
related to reaching, such as manipulation, may not be right lateralized until after 16 months in daily nursery school activity
(Provins, Dalziel and Higgenbottom, 1987). (e) It is uncertain when
right preference in bimanual reaching with one hand leading emerges.
Estimates range between 7 and 13 months (Goldfield and Michel, 1986;
Michel et al., 1986). (f) Bimanual organization toward an object
on a stand at around 5 months may show right hand object grasping
after left hand reaching for the support, or it may show the opposite, depending on the nature of the situation (Bresson, Maury,
Piérault-Le-Bonniec and de Schonen, 1977; Ramsay and Willis, 1984).
(g) Such behavior at one year seems to involve reaching for the
support with the left hand so that the right one is free for the
object (Michel et al., 1986). (h) Finally, sex differences in
infant reaching are not usually evident. However, when found, they
seem to follow a particular pattern. Humphrey and Humphrey (1987)
found that 5- to 8-month-old girls but not boys showed a right hand
preference for reaching. From 9 to 12 months, both sexes were
equally right lateralized. They argued that the results could
reflect an earlier development of the left cerebral cortex in infant
girls. Other studies support their conclusions. Carlson and L.
Harris (1985) found a similar advantage for familial right-handed
infant girls in right hand reaching. Michel et al. (1986) noticed
an analogous sex difference favoring girls in about the same age
period in right hand manipulatory activity with blocks. Trevarthen
(1986) also observed an earlier female right side lateralization in
this age period - this time positive gesturing to the mother was
involved. Lewkowicz and Turkewitz (1982, 1983) investigated latency
to reach for an object with and without interfering stimuli presented to the ears. At 8 months, female infants showed the expected
adult pattern of interference due to speech to the right ear and
music to the left ear. In contrast, males showed the opposite pattern at both 6 and 8 months. Note that Shucard, Shucard and Thomas
(1984) reported a sex difference favoring girls in auditory evoked
potentials at 6 months. However, their results did not involve
lateralization, per se. If all these data concerning early sex
differences in left hemisphere specialization are replicated, de
Lacoste's hypothesis that the foetal corpus callosum may be involved
in such sex differences should be investigated (de Lacoste and
Woodward, 1988).

3.4. Longitudinal relations between the neonatal and toddler or
     child periods

Toddler and childhood lateralization has been related both to early
(a) lateralized behavior and (b) nonlateralized characteristics.
The first kind of research is usually based on the finding that neonate head turning is highly right lateralized and stable. Consequently, it has been suggested that it is a causal precursor to
later handedness, with the majority right side head-turners ending

up right-handed and the minority left side turners emerging left-handed. Michel and Harkins (1986) found that side of neonate head turning preference predicted (a) side of hand looking up to 8 weeks, (b) hand activation at 12 weeks, and (c) reaching up to 18 months. Coryell (1985) found a link between (a) neonatal head turning and hand looking preference in the first 12 weeks and (b) handedness as reported by parents between 3 1/2 and 6 years. Similarly, Young et al. (1983b) noted a correlation between degree of right lateraliza-tion in 1-month target directed activity and in 18-month tapping, among other findings.

The Molfeses have performed the most rigorous research involving longterm relations stemming from lateralization early in life. They examined a variety of measures in the newborn period, including the lateralized ones based on auditory evoked responses (AERs) discussed in section 3.2. These measures were related to language skills 3 years later (D. Molfese and V. Molfese, 1985; D. Molfese and Betz, in press). Specifically, newborns with left hemisphere AERs which discriminated between different consonant sounds developed better language than those without such AERs. Moreover, the advanced language group at 3 years showed certain neonatal left hemisphere AERs which discriminated between different consonant-based speech sounds and right ones which discriminated between certain nonverbal sounds. In contrast, the low language group did not evidence any neonatal AER lateralization.

Nonlateralized characteristics early in life that have been related to later lateralization include prematurity and risk status since they may affect the developing central nervous system and its late-ralization. Konishi and associates (Konishi, Mikawa and Suzuki, 1986; Konishi et al., 1987) found that prematurity led to more right lateralization in neonate head turning and in 9- and 18-month reaching, especially in infants who were nursed supine. The healthy status of the preterm and term subjects in this study may have some-how played in these unexpected results, which need statistical con-firmation and replication. Fox (1985) reported data showing a pattern somewhat opposite to Konishi's. Healthy preterms and sick terms in comparison to at risk preterms and healthy terms were more left-handed on tapping tasks at 24 months. This time, the results for the at risk preterms seem anomalous. Clearly, the early late-rality of prematures needs further investigation. Ross, Lipper and Auld (1987) compared at risk preterms with healthy terms on handed-ness as observed by their parents when they were 3 years. The for-mer were less right-handed. However, these results are difficult to compare to Fox's since it is impossible to determine whether the prematurity or health difference between the groups accounted for the results. Ross et al. also found that if left-handed, the prema-tures had more language and cognitive problems at age 3. They con-cluded that these data support the position that birth complications may induce cerebral insult and thus (a) consequent alteration of lateralization and (b) simultaneous change in mental development (Bakan, Dibb and Reed, 1973; Satz, 1973).

This latter theory is controversial since the data with fullterms do not always support it, especially with respect to part "a" (e.g., Nachshon and Denno, 1986). When more direct measures of birth stress are examined, such as maternal retrospective reports or hos-

pital files on newborns in prospective studies, the results are
somewhat more positive. For example, Coren, Searleman and Porac
(1982) and Orsini, Satz and Zemansky (1985) found that birth stress
is associated with later left handedness. However, Ehrlichman,
Zoccolotti and Owen (1982) and Schwartz (1985) did not find such an
association using similar measures. The most unequivocal results in
favor of the hypothesis are based on measures of eye preference.
Coren et al. (1982), Ehrlichman et al. (1982), Gur, Levy and Van
Auken (1979), and Nachshon and Denno (1987; in press) all found an
association between higher birth stress and later left eye preference. Ehrlichman et al. (1982) argued that hand preference compared to eye preference is more subject to influences such as parent
or teacher environmental pressures. Thus, its relation to birth
stress may be obscured compared to the case for eye preference.

3.5. Other longitudinal relations

Studies with neonates' head turning preference are also showing that
birth stress can influence laterality (e.g., Feldman, 1983; Fox and
Lewis, 1982; Liederman and Coryell, 1982). For example, Feldman
(1983) observed neonates of mothers preselected for being at risk
for having low birth weight offspring. Neonates were categorized as
right, left, or inconsistent head-turners. Neurological score,
birthweight, and gestational age helped distinguish the groups, with
more risk apparent in the latter two head turning groups. Our conclusion must be that early influences may affect the developing central nervous system and its lateralization, and may thus have long-
term consequences in lateralization and behavior. However, only
appropriate methods can uncover this subtle effect.

Other research relates infant lateralization of behavior in the
second year to later language and similar skills. Bates, O'Connell,
Vaid, Sledge and Oakes (1986) found that the degree of right side
preference in 13-month, nonsymbolic, manual activity with objects
(e.g., pick up, put down) correlated with 20- and 28-month
analytic/receptive language. Gottfried and Bathurst (1983; Kee,
Gottfried, Bathurst and K. Brown, 1987) observed that girls consistent in their drawing handedness every 6 months between 18 and 42
months showed better scores on various intellectual indices (e.g.,
cognitive, verbal, memory) in the age period concerned. Moreover,
girls inconsistent in handedness did not show left hemisphere language specialization at 5 to 6 years, as determined by a time sharing task involving tapping and nursery rhyme recitation. Also,
they were less right lateralized for tapping. The sex difference in
these results fits with earlier suggestions that the left hemisphere
of girl infants may mature earlier. That is, girls can show a relationship between lateralization, the left hemisphere, and cognitive-
language skills because their left hemisphere may mature earlier
than boys and thus be primed for such linkages. Moreover, individual differences in such relations can only be evident in girls for
they are probably undergoing such priming more than boys.

Finally, two studies relate neonatal lateralization measures to
intellectual development at 12 months. Feldman (1983) found that in
a sample of at risk newborns, head turning preference was related to
1-year gross motor development in boys and to object permanence, an
index of sensorimotor intelligence, in girls. This sex difference

is similar to the ones of Gottfried and Bathurst that were just discussed, and can thus be interpreted in the same way. In another
study, deviations from optimal left but not right hemisphere blood
flow in premature neonates were associated with lower Bayley developmental quotient scores at 1 year (Ment, Scott, Lange, Ehrenkranz,
Duncan and Warshaw, 1983).

3.6. Conclusions

Previously, we have argued that the nature-nurture distinction in
developmental psychology is too coarse, and that multiple interacting influences on behavior need to be considered. In this
regard, it should be noted that clear environmental influences on
lateralization development have not yet been discussed. However,
evidence is accruing that classic environmental factors need to be
taken into account when explaining such development. Denenberg
(1981) has argued that experience can induce or augment lateralization in young rats. Young et al. (1983b) have a similar hypothesis concerning the augmentation of lateralization by relevant
social experience in young human infants. Turkewitz (in press) has
even discussed a possible role for foetal experiences on hemispheric
specialization. Postural positioning in the hospital after birth
can affect head turning (L. Harris and Fitzgerald, 1983) and perhaps
later behavior (Konishi et al., in section 3.4). Even the notion of
imitation of maternal hand preference has been invoked to help
explain some data with infants. Harkins and Michel (in press) found
that left-handed mothers, in particular, had 10-month-olds left-
preferring in reaching and unimanual actions, and argued that imitation may explain the relationship.

In summary, neonates seem to possess a pattern of lateralization of
brain processes somewhat akin to the adult. Each hemisphere appears
to have its specialized skills which influence behavior lateralization. Moreover, there may be longterm consequences in later lateralization and in intellectual-language skills stemming from individual differences in early lateralization, or from factors which may
affect that lateralization. Such factors cover a range of variables
including sex, risk, and more direct environmental experiences.
L. Kamptner, Kraft and Harper (1984) have even shown that individual
differences in a measure of left hemisphere lateralization (dichotic
word listening) were associated with social interactions and vocali-
zations in a sample of 2- to 5-years-olds. Thus, it is essential
that we fully apprehend the development of lateralization, for its
consequences may concern much of what makes us human. To this end,
in the next section we survey the major contemporary theories of how
hemispheric specialization develops.

4. HEMISPHERIC SPECIALIZATION DEVELOPMENT

4.1. Introduction

There is general agreement in the field that Lenneberg's (1967) developmental model of hemispheric specialization is no longer tenable
(e.g., Curtiss, 1986). He argued that the two sides of the brain
are congenitally equipotential for language and that over the first
two years of life the left hemisphere becomes progressively specia-

lized for that function. The evidence cited in the previous section, for example, counters Lenneberg's proposal. Some theorists
have adopted an opposite but equally polarized view - that hemispheric specialization does not develop since it is fully present in
some ways at birth (Kinsbourne and Hiscock, 1987; Witelson, 1987).
However, we shall see that this approach has a limited range of
reference and may not apply to infancy, the period of concern to us
here. Thus, reality lies somewhere between the opposite views of
(a) a gradual developmental increase in hemispheric specialization
which begins with a nonlateralized neonatal brain, and (b) no
developmental increase in hemispheric specialization since there is
a fully lateralized neonatal brain. This intermediate position on
lateralization development can be labelled "progressive" lateralization. We are the first to show that the progressive school of
thought is not monolithic, but can be decomposed into several complementary points of view. These are the progressive addition,
progressive stages, and progressive transfer approaches to lateralization development. The labels characterizing these approaches
were derived from examination of the works of their key exponents
(the Molfeses, Ramsay, and Michel, respectively), as shall be shown
in the next sections.

It is worthwhile noting exactly what is included and excluded in
this section before beginning. (a) We emphasize major approaches to
the normal development of hemispheric specialization which include
the infancy period in one way or another. The reader is referred to
Bullock, Liederman and Todorovic (1987), Hécaen (1984), Kinsbourne
and Hiscock (1987), and Witelson (1987) for accounts including pathological effects and their consequences. (b) The question of
increased communication between the hemispheres is not examined
since the evidence in infancy is sparse and perhaps contradictory
(see Michel, Ovrut and Harkins, 1984; de Schonen and Bry, 1987).
Moreover, such an increase in interhemispheric communication can be
seen as orthogonal to the primary issue of development within the
hemispheres. That is, a regressive lateralization in development
may occur in the sense of a lessening isolation of the hemispheres
(Kershner, 1985; Levy, 1985). However, the inverse of progressive
lateralization in the way it was introduced above is not implied.
(c) Possible differences within the hemispheres are generally ignored, as a global perspective is sought. Thus, the issues of
anterior-posterior differences, specific regional differences (e.g.,
Kirk, 1985), etc., are generally not considered. (d) Peripheral
(e.g., muscular) asymmetries and their relation to more central ones
are excluded even though important (see Thelen, Skala and Kelso,
1987; Peters, 1983). (e) Finally, we focus especially on the development of left hemispheric specialization in the right-side preferring individual, except where indicated. We now turn to the
theories. Note that they do not fall so clearly into the categories
that are used to catalogue them; there is some overlap. Nevertheless, it is felt that the labels do capture the essence of each
theory, and the important ways that they overlap are discussed.

4.2. Invariant hemispheric specialization

4.2.1. The theory as applied to infancy

When originally introduced, the concept of invariant, unchanging lateralization in development was broadly conceived. For example, Kinsbourne and Hiscock (1983) argued that "the degree of lateralization remains constant across the lifespan" (p.215). There may be subcortical-cortical shifting and strategy changes in hemisphere deployment during certain tasks, but the brain is lateralized invariantly from "the time of birth". Kinsbourne and Hiscock (1987) have added that there may be early asymmetries which serve as precursors of later hemispheric specializations, but which "serve no immediate purpose" (p.232). However, in this most recent statement of their position, Kinsbourne and Hiscock have restricted their invariant lateralization hypothesis to the period beyond infancy. For the infancy period, they cited the kind of research mentioned in section 4.4 concerning predictions of later handedness from neonatal head turning (e.g., Michel, 1983). Then they argued that these data are not incompatible with some form of progressive lateralization. For example, slight or inconsistent early asymmetries may develop into more marked, stable ones.

Witelson (1987) also defended the view that "hemisphere specialization exists from birth onward and does not undergo further change in either its nature or degree" (p.653). As development proceeds, more brain areas become involved in lateralization, more cognitive skills are acquired and become lateralized, and changes in strategies of hemispheric activation on certain tasks may occur. However, these are secondary epiphenomena in relation to constant hemispheric processes. Nevertheless, when reviewing the infancy data, Witelson suggested that the issue of change in the degree of lateralization "remains open". Thus, we see that no unequivocal statement about the invariance of lateralization in infancy has been made by major proponents of this position. Moreover, there are logical inconsistencies in this hypothesis, as pointed out by Bullock et al. (1987). First, only data primarily concerning cortical functioning are considered relevant by Witelson. Second, only lateralization of matured skills is examined. The exclusion of data suggestive of (a) subcortical functioning or (b) transitions to stable behavior seems to deny much of what infancy and lateralization in infancy are about.

What is the mechanism underlying the notion of invariant lateralization since birth ? Kinsbourne and Hiscock (1987), in particular, described a very specific mechanism in neonatal lateralization and how it influences subsequent lateralization in an invariant way. They suggested that tonic brainstem arousal mechanisms are lateralized from birth for channelling speech-related stimuli to the left side of the brain and various nonverbal stimuli to the right side. Such a mechanism leads to differential hemispheric activation and consequent lateral preferences in behavior in a constant way throughout the lifespan. In support of the theory, Levine, Liederman, and Riley (1988) found an asymmetry in the brainstem auditory evoked potential, and note that the auditory brainstem is almost fully myelinated before birth.

4.2.2. Comments on the theory

Kinsbourne (1978) has related early left- and right-side brain
functioning to more general tendencies. He argued that the left and
right hemispheres are specialized for approach and withdrawal, respectively, since they seem to control positive and negative emotivi-
ty, respectively, as well as speech and various nonverbal processes.
To test the hypothesis, Fox and Davidson (1986, 1988) have examined
frontal and parietal electroencephalogram (EEG) activity during
elicited facial signs of emotion in newborns and in 10-month-olds.
In the former, a disgust-inducing situation (pipette on tongue to
present water) provoked right brain side activation, whereas sucrose
showed the opposite effect (Fox and Davidson, 1986). EEG activity
during mother and stranger approach and mother departure was analyzed in the 10-month-olds. Full smiles involving the cheeks and eyes
were elicited by the mother and were associated with left frontal
activation. Less evident smiling with the cheeks only was elicited
by the stranger and was associated with right frontal activation.
Similarly, a more controlled negative expression without crying was
left hemisphere active, while a less controlled one with crying was
right hemisphere active (Fox and Davidson, 1988).

An alternate explanation to the approach-withdrawal hypothesis of
hemispheric specialization flows from Young et al.'s (1983b) inhibition hypothesis. On the one hand, the link between withdrawal and
right hemisphere skills such as spatial integration is not clear.
On the other hand, approach and withdrawal are descriptive terms
about behavior rather than explanatory ones about mechanisms. To
approach effectively, a balance of activation of social skills and
inhibition of interfering tendencies would seem important. Thus,
such behavior should be left hemisphere controlled according to
Young et al.'s (1983b) inhibition theory, since that hemisphere
seems specialized for complex inhibition activity. In contrast, to
control withdrawal, a more global inhibition of activity seems
required, consistent with our prior emphasis that the right hemisphere controls less complex inhibitory skills (see section 2.2).

There are other theorists who emphasize prenatal and neonatal biological factors in the emergence of lateralization of brain function. For example, Geschwind and Galaburda (1985a, 1985b;
Galaburda, Corsiglia, Rosen and Sherman, 1987) describe individual
differences in lateralization of foetal brain structure and in how
the male sex hormone testosterone affects this lateralization. The
planum temporale, in particular, is larger on the left side (see
section 3.2), but to different degrees in the individual even foetally. Moreover, testosterone may act to accelerate growth of the
right side of the brain by interfering with neuronal loss, and this
process can occur at different rates in the individual during foetal
life. Finally, when foetal brain development is adversely affected,
problems in neuronal organization, loss, and migration may result.
This in turn may upset both normal lateralization and behavior. For
example, severe childhood dyslexics upon postmortem analysis showed
cytoarchitectural anomalies in the left hemisphere. However,
Kinsbourne and Hiscock (1987) question both the notion that testosterone can influence foetal brain asymmetries and the implication
that all dyslexics manifest neuropathologies. Nevertheless, for our
purposes, the Geschwind-Galaburda model resembles Kinsbourne and

Hiscock's (1987) invariant lateralization hypothesis, for both approaches suggest that early biological factors deterministically fix
later lateralization. Kinsbourne first presented his theory in
1975, and since then other hypotheses have emerged on the nature of
the development of lateralization. We now examine them.

4.3. Progressive additions in lateralization

Most other theorists do not deny that basic biological processes
early in life play a role in the development of cerebral lateralization. However, they dispute that these early factors are exclusive and primary, and that all later acquisitions concerning lateralization are secondary epiphenomena. For example, we have seen
that the Molfeses' research (V. Molfese and Betz, 1987; D. Molfese
and Betz, in press) suggests that there are neonatal asymmetries in
response to various components of speech sounds (in section 3.2).
Also, we have described their research showing that individual differences in neonatal AER lateralization to speech and nonspeech
sounds help predict the quality of preschool language behavior (in
section 3.4). Such data are consistent with the invariant lateralization hypothesis (Hahn, 1987). Yet the Molfeses' program of
research has uncovered more about the development of brain lateralization.

The essence of the Molfeses' other work is captured in the following
quote. "Structural as well as some functional asymmetries exist
between the two hemispheres at birth. With age, additional structural and functional asymmetries develop" (V. Molfese and Betz, 1987,
p.266). That is, the Molfeses and colleagues describe successive
steps in the development of cerebral lateralization beyond the infancy period. These findings are not compatible with the invariant
lateralization hypothesis, for which reason this research is presented in some detail.

The Molfeses' investigation of neonatal left brain side activity to
speech sounds has focussed on place of articulation. For example,
they showed that there are left hemisphere advantages in processing
syllables with consonants similar in all major sound parameters except for changes in the place cue, in particular (b, g differ in
second formant transition; see section 3.2 for the specific results). Other types of stimuli have been shown to elicit more right
side electrophysiological activity. Categorical voiced onset time
(VOT) involves the timing between laryngeal pulsing (vocal fold
vibration) and onset of consonant release. For certain sounds such
as [ba] and [pa], the exact time difference between the pulsing and
release is important in distinguishing the consonants. For example,
even very young infants discriminate classes of [ba] and [pa] sounds
categorically. When the pulsing is delayed for 20 ms or less, relative to consonant release, a [ba] is perceived, whereas higher values such as 40 ms or more produce the perception of [pa]. The
Molfeses exposed infants to such sounds, beginning from the newborn
period, and it was only as about 3 months that a lateralized AER was
evident. Moreover, the right rather than the left hemisphere was
involved. One later portion of the AER on this side discriminated
between the different speech sounds in a categorical way.

When V. Molfese and Betz (1987) examined the pattern of results

across all the preterm, term, child, and adult samples that they
tested, they concluded the following. For place of articulation
stimuli, early left lateralized processes involving only speechlike
qualities (e.g., in formant structure) may disappear with development or may be replaced by more general lateralized processes (e.g.,
sensitivity to both nonspeech and speech formant structure). In
contrast, for the speech cue of VOT, AER lateralization is to the
right and is present only after the neonatal period, i.e., at 3
months for one component, as we have seen. Moreover, new right AER
lateralization emerges in adulthood.

V. Molfese and Betz (1987) also attempted to explain how earlier and
later lateralizations relate to each other. First, earlier lateralizations are considered as quite distinct from later ones in that
they are not seen as "markers" of the later ones. Second, earlier
ones are considered distinct from later ones even when they co-occur
during development since they may be parallel and not structurally
related. Thus, as new elements emerge in the development of cerebral lateralization, they can remain quite divorced from other lateralized functions, adding to them in an independent way. This perspective contrasts with that of the invariant lateralization school
introduced previously where all lateralizations subsequent to birth
are considered secondary unlateralized epiphenomena which map onto
an unchanging lateralized process. In short, the Molfeses depict
the development of lateralization in the brain as a series of steps
where some can be quite independent, adding to the developmental
process.

The Molfeses' account of the development of lateralization is mostly
a descriptive one. For example, they attempt little discussion of
why certain place of articulation parameters should be left lateralized in the brain while other VOT ones should be right lateralized.
D. Molfese and Best (in press) do indicate that the VOT results are
consistent with clinical findings and so are not unique to their
laboratory. May I tentatively suggest that the place of articulation - VOT differences in hemispheric specialization are congruent
with Young et al.'s (1983b) theory of hemispheric specialization for
inhibition. That is, the left hemisphere may better handle the place of articulation speech cues since they require more subtle discrimination of detail and thus may need more complex inhibitory
skills compared to the categorical VOT speech cues.

4.4. Progressive stages in lateralization

4.4.1. Synchronies in lateralization and language

Ramsay (1980-1985) would not disagree with the position of both the
invariant lateralization and progressive addition lateralization
approaches that early lateralization can be found and can be a predictive precursor of later lateralized events. However, instead of
depicting a newly evident lateralized behavior as potentially isolated from the others existing at the time of its emergence, Ramsay
envisages such behavior in a larger perspective and has even related
lateralization development to cognitive Piagetian development. He
has documented several temporal relations in the infancy period
between an advance in language development and a parallel advance in
manual lateralization. One set of findings concerns the onset of

duplicated syllable babbling (e.g., dada) at around 6 months, while a second concerns the onset of dissimilar consonant-vowel (CV) syllables (e.g., doggie) at around 1 year. The latter research is described first.

Ramsay (1980a) followed infants longitudinally from 10 months of age until they demonstrated a hand preference in manipulating toys. He also collected mothers' reports of the infants' use of dissimilar CV syllables. In a second study, a cross-sectional sample of 11- and 12-month-olds was investigated (with the number of handed and non-handed boys and girls equal). Of several syllable structures examined in the studies, only the different consonant-vowel variety related to manual behavior. It emerged after handedness in the longitudinal sample, and was present only in handed children in the cross-sectional sample (except in the case of some boys, left-handers, or infants who were both). Walking, indicative of general motor development, did not relate to these results. Thus, an articulatory advance seemed related to one in manual preference.

In 1980, Ramsay also began his work with younger infants (Ramsay, 1980b). He found that 7-month-olds attempted to move the moveable portion of a toy with the right hand and, according to maternal report, also babbled duplicated syllables. Ramsay (1983) extended these findings, showing that at about 6 months of age toy contact became right-lateralized only at the time of or after the onset of babbling duplicated syllables. Ramsay (1984) used weekly follow-ups to verify these data. Beginning at 5 months of age, boys and girls were tested in their homes on unimanual manipulation tasks at weekly intervals until 8 weeks had elapsed since duplicated syllable babbling onset. The infants began to prefer their right hand on the week of babbling onset, not before. However, they temporarily lost this advantage several weeks later (see section 2.6). In 1984, Ramsay and Willis observed that reaching compared to manipulation does not show the same relation to duplicated syllable babbling onset. Although unilateral reaching was dependent on this onset, it emerged as right-handed only 5 weeks after it, and then only for a short-lived time. In 1985, Ramsay performed a follow-up which lasted 14 weeks after duplicated syllable babbling onset. He noticed fluctuations in hand preference for toy contact and for banging, relative to original hand preference, not only at 4 weeks but also at 8 weeks (Ramsay, 1985a). Moreover, individual infants showed considerable variation "in the occurence and/or timing of these fluctuations" (p.322).

For Ramsay, the research suggests that there are successive stages or reorganizations in the expression of hemispheric specialization, and that these stages concern the articulatory, structural level rather than the phonemic, phonological, or linguistic level. "Developmental changes at the manual level are dependent on these changes. Different types of handedness might index successive levels of hemisphere specialization, or asymmetrical brain organization, for articulatory control" (Ramsay, 1984, p.65). However, Ramsay is not always consistent in emphasizing the primacy of articulatory advances in hemispheric specialization, for he also alluded to one common development in articulatory and manual lateralization. He argued that changes in left hemisphere specialization that take place in the course of infancy concern maturation

of multiple, related (common) motor programs responsible for sequencing the separate constituent movements of (a) the vocal apparatus
during articulation, (b) manual behavior, and so on. Also, we saw
that in his 1980 study with 1-year-olds, the lateralized manual
behavior and not the articulatory advance emerged first in development.

4.4.2. General implications

In his most recent study relating duplicated syllable babbling onset
and manual laterality, Ramsay (1985b) examined midline block banging
for 14 weeks after babbling onset in the subjects studied in Ramsay
(1985a). Block banging emerged and/or increased in frequency synchronously with unimanual handedness fluctuations. Given the nonlateralized nature of bimanual midline block banging, Ramsay suggested that the developmental moments of its increase may reflect the
particular points in time when the dominant (left) hemisphere is
gaining progressively better control of the nonpreferred hand
through interhemispheric processes. Thus, he postulated that other
signs of better integrated hemisphere functioning (e.g., aspects of
left hemisphere syllable mediation integrated with right hemisphere
intonation mediation) should be predicted by increases in midline
block banging. Finally, Ramsay related the emergence of bilateral
block banging to substage 4 of Piaget's sensorimotor theory of intelligence (Piaget, 1936). Unilateral banging resembles the stereotypies described in Piaget's third substage, while bimanual collaboration resembles the trial and error variations seen in substage 5.
Thus, bilateral block banging may be a transition between the two
substages, especially given its emergent means-end intentionality,
which is so characteristic of Piaget's substage 4 in sensorimotor
thought.

Ramsay and Weber (1986) have extended the comparison between manual
activity and sensorimotor intelligence to include the transition to
the 6th substage. They found that 17- to 19-month-olds but not 12-
to 13-month-olds removed a toy from a box with completely differentiated hand roles. Only the older subjects reached for the box with
one hand, then retrieved the toy with the other. According to the
authors, this suggests a transition to foresightful planning.

Ramsay (1985b) and Ramsay and Weber (1986) are not clear exactly how
lateralization in manual behavior relates to Piaget's substages of
cognitive development. However, in 1984, Ramsay explained how (a)
developmental synchronies across left and right hemisphere specializations may be related to (b) Piagetian sensorimotor substages in
intellectual development. The former were considered the "base" of
the latter, and those in turn were thought to be "predicted" by the
former, at least "to the extent that the behaviors observed depend
on hemispheric specialization or asymmetrical brain organization"
(p.69). Thus, levels in cognitive development are seen to depend
on levels in hemispheric specialization development as indexed by
manual asymmetries. And as we have seen, these in turn are most
probably related to advances in language development according to
Ramsay (1984). We now describe the work of Bates et al. (1986) to
better see how language can play this role.

Bates et al. (1986) argued that when infants or toddlers are in the process of competing with language they co-opt more left hemisphere resources than usual. In consequence, normal right-handed manual preferences controlled in the left hemisphere are interfered with, producing the fluctuations and cycles in laterality evident in Ramsay's work. In support of the hypothesis, Bates et al. found that toddlers were more right-handed in language-related gestures than nonsymbolic ones, presumably because the former relative to the latter behaviors compete less with language for left hemisphere resources. Also, toddlers at 20 months who seemed in transition between the two-word and grammar phases of language acquisition were more right-handed than age-mates behind or ahead of them in language development. This finding fits the argument that children not facing complex language acquisition will be more right-handed because of more available left hemisphere resources. Archer, Campbell and Segalowitz (1988b) reported similar results. They found that 2-year-old boys showed a spurt in language production and a simultaneous alteration in handedness. Thus, Archer et al. (1988b) and Bates et al. (1986) side with Ramsay's view that emphasizes that advances in language and its lateralization come to affect manual lateralization. We can conclude that the sequence in development at any one stage which is being described by Ramsay and his supporters concerns an advance in language, then one in hemispheric specialization, and then another in cognition. We will return to this question in section 5.4.

4.5. Progressive transfers in lateralization

A group of theorists on the development of lateralization have described how each step in this process lays the groundwork for the subsequent step through its experiential consequences. Michel (1983, 1987, in press) consistently maintains that "adultlike hemispheric specialization has not yet been adequately demonstrated for infants" (in press, p.7; Evaluation of his criticisms of the research in the area, such as the studies by the Molfeses, is beyond the scope of the present work). This sets the stage for his argument that neonatal head orientation preferences at birth induce lateral asymmetries in hand regard and then in hand activity in the first months (Coryell and Michel, 1978). Subsequently, this leads to the right-hand preference in visually-directed reaching evident at about the middle of the first year. In turn, hand differences in visual and proprioceptive stimulation produced by these movements occur. Thus, one hand (usually the right) gets a pattern of self-generated experience supportive of better sensorimotor skill. This eventually helps lead to later (right) handedness. In short, as each manual skill lateralizes (to the right), it permits the development of a transfer of preference to the subsequent skill.

The data in support of the theory have been presented in section 4.4, and are not in dispute. Michel (1987) goes on to argue that since the head orientation and manual preference lateralities are based on distinct neural mechanisms, the "same lateral asymmetry in CNS functioning" cannot be involved. However, I contend that even if subcortical and cortical structures are exclusively involved in the respective lateralities, there still may be an underlying commonality in their functioning. For example, Young et al.'s (1983b) inhibition hypothesis of left hemisphere specialization readily could be applied to both types of laterality. There may be more

than just experiential links between successive behavioral lateralities, since common underlying central functions may somehow be
playing a role. Michel (1987) also argued that since centering the
young infant's head at the midline eliminates asymmetries in manual
activity, the neural bases underlying the head and manual lateralities must be independent. However, again one cannot rule out a
superordinate unifying mechanism which may be involved.

Turkewitz (in press) has also presented a theory of hemispheric
specialization development which describes several steps where
experience plays a critical role. He argues that before the last
weeks of foetal development, the right hemisphere is larger or more
mature, and is thus predisposed to activate more to the prevailing
environment, which consists of nonverbal noises. This then leads to
the left hemisphere's specialization for language, since it is available for processing in the last weeks of pregnancy when the foetus
can hear the mother's speech; moreover, the planum temporale on that
side is larger in this age period, facilitating this specialization.
Then after birth, when the newborn sees a face, it is usually spoken
to simultaneously. The speech activates the left hemisphere, thus
allowing the available right hemisphere to specialize in the processing of the face. However, all the infant sees of the face at this
point are holistic configurations. Then, as the young infant grows,
faces become less associated with speech. This frees the left hemisphere to become specialized for the task of analyzing the face's
detail once this skill develops. Thus, each hemisphere comes to
possess different roles in the processing of facial information, and
the development of this circumstance begins with foetal experience
of noise in the right hemisphere ! Finally, the female's brain may
be less lateralized than that of the male's because its left hemisphere may be larger than that of the male's during this initial
phase, thus reducing the right hemisphere's relative advantage. All
these interesting speculations need to be directly verified.

Kosslyn (1987) has extrapolated a developmental theory of hemispheric specialization from his research with adults. He posits that
each neonatal hemisphere innately possesses its own control subsystem which catalytically "snowballs", serving as a "seed". The left
hemisphere is innately biased to govern a bilateral speech output
controller. With exercise, the speech subsystem develops more effective relevant links in its network while the corresponding subsystem on the right side gets degraded feedback and less exercise.
Secondary subsystems feeding the left side speech controller (e.g.,
for associated memory of phonemic instructions) in turn become more
lateralized, leading to left hemisphere specialization for categori-
.cal representation, etc. On the right side, the innate subsystem
concerns control of bilateral, rapid, systematic search scans of
attention over scenes. Secondary lateralization involves associative memory for shape encoding, navigational space, etc. As with
Turkewitz (in press), these interesting conjectures need research
support. Rourke (1987) also presented a theory of the development
of hemispheric specialization where the left hemisphere becomes
progressively more lateralized through experience. Basing himself
on Goldberg and Costa's (1981) approach to hemispheric specialization, described in section 2.1, Rourke argued that the left hemisphere better applies existing codes, and that the right hemisphere
better deals with novel information processing demands. Thus, the

developing individual first uses the right hemisphere in novel situations, and then shifts hemispheric activation in similar situations in the future to the left side once the appropriate code has
been assembled by that side. Again, appropriate tests of the hypothesis are needed.

4.6. Conclusions

Traditional lists of theories of lateralization development include
the equipotential, invariant, regressive, and progressive views.
The first is uniformly rejected today; proponents of the second are
hesitant about its status in infancy; and the third really concerns
interhemispheric development, as we have seen in section 4.1. As
for the fourth position, it has been shown that it is comprised of
three distinct views, as typified by the work of the Molfeses,
Ramsay, and Michel. These approaches concern additions, stages, and
transfers in the development of hemispheric specialization, respectively. We now try to relate these three views of progressive development of hemispheric specialization, along with the invariant
lateralization theory, to the general model of phenotypic development described in section 1.4. It will be recalled that four types
of ontogenesis were considered possible for newly emergent behavior
in the growing individual. It could or could not be related in a
structure to other behavior; moreover, for each of these options
individual differences might or might not be present (see Table 1).

Both the invariant lateralization and progressive stage theories
conceive of emergent developing lateralizations as part of larger
wholes. In the former, new behaviors susceptible to lateralization
map onto the one unchanging process which englobes all prior lateralized behavior. In the latter, lateralized behavior is perceived as
related to Piagetian cognitive developmental stages. In terms of
individual differences, the invariant position acknowledges, in
particular, that the dominant (language) hemisphere sometimes may be
the nonstandard right one, and that pathologies and different qualities may arise in normal development. However, Ramsay's view of
progressive stages in lateralization development explicitly emphasizes individual differences (Ramsay, 1984; see section 4.4).
Moreover, language acquisitions are considered as prime movers of
hemispheric specialization, and individual differences are inevitable here. As for the addition and transfer theories of progressive
lateralization, both emphasize that the development of isolated
asymmetries can occur. For the former, the Molfeses describe how
successive independent additions in lateralization develop. For the
latter, Michel shows that there are single lateralized acquisitions
which set in motion experiences leading to subsequent single lateralizations. With respect to individual differences, both discuss the
left-handed or left-turning minority, as the case may be, and/or the
role of better or fully present neonatal lateralizations in subsequent development. However, one can conclude that Michel's transfer
view of lateralization development allows for more individual differences since it is dependent on experiences.

In short, the various approaches to lateralization development under
scrutiny collectively seem to be discussing much of what developing
behavior is about in general. Each of the four approaches seems to
have its niche in the 2 x 2 grid in Table 1 which depicts the four

major views of emergent phenotypic development. Moreover, attempts
have been made to relate diverse experiences to the development of
lateralization. However, it seems apparent that the threshold is
just being crossed, and more research and thought are needed. Can
the field create one coherent theory which amalgamates the various
positions on lateralization development ? Is it possible to directly relate the various genotypic and experiential influences on development to this coherent theory ? In the next section, I present an
updated view of the multiple inhibition theory of left hemisphere
specialization (Young et al., 1983b). It describes a sequence of
structured stages in lateralization development, but accepts that
both isolated emergent lateralized behavior and individual differences are important in that development.

5.   LATERALIZATION DEVELOPMENT, COGNITION, AND THE BRAIN

5.1. Contemporary neo-Piagetian cognitive development

In the inhibition hypothesis of lateralization development that will
be presented shortly, advances in cognitive development are considered cardinal, similar to Ramsay (in section 5.4). However, instead
of adopting the classical Piagetian position on stages in cognitive
development, contemporary neo-Piagetian theorists were consulted.
Also, instead of focussing just on the latter part of infancy, a
lifespan perspective was adopted. Finally, as we shall see, the
relationship between the development of lateralization, language,
and cognition espoused here is different from the one proposed by
Ramsay. Before beginning, the reader is reminded that there is no
one universally accepted definition of a stage (Case, 1987). Also,
current conceptions of stages in cognitive development emphasize
that they are not extensive, all-encompassing structures, but that
they are a more limited family of semi-independent agencies liable
to individual differences (see section 1.4).

It is possible to elaborate upon Piaget today without trying to revise his view of what are the stages in cognitive development (e.g.,
Chapman, 1988; Inhelder, de Caprona and Cornu-Wells, 1987; Sugarman,
1987). However, others are presenting novel views of what are the
developing cognitive stages. The major theorists in this regard are
Case (1978, 1985; Case, Hayward, Lewis and Hurst, 1988; Case, Reid,
McKeough, Dennis and Marini, 1987), Fischer (1980; Fischer and
Lamborn, in press; Fischer, Shaver and Carnachan, in press; beginning with Watson and Fischer, 1977), and Mounoud (1976, 1986;
Mounoud and Vinter, 1985). Their work will be focussed upon, since
others usually do not include the whole lifespan (e.g., Chapman,
1987; Halford, 1987) and/or do not consider cyclic recursions or
repetitions of substages in cognitive development (e.g., Pascual-
Leone, 1987), which are essential to my view, as we shall see in
section 5.2. These neo-Piagetian revisions of the traditional
Piagetian cognitive stages are not without their limits (c.f.,
Breslow, 1986; Sternberg, 1987), but some of these limits are common
to the Piagetian enterprise, in general (e.g., the mechanisms of
stage transformation; note that this important topic is treated at
length by Fischer and Case).

Case (1987) effectively compared the various neo-Piagetian stage

theorists on a number of parameters. He maintained that the theorists show points of agreement concerning the nature of the stages,
with differences "not particularly fundamental". However, in Table
2 a summary of the theories of Case, Fischer, and Mounoud are presented, and important differences seem evident along several dimensions. Each theory describes a number of cognitive developmental
stages which pass through several substages. Moreover, these substages are cyclic recursions, bearing the same label each time they
reappear. Beyond these surface similarities, the theories differ in
(a) the number of stages, (b) the number of cyclic substages within
them and, consequently, (c) the number of total substages added over
all the stages. More important, the nature of the various stages
and substages differs from one theory to the next. Finally, large
age differences are evident; this applies even to when the first and
last stages begin.

Fischer and Case both describe a 13 level theory involving four stages with three substages each, plus an extra level. In both theories, the cyclic substages begin with single entities (set, unifocal
levels for Fischer and Case, respectively), which come to coordinate
in pairs (mapping, bifocal levels), and then become even more complex (system, elaboration levels). Moreover, the initial single
entity substage in each cycle (except the first one in Fischer) are
really extensions of the previous substage, as a single entity level
(set, unifocal) is a compound (system of systems, consolidation) of
the prior complex level. A major difference between Fischer's and
Case's theories concerns the modal ages when the levels are supposed
to emerge (ages listed in Table 2 derived from their recent works).
The only time that similar substages are seen to develop at comparable ages across the two theories is in the sensorimotor period between 4 and 12 months. In contrast, the 2-year-old uses representational single entity sets in Fischer, but uses interrelational coordinated bifocal relations in Case. Another example is that the
16-year-old uses abstract thought in both Fischer and Case, but at a
coordinated mapping level in Fischer and at a complex elaboration
level in Case. Such inconsistencies may speak to basic lacunae in
the theories. Mounoud presents a clearer dividing line between the
various levels, since 15 levels are seen to derive from the repetition of five substages in each of three stages with no extra compound substage equivalent to the single entity substage. In
Mounoud's system, initial global codes emerge and then are applied
separately. Following this, codes are globally related. Then, the
relations are partly analyzed, leading to complete synthesis (this
summary is a simplification from Mounoud's recent tables).

In terms of the major stages, the four that Fischer describe concern
reflexive, sensorimotor, representational, and abstract behavior or
thought. [The last three stages resemble Piaget's ones of sensorimotor, combined preoperational-concrete operational, and formal operational thought]. Case excludes the reflexive stage, and splits
the representational one, calling the resultant stages interrelational and dimensional; these are akin to Piaget's preoperational
and concrete operational stages. Mounoud differs extensively from
these theorists and from Piaget, as he proposed a sequence of perceptual, conceptual, and semiotic stages.

Table 2. Some Contemporary Neopiagetian Theories of Cognitive Development.

Fischer (1980 on)			Case (1985 on)			Mounoud (e.g., 1986)		
Stage	Substage	Age	Stage	Substage	Age	Stage	Substage	Age
Reflex	Set	1 mo-		Precoord.(a)	0 mo-	Perceptual	Global(b)	0 mo-
	Map	2-		Unifocal	4-		Applic.	1-
	System	3-		Bifocal	8-		Related	4-
Sensori-motor	Set	4-	Sensori-motor	Elabor.	12-		Analysis	8-
	Map	8-					Synthesis	12-
	System	12-		Unifocal	18-	Conceptual	Global	18-
Represen-tational	Set	2 yr-	Interrela-tional	Bifocal	2 yr-		Applic.	3 yr-
	Map	5-		Elabor.	3 1/2-		Related	5-
	System	7-		Unifocal	5-		Analysis	7-
			Dimensional	Bifocal	7-		Synthesis	9-
				Elabor.	9-			
Abstract, Formal Operatio-nal	Set	12-	Abstract, Vectorial	Unifocal	11-	Semiotic	Global	10-
	Map	16-		Bifocal	13-		Applic.	11-
	System	20-		Elabor.	16-19		Related	13-
	System of System	26+					Analysis	15-
							Synthesis	16-18

(a) Precoord. = Precoordination; Elabor. = Elaboration.
(b) Global = Global code; Applic. = Code applied; Related = Codes related.

5.2. A new theory of neo-Piagetian cognitive development

The current theory borrows from Fischer, Case, and Mounoud. It
shares their fundamental assumption that cognitive development witnesses a repetition of identical structural steps from stage to
stage, in a cyclic recursion of substages. This concept is related
to Piaget's notion of "vertical decalage", but is more stringent and
operational than its forebear (Case, 1987; Fischer, 1980). The notion of cyclic recursion speaks to a parsimony or conservation in
development, consonant with a belief in biological influence on its
course. Despite, this shared starting point with prior theories,
the current theory differs extensively from them. However, it resembles each of them in terms of their most salient contributions.

(a) It retains Fischer's four stages. On the one hand, Fischer is
the only theorist of the three concerned here to include a reflexive
stage, which is needed to best describe earliest development. On
the other hand, Fischer does not separate Piaget's preoperational
and concrete operational stages, which is important (see end of
point "b" below). A major difference between our approach and that
of Fischer's is that we label his third stage "perioperational"
instead of representational for two reasons. First, all agree that
representational thought is considered to emerge at the end of the
prior sensorimotor stage. Second, by using the label perioperational, with its meaning of "around" or "about", a way has been
found to keep Piaget's preoperational and operational stages under
one rubric, like Fischer. Note that a major change here is that the
reflex stage is considered to begin prenatally. The development of
reflexes in the preterm infant and in foetal stage justifies this
modification of Fischer (Willis and Widerstrom, 1986).

(b) The current theory builds on Case's age ranges for the levels he
presented. Case is the theorist who best respected Piaget's original age ranges for the stages the latter described. That is, except
where Case collapsed Piaget's first two sensorimotor substages into
the precoordination level, Case added new levels solely by an apparent splitting of Piaget's original stages and their respective age
ranges. Perhaps this is why in Case there is an orderly increase in
the age range of successive levels (one to several levels involving
1/3, 1/2, 1, 1 1/2, 2, and then 3 years, in turn). This stable progression in normative age from level to level accords with the implicit assumption of biological influence in cyclic substage recursions (just discussed above). However, a major change here is that
the particular cognitive levels hypothesized by Case to emerge at
each age range were not retained in the current theory. This is (1)
partly due to his differences with Fischer on the major stages and
(2) partly due to his differences with Mounoud on the nature of
cyclic recursions. With respect to (1), Case's model of the major
stages excludes a reflexive stage, unlike Fischer, who we have
chosen to emulate in this regard, as we have just seen. Moreover,
Fischer combines Piaget's preoperational and concrete operational
stages into the representational stage, but he does not really drop
the essence of either the preoperational or concrete operational
stages of Piaget; he simply has changed their organization. With
respect to (2), recall the belief that I share with Mounoud that we
need more than a three substage model (found in both Fischer and
Case) in the cyclic recursions under discussion. This, when

combined with the need for stages encompassing the reflexive to
abstract periods, renders Fischer's model of the major stages the
only one that could accomodate all of our concerns.

(c) The current theory was constructed upon a five step substage
cycle with no compound substage included, like Mounoud. This seemed
justified, in part, by the possible confusion in Fischer and Case
about whether single entity levels are really just compound levels,
and perhaps not the beginning of new distinct cycles. I did not
directly borrow the specific descriptions of the five substages used
by Mounoud. However, the general pattern of this five substage cycle was incorporated into my model presented below. In Mounoud, the
pattern seems to be the following. After an initial substage develops, it becomes expanded in its usage, but only in the next substage is there a major qualitative improvement. Then, this latter
advance is itself expanded, leading to a final qualitative improvement. This pattern seems more general and less quantitative compared to the pattern in Fisher and Case, where there is a (a) single
entity, (b) pair, then (c) complex series. Thus, I adopted an
approach similar to Mounoud's of having more qualitative advances
alternating with their expansion. Note that for the developing
individual an expansionary substage may not be less important than
one involving more qualitative change. In fact, it may be just the
opposite since in an expansion substage major consolidation may take
place (this point is elaborated in section 5.5).

A five step cyclic recursion of cognitive substages seemed prefe-
rable for more than the prior reasons. Such a cycle could preserve
intact much of Piaget's account of the sensorimotor stage. Piaget
described a six step progression in sensorimotor cognition based on
careful observation of his children. Despite revisions of Piaget's
version of the sensorimotor stage, such as the ones discussed here,
others researchers are more traditional. They still work with an
intact six substage model, even if not as all-inclusive as Piaget
suggested. Examples with respect to human infants are numerous (cf.
references in Doré and Dumas, 1987; P. Harris, 1983). Moreover,
most investigations of the comparative development of sensorimotor
intelligence in nonhuman primates have been based on the traditional
Piagetian model (e.g., Doré and Dumas, 1987; Russon, in press).
When examining Piaget's account of infant sensorimotor intelligence,
what I find outstanding is his description of the changes in purpose
in behavior. The shift from reflexive to groping to directed to
planned behavior that Piaget depicts seems to be the heart of his
work. Consequently, I have emphasized this aspect of his model of
sensorimotor development in Table 5 below, where his model is integrated into my own. However, there is one major change in Piaget's
approach to the sensorimotor stage that has been made, and it can be
readily justified. I have placed his first sensorimotor substage,
which begins at birth, at the end of my reflexive stage, seen to
develop prior to the sensorimotor stage. Thus, the last five substages in Piaget's account of sensorimotor intelligence are kept as
a unit. Since Piaget's first sensorimotor substage involves reflex
exercise for the most part, this decision seems well founded.

With this initial logic, I proceeded to determine what five step
cyclic recursion best fit Piaget's original description of the last
five substages of the sensorimotor stage. I also kept in mind that

the five step cycle had to simultaneously fit simpler reflexive
behaviors which developed earlier and more complex thought which
emerged later. Moreover, I tried to assure that the five step recursion was phrased in terms general enough to permit a variety of
examples at any one level, including those concerning manual specialization. Note that, to my knowledge, not one of Fischer, Case, and
Mounoud emphasized the data in the sensorimotor period in infancy as
a starting point for determining the cyclic recursions of substages
in their theories. Rather, if anything, they analyzed the behavior
of the preschool and/or older child, and worked backward to infancy
from there (e.g., Case, 1978, p.38; Ficher, 1980, footnote 4,
p.486; Mounoud and Bower, 1974/1975, in Fischer, 1980, p.518).

5.3. The details of the theory

Given this basis, it is postulated that cognitive development passes
through a 20 level progression (see Table 3). There are four major
stages (reflexive, sensorimotor, perioperational, abstract), each
with five substages. In the first substage, a coordination of pairs
of cognitive control units is found. However, the units are not
fixed in one temporal order or tied to very specific stimuli releasers. In the second substage, hierarchization of paired units takes
place through specification of (a) their temporal sequencing and (b)
their releasers. (The second aspect of hierarchization is not relevant at later cognitive stages). In the next substage of systematization, the units separately acquire refinements which permit better
on-target behavior (e.g., at the behavior's onset, end-point).
Then, paired units can themselves be chained or somehow combined in
a process called multiplication. Finally, in the fifth substage of
integration, multiple units can differentiate through more flexible
branching in their application. These substages show an alteration
of qualitative and expansionary advances, following Mounoud. On the
one hand, the coordination, systematization, and integration substages produce major discontinuous shifts in cognitive skills, and not
just a juggling of component units. On the other hand, the hierarchization and multiplication substages, which are sandwiched between
the other three, involve rearrangement of existing components without adding extra behavioral skills, per se. Note that coordination
is considered a qualitative advance and not simply a quantitative
juggling of two units, since the whole gestalt formed in its combination goes beyond its constituent parts.

There may be sublevels within any one level, depending on the task
to which the theory is applied, like in Fischer. However, it is
only these 20 levels that are related to underlying development of
lateralization in the brain according to the current theory, as
shall be shown in section 5.5. Also, there may be a twenty-first
level in cognitive development, but it may be more communal, e.g.,
related to how we interface with computers, rather than being related to the individual brain. This possibility of a twenty-first
cognitive level fits with the following: The 4 stage x 5 substage
revision proposed here of contemporary neo-Piagetian theories is not
the only one that could accommodate some of the inconsistencies in
these theories. For example, one could envisage a 7 stage x 3 substage model which would keep Case's model as its starting point. It
would replace the precoordination level with two three-level stages
concerning simpler and complex reflexive behavior, respectively, and

add one advanced three-level stage in adulthood. However, this possibility would still leave us with a three substage cyclic recursion, which is not the best option, as we have just seen.

How could one directly test which theory (Fischer, Case, Mounoud,
current) best accounts for cognitive development ? Researchers typically set up studies which support their own theory without trying
to negate competing views. For example, Fischer and Case have quite
different conceptions of what levels in cognitive development can be
found at any one age (see Table 2), yet fail to show how their data
can or cannot be accounted for by the views of the other. Given
their relatively quantitative, geometric conception of cyclic substage recursions (single entity, coordinate, compound; see section
5.1), Fischer and Case readily divise series of increasingly difficult tasks linked to the cognitive levels that they propose, and
show an orderly increase with age in performance. However, do the
results reflect an imposition of a structure on the child or the
child's natural course in development ? One must begin with an
ecological investigation of cognition, as did Piaget with his
children in the infancy period, and then compare the various theories with the observations so derived. This approach should be
complemented by the use of tasks which are not biased a priori
against supporting any one of the competing theories. Only with
such a research strategy will the issues dividing the theories be
resolved.

Table 3.   A Neo-Piagetian Theory of Cognitive Development
           Consisting of 20 Levels.

Level	Stage	Substage	Age Range
1	Reflex	Coordination	earlier foetal life
2		Hierarchization	quite premature
3		Systematization	somewhat premature
4		Multiplication	fullterm newborn
5		Integration	0-1 month
6	Sensori-	Coordination	1-4 months
7	motor	Hierarchization	4-8 months
8		Systematization	8-12 months
9		Multiplication	12-18 months
10		Integration	18-24 months
11	Perioper-	Coordination	2-3 1/2 years
12	ational	Hierarchization	3 1/2-5 years
13		Systematization	5-7 years
14		Multiplication	7-9 years
15		Integration	9-11 years
16	Abstract	Coordination	11-13 years
17		Hierarchization	13-16 years
18		Systematization	16-19 years
19		Multiplication	youth
20		Integration	adult

5.4. Cognition and the brain

Fischer and Case have both attempted to relate cognitive growth to changes in brain development. Fischer (1987) described Goldman-Rakic's (1987) work showing that in infant rhesus monkeys, concurrent cortical synaptogenesis or synapse formation may be related to the onset of stages in cognitive skills akin to Piagetian object permanence. Fischer suggested that a similar parallel is evident in humans, at least when EEG and head growth spurt data are examined. Russon (in press) observed that infant chimpanzee peer play reflects Piagetian sensorimotor development, and that this in turn may be related to concurrent cortical synaptogenesis. Aside from synaptogenesis, synapse pruning and myelin formation may be involved in cognition-brain relations, according to Fischer. Given Aboitiz's (1988) view of the evolution of the brain, one can add that synaptic stabilization or connectivity may be involved, as well. Like Fischer, Case (1985) mentioned myelinization in his search for a correspondence between cognitive development and brain development. Case et al. (1987) have argued that a stage may have more than just CNS underpinnings related to myelinization. They suggested that there are structural, cross-domain parallels in separate multiple intelligences. Each of the latter may have a distinct neurological substrate, but a central entity may impose organizational limits on each one, creating similarities across them.

Others have tried to link cognitive and brain development. Hooper and Boyd (1986) showed how Luria's (1973) view of the brain contains within it an implicit theory of neurodevelopmental stages which seem to parallel the classic Piagetian cognitive stages. Luria's stages 1 and 2 concern maturation of the arousal, primary sensory, and primary motor areas, presumably important in sensorimotor development. Stage 3 involves secondary cortical areas, which should underlie preoperational representational thought. In Stage 4, tertiary parietal areas mature, and the complex thought that they permit resembles Piaget's concrete operations. Finally, in the last stage, tertiary prefrontal areas mature and interrelate with other regions, allowing formal operations. A somewhat similar approach has been presented by J. Brown (1978) who described four levels in the development of the brain, and linked them to cognitive behavior. The levels are subcortical sensorimotor, limbic presentational, neocortical representational, and later neocortical symbolic. Also, Diamond (1987; in Corbetta and Mounoud, in press) has argued that portions of the frontal cortex mature as early as 9-12 months and come to permit the cognitive behaviors of that age range.

Implicit in all these approaches is the notion that advances in cognitive development are dependent on advances in brain development. The latter are no longer depicted solely in terms of specific brain region maturation, since cross-region synaptic and myelin processes may be involved, as well. In the theory presented in the next section, the role of a general CNS function is emphasized more than particular regions or particular CNS growth factors. That is, I suggest a role for inhibition as a neurological function underlying cognitive and other development. Perhaps this inhibitory function is the organizing "central entity" to which Case et al. (1987) referred. At the structural level, the left hemisphere is underscored. Recall that several times in the course of the chapter, an

"inhibition" interpretation was used to explain suggested differences between the hemispheres (e.g., approach-withdrawal, section 4.2;
place of articulation-VOT, section 4.3).

If there is one central neural function underlying much of the apparently dissimilar processes in the lateralized brain, then it may be
premature to try to determine which of the latter have primacy or
cause the remainder. It will be recalled that the progressive stages view of lateralization development attributed the impetus for
hemispheric specialization and cognitive development to language
acquisitions (see section 4.4). In our view there are structural
and functional underpinnings involving inhibition which develop.
Consequent advances in language, cognition, and other behavior flow
from these inhibitory changes. These consequent advances may evidence feedback growth cycling amongst themselves and even with respect to the underlying inhibitory changes. Moreover, experience can
profoundly affect all the components in this process. Therefore,
in our view, in contrast to the progressive stages view of lateralization development, language does not seem to be a causal impetus
in the growth of stages in hemispheric specialization and cognition.

5.5. Progressive inhibition in lateralization development

Tables 4 to 6 outline a model of lateralization development which
incorporates many of the concerns presented in the prior sections.
The tables depict in turn lateralization development in the reflex,
sensorimotor, perioperational, and abstract stages of cognitive
growth. The left side of each table describes general and behavioral changes, and emphasizes the left hemisphere and right upper
limb. The right side of each table suggests changes in neuronal
inhibition and structure which should relate to the developments on
the left side of the table. Piaget emphasized how the schema is
gradually tranformed into operations in the course of ontogenesis.
However, Case (1987) documents how the various neo-Piagetians have
differing perspectives on what are the basic cognitive control units
(fundamental (mental) structures which organize specific behaviors
or thoughts), and how they differentiate with development. Examination of Tables 4 to 6, where my own Piagetian theory is presented in
detail, shows that at every one of the 20 levels, a new cognitive
control unit is hypothesized to evolve (these are underlined in the
left hand columns).

At each level in the proposed theory in Tables 4 to 6, the advances
in motor, sensorimotor, and cognitive skill suggest an increasing
role of inhibitory mechanisms. There especially seems to be an
increase in executive, sequential, and hierarchical abilities in the
development of lateralized manual behavior, and all these abilities
can be construed as the result of an increasing skill and timing in
inhibition deployment. Even the general progression through the
cyclic neo-Piagetian substages seems to be marked by an increasing
inhibitory control. For example, the substage of hierarchization
sees limits imposed on how the coordinations formed in the prior
substage are manifested. Also, the passage from each of the four
major neo-Piagetian stages to the next appears marked by an increasing "distancing" (Sigel, 1970), which can be interpreted as an
increasing intervening inhibition. In terms of central development, with each level it appears that there is an expanded recruit-

Table 4. Reflex Levels in the Development of Left Brain Specialization.

Behavioral Specialization (e.g., in right arm-hand)	Central Specialization (and inhibition therein)
1. Pairs of single reflexive behaviors (reflex pairs) not yet linked to activating mechanisms are evident, but do not manifest in fixed order (e.g., in proximal arm flexion and extension, in distal fingers open and flex; either example in reverse).	At first, reflex centers mature without stimulus sensitive activating mechanisms; nevertheless, they discharge, and this occurs even in pairs through lateral inhibition-activation interplay.
2. Reflexive behavior hierarchies manifest in two ways. First, they become subordinated to specific stimulus sensitivities in firing. Second, reflexive behavior pairs become fixed in sequence, but with second component only fortuitously on target (e.g., in proximal ipsilateral arm extension in tonic neck reflex, in distal finger opening to facilitate flexing on contact).	Fixed order established in reflex pairs by one-way inhibitory suppression of direction in their functional linkage. Also, full stimulus-provoked reflex arcs develop through control by inhibition-disinhibition timing.
3. Each component of reflex pair can become associated with simultaneously occurring movement, either reflexive or not, in order to assure better targeting of second component, thus creating primitive patterns. At this	Above process expands to include other components at second or both phases of movement. This may involve coupling with other reflexes and/

point, the primarily reflex related _primitive schemas_ are being formed (e.g., in looking directed tonic neck reflex with subsequent proximal arm extension on appropriate side, in fingers open and move slightly before flexing to grip after noncentered contact).

4. Patterned, _schema_ controlled, ballistic, preprogrammed behavior (i.e., sequential multiples of above) triggered, but not always directly to (on) target; in proximal activity (e.g., prereach agitation in front of target appropriately alternated across limbs as target moves) and/or in distal activity (e.g., fingers serially extend and flex upon sheet contact on back of hand, with arm and hand agitation producing turning).

5. Patterned behaviors above begin to _differentiate_ with practice, as continual monitoring of own movement and/or moving target render movement more smooth, flexible. _Independent schemas_ no longer are dominated by reflexes (e.g., in proximal reaching adjustment to moving object, in distal fingers grasp target).

or interdigitation with extra-reflex neuronal centers primarily sensory-perceptual in nature.

Level 3 units coordinated sequentially in time by inhibition-activation balancing.

Movement becomes partly reflex-free as neuronal clusters incorporate via inhibition-activation balancing extra-reflex neuronal centers involved in control of spatio-temporal changes.

Note: Each level: (a) Describes the neopiagetian level on which it is based; (b) gives the cognitive control unit seen to develop at the level (underlined); (c) provides manual examples consistent with the nature of the level; (d) suggests corresponding central advances which may underlie its development.

Table 5. Sensorimotor Levels in the Development of Left Brain Specialization.

Behavioral Specialization (e.g., in right arm-hand)	Central Specialization (and inhibition therein)
6. Through schema coordination parallel and back and forth in nature after behavior onset (e.g., vision and appropriate movement), behavior patterns come under even more moment to moment control (e.g., in watching arm during proximal reach to target, in watching hand while distal fingers serially touch target).	By recruitment process similar to that in step 5, larger neuronal clusters form. They require intra-cluster inhibition-activation synchrony so that movement sequence is controlled for fine interference by perseverations, and intruding similar movements.
7. With schema coordination hierarchies, after beavior onset, goal can be established in context (primary releasing stimuli defined), and one schema in above schema coordination becomes primary; thus, there is directed target groping subserved by dominant-subordinate linkage of two schemas (e.g., in visually directed proximal reaching, in watching as distally manipulate target, in simple bimanual collaboration involving (right hand) reach then (left hand) grasp).	Neuronal cluster interdigitation goes one step beyond as pairs form a hierarchy with one subsumed to another by inhibition-activation regulation. The fine interference control described above also applies here.

8. *Linked schemas above related more systematically, allowing primitive representation of target, permitting intentional end-focussed goal from behavior onset (e.g., in proximal reach for hidden object, in two step movement to target, in distal exploratory manipulation either (a) alone or (b) in complex bimanual coordination, with complementary (left hand) stabilization).*

Above process expands to permit larger zone-area mobilization. Neuronal cluster hierarchies are synchronized to permit inhibitory control of gross interference at outset and throughout by unrelated neuronal clusters.

9. *Through multiplicative embedding of one simple intention or means in another, or in multiplicative combining of two means or ends, linear plans formulated (e.g., in proximal diagonal movement to target, in cooperative distal hand use in resolving an embedded hiding, in trial-and-error exploration of means-ends relationship between distal manual activity and effects on objects).*

Widespread expansion into extra zone-area surround is a major step, ensuring that the gross interference control described above comes to include multiple surround neuronal clusters.

10. *Organized sequences above begin to differentiate into hierarchic branching of embedded secondary sequential plans followed by return to primary one, which is the structure of a priori symbolic plans (e.g., in proximal hitting of rolled ball back to thrower, in resolution of an embedded hiding with a tool distally manipulated in the hand or in double embedded hiding resolution, in using distal hands to set apart one subset of a group and then another).*

The range of interference control now extends cross zone-area, i.e., intrahemispherically to some extent, as the inhibition-activation balancing continues to expand.

Table 6. Perioperational and Abstract Levels in the Development of Left Brain Specialization.

Behavioral Specialization (e.g., in right arm-hand)

11. *Symbol plan coordination found, as the child simultaneously holds in mind several symbol plans (e.g., in proximal hitting of rolled ball to side target, in using distal hands to simultaneously sort two subsets of a group of objects, in using memory to begin to learn to draw, write).*

12. *The above pairs develop a dominant-subordinate symbol plan hierarchization (e.g., in proximal symbolic fantasy gesturing to help explicate a sentence, in speeded distal tapping interfered with or being subordinate to spared language in dual, time sharing tasks). This hierarchization also refers to the child placing own plan as dominant in relation to perception of those of parents, others (as in egocentric notions of good drawing, lettering).*

13-15. *The above symbol plan hierarchies expand as they integrate other symbols into symbol plan systems. There is an increasing ability to hold things in mind while solving problems or even undue past learning about a problem, trying to use a primitive logic. In the next step, these systems are intercoordinated, inversed, alternated, ordered, etc.*

Central Specialization (and inhibition therein)

The process in level 10 radiates across the hemisphere, permitting cross zone-areas to begin to form interlinked pairs.

Zone-areas in the same hemisphere form inhibition barriers between them to better control interference during their interrelating and simultaneous functioning.

Interhemispheric communication-collaboration (controlled in left hemisphere) by commissural (corpus callosum) inhibition-activation coordination allows brain-wide mobilization. Several phases probably occur,

Such a structure allows a better logic, leading to rule-governed, skillful application (e.g., in art activity, writing, manual dexterity in music). Piaget's concrete operations develop in this context. Next, this process refines, as the child can use logic in imagination in restricted contexts.

16. A coordination of logic in imagination is found, (e.g., in solving problems by allowing one variable at a time free to vary). This can lead to novel, abstract, formal thought in restricted contexts (e.g., genuine craft, interpretation in painting, music).

17-20. Abstract approaches explored. First, there is their pair-wise comparison, or abstract hierarchization (with that of a mentor, between themselves, etc). Then, one may find abstract systematization of the approaches, leading to a better desired outcome. Third, dialectical relativist abstraction could lead to changing inter-approach multiples, and thus superior creativity. Lastly, an empathic, abstract universality may prevail (e.g., in painting, music, theorizing).

involving intrahemispheric incorporation of emerging anterior areas into the process. The frontal regions, for example, are known for inhibition of action to allow for evaluation.

The process in level 15 expands to include integration of major anterior (frontal) areas. Welsh and Pennington (1988) describe how these may emerge.

Interhemispheric integration (controlled in the left hemisphere) occurs by optimal synchronization of inhibition-activation coordination. Several phases may occur, and in the last one the integration may include inhibition of major self-reinforcing systems.

ment or incorporation of neuronal clusters by an inhibition/ activation coordination. The left side of the brain seems ideally suited for the unilateral cerebral control of these behaviors because of its underlying neuronal organization. That is, its neural networking is more focal, dense, and rich in intraconnectivity (Goldberg and Costa, 1981; see section 4.5). This finding may be at the base of its hypothesized superiority in inhibition skills, especially as it relates to a coordination with activation.

Inspection of the left side of Tables 4 to 6 shows that major gains in inhibitory behavior control are found in the first, third, and fifth substages. It will be recalled that cognitive gains generally seem qualitatively different in these substages compared to the others (see section 5.2). In the reflexive stage, this increasing inhibitory control in the first, third, and fifth substages concerns the fingers, fingers and palm, and fingers and thumb, respectively. In the sensorimotor stage, there is successive increasing control of fine motor/arm, gross motor/arms, and fuller body plans in behavior. In the perioperational stage, the control concerns the single hemisphere, then both hemispheres, and then the hemispheres of the self and other together. Finally, in the last stage, the self, then the self and the other's self together, and then all selves seem involved. In short, the net of inhibitory control seems to expand throughout the lifespan, passing from basic body parts to the hemispheres and the self and others.

Even though major gains in inhibitory control seem to be made mostly in the qualitative substages, the expansionary substages are not less important in cognitive development. In fact, during the second expansionary substage of each five step recursion of substages (i.e., the fourth substage of multiplication), the most important advances in cognitive development in general appear to take place. Thus, in the four stages in the current theory (concerning reflexes, sensorimotor, perioperational, and abstract behavior, respectively), the multiplication substage witnesses in turn the emergence of schemas, plans, concrete operations, and relativistic abstract thoughts. In section 6.4, it shall be shown that the expansionary substages are also important in socioemotional development.

5.6. Relations with neo-Piagetian cognition

The progressive inhibition theory of lateralization development being presented is mostly the product of a search for logic at the theoretical level. It is an inevitable outcome of the juxtaposition of my analyses, in particular, of (a) lateralization development and the role of inhibition therein, and (b) neo-Piagetian cognitive development (also see section 5.1 in this regard). That is, a cyclic recursion of neo-Piagetian cognitive substages was established based on Piaget's infancy investigations. The theory worked vertically from this juncture in terms of age (backwards and forwards), and horizontally from this juncture in terms of topic (from cognition to examples dealing with lateralization, and, as we shall see in section 7 with socioemotional behavior). The examples used were selected, filtered, etc., in order to fit this pre-existing theoretical foundation. In fact, the specific changes in ontogenesis hypothesized at the central (inhibitory) level in the current theory (see the right side of Tables 4 to 6) are highly

speculative. The kind of data necessary to support this aspect of
the theory will probably be derived from the growing work in neural
networking (e.g., see Grossberg in Bullock et al., 1987), cerebral
cytoarchitecture (Geschwind and Galaburda, 1985a, 1995b), cortical
synaptogenesis (see Fischer, 1987), EMG research, biomechanics, and
kinesics (Thelen et al., 1987), etc.

As for the changes in behavior predicted to emerge in the course of
ontogenesis (the left side of Tables 4 to 6), many of the examples
were derived from research on the topics of (1) lateralization and
(2) cognitive development. As cases in point, for the former
Lewkowicz and Turkewitz (1983) report different lateralities for (a)
head turning in various stages of prematurity and (b) before and
after 12 hours of age, in support of the notion that there are such
differences in levels 2 to 5 of the current theory. Recent work on
(a) the tonic neck reflex and (b) early reaching (see Young,
Segalowitz, Corter and Trehub, 1983d) form the basis of examples in
levels 2 to 4 and 5 to 7, respectively. Various kinds of bimanual
behavior have been presented in section 3.3, and they are integrated into levels 7 to 9. Case et al. (1987) describe a series of
ball-target tasks, and these are mentioned in levels 9 to 11.
Kinsbourne and Hiscock (1983) discuss how time sharing tasks can be
executed by three-year-olds, and these data are incorporated into
level 12. As for the cognitive portion of the theory, some examples
follow. The last three steps that Piaget observed in the development of object permanence are included in levels 8 to 10, while
other aspects in his first three sensorimotor substages are included
in levels 5 to 7. Corbetta and Mounoud (in press) describe the
development of object grouping, and this is incorporated in levels
10 and 11.

The last comment in this section concerns the exact temporal relationship between lateralization and cognitive development, as depicted in the left side of Tables 4 to 6. Despite the specific predictions about what behaviors develop during each age period, it is
difficult to foresee when they exactly become lateralized to the
right side. Laterality in behavior is not necessarily stable; it
can vary with experience; it can shift in development as a different
function might come to guide a task previously served by another;
etc. (e.g., Rourke, 1987). The modal pattern probably is that the
behaviors in Tables 4 to 6 are not fully lateralized when they first
appear, and that they become so as the behaviors are consolidated in
the individual's repertoire. However, the use of appropriate, optimal tasks should help reveal the predicted laterality of each behavior in the tables (almost) as soon as it manifests in development.

6. OVERALL CONCLUSIONS AND IMPLICATIONS

6.1. Overall conclusions

The theory of progressive inhibition in lateralization development
that has just been presented should be examined against the background of the general model of development introduced in sections
1.4 and 4.6. That model suggested that the developing phenotype
manifests four patterns of growth. Emergent developing behavior may
or may not be related to others, and for each of these options indi-

vidual differences may or may not be found. The current theory emphasizes structured stages of related behaviors in development, but these need not include all behavior at any one time, nor need they be constant across individuals (e.g., Young, 1977b, has studied individual differences in conservation justifications in Piaget's concrete operational thought). There is an underlying central inhibitory function that guides lateralization development and related acquisitions. However, ontogenetic unfolding is dependent on too many diverse genetic and experiential effects to be inclusive across all behaviors and constant across all individuals. Moreover, the feedback interplay both among these behaviors and between them and the central inhibitory function are important in this regard, as discussed at the end of section 5.4. Thus, in terms of a major theme in this volume, neo-Piagetians should examine how multiple biological and experiential phenomena interact to affect the developing cognitive phenotype. Perhaps the current theory can help here. That is, the theory outlined above of progressive stages of inhibition in left hemisphere lateralization may be important in cognitive stage transitions.

A valid theory not only answers questions; it also creates them. The initial ones that come to mind follow. What is the complementary role of the right brain side at any one level in this progressive inhibition theory ? Which specific brain location-area-zones are involved in the lateralization at each level ? Among right-handers (or preferers, to be more general), are the levels equally lateralized in terms of each one's degree and depth and their intercoordination with others ? Are they equally lateralized in terms of the proportion of the population manifesting the lateralization ? Are there other individual differences in ontogenesis related to the theory (e.g., males vs. females, section 3.3; cultural and experiential differences, section 2.1; effects of postural differences; presence or absence of pathological sequelae) ? Does the development of each level (each individual) involve any disruption or displacement of prior levels ? In the extreme form of this question, does each level always begin and end on the left side or are there shifts in lateralization ? Do the levels equally predict later behavior ? How do emerging behaviors (e.g., vocal-language functions) map onto the lateralized base at each level, and does this process differ among individuals ? Can the theory be applied to the work on primate manual behavior and its evolution (for example, MacNeilage, Studdert-Kennedy and Lindblom, (1987) present a four step sequence in the evolution of manual asymmetries (ancestral prosimians, monkeys, great apes, hominids), and levels 9 to 12 of the current theory should describe the maximum competencies of the adult members of the species in the sequence) ? It is hoped that answers to these questions will be forthcoming and will result in a more accurate theory of lateralization development.

6.2. Implications for emotional development

Among the preceding questions, the one that currently is of most interest to me is the second last one. In particular, I am investigating to what extent the various proposed levels in my theory are coordinated with developmental acquisitions in socioemotional behavior. There is a rich tradition of similar efforts (e.g., Décarie, 1962; Wolff, 1960). The working hypothesis behind this extension of

my theory is that there are independent socioemotional behavior systems which develop in concert with the various levels proposed here-
in. For example, a six step progression in the ontogenesis of primary emotions is envisaged, and these steps are considered as parallel acquisitions to the levels in Table 3 equivalent to the six

Table 7. Emotional Levels Corresponding to Levels 5 to 10
          in Table 3.

Type	Activity	Evaluation	
		Goal Compatible (Positive hedonic tone)	Interfering (Negative tone)
Arriving	Active	Arrives at positively (Quiescence)	Arrives at negatively (or not) (Distress)
	Reactive	Arrived at positively (Relief, Startle)	Arrived at negatively (Disgust)
Possessing	Active	Possesses positively (Pleasure)	Possesses negatively (Unpleasure)
	Reactive	Possessed positively (Contentment)	Possessed negatively (Discontentment)
Approaching	Active	Approaches positively (Interest)	Approaches negatively (Anger)
	Reactive	Approached positively (Delight)	Approached negatively (Fear)
Giving	Active	Gives positively (Affection)	Gives negatively (Petulance)
	Reactive	Given positively (Comfort)	Given negatively (Wariness)
Desiring	Active	Desires positively (Eagerness)	Desires negatively (Greed)
	Reactive	Desired positively (Coyness)	Desired negatively (Defiance)
Evaluating	Active	Evaluates positively (Appreciation)	Evaluates negatively (Dislike, Contempt)
	Reactive	Evaluated positively (Pride)	Evaluated negatively (Shame)

Piagetian sensorimotor substages (levels 5 to 10). Case and Fischer
are also developing neo-Piagetian theories of emotional development
(e.g., Case et al., 1988; Fischer et al., in press). Extensions of
my neo-Piagetian model seem complementary to their work, since I emphasize that there are many primary emotions and show the point of
emergence of each in development. In contrast, both Case and
Fischer analyze only several emotions; however, unlike myself, they
show how emotions are modified as the child passes from one cognitive level to the next. Nevertheless, Case's and Fischer's neo-Piagetian approaches to emotional development are only as viable as
their perspectives on cognitive development, per se.

The specific model of emotional development in infancy which derives
from my neo-Piagetian theory of cognitive development is presented
in Table 7. At the point of onset of each of the six neo-Piagetian
levels concerned (5-10), a class or type of emotion comes to manifest. Moreover, there are four emotions possible at each of the
levels, since emotions are seen to vary along two other axes (each
with two poles). First, they can reflect compatibility with ongoing
goals, and thus be positive in hedonic tone for the most part, or
they can be incompatible or interfering and negative in tone.
Second, for each of these two options, emotions can reflect an active organism or one that is reacting to the environment.

The six classes of emotion are now more specifically described. In
general, they concern arriving at an end, possessing, approaching,
giving, desiring, and evaluating, respectively. Thus, 24 (6 x 2 x
2) primary emotions are posited to develop in infancy. The 24 cells
in Table 7 can be seen as blueprints. For when the specific
points along the three dimensions of the model come to intersect,
the primary emotions do not inevitably manifest. There are many
situational, individual, etc., factors which can come into play.
Moreover, there may be several variants of each of these emotions
(e.g., in terms of intensity), some examples of which are given in
the table. Also, these primary emotions change in nature at the
levels succeeding the one in which they first appear; they blend or
combine; etc. Note that the current view of what are the primary
emotions differs noticeably from other points of view. Traditional
approaches, such as Ekman's (Ekman and Friesen, 1986; Fridlund,
Ekman and Oster, 1987), normally include 10 or fewer primary emotions. However, the terms of reference of these traditional approaches are limited compared to the present one, since they only include primary emotions thought to be expressed by specific, innately
programmed facial expressions, in particular.

Neonatal emotions involve arriving at relevant ends although without
necessarily obtaining them, since behavior at the corresponding neo-
Piagetian level especially concerns a continual monitoring of movement and/or target, but with little successful target attainment
(see Table 4). Note that neonatal emotions can also be seen as the
inverse of arriving, i.e., as leaving (e.g., in leaving disequilibrium or equilibrium, leading to quiescence and distress, respectively). First month emotions reflect possession, since behavior at
the corresponding sensorimotor level more often leads to target
attainment, and the environment becomes more concerned about such
attainment (see Table 5). In the next months, emotions index more
definite approach in order to attain targets both in terms of the

infants' behavior and in terms of his/her perception of environmental activities. This reflects the beginning of purpose and directed groping evident in the infant's new cognitive skills. At
about 8 months, infants show giving and understanding when given to
in their emotions. This can take place since, at the cognitive
level, there are primitive representations and purposes which allow
the guiding of behavior from its outset to quasi-independent targets. The one-year-old can emote by desiring or sensing being
desired, since cognitively the infant can embed or multiply in a
sequence, and thus better see relations between a target and her/
himself. Finally, the toddler in the second year of life possesses
powerful symbols which can help him/her evaluate emotionally or
sense being evaluated. This sequence in the development of the
emotions may have import in related areas of ontogenesis; I imagine
that phases in the development of attachment to the caretaker are
related to the six steps described for the development of the primary emotions and their cognitive underpinnings.

6.3. Socioemotional systems

All of the many socioemotional systems hypothesized to relate to the
levels in the current neo-Piagetian model are now introduced in
order to reveal the full scope of the theory that can be derived
from the present train of thought. Except for the emotional system
just discussed, each is structured along three bipolar dimensions:
(a) Goal compatibility-incompatibility and (b) activity-reactivity,
like for the emotions, and (c) figure-ground. The latter refers to
whether behavior is targeted (i) directly to the primary object of
concern (e.g., toy, self, parent), or (ii) to (a) the object's
context (e.g., distance, situation), (b) secondary others (e.g.,
peers), (c) only indirectly to the primary object (e.g., using
reinforcement with it), etc. In this sense, some of the emotions in
Table 7 relate to figure (e.g., possession), while others relate to
ground (e.g., approach). The pole of reactivity in the dimension of
activity-reactivity concerns more than a passive organism, for it
also can involve behavior related to the consequences or responses
of the organism to its activity. The socioemotional systems are
specifically depicted in Table 8, at least for positive, goal-
compatible behavior. [Examples of negative behavior are given for
the second system in the table]. The 12 systems listed are thought
to manifest one after the other in concert with the emergence of the
three qualitative substages which develop in each of the four major
neo-Piagetian stages (the first, third, and fifth ones in each five
step cyclic recursion of substages, see section 5.2). However, the
systems may rapidly expand at points subsequent to their initial
appearance.

The relationship of each of the socioemotional systems to its corresponding neo-Piagetian level is now briefly described. Reflex
pairs (see Table 4, level 1) can only permit behavior involving distance maintenance or alteration, and thus are not truly social (this
system and the next one are derived from Plutchik, 1980). Primitive
schema-controlled behaviors (level 3) are more target oriented, so
that acts can concern outcome in social situations, but these are
purely functional and again not truly social. With reflex-
independent schemas (level 5), the first emotions can develop, as
described in the prior section (6.2). Schema coordination (Table 5,

Table 8. Socioemotional Systems Concerning Goal Compatibility Corresponding to Qualitative Neo-Piagetian Substages (Each 1st, 3rd, 5th One).

System Name	Dimension			
	Figure		Ground	
	Active	Reactive	Active	Reactive
Distance Acts	Incorporate (zero distance)	Try to induce distance reduction	Reduce actual distance	Maintain minimum distance
Outcome Acts	Explore, take (vs. aggress)	Attract (vs. protect)	Approach (vs. avoid)	Orient (vs. reject)
Emotional Acts	Possesses (pleasure), etc.	Possessed (contentment), etc.	Approaching (interest), etc.	Approached (delight), etc.
Dyadic Acts	Modelling (eliciting imitation)	Imitating (built on neo-natal skill)	Classical Pavlovian conditioning	Shaping, operant conditioning
Sociability Acts	Secure with caretaker	Adapt to her departure	Seek out strangers	Adapt to their approach

(Following Table 8.)

Interactional Acts	Join, play (no asymmetry in relation)	Let join, play	Lead or seek lead	Let (seek) lead
Superordinate Acts	Coherence over all units	Accentuated by cohesion over related units	Syntax among neighboring units	Style (e.g., rhythm) coordinates with syntax
Gender Acts	Same-sex parent identification accelerates	Complementary reaction: Opposite sex	Same-sex peer identification accelerates	Complementary reaction: Opposite sex
Role Acts	In family, with friends	Even when imposed	In school, peer clubs	In wider community
Conscious Acts	Esteem for self, identity	Unrepression of unconscious	Esteem for others, ecology	Open to abstract learning
Nurturing Acts	Love romantic partner	Love children (with partner)	Daily responsibility, work	Also beyond this
Universal Acts	Encourage self for self	Encourage other for self	Encourage self for other	Encourage other for other

level 6) allows the first truly social dyadic interactions, since
elemental coordination between a baby's schema and that of an adult
becomes possible. This process may even come to include imitations
in the very young infant (built upon neonatal skills in imitation,
following Meltzoff, 1985). Primitive representations (level 8) cul-
tivate truly sociable behavior, as the infant can be secure with
mother and liked stranger and adapt to their coming and going. The
symbolic plans of the toddler (level 10) open up a new social dimension, for they permit prolonged interaction, either for its own
sake, as in play, or with the seeking of control. The young child
comes to coordinate plans (Table 6, level 11), and her/his behavior
becomes complexly organized. Whether one analyzes conversations,
monologues, stories, etc., the beginning of superordinate structures
are now evident. The target whole has an overall coherence to some
extent, which is accentuated by cohesive relations between its parts
(e.g., Halliday and Hasan, 1976). Even groups of neighboring units
display more rules, as in the development of verbal syntax and its
coordination with intonation in the utterances forming the base of
the whole. The plan systems of middle childhood (level 13) enable
the child to increasingly relate him/herself to the personalities,
styles, habits, etc., of valued others. This process carries the
child beyond the initial phases of gender identification which
begins earlier in life. In particular, identification with parents'
and friends' characteristics accelerates. With the growth of logic
in imagination (level 15), the child can better imagine his/her role
in the untested world around him/her, and organized institutions
become a focus. In the abstract stage, socioemotional behavior
based on conscious awareness (level 16), nurturing (18), and more
universal (20) acts can begin to develop.

6.4. Relations with Erickson

The relationship of these proposed socioemotional systems to those
derived from other approaches may be worth investigating. For example, the current approach to socioemotional development is considered congruent with Erikson's (1963) psychodynamic perspective. For
the development of personality and social relations, he describes
eight stages which are thought to emerge in age ranges that are
coincident with many of the expansionary substages of the current
theory. It will be recalled that these substages are the second and
fourth ones in each five step cyclic recursion of neo-Piagetian substages, and concern hierarchization and multiplication (see section
5.2). For example, Erickson's first stage of trust vs. mistrust is
seen as especially emerging at around 6 months, just when the sensorimotor substage of hierarchization has developed. An example involving the multiplication substages concerns the Ericksonian stage
of industry; it appears in middle childhood, an age period where
perioperational multiplication is manifesting in the current theory.

This correspondence between Erickson's eight stages and the expansionary substages of the current theory does not manifest a one-to-
one relationship. On the one hand, the reflex expansionary substages of the current theory develop before any Ericksonian stage. On
the other hand, the last three stages of Erickson's theory seem to
develop during the abstract multiplication level of the current
theory, but also afterwards (i.e., Erickson's last three stages may
not be either universal or biologically-based, unlike the others).

It is worth noting that the first five stages of Erickson are the
ones closely identified with Freud's five stages, and these are precisely the ones with the clearest one-to-one relation to successive
expansionary substages of the current theory. As a general conclusion, it seems that the specific socioemotional acquisitions during
qualitative substages of the current theory which precede expansionary substages prepare the groundwork for spurts in key areas of
personality development during those expansionary substages. This
leads to points in development where there are alternations in the
emergence of socioemotional systems as defined by the current theory
and more general stages as defined by Erickson.

Exactly how such Ericksonian spurts may depend on the socioemotional
systems of the current theory (and thus underlying neo-Piagetian
acquisitions) is worth investigating. For example, Erickson's substage of autonomy may peak in the second year of life since, on the
one hand, the necessary (but insufficient) security with the caretaker blossoms in the prior age period. On the other hand, in the
second year the underlying cognitive acquisition of sensorimotor
multiplication develops, and its plans involving combined or embedded means may permit the previously developed sense of security with
the caretaker to evolve into a sense of autonomy from her/him. That
is, this cognitive acquisition may permit the infant to explore
means-end relationships, promoting autonomy in optimal circumstances. Similarly, the 3-year-old may enter into Erickson's stage of
initiative since the prior period sees the beginning of the development of coordinated plans at the cognitive level. Consequently, in
terms of socioemotional systems, one sees a superordinate coherence
across behaviors. At the cognitive level, the 3-year-old child can
come to hierarchize these superordinate coordinations. Thus, in
terms of Erickson, the 3-year-old's perspective may be hierarchically positioned as dominant (in initiative) over those of others (even
at the oedipal level, if one abstracts from Freud). As a final note, it is possible that there are as yet unthought of socioemotional
systems that develop with the expansionary substages of neo-
Piagetian cognitive development. Moreover, these possible systems
may obviate the need for our parallel between the current theory and
Erickson's stages if these systems are structured to resemble
Erickson's stages.

This extension of the current theory in order to integrate the far
reaching views of Erickson hopefully underscores the full potential
scope of the current theory. It begins with a discussion of development, in general. Then, it emphasizes the role of inhibition in
lateralization development. Next, it presents a novel neo-Piagetian
model in order to show that developmental stages englobing cognitive, lateralization, and central acquisitions progressively emerge in
ontogenesis. Finally, it terminates with implications for socioemotional behavior, even at the Ericksonian level. In short, the current theory has many different components, but hopefully it will be
assimilated and employed as a whole.

ACKNOWLEDGEMENTS

Special thanks to Ronald Cohen and Graham Reed for their many
helpful and constructive comments.

REFERENCES

Aboitiz, F. (1988). Epigenesis and the evolution of the human brain. *Medical Hypotheses, 25,* 55-59.

Albert, M., & Sandson, J. (1986). Perseveration in aphasia. *Cortex, 22,* 103-115.

Archer, L., Campbell, D., & Segalowitz, S. (1988a). A prospective study of hand preference and language development in 18- to 30-month-olds: I. Hand preference. *Developmental Neuropsychology, 4,* 85-92.

Archer, L., Campbell, D., & Segalowitz, S. (1988b). A prospective study of hand preference and language development in 18- to 30-month-olds: II. Relations between hand preference and language development. *Developmental Neuropsychology, 4,* 93-102.

Bakan, P., Dibb, G., & Reed, P. (1973). Handedness and birth stress. *Neuropsychologia, 11,* 363-366.

Barnes, C., Cornwell, K., Fitzgerald, H., & Harris, L. (1985). Spontaneous head positions in infants during the first 9 postnatal months. *Infant Mental Health Journal, 6,* 117-125.

Bates, E., O'Connell, B., Vaid, J., Sledge, P., & Oakes, L. (1986). Language and hand preference in early development. *Developmental Neuropsychology, 2,* 1-15.

Bateson, P. (1987). Biological approaches to the study of behavioral development. *International Journal of Behavioral Development, 10,* 1-22.

Best, C. (in press). The emergence of cerebral asymmetries for perceptual and cognitive functions in infancy. In: D. Molfese & S. Segalowitz (Eds.), *Developmental implications of brain lateralization.* New York: Guilford.

Best, C., & Queen, H. (1989). Baby, it's your smile: Right hemiface bias in infant emotional expressions. *Developmental Psychology, 25,* 264-276.

Bigsby, R. (1983). Reaching and asymmetrical tonic neck reflex in pre-term and full-term infants. *Physical Occupational Therapy in Pediatrics, 3(4),* 25-42.

Bradshaw, J., & Nettleton, N. (1981). The nature of hemispheric specialization in man. *The Behavioral and Brain Sciences, 4,* 51-63.

Breslow, L. (1986). Lumping and splitting in developmental theory: comments on Fischer and Elmendorf. In: M. Perlmutter (Ed.), *Cognitive perspectives on children's social and behavioral development. The Minnesota Symposia on Child Psychology, Vol. 18.* Hillsdale, N.J.: Erlbaum, pp.179-187.

Bresson, F., Maury, L., Piéraut-le-Bonniec, G., & de Schonen, S. (1977). Organization of asymmetric functions in hands collaboration. *Neuropsychologia, 15,* 311-320.

Bresson, F., & de Schonen, S. (1983). Le développement des dissymétries hémisphériques et comportementales au cours de la première année. *La Médecine Infantile, 90,* 281-289.

Brésard, B., & Bresson, F. (1987). Reaching or manipulation: Left or right ? *The Behavioral and Brain Sciences, 10,* 265-266.

Brown, J. (1978). Lateralization: A brain model. *Brain and Language, 5,* 258-261.

Brown, T. (1988). Ships in the night: Piaget and American cognitive science. *Human Development, 31,* 60-64.

Bruno, R., & Auerbach, C. (1983). Differential left hemisphere

activation during the voluntary control of skin resistance level. *Biofeedback and Self-Regulation, 8,* 505-516.
Bruyer, R., & Guerit, J. (1983). Hemispheric differences in the voluntary inhibition of movement. *Brain and Cognition, 2,* 251-256.
Buck, R., & Duffy, R. (1980). Nonverbal communication of affect in brain-damaged patients. *Cortex, 16,* 351-362.
Bullock, D., Liederman, J., & Todorovic, D. (1987). Reconciling stable asymmetry with recovery of function: An adaptive systems perspective on functional plasticity. *Child Development, 58,* 689-697.
Carlson, D., & Harris, L. (1985). Development of the infant's hand preference for visually directed reaching: Preliminary report of a longitudinal study. *Infant Mental Health Journal, 6,* 158-174.
Case, R. (1978). Intellectual development from birth to adulthood: A neo-Piagetian interpretation. In: R. Siegler (Ed.), *Children's thinking: What develops ?* Hillsdale, N.J.: Erlbaum.
Case, R. (1985). *Intellectual development: Birth to adulthood.* Orlando, Fla: Academic Press.
Case, R. (1987). Neo-Piagetian theory: Retrospect and prospect. *International Journal of Psychology, 22,* 773-791.
Case, R., Hayward, S., Lewis, M., & Hurst, P. (1988). Toward a neo-Piagetian theory of cognitive and emotional development. *Developmental Review, 8,* 1-51.
Case, R., Reid, D., McKeough, A., Dennis, S., & Marini, Z. (1987). Dialectical cycles in the development of multiple intelligences. Paper presented at the biennial meeting of the Society for Research in Child Development, Baltimore.
Chapman, M. (1987). A longitudinal study of cognitive representation in symbolic play, self-recognition, and object permanence during the second year. *International Journal of Behavioral Development, 10,* 151-170.
Chapman, M. (1988). *Constructive evolution: Origins and development of Piaget's thought.* New York: Cambridge University Press.
Cook, N. (1984). Callosal inhibition: The key to the brain code. *Behavioral Science, 29,* 98-110.
Corballis, M., & Morgan, M. (1978). On the biological basis of human laterality: 1. Evidence for maturational left-right gradient. *The Behavioral and Brain Sciences, 2,* 261-269.
Corbetta, D., & Mounoud, P. (in press). Early development of grasping and manipulation. In: C. Bard, M. Fleury, & L. Hay (Eds.), *Development of eye-hand coordination across the lifespan.*
Coren, S., Searleman, A., & Porac, C. (1982). The effects of specific birth stressors on four indices of lateral preference. *Canadian Journal of Psychology, 36,* 478-487.
Cornwell, K., Fitzgerald, H., & Harris, L. (1985). On the state-dependent nature of infant head orientation. *Infant Mental Health Journal, 6,* 137-144.
Cornwell, K., Barnes, C., Fitzgerald, H., & Harris, L. (1985). Neurobehavioral reorganization in early infancy: Patterns of head orientation following lateral and midline holds. *Infant Mental Health Journal, 6,* 126-136.
Coryell, J. (1985). Infant rightward asymmetries predict right-handedness in childhood. *Neuropsychologia, 23,* 269-271.
Coryell, J., & Michel, G. (1978). How supine postural preferences of infants can contribute toward the development of handedness.

Infant Behavior and Development, 1, 245-257.
Curtiss, S. (1986). The development of human cerebral lateralization. In: D. Benson & E. Zaidel (Eds.), *The dual brain: Hemisphere specialization in humans.* New York: Guilford, pp.97-116.
Dawson, G. (in press). Cerebral lateralization in autism: Clues to its role in language and affective development. In: D. Molfese & S. Segalowitz (Eds.), *Developmental implications of brain lateralization.* New York: Guilford.
Décarie, T. (1962). *Intelligence et affectivité chez le jeune enfant.* Neuchâtel: Delachaux et Niestlé.
Denenberg, V. (1980). General systems theory, brain organization, and early experiences. *American Journal of Physiology, 238,* R3-R13.
Denenberg, V. (1981). Hemispheric laterality in animals and the effects of early experience. *The Behavioral and Brain Sciences, 4,* 1-21.
De Renzi, E., Gentilini, M., & Bazolli, C. (1986). Eyelid movement disorders and motor impersistence in acute hemisphere disease. *Neurology, 36,* 414-418.
Doré, F., & Dumas, C. (1987). Psychology of animal cognition: Piagetian studies. *Psychological Bulletin, 102,* 219-233.
Ekman, P., & Friesen, W. A new pan-cultural facial expression of emotion. *Motivation and Emotion, 10,* 159-168.
Erickson, E. (1963). *Childhood and society.* New York: Norton.
Fagot, J., & Vauclair, J. (1988). Handedness and bimanual coordination in the lowland gorilla. *Brain, Behavior and Evolution, 32,* 89-95.
Fagot, J., & Vauclair, J. (in press). Handedness and manual specialization in the baboon. *Neuropsychologia.*
Ehrlichman, H., Zoccolotti, P., & Owen, D. (1982). Perinatal factors in hand and eye preference: Data from the Collaborative Perinatal Project. *International Journal of Neuroscience, 17,* 17-22.
Feldman, J. (April, 1983). Implications of the laterally asymmetric head position bias in newborns for behavioral development at 1 year. Paper presented at the biennial meeting of the Society for Research in Child Development, Detroit.
Fischer, K. (1980). A theory of cognitive development: The control and construction of hierarchies of skills. *Psychological Review, 87,* 477-531.
Fischer, K. (1987). Relations between brain and cognitive development. *Child Development, 58,* 623-632.
Fischer, K., & Lamborn, S. (in press). Mechanisms of variation in developmental levels: Cognitive and emotional transitions during adolescence. In: A. de Ribaupierre (Ed.), *Transition mechanisms in cognitive-emotional child development: The longitudinal approach.* New York: Cambridge University Press.
Fischer, K., Shaver, P., & Carnachan, P. (in press). From basic- to subordinate-category emotions: A skill approach to emotional development. In: W. Damon (Ed.), *Child development today and tomorrow. New directions for child development, no. 40.* San Francisco: Jossey Bass.
Flor-Henry, P. (1983a). Functional hemispheric asymmetry and psychopathology. *Integrative Psychiatry, 4,* 46-59.
Flor-Henry, P. (1983b). Hemisyndromes of temporal lobe epilepsy: Review of evidence relating psychopathological manifestations in epilepsy to right- and left-sided epilepsy. In: M. Myslobodsky

(Ed.), *Hemisyndromes: Psychobiology, neurology, psychiatry*.
New York: Academic Press, pp.149-174.

Flor-Henry, P. (1985). Observations, reflections and speculations
on the cerebral determinants of mood and on the bilaterally
asymmetrical distributions of the major neurotransmitter systems.
In: W. Dewhurst & G. Baker (Eds.), *Pharmacotherapy of affective
disorders: Theory and practice*. London: Croom Helm, pp.151-
184.

Fogel, A., & Hannan, T. (1985). Manual actions of nine- to fifteen-
week-old human infants during face-to-face interaction with their
mothers. *Child Development, 56*, 1271-1279.

Fox, N. (1985). The relationship of perinatal birth status to
handedness: A prospective study. *Infant Mental Health Journal,
6*, 175-184.

Fox, N., & Lewis, M. (1982). Motor asymmetries in preterm infants:
Effects of prematurity and illness. *Developmental Psychobiology,
15*, 19-23.

Fox, N., & Davidson, R. (1984). Hemispheric substrates of affect:
A developmental model. In: N. Fox & R. Davidson (Eds.), *The
psychobiology of affective development*. Hillsdale, N.J.:
Erlbaum, 353-381.

Fox, N., & Davidson, R. (1986). Taste-elicited changes in facial
signs of emotion and the asymmetry of brain electrical activity
in human newborns. *Neuropsychologia, 24*, 417-422.

Fox, N., & Davidson, R. (1988). Patterns of brain electrical
activity during facial signs of emotion in 10-month-old infants.
Developmental Psychology, 24, 230-236.

Fridlund, A., Ekman, P., & Oster, H. (1987). Facial expression of
emotion: Review of literature, 1970-1983. In: A. Siegman &
S. Feldstein (Eds.), *Nonverbal behavior and communication
(2nd ed.)*. Hillsdale, N.J.: Erlbaum, pp.143-224.

Galaburda, A., Corsiglia, J., Rosen, G., & Sherman, G. (1987).
Planum temporale asymmetry, reappraisal since Geschwind and
Levitsky. *Neuropsychologia, 25*, 853-868.

Geschwind. N. (1975). The apraxias: Neural mechanisms of disorders
of learned movement. *American Scientist, 63*, 188-195.

Geschwind, N., & Galaburda, A. (1985a). Cerebral lateralization.
Biological mechanisms, associations, and pathology: A hypothesis
and a program for research. I. *Archives of Neurology, 42*, 428-
459.

Geschwind, N., & Galaburda, A. (1985b). Cerebral lateralization.
Biological mechanisms, associations, and pathology: A hypothesis
and a program of research. III. *Archives of Neurology, 42*, 634-
654.

Gesell, A., & Ames, L. (1947). The development of handedness.
Journal of Genetic Psychology, 70, 155-175.

Glick, S., Ross, D., & Hough, L. (1982). Lateral asymmetry of
neurotransmitters in human brain. *Brain Research, 234*, 53-63.

Goldberg, E., & Costa, L. (1981). Hemispheric differences in the
acquisition and use of descriptive systems. *Brain and Language,
14*, 144-173.

Goldfield, E., & Michel G. (1986). The ontogeny of infant bimanual
reaching during the first year. *Infant Behavior and Development,
9*, 81-89.

Goldman-Rakic, P. (1987). Development of cortical circuitry and
cognitive function. *Child Development, 58*, 601-622.

Gottfried, A., & Bathurst, K. (1983). Hand preference across time is related to intelligence in young girls, not boys. *Science*, *221*, 1074-1076.

Gratch, G., & Schatz, J. (1988). Evaluating Piaget's infancy books as works-in-progress: The case of prehension. *Human Development*, *31*, 82-91.

Griener, J., Fitzgerald, H., & Cooke, P. (1986). Speech fluency and hand performance on a sequential tapping task in left- and right-handed stutterers and non-stutterers. *Journal of Fluency Disorders*, *11*, 55-69.

Gruzelier, J. (1983). A critical assessement and integration of lateral asymmetries in schizophrenia. In: M. Myslobodsky (Ed.), *Hemisyndromes: Psychobiology, neurology, psychiatry*. New York : Academic Press, pp.265-326.

Gruzelier, J., & Hammond, N. (1979). Gains, losses and lateral differences in the hearing of schizophrenic patients. *British Journal of Psychology*, *70*, 319-330.

Gruzelier, J., & Hammond, N. (1980). Lateralized deficits and drug influences on the dichotic listening of schizophrenic patients. *Biological Psychiatry*, *15*, 759-779.

Gur, R., Levy, J., & Van Auken, C. (1979). Eyedness, handedness and perinatal stress. Paper presented at the annual meeting of the International Neuropsychological Society, New York.

Haaland, K. (1984). The relationship of limb apraxia severity to motor and language deficits. *Brain and Cognition*, *3*, 307-316.

Hahn, W. (1987). Cerebral lateralization of function: From infancy through childhood. *Psychological Bulletin*, *101*, 376-392.

Halford, G. (1987). A structure-mapping approach to cognitive development. *International Journal of Psychology*, *22*, 609-642.

Halliday, M., & Hasan, R. (1976). *Cohesion in English*. London: Longman.

Hannan, T. (1987). A cross-sequential assessment of the occurrences of pointing in 3- to 12-month-old human infants. *Infant Behavior and Development*, *10*, 11-22.

Harkins, D., & Michel, G. (in press). Evidence for a maternal effect on infant hand-use preferences. *Developmental Psychobiology*.

Harris, L. (1983). Laterality of function in the infant: Historical and contemporary trends in theory and research. In: G. Young, S. Segalowitz, C. Corter & S. Trehub (Eds.), *Manual specialization and the developing brain*. New York: Academic Press, pp.177-247.

Harris, L., & Fitzgerald, H. (1983). Postural orientation in human infants: Changes from birth to three months. In: G. Young, S. Segalowitz, C. Corter & S. Trehub (Eds.), *Manual specialization and the developing brain*. New York: Academic Press, pp.285-305.

Harris, P. (1983). Infant cognition. In: M. Haith & J. Campos (Eds.), *Handbook of child psychology (4th ed.). Vol. 2. Infancy and developmental psychobiology*. New York: Wiley, 689-782.

Hécaen, H. (1984). *Les gauchers: Etude neuropsychologique*. Paris: Les Presses Universitaires de France.

Hoff-Ginsburg, E. (1986). Function and structure in maternal speech: Their relation to the child's development in syntax. *Developmental Psychology*, *22*, 155-163.

von Hofsten, C. (1982). Eye-hand coordination in the newborn. *Developmental Psychology*, *18*, 450-461.

von Hofsten, C. (1984). Developmental changes in the organization
    of prereaching movements. *Developmental Psychology, 20,* 378-388.
Hooper, S., & Boyd, T. (1986). Neurodevelopmental learning
    disorders. In: J. Obrzut & G. Hynd (Eds.), *Child
    neuropsychology, Vol. 2. Clinical practice.* Orlando, Fla:
    Academic Press, pp.15-58.
Hopkins, B., Lems, W., Janssen, B., & Butterworth, G. (1987).
    Postural and motor asymmetries in newlyborns. *Human Neurobiology,
    6,* 153-156.
Hudson, A. (1968). Perseveration. *Brain, 91,* 571-582.
Humphrey, D., & Humphrey, G. (1987). Sex differences in infant
    reaching. *Neuropsychologia, 25,* 971-975.
Ingram, D. (1975). Motor asymmetries in young children.
    Neuropsychologia, 13, 95-102.
Inhelder, B., de Caprona, D., & Cornu-Wells, A. (Eds.). (1987).
    Piaget today. Hillsdale, N.J.: Erlbaum.
Jasper, H., & Raney, E. (1937). The physiology of lateral cerebral
    dominance: Review of literature and evaluation of the test of
    simultaneous bilateral movement. *Psychological Bulletin, 34,*
    151-165.
Johnston, T. (1987). The persistence of dichotomies in the study of
    behavioral development. *Developmental Review, 7,* 149-182.
Kagan, J., Reznick, J., & Snidman, N. (1988). Biological bases of
    childhood shyness. *Science, 240,* 167-171.
Kamptner, L., Kraft, R., & Harper, L. (1984). Lateral
    specialization and social-verbal development in preschool
    children. *Brain and Cognition, 3,* 42-50.
Kamptner, N., Cornwell, K., Fitzgerald, H., & Harris, L. (1985).
    Motor asymmetries in the human infant: Stepping movements.
    Infant Mental Health Journal, 6, 145-156.
Kaufman, A., Zalman, R., & Kaufman, N. (1978). The relationship of
    hand dominance to the motor coordination, mental ability, and
    right-left awareness of young normal children. *Child Development,
    49,* 885-888.
Kee, D., Gottfried, A., Bathurst, K., & Brown, K. (1987).
    Left-hemisphere language specialization: Consistency in hand
    preference and sex differences. *Child Development, 58,* 718-724.
Kershner, J. (1985). Ontogeny of hemispheric specialization and
    relationship of developmental patterns to complex reasoning
    skills and academic achievement. In: C. Best (Ed.), *Hemispheric
    function and collaboration in the child.* Orlando, Fla: Academic
    Press, pp.327-360.
Kiessling, L., Denckla, M., & Carlton, M. (1983). Evidence for
    differential hemispheric function in children with hemiplegic
    cerebral palsy. *Developmental Medicine and Child Neurology, 25,*
    727-734.
Kinsbourne, M. (1975). The ontogeny of cerebral dominance. *Annals
    of the New York Academy of Sciences, 263,* 244-250.
Kinsbourne, M. (1978). Biological determinants of functional
    bisymmetry and asymmetry. In: M. Kinsbourne (Ed.), *Asymmetrical
    function of the brain.* New York: Cambridge University Press.
Kinsbourne, M. (in press). Sinistrality, brain organization and
    cognitive deficits. In: D. Molfese & S. Segalowitz (Eds.),
    Developmental implications of brain lateralization. New York:
    Guilford.
Kinsbourne, M., & Hiscock, M. (1983). The normal and deviant
    development of functional lateralization of the brain. In: M.

Haith & M. Campos (Eds.), *Handbook of child psychology (4th ed.)*, *Vol. 2. Infancy and developmental psychobiology*. New York: Wiley, pp.157-280.

Kinsbourne, M., & Hiscock, M. (1987). Language lateralization and disordered language development. In: S. Rosenberg (Ed.), *Advances in applied psycholinguistics. Vol. 1. Disorders of first language development*. New York: Cambridge University Press, pp.220-263.

Kirk, V. (1985). Hemispheric contributions to the development of graphic skill. In: C. Best (Ed.), *Hemispheric function and collaboration in the child*. Orlando, Fla: Academic Press, pp. 193-228.

Konishi, Y., Mikawa, H., & Suzuki, J. (1986). Asymmetrical head-turning of preterm infants: Some effects on later postural and functional lateralities. *Developmental Medicine and Child Neurology, 28*, 450-457.

Konishi, Y., Kuriyama, M., Mikawa, H., & Suzuki, J. (1987). Effect of body position on later postural and functional lateralities of preterm infants. *Developmental Medicine and Child Neurology, 29*, 751-757.

Kosslyn, S. (1987). Seeing and imagining in the cerebral hemispheres: A computational approach. *Psychological Review, 94*, 148-175.

Lacoste, M. de, & Woodward, D. (1988). The corpus callosum in nonhuman primates: Determinants of size. *Brain, Behavior and Evolution, 31*, 318-323.

Lenneberg, E. (1967). *Biological foundations of language*. New York: Wiley.

Levine, R., Liederman, J., & Riley, P. (1988). The brainstem auditory evoked potential asymmetry is replicable and reliable. *Neuropsychologia, 26*, 603-614.

Levy, J. (1983). Commentary on Flor-Henry 1983a. *Integrative Psychiatry, 4*, 52-53.

Levy, J. (1985). Interhemispheric collaboration: Single-mindedness in the asymmetric brain. In: C. Best (Ed.), *Hemispheric function and collaboration in the child*. Orlando, Fla: Academic Press, pp.11-31.

Levy, J., Heller, W., Banich, M., & Burton, L. (1983). Are variations among right-handed individuals in perceptual asymmetries caused by characteristic arousal differences between hemispheres ? *Journal of Experimental Psychology: Human Perception and Performance, 9*, 329-359.

Lewkowicz, D., & Turkewitz, G. (1982). The influence of hemispheric specialization in sensory processing on reaching in infants: Age and gender related effects. *Developmental Psychology, 18*, 301-308.

Lewkowicz, D., & Turkewitz, G. (1983). Relationships between processing and motor asymmetries in early development. In: G. Young, S. Segalowitz, C. Corter & S. Trehub (Eds.), *Manual specialization and the developing brain*. New York: Academic Press, pp.375-393.

Liederman, J. (1983). Mechanisms underlying instability in the development of hand preference. In: G. Young, S. Segalowitz, C. Corter & S. Trehub (Eds.), *Manual specialization and the developing brain*. New York: Academic Press, pp.71-92.

Liederman, J. (1987). Neonates show an asymmetric degree of head rotation but lack an asymmetric tonic neck reflex asymmetry:

Neuropsychological implications. *Developmental Neuropsychology,*
3, 101-112.
Liederman, J. (in press). Misconceptions and new conceptions about
early brain damage, cerebral laterality and behavioral outcome.
In: D. Molfese & S. Segalowitz (Eds.), *Developmental
implications of brain lateralization.* New York: Guilford.
Liederman, J., & Coryell, J. (1981). Right-hand preference
facilitated by rightward turning biases during infancy.
Developmental Psychobiology, 14, 439-450.
Liederman, J., & Coryell, J. (1982). The origin of left hand
preference: Pathological and non-pathological influences.
Neuropsychologia, 20, 721-725.
Liederman, J., & Foley, L. (1987). A modified finger lift test
reveals an asymmetry of motor overflow in adults. *Journal of
Clinical and Experimental Psychology, 9,* 498-510.
Lokker, R., & Morais, J. (1985). Ear differences in children at two
years of age. *Neuropsychologia, 23,* 127-129.
Lomas, J. (1980). Competition within the left hemisphere between
speaking and unimanual tasks performed without visual guidance.
Neuropsychologia, 18, 141-149.
Luria, A. (1962/1966). *Higher cortical functions in man.* Trans. B.
Haigh. New York: Basic.
Luria, A. (1973). *The working brain.* New York: Basic.
Luria, A., Homskaya, E., Blinkov, S., & Critchley, M. (1967).
Impaired selectivity of mental processes in association with a
lesion of the frontal lobe. *Neuropsychologia, 5,* 105-117.
MacNeilage, P., Studdert-Kennedy, M., & Lindblom, B. (1987).
Primate handedness reconsidered. *The Behavioral and Brain
Sciences, 10,* 247-263.
McCormick, C., & Maurer, D. (1988). Unimanual hand preferences in
6-month-olds: Consistency and relation to familial handedness.
Infant Behavior and Development, 11, 21-29.
McDonnell, P., Anderson, V., & Abraham, W. (1983). Asymmetry and
orientation of arm movements in three- to eight-week-old infants.
Infant Behavior and Development, 6, 287-298.
McGraw, M. (1943). *The Neuromuscular maturation of the human
infant.* New York: Columbia University Press.
Mehler, J. (1985). Language related dispositions in early infancy.
In: J. Mehler & R. Fox (Eds.), *Neonate cognition: Beyond the
blooming buzzing confusion.* Hillsdale, N.J.: Erlbaum, pp.7-28.
Melekian, B. (1981). Lateralization in the newborn at birth:
Asymmetry of the stepping reflex. *Neuropsychologia, 19,* 707-711.
Meltzoff, A. (1985). Perception, action, and cognition in early
infancy. *Annales de Pédiatrie, 32,* 63-77.
Ment, L., Scott, D., Lange, R., Ehrenkranz, R., Duncan, C., &
Warshaw, J. (1983). Postpartum perfusion of the prenatal brain:
Relationship to neurodevelopmental outcome. *Child's Brain, 10,*
266-272.
Michel, G. (1983). Development of hand-use preference during
infancy. In: G. Young, S. Segalowitz, C. Corter & S. Trehub
(Eds.), *Manual specialization and the developing brain.* New York:
Academic Press, pp.33-70.
Michel, G. (1987). Self-generated experience and the development of
lateralized neurobehavioral organization in infants. In: J.
Rosenblatt, C. Beer, M. Busnel & P. Slater (Eds.), *Advances in
the study of behavior. Vol. 17.* New York: Academic Press, pp.
61-83.

Michel, G. (in press). A neuropsychological perspective on infant
sensorimotor development.
Michel, G., & Harkins, D. (1986). Postural and lateral asymmetries
in the ontogeny of handedness during infancy. *Developmental
Psychobiology, 19,* 247-258.
Michel, G., Ovrut, M., & Harkins, D. (1984). Intermanual transfer
of tactile discrimination. *Infant Behavior and Development.
Special International Conference on Infant Studies Issue, 7,* 247.
Michel, G., Ovrut, M., & Harkins, D. (1986). Hand-use preference
for reaching and object manipulation in 6- through 13-month-old
infants. *Genetic, Social, and General Psychology Monographs,*
409-427.
Milner, B., & Petrides, M. (1984). Behavioural effects of
frontal-lobe lesions in man. *Trends in Neurosciences, 7,* 403-407.
Mintz, M., & Myslobodsky, M. (1983). Two types of hemisphere
imbalance in hemi-Parkinsonism coded by brain electrical activity
and electrodermal activity. In: M. Myslobodsky, (Ed.),
Hemisyndromes: Psychobiology, neurology, psychiatry. New York:
Academic Press, pp.213-239.
Molfese, V., & Betz, J. (1987). Language and motor development in
infancy: Three views with neuropsychological implications.
Developmental Neuropsychology, 3, 255-274.
Molfese, D., & Molfese, V. (1979). Hemisphere and stimulus
differences as reflected in the cortical responses of newborn
infants to speech stimuli. *Developmental Psychology, 15,* 505-511.
Molfese, D., & Molfese, V. (1980). Cortical responses of preterm
infants to phonetic and nonphonetic speech stimuli. *Developmental
Psychology, 16,* 574-581.
Molfese, D., & Molfese, V. (1983). Hemisphere specialization in
infancy. In: G. Young, S. Segalowitz, C. Corter & S. Trehub
(Eds.), *Manual specialization and the developing brain.* New York:
Academic Press, pp.93-109.
Molfese, D., & Molfese, V. (1985). Electrophysical indices of
auditory discrimination in newborn infants: The bases for
predicting later language development ? *Infant Behavior and
Development, 8,* 197-211.
Molfese, D., & Betz, J. (in press). Electrophysiological indices of
the early development of lateralization for language and
cognition and their implications for predicting later
development. In: D. Molfese & S. Segalowitz (Eds.),
Developmental implications of brain lateralization. New York:
Guilford.
Mori, E., & Yamadori, A. (1985). Unilateral hemispheric injury and
ipsilateral instinctive grasp reaction. *Archives of Neurology,
42,* 485-488.
Mounoud, P., & Bower, T. (1974-1975). Conservation of weight in
infants. *Cognition, 3,* 29-40.
Mounoud, P. (1976). Les révolutions psychologiques de l'enfant.
Archives de Psychologie, 44(171), 103-114.
Mounoud, P. (1986). Similarities between developmental sequences at
different age periods. In: I. Levin (Ed.), *Stage and structure:
Reopening the debate.* Norwood, N.J.: Ablex, pp.40-58.
Mounoud, P., & Vinter, A. (1985). A theorical developmental model:
Self-image in children. In: V. Shulman, L. Restaino-Baumann & L.
Butler (Eds.), *The future of Piagetian theory: The neo-
Piagetians.* New York: Plenum, pp.37-69.
Nachshon, I., & Denno, D. (1986). Birth order and lateral

preferences. *Cortex, 22*, 567-578.
Nachshon, I., & Denno, D. (1987). Birth stress and lateral
preferences. *Cortex, 23*, 45-58.
Nachshon, I., & Denno, D. (in press). Hemisphere dysfunction in
violent offenders. In: S. Mednick & T. Moffitt (Eds.), *Biology
and antisocial behavior*. Cambridge: Cambridge University Press.
Orsini, D., Satz, P., & Zemansky, M. (1985). Laterality and early
CNS damage. Paper presented at the 13th annual meeting of the
International Neurological Society, San Diego .
Pascual-Leone, J. (1987). Organismic processes for neo-Piagetian
theories: A dialectical causal account of cognitive development.
International Journal of Psychology, 22, 531-570.
Penfield, W., & Jasper, H. (1954). *Epilepsy and the functional
anatomy of the human brain*. Boston: Little Brown.
Peters, M. (1983). Differentiation and lateral specialization in
motor development. In: G. Young, S. Segalowitz, C. Corter &
S. Trehub (Eds.), *Manual specialization and the developing brain*.
New York: Academic Press, pp.141-159.
Peters, M. (1988). Footedness: Asymmetries in foot preference and
skill and neuropsychological assessment of foot movement.
Psychological Bulletin, 103, 179-192.
Peters, M., & Petrie, B. (1979). Functional asymmetries in the
stepping reflex of human neonates. *Canadian Journal of
Psychology, 33*, 198-200.
Piaget, J. (1936). *La naissance de l'intelligence*. Neuchatel,
Switzerland: Delachaux et Niestlé.
Pietro, M., & Rigrodsky, S. (1986). Patterns of oral-verbal
perseveration in adult aphasics. *Brain and Language, 29*, 1-17.
Plutchik, R. (1980). *Emotion: A psychoevolutionary synthesis*.
New York: Harper.
Provins, K., Dalziel, F., & Higginbottom, G. (1987). Asymmetrical
hand usage in infancy: An ethological approach. *Infant Behavior
and Development, 10*, 165-172.
Ramsay, D. (1980a). Beginnings of bimanual handedness and speech
in infants. *Infant Behavior and Development, 3*, 67-77.
Ramsay, D. (1980b). Onset of unimanual handedness in infants.
Infant Behavior and Development, 3, 377-385.
Ramsay, D. (1983). Unimanual hand preference and duplicated
syllable babbling in infants. In: G. Young, S. Segalowitz, C.
Corter & S. Trehub (Eds.), *Manual specialization and the
developing brain*. New York: Academic Press, pp.161-176.
Ramsay, D. (1984). Onset of duplicated syllable babbling and
unimanual handedness in infancy: Evidence for developmental
change in hemispheric specialization ? *Developmental Psychology,
20*, 64-71.
Ramsay, D. (1985a). Fluctuations in unimanual hand preference in
infants following the onset of duplicated syllable babbling.
Developmental Psychology, 21, 318-324.
Ramsay, D. (1985b). Infants' block banging at midline: Evidence
for Gesell's principle of 'reciprocal interweaving' in
development. *British Journal of Developmental Psychology, 3*,
335-343.
Ramsay, D., & Willis, M. (1984). Organization and lateralization of
reaching in infants: An extension of Bresson et al.,
Neuropsychologia, 22, 639-641.
Ramsay, D., & Weber, S. (1986). Infants' hand preference in a task
involving complementary roles for the two hands. *Child*

Development, 57, 300-307.
Rogers, L. (1980). Lateralisation in the avian brain. *Bird Behaviour, 2,* 1-12.
Rose, S. (1984). Developmental changes in hemispheric specialization for tactual processing in very young children: Evidence from cross-modal transfer. *Developmental Psychology, 20,* 568-574.
Ross, G., Lipper, E., & Auld, P. (1987). Hand preference of four-year-old children: Its relationship to premature birth and neurodevelopmental outcome. *Developmental Medicine and Child Neurology, 29,* 615-622.
Rossor, M., Garrett, N., & Iversen, L. (1980). No evidence for lateral asymmetry of neurotransmitters in post-mortem human brain. *Journal of Neurochemistry, 35,* 743-745.
Rourke, B. (1987). Syndrome of nonverbal learning disabilities: The final common pathway of white-matter disease/dysfunction ? *The Clinical Neuropsychologist, 1,* 209-234.
Russon, A. (in press). The ontegeny of peer social interaction in infant chimpanzees: A description and comparative analysis. In: S. Parker & K. Gibson (Eds.), *Comparative developmental psychology of language and intelligence in primates.* Cambridge: Cambridge University Press.
Satz, P. (1973). Left-handedness and early brain insult: An explanation. *Neuropsychologia, 11,* 115-117.
Scheibel, A. (1984). A dendritic correlate of human speech. In: N. Geschwind & A. Galaburda (Eds.), *Cerebral dominance: The biological foundations.* Cambridge, Mass.: Harvard University Press, pp.43-52.
Schonen, S. de, & Bresson, F. (1984). Développement de l'atteinte manuelle d'un objet chez l'enfant. *Comportements, 1,* 99-114.
Schonen, S. de, & Bry, I. (1987). Interhemispheric communication of visual learning: A developmental study in 3-6-month old infants. *Neuropsychologia, 25,* 601-612.
Schwartz., M. (1985). Perinatal stress factors and laterality: A preliminary report. Paper presented at the 13th annual meeting of the International Neurological Society, San Diego.
Segalowitz, S. (1986). Some implications of lateralization for developmental psychology. In: J.-L. Nespoulous, P. Perron & A. Roch Lecours (Eds.), *The biological foundations of gestures: Motor and semiotic aspects.* Hillsdale, N.J.: Erlbaum, pp.203-213.
Seidman, S., Allen R., & Wasserman, G. (1986). Productive language of premature and physically handicapped two-year-olds. *Journal of Communication Disorders, 19,* 49-61.
Shucard, D., Shucard, J., & Thomas, D. (1984). The development of cerebral specialization in infants. In: R. Emde & R. Harmon (Eds.), *Continuities and discontinuities in development.* New York: Plenum Press, 293-314.
Sigel, I. (1970). The distancing hypothesis: A causal hypothesis for the acquisition of representational thought. In: M. Jones (Ed.). *The effects of early experience.* Miami: University of Miami Press.
Sternberg, R. (1987). A day at developmental downs: Sportscast for race #2 - Neo-Piagetian theories of cognitive development. *International Journal of Psychology, 22,* 507-529.
Subirana, A. (1964). The relationship between handedness and language function. *International Journal of Neurology, 4,*

215-234.

Sugarman, S. (1987). *Piaget's construction of the child's reality.*
New York: Cambridge University Press.

Swartzburg, M. (1983). Hemispheric laterality and EEG correlates of
depression, research communications in psychology. *Psychiatry and
Behavior, 8,* 187-205.

Thelen, E., Kelso, J., & Fogel, A. (1987). Self-organizing systems
and infant motor development. *Developmental Review, 7,* 39-65.

Thelen, E., Skala, K., & Kelso, J. (1987). The dynamic nature of
early coordination: Evidence from bilateral leg movements in
young infants. *Developmental Psychology, 23,* 179-186.

Tournay, A. (1924). L'asymétrie dans le développement sensitivo-
moteur de l'enfant. *Journal de Psychologie Normale et
Pathologique, 5,* 135-144.

Trehub, S., Corter, C., & Schosenberg, N. (1983). Neonatal
reflexes. A search for lateral asymmetry. In: G. Young, S.
Segalowitz, C. Corter and S. Trehub (Eds.), *Manual
specialization and the developing brain.* New York: Academic
Press, 257-274.

Trevarthen, C. (1986). Form, significance, and psychological
potential of hand gestures of infants. In: J.-L. Nespoulous, P.
Perron & A. Roch Lecours (Eds.), *The biological foundations of
gestures: Motor and semiotic aspects.* Hillsdale, N.J.: Erlbaum,
pp.149-202.

Turkewitz, G., (in press). Perinatal influences on the development
of hemispheric specialization and complex information processing.
In: M. Weiss & P. Zelazo (Eds.), *Infant attention.* Norwood,
N.J.: Ablex.

Verfaellie, M., & Heilman, K. (1987). Response preparation and
response inhibition after lesions of the medial frontal lobe.
Archives of Neurology, 44, 1265-1271.

Wada, J., Clarke, R., & Hamm, A. (1975). Cerebral hemispheric
asymmetry in humans. *Archives of Neurology, 32,* 239-246.

Watson, M., & Fischer, K. (1980). Development of social roles in
elicited and spontaneous behavior during the preschool years.
Developmental Psychology, 16, 483-494.

Weinberger, D., Luchins, D., Morihisa, J., & Wyatt, R. (1982).
Asymmetrical volumes of the right and left frontal and occipital
regions of the human brain. *Annals of Neurology, 11,* 97-99.

Welsh, M., & Pennington, B. (1988). Assessing frontal lobe functioning in children: Views from developmental psychology.
Developmental Psychology, 4, 199-230.

West, M., & King, A. (1987). Settling nature and nurture into an
ontogenetic niche. *Developmental Psychology, 20,* 549-562.

Willis, W., & Widerstrom, A. (1986). Structure and function in
prenatal and postnatal neuropsychological development: A dynamic
interaction. In: J. Obrzut & G. Hynd (Eds.), *Child
neuropsychology. Vol. 1. Theory and research.* Orlando, Fla:
Academic Press, pp.13-53.

Witelson, S. (1987). Neurobiological aspects of language in
children. *Child Development, 58,* 653-688.

Wolff, P. (1960). The developmental psychologies of Jean Piaget and
psychoanalysis. *Psychological Issues, 2(1).*

Wolff, P., & Cohen, C. (1980). Dual task performance during
bimanual coordination. *Cortex, 16,* 119-133.

Wolff, P., Gunnoe, C., & Cohen, C. (1983). Associated movements as
a measure of developmental age. *Developmental Medicine and Child*

Neurology, 25, 417-429.
Yeudall, L. (1985). A neuropsychological theory of stuttering. *Seminars in Speech and Language, 6,* 197-223.
Young, A., Lock, A., & Service, V. (1985). Infants' hand preferences for actions and gestures. *Developmental Neuropsychology, 1,* 17-27.
Young, G. (1977a). Manual specialization in infancy: Implications for lateralization of brain functions. In: S. Segalowitz & F. Gruber (Eds.), *Language development and neurological theory.* New York: Academic Press, pp.289-311.
Young, G. (1977b). Use of negation to justify correct judgments of conservation by boys. *Perceptual and Motor Skills, 44,* 287-292.
Young, G., Corter, C., Segalowitz, S., & Trehub, S. (1983a). Manual specialization and the developing brain: An overview. In: G. Young, S. Segalowitz, C. Corter & S. Trehub (Eds.), *Manual specialization and the developing brain.* New York: Academic Press, pp.3-12.
Young, G., Bowman, J., Methot, C., Finlayson, M., Quintal J., & Boissonneault, P. (1983b). Hemispheric specialization development: What (inhibition) and how (parents). In: G. Young, S. Segalowitz, C. Corter & S. Trehub (Eds.), *Manual specialization and the developing brain.* New York: Academic Press, pp.119-140.
Young, G., Segalowitz, S., Misek, P., Alp, I., & Boulet, R. (1983c). Is early reaching left-handed ? Review of manual specialization research. In: G. Young, S. Segalowitz, C. Corter & S. Trehub (Eds.), *Manual specialization and the developing brain.* New York: Academic Press, pp.13-32.
Young, G., Segalowitz, S., Corter, C., and Trehub, S. (1983d). *Manual specialization and the developing brain.* New York: Academic Press.
Yu-Yan, M., Cun-Ren, F., & Over, R. (1983). Lateral symmetry in duration of grasp by infants. *Australian Journal of Psychology, 35,* 81-84.

DEVELOPMENTAL PSYCHOLOGY
Cognitive, Perceptuo-Motor, and Neuropsychological Perspectives
C-A. Hauert (Editor)
© Elsevier Science Publishers B.V. (North-Holland), 1990

DEVELOPMENT IN INFANCY:
A QUARTER CENTURY OF EMPIRICAL AND THEORETICAL PROGRESS

George BUTTERWORTH
Department of Psychology
University of Stirling
Stirling, Scotland

This chapter attempts a synthesis and offers a commentary on the contributions to part II, on infant development. The papers are reviewed with respect to four issues:

i) The problem of the origins of development. This section contrasts the traditional, parsimonious, Piagetian account which argues that logico-mathematical development originates in sensori-motor schemes with alternative hypotheses. The chapters by Langer and McKenzie are reviewed with respect to the possibility that cognitive development may originate in processes of sensory perception.
ii) The relationship between perception and actions in development. The main issue here concerns the contrast between relatively mechanistic approaches to the origines and control of action (reflexes) and contemporary dynamic approaches. The review by Jouen and Lepecq is considered with reference to recent research on proprioception. The dynamic approach cuts across the traditional dichotomy between sensori and motor processes by emphasising the equipotentially of different kinds of information for motor control.
iii) Engines of development. A third problem concerns the processes which drive development along. Here the question concerns the necessary foundation for cognitive development. Does action drive cognition or does cognitive development occur in a relatively modularised form, independent of physical activity, and perhaps based on perceptual processing and memory formation ?
iv) Biological processes. This section considers the chapter by Young in which it is attempted to relate Piagetian theory to brain structure and function. Contemporary research on adult brain function has shifted from the traditional assumption that the mid-brain is developmentally "primitive" while the cortex is advanced, toward an emphasis on the nature of their collaboration. Midbrain structures are involved in perception and cognition in sophisticated ways. By the same token, hemispheric functioning may best be understood in terms of their collaboration, rather than as the dominance of one cerebral hemisphere by the other.

The main conclusion is that 25 years of research on infant
development have led to a radical reconsideration of
infant competence with the realisation of how wonderfully
adapted to the ecology the baby actually is.

1. INTRODUCTION

The study of development in infancy is undoubtedly one of the areas
of psychology where fundamental advances have been made during the
past quarter century. Although there have been periods of active
investigation of babies in the late nineteenth and early twentieth
century, there has never before been such a prolonged and intensive
preoccupation with basic human, psychological processes as revealed
by the contemporary study of babies. The specific aspects of infancy covered in this book are restricted to aspects of sensori-motor
and cognitive development but it is worth mentioning that current
concerns extend well beyond these boundaries. A comprehensive overview may be found in Volume II of the Handbook of Child Psychology
(Haith and Campos, 1983) which covers developmental psychobiology,
perception, cognition and applications to developmental risk factors. An equally weighty Handbook of Infant Development, now in
its second edition, covers twenty seven areas of infant development,
ranging from language, perception and cognition to temperament and
clinical applications (Osofsky, 1987). In addition, four volumes of
the series "Advances in Infancy Research" (Lipsitt and Rovee-
Collier, 1986) have now been published, as well as a number of spe-
cialised journals (Infant Behaviour and Development; Early Human
Development) each attesting to a lively and very broad range of investigation. The study of infant development as an activity within
psychology has perhaps reached the point where it defies synthesis,
with as many competing views as characterise the discipline as a
whole. The material under consideration here is restricted to four
areas of study, and this may render an overview somewhat artificial.
Yet, the focus on sensori-motor and cognitive development brings
certain issues to the fore. Each contribution raises basic questions of the origins of behaviour; questions of the relationship
between inborn, biological processes and developmental change; and
questions concerning the relationship between the various possible
"engines" driving development. These topics will offer a framework
for an attempt at synthesis of the various chapters presented in
part II.

Piaget's trilogy on infant cognitive development (Piaget, 1951,
1953, 1954) provided the most coherent overall framework for students of infancy in the past quarter century. Thus, one approach
toward a synthesis would be to consider his theory in the light of
new evidence. Not all aspects of the theory need be rejected, even
if major changes are required. At the root of the Piagetian synthesis are two fundamental assumptions about the origins of cognitive processes; first that there is continuity between biology and
the acquisition of knowledge and secondly that knowledge is rooted
in action. As empirical evidence has accumulated, these assumptions
have both been elaborated and modified.

2. ON THE ORIGINS OF DEVELOPMENT

Jonas Langer has carried out the most extensive programme of empirical research on the development of logic in action since Piaget's
own pioneering observations (Langer, 1980, 1986). Langer distinguishes between acting and knowing, and suggests that to know is to act
but that action without knowledge is mere movement. Knowledge originates from but does not consist in the biopsychological functioning of the newborn. The sensori-motor schemes of sucking, looking,
grasping, etc. with which we are innately endowed lie at the root of
knowledge. So far, this agrees with Piaget's own position on the
origins of development. However, Langer raises other possibilities
for the development of cognitive processes. First, he outlines the
traditional Piagetian position on physical cognition, that knowledge
of space, time, causes and objects is obtained in infancy as "things
of action". Logico-mathematical knowledge depends on the development of representation and, in an extreme view, on the acquisition
of language. A second possibility, which he attributes to the
Gestalt psychologists, is that physical and logico-mathematical
knowledge has its origins in perception and this would imply innate
bio-psychological perceptual mechanisms. These he contrasts as the
"symbolist" and "perceptual" derivationist hypotheses. A third possibility, based on Langer's own extensive data, is that logico-
mathematical cognition is an original development, not derivative of
representation, with its own sensori-motor ontogenesis. Langer's
position seems similar to contemporary "modularity" theories (Fodor,
1983) in that action during infancy is thought to generate independent "modules" on physical and logico-mathematical cognition. Both
types of knowledge are evident in action long before language or
representation (in Piaget's useage) have been acquired and thus,
some logico-mathematical knowledge and its underlying logic, however
elementary, must be available in infancy.

There can be little disagreement with Langer that the emerging logic
of action evident in the elementary activities of the baby cannot be
derivative of language; this conclusion seems inescapable given both
the human and primate evidence. However, a great deal more uncertainty attaches to the question of the original relation between
perception and cognition and to the constructive role of action in
development. This uncertainty may be expressed in two ways. First
while the constructivist perspective may be correct to associate
knowledge with the ability intentionally to execute a particular sequence of actions it may nevertheless be mistaken to reduce actions
prior to the "gnostic" kind to "mere movement". A second, and related issue concerns the nature of the structures inherent in perception and their contribution to development.

In her chapter Beryl McKenzie reviews a great deal of evidence relevant to these issues which shows that many aspects of perceptual
functioning such as perceptual constancy, traditionally considered
to be constructed in development, may be a part of our innate endowment. Both of the issues above i.e., the status of action prior
to knowledge and the status of perception in the acquisition of
knowledge, have been addressed most clearly in the work of Eleanor
Gibson and her students. This dynamic approach to perception is
characteristic of much of the most recent work on perception and
action in infancy (see Butterworth, 1981, 1986). This approach to

infant perception may be distinguished from earlier positions, such
as the Gestalt school, in the emphasis placed on the dynamic,
spatio-temporal properties of perception. Whereas Gestalt approaches tended to stress the holistic properties of static visual
forms, contemporary Gibsonian theory emphasises the information
available to perceptual systems inherent in the dynamic relation
between the infant and a structured environment. The dynamic approach also stresses the inter-relationships between the senses as
sources of information about the real world. Perceptual systems
function (at least in their original state) without benefit of fore-
knowledge. However, the biological and evolutionary assumption is
that perceptual systems are pre-adapted for certain kinds of information and from this, knowledge about specific objects may flow.
Knowledge may be acquired not only as a consequence of action but
also by attending to the information generally available in the environment (see also Gibson, 1966, and Reed and Jones, 1982). The
evidence for infant perceptual competence forms a great part of the
literature of the last quarter century (Gibson and Spelke, 1983, and
Harris, 1983). Spelke (1983) goes so far as to argue that general
concepts of objects such as substantiality, boundedness in space,
permanence, causality are innate (but note, this does not mean that
specific knowledge about particular objects is inborn, this still
requires extensive experience and laying down of memory in development). The important point for a reconsideration of Piaget's theory
is that the status of inherent structure within perception is greatly enhanced in its role in the acquisition of knowledge. Such a reconceptualisation does not imply that there are innate ideas; ideas
about particular objects or classes of objects will require extensive experience of the world and developmental processes that will
enable reflection upon stored experience.

3. PERCEPTION AND ACTION

Similar points can be made about the status of action in development. Contemporary theories of action acknowledge much more structure than the traditional Piagetian viewpoint. The inherent richness of action is one of the main implications of the review by
Jouen and Lepecq on early postural and locomotor development. From
the perspective of a dynamic approach to perception and action it is
a misconception to consider the initial state of motor organisation
as "primitive" or merely mechanically "reflexive". Contemporary
approaches to early motor organisation consider the repertoire of
movements available to the young infant as pre-programmed motor
synergies, particular coalitions of action, some with pre-adaptive
or fully adaptive functions. Recent study of pre-natal activity
patterns using real time ultra-sonic scanning techniques has revealed that the fetus of 12 weeks has as many as fifteen distingui-
shable movement patterns. These include hand-face coordination,
"stepping" movements, breathing movements, hiccups and other rhythmic behaviours (de Vries, Visser and Prechtl, 1984). Study of the
so called "stepping reflex" has revealed how very unstereotyped and
"intelligent" are even such basic movement synergies. Thelen (1984)
has shown that such movement patterns involve equifinality, or goal
directed cooperation, among radically different muscle groups, depending whether the infant is supine or held in a vertical posture.
It is as if walking movements are a set goal that can be achieved by

infinitely many temporary coalitions among the constituent muscles. It is simply an inadequate characterisation of such movement patterns to dismiss them as merely reflexive. On the other hand, such coordinated movement patterns should not be taken to mean that babies innately know how to walk, any more than perceptual competence should be taken to imply innate knowledge about particular objects of experience. In both the motor and perceptual case, there is much more a priori function than Piaget had supposed but it still makes sense to distinguish a priori function from specifically structured "a posteriori", knowledge.

The most difficult theoretical problem is to find a way of reconceptualising the relation between motor and sensory processes in contemporary terms to arrive at a new view of the origins of knowledge. The dynamic approach to perception and action offers such a possibility since it tends to cut across many of the traditional dichotomies. For example, Jouen and Lepecq discuss visual proprioception as one source of information for postural stability. Visual proprioception refers to the information available for self movement in the optic flow pattern at the eye. Much recent evidence shows that such "exteroceptive" information complements "interoceptive" information derived from joints, muscle spindles and the vestibular system in maintaining postural stability. Postures acquired early in development, such as head control, rely on visual proprioception as do later postures such as sitting or standing unsupported. The important theoretical point is that the dynamic, information based approach cuts across the dichotomy of sensory and motor processes by emphasising the equipotentiality of different kinds of information for maintaining control. Visual proprioception may be considered a pre-structured feedback loop that is highly informative about postural stability and as such, it may be considered as one of the engines that drive development from functional "a priori" to structural "a posteriori" since it both specifies when a stable posture has been attained and provides specific feedback concerning the mismatch between intended and actual outcomes. Monitoring such discrepancies in maintaining postural control may accumulate as knowledge of the stability of the body with repeated experience.

4. ENGINES OF DEVELOPMENT

The hypothesis that information available to perceptual systems, through repeated encounters, may give rise to knowledge is one approach to the problem of the causes of development. Registration and storage of information in memory, may give rise to qualitatively new forms of "anticipatory", "feed-forward" perception that may accurately be characterised as dependent upon particular knowledge. Such a hypothesis would stress continuity between perceptual and conceptual processes, the engine of development being the accumulation of information through experience. On this view, action would not construct information within experience, rather it would draw attention to different types of information, more or less relevant to the act. Such a theory would be radically different from Piaget's in the status it accords perception and in the characterisation of action. However, it would share the general framework of evolutionary epistemology and the conviction that knowledge arises through experience.

It must be admitted, however, that the evidence is not yet in; this
is merely to suggest that perception may be one of the engines of
cognitive development, at the root of physical and logico-
mathematical reasoning. It remains possible, as Langer suggests,
that development may be modular and sensory perception may simply be
a module within a modularised, relatively independent system of
physical knowledge, logico-mathematical knowledge and the sensory
control of action.

5. BIOLOGICAL PROCESSES: THE DEVELOPMENT OF THE NERVOUS SYSTEM IN
   INFANCY

A theory of cognitive development rooted in a biological, evolutionary, epistemology, such as Piaget's, should be an ideal vehicle for
the task of relating psychological structures to the developing
brain. Indeed, there has been notable progress in this enterprise,
especially in the study of frontal lobe functions and their relation
to perseverative error in infant manual search (see Diamond, 1988,
for a review). Such research proceeds by intensive comparisons
between species and within human ontogeny. It reveals remarkable
commonalities in perseverative responding between men and monkeys,
and in the ability to solve detour problems between humans and other
primates. It confirms the view from neuropsychology that prefrontal areas of the brain are implicated in planning and the spatial control of action (Jeannerod, 1988). This research also
reveals profound differences in the developmental timetable for
these acquisitions between species. Hence, it is extremely difficult to establish the relation between cognitive development and
brain development in an unambiguous way since species differences
may be attributed to differences in rates of maturation or myelini-
sation or simply to the more rapid accumulation of experience in
species with motor precocity.

The chapter by Young offers an extremely comprehensive overview of
the literature on lateralisation and hemispheric specialisation and
there seems little doubt that motor asymmetries, consistent with
right hemisphere dominance, can be observed from birth. Laterality
waxes and wanes and lateralised hand movements, for example, enter
into multiple coalitions with non-lateralised actions, such as voca-
lisation (Ramsay, 1985). It is tempting to interpret such data on
continuity and discontinuity in laterality in a stage theoretic
fashion. There is a danger however, that enthusiasm for hemispheric
lateralisation as the basic cause may give rise to grand theories of
inter-hemispheric inhibition that may prove untenable when all the
evidence is in. A similar enthusiasm for dichotomous explanation
led to the widespread assumption that the neonate is a mid-brain
organism, effectively decorticate.

However, contemporary neuropsychological research suggests extensive
involvement of sub-cortical processes in cognition, face perception
and memory (Weiskrantz, 1980). This reconceptualisation shifted the
focus of discussion toward the nature of the collaboration between
mid-brain and cortical systems in cognitive functioning. By the
same token, the essential question for theories of inter-hemispheric
functioning may concern the nature of their collaboration and the
consequent implications for development (Best, 1985).

The grand reconceptualisation of Piaget's theory espoused in the latter part of Young's chapter seems premature given the uncertainties outlined earlier about the status of constituent cognitive processes and their respective contributions to development. If infant perceptual competence is an important theoretical consideration for theories of cognitive growth, then there are a variety of ways in which perceiving and knowing may interact. There is a great attraction to the biological idea of a repeated, recursive growth cycle which gives rise to a universal sequence of stages. There may even be some truth to the theory. However, neither cognitive development in infancy nor theories of brain functioning and development are sufficiently secure for us to be able unequivocally to relate one to the other. The detailed study of neurogenesis holds great promise for understanding infant perception and cognition and we may look forward to advances from neuro-biology to assist developmental psychologists in this endeavour (Changeux, 1985; Edelman, 1988).

6. CONCLUSION

In conclusion, the task of synthesis is not an easy one, even when only four areas of infant cognitive development are under consideration. There is little doubt that many advances have been made in the study of cognitive development in babies during the previous quarter century. The major changes have arisen through a combination of hard, empirical work and imaginative theorising. Our eyes have been opened to the wonderfully adapted, competent infant and this change in our understanding seems permanent. Perhaps the next quarter century will see a truly post-Piagetian synthesis on cognitive development in babies; the papers here show that we may be on the threshold of such an advance.

REFERENCES

Best, C.T. (1985). *Hemispheric function and collaboration in the child*. New York: Academic Press
Butterworth, G.E. (1981). The origins of auditory-visual perception and visual proprioception in human development. In: H.A. Pick Jr. & Walk (Eds.), *Perception and experience, Vol 2*. New York: Plenum, 37-66.
Butterworth, G.E. (1986). Events and encounters in infant perception. *The New Psychologist 1986, 3-8*. Reprinted in: J. Oates & S. Sheldon (Eds.), *Cognitive development in infancy*, 1987. Hove: Lawrence Erlbaum, 95-104.
Changeux, J.P. (1985). *Neuronal man*. Oxford: Oxford University Press.
De Vries, J.I.P., Visser, G.H.A., and Prechtl, H.F.R. (1984). Fetal motility in the first half of pregnancy. In: H.F.R. Prechtl (Ed.), *Continuity of neural functions from prenatal to postnatal life*. Spastics International Medical Publications, 46-64.
Diamond, A. (1988). Differences between adult and infant cognition; is the crucial variable presence or absence of language ? In: L. Weiskrantz (Ed.), *Thought without language*. Oxford: Oxford University, 337-380.
Edelman, G. (1988). *Topobiology: An introduction to molecular embryology*. New York: Basic Books.

Fodor, J. (1983). *The modularity of mind.* Cambridge: Bradford Books.

Gibson, E.J., & Spelke, E. (1983). The development of perception. In: J. Flavell & E. Markman (Eds), *Cognitive development: Vol III, Handbook of Child Psychology.* New York: Wiley.

Gibson, J.J. (1966). *The senses considered as perceptual systems.* London: George Allan and Unwin.

Haith, M.M., & Campos, J.J. (1983). *Infancy and developmental psychobiology. Volume II. Handbook of child psychology.* New York: Wiley.

Harris, P.L. (1983). Infant cognition. In: M.M. Haith and J.J. Campos (Eds.), *Infancy and Developmental Psychobiology. Volume II. Handbook of Child Psychology.* New York: Wiley, 435-572.

Jeannerod, M. (1988). *The neural and behavioural organisation of goal directed movements.* Oxford: Clarendon Press.

Langer, J. (1980). *The origins of logic: Six to twelve months.* New York: Academic Press.

Langer, J. (1986). *The origins of logic: One to two years.* New York: Academic Press.

Lipsitt, L., & Rovee-Collier, C. (1986). *Advances in infancy research, Vol. 4.* New Jersey: Ablex.

Osofsky, J.D. (1987). *Handbook of infant development.* 2nd edition. New York: Wiley.

Piaget, J. (1951). *Play dreams and imitation in childhood.* New York: Norton.

Piaget, J. (1953). *The origins of intelligence in the child.* New York: International Universities Press.

Piaget, J. (1954). *The construction of reality in the child.* New York: Basic Books.

Ramsay, D. (1985). Fluctuation in unimanual hand preference in infants following the onset of duplicated syllable babbling. *Developmental Psychology, 21,* 318-324.

Reed, E., & Jones, R. (1982). *Reasons for realism: Selected essays of J.J. Gibson.* New Jersey: Lawrence Erlbaum.

Spelke, E. S. (1983). Cognition in infancy. Occasional paper N° 23, Center for Cognitive Science: Massachussets Institute of Technology.

Thelen, E. (1984). Learning to walk: Ecological demands and phylogenetic constraints. In: L.P. Lipsitt & C. Rovee-Collier (Eds.), *Advances in infancy research, Vol III,* 213-257.

Weiskrantz, L. (1980). Varieties of residual experience. *Quarterly Journal of Experimental Psychology, 32(3),* 365-386.

PART III

CHILDHOOD AND ADOLESCENCE

RECENT APPROACHES

DEVELOPMENTAL PSYCHOLOGY
Cognitive, Perceptuo-Motor, and Neuropsychological Perspectives
C-A. Hauert (Editor)
© Elsevier Science Publishers B.V. (North-Holland), 1990

CHILD COGNITIVE DEVELOPMENT: THE ROLE OF CENTRAL
CONCEPTUAL STRUCTURES IN THE DEVELOPMENT OF SCIENTIFIC
AND SOCIAL THOUGHT

Robbie CASE and Sharon GRIFFIN

Centre for Applied Cognitive Science
Ontario Institute for Studies in Education
Toronto, Ontario, Canada

*Children's cognitive development is described in this
chapter from the perspective of an evolving neo-Piagetian
theory of intellectual development. A series of studies
designed to test the theory in a variety of content domains, with a variety of tasks, is reported. The findings
of eleven studies provide support for the developmental
progression proposed in the theory and also permit the
authors to characterize this progression more precisely.
It is suggested that the findings can best be explained by
postulating the existence of two central conceptual structures, namely: A structure for representing quantitative
problems which mediates age-level performance on a variety
of scientific tasks, and a structure for representing
social problems which mediates age-level performance on a
variety of social tasks. Modifications to the theory which
are entailed by these postulates are discussed in the final
section. Similarities and differences between the proposed
central conceptual structures and Piaget's "structures
d'ensemble" are also considered.*

1. INTRODUCTION

In the late 1970's and early 1980's, a number of "neo-Piagetian"
theories of cognitive development were advanced. Each of these, in
its own way, attempted to retain the strengths of classic Piagetian
theory while overcoming some of its weaknesses (see Case, 1978;
Fischer, 1980; Halford, 1982; Mounoud, 1986; Pascual-Leone and
Goodman, 1979). One such theory was proposed by the senior author
(Case, 1985). In keeping with the Piagetian tradition, this theory
suggested that there are four major stages of development from birth
to adulthood; and that stage transition entails the coordination and
hierarchic integration of two control structures which are assembled, independently, during the previous stage. The theory also
suggested that, within each stage, there are three substages; and
that substage transition is regulated by an age-related growth of
working memory, from one to four units. Finally, the theory suggested that working memory growth itself is controlled by changes in
operational efficiency, which take place in response to practice as

Figure 1:   A neo-structural model of intellectual development.
            [Note: The general form of notation in this figure is
            taken from Fischer (1980). The specific notation for
            substage 3 is taken from Pascual-Leone (1969).]

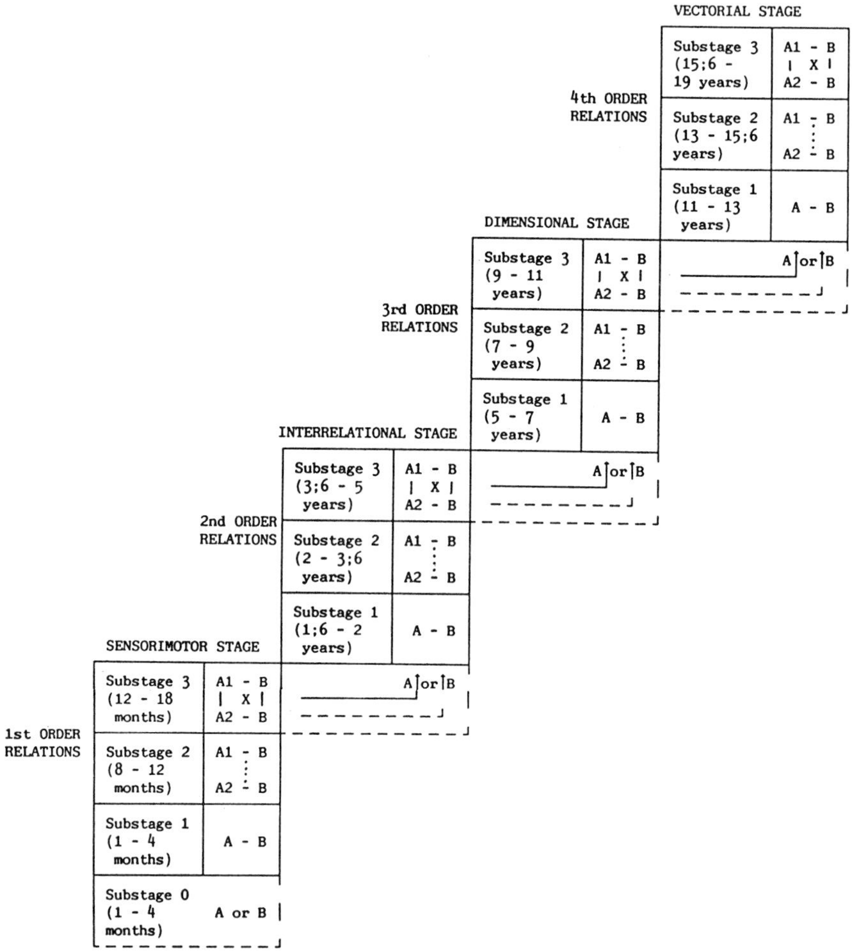

VECTORIAL STAGE

4th ORDER RELATIONS	Substage 3 (15;6 - 19 years)	A1 - B | X | A2 - B
	Substage 2 (13 - 15;6 years)	A1 - B : A2 - B

DIMENSIONAL STAGE

	Substage 1 (11 - 13 years)	A - B
3rd ORDER RELATIONS	Substage 3 (9 - 11 years)	A1 - B | X | A2 - B A⌉or⌈B
	Substage 2 (7 - 9 years)	A1 - B : A2 - B

INTERRELATIONAL STAGE

	Substage 1 (5 - 7 years)	A - B
2nd ORDER RELATIONS	Substage 3 (3;6 - 5 years)	A1 - B | X | A2 - B A⌉or⌈B
	Substage 2 (2 - 3;6 years)	A1 - B : A2 - B

SENSORIMOTOR STAGE

	Substage 1 (1;6 - 2 years)	A - B
1st ORDER RELATIONS	Substage 3 (12 - 18 months)	A1 - B | X | A2 - B A⌉or⌈B
	Substage 2 (8 - 12 months)	A1 - B : A2 - B
	Substage 1 (1 - 4 months)	A - B
	Substage 0 (1 - 4 months)	A or B

well as maturation.

The central postulates of this theory are displayed in graphic form in Figure 1. As the figure indicates, the control structures constructed in the final substage of each major stage serve as the building blocks for the next developmental stage. When two of these building blocks are coordinated, a new unit of thought is produced which is qualitatively distinct from those which preceded it. This unit, in turn, is then coordinated with other similar units as children progress through this stage, until a complex structure has been assembled. In subsequent major stages, this entire assembly process is repeated, in a recursive fashion.

A concrete example will help to illustrate the nature of this process. Consider, therefore, the following changes that take place within the context of Western industrial culture between 4 and 10 years of age. By the age of 4, if they are allowed to play with a balance beam, most children soon realize that the side with the big stack of weights goes down, while the side with the little stack of weights goes up (Liu, 1981; Marini, 1984). The same children can also count small sets of objects, and realize that the set with the bigger number contains more objects, while the set with the smaller number contains fewer (Case and Sandieson, 1986). While they can execute either of these operations in isolation, they are unable to execute them in a coordinated fashion in order to solve beam problems which require that counting be used as a means to weight estimation (Marini, 1984).

Six-year-olds, in contrast, are able to coordinate their control structure for counting with their weight estimation structure, and solve beam problems in which the number of weights on each side differs slightly, and counting is thus required to estimate the size (and weight) of each array (Siegler, 1976). As a consequence, their performance takes on a qualitatively different character, and they enter the "dimensional" stage.

Although they are quite adept at making isolated dimensional evaluations, 6-year-olds cannot solve balance beam problems of a more complex nature. For example, when the number of weights on each side is kept constant and the distance of these weights from the fulcrum is varied, the majority of 6-year-olds fail. Eight-year-olds, however, are able to decenter from the weight dimension and shift their focus to the distance dimension in order to solve problems of this sort (Siegler, 1976).

Finally, 10-year-olds are able to solve certain problems in which the number of weights *and* the distance from the fulcrum both vary, and some sort of compensation between these variables is required (Inhelder and Piaget, 1958; Marini, 1984).

In the context of the theory which is illustrated in the figure, these findings are interpreted by suggesting that 4-year-olds are able to assemble and employ, at any one time, only one of the problem-solving structures which are used, in a coordinated fashion, at the 6-year-old level. With an increase in working memory capacity, 6-year-olds are able to coordinate two such structures and construct a superordinate structure which is qualitatively distinct

from its predecessors, and which permits them to quantify elements
along a dimension. With the construction of this new structure,
they make the transition to the first substage of the dimensional
stage. Then, with an additional increase in working memory, 8-year-
olds make the transition to substage 2 and are able to employ this
quantification procedure twice, in a loosely coordinated fashion.
Finally, at the 10-year-old level (i.e., substage 3), with four
units of working memory, children are able to employ more complex
quantification procedures and effect an integration of two quantitative variables. In keeping with this interpretation, the substages are labelled pre-dimensional, unidimensional, bidimensional,
and elaborated bidimensional thought.

In the time which has elapsed since the theory that is illustrated
in Figure 1 was first proposed, a number of studies have been conducted to apply it to the area of instruction (e.g., Case, Sandieson
and Dennis, 1987), as well as to cognitive development in several
distinct domains (e.g., Case, Marini, McKeough, Dennis and Goldberg,
1986). Most of these studies have focussed on learning and development in middle childhood and have assessed mental functioning across
the age range of 4 to 10 years. Our efforts to interpret these studies have produced a gradual and subtle shift in the way we look at
children's cognitive development. In the present chapter, we describe the data which provoked this shift, and the conceptions which
have evolved as a result.

The chapter is organized in three sections. In the first section,
we describe studies which assessed some aspect of logical-
mathematical cognition, using tasks which varied widely in surface
content and in procedural demands. In the second section, we describe studies which assessed some aspect of social cognition, using
tasks which once again spanned a variety of surface content and procedural demands. Finally, in the third section, we compare and contrast our current theoretical conceptions with our previous ones, as
well as with the classic Piagetian theory of cognitive development.

2. LOGICO-MATHEMATICAL COGNITION

Study 1

In the first study, the question that was asked was, "Is the developmental progression on the balance beam specific to that task, or
is it more general and present in children's performance across a
diversity of tasks ?" To answer this question, Marini (1984; in
press) assessed children's performance on four tasks which were
similar in task structure but which differed widely in surface
content. Two of these tasks had content which is generally classified as logical-mathematical. The first of these was the balance
beam task. The second was Siegler's (1978) version of Piaget's
projection of shadows task, which required children to estimate
which of two shadows would be larger, when the size of two bars
and/or the distance of the bars from the screen was varied. The
remaining two tasks contained a mathematical requirement but had
content which is generally classified as social. The first of these
required children to determine which of two children would be
happier, when the number of marbles they received and/or the number

of marbles they hoped for was varied. The final task required
children to determine which of two children should get the bigger
reward, when the number of products they produced and/or the number
of days they worked was varied.

Each task contained problems at four postulated levels. At level 0
(i.e., substage 0), the problems presented global, perceptually-
salient variations along one task variable, while the second variable was kept constant. At level 1 (i.e., substage 1), the problems
presented finer variations along the first task variable, so that
counting was required to determine the relative size of each display. At level 2 (i.e., substage 2), small variations along the
second variable were introduced, and the first was kept constant.

Figure 2:   *Mean scores of four age groups on four different*
              dimensional tasks. (From Marini, 1984).

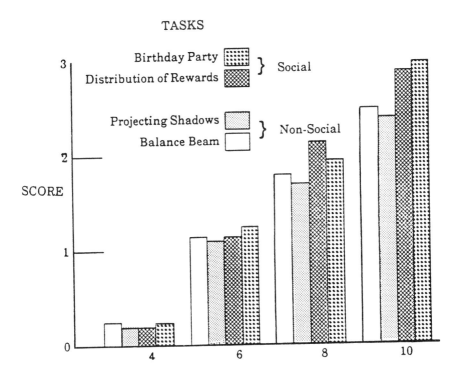

Children were thus required to shift their focus from the first variable to the second, and to make two quantitative comparisons. Finally, at level 3 (i.e., substage 3), variations along both variables were present in each problem. Children were then required to make two quantitative comparisons *and* effect some sort of compensation between the resulting products.

Marini assigned scores of 0, 1, 2, and 3 to successful performance at each of these levels, and administered the four tasks to 20 children at each of four ages: 4, 6, 8, and 10 years. The results (presented in Figure 2) indicate a near perfect linear progression on each task, with no significant deviations from the predicted form. The performance of each age group was highly consistent across tasks and, when the cross-task performance of individual children was analyzed, it was found that a majority of children performed at the predicted level on the majority of tasks. An analysis of variance indicated a strong and highly significant age effect and no significant task effects. Marini's findings thus presented strong evidence that the developmental progression on the balance beam task is present in children's performance on other tasks as well, even those with widely varying surface content.

Since such findings are not typical of those in the developmental literature, at first glance they might appear to constitute a strong confirmation of the theory by which they were predicted. There is, however, a straightforward counter-interpretation of the data. This argument holds that the reason no decalage was found across tasks was that all variables which have been found to produce decalage in the literature were held constant across the four tasks. These include the following:

1. Background experience in the task in question. This had clearly been provided by the culture for the two social tasks and was ensured, for the two physical tasks, by a warm-up play period and practice trials.

2. Stimulus arrays. In each case two clear "sides" were present in the array, each of which contained two sets of countable objects.

3. Type of operation. The general type of operation required by the tasks was, in each case, the same (i.e., counting).

4. Operational difficulty. The difficulty of executing the counting operation was also controlled, by using the same number of objects for each variable and for each trial, across the four tasks.

5. Question format. In each case the question format was very similar, namely: "Will this side have the larger X (tilt, shadow, degree of happiness, number of candies) or will this side, or will they be the same ?"

6. Response format. In each case the response format was also identical. Children simply had to pick one of the three alternatives posed by the question, and then provide a simple quantitative justification.

7. Instruction. In no case had children been provided with any
direct instruction in the underlying rationale for dealing
with any of the problems.

Given that virtually every variable that has been postulated as
being of developmental relevance by those who have challenged the
validity of stage theory was held constant across the four tasks,
while general experience was allowed to vary so widely across the
four age groups, it could be argued that what is remarkable is not
that there was a strong age effect but no task effect. What is
remarkable is that there was any variability from task to task at
all !

The above argument clearly has some merit, and must somehow be contended with. In the next set of studies, therefore, we investigated
a set of tasks which children encounter more frequently and directly
in their everyday life, and where the above set of factors vary
naturally, in a less systematic fashion.

Study 2

In the second study, Capodilupo (1985; in press) used a task in
which the stimulus content and the sort of response required differed considerably from the tasks used by Marini. She also selected
children who had no prior knowledge of the stimuli or the responses,
and provided them with direct training in each. The task in question was a musical sight-reading task.

At the first level (i.e., pre-dimensional thought), Capodilupo's
tasks required a global discrimination between two notes on the
musical staff (C and F) and the ability to map these on to two key
positions on the piano. Both notes and keys were made perceptually
salient, and the overall task was embedded in a familiar script in
order to help children master it. At the next level (i.e., unidimensional thought), children had to learn to sight read sequences
of notes on a staff, and to map the quantitative intervals on the
staff on to corresponding quantitative intervals on the keyboard.
The tasks constructed for this level presented children with various
combinations of middle C, D, E, and F, and the middle two notes were
conventionally notated, with no conspicuous markers. Once again,
the task was presented within the context of a familiar script,
which was maintained at the next two levels as well.

At the next level (i.e., bidimensional thought), Capodilupo predicted that an ability to deal with two quantitative dimensions would
enable 8-year-old children to learn to sight read notes which were
raised one semitone, with a sharp notation: That is, to count the
number of places on the staff, map this onto the appropriate quantitative interval on the keyboard, and then progress a further unit
"up" in the appropriate direction. For the final level (i.e., elaborated bidimensional thought) it was predicted that an ability to
simultaneously integrate two dimensional variables would permit 10-
year-olds to learn to sight read closed intervals (i.e., two notes
which must be played simultaneously) in which one or both notes
were sharpened. In the tasks constructed for each of these upper
levels, the number of sharps was gradually increased from one to
six. Each level consisted of several training tasks constructed to

facilitate mastery, followed by eight test tasks.

This graded sequence of tasks was administered, individually, to 40 children who had no previous musical sight-reading experience. The entire sample was comprised of 10 children at each of the ages of 4, 6, 8, and 10 years. Each child was led through a training program until he or she failed more than 50% of the test items at any level, at which point training was discontinued. With a 75% pass rate used as a criterion for success, children were assigned a score of 0, 1, 2, or 3 according to the level which represented their highest level of successful performance. When the mean scores achieved by four age groups were computed (see Figure 3), they were found to form a near perfect linear progression, with each age group achieving success at the level predicted by the theory. Moreover, when the success rate of individual children was computed, it was found that a majority of children in each age group passed tasks at the predicted level, and failed to achieve success at a level beyond the one predicted by the theory.

Figure 3:   Mean scores of four age groups on a musical sight-reading task. (From Capodilupo, 1985).

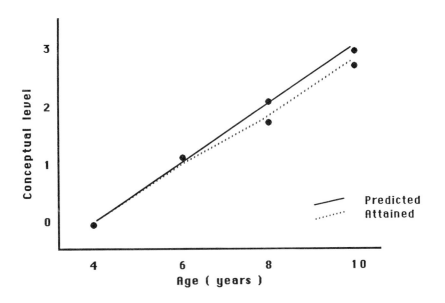

These findings not only extend the range of tasks on which the postulated dimensional progression has been found, but they also extend the range of circumstances in which this progression has been demonstrated. Specifically, they extend the range to include tasks where the stimulus and response formats are quite different from those used in Marini's study, and where the same experience (in the format of explicit training) is provided to each age group. In the next two studies, the range of content for which dimensional thought was investigated was extended further. In addition, such factors as experience, operational difficulty, and question format were allowed to vary more widely, in a naturalistic fashion.

Studies 3 and 4

The everyday problems encountered in learning to "tell the time" and "handle money" constituted the two sets of tasks which were investigated in these two studies. For each skill domain, the range of problems children might encounter in their everyday lives was considered. These were then used to construct a set of developmental predictions for age level performance at the ages of 4, 6, 8 and 10 years (Case, Sandieson and Dennis, 1987; Griffin, Case and Sandieson, in press). In order to accommodate the variety of problems children could be expected to encounter in each domain, several predictions were advanced for each age level. The most salient of these are described below.

In the domain of time-telling, it was reasoned that 4-year-olds would be able to solve problems that require them to make global distinctions within a time dimension, provided that the features to be distinguished are perceptually salient. Thus, for example, they should be able to recognize that certain events (e.g., driving to the cottage) take a long time and other events (e.g., blinking an eye) take a short time. They should also recognize that certain, long events take "hours" and other, short events take "minutes". Finally, they should be able to recognize global differences in clock patterns and, when the numbers are small, identify changes in certain "hour" patterns on the clock (i.e., 1 o'clock becomes 3 o'clock when the hour hand is moved from 1 to 3).

At the 6-year-old level, it was predicted that children would be able to coordinate their counting procedure with their procedure for making global time distinctions, in order to seriate elements along a time dimension. Thus, they should now be able to compare two or three numerical values along one time dimension and recognize, for example, that 2 o'clock comes before 3 o'clock and that 7 o'clock is three hours later than 4 o'clock. They should also be able to identify most of the hour times on a clock and compare hour values, provided that the minute hand is straight up and presents no misleading cues.

At the 8-year-old level, it was predicted that children would be able to seriate elements along two time dimensions, would be able to shift their focus from one dimension to another, and would be able to solve time-telling problems that require them to read "hours" *and* "minutes" on a clock. Because a fully integrated use of two dimensional procedures is not postulated in the theory until the final dimensional substage (i.e., 10 years), it was expected that 8-year-olds would only be able to read hour *and* minute values on a clock if no compensation between these values was required. Thus, it was predicted that 8-year-olds would be able to read clock times in which two dimensions (e.g., hours and minutes-by-five) could be "read off" the clock in a straightforward fashion, but not clock

times in which the hour value had to be adjusted, in an on-line
fashion, to accommodate the minute reading. The latter task was
assumed to require a level of operational complexity which is consistent with that postulated for the 10-year-old level.

Using the same line of reasoning, it was predicted that 8-year-olds
would be able to compare time values along two dimensions instead of
one and recognize, for example, that two hours and one minute is a
longer time to wait than is one hour and fifty-six minutes. When
value comparison problems require children to focus on two dimensions *and* effect a compensation between these dimensions (e.g., Is
one hour and thirty minutes longer than 90 minutes ?), it was predicted likewise that the compensation demands of the task could not
be met until the 10-year-old level. Finally, it was predicted that
8-year-olds would be able to read clock times which required computation of two variables, "hours" and "minutes by five" (e.g., 4:15),
while 10-year-olds, in contrast, would be able to read clock times
which required computation of three variables, "hours", "minutes by
five", and "minutes by one" (e.g., 4:18).

In the domain of money-handling, a set of formally equivalent predictions was advanced. It was reasoned that 4-year-olds would be
able to solve problems that require them to make global distinctions
within a monetary dimension, provided that the features to be distinguished are perceptually salient. Thus, for example, they should
be able to recognize that a quarter is worth more than a nickel, because a quarter is bigger; conversely, they should be apt to mis-
takenly identify a nickel as worth more than a dime because, in this
case, a nickel is also bigger. They should also be able to imple-
ment simple, automatic counting routines and use these routines to
compute the quantity of a small (i.e., five or under) array of coins
or bills. Finally, they should be able to determine the sum of two
small arrays (e.g., when one penny is added to an array of two pennies) by simply starting at one and counting the new array.

At the 6-year-old level, it was predicted that children would be
able to coordinate their counting procedure with their procedure for
making global monetary distinctions in order to seriate elements
along a monetary dimension. Thus, they should now recognize that a
dime is worth more than a nickel, because ten is a larger number
than five; that a $1 bill is worth less than either a $5 bill or a
$10 bill; and that *one* $5 bill has a greater monetary value than *two*
$1 bills. An ability to seriate numbers along a dimension should
also enable 6-year-olds to compute quantity without starting at one
and counting the entire set of coins or bills. They should now recognize, in the absence of countable objects, that when one penny is
added to a set of three pennies, the sum is four because four is the
next number in the sequence. Finally, it was predicted that children would now be able to handle numbers greater than five, provided
they are confined to one place value. Within this constraint, they
should be able to add or subtract numbers greater than five, using
what has been termed the "count-on" procedure (Fuson, 1982).

At the 8-year-old level, it was predicted that children would be
able to seriate elements along two monetary dimensions, shift their
focus from one dimension to the other, and solve money problems
which required them to deal with both dollars and cents. Thus, for

Table 1:   Sample of problems included in the time-telling test
            and percentage of children passing at four age levels.

Problem	Percentage Passing 4yr 6yr 8yr 10yr			

Level 0

This clock says 7 o'clock (demonstrate). Now   73   92   100   100
I'm going to change it, now its 5 o'clock.
What time is this, 4:00 ?

Suppose you have to wait for 7 hours. Is that   91   92   100   100
a short time or a long time ?

If you blinked your eyes like this, would that   64   69   100   100
take a short time or a long time ?

Level 1

What time is this, 9:00 ?   18   100   100   100

If I tell you I'll meet you at 6 and I get   45   85   100   100
there at 5 o'clock. Am I early or late ?

If you wait for one minute, and then you wait   9   92   100   100
for two more minutes, how many minutes have
you waited altogether ?

Level 2

What time is this, 2:15 ?   0   0   69   100

Which is longer: 1 hour and 50 minutes or 2   0   15   61   100
hours and 1 minute ?

If I wait for 60 minutes and then I wait another   0   8   77   89
60 minutes, how long have I waited altogether ?

Level 3

What time is this, 11:37 ?   0   0   38   83

My friend walked to school and it took him 90   0   0   8   67
minutes. On the way back it took him an hour
and a half. Can you explain ?

If I walk for 1 hour and 25 minutes and then I   0   0   15   50
walk for 2 hours and 55 minutes, how long have
I walked altogether ?

Table 2:   Sample of problems included in the money-handling test
            and percentage of children passing at four age levels.

| Problem | Percentage Passing |
	4yr 6yr 8yr 10yr

Level 0

I'm going to give you 1, 2 pennies. When I   83 100 100 100
give you 1 more (do so), how many do you have ?

I have 2 piles of money here. (Show 2 pennies   92 100 100 100
and 18 pennies.) Which is worth more ?

Joe wanted to buy a candy. It costs 2 cents. He   58   78 100 100
pays this much (show 3 cents). Is this right ?

Level 1

(Con't. from above) What should I do ? Give him   17   60 100 100
back money or ask for more? How much ?

If I give you 1 cent and then I give you 2   25 100 100 100
cents, how much did I give you altogether ?

Here are 3 bills $5, $1, $10 (show picture).   17   80 100 100
Which one is worth the most ?   Next ?

Level 2

If I give you 25 cents and then give you 6   0   0   87 100
more cents, how much have I given you ?

Here are two amounts of money. Which is worth   0   33   87 100
more ? (a) $1, 20 pennies (b) $5, 1 penny.

You want to buy a toy. It costs 19 cents. You   0   0   60   93
pay 25 cents. How much should you get back ?

Level 3

How much money is this altogether ? (Show)   0   0   40   87
$1, $2, $5, 25 cents, 10 cents, 2 cents.

You want to buy a tape recorder. It costs $100.   0   0   26   80
You have $19. How much more money do you need ?

Which of these is worth the most ? Why ? (Show)   0   0   53   80
(a) 7 $1 bills, 2 quarters; (b) $5, $2, 1
quarter, 3 dimes; (c) 5 $1 bills, 3 quarters.

example, they should be able to recognize that $5 and 1 penny is worth more than $1 and 20 pennies because, although there are more pennies than dollars, dollars have a larger monetary value. It was predicted, as well, that an ability to handle two dimensions would enable children to deal with two place values and consequently, with numbers up to 99. Addition and subtraction with double digit numbers was therefore deemed possible at this age level, provided that the individual numbers were sufficiently small to permit children to "count on" without having to make any two-column computations.

At the 10-year-old level, it was predicted that children would be able to seriate or quantify elements along two monetary dimensions *and* coordinate the products. Thus, for example, they should be able to compute the total of several sets of dollars and cents, by first quantifying the dollar values, then quantifying the cents values, and finally integrating the products appropriately. They should also be able to solve problems in which dollars and cents are expressed in an integrated fashion (i.e., $9.34) and deal with three place values.

To test these predictions, an assortment of 38 time-telling problems and 25 money-handling problems was assembled. These problems were then assigned to one of four developmental levels, on the basis of the theoretical analyses described above. An illustrative sample of the problems included in each task battery, at each postulated level, is provided in Tables 1 and 2. Note that, in contrast to the first study reported above (Marini, 1984), task factors varied widely in these test batteries, both across and within task levels.

These task batteries were administered, individually, in two separate studies, to populations of children drawn from a middle class district of a large metropolitan city. The time-telling sample included 11 four-year-olds, 13 six-year-olds, 13 eight-year-olds, and 18 ten-year-olds. The money-handling sample included 12 four-year-olds, and 15 children at each of the ages of 6, 8, and 10 years. Performance on each test was scored by assigning a score of 0 for each item passed at the pre-dimensional level (i.e., conceptual level 0), a score of -1 for each item failed at this level, and a score of 1 for each item passed at the remaining three levels. Developmental level scores were derived by computing the child's mean score for each level and by summing across levels.

When the percentage of children passing each task at each of four hypothesized developmental levels was computed, a good deal more cross-task variability was apparent on both test batteries than was found in the first study reported above. However, as illustrated in Tables 1 and 2, it was also the case that a majority of children passed a majority of tasks at the predicted level. On both the money-handling and the time-telling tests, the mean developmental level scores achieved by the four age groups (see Table 3) showed a pattern that was strikingly similar to the one found by Marini, and which conformed closely to theoretical expectations. On each test, a Guttman scale analysis revealed the presence of a strong developmental progression. With the criterion for passing a level set at 60%, the coefficient of reproducibility was 1.00 on both tests, and the coefficient of scalability was .98 on the time-telling test and 1.00 on the money-handling test.

Table 3:   Mean scores of four age groups on the time-telling and
           money handling tests. (Predicted scores in brackets).

Age	Time-telling	Money-handling
10 yrs.	2.7 (3.0)	2.9 (3.0)
8 yrs.	2.0 (2.0)	1.8 (2.0)
6 yrs.	0.9 (1.0)	0.7 (1.0)
4 yrs.	0.0 (0.0)	-0.1 (0.0)

The strong developmental progressions present in these findings once
again provide support for the theory's age level prediction. Moreover, it is important to remember that these progressions were found
in spite of wide fluctuations in task factors which exerted some
influence on the percentage of children passing tasks at each developmental level.

Table 4 presents the mean scores achieved by each age group on several sets of tasks, which preserved the postulated structure across
three or four levels, and which differed in task demands (e.g., in
type of operation required). Although cross-set variability is present in these findings, at each age level this variability is contained to a modest range and is never greater than that predicted by
the theory (i.e., 4/10th of a point). When the size of the effects
was computed, with omega squared used to determine source of variation, age level was found to account for a major proportion of the
variance in each study (e.g., 87% in the money-handling study) and
set for a very minor proportion of the variance (e.g., 11% in the
money-handling study)(Griffin, Case and Sandieson, in press). Each
set was also found to form a near-perfect Guttman scale, with reproducibility coefficients ranging from .99 to 1.00 and scalability
coefficients ranging from .97 to 1.00. In a final analysis of this
data, it was found that the performance of individual children was
also reasonably consistent across sets.

Given the above findings, it seems clear that the pattern which was
obtained in Marini's study was not purely an artifact, which resulted from the fact that so many variables of developmental relevance
had been controlled. How, then, can this developmental trend best
be characterized and explained ? One way to characterize the trend
was offered in the introductory paragraphs. In this conception,
logical-mathematical development is construed as a progressive, age-
related increase in the complexity of the control structures children are able to assemble to solve logical-mathematical problems.
Structural complexity, in turn, is seen as being regulated by an
age-related working memory constraint, which can exert its effect on
any of three components of a control structure, namely: (a) The
initial representation of the problem, (b) the set of goals which
are set up to solve the problem, or (c) the procedures which these
goals imply.

Table 4:   Mean scores of four age groups on six time-telling and
money-handling task sets. (Predicted scores in brackets).

Age	Time-telling Sets			Money-handling Sets		
	Set 1 *(Add-on)	Set 2 (Compare Values)	Set 3 (Read Clock)	Set 1 *(Add-on)	Set 2 (Compare Values)	Set 3 (Make Change)
10 yrs.(3.0)	2.4	2.6	2.8	2.9	2.8	2.7
8 yrs.(2.0)	1.9	1.6	2.0	2.3	2.4	1.9
6 yrs.(1.0)	1.0	0.9	1.0	1.0	1.1	0.7
4 yrs.(0.0)	0.1	0.2	-0.2	0.1	0.1	0.1

*Type of operation required.

After examining sets of time-telling and money-handling tasks in
which one or another of these components was allowed to vary independently of the others, Case and Sandieson (1987) suggested that
the requirement for setting up an initial representation was the one
that posed the greatest developmental difficulty. Since a wide variety of tasks typically passed at a given age-level had similar
representational requirements --and varied more widely in procedural
requirements-- it appeared that what all these tasks had in common
was the requirement for setting up a particular *form of representation*. Accordingly, it was suggested that the developmental trend
could be characterized more precisely by specifying the way in which
each age group represents these sorts of tasks. The developmental
progression depicted in Figure 4 was therefore proposed.

What this figure is meant to suggest is that, at the age of 4 years,
children tend to represent all possible variables in a global or
polar fashion, so that they can make mappings of the sort "Big
things are worth a lot; little things are worth a little". At the
age of 6 years, children tend to represent variables in a continuous
fashion (i.e., as having two poles and a number of point in between). Moreover, they realize that these points can be treated as
lying along a mental number line, such that values which have a
higher numeric value also have a higher real value associated with
them. At the age of 8 years, children can think in terms of two
independent quantitative variables (e.g., hours and minutes on a
clock, dollars and cents), but cannot yet make successful comparisons between variations along each. Finally, at the age of 10
years, children can make these sorts of comparisons by thinking in
terms of the "trade-offs" between two quantitative variables.

As the above conception was developed, we realized that it was similar in many respects to Piaget's "structure of the whole" and therefore subject to the criticisms which had been directed at this no-

Figure 4:   Conceptual representation hypothesized to underlie
             children's progress on quantitative problems.

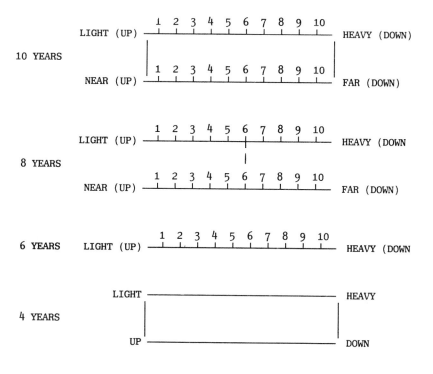

tion in several decades of North American research. We therefore
felt obligated to re-examine these criticisms, and to determine the
extent to which they applied to our emerging conception.

The first argument against Piaget's general operational structures
is a rational one. This argument holds that Piaget's logical structures may explain development reasonably well *from the perspective
of the observer*. However, since it is unlikely that children them-

selves represent problems in a logical form, or have anything remo-
tely resembling the sorts of mathematical groups Piaget described *in
their minds*, his explanation sheds little light on the operations
children actually employ in their problem-solving behavior.

When the representational structures we propose are examined, this
argument loses a lot of its force. Although the structures we
propose correspond in form to Piaget's structures, they have been
made sufficiently concrete so that it is not hard to imagine that
they actually correspond to children's internal representations.
Summing up a decade of mathematics research, for example, Resnick
(1983) concluded that 6-year-old children solve most addition and
subtraction problems by using something like a "mental number line".
In interview situations on our tasks, children themselves corroborate this interpretation, often explaining their performance by
referring to images of countable objects lined up in a row.

The next set of arguments against Piaget's general structures are
empirical ones. The first is that, when tests are characterized in
terms of the logical grouping they entail, massive decalage and
insignificant cross-task correlations emerge. In the studies reported above, however, the absence of decalage was a robust and major
finding. Moreover, at least in the study reported by Marini, the
cross-task correlations were also substantial, even after age had
been partialled out (r=.56). Thus, these criticisms also seem
inapplicable.

A final argument against Piaget's concept of general structure deals
with the issues of instruction and generalization. This argument
holds that, if general operational structures exist, they should be
very difficult to teach. However, if and when instruction *is* successful, there should be transfer to a broad range of tasks which
require the same underlying logical structure. In the case of our
emergent notion regarding central conceptual representations, the
first of these two arguments is not applicable, since there is no
suggestion that these structures are assembled by a process that is
exclusively auto-regulative, or that their assembly necessarily
takes a long time. Given the appropriate experience and working
memory, the representations in question should be able to be learned
without undue difficulty. The argument concerning generalization,
however, does pose a problem. Given that children understand the
specific requirements of any task, it would appear that acquisition
of a new conceptual structure --if it is indeed a "central" one--
should make for very broad transfer. Since the absence of generalization is the single most robust research finding in the learning
literature of this century, we felt that this prediction would have
to be tested empirically.

Study 5

In order to teach the central conceptual structure postulated for
6-year-old logical-mathematical thought, Case and Sandieson (in
press) first specified it's constituent elements. As depicted graphically in Figure 5 with respect to the balance beam task, an ability to represent elements in a dimensional fashion may be seen to
be comprised of the following elements: (a) A knowledge of the
number sequence from 1 to 10 and an awareness of each number's po-

sition in the sequence, (b) a knowledge of the one-to-one manner in which this sequence is mapped on to objects when counting, (c) an understanding of the cardinal value of each number (i.e., that when touching the third object and saying "3", one has formed a set whose size is indicated by this number), (d) an understanding of the generative rule· which relates adjacent cardinal values (e.g., that 3 represents a set that's just like 2 except that 1 object has been added, or that 3 represents a set that's just like 4 except that 1 has been subtracted), and (e) an understanding of the consequence of this fact: Namely that each successive number represents a set which contains more objects, and thus has a greater value along any particular dimension. The first three elements specified above are known to develop in the pre-school years (Gelman, 1978).

Figure 5:   Hypothesized 6-year-old structure for solving
            quantitative problems.

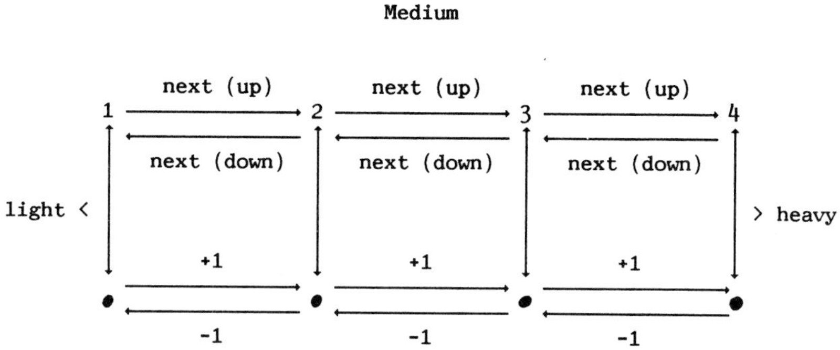

Medium

With the elements thus specified, Case and Sandieson next constructed training activities to teach each component of the structure: (a) Instruction in the number sequence was provided with a series of contextual counting exercises in forwards and backwards counting (e.g., "We're going on a rocket and we have to count down 5, 4, 3, 2, 1, blast-off"); (b) Understanding of one-to-one correspondence was taught in the context of object-collecting activities (e.g., "We're going on a picnic and there are 1, 2, 3, 4, 5 of us so get 5 forks, 5 knives, etc."); (c & d) Instruction in the relationship between adjacent cardinal values was provided with a series of highly motivational add-on and take-away exercises (e.g., "We have 3 cookies and the good/bad fairy comes along and adds 1/gobbles 1 up. Let's count how many we have now"); (e) Finally, instruction in making relative quantity assessments was provided with a series of exercises in which children were required to draw some polar conclusion (e.g., which army will win/lose) as a function of the number of things present (e.g., the number of soldiers in each army).

This training program was used with a group of 12 lower class children who were between the ages of 4 and 5 years, in a series of 15 fifteen-minute sessions. A control group of children received activities of equal duration and motivational value which focussed exclusively on efficient counting and number recognition, and which included no training in the remaining components of the conceptual structure described above. At the beginning of the study, children's counting skills were roughly equivalent to those of middle class 2 1/2-year-olds, using the criteria established by Case and Khanna (see Case, 1985, p.176). At the end of the study, each child was given a test of counting and number knowledge, as well as four tasks from the studies reported above. These included: (a) The balance beam task; (b) Marini's birthday party task; (c) the time-telling task; and (d) the money-handling task. Note that no direct instruction was included in the training program for any of these tasks.

The results of this study and a subsequent replication were identical (see Table 5). Both groups of children made significant improvements on the number knowledge post-test. However, in contrast to the control group, the treatment group showed substantial transfer to each transfer task, with success rates ranging from a low of 33% passing the balance beam task to a high of 80% passing the birthday party task *at the 6-year-old level*. These findings

Table 5: *Percentage of children passing transfer tasks in two quantification training studies.*

Transfer Tasks	Treatment Group Pre-test Post-test		Control Group Pre-test Post-test	
Balance beam task				
Study 1	0	33 (57)*	0	0
Study 2	0	36 (57)	0	7
Birthday party task				
Study 1	16	75(100)	0	0
Study 2	0	64 (86)	0	7
Time-telling task				
Study 1	0	50 (86)	0	0
Study 2	0	43 (78)	11	29
Money-handling task				
Study 1	0	80 (92)	0	14
Study 2	0	79(100)	0	29

* *Figures in brackets indicate percentages for the subsample who mastered the training activities.*

present a sharp contrast to the training results which are typical
in the literature, and which traditionally report few or no transfer
effects. Given the range of generalization which was found, the
findings suggest that the postulated central conceptual structure
is, indeed, psychologically real and plays an important role in mediating transfer.

With the above findings, the last argument against the notion of a
central conceptual structure appeared to have been surmounted, and
we began to wonder whether there might not be one or more other central conceptual structures which mediate age-level performance in
other domains. To answer this question, we turned our attention to
the social domain and examined recent findings which had been collected by members of our research group, and by our colleagues at
the Ontario Institute for Studies in Education. These findings are
the subject of the next section.

3. SOCIAL COGNITION

Study 1

The first study we examined provided an index of the level of social
understanding present in children's thought in the predimensional
substage (i.e., the age of 3-4 years). Using a graded sequence of
tasks to assess the development of children's empathic understanding
across the preschool years, Bruchkowsky (1984) found that a majority
of 4-year-olds were able to predict how two puppets would feel, on
the basis of the gifts each wanted (e.g., both want a bike) and the
gifts each received (e.g., one receives a bike and the other receives a doll). More specifically, 4-year-olds were able to respond to
the task questions, "How will this doll feel ?" and "How will this
(other) doll feel ?", with the prediction that one would feel happy
because she got what she wants, and the other would feel sad because
she didn't get what she wants. These findings indicate that 4-year-
olds are able to assign feelings to others on the basis of the relationship between a specific event and a specific internal state
(i.e., a desire or "want"). They suggest, in short, that 4-year-
olds have a fairly sophisticated understanding of social experience.
They understand that people have feelings; they understand that
people have desires; and they understand the ways in which particular desires, events, and feelings are related.

Study 2

In the next study, children's social understanding was assessed
across the age range of 4 to 10 years, with a different research
focus and a different set of tasks. In order to investigate young
girls' understanding of their mother's role, Goldberg-Reitman (1984;
in press) presented 10 girls at three age levels (4, 6, and 10
years) with a series of illustrated story events, depicting a female
child in hazardous, difficult, and neutral situations. Subjects
were asked to predict what a mother would do in response to each
situation (e.g., a child is falling off a roof), and to provide a
rationale for their prediction.

The results indicated no age-level differences in children's ability to predict an appropriate maternal response (e.g., a mother will catch her child) but significant age-level differences in the rationales provided. A majority of 4-year-olds explained the mother's action by exclusive reference to the antecedent event (e.g., because the child is falling). A majority of 6-year-olds explained the same maternal action by reference to the mother's internal state (e.g., because the mother doesn't *want* her child to get hurt). A majority of 10-year-olds explained the same maternal action by reference to two internal states (e.g., because the mother *loves* her child and doesn't *want* her to get hurt). These three response categories corresponded to three levels of structural complexity suggested by the theory and children answering at each of these levels received a score of 0, 1, or 2 respectively. Figure 6 displays the mean scores achieved by three age groups at three conceptual levels, and indicates the presence of a near perfect linear progression.

Figure 6: Mean scores of three age groups on explanations provided for a mother's role. (From Goldberg-Reitman, 1984).

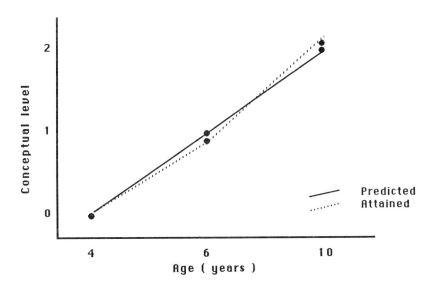

How is one to explain these results ? On the surrace, Bruchkowsky's results provide clear evidence that 4-year-old children understand the relations between a single event and certain internal states (i.e., desires and feelings). Goldberg-Reitman's results provide equally clear evidence that 4-year-olds also understand the relations between events. They are able to predict a subsequent event

on the basis of a previous event and they are able to explain an
event by reference to an antecedent event. What Goldberg-Reitman's
findings also show, however, is that the performance of 4-year-olds
is distinguished from that of 6- and 10-year-olds by the *absence* of
any internal state references in explaining a mother's behavior.
Thus, it appears that, although 4-year-olds have a *knowledge* of internal states, they do not *use* this knowledge to explain the relations between events (i.e., event-sequences). It is only when
children reach the age levels postulated for dimensional thought
(i.e., 5-10 years), that this knowledge is actively used.

Using the theory illustrated in Figure 1, we can interpret the findings of these first two studies by suggesting that 4-year-olds are
able to represent only one set of relations at a time. They can represent the causal relations which obtain between any two or three
events *or* they can represent the "intentional" relations which obtain between a single object or event and specific internal states.
Until the age of 5-6 years, however, they are unable to represent
these two sets of relations in a coordinated fashion so that one can
be used to predict and explain the other. This interpretation is
further supported by the data from two further studies.

Study 3

In a follow-up to her first study on empathy, Bruchkowsky (1989; in
press) conducted a second study in which she presented 4- to 10-year
old children with three short videotaped vignettes. In each vignette the central character was a young girl, who was in one mood at
the start and in a radically different mood at the end, as a function of some clearly demarcated event. The first vignette showed a
young girl who was bored, frustrated, and alone on her birthday, and
who then reacted with surprise and delight when a friend arrived unexpectedly and presented her with a gift. The second vignette showed a young girl who was happily engaged in building a giant castle
out of blocks, and then reacted with anger when the castle was des-
troyed by a spiteful peer. The third vignette showed a young girl
who was playing joyfully with her dog, and who then reacted with
grief and tears when the dog ran out on the street and was killed by
a truck. (For obvious reasons, this latter event was simulated, not
actually seen). These vignettes were shown to 24 children at each
of three age levels (i.e., 4, 6, & 10 years), and the children themselves were videotaped as they watched each episode.

The study examined a variety of interesting issues relating to
children's emotional display and coping mechanisms. However, the
most important issue from the present point of view was how children
at different ages conceptualized the events that they witnessed. To
address this issue, Bruchkowsky asked each child the following questions after each vignette was over: "How do you think the little
girl in the film was feeling ?" and "Why do you think she was feeling that way ?"

When directly probed, 4-year-olds had no trouble identifying the
feeling of the protagonist at the end of the episode (i.e., happy,
angry, sad). When asked to explain either feeling, however, they
responded in much the same fashion as had Goldberg's subjects to the
request to explain a mother's actions. That is to say, they refer-

red exclusively to the central event that had taken place, to which
the protagonist's mood change had been a response (e.g., "Her friend
came over" or "The girl knocked down her castle" or "Her dog died").
By contrast, 6-year-olds provided an explanation that went beyond
this, and that mentioned some internal state in the protagonist as
well. Typically, the internal state was one which, in combination
with the external event, was jointly responsible for producing the
feeling (e.g., "Her friend came over and she really wanted her to").
Finally, 10-year-olds mentioned a more extensive sequence of internal events, which normally included two rather than just one internal states.

When the findings of the above three studies are considered in conjunction, they suggest a developmental progression which is similar
in its general *form* to that which is observed on quantitative tasks.
On both sets of tasks (i.e., social tasks and quantitative tasks),
two qualitatively different sorts of understanding are integrated at
the 6-year-old level to form a new sort of "explanatory" unit, and
two or more units of this sort are subsequently integrated during
the period from 6 to 10 years. However, the *content* of children's
understanding, and the structures from which they derive, is clearly
quite different. A further clue as to the nature of this content is
provided by a study in a domain that is superficially quite different from the study of empathy, namely the comprehension of "speech
acts".

Study 4

As part of a larger investigation of children's understanding of
"speech acts" and "intentional attitudes", Astington (1985) examined
children's comprehension of the following expressions: *Intends to,
plans to, is going to* and *thinks (s)he will*. To assess age-level
understanding, she embedded each intentional expression in several
sentences (e.g., "The boy *plans to* slide down") and asked children
to choose, from pairs of pictures, the one that illustrated the sentence. In the sample pair of pictures depicted in Figure 7, it is
apparent that the top picture (the boy is climbing up the ladder)
expresses the intentional concept and the bottom picture (the boy is
sliding down) expresses a current action, rather than an intention.
Fourteen pairs of pictures and fourteen sentences which expressed
either an intention *or* a current action, were presented to 24 children at each of four age levels: 5 (mean = 4.10), 7 (mean = 6.11), 9
and 11 years.

The results indicated that almost all children at all age levels
were able to correctly choose the picture which expressed current
action when presented with sentences which omitted an intentional
expression. When an intentional expression was included in the sentence, however, significant age-level differences were found. A
majority of 4- to 5-year-olds failed to choose the picture expressing an intention and chose the picture expressing current action
instead. In contrast, a majority of the older age groups correctly
identified the picture expressing the intentional concept.

These findings indicate that 4- to 5-year-olds (i.e., the pre-
dimensional substage) make no distinction between an expression of
intention and an expression of current action. Moreover, in a for-

Figure 7:   Sample of tasks used to assess children's comprehension
of intentional expressions. (From Astington, 1985).

ced choice situation, they relate intentional expressions to the
(subsequent) actions which fulfill them rather than the (antecedent)
actions which express them. An analysis of the conceptual demands
of this task suggests that it requires children to consider the temporal relations between two events *in relation to* the intentional
relations expressed in the sentence. The 4- to 5-year-old's failure
to recognize that the antecedent event provides the best expression
of the intentional attitude embedded in the sentence can thus be
interpreted as an inability to represent these two sets of relations
in a coordinated fashion. In contrast, the success of the older age
groups provides evidence that children in the dimensional stage *can*
effect this coordination and thus represent a sequence of external
events along an internal or intentional continuum.

Study 5

The fifth study provided a direct assessment of children's ability
to construct relations between socially significant events, at 4, 6,
8 and 10 years of age. With a research focus on the structure of
children's narratives, McKeough (1986) gave 20 children at each of
the above age levels the following instructions: "Tell me a story
about a little boy or girl who has a problem and what they do to fix
it." In a separate condition, children were also shown a sad face
and a happy face and were given the following prompt: "This is Joe.
Tell me what happened to make him unhappy and what he did to get
happy again." The happy and sad faces were then removed and children's stories were recorded verbatim.

The results indicate that a majority of 4-year-olds were able to
produce one-half of the story structure. They were able to tell a
story about what happened to make a child unhappy, and occasionally
they told a story about what happened to make a child happy. Only a
small minority of this age-group, however, produced a story in
which, in the first part, a child had an experience which made him

or her unhappy and, in the second part, became happy again. At the 6-year-old level, in contrast, the majority of children produced the full story structure, at least in a "bare-bones" fashion. This structure was further elaborated in the stories produced by the majority of 8- and 10-year-olds, by the inclusion of an additional problem episode (i.e., a subplot) or a series of failed attempts, which intervened between the original problem and its solution. Although the 8- and 10-year-old performance is further distinguished in this study and provided support for the age-level postulates of the theory, comparable findings are not available for the other studies reported in this section. This distinction is therefore omitted from further discussion.

These three response categories corresponded to three levels of structural complexity suggested by the theory and children's productions were assigned scores of 0, 1, or 2 accordingly. Specifically, a score of 0 was assigned if the story described a problem *or* a solution or any situation which could be construed as such, within broad definitional parameters. A score of 1 was assigned if the story described both a problem *and* a solution, in a coordinated fashion. A score of 2 was assigned if the story described a problem, an additional problem which intervened between the first problem and its solution, and an ultimate resolution. Figure 8 shows the mean scores achieved by three age groups at three conceptual level and indicates, once again, the presence of a near-perfect linear progression.

These findings suggest that 4-year-olds are perfectly capable of generating a script (i.e., a sequence of two or three events) for unhappiness. They know what happens first, what happens next, and what happens last to produce unhappiness. They are also capable of generating a script for happiness which shows the same understanding of temporal sequence. What they appear incapable of doing, however, is generating a story in which these two scripts are combined: In which the first event(s) depict unhappiness and the last event(s) depict happiness, and where the connecting link between the two is the child's internal state (i.e., a feeling of unhappiness and a desire or plan for how to deal with it). At the 6-year-old level, this capacity is demonstrated in children's story productions while, at the 8- and 10-year-old levels, two or more links of this sort are created and integrated. On the basis of these findings, we hypothesize that children in the predimensional substage, in contrast to children in the dimensional substages, are unable to represent events as lying along an internal state continuum and/or relate this continuum to an event-sequence.

The findings of the above two studies shed light on the sorts of understandings which are integrated in this domain at the 6-year-old-level, and permitted us to add more content to the developmental progression which had been apparent, in its general form, in the studies reported earlier. When the findings of all five studies are considered in conjunction, we believe they can best be explained by postulating the presence of a second central conceptual structure, which can be described as follows:

Four-year-olds tend to represent any unit of social experience (i.e., a behavioral event) in terms of its temporal relationship to

Figure 8:   Mean scores of three age groups on a story
             production task. (From McKeough, 1986).

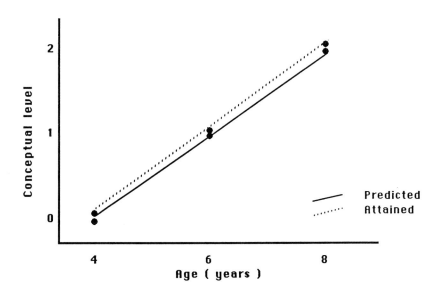

other behavioral events *or* in terms of its relationship to an internal state. Thus they can take any given event, focus on external
happenings, and tell you what happened before and what is likely to
happen next, and next. Alternatively, they can take any given
event, focus on internal happenings, and tell you what internal state (e.g., feeling or desire) is likely to be present. At this age-
level, however, children are not able to coordinate these two foci
in order to represent a sequence of events *in relation to* a sequence
of internal states. Thus, while they can see any local occurrence
(e.g., reaching for an object) as being caused by an internal wish
(e.g., for the object), they do not see entire event-sequences in
the same fashion.

Six-year-olds, in contrast, tend to represent event-sequences as
lying along (or parallel to) an internal state continuum. Thus, as
depicted in Figure 9, they are now able to recognize that changes in
the flow of external events are related to changes in the internal
states of the participants. For any particular event-sequence
(e.g., a problem followed by a resolution), they are able to recognize: (a) That two or more internal states are present; (b) that
the relations between these states (e.g., unhappiness turns to
happiness) can be predicted and explained as a function of a beha-

vioral event (e.g., a problem-solving action); and (c) that the
relations between events can be predicted and explained as a function of an internal state (e.g., a desire to get happy again).

Figure 9: *Hypothesized 6-year-old structure*
for solving social problems.

Middle

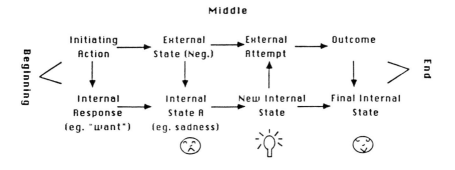

At the 8-year-old level, children tend to represent event-sequences
as lying along (or parallel to) two internal state continua. Thus,
they are now able to recognize that the relations between events
(e.g., a mother moves to catch her child who is falling off a roof)
can be explained as a function of two distinct internal states
(e.g., a mother's *wants* for her child and a mother's *feelings* towards her child). They are also able to recognize that the relations between events can be made more dramatic by introducing a subplot which embeds a second source of unhappiness within the major
unhappiness to happiness sequence and heightens the final internal
state experience. Finally, they are able to understand that feelings can be intentionally disturbed (e.g., a girl's feelings can
change from happy to angry as a result of a protagonist's *desire*
to hurt her feelings by destroying her castle).

Since this postulate proposes a *second* general conceptual structure,
one must once again confront the arguments which have been directed
at Piaget's similar notion. In particular, the criticism that this
structure exists only in the mind of the psychologist and not in the
mind of the child must be dealt with. This criticism can be addressed by examining the results of a study by Griffin (1988), in which
children's representations for their own internal states and processes were examined.

Study 6

To investigate the representations children construct for "self"

across the age range of 4 to 8 years, Griffin (1988; in press) examined the meanings children assign to several internal states. Of
particular relevance to the present discussion are her findings for
two internal states, happiness and sadness, which can be safely
assumed to be present in children's experience well before the age
of 4 years, and which the culture acknowledges and provides a voca-
bulary for describing. To elicit children's representations for
happiness and sadness, Griffin first provided a facilitating context. Twenty children, at each of the age-levels of 4, 6, and 8
years, were introduced, individually, to a cabbage-patch-kid doll
and were told:

> "This is my friend Wilbert. He's 4 (6 or 8) years
> old, the same age as you. He really needs your
> help. He's tired of being a cabbage-patch kid and
> wants to be a real 4- (6- or 8-) year-old kid.
> But --if he's going to be real-- he needs to know
> as much as real kids know. He needs, especially,
> to know what words mean. Today, Wilbert heard a
> new word he's never heard before. He has no idea
> what it means. The word is "happy". You're a real
> 4- (6- or 8-) year-old kid and you know what this
> word means. Can you tell Wilbert what it means to
> be happy ?"

Using a structured interview technique, this opening question was
followed by three other questions, namely: "What else can it
mean ?"; "What is happening when you are happy ?"; "When you are
happy doing X (child's example), where does the happiness come
from ?" The four questions were repeated for "being sad", with the
doll serving throughout as a motivating device. Children's responses to each question were recorded verbatim.

The results showed that 4-year-olds represent happiness and sadness
in terms of their relationship to specific external events, and explain these terms by exclusive reference to such events (e.g., Happy
means a birthday party; Sad means Mommy leaves). Furthermore, 4-
year-olds locate these internal states in the external world of actions, objects, or events, rather than within themselves (e.g.,
Happiness comes from the sky/from my toys/from playing/from
laughing/from the birthday party).

By contrast, six-year-olds represent happiness and sadness in terms
of their relationship to a continuum of internal events or processes
which is distinct from, but functionally related to, an external
event-sequence. Thus, they define each internal state as a *feeling*
about an event, as a *change in feeling state* when one event follows
another, or as the state that results when a particular set of
events does not correspond to their own *wants* (e.g., Sad means I
don't *want* Mommy to go out and she leaves). Furthermore, they now
locate their internal states within themselves (e.g., Sadness comes
from my heart/my brain/from thinking/from feeling).

Finally, the results showed that eight-year-olds can think in terms
of two internal continua, and explain happiness or sadness by a coordinated reference to two distinct internal state categories.
Thus, they explain happiness, for example, as a *change in feeling*

state which occurs when a *want* is satisfied (e.g., Happy means when I get to do something that I've been *wanting* for a long time, like going to Florida, then my *feelings* go up to really happy and I feel really excited and stuff). At this age-level, children again located these states within themselves. Figure 10 presents the mean scores achieved by the three age groups, when children's explanations for happiness and sadness, at each of the above levels, were assigned scores of 0, 1, and 2 respectively. As can be seen, age by conceptual level performance formed a near-perfect linear progression for both internal states assessed.

Figure 10:   *Mean scores of three age groups on explanations provided for happiness and sadness. (From Griffin, 1988).*

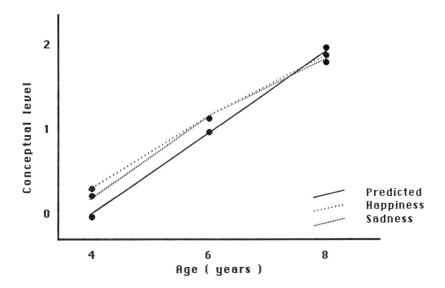

We believe these results provide another illustration of the same structural trend that was evident in the earlier studies. More important for the present argument, we believe they also provide support for the notion that the form we have used to represent this structure is similar to the form children use themselves. Children's verbalizations, in response to very general interview questions, suggest that the postulated structures are actually in the minds of the children, not just in our minds or in the logical structure of the tasks we have presented. In this connection, it is perhaps worthwhile to mention that a number of children actually illustrated the full structure we have postulated by describing a *continuum* of internal states and its relationship to a *sequence* of events. Thus, for example, one six-year-olds defined happiness in the following manner, "Happy means, well, like I'm all alone and then my feelings turn from sad to happy when I get to have a friend over".

If the postulated structures really are in children's own minds, in a fashion which has a similar form to the one we have suggested, the next classic question to be considered is whether the structures really are central. In this regard, one can ask whether they are actually used by children in thinking about a wide variety of tasks that we normally think of as belonging to different domains, or whether they are constructed separately for each domain, in response to the particular constraints which the domain entails in combination with their own general developmental constraints. Although the data on cross-task consistency can not answer this question with any certainty, they can certainly provide evidence of a disconfirmatory sort, as the data on decalage and the many critiques of Piaget's theory have demonstrated. The next datum we decided to examine, therefore, was the extent to which cross-task consistency was present when children's thinking was analyzed from the perspective of our emerging theoretical construct.

Table 6 presents the results from the studies that have been cited so far, when aggregated across the various items that were used, and scored for the level of central conceptual representation they entail. As is apparent, a majority of children in each age group scored at the predicted level on the majority of tasks although, at any age level, there was some variation from task to task as a function of its specific requirements.

Another way to examine the question is to look at the data from individual children to whom several different tasks have been administered. Griffin's (1988) study provided measures of: (a) Children's definitions of happiness and sadness, (b) their localization of each of these feelings inside or outside themselves; and (c) the level of structure they introduce into their narratives on McKeough's story-telling task. When cross-task consistency was computed for individual children, it was found that 50% of the 4-year-olds, 35% of the 6-year-olds, and 55% of the 8-year-olds performed at the same level across all five tasks. The typical pattern for the remaining children was one in which children performed at the same level on three or four tasks and at one level removed on the remaining task(s). Only 7 children in the total sample of 60 showed a two-level split across any pair of tasks.

When cross-task consistency was computed for selected combinations of tasks, the consistency estimates were much higher. A majority of children (70-85% of each age group) performed consistently in the definitions they provided for two distinct internal states (i.e., happiness and sadness). A majority of children (60-75% of each age-group) performed consistently across these two tasks and McKeough's story task. Finally, a majority of children (70-90% of each age-group) performed consistently in the definitions they provided for each internal state and their localization of these states inside or

Table 6:   *Percentage of children in three age groups passing each*
          of three conceptual levels (0, 1, 2), on five different
          tasks of social cognition.

Age	Level	*Studies*				
		Mother's role (Goldberg)	Empathy (Bruchkow.)	Intentional expressions (Astington)	Narrative structure (McKeough)	Internal states (Griffin)
8-10	2*	90	68	71	75	90
	1	100	88	80	100	100
	0	100	100	100	100	100
6	2	10	30	20	10	22
	1*	81	58	71	90	88
	0	100	100	100	100	100
4	2	0	0	0	0	2
	1	20	26	16	5	22
	0*	89	53	84	75	75

* indicates conceptual level hypothesized for age group.

outside themselves (e.g., children who defined happiness and sadness by exclusive reference to external events also located these internal states in the external world, rather than within themselves).

In summary, while the existing data clearly needs to be supplemented by further data of the sort that are available for children's quantitative structures (i.e., data on training and transfer), it would appear that they already point in the same direction. That is to say, they suggest that children's responses to particular social tasks at any age level are not simply a function of the individual constraints and procedures which these tasks entail, in combination with whatever relevant background experience or training children have had with regard to them. Rather, they are a function of the central conceptual structures which children possess at this age, and which they use to invest the tasks they are set with meaning.

4. CONCLUSION

At the beginning of this chapter, we mentioned that there has been a gradual and subtle shift in the way we view the process of cognitive development, as a result of the work we have done over the past five years to test the neo-Piagetian theory that was proposed earlier (Case, 1985). We would like to conclude by clarifying the nature of

this shift, and the way our present view relates to the one we held
earlier. We would also like to specify --as clearly as we are able
at the present moment-- the relationship that exists between our
emerging view of cognitive development and the classic view proposed by Piaget and his colleagues.

Definition of a Central Conceptual Structure

In the present chapter we have given an illustration of two central
conceptual structures, and the role we believe they play in the
development of children's logico-mathematical and social thought.
Although the nature of the general class to which these two structures belong may be obvious, it seems worthwhile to specify the
criterial properties of this class more explicitly. By a *structure*
we mean an internal mental entity which consists of a number of
nodes, and the relations among them. By *conceptual* we mean that the
nodes and relations are semantic, rather than syntactic: That is to
say, they consist of "meanings", "representations", or "concepts"
that the child assigns to external entities in the world, rather
than devices for parsing such meanings. Finally, by *central* we mean
structures which (a) form the core of a wide range of more specific
concepts, and (b) play a pivotal role in enabling the child to make
the transition to a new stage of thought where these more specific
concepts are constructed and coordinated. A central conceptual
structure is thus an internal network of concepts and conceptual relations, which plays a central role in permitting children to think
about a wide range of (but not all) situations at a new epistemic
level, and to develop a new set of control structures for dealing
with them.

Changes Required by This Notion to our Early Theory of Children's
Development

No matter how compatible a new concept may be with an existing network of concepts, its addition to that network invariably requires
certain changes in the existing structure. So it is with regard to
the addition of the notion of a central conceptual structure. Its
addition into our existing theory of children's cognitive development requires certain adjustments and adaptations.

In our earlier work, we defined a control structure as a tripartite
entity consisting of a problem representation, a nested goal set,
and a strategy for attaining a goal set of this sort (see footnote
1). In addition, we suggested that the assembly of any given control structure was constrained by the size of a child's working memory, which in turn was determined by his level of maturation and
the degree to which certain key operations had been automatized.
Finally, we suggested that each new control structure led to a
change in children's knowledge of the external world, and the new
knowledge thus constructed served, in turn, as the base from which
further control structures would be constructed (Case, 1985, p.93).

Viewed solely from the foregoing perspective, the notion of a central conceptual structure would appear to constitute no more than a
natural addition to an existing set of propositions, which flows
directly from an attempt to specify one of the propositions in greater detail, and which requires no change in the existing set. In

particular, the new construct would appear to flow directly from an attempt to model the knowledge that is acquired at any level of development --and whose coordination in working memory leads to new control structures-- in a slightly more detailed and formal fashion.

Although they may not be obvious, however, certain accommodations are required by this addition as well. The most important of these are the following:

1. *Nature of Children's Problem Representations.* In our previous attempts to model the process of intellectual development, we treated children's "problem representations" as consisting of an ordered set of task features, to which their attention was directed as a function of the particular problem question they had been posed, and the particular perceptual and/or social context which made this question meaningful. The first change that the above conception implies is that children's problem representations can no longer be viewed in this relatively atomistic fashion. Rather, they must be seen as having their own internal structure, which very often exists prior to a problem being posed, and which exerts an independent effect on the way the problem is interpreted across a broad range of perceptual and social situations.

2. *Relationship of Different Control Structures to Each Other.* In our previous description of children's growing intellectual competence, we described children's control structures as belonging to a number of broad and culturally-conventional categories such as spatial, linguistic, social, and scientific functioning. However, we had no basis for distinguishing, a priori, among these various categories, or for presuming that developmental sequences within any category would be any more closely related than those across categories, once the effects of common operational requirements were taken into consideration. The second change which is required by the addition of the above notion is that control structures can no longer be seen in this independent, unrelated fashion. Rather, they must be seen as being part of a network of related control structures, which are tied together by a common conceptual core.

While certain of these core networks may well be isomorphic with the conventional categories that we utilized earlier, others may be different. In fact, this was the case in the first example provided in the present chapter. At the outset of our investigation, we thought of scientific reasoning on the balance beam, social reasoning about distributive justice, the sight reading of music, and learning to tell the time or deal with money as belonging to different domains. What we can now see, however, is that these are all part of one common conceptual domain, in which children's increasing competence is directly controlled by their growing understanding of *number*.

3. *Importance of Working Memory in Determining the Upper Bound of Children's Functioning.* In our previous work we implicitly assumed that the size of children's working memory was the *only* important constraint of a general sort which set a limit on their construction of new control structures. With the addition of the new construct, however, we have come to realize that there are other important general constraints of a conceptual nature. These constraints are less general than those imposed by working memory, in that they do

not apply across the full range of structures which a child might
assemble. However, they are also a good deal more general than
those imposed by any specific set of task requirements.

4. *Locus of Action of Working Memory Limitations.* In our earlier
work, we were not explicit in specifying the point in the process of
structural assembly at which working memory limits were most frequently encountered. If anything, however, we implied that this
bottleneck would most likely occur with regard to the goals a child
can set up regarding the operations (s)he intends to carry out in
the immediate future, or the pointers (s)he can store regarding operations already executed. The final change which the addition of
the new construct suggests is that these latter limitations should
be viewed as relatively elastic. While they are not trivial, it
seems likely to us that the problems associated with assembling a
set of goals and procedures for accomplishing a complex new objective that is well understood may be relatively easy to circumvent.
The reason for this is that the conceptual structure which represents the problem will act as a retrieval and organizing device
which will enable the child to keep coming back to each problematic
element, even after the importance of one or another of these elements has been temporarily forgotten. By contrast, when such an
organizing device is not yet in place, even simple goals and procedures may be difficult to orchestrate, because the temporary deletion of even one key element will change (and distort) the overall
conceptual shape which the problem assumes.

In summary, it may be seen that the notion of a central conceptual
structure re-introduces a strong structural element into our neo-
Piagetian theory, after a period in which this element was de-
emphasized in favour of considerations which were more functional
in nature.

*Similarities Between the Notion of a Central Conceptual Structure
and the Piagetian Notion of a "Structure of the Whole"*

The primary difference between our earlier view of cognitive development and the classic Piagetian view was our emphasis on the importance of functional factors such as working memory and automati-
city, and our attention to the specific situational and task factors
in which this working memory had to be deployed. With the re-
introduction of a strong structural element to the theory, a question that naturally arises is the extent to which the new theory
entails a return to the classic Piagetian position. In particular,
a question that arises is whether there is any difference between
the present notion of a central conceptual structure and the classic
notion of an "operative structure," or a "structure of the whole."

To some extent we have already addressed this question in our consideration of the arguments that were levelled at Piaget's notion of a
structure of the whole, and the reasons we do not think they apply
to our own notion of a central conceptual structure. Nevertheless,
it seems worthwhile to conclude by making a somewhat more formal
comparison of the points of similarity and difference between the
two constructs.

The following properties are all ones which Piaget ascribed to his structures of the whole, which we would also ascribe to the central conceptual structures we have hypothesized. Both sets of structures may be defined as *internalized sets of operations* which:

- Transcend any particular task.

- Are arranged into coherent systems.

- Change only gradually in their constituent make-up.

- Have different characteristic forms.

- Define different major stages and substages of development.

- Are used to make sense of, or learn new things about, the external world.

In addition, we would endorse many of the classic Piagetian suggestions concerning the *origins* of such structures. Each higher-order structure, we would agree:

- Is assembled out of lower order structures

- which become differentiated, and coordinated

- via autoregulative processes (e.g., equilibration; reflexive abstraction)

- which are activated by the universal human experience of trying to make sense of, or abstract invariants from, the normal flux of human experience.

Differences Between the Notion of a Central Conceptual Structure and the Piagetian Notion of a "Structure of the Whole"

The following set of properties do not appear to be ones which are the same as --or even necessarily compatible with-- the classic Piagetian notion. The structures we have proposed:

- Are organized sets of concepts and conceptual relations, not logical relations.

- Are universal with regard to sequence but potentially specific with regard to their form, and incidence of occurrence.

- Are applicable to a broad range of content, but only within a specific domain.

- Are acquired via socially facilitated processes (i.e., processes which call the subject's attention to certain factors, and encourage certain kinds of constructions rather than others).

- Are potentially teachable, in a rather direct fashion.

In summary, the structures with which we have become interested are
semantic, not syntactic ones, which --while they may well have certain logical characteristics (e.g., reciprocity)-- are not developmentally constrained by these properties. Moreover, the underlying
processes which we presume to be at work, while they may well have
certain universal autoregulative features, are nevertheless ones
with a strong social component as well. The result is that children
are seen as re-constructing the conceptual inventions of prior gene-
rations with the aid of the current generation, rather than as abstracting universal logical invariants exclusively from their own
epistemic activity.

ACKNOWLEDGEMENTS

Preparation of this chapter was facilitated by a grant from the
James S. McDonnell Foundation. The studies that are reported were
made possible by grants from the Social Sciences and Humanities
Council of Canada and the Ontario Ministry of Education.

FOOTNOTE AND REFERENCES

1. A control structure is defined as a tripartite problem-solving
structure, which includes: (a) A representation of the problem
situation, (b) a representation of the goal which the situation
entails, and (c) a representation of the procedures that will take
the child from the current situation to the goal state.

Astington, J.W. (1985). Children's understanding of promising.
    Unpublished doctoral thesis, University of Toronto.
Bruchkowsky, M. (1984). The development of empathic understanding
    in early childhood. Unpublished master's thesis, University of
    Toronto.
Bruchkowsky, M. (1989). Affect and cognition in the development of
    empathy in children. Unpublished doctoral dissertation,
    University of Toronto.
Bruchkowsky, M. (in press). The development of empathy in early and
    middle childhood. In: R. Case (Ed.), *The mind's staircase:
    Stages in the development of human intelligence*. Hillsdale,
    NJ: Erlbaum.
Capodilupo, S. (1985). Sight reading of musical notation: A neo-
    Piagetian investigation. Unpublished masters thesis, University
    of Toronto.
Capodilupo, A. (in press). Development and learning: A neo-
    structural analysis of children's response to instruction in the
    sight reading of musical notation. In: R. Case (Ed.), *The mind's
    staircase: Stages in the development of human intelligence*.
    Hillsdale, NJ: Erlbaum.
Case, R. (1978). Intellectual development from birth to adulthood:
    A neo-Piagetian investigation. In: R. Siegler (Ed.), *Children's
    thinking: What develops ?* Hillsdale, NJ: Erlbaum.
Case, R. (1985). *Intellectual development: Birth to adulthood*.
    New York: Academic Press.
Case, R., Marini, Z., McKeough, A., Dennis, S., & Goldberg, J.
    (1986). Horizontal structure in middle childhood: Cross-domain

parallels in the course of cognitive growth. In: I. Levin (Ed.), *Stage and structure: Reopening the debate.* New York: Ablex.
Case, R., & Sandieson, R. (1986). Horizontal and vertical enrichment: A developmental approach to the teaching of central conceptual skills (Second Year Report). Toronto: Ontario Institute for Studies in Education.
Case, R., & Sandieson, R. (1987). *General conceptual constraints on the development of specific procedural knowledge (and vice-versa).* Paper presented at American Educational Research Association, Washington, D.C.
Case, R., Sandieson, R., & Dennis, S. (1987). Two cognitive developmental approaches to the design of remedial instruction. *Cognitive Development, 1,* 293-333.
Case, R., & Sandieson, R. (in press). New data on learning and its transfer: The role of central numerical structures in the development of children's scientific, social, and temporal thought. In: R. Case (Ed.), *The mind's staircase: Stages in development of human intelligence.* Hillsdale, NJ: Erlbaum.
Fischer, K.W. (1980). A theory of cognitive development: The control and construction of hierarchies of skills. *Psychological Review, 87,* 477-531.
Fuson, K.C. (1982). An analysis of the counting-on solution procedure in addition. In: T.P. Carpenter, J.M. Moser & T.A. Romberg (Eds.), *Addition and subtraction: A cognitive perspective.* Hillsdale, NJ: Erlbaum.
Gelman, R. (1978). Counting in the pre-schooler: What does and what does not develop ? In: R.S. Siegler (Ed.), *Children's thinking: What develops ?* Hillsdale, NJ: Erlbaum.
Goldberg-Reitman, J. (1984). Young girls' understanding of their mother's role: A developmental investigation. Unpublished doctoral thesis, University of Toronto.
Goldberg-Reitman, J. (in press). Young girls' conceptions of their mother's role: A neo-structural analysis. In: R. Case (Ed.), *The mind's staircase: Stages in the development of human intelligence.* Hillsdale, NJ: Erlbaum.
Griffin, S.A. (1988). Children's awareness of their inner world. Unpublished doctoral dissertation, University of Toronto.
Griffin, S.A. (in press). The development of intrapersonal intelligence in middle childhood: A neo-structural analysis. In: R. Case (Ed.), *The mind's staircase: Stages in the development of human intelligence.* Hillsdale, NJ: Erlbaum.
Griffin, S.A., Case, R., & Sandieson, R. (in press). Synchrony and asynchrony in children's everyday mathematical knowledge: Towards a representational theory of children's intellectual growth. In: R. Case (Ed.), *The mind's staircase: Stages in the development of human intelligence.* Hillsdale, NJ: Erlbaum.
Halford, G.S. (1982). *The development of thought.* Hillsdale, NJ: Erlbaum.
Inhelder, B., & Piaget, J. (1958). *The growth of logical thinking from childhood to adolescence.* New York: Basic Books.
Liu, P. (1981). An investigation of the relationship between qualitative and quantitative advances in the cognitive development of preschool children. Unpublished doctoral dissertation, University of Toronto.
Marini, Z. (1984). The development of social and physical cognition in childhood and adolescence. Unpublished doctoral dissertation, University of Toronto.

Marini, Z. (in press). Synchrony and asynchrony in cognitive
    development: Re-analyzing the problem of decalage from a neo-
    structural perspective. In: R. Case (Ed.), *The mind's staircase:
    Stages in the development of human intelligence.* Hillsdale, NJ:
    Erlbaum.
McKeough, A. (1986). Developmental stages in the narrative
    compositions of school aged children. Unpublished doctoral
    dissertation, University of Toronto.
Mounoud, P. (1986). Similarities between developmental sequences at
    different age periods. In: I. Levin (Ed.), *Stage and structure.*
    New York: Ablex.
Pascual-Leone, J. (1969). Cognitive development and style: A
    general theoretical integration. Unpublished doctoral
    dissertation, University of Geneva.
Pascual-Leone, J., & Goodman, D. (1979). Intelligence and
    experience: A neo-Piagetian approach. *Instructional Science, 8,*;
    301-367.
Resnick, R.B. (1983). A developmental theory of number
    understanding. In: H. P. Ginsburg (Ed.), *The development of*;
    mathematical thinking. New York: Academic Press.
Siegler, R.S. (1976). Three aspects of cognitive development.
    Cognitive Psychology, 8, 481-520.
Siegler, R.S. (1978). The origins of scientific reasoning. In:
    R. Siegler (Ed.), *Children's thinking: What develops ?*
    Hillsdale, NJ: Erlbaum.

DEVELOPMENTAL PSYCHOLOGY
Cognitive, Perceptuo-Motor, and Neuropsychological Perspectives
C-A. Hauert (Editor)
© Elsevier Science Publishers B.V. (North-Holland), 1990

CHILD COGNITIVE DEVELOPMENT: OBJECT. SPACE, TIME,
LOGICO-MATHEMATICAL CONCEPTS

Jacques Crépault(1) and Anh NGUYEN-XUAN

Psychologie cognitive du traitement
de l'information symbolique
Université de Paris 8 / CNRS UA218
Paris - St.-Denis, France

*This chapter presents a detailed look at the intellectual
development of logico-mathematical concepts for classes
and relations and of temporal concepts and reasoning from
childhood through adulthood. These two areas are explored
using different perspectives: An information processing
approach and a renewed "structural" approach of knowledge
transformation for physical cognition. In the latter,
there is an emphasis on "stable" and "unstable" cognitive
systems. Our basic hypothesis is that there are two main
types of knowledge which are applied in a given situation:
(1) General states of knowledge which are applied to several fields of cognition and (2) states of inferred knowledge which are more specific and built from various task
domains. To explain our approach for studying cognitive
development, the main findings from a series of studies on
logico-mathematical concepts and time reasoning, and some
conceptual tools used in qualitative models are presented.*

(1) Preparation of part of this chapter and the research reported
was supported by grant No A6301 from the Natural Sciences and
Engineering Research Council (Canada) and the "Conseil de la
recherche" of Université de Moncton (New-Brunswick, Canada).

1.   INTRODUCTION

This chapter concerns the cognitive development of logico-
mathematical concepts dealing with classes and relations and the
development of physical cognition, particularly temporal concepts
and qualitative reasoning from childhood through adult age. These
two areas will be approached differently. Logico-mathematical concepts will be analysed with an information processing approach (part
2), while knowledge representation of temporal concepts and reasoning will be studied within the framework of a renewed "structural"
approach of knowledge transformation for physical cognition (part
3). In the latter, there is an emphasis on "stable" and "unstable"
states of knowledge.

At present, the information processing approach dominates cognitive psychology and has also become popular in the study of cognitive development. It allows a more precise analysis of some difficult questions which the classical structural approach has not been able to satisfactorily address, such as "horizontal decalage" or the "mechanisms of knowledge acquisition" (Baylor and Lemoyne, 1976; Wallace, Klahr and Bluff, 1987; Gilliéron, 1976; Nguyen-Xuan, 1986; Siegler, 1983). While several theories of cognitive development are based on this approach, no single theory replaces Piaget's monumental theory which remains the only existing general theory to explain cognitive development in a synthetic manner. In fact, this book is organized under the framework of Piagetian concepts and while the conceptual tools presented below are quite different from the ones discussed by Piaget, the cognitive skills they examine are still the ones defined by Piagetian theory.

What do we know about the development of temporal reasoning from childhood through adulthood from the point of view of cognitive psychology ? For the last fifteen years, the study of the development of temporal reasoning, which is based on Piaget's classical works (Piaget, 1946a, 1946b, 1950, 1966), has been subjected to several different methodologies. These include the method of rule-type assessment or "decision-tree methodology" (Richards, 1982; Siegler and Richards, 1979), the method of functional measurement within the framework of information integration theory (Wilkening, 1982, 1988; Wilkening and Anderson, 1982), the method based on the facet model (Levin, 1977, 1982) and the "neo-Piagetian" method (Montangero, 1977, 1983, 1984). These new paradigms allow for the renewal of Piaget's methodology and raise new questions concerning the development of time reasoning. In part 3, we present the main findings of this series of research, as well as some conceptual tools to establish our approach towards cognitive development which is based on a notion of alternate stable and unstable states of knowledge. Are certain states of knowledge more stable than others ? What criteria should one use to distinguish stable and unstable cognitive systems ? Recent studies of theoretical models suggest that problems of "structural stability" have rarely been tackled (Case, 1985, 1987a; Chapman, 1987; Fischer and Farrar, 1987; Halford, 1987; Kerkman and Wright, 1988; Mounoud, 1986; Nguyen-Xuan, Cauzinille-Marmeche, Frey, Mathieu and Rousseau, 1983; Wallace et al., 1987). Thus what is the relation between the notion of stage and the concept of structural stability ? To answer these questions, we will present a conceptual framework for studying the development of physical cognition and qualitative reasoning.

2. THE LOGICO-MATHEMATICAL CONCEPTS OF CLASS AND RELATION

In this section, we discuss the information processing approach for studying the development of logico-mathematical concepts and how it can explain the development of these concepts. Detailed examples will be taken from our own research on the concepts of "class" and "relation". These are central concepts in the development of logical thinking from the "sensori-motor" stage through the "formal operation" stage. In Piagetian theory, they are the building blocks of the "grouping structures" that characterize the "concrete operations" stage.

2.1. Methodological aspects

A theory of cognition based on the information processing approach
is characterized by three general features. First, cognition is information processing, i.e. manipulating symbols. Second, many of
the psychological concepts stem from the pioneering research of
Atkinson and Shiffrin (1968), and Newell and Simon (1972), on reasoning and memory processes. Third, a close relationship is established between the characteristics of a task (the "task environment"),
the type of knowledge that is necessary for successfully performing
the task (the "information processing demands"), and the types of
knowledge that lead to what are considered to be the different kinds
of "bad" performances. The best known of the information processing
theories are those proposed by Case (Case, 1985, 1987a), Klahr and
Wallace (Klahr and Wallace, 1976; Wallace et al, 1987), Siegler
(1981, 1983, 1986) and Sternberg (1984). Case and Sternberg use the
information processing approach at a general level while Klahr and
his colleagues and Siegler attempt to make their theories very precise by building computer models to simulate the thinking process
and the acquisition of knowledge. Our approach is closer to Klahr's
and Siegler's than to Case's or Sternberg's.

2.1.1. Task environment and information processing demands

The information processing approach emphasizes the close relationship between task environment and information processing demands.
We will use the addition task as an example to show the link between
these two aspects, to precisely define the concept of "information",
and to say a word about the characteristics of experimental situations.

Let us examine an experimental situation where subjects are given a
series of addition problems where the two addents are always one-
digit numbers, such as "How much is four plus five ?". The questions are presented orally, the subject must find the answer as
quickly as possible, and he/she is not allowed to count using her
fingers. A normal adult answers each question correctly and rapidly. In all likelihood, adults use memorized "number facts" because
normal adults typically know the sum of every pair of one-digit
numbers: The adult possesses an "addition table" for one-digit
numbers. However, nobody would suppose that four-to-five-year-old
children use addition tables. More likely, they use some technique
of mental counting, or perhaps they will make mistakes because they
have neither completely mastered the addition table nor one of the
counting techniques (Siegler and Shrager, 1984).

Now, let us examine mental addition problems where the addents are
two-digit numbers. The two types of problems, adding one-digit
numbers and adding two-digit numbers, are structurally isomorphic.
If a series of two-digit number problems are given to adults, there
are more mistakes but performance is still honorable. Since people
do not normally memorize numerical facts for addition problems with
large numbers, correct answers are probably not produced by simply
retrieving numerical facts. Hence, it is necessary to examine the
two-digit number problems in terms of the information processing demands that differ from those assumed for the addition of one-digit
numbers. For example, besides knowledge of the addition table, one

must suppose some additional knowledge, such as "a two-digit number is the made up of a one-digit number representing tens and a one-digit number". This knowledge leads to the application of the addition table to the tens and to the single digits separately, then to the integration of the two obtained results into a single number.

The concept of "information" can be defined as follows with the terms "task" and "problem" being synonymous. Solving a problem is the act of producing new information from available information. A problem is defined by an initial state and a goal state. The initial state is defined by a set of properties that determine the available information. The goal state is defined by a set of properties which represent the information that must be produced. The goal state is obtained by applying operators that modify the properties of the initial state. The operators can be motor manipulations (e.g., raising one's fingers), but the most important ones are mental (search of numerical facts in memory, analysing a number into two simpler ones, etc.).

In the examples presented above, the properties of the initial state are not the same depending on whether or not finger counting is allowed. In the case where it is permitted, control of the counting process can be based on the finger configuration. In the other case, control can be based only on an internal representation. In other words, the information that is available and that has been used is not identical in the two problems. Note that, depending on what knowledge he/she actually possesses, the subject may or may not be able to take into account all the pieces of available information. For example, in the balance-scale task used by Siegler (1981), information about the distance of the weights from the fulcrum is available, but small children do not use this information.

This example shows that the task environment cannot be defined independent of the information processing demands, and vice versa. It also illustrates two important characteristics of the information processing approach:

1) Two tasks considered structurally isomorphic can be different in terms of the information processing demands, and consequently can be processed differently by the same subject.

2) One cannot theorize about the acquisition of knowledge (e.g., the logico-mathematical concepts of "number", "conservation", "class", etc.) without defining precisely the context in which the knowledge should be used i.e., the category of tasks in which the observed behaviors can be explained in reference to the knowledge.

The definition we have proposed for the concept "information" leads to two relevancy criteria for distinguishing between different problem situations:

1) A situation where all the information is given in the problem statement is less relevant than a situation where the subject has to look for additional information to arrive at the final goal.

2) A situation where the cognitive processing is entirely internal is less relevant than a situation where part of the processing con-

sists of manipulating objects in the external environment.

A problem situation that allows a rich harvest of data is one where the subject has to actively search for additional information, and where many overt behaviors can be observed. If the problem situation is such that all the information is given from the outset and the subject's answer is the only overt behavior, then it is necessary to give the subject a set of problems where the information processing demands are varied. The analysis of the subject's behavior can then be based on the pattern of her answers to the whole set of problems, and not simply on some numerical score.

2.1.2. Logical thinking and inference rules: An approach based on the concept of "just sufficient knowledge"

The knowledge that will be attributed to a subject is closely linked to the way the task is analyzed. Therefore, we shall introduce the concept of "just sufficient knowledge" for carrying out a task, which is quite similar to the concept of information processing demands. On this basis, we will approach the question of how the age related changes of the logico-mathematical concepts can be studied.

Our approach can be summarized as follows. Given a problem situation which is defined by an initial state, a goal state and available information, a minimum set of inference rules (or operators) can be defined. A subset of these rules are "logical" inference rules, the remaining rules are inference rules we can qualify as "pragmatic" because they are domain specific. Cognitive development can then be examined either in respect to domain specific knowledge or in respect to the rules that are general across domains.

This minimum set of rules is just sufficient for producing a behavior judged as "optimal", for example, a correct answer to a problem. From the minimum set of rules for optimal behavior in a given problem situation, research can proceed in two directions: 1) Determining the way the set of rules can be "weakened" in order to produce the set of observed non-optimal behaviors; 2) determining the way the set of rules can be strenghtened to produce optimal behaviors in classes of problems that are known to be successfully solved only later in the course of development. Note that some higher-order rules (some kind of "meta-rules") should be assumed which activate and coordinate the two types of rules. We will not discuss this issue because it is closely linked to complex questions about the processes of building a problem representation which fall outside the limits of this chapter.

To illustrate our approach, we will consider the well known "seriation" task. Within the framework of Piagetian theory the length seriation task (ranking a set of sticks by length) and the weight seriation task (ranking a set of objects by weight, using a Roberval balance) are "structurally isomorphic". Piaget described seriation behavior as "operational" when the subject used a method called "the extremum". This method consists of reaching an iterative series of goals. That is, first, the subject finds the longest (or the heaviest) of the yet unranked set of objects and places it down. Then he/she finds the next longest (or heaviest) from the unranked set and places it down next to the first one and so on.

This iterative goal can be formulated in general terms by using the
variable X instead of the constants "long" or "heavy": "Find the
most X of the yet unranked set of objects, then put it in line next
to the preceding most X".

We need to assume two important pragmatic rules. One rule is specific to the length domain and the other to the weight domain:

   E1: If a set of sticks are assembled and held upright on the
        table, the stick that overlaps is longer than all the others.

   Ew: If each of two objects are put on each of two trays of a
        balance scale and if the balance tilts, the object on the
        inclining side is heavier.

To reach the goal "find the longest of the yet unranked set of
sticks", we need assume, in addition to rule E1, the following
logical inference rule R1:

   R1: If an object is more X than all the others, then it is the
        most X.

In the case of weight seriation, since the relation "more X than"
can be obtained by observation only for a couple of objects at the
same time, to reach the goal "finding the heaviest of the yet unranked set of weights", we need assume another rule in addition to Ew
and R1, namely R2:

   R2: If an object is more X than any of the other objects, then it
        is more X than all the other objects.

Now, how can one find the object which is "more X than any of the
others" ? Suppose that we observed two subjects S1 and S2. Both
subjects concluded that object W1 was the heaviest of a set of five
objects, but their sequences of weighting were not identical. S1
made six weightings and S2 made four, as shown below:

           S1: W3>W4; W3>W5; W2>W3; W1>W2; W1>W3; W1>W4
           S2: W3>W4; W3>W5; W2>W3; W1>W2.

S1 compared object W1 with each of the others, and W1 was heavier
than any of the other objects. The just sufficient knowledge in
terms of the logical inference rules which are needed to explain
S1's behavior, are the rules R1 and R2. Nevertheless, these two rules are not sufficient for explaining S2's behavior because S2 found
that W1 was heaviest without comparing it to each of the other objects. Hence, it is necessary to attribute at least one more logical inference rule R3 to S2:

R3: If an object Wt is more X than an object Wu, and Wu is more X
     than an object Wv, then Wt is more X than Wv.

R3 is used to generate mentally the information "W1>W3" and "W1>W4",
instead of looking for this information in the external environment
by weighing the pairs (W1,W3) and (W1,W4).

2.2. The concepts of class and relation

The approach presented above implies that it does not make sense to speak of the acquisition of a logico-mathematical concept without referring to a precise category of tasks. The categories used by Piaget and many other as being the most relevant for studying the acquisition of class and relation are the problems called "class-inclusion", "multiple classification" and "seriation". For about fifteen years, the two situations which stimulated the most research were "class inclusion" and "seriation" (Bideaud, 1988; Lautrey, Bideaud and Pierre-Puységur, 1986). These tasks raise the problem of "horizontal decalage" which therefore makes questionable the concept of a "general structure" and thus the Piagetian notion of "stage".

We shall not discuss the class-inclusion task since it has been extensively studied; we refer the reader to the review by Winer (1980). Moreover, according to the criteria presented in the preceding section for differentiating experimental situations by their degree of relevancy for studying cognitive processes, this type of problem is perhaps the least interesting because all the information is provided from the outset. Klahr and Wallace (1976) and Wilkinson (1976) proposed computer models which described very precisely the processes of reasoning in various class-inclusion problems. Research done by Markman (1973) on the relationships between the inclusion relation and the concept of "collection" showed that for the class-inclusion problems, domain specific knowledge must also be taken into account. Subsequent research on the class-inclusion task studied the role of "empirical knowledge" in various class-inclusion problems (cf. e.g., Bideaud, 1988; Bideaud and Lautrey, 1983). But this research lacks a theoretical basis that could lead to both a clear definition of a criterion for judging when a child has mastered the logical class inclusion relation and an explicit hypothesis concerning the role of empirical knowledge in the construction of the concept of class. From the point of view of the logical construction of the class-inclusion relation, the most relevant analysis remains that proposed by Inhelder, Sinclair and Bovet (1974).

2.2.1. The concept of multiple classification

In the grouping described by Piaget (Piaget, 1941, 1972) as the "bi-univocal multiplication of classes", there are two operations which have operational status i.e., that of an inference rule.

1) "Logical multiplication" where given two criteria of classification, A and B, which have respectively n and m modalities (A1, A2, .., An, and B1, B2, .., Bm), the result of the multiplication of A and B is the set of (n x m) classes defined by the entire set of pairs (Ai,Bj).

2) "Logical division", which is the inverse of the preceding operation and which has the meaning of an abstraction: Given a set of objects identified by two characteristics A and B such as (A1Bj, A2Bj, ..., AnBj), the abstraction of Bj from the set of objects results in the set of modalities (A1, A2, ..., An).

The "bi-univocal multiplication of classes" is considered by Piaget

as the most general of the four grouping structures of classes.
However, this grouping has not led to much research. Multiple classification problems that have been used are much more varied than
the class-inclusion and seriation tasks. From a structural perspective, the problems used in experiments on multiple classification
can be divided into three groups. These three situations will be
described briefly below. A more detailed analysis of some problems
in the third group will be presented within a framework of computer
models.

2.2.1.1. The multiple classification problems

1) The first group of problems can be characterized as dealing with
the "logical multiplication" operation: Two series of modalities of
two classification criteria A and B are given, and the subject has
to identify or create objects AiBj. Two categories of problems can
be distinguished. (a) The subject is given a double entry table
whose cells are empty but whose rows and columns are labelled (e.g.,
the rows are labelled with colour spots and the columns with geometrical drawings), together with a set of objects (e.g., coloured
geometrical objects). He/she has to place the objects into the
cells of the table so that they are "correct" according to the labels of the table headings (Bastien, 1987; Bastien, de Oliviera and
Pinelli, 1982). (b) The subject receives two series of modalities
belonging to two criteria of classes A and B (e.g., transparent
plastic bags bearing various line drawings and pieces of paper of
different colours). He/she is asked to produce all the possible
"handkerchiefs" (Maury and Rogalski, 1970). As expected, the second
task is more difficult than the first because the second task requires a combinatorial procedure for controlling the completeness of
the product set. This procedure is not necessary in the first task
because the product set is complete when all the cells of the
double-entry table are filled up. Thus, although both tasks deal
with the logical multiplication operation, the two task environments
do not provide the same type of information. Hence the information
processing demands in the two tasks are not identical.

2) The second group of problems can be characterized as dealing with
the "logical division" operation. These are called "shifting
tasks". The subject is given a set of objects and some boxes and
asked to place the objects into the boxes and explain the principle
used to partition the objects. The experimenter then asks the subject whether another way for partitioning (either the same set of
objects or the same set plus some additional objects) can be found.
As in the class-inclusion task, empirical knowledge (i.e., knowledge
of the specific content) plays a very important role in this task.
Young children (6 years) carry out the shifting task successfully
(Laflaquière, 1979) when the material is based on colour and shape;
it is more difficult with other materials (Piaget and Inhelder,
1959; Smith and Baron, 1981).

3) The third group of problems can be characterized as dealing with
both the "logical division" and "logical multiplication" operations.
There are two major types of situations that use both a double entry
table without labels on the margins. (a) The subject has to fill in
a double entry table with objects representing the product of two
sets of modalities, shapes and colours. At the beginning, the table

is either empty or holds just one object placed in a cell (Bruner, Olver and Greenfield, 1966; Piaget and Inhelder, 1959; Nguyen-Xuan and Rousseau, 1979). (b) The subject is given a double entry table in which some cells are already filled with objects so that there is only one way to fill the empty cells and arrive at a correct double classification. The subject is either asked to place additional objects into the table or to choose an object from a pile to fill one or several empty cells (Piérault-le-Bonniec, 1972; Cauzinille, Mathieu and Nguyen-Xuan, 1982).

We presented both types of tasks to subjects aged 4;6 and 7;6 years (Nguyen-Xuan et al., 1983). Two global results should be mentioned: 1) Within category (b), the difficulty of the problem varied as a function of the configuration of the objects already placed in the table. 2) The most difficult problem of category (a) was easier than the most difficult problem of category (b). These differences have been explained by analysing the problems in terms of "knowledge that is just sufficient for solving the problem". An analysis of some of the category (b) problems is presented below. This analysis will lead to a developmental model of the multiple classification concept and specifically, the development of the understanding of a double entry table.

2.2.1.2. Just sufficient knowledge to solve double classification problems

The type of problem to be analysed is the following. The child is given a 3x3 double entry table without a margin label in which some cells are already filled with an object, and a pile of 27 objects of three different colours and shapes. He/she is asked to choose an object from the pile to fill an empty cell designated by the experimenter and marked with the sign "?". We used five different patterns of already-filled cells where a pattern is characterized by the number of objects (0, 1 or 2) in the two arrays (i.e., the row and the column) in which the intersecting cell is the empty cell to be filled. The five types of problems are consequently called P10, P11, P12, P20, P22 and their generic name will be Pij (see Figure 1). The whole set of problems belonging to the same type can be generated from any element of the set by permutation(s) of rows and/or columns, and/or transpositions of the matrix. The subjects were given one or two series of 10 Pij problems, each containing two of each of the five types of problems. The classification criteria used in these Pij problems are "shape" and "colour" with, respectively, the modalities: Triangle, square, circle; and red, blue, yellow.

To model the problem solving processes at different developmental levels, we made seven assumptions about the knowledge the subject might have. They are presented below in the order they are assumed to be acquired. The first five can be thought of as pragmatic knowledge related to the situation of filling in a double entry table. Only the remaining two can be considered as directly related to the logical concept of multiple classification. C7 is knowledge of the relation between the sub-classes (e.g., "red", "blue"...) and their super-class (e.g., colour). C6 is knowledge about class multiplication. Note that this knowledge about class multiplication is limited to modalities (e.g., "red" and "round") and does not necessa-

Figure 1:   Examples of problems Pij.

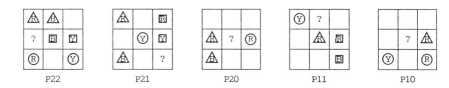

P22   P21   P20   P11   P10

rily imply that the child knows "red" and "blue" are equivalent under the class "colour". To simplify the presentation, we define the
seven assumptions in reference to the double entry table situation.
In these definitions, "similar" means that there is some common characteristic.

C1.   The objects in two adjacent cells are similar in some way.
C2.   The objects in different cells belonging to the same row or
        to the same column are similar in some way.
C3.   The objects in the cells belonging to the same row are
        similar in some way, but not identical.
C4.   An object has a shape and a colour: But "red" and "blue"
        do not make an object. Consequently, while looking for an
        object which is known to be red (or blue, or green), search
        space is limited to the modalities "round" or "square" or
        "triangle", and not the entire set of modalities describing
        the entire set of objects.
C5.   Two different cells cannot be filled in by identical
        objects.
C6.   An object in a given cell is similar in some way to the
        objects in the same row and similar in some way to the
        objects in the same column.
C7.   The parallel arrays of a table must be characterized by the
        modalities (e.g., "red", "blue"...) belonging to some
        common classification criterion (e.g., "colour").

The assumptions about the strategy for solving the Pij problems are:
1) Determine the characteristic(s) of the object to be placed in the
cell marked "?" by examining the objects already placed in the
table; 2) take the first object from the pile that bears the charac-
teristic(s) that has (have) been determined in the preceding stage.

We built 6 production systems called SP1, SP2, SP3, SP4, SP5, and
SP6. The functioning of these systems predicts all the observed individual protocols. A protocol is the pattern of choices that a
subject makes across a set of problems. A set is comprised of two
problems from each of the five different types, thus each set is
made up of 10 problems. We present below the just sufficient knowledge for each of the six production systems:

        (SP1: C1); (SP2: C2); (SP3: C3); (SP4: C3, C4, and C5);
        (SP5: C3, C4, C5, and C6); (SP6: C3, C4, C5, C6, and C7).

Except for two cases, it was possible to categorize each protocol with one of these production systems. Two criteria were used for identifying a production with a protocol: (1) For a given Pij problem, a given production system deduces, rightly or wrongly, the characteristic(s) of the object that will fill in the cell marked "?" from the pattern of already placed objects. The objects bearing this (these) characteristic(s) compose the set of objects that are accepted as correct by the system for this problem. A protocol is identified with a production system if the object chosen by the subject for any problem Pij is within the set of objects accepted by the system for this problem. (2) If a protocol can be identified with more than one production system, then choose the most sophisticated system (as defined by the seven above mentioned assumptions C1 to C7). There is a good correspondance between age and level of "sophistication" (increasing from SP1 to SP6) of the systems, as well as intra-individual consistency. 56 subjects (from 4;6 to 7;6) were given two series of 10 problems, hence each subject produced two protocols. For 40 subjects, both protocols were classified by the same production system. For 15 subjects, the two protocols were identified with two different production systems. Nevertheless, the production system of the second protocol was always the most sophisticated of the two production systems. One subject could not be classified.

Figure 2 presents an example of the sets of objects accepted by the production systems SP1, SP2, SP3, SP4 and SP5 for five exemplars of Pij problems. SP6 is not presented because for any problem Pij in which the objects are characterized by only two class criteria (e.g. coloured geometric objects), only the logically correct answer is accepted. Of course, the set of objects accepted by a system varies between problems belonging to the same type. It should be noted that although both SP1 and SP2 do not systematically find the logically correct solution to any problem, the set of accepted answers are different.

Technically, the main relations between the six systems are the following (cf. details in Nguyen-Xuan et al., 1983). System SP4 is built first and includes 20 production rules. System SP3 uses eleven of these twenty rules. Systems SP1 and SP2 include, respectively, five and eleven rules. Some of these rules belong to SP4 and others are rules of SP4 where the condition side is modified. The system SP5 is made up from SP4 by adding two new rules, by modifying the condition side of three rules, and by modifying the action side of one rule. The system SP6 is made up from SP5 by adding three new rules and by modifying the action side of one rule.

Two results should be pointed out. 1) Knowledge C7 is the only one that establishes an equivalence relationship between subclasses in respect to a superclass i.e., "blue, red ... are all colours". Although this is quite elementary knowledge, it is assumed to exist only for the most sophisticated system, system SP6. 2) By assuming C4, which is rather pragmatic in nature, the object to be put in an empty cell can be defined by applying the "logical division" operation only once. Indeed, the process of determining the characteristics of the object to be put in an empty cell is to first apply the class division operation to find the modality common to all objects in the same row (or column). Let us suppose that the result is "red". Next simply match the lacking feature (the shape) with some

Figure 2:   Patterns of compatible answers for the five problems of
the Figure 1:   The striped cells of a matrix represent
the choices the systems SP1, SP2, SP3, SP4, and SP5
would accept for each problem.

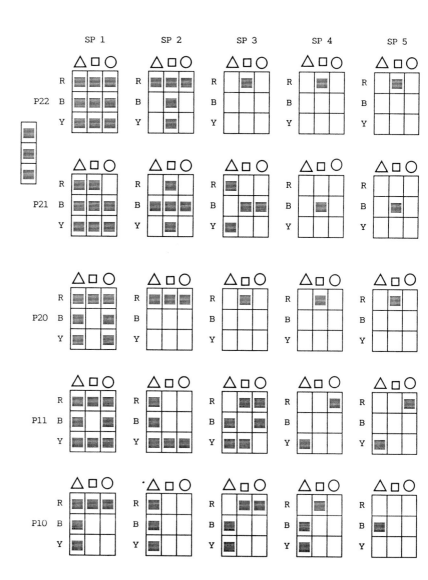

object that is in the same column (or row).

In conclusion, Piaget assumed that double classification tasks imply applying twice the "direct" and "inverse" operations of the grouping "bi-univocal multiplication of classes". Our model, based on the concept of "just sufficient knowledge", shows that when the objects are defined by only two criteria (e.g., shape and colour), they can be double classified successfully by applying the logical division only once. This is because we take into account the pragmatic knowledge of the kind "red and blue do not make an object". Of course, if the objects are defined by more than two criteria, and if the task is to double classify them, the operations "direct" and "inverse" will be needed twice. That is what we have shown (Nguyen-Xuan et al, 1983) by giving the same children double classification tasks with objects made up of either two or three criteria. This illustrates again the idea that structurally isomorphic tasks may require different inference rules depending on the nature of the information that is available.

2.2.2. The relation of order and the construction of a series

The seriation problems are considered by Piaget as excellent situations to study the mastery of the grouping known as "addition of asymetrical relations" (Piaget, 1941, 1972). Any seriation problem can be described as follows. To begin, there is a set of unranked objects that can be organized by an order relation and the goal state is an arrangement of the objects in a spatial configuration consistent with this order relation. Pioneering research by Baylor and his colleagues has shown how the information processing approach can explain the phenomenon of horizontal decalage (e.g., Baylor and Gascon, 1974; Baylor and Lemoyne, 1976). Subsequent, other research has studied the seriation behaviors in more detail to detect or model the different methods used by children (e.g., Gilliéron, 1976; Young, 1976; Retschitzki, 1978). Several methods have been detected, but the two established by Piaget ("search for the extremum" and "insertion") remain the most stable. Frey (1964) and Nguyen-Xuan (1976) insisted on the importance of distinguishing between procedures which effectively apply the transitive inference rule and those which do not. For example, they demonstrated that applying the method "search for the extremum" implies an understanding of the transitivity property of the order relation, but it does not necessarily imply the use of the transitive inference rule. As is shown in section 2.1.2, the subject can find "the most X" either by using the transitive inference rule R3 to generate information, or without using this rule. In the latter case, the information must be searched for in the external environment. Moreover, Frey (1964) demonstrated that of all the "operations" for the "addition of asymetrical relations" grouping, only what Piaget called the "transitive operation" has the status of an "operation" for a logician. Hence, the seriation task involves a unique operation in the logical sense.

2.2.2.1. Inference rules and order relation

The issue we will discuss in this section deals with the transitive inference rule and its reciprocal. We will consider the weight seriation task because it is a situation where the information about "the most X" cannot be obtained with a single request as in the

length seriation task. The complete transitive inference rule can
be expressed as follows:

If X>Y and Y>Z, then X>Z and (Y between X and Z).

The reciprocal of this rule is:

If X>Z and (Y between X and Z), then X>Y and Y>Z.

The reciprocal rule is considered understood by the subject when
he/she "efficiently" uses the insertion method i.e., he/she does not
make a redundant weighting. Indeed, while searching the place of a
new element N, the subject must know that the place of N is between
two adjacent elements X and Y so that X>N and N>Y. Thus, its place
is determined as soon as X and Y have been identified. This comprehension is not necessary for the seriation method "search for the
extremum". If this "extremum" method is considered by Piaget as the
"operational method", then the "insertion" method is the most general (Frey, 1964; Nguyen-Xuan, 1976) and the frequency of its use
increases with age (Gilliéron, 1976; Nguyen-Xuan and Hoc, 1987).

However, it is necessary to differentiate between understanding an
inference rule and effectively using it. In the seriation task, if
the subject uses the insertion method without weighting redundantly,
he/she demonstrates that he/she understands the reciprocal of the
complete transitive inference rule. However this does not insure
that this reciprocal rule can be effectively applied. Unfortunately, in the classical seriation situation, one cannot observe whether
or not it is applied because it is not necessary in any case.
Therefore, to observe the use of the reciprocal rule, we built a
seriation task called IB (for "insensible balance", c.f. Frey and
Nguyen-Xuan, 1983). This task, described below, is formally related
to a task used by Piaget (1974) in his study on how children resolve
contradictions.

To make it very clear to the subject, the IB task is presented after
two phases of an exercise. 1) The subject is asked to solve the
classical problem of weight seriation by means of a Roberval balance. The objects are 11 boxes, which are filled before him with 1, 2
... 10, 11 metal nails. 2) The initial balance is replaced by a
less sensitive one that operates in a way such that if two boxes
containing nails differing in number by only one are placed on each
of the two trays, the trays remain balanced. This is demonstrated
with several pairs of open boxes with which the subject is asked to
predict whether or not the insensible balance will tilt. 3) IB
task: The experimenter takes 11 new empty match boxes and, in front
of the subject, introduces respectively 1, 2, 3, ... 10, 11 nails
into the 11 boxes. He closes them and mixes the boxes. The subject
has to rank order the boxes according to their weight by using the
insensible balance.

It should be noted that the initial and goal states of the IB problem are the same as those in the classical seriation problem. The
characteristic of the IB situation, which differentiates it from the
classical situation, is that in the IB task, there are two different
types of information: 1) The balance inclines on the X side, which
means that "X is heavier than Y" and that "X and Y are not adjacent

in the final series"; 2) the balance does not incline, which means
"X and Y are adjacent".

In order to reach the goal "find a total order" i.e., characterize
every pair (X,Y) with the relation "heavier than", the subject must
coordinate the two types of information by applying inference rules
that are not necessary in the classical weight seriation task. Indeed, since the balance is not sensitive enough, the relation X>Y
cannot be determined for all the pairs (X,Y) based on the pragmatic
inference rule "if the balance inclines on the side of box X, then X
is heavier than Y". The following are two examples of logical inference rules needed for the insensible balance situation, but useless
for the classical seriation task:

- If X is contiguous to Y and Y is contiguous to Z,
  then Y is between X and Z.

- If X is heavier than Z and Y is between X and Z,
  then X is heavier than Y and Y is heavier than Z.

The Insensible Balance problem has, in fact, a very rich structure
compared to classical seriation problems. We present below a formalization taking into account the temporal dimension of the process
of solving the IB problem. This formalization makes explicit some
interesting inference rules and is useful as a tool for analyzing
the individual protocols in the IB task.

2.2.2.2. Formalization of the Insensible Balance task

Let us consider a set of n objects to be ranked in a total order by
the subject. The subject weighs different pairs of objects. The
result of a weighting will be termed "information obtained by request". Other pieces of information can be inferred by applying
inference rules which will be defined. *At a given stage of the resolution process*, each pair of objects can be defined according to
two types of binary relations, "order" and "contiguity", as follows:

1) Considering one pair of objects according to the relation "order", either the order between X and Y is determined or not yet determined. This will be noted by "X>Y" and "X?Y", respectively.

2) Considering the pair (X,Y) according to the relation "contiguity",
three cases are possible: a) X and Y are contiguous; b) X and Y are
not contiguous; c) the contiguity has not yet been determined. This
will be noted by, respectively, "X.Y", "X,X" and "X;Y ".

The four *elementary* inference rules, which have as premises two binary relations and as a conclusion one or two binary relations, are:

1. X>Y and Y>Z --> X>Z and X,Z
2. X.Y and Y.Z --> X,Z
3. X>Y and Z.X --> Z>Y
4. X>Y and Z.Y --> X>Z

There are six combinations of the two relations "order" and "contiguity". They will each be given a name which will be adopted in the
discussion that follows ("undetermined" signifies that no informa-

tion is available at that very moment):

* Ordered and contiguous: ⟨X.Y⟩, object called CHAIN;
* Ordered and non-contiguous: ⟨X,Y⟩, object called SERIES;
* Ordered and of undetermined contiguity: ⟨X;Y⟩, object called
  SLOPE;
* Order undetermined and contiguous: [X.Y], object called STONE;
* Order undetermined and non-contiguous: [X,Y], object called GROUP;
* Order and contiguity undetermined: [X;Y] object called MAGMA.

The same names "Chain", "Series", "Slope", "Stone", "Group" or
"Magma" can be given to a set comprised of m (where m≥2) elementary
objects (e.g. match boxes), which will be called an "Assemblage".
For instance, an Assemblage-Chain of 4 elements ⟨X.Y.Z.U⟩; or an
Assemblage-Stone of five elements: [X.Y.Z.U.V]. The above four
elementary inference rules can be used for transforming the Assemblages. For example, if the information {A.B, B.C, C.D, D.E} is
obtained by request, a Stone is determined: [A.B.C.D.E]. If later
the information A>C is obtained by request, the elementary inference
rules allow one to infer other pieces of information about the pairs
of this set of five elements, and the Stone becomes a Chain:
⟨A.B.C.D.E⟩. The notion of "Assemblage" is interesting because it
allows one to define macro-rules of inference which can manipulate a
set of objects. For example:

        [A.B.C.D] & A>C --> ⟨A.B.C.D⟩,
        macro-rule for transformation: Stone --> Chain.

        [A.B.C] & ⟨D.E.F⟩ & D.A --> ⟨C.B.A.D.E.F⟩,
        macro-rule for transformation: Stone & Chain --> Chain.

By extension, and considering by convention that an elementary object (e.g. a match box) is a degenerated Stone, more complex objects
can be defined which will be called "Lists". A List is an Assemblage, the elements of which are Assemblages or Lists. The notion of a
List is interesting because it allows one to describe, in a conden-
sed manner, the successive structures of the elementary objects'
set, as the subject proceeds with the information request (i.e., the
sequence of weightings). It also helps one to identify the macro-
rules applied by the subject.

In an exploratory experiment, we gave 24 subjects, aged 10 to 12
years, the Insensible Balance problem (two trials). Earlier, all
the subjects had succeeded in solving the classical problem of
weight seriation. The two most interesting results are: 1) All the
subjects succeeded in finding, at least once, the correct solution
through a verification process based on the following knowledge: In
the final series, except for the two extremes of the series, every
object X must be between two objects Y and Z such that X.Y and X.Z;
i.e., the balance does not incline if the two trays bear either,
respectively, X and Y, or Y and Z.   2) The subjects are differentiated by their application of the macro-rules which transform the
Assemblages. We found that the manipulations of the Stone cause the
most problems; for instance, the two above mentioned macro-rules are
among the most difficult. This is probably because these rules for
transforming Assemblage-Stones consist of a complex coordination of
the contiguity and order relations. The result of this coordination

is an order relation which cannot be obtained by request (i.e., by using the balance).

Figure 3:   Examples of protocoles for the IB problem.

SUJET 1	(1)	(2)	(3)	(4)	(5)
Information	B>D	C.B	A.B	D.E	D.A
Established list	<B,D>	<[B.C],D>	<[A.B.C],D>	<[A.B.C],[D.E]>	<C.B.A.D.E>
Subject's arrangment of objects	B,D B D ⟶	C C B D ⟶	A C B A D ⟶	E C B A D E ⟶	C B A D E

SUJET 2	(1)	(2)	(3)	(4)	(5)
Information	A.B	C.B	D.E	B>D	D.A
Established list	[A.B]	[A.B.C]	<[A.B.C],[D.E]>	<[A.B.C],[D.E]>	<C.B.A.D.E>
Subject's arrangment of objects	A B ⟶	C A B C ⟶	D,E A B C D E ⟶	A B C D E ⟶	D A B C E

The example in Figure 3 shows that for the same set of five objects and given the same set of information, the Lists that are gradually established are different; thus, the macro-rules applied to transform the Assemblages making up each List are different. The subject S1 found the right solution, but he/she never had to apply the macro-rule for transforming two Stones of a Series-List into a Chain. The order of information he/she obtained by request is such that the spatial disposition he/she chose for the Stones is compatible with the correct solution, whereas subject S2 arranged the objects in a way that the solution could only be found if he/she applies this inference rule.

This example also allows us to emphasize two important characteristics of the method we proposed for analysing the individual protocols:

1) By taking into account the temporal dimension i.e., considering the order in which the information has been obtained by request, our model of analysis demonstrates that, in fact, the two subjects S1 and S2 faced progressively different scenarios.

2) A precise method of individual protocol analysis may disclose a complete consistency in the subject's behaviors, whereas a more global analysis based on the same behaviors may lead to the conclusion that the subject is "unstable". For instance, let us suppose that the two protocols of Figure 3 belong to the same subject, who twice tried to resolve the Insensible Balance problem. If the whole set of information obtained by request is considered without taking

into account the order in which the pieces of information were obtained, the two sets are identical. Hence, the subject would have
been considered "unstable" because although he/she had processed the
same set of information in both trials, he/she found the correct solution on the first but failed on the second. Our model of analysis
demonstrates, however, that in the first trial, the subject did not
need to use inference rules manipulating Stones and that he/she did
not know how to use them in the second trial.

2.3. Conclusion

Developmental research which focusses on cognitive processes shows
that our understanding of a child's knowledge as well as the way
he/she uses his/her knowledge in different domains can be refined.
We have tried to demonstrate that this leads to a new way of asking
questions and looking at the child. Particularly, we showed that:

1) If the "information processing demands" are analysed in terms of
"just sufficient knowledge", it is possible to distinguish between
"logical" knowledge, which applies to various domains, and pragmatic
knowledge, which is domain specific. It is then possible to define
more precisely the operations linked with "logico-mathematical" concepts in order to examine their coordination and to study the construction of new "logical" knowledge.

2) The concept of "instability of behaviors during transition periods", just like the concept of "decalage" (vertical and horizontal), is useful for understanding cognitive development. However,
this "instability" could be examined from a positive point of view.
The information processing approach looks for mechanisms that produce successful as well as unsuccessful behaviors, emphasizes the analysis of the task environment while studying a child's knowledge and
assumes that the child is consistent. This perspective leads to
distinguishing between an apparently unstable behavior and a basically unstable one. The first type of instability can be explained
in terms of variability in behavior due to the variability of tasks
or scenarios within a task. The second type of instability can be
explained in terms of a "random choice" between available behaviors
(for instance, Siegler's model for the child's knowledge on addition, 1986), or else in terms of the co-existence of two contradictory inference systems (Piaget, 1974).

3. PHYSICAL COGNITION AND QUALITATIVE REASONING

3.1. Preliminary questions

The importance ascribed to ordinal relations like "more than", "less
than" and "same as" in the developmental psychology literature is
striking. But it is not surprising when one considers that several
neo-Piagetian models of cognitive development (Case, 1987a; Siegler,
1981) asssume that the child first establishes rules or representational systems of a qualitative type before being able to reason
with those of a quantitative type. This hypothesis is compatible
with the Piagetian model which stipulates that the "scheme of proportionality requires a qualitative operational system as a necessary and sufficient condition" (Inhelder and Piaget, 1955). However,

what is the status of qualitative/quantitative relations from the
subject's point of view ?

It should be emphasized that most of the work on physical cognition
is limited to particular classes of situations. For example, for
time reasoning, the classical paradigm consists of judging the relative duration of two lights in three types of problems: 1/ Where
the events to be compared start and stop simultaneously, 2/ where
the events start one after the other and stop simultaneously, and 3/
where the events start simultaneously and stop one after the other
(Levin, 1977, 1982; Levin, Goldstein and Zelniker, 1984; Montangero,
1977; Richie and Bickhard, 1988). For physical reasoning, the balance beam paradigm is limited to one type of problem i.e., the horizontal position of the beam (Case, 1985; Ferretti and Butterfield,
1986; Kerkman and Wright, 1988; Siegler, 1981; Strauss and Ephron-
Wertheim, 1986). Generalizations from the proposed models beyond
the classical experimental situations is questionable. One question
is whether one can make predictions when the information is presented in the form of a hypothetical statement problem ?

In many situations, such as problems with three variables , the
steps preceding the mastery of the quantitative relations are characterized by the use of undetermined relations (Inhelder and Piaget,
1955). For instance, in the balance beam problem the relations
"heavier" and "less distant" (on side X) lead to a state of indecision. Therefore, three states of the physical system are possible.
In the time domain, the relations "started before" and "longer duration" (for lamp X) lead to three possible relations concerning the
extinction order of the lights; namely, where X is before Y. In the
space domain, the relations "beyond point 1" and "beyond point 2"
(concerning stick X) allow one to infer three possible relations
concerning their relative lengths. In the kinematic domain (time-
distance-speed problems) the relations "more distance" and "more
time" (for some mobile X) lead to a state of indecision concerning
their relative speeds.

However, certain pairs of relations can be decided, for example,
"more distance" and "less time" for the mobile X. For problems with
three variables, twenty one couples of relations are decidable (they
lead to a single correct answer) and six couples of relations are
not decidable because there are three possible answers. Note that
the undecidable relations change into decidable ones within a metric. Here are some examples of decidable relations concerning the
previously mentioned domains of knowledge: "Heavier" and "more
distant" (on side X, balance beam problem); "started before" and
"stopped after" (duration-succession problem), "behind point 1" and
"in front of point 2" (length-position problem); "more distance" and
"less time" (time-distance-speed problem). What do we know about
the stages preceding this metrical phase or "product of measures"
(Vergnaud, 1983) ? What is the status of the undetermined relations ? What is the relationship between the process of decidabili-
ty/undecidability and cognitive systems ?

3.2. Some conceptual tools

The proposed model is part of a series of theoretical studies concerning the development of temporal reasoning (Crépault, 1978a,

1978b, 1980, 1983, 1988b). The model applies to situations that
have "three variables" e.g., time, distance, velocity (in the case
of kinematic events); duration, initial order, final order (in the
case of non-kinematic events); weight, distance, beam position (in
the case of balance beam problem), etc.

The theoretical model is based on a class of experimental situations
dealing with the composition of two distinct motions where time and
velocity have to be judged on the basis of a ribbon of paper marked
with dots and dashes. These marks are produced by a pencil that
touches the paper with a certain rhythm. The pencil motion is coupled with a translation motion of the ribbon of paper. The verbal
information from the experimenter specifies the type of composition:

1/ Type I problems: Periodical frequency (the pencil beats at the
same rhythm) while the speed of the paper ribbon varies;

2/ Type II problems: The pencil beats with a variable frequency
while the paper ribbons advances at a constant velocity.

For type I problems, the pencil marks the paper at regular intervals
while the ribbon moves faster and faster. At the beginning this
produces dots close to one another, followed by dashes at wider and
wider intervals, when the speed of the paper increases. Subjects
knew that the "pencil's frequency" was constant. They had to judge
whether the ribbon moved faster (and whether it took more time) between two close successive dots or between two successive dashes that
were wide apart. It should be noted that duration is defined by, on
one hand, the indication of the periodical frequency (the "pencil's
duration") and, on the other hand, by the ribbon's motion (the "ribbon's duration").

The results of these experiments demonstrate that most subjects,
from eleven year olds through adults, make different judgements based on the duration defined according to the frequency indication
("pencil's duration") and the duration defined according to the
translation indication (the time interval concerning the shifting of
the ribbon between two marks); for example, the subjects believe
that the "pencil's duration" is constant, and that the "ribbon's
duration" (translation-mark) varies according to the velocity or the
distance. The errors observed, which mostly concern the "ribbon's
duration", suggest that there is a special status for the relations
between speed and time; namely, "faster" means "less time", and "same speed" means "same time".

Based on the empirical data, different levels of organisation of kinematic relations have been established (Crépault, 1989). At the
first level (L-1), the inverse relationship between velocity and
distance (where "faster entails less distance") is associated only
with the direct relationship between distance and time ("more time
entails more distance"). A second level (L-2) is characterized by
the use of the direct relationship between speed and distance, this
relationship being associated with the direct or inverse relationship between distance and time. At a third level (L-3 where "pencil's duration" is constant), the inverse relationship between distance and time ("more time entails less distance") is coordinated
with the direct relationship between velocity and distance. A

fourth level (L-4) is characterized by the use of a common duration either for the type I problems or type II problems; for example, the "pencil's duration" and "ribbon's duration" are constant for the type I problem and variable for the type II problems. Finally, at the last level (L-5), subjects give correct answers concerning velocity, "pencil's duration" and "ribbon's duration" for type I and type II problems. Very few adolescents and adults reach this last level. Note that levels L-2 and L-4 are relatively unstable in time (for a series of experimental situations). The subjects in L-2 move mainly to level L-1 or L-3 and the subjects in L-4 go partly back to level L-3 (Crépault, 1989).

3.2.1. States of general knowledge and inferred knowledge

Our main hypothesis is that there are two main types of knowledge that the subject applies to a given situation. On one hand, there are general states of knowledge (GK) which are applied to several fields of cognition (e.g. kinematic cognition, spatial cognition, temporal cognition, etc.). On the other hand, states of inferred knowledge (IK) are based on general knowledge and the situation (e.g. the instructions, the experimental interview, the questions, etc.). These two types of knowledge are interdependent i.e., part of the general knowledge can be substituted by inferred knowledge and thus produce new general knowledge.

What is the relationship between general knowledge, inferred knowledge, and the "logical" and "empirical" inference rules ? In the case of the proposed model, the two types of rules are basic components of general knowledge and inferred knowledge. A "logical component" can be defined as a component independent of content: For example, couples of relations defined in terms of decidable or undecidable relations (dyadic relations). However, an empirical component of GK/IK can be defined as a component characterized by both the specific knowledge of one domain (e.g. temporal, kinematic, spatial, etc.), and the specific knowledge related to the task.

3.2.2. Stable and unstable cognitive systems

Two basic mechanisms between GK and IK must be assumed:

1) When general and inferred states of knowledge are compatible, the system is called "structurally stable" because newly constructed "theoretical objects" are similar to the "initial theoretical objects" in the state of knowledge.

2) When general and inferred states of knowledge are incompatible, the system is called "structurally unstable" because inferred and initial "objects" are contradictory.

In the case of unstable systems, the model applies two mechanisms to eliminate certain knowledge states:

- Inferred states of knowledge are eliminated but the general knowledge states remain. In this case, the inferred relation could be more "fragile" than one that is part of the initial system.

- Inferred knowledge states replace part of the general knowledge
state. In this case, a new organization of general knowledge
is created that is structurally stable.

The following is an example of two types of processes for kinematic
relations. We assume that the subject's general knowledge state is
defined by three "theoretical objects" consisting of symmetrical relations of two dimensions (dyadic relations):

1) Direct relation between velocity and distance. Faster entails
more distance, or less fast entails less distance. This relation
can be symbolized as follows: V+ → D+ and symetrically D+ → V+;
hence D+ ←→ V+ which in this paper will be written V+D+;

2) Inverse relation between velocity and time: V+ → T-, V- → T+;

3) Direct relation between distance and time: T+ → D+, T- → D-.

The model uses a composition of the couples "V+T-" and "T-D-" (GK);
this leads to a new relation (IK) through the transitive inference
rule: Inverse relationship between velocity and distance (V+D-).
Note that this last relation (V+D-: IK) is, of course, incompatible
with the initial relation (V+D+: GK). The cognitive system
(V+D+/V+D-,T-D-,V+T-) is then structurally unstable.

Two possibilities arise:

Either the inverse relationship between velocity and distance is
eliminated (IK) and the direct relationship between velocity and
distance remains (type I mechanism), or the direct relationship
between velocity and distance (type II mechanism) is substituted by
the inverse relationship between velocity and distance. In the latter case, the system is then structurally stable (e.g. V+D-, V+T-)
and the couples T-D- and V+T- generate the relation V+D- which is
compatible with the initial relation.

3.2.3. Status of the decidable and undecidable relations

Generally, the stable and unstable cognition systems are defined by
any combination of three couples of decidable or undecidable relations, dR and uR, respectively. How are these relations coordinated ?

The model assumes a dyadic composition of relations i.e., variables
are composed two by two. For example, for kinematic relations, the
direct relationship between velocity and distance is independent of
the third variable (time). The distinction we made between decidable and undecidable relations reflects decidable and undecidable
wordings. It should be remembered that, in the case of problems
with three variables (qualitative relations), one can define either
decidable wordings (21 couples of relations) or undecidable wordings
(6 couples of relations). In the first case, the obtained information allows the inference of only one correct relation, whereas in
the second case, three relations are possible (indeterminate relations).

In the case of the physical model (when the composition of variables

is three by three), the undecidability naturally concerns the third
variable. For example, for temporal relations, the couple "started
before-stopped before" ("the red lamp one goes on before the green
light" and "the red lamp goes out before the green light") entails
three possible answers related to duration: "More time", "less
time" or "same time". In the case of the proposed model, the decidable (dR) or the undecidable (uR) relations are defined by relation
couples of two variables (e.g. "before 1" entails "before 2", "before 1" entails "less time", etc.). Thus considering, for example,
temporal inequality relations, six decidable and six undecidable relations are obtained. This is also true for other fields of physical knowledge.

3.2.4. Theoretical objects and inferential schemes

The concept of theoretical objects is defined by a series of inferential schemes: Relative couples of the three variables. In fact,
each object is characterized by four inferential schemes (e.g.,
"more X → less Y", "less X → more Y", "more Y → less X ", "less Y →
less X"). In kinematics (Crépault, 1978b, 1983), five theoretical
objects are postulated:

1) The direct relationship between time and distance (object Tx):
More time entails more distance, or less time entails less distance
and vice-versa;

2) The inverse relation between time and distance (object Tx*):
More time entails less distance or less time entails more distance
and vice-versa;

3) The inverse relationship between velocity and time (object Tv*):
Faster entails less time or less fast entails more time and vice-
versa;

4) The direct relationship between velocity and distance (object
Vx): Faster entails more distance or less fast entails less distance and vice-versa;

5) The inverse relationship between velocity and distance (object
Vx*): Faster entails less distance or less fast entails more distance and vice-versa.

The theoretical objects (1), (3) and (4) are undecidable relationships whereas the objects (2) and (5) are decidable relationships.
It is important to remember that the object Tv* (operator's status)
allows one to build new theoretical objects (inferred relations) based on the "initial objects"; the operator transforms a decidable
relation in an undecidable relation and vice-versa. The inferred
states of knowledge are deduced from these theoretical objects and
within the defined general framework, the general states of knowledge represent a subset of two theoretical objects plus the operator.

3.2.5. Stable and unstable cognitive systems and decidable/
undecidable relations

3.2.5.1. Definition of the stable cognitive systems

Stable cognitive systems are defined by the following basic components:

      1) {dR, uR, uR} (three possible systems)
      2) {dR, dR, dR} (one system only).

The first general system is characterized by a decidable (dR) and
two undecidable relations; three "subsystems" are thus possible:
{dR1, uR2, uR3}, {dR2, uR1, uR3} or {dR3, uR1, uR2}. The second
general system deals with three decidable relations: {dR1, dR2,
dR3}. In the case of the four proposed subsystems, the deduced relation (inferred knowledge) based on two couples of relations is
part of the subsystem (0: operation of composition):

      - dR 0 uR = uR
      - uR 0 uR = dR
      - dR 0 dR = dR

Note that each system includes two subsystems (cf. 3.3.1).

The following are some examples of stable systems. We consider the
system {dR1, uR2, uR3} in the domain of kinematic relations and assume that the relation dR is defined by the theoretical object Vx*
(inverse relationship between velocity and distance). Furthermore,
the two uR relations are defined respectively by the theoretical
objects Tx (direct relationship between time and distance) and the
operator Tv* (inverse relationship between time and velocity).

The objects Vx*, Tx and the operator Tv* (inverse relationship between velocity and time) constitute the gamma state.

Within a stable system, the composition of the object-operator Tv*
with the object Tx allows for the construction of a new object Vx*
(the inverse relationship between velocity and distance) which is
compatible with the initial object. In other words, in the first
step, the inferential schemes "faster entails less time" and "less
time entails less space" are activated. In the second step, these
two schemes are combined to produce the inverse relationship between
velocity and distance ("faster entails less distance"), the latter
being compatible with the initial relation. Within the system {dR,
uR, uR}, the beta state made up of the objects Vx, Tx* and the operator Tv* can also be defined.

What predictions can a stable system make ? How does one arrive at
a judgment concerning a subject's level of knowledge ? If the subject's answer is of the type: "Faster: Less distance" (answer B),
according to the model, all but one single theoretical object (Vx*)
can be predicted. Since the object Vx* is specific to the gamma
state (structurally stable), answer B is an expression of the transformation laws of gamma. As a result, only answers like: "More
time: More distance" can be predicted. Concerning the inverse relationship between time and distance (object Tx*), which is an

object specific to the beta state, the reasoning is analogous (Crépault, 1978a, 1989). Based on this last answer, the model predicts only answers like: "Faster: More distance". Once the subject's first answers are known, the model can predict a series of answers.

3.2.5.2. Definition of unstable cognitive systems

The possible unstable cognitive systems are defined as follows:

(c) {dR, dR, uR} (three possible systems)
(d) {uR, uR, uR} (only one system).

System (c) is characterized by two decidable relations (dR) and one undecidable relation (uR). System (d) is characterized by three undecidable relations.

Examining the formal properties of the system {uR1, uR2, uR3}, it must be noted that two undecidable relations entail a new decidable relation:

uR1 0 uR2 = dR3.

The relation dR3 is then incompatible with the "initial relation" uR3. The system then becomes transformed:

{uR1, uR2, uR3} --> {uR1, uR2, uR3/dR3} -->
{uR1, uR2, uR3} (unstable) or {uR1, uR2, dR3} (stable).

The following are some examples of unstable systems. Consider the system {uR1, uR2, uR3} within the context of kinematic relations. The relations uR can be assumed to correspond with the following theoretical objects: Vx, Tx and Tv* (the alpha state).

Within the level of knowledge alpha, the relation deduced from the inverse relation velocity-time (operator Tv*) and the direct relation velocity-distance (object Vx) leads to the new inverse relationship between time and distance (Tx*) which is incompatible with Tx (the initial theoretical object).

Two mechanisms of elimination are possible at this point: Either the object Tx is eliminated which would then transform the system from the alpha state to a structurally stable state (beta) or the object Tx* is eliminated (inferred relation) and the original general state of knowledge is maintained.

Finally, one would expect that the number of alpha-state behaviors (unstable states of knowledge) to be reduced by one half at each trial, since two states are possible, based on alpha.

3.2.5.3. Remarks

Although the theoretical system looks like a mathematical structure, the postulated system has many non-mathematical characteristics. First, in mathematics, structures are non-temporal. The same applies to the structures of "grouping" and the INRC group (Piaget, 1941, 1972), which are the structures that underlie operational

thinking. From our perspective, the concept of structure or system
has a temporal component. Moreover, in the course of the knowledge
structure's transformation, the system applies a dialectic process
between general and inferred states of knowledge. The inferred
states of knowledge transform the subject's general knowledge which,
in turn, becomes integrated into the subjet's general knowledge.
Briefly, the built up states of knowledge are new at each step, except in the case of structurally stable system where the inferred
relations (IK) are compatible with the initial relations (GK).

3.2.6. Developmental filiation of the cognitive systems

According to our main developmental hypothesis, development is characterized by alternating structurally stable and unstable cognitive
systems. This is analogous to the equilibration process (Piaget,
1975; Piaget and Garcia, 1983, 1987). One of the basic problems of
developmental cognitive psychology concerns the description and explanation of the mechanisms of transition from one cognitive level
to another (Klahr, 1984; Wallace et al., 1987).

Are certain states of knowledge unstable ? According to Piaget's
classical experiments on conservation the "intermediary levels" seem
to reflect this character of conceptual instability. Likewise, the
third relevant rule postulated by Siegler (1981) for the balance
beam problem is of the same nature. The recent neopiagetian models
(see Case, 1987b) generally postulate a certain degree of coherence
at each level of development. In our perspective, the behaviors of
the intermediary level correspond to an unstable cognitive system
i.e., an incompatibility between general states of knowledge and inferred states of knowledges. But as opposed to Piaget, we assume
that the knowledge states are reorganized at another level with
their own "structure". We would thus have a succession of cognitive
systems that are not necessarily hierarchically ordered, for example, like those found in information processing models (Fischer and
Farrar, 1987; Nguyen-Xuan et al., 1983; Siegler, 1981; Case, 1985).
In fact, it is suggested that certain relations are privileged (such
as the operator's status) in the course of cognitive development and
the operator is found in both structurally stable and unstable cognitive systems (Crépault, 1983, 1989). An important aspect of the
model is that the operator can become a "conceptual obstacle" that
gets eliminated in the course of development to allow a triadic
construction of ordinal relations (a structural change from dyadic
to triadic relations).

3.2.7. Structural pole and functional pole

So far, we have theoretically defined the structural components of
the model in terms of stable/unstable systems. A precise description for its subsystems (three couples or relations each) can be
defined:

Beta1 = V+D+, V+T-, D+T-;

and

Beta2 = V-D-, V-T+, D-T+;

Note that Beta1 and Beta2 represent the components of the theoretical object Tx*.

The functional component concerns the processes applied at the level of subsystems. We assume that, in the case of the hypothetical wordings, two "elements" belong to different subsystems. Which subsystem is released ?

Two types of rules (meta-rules) can be postulated:

1) Primary rules permitting one to select the subsystems for at least two classes of problems;

2) Secondary rules selecting subsystems for the third class of problems (Crépault, 1988).

For example, we assume that the final succession orders (e.g., "the red lamp turns off after the green lamp") have priority. It can then be possible to apply the subsystems for the problems of type T1f & T2f (information on succession orders: E.g., lamp R turns on after..." and "lamp R turns off before..."). The problems of type T1 & ΔT assume a second rule e.g., the secondary rule "ΔT". Note that in certain cases, the primary rule is sufficient (e.g., subsystems SAP of SAV, 3.3.1).

3.3. Applications of the model regarding the relations duration-successions

Up until now, most research on the development of temporal reasoning as a part of kinematics (time-distance-velocity relations), was limited to one particular class of problems (Levin, 1977, 1982; Levin, Goldstein and Zelniker, 1984; Levin, Wilkening and Dembo, 1984; Montangero, 1977, 1984).

The classical experimental paradigm consists of presenting a child with information concerning the temporal order of two displayed lamps that are each switched on and off. This leads to three problem types: Those that involve synchronicity, end-problem types, and beginning types in which the subject is asked to judge the lights' relative duration. An important result of these studies is the observation that a young child, in favourable situations, can set up a notion of duration that is partly compatible with the logical model and takes into account initial and/or final succession orders. Moreover, recent data (Levin et al., 1984; Montangero, 1981) suggest that children more often compare durations correctly when durations differ in ending times rather than in beginning times. Although a young child gathers information concerning temporal orders (high recall) for end-problem and beginning problem types, he/she finds it very difficult to integrate initial and final temporal successions: "Children may recall beginnings just as well as endings but nevertheless perform better on end-differing duration problems because they fail to integrate information about both beginnings and endings in the process of inferring duration" (Levin et al., 1984, p.263). For example, a young child infers correct information from duration comparisons if there are simultaneous endpoints and no-simultaneous beginning points: "... very young children, nursery school children or kindergarteners, are able to infer rela-

tive durations from differences in starting times or ending times
..." (Levin, 1982, p.82). What happens if the information is given
in the form of a hypothetical situation ?

3.3.1. The temporal subsystems SAFI and SBEI

Below we present some examples of structurally stable cognitive systems concerning temporal reasoning, particularly the relations between duration (ΔT), the initial succession order (T1) and the final
succession order (T2) in non-kinematic cases.

Below are some examples of situations presented to subjects in written form.

1) Judging relative durations:

"Lamp R turns on before lamp V" and "Lamp R turns off before lamp V"
(undecidable situations BE1 & BE2);

"Lamp R turns on before lamp V", "Lamp R turns off after lamp V"
(decidable situations BE1 & $\Delta T+$).

2) Judging the final succession order:

"Lamp R turns on after lamp V" and "Lamp R shines for less time"
(undecidable situations AF1 & $\Delta T-$);

"Lamp R turns on after lamp V" and "Lamp R shines for more time"
(decidable situations AF1 & $\Delta T+$).

3) Judging the initial succession order:

"Lamp R shines for more time" and "Lamp R turns off later" (undecidable situations $\Delta T+$ & AF2);

Based on the model, what can be predicted ? Note that the model, at
its first level, is only concerned with inequality relations (e.g.,
"before", "after", "more time", etc.).

The following are some characteristics of the postulated theoretical
systems.

System S-I (see Figure 4) is characterized by non-differentiation
between the initial succession order (AF1) and the final succession
order (AF2).

The symbols uR and dR indicate undecidable and decidable relations,
respectively, that are associated with each couple of dyadic relations. Two subsystems can be distinguished: SAFI and SBEI. The
symbols AF and BE mean the relations "after" and "before".

Note that the above scheme is an abbreviated form of the three couples of temporal relations. For example, the sub-system SAFI is an
abreviated form of the following couples: (AF1-AF2), (AF1-$\Delta T+$),
(AF2-$\Delta T+$). The composition of (AF2-$\Delta T+$) and (AF1-$\Delta T+$), which are
general states of knowledge, generate a new relation (AF1-AF2) which
is an inferred state of knowledge compatible with the initial rela-

tion. The same composition mechanism applies to the sub-system SBE (duration, initial succession order, final succession order).

Figures 4 and 5: See text.

System S-I

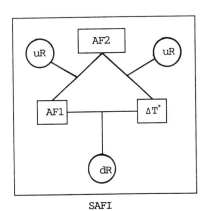 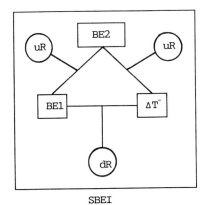

System S-II

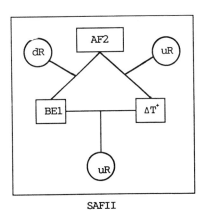 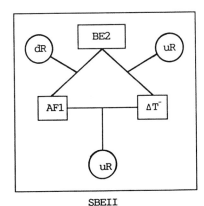

3.3.2. The temporal subsystems SAFII and SBEII

Within the system S-II (see Figure 5) the succession order is differentiated. The subsystems SAFII and SBEII also represent three couples of dyadic relations (duration, initial succession order, final
succession order): [AF2 - BE1], [AF2 - ΔT+], [BE 1 - ΔT+]. The
system is also structurally stable i.e., the inferred relation is
compatible with the initial relation (general states of knowledge).

3.3.3. The temporal subsystems SAFIII and SBEIII

The SIII system is analogous to the first in that there is a non-
differentiation of the temporal succession order. However, the duration which is inferred from the initial succession order is compatible with the physical model. Naturally, the basic structure of
SIII is common to the systems SI and SII.

3.3.4. Some predictions of the model

To conclude this section, we present some examples of predictions
based on the model (Crépault, 1988) of hypothetical undecidable situations (e.g. "After 1 & After 2", "Less time & After 1") and of
decidable hypothetical situations (e.g. "Before 1 & After 2", "More
time & After 2").

For dyadic relations, the model predicts only one answer to each situation. We suppose that a subject responds by giving a series of
correct answers to all the decidable hypothetical situations. Elsewhere (Crépault, 1988a), we have demonstrated that at least nine
models can be built, through the structural pole/functional pole
distinction, allowing one to render an account of the exact pattern
(for six problems).

The following is a short description of the systems SI, SII, and
SIII and the primary (R-1) and secondary rules (R-2):

   (1)   Subsystems SAFI and SBEI (two models)

         R-1: T2;   R-2: SAF
         R-1: T.O.; R-2: T2 (T.O.: temporal order)

   (2)   Subsystems SAFII and SBEII (three models)

         R-1: ΔT; R-2: T2
         R-1: ΔT; R-2: SAF
         R-1: ΔT; R-2: SBE

   (3)   Subsystems SAFIII and SBEIII (four models)

         R-1: T1; R-2: SAF
         R-1: T1; R-2: SBE
         R-1: T1; R-2: ΔT
         R-1: T1; R-2: T2

Note that each model allows one to predict distinct individual configurations based on six undecidable situations. Thus it is possible to choose specific answers to each sub-system. For example, in

the case of the situations "ΔT+ & AF2" and "ΔT- & BE2", the systems
SI and SII predict the respective answers "AF1, BE1" and "BE1, AF1".
The system SIII predicts the specific answers "ΔT-" and "ΔT+" for
situations "AF1 & AF2" and "BE1 & BE2".

The answers within one system can also be analysed. For example,
based on the rules R-1 and R-2, the system SI predicts eighteen patterns of answers, three of them leading to identical answers. The
model thus allows one to make predictions concerning the sequence of
answers based on the "cognitive systems" available.

From a developmental viewpoint, intersystem transformations (structural changes) and intrasystem transformations (functional changes)
can be taken into account. It can be hypothesized that subjects of
a certain age act within a system based on several functional rules.
From this perspective, there is one common structure and several
"developmental trajectories".

3.4. Models, tasks, and cognitive development of temporal reasoning

3.4.1. Introduction

In the psychological literature, two relatively independent lines of
research on the development of time notions in children can be distinguished.

The first is a series of essentially empirical studies on the development of time conventions; that is, how children use temporal
words like 'yesterday' and 'tomorrow' and how do they understand
seriation of historical events, etc. (Friedman, 1978). These studies are limited to an analysis of success or failure. More recently, the development of time conventions has been viewed as a analysis of the structure and processes concerned (Friedman, 1982).
According to Friedman, the comprehension of time conventions is based on several components: (1) The temporal succession order, (2)
the duration of each element, and (3) the notion of cycle.

The second line of research stems from Piaget's classical studies on
time (1946a, 1946b). Work on time was continued for twenty years by
the 'Centre d'Epistémologie Génétique' (Bovet, Gréco, Papert and
Voyat, 1967; Grize, Henry, Meylan-Backs, Orsini, Piaget and van den
Bogaert-Rombouts, 1966). This research led Piaget (1966) to specify
his concepts divergence and convergence with Fraisse (1967, 1982).
Piaget and his collaborators' work was continued by Montangero
(1977, 1984), mainly with children from 5 to 9 years old, to study
the substages that lead up to "operational duration".

In his first studies, Montangero (1977) suggested that one could
distinguish two types of inferences concerning children's behaviors:
The "logical" and the "physical" mode. In the physical mode, reasoning is based on the contents of the event, for example, work achieved (distance, number of objects displaced, etc.) and velocity.
However, in the case of the logical mode, reasoning is not based on
any physical reference or content of events, but on temporal succession orders that deduce duration.

In a recent article concerning the "meaning" of the notion of dura-

tion, Montangero (1985) suggested that one makes a distinction between three subsystems. Each subsystem includes three variables.
The first relates to the temporal succession order and duration.
The second deals with displacement velocity, its results (e.g., the
amount of space covered) and duration. The third is concerned with
"speed-frequency", the discontinuous quantity produced (expressed in
terms of number) and the time of change. According to Montangero,
complete understanding of duration requires at least the knowledge
of the duration with the components of the three subsystems.

The results of several experiments (Gurtner and Montangero, 1986;
Montangero, 1977, 1979, 1981, 1983, 1985) demonstrate common general
behaviors for the three subsystems as well as specific behaviors
which seem to justify the differentiation of the subsystems. Much
of the covariation established between two variables corresponded to
the relations within the "physical model" when the third variable is
constant.

3.4.2. Acquisition situations and order of kinematic notions

It must be recalled that according to Piaget's hypothesis, the pre-
notion of velocity-overtaking precedes that of duration (Piaget,
1946a; Piaget and Garcia, 1983), whereas, on an "operational level",
velocity is based on duration and vice-versa (Piaget, 1966). Until
recently, subjects were usually asked to judge duration or velocity
according to the motion of the mobile on straight and parallel trajectories (partially or totally synchronised motions) (Acredolo and
Schmid, 1981; Acredolo, Adams and Schmid, 1984; Bentley, 1987;
Fraisse, 1982; Levin, 1977; Richards, 1982). This method one allowed to gather important data concerning temporal reasoning in children. For example, young children claim that the instant of departure and arrival are simultaneous, but believe that the durations
are not equal.

What can be said about the acquisition order of kinematic notions ?
Does it depend on the nature of situations and/or the processing of
observation data (Crépault, Jaquet, Levin, Montangero, Pouthas and
Wilkening, 1983), e.g. the method of functional measurement
(Wilkening, 1982), the method of rule assessment (Richards, 1982),
or the method of the facet model (Levin, 1977, 1982) ? Using the
method of rule assessment, Siegler and Richards (1979) showed a
clear difference between correctly answering questions on duration
(around 17% correct for 11-12 year olds) and on distance and velocity (58% and 83%, respectively for 11-12 year olds). Acredolo and
Schmid (1981) have referred to Siegler and Richard's experiment and
added ten new situations also characterized by straight and parallel
trajectories. The results regarding the notion of duration are
equally mediocre for 13 year old: Less than 20% correct responses.
Therefore, it seems that the notion of duration is acquired later
than velocity. An important point must be emphasized: Nearly all
adults answer duration questions correctly in this experimental
situation (through the use of rule R-III, according to Siegler and
Richards, 1979). Therefore, the question is, what happens between
the age of 11-12 years and adulthood.

This lead us to the question of what do we know about qualitative
reasoning in adults ? Research on physical cognition in adults is

quite recent. A number of studies demonstrate that the "Newtonian model" is relatively uncharacteristic of the typical adult's spontaneous reasoning reasoning (Crépault, 1989; Kuhn, Amsel and O'Loughlin, 1988; Levin and Simon, 1986; McCloskey, 1983; Saltiel, 1981; Trowbridge and McDermott, 1980). Recent research by Levin and Simon (1986) on circular motions (synchronous duration) with subjects who were between eight years old and adult age shows that the notion of velocity is acquired later than that of duration and that it creates serious conceptual difficulties for adult science students. These results can be related to Saltiel's (1981), Saltiel and Malgrange's (1979) findings which demonstrate, through the use of Galilean reperage problems, that 60% of science students make at least one mistake answering questions about velocity and 80% answering questions about distance covered. Caramazza, McCloskey and Green (1981) also describe adults' difficulties --with or without knowledge in physics-- in creating a picture of a projectile's trajectories in the case of a pendulum. Only 25% of the subjects produce a picture that conforms to the Galilean model. What then is the final point of cognitive development ? Also, what is the status of the concept of "stage" in research with adults ?

3.4.3. Development of temporal reasoning

How will an adolescent process information when his reasoning is based on traces representing the composition of two distinct motions or hypothetical kinematic situations ? With this question in mind, we designed a series of experiments to shed some light on several aspects of kinematic reasoning in children as well as adults.

The proposed model should allow us to make predictions concerning the sequence of the subjects' answers (the micro-developmental component), and answer patterns as a function of age (the macro-developmental component).

The experimental situations can be divided into two classes (Crépault, 1979a, 1979b, 1981a, 1981b, 1982, 1989):

(1) Spatial type situations

These present a double reference system:

(a) Type I: Composition of a periodic motion and a motion of varied translation;

(b) Type II: Composition of a non periodic motion and a motion of uniform translation;

(c) Undecidable type: Undetermined frequency and velocity.

A certain number of duration transformations are defined: Order 1, order 2 (relation between partial duration and velocity) and order 3 transformations (transformation relation between partial duration, total duration and velocity).

(2) Non spatial type situations (hypothetical statement problems)

The hypothetical statement problems consist of the conjunction of

either two comparative relations (e.g., V+T=, T+D+, V-D-, etc...) or
three comparative relations (e.g., V+T+D+, V+T=D+, V=T+D+, etc...).
The subject is asked to judge the compatibility of the statements.
If they are compatible, then the subject is asked to give an inference about the third variable. In the second verbal problem (which
is three sentences long), the subject may transform the "initial
statement", if incompatible, into a "compatible statement".

The results (Crépault, 1988b) showed that the model's predictions
are in accordance with the data for the limited domain of relations
between partial duration and velocity (order 1-transformations and
order 2-transformations), mainly in type I situations (periodic frequency). With undecidable situations and order 3 transformations
(relations between partial or total duration), the data are partially compatible with the predictions of the model. A new model --the
bi-state model (see Crépault, 1988b)-- was then proposed that takes
into account the limitations of the initial model.

The following are some levels of organization of kinematic relations
(spatial type situations) resulting from a series of experiments.

(1) The behaviors of 9-10 year-old children are, generally, very
homogeneous in the three types of situations (problems of double
reference): Coexistence of the inverse relationship between velocity and distance and the direct relationship between distance and
time, which was independent of the used mark (reference). The behavior of our young subjects is in accordance with the predicted
transformations of the model for the gamma-state (Vx*, Tx, Tv*), a
structurally stable state.

2) At 11-12 years of age, the behaviors are much less homogeneous.
The velocity-frequency relation is differentiated from the velocity-
displacement relation for the three types of situations. For the
model, the transformations of the alpha-state (Vx, Tx, Tv*), a
structurally unstable state, allow one to render many of the subjects' responses as "errors".

3) Towards 13-14 years of age , most subjects in spatialised frequency (type I) situations, infer a relation of temporal equality
compared with the frequency mark. Likewise, towards 13-14 years of
age the notion of undecidability is acquired immediately. The "errors" observed are relatively homogeneous: They concern the inverse
relationship between distance and time (type I) and constant duration according to the translation mark (type II). It seems that the
transformation of the beta-state accounts for most of the "errors"
(Vx, Tx*, Tv*).

4) For subjects who are approaching 15-16 years of age, subjects
give an exact answer regarding duration (type I or type II), according to the mark-frequency and the mark-translation. Note that very
few subjects give an exact pattern for both problems (type I and
type II).

The data from a three year longitudinal study (Crépault, 1989)
which had four groups of subjects aged 9 years (N=56), 11 years
(N=59), 13 years (N=55) and 15 years (N=30), showed that:

1) More than 75% of the "gamma" subjects (level I) advance by one level, 50% by two levels and less than 20% by three levels;

2) Most of the "alpha" subjects (level II) progress by one level, passing from alpha to beta;

3) Very few beta subjects (level III) progress by even one level after two or three years;

4) Finally, most of the "phi" subjects (level IV) regress to the third level (beta-state) after two or three years.

Briefly, the transformations associated with the first construction levels (L-I, L-II) are compatible with the model's predictions. However, as soon as subjects have reached the beta-state (L-III), a structurally stable level, they are inclined to remain there. One may ask why do subjects who give an exact pattern regress in time ? Is this phenomenon specific to the nature of the situation ? It should be noted that very few subjects act isomorphically (level V: Double "phi"-state) in type I situations (constant frequency) and type II situations (variable frequency). Thus, perhaps we could find a tryadic relation system that allows one to pass from one physical system to another with the latter subjects.

Can the model be generalized to other contents ? In a recent study (Crépault, 1985), we analysed the patterns of answers predicted by the one-state model (Crépault, 1983) concerning the hypothetical statement problems for kinematic information (type V+ or D+ situations), where two pieces of information were given concerning the relative starting orders (started before, after, or simultaneously) and the relative stopping orders (stopped before, after, or simultaneously). The judgements concern the time intervals and either velocity or distance. The results showed that more than 70% of behaviors (N=180, three age groups) are predicted by the model.

In another study (Crépault and Pelletier-Doucet, 1984), we used a situation similar to Gréco's (1967). The difference between the two was that information was presented verbally (with written sentences) and judgements concerned duration or succession orders, while "velocity" and "distance" were undetermined relations. The results showed that 80% (N=90, three age groups) of the answer patterns are compatible with the prediction of the one-state mode.

How is time treated outside the kinematic context ? Do the difficulties persist with adolescents and even adults ? Recent work (Levin et al., 1984; Richie and Bickhard, 1988) shows that young children can build primary notions of duration relatively early (e.g., correct judgements in the case of duration of shining). What happens if the given information is hypothetical ?

Crépault's results (1988) demonstrate that most adolescents (14-15 year olds) fail when dealing with double temporal decalage (e.g., AF1 & ΔT=, judgement on T2), whereas nearly all adults answer correctly. However, undecidable situations where there are three possible answers present conceptual difficulties for adults.

How does one explain the enormous decalage between the early success

of a young child regarding duration of a physical display and the
relatively weak result of adolescents in the case of hypothetical
statements ? It is important to bring the characteristics of the
task into the relation as well as the subject's available states of
knowledge (whether they be general, inferred, empirical and specific
task knowledges or relevant knowledge to a field of concepts, etc.).
However, regarding future research, it would be interesting to see
if the notions of stability and instability can be applied to other
contents.

The question is to know whether these phenomena of "regression", at
a certain level of development also characterize different fields of
knowledge.

4. CONCLUSION

The two approaches presented in this chapter enable us to address
the following two issues. 1) How useful is the notion of "stage",
which is defined according to the theoretical criterion of a "general structure" but rejected by numerous empirical data ? 2) What
meaning should be given to the notion of "linear or complex age-
related change" when developmental change is not described in terms
of a quantitative measure (e.g., the relationship between age level
and percentage of success), but in terms of qualitative models ?

Piagetian theory formalizes the "operational" behaviors in terms of
logical structures. Since a logical structure cannot be inconsistent, only the stable states of the child's knowledge can be described in terms of logical structures. The "non-operational" or non-
consistent behaviors are merely compared to the "operational" ones
and considered in terms of "failure" (non-compensation, non-transi-
tivity, etc.). Hence the theory does not offer homogeneous tools
for describing a sequence of developmental changes in the non-
operational behaviors that precede a stable stage. Moreover, empirical data showing "horizontal decalages" invalidate the hypothesis
of a "general structure". However, there are at least two parsimonious reasons for considering the concept of "stage" as a heuristic
concept for theories of cognitive development. The first is economy
of theory. If stages can be defined for cognitive development in
general, then it is not necessary to have a theory of developmental
change for each field of knowledge. The second reason is economy in
gathering observations. If one can define the stages, one necessarily has a unifying theory of cognitive development which enables
one to know more precisely what and how to observe --hence, an economy of experimental work !

To achieve this unification theory, one possibility is to refine
Piagetian concepts by considering recent work on adults and Artificial Intelligence to generate hypotheses about learning and development (Wallace et al., 1987), representation of knowledge (Anderson,
1983), mental models (Johnson-Laird, 1983) and temporal reasoning
(Shoham, 1988).

In the framework of qualitative models, the notion of "age-related
change" can be considered as follows. The qualification "linear"
can be applied to models in which the description of a level L is

included in the description of a level L+1 (one of the basic postulates of neo-Piagetian models, Case, 1987b). This applies to the production systems which we built in our research on the multiple classification problems. On the other hand, the models that describe behavior in terms of "structural stability/instability" allow for a new interpretation of the phenomenon "complex age related change" by supposing that the cognitive systems do not necessarily form a hierarchy according to age.

One must not forget that the richness of the human mind eludes the schematic approximations of all models of human thought, including those of young minds.

REFERENCES

Acredolo, C., & Schmid, J. (1981). The understanding of relative speeds, distances, and durations of motions. *Developmental Psychology, 17,* 490-493.
Acredolo, C., Adams, A., & Schmid, J. (1984). On the relationships between speed, duration and distance. *Child Development, 55,* 2151-2159.
Anderson, J.A. (1983). *The architecture of cognition.* Cambridge, Mass.: Harvard University Press.
Atkinson, R.C., & Shiffrin, R.M. (1968). Human memory: A proposed system and its control processes. In: K.W. Spence & J.T. Spence (Eds.), *Advances in the psychology of learning and motivation research and theory. Vol. 2,* pp.90-195. New York: Academic Press.
Bastien, C. (1987). *Schèmes et stratégies dans l'activité cognitive de l'enfant.* Paris: Presses Universitaires de France.
Bastien, C., de Oliveira, A., & Pinelli, P.M. (1982). Un conflit d'ordres: Organisation du produit de deux ensembles. *Enfance, 1-2,* 10-14.
Baylor, G.W., & Gascon, J. (1974). An information processing theory of aspects of the development of weight seriation in children. *Cognitive Psychology, 6,* 1-40.
Baylor, G.W., & Lemoyne, G. (1976). Experiment in seriations with children: Toward an information processing explanation of decalage. *Canadian Journal of Behavioral Sciences, 7,* 4-29.
Bentley, A.M. (1987). Swazi children's understanding of time concepts: A Piagetian study. *Journal of Genetic Psychology, 148,* 443-453.
Bideaud, J. (1988). *Logique et bricolage chez l'enfant.* Lille: Presses Universitaires de Lille.
Bideaud, J., & Lautrey, J. (1983). De la résolution empirique à la résolution logique du problème d'inclusion: Evolution des réponses en fonction de l'âge et des situations expérimentales. *Cahiers de Psychologie Cognitive, 3,* 295-326.
Bovet, M., Gréco, P., Papert, S., & Voyat, G. (1967). *Perception et notion du temps.* Paris: Presses Universitaires de France.
Bruner, J., Olver, R.R., & Greenfield, P.M. (1966). *Studies in cognitive growth.* New York: Wiley.
Caramazza, A., McCloskey, M., & Green, B. (1981). Naive beliefs in "sophisticated" subjects: Misconceptions about trajectories of objects. *Cognition, 9,* 117-123.

Case, R. (1985). *Intellectual development: Birth to adulthood.*
New York: Academic Press.
Case, R. (1987a). The structural process of intellectual
development. *International Journal of Psychology, 22,* 571-607.
Case, R. (1987b). Neo-Piagetian theory: Retrospect and prospect.
International Journal of Psychology, 22, 773-791.
Cauzinille, E., Mathieu, J., & Nguyen-Xuan, A. (1982). Le niveau
d'inférence de la structure d'un tableau à double entrée: La
construction d'un produit. *Enfance,* 1-2, 14-22.
Chapman, M. (1987). Piaget, attentional capacity, and the
functional implications of formal structure. In: H.W. Reese
(Ed.), *Advances in child development and behavior,* pp.289-334.
London: Academic Press.
Crépault, J. (1978a). Le raisonnement cinématique chez le préadolescent et l'adolescent. I. Esquisse d'un modèle théorique:
Concepts de base. *Archives de Psychologie, 178,* 133-183.
Crépault, J. (1978b). Le raisonnement cinématique chez le préado-
lescent et l'adolescent. II. Predictions du modèle théorique pour
une classe de situations. *Archives de Psychologie, 179,* 185-203.
Crépault, J. (1979a). Organisation et genèse des relations temps,
espace et vitesse. In: P. Fraisse et al. (Eds.), *Du temps
biologique au temps psychologique,* pp.227-253. Paris: Presses
Universitaires de France.
Crépault, J. (1979b). Influence du repérage sur la durée. Etude
génétique des inférences cinématiques. *Année Psychologique, 79,*
43-64.
Crépault, J. (1980). Compatibilité et symétrie. Etude génétique
chez des sujets de 11 et 13 ans. *Année Psychologique, 80,* 81-97.
Crépault, J. (1981a). La notion d'indécidabilité. Validité et
limite du modèle théorique uni-état. *Cahiers de Psychologie
Cognitive,* 1, 3-33.
Crépault, J. (1981b). Etude longitudinale des inférences
cinématiques chez le préadolescent et l'adolescent. Evolution ou
régression. *Canadian Journal of Psychology, 35,* 244-253.
Crépault, J. (1982). Psychogenèse du raisonnement cinématique.
Processus d'inférence chez le préadolescent et l'adolescent.
Thèse de doctorat d'Etat, Université de Paris 8.
Crépault, J. (1983). Modèles, raisonnements et notions de temps
chez l'adolescent. *Cahiers de Psychologie Cognitive, 3,* 387-392.
Crépault, J. (1985). Reasoning and time concepts in adolescent.
Actes de l'International Society for the Study of Behavioral
Development. *European Bulletin of Cognitive Psychology, 5,* 438-439
Crépault, J. (1988). The development of temporal reasoning in
children, adolescents and adults. The relation between duration
and succession. Paper presented at the meeting of the European
Society for the Study of Behavioral Development, Budapest,
Hungary.
Crépault, J. (1989). *Temps et raisonnement. Développement cognitif
des processus d'inférence de l'enfant à l'adulte.* Lille: Les
Presses Universitaires de Lille.
Crépault, J., & Pelletier-Doucet, E. (1984). Raisonnements
temporels et modèles. *Canadian Psychology, 25(2),* 114.
Crépault, J., Jacquet, A.Y., Levin, I., Montangero, J., Pouthas, V.,
& Wilkening, W. (1983). La psychogenèse du temps: Cinq
approches. *Cahiers de Psychologie Cognitive, 4,* 361-418.
Ferreti, R.P., & Butterfield, E.C. (1986). Are children's rule-
assessment classifications invariant across instances of problem

types ? *Child Development*, *47*, 1419-1428.

Fischer, K.W., & Farrar, M.J. (1987). Generalizations about generalisation: How a theory of skill development explains both generality and specificity. *International Journal of Psychology*, *22*, 643-677.

Fraisse, P. (1967). *Psychologie du temps*. Paris: Les Presses Universitaires de France.

Fraisse, P. (1982). The adaptation of the child to time. In: W.F. Friedman (Ed.), *The developmental psychology of time*, pp.113-140. New York: Academic Press.

Frey, L. (1964). Sériation et transitivité. *Cahiers de Psychologie*, *7*, 143-157.

Frey, L., & Nguyen-Xuan, A. (1983). Un schéma d'analyse des processus de classement. In: J. Caron (Ed.), *La Pensée naturelle: Structure, procédure et logique du sujet*, pp.147-155. Rouen: Presses Universitaires de France.

Friedman, W.J. (1978). Development of time concepts in children. In: H.W. Reese & L.P. Lipsitt (Eds.), *Advances in child development and behavior*, vol. 12, pp.267-198. New York: Academic Press.

Friedman, W.J. (1982). Conventional time concepts and children's structuring of time. In: W.F. Friedman (Ed.), *The developmental psychology of time*, pp.171-206. New York: Academic Press.

Gilliéron, C. (1976). Décalage et sériation. *Archives de Psychologie*, *44*, Monographie 3.

Gréco, P. (1967). Comparaison "logique" de deux durées et jugements corrélatifs de distance et de vitesse chez l'enfant de 6 à 10 ans. In: *Perception et notion de temps*, EEG, vol.21, pp.3-103. Paris: Les Presses Universitaires de France.

Grize, B., Henry, K., Meylan-Backs, M., Orsini, F., Piaget, J., & Van Den Bogaert-Rombouts, N. (1966). *L'épistémologie du temps*. Paris: Les Presses Universitaires de France.

Gurtner, J.L., & Montangero, J. (1986). Représentation du temps global, incluant temps d'activité et temps d'arrêt, chez l'enfant préoperatoire. Etude génétique. *Cahiers de Psychologie Cognitive*, *6*, 339-354.

Halford, G.S. (1987). A structure-mapping approach to cognitive development. *International Journal of Psychology*, *22*, 609-642.

Inhelder, B., & Piaget, J. (1955). *De la logique de l'enfant à la logique de l'adolescent*. Paris: Les Presses Universitaires de France.

Inhelder, B., Sinclair, H., & Bovet, M. (1974). *Apprentissage et structure de la connaissance*. Paris: Les Presses Universitaires de France.

Johnson-Laird, P.N. (1983). *Mental models*. Cambridge, Ma: Harvard University Press.

Kerkman, D., & Wright, J.C. (1988). An exegesis of two theories of compensation development: Sequential decision theory and information integration theory. *Developmental Review*, *8*, 323-360.

Klahr, D. (1984). Transition processes in quantitative development. In: R.J. Sternberg (Ed.), *Mechanisms of cognitive development*, pp.101-140. New York: Freeman.

Klahr, D., & Wallace, J.G. (1976). *Cognitive development. An information-processing view*. Hillsdale, N.J.: Erlbaum.

Kuhn, D., Amsel, E., & O'Loughlin, M. (1988). *The development of scientific thinking skills*. London: Academic Press.

Laflaquière, A. (1979). Etude génétique des conduites de

classification. *Enfance*, *1*, 15-30.

Lautrey, J., Bideaud, J., & Pierre-Puységur, M.A. (1986). Aspects génétiques et différentiels du fonctionnement cognitif lors de tâches de sériation. *L'Année Psychologique*, *86*, 489-526.

Levin, I. (1977). The nature and development of time concepts in children: Reasoning about duration. *Child Development*, *48*, 435-444.

Levin, I. (1982). The nature and development of time concepts in children: The effets of interfering cues. In: W.J. Friedman (Ed.), *The developmental psychology of time*, pp.47-85. New York: Academic Press.

Levin, I, & Simons, H. (1986). The nature of children's and adult's concepts of time, speed, and distance ant their sequence in development: Analysis via circular motion. In: I. Levin (Ed.), *Stage and structure*, pp.77-105. Norwood, N.J.: Ablex.

Levin, I., Goldstein, R., & Zelniker, T. (1984). The role of memory and integration in early time concepts. *Journal of Experimental Child Psychology*, *37*, 262-270.

Levin, I., Wilkening, F., & Dembo, Y. (1984). Development of time quantification: Integration and nonintegration of beginnings and endings in comparing duration. *Child Development*, *55*, 2160-2172.

Maury, L., & Rogalski, J. (1970). Produit cartésien et complément. Etude génétique. *L'Année Psychologique*, *1*, 53-71.

Markman, E.M. (1973). Empirical versus logical solution to part-whole comparisons problems concerning classes and collections. *Child Development*, *49*, 168-177.

McCloskey, M. (1983). Naive theories of motion. In: D. Gentner & A.L. Stevens (Eds.), *Mental models*, pp.299-324. Hillsdale, N.J.: Erlbaum.

Montangero, J. (1977). *La notion de durée chez l'enfant de 5 à 9 ans*. Paris: Les Presses Universitaires de France.

Montangero, J. (1979). Les relations du temps, de la vitesse et de l'espace parcouru chez le jeune enfant. *Année Psychologique*, *79*, 23-42.

Montangero, J. (1981). Les relations entre durée et succession. Etude d'une prélogique enfantine appliquée au temps. *Année Psychologique*, *81*, 287-308.

Montangero, J. (1983). Organisation de significations temporelles et rôles d'indices perçus. *Cahiers de Psychologie Cognitive*, *3*, 407-411.

Montangero, J. (1984). Perspectives actuelles sur la psychogenèse du temps. *L'Année Psychologique*, *84*, 433-460.

Montangero, J. (1985). The development of temporal inferences and meanings in 5 to 8 year old children. In: J.A. Michon & J.L. Jackson (Eds.), *Time, mind and behavior*, pp.279-287. New York: Springer-Verlag.

Mounoud, P. (1986). Similarities between developmental sequences at different age. In: I. Levin (Ed.), *Stage and structure*, pp.40-58. Norwood, N.J.: Ablex.

Newell, A., & Simon, H.A. (1972). *Human problem solving*. Englewood Cliffs, N.J.: Prentice-Hall.

Nguyen-Xuan, A. (1976). Suite aux automates de sériation de Frey. *Cahiers de Psychologie*, *19*, 101-108.

Nguyen-Xuan, A. (1986). Modèle de fonctionnement en psychologie du développement: Pour quoi faire ? In: R. Ghiglione (Ed.), *Comprendre l'homme, construire des modèles*, pp.95-111. Paris: Editions du CNRS.

Nguyen-Xuan, A., & Rousseau, J. (1979). Un apprentissage de classi-
fication multiple. *Cahiers de Psychologie*, *22*, 99-107.
Nguyen-Xuan, A., & Hoc, J.M. (1987). Learning to use a command
device. *European Bulletin of Cognitive Psychology*, *7*, 5-31.
Nguyen-Xuan, A., Cauzinille-Marmèche, E., Frey, L., Mathieu, J., &
Rousseau, J. (1983). Fonctionnement cognitif et classification
multiple chez l'enfant de 4 à 7 ans. *Monographie Française de
Psychologie*, N°60. Paris: CNRS.
Piaget, J. (1941). Le mécanisme du developpement mental et du
groupement des opérations. *Archives de Psychologie*, *112*, 215-
285.
Piaget, J. (1946a). *Le développement de la notion de temps
l'enfant*. Paris: Les Presses Universitaires de France.
Piaget, J. (1946b). Problèmes du temps et de la fonction. In:
Epistémologie du temps. *Etudes d'épistémologie génétique*, vol.
20, pp.2-66. Paris: les Presses Universitaires de France.
Piaget, J. (1972). *Essai de logique opératoire*. Paris: Dunod.
(2nd edition by J.B. Grize).
Piaget, J. (1974). Recherches sur la contradiction. I. Les
différentes formes de la contradiction. *Etudes d'épistémologie
génétique*, Vol. *31*. Paris: Les Presses Universitaires de
France.
Piaget, J. (1975). L'équilibration des structures cognitives.
Etudes d'épistémologie génétique, Vol. *33*. Paris: Les
Presses Universitaires de France.
Piaget, J., & Inhelder, B. (1959). *La genèse des structures
logiques élémentaires: Classification et sériation*. Neuchâtel:
Delachaux et Niestlé.
Piaget, J., & Garcia, R. (1983). *Psychogenèse et histoire des
sciences*. Paris: Flammarion.
Piaget, J., & Garcia, R. (1987). *Vers une logique des
significations*. Genève: Murionde.
Piéraut-le-Bonniec, G. (1972). Recherche sur l'évolution génétique
des opérations de classification. *Archives de Psychologie*, *41*,
89-117, 1.
Retschitzki, J. (1978). L'évolution des processus de sériation:
Etude génétique et stimulation. *Archives de Psychologie*, *46*,
Monographie N°5.
Richards, D.D. (1982). Children's time concepts: Going the
distance. In: W.J. Friedman (Ed.), *The developmental psychology
of time*, pp.13-45. New York: Academic Press.
Richie, D.M., & Bickhard, M.H. (1988). The ability to perceive
duration: Its relations to the development of the logical
concept of time. *Developmental Psychology*, *24*, 318-323.
Saltiel, E. (1981). Kinematics concepts and natural reasoning:
Study of comprehension of galilean frames by science students.
European Journal of Science Education, *3*, 110-111.
Saltiel, E., & Malgrange, J.L. (1979). Les raisonnements naturels
en cinématique élémentaire. *Bulletin de l'Union des Physiciens*,
616, 1325-1355.
Shoham, Y. (1988). *Reasoning about change: Time and causation
from the standpoint of artificial intelligence*. Cambridge: The
MIT Press.
Siegler, R.S. (1976). Three aspects of cognitive development.
Cognitive Psychology, *8*, 481-520.
Siegler, R.S. (1981). Developmental sequences within and between
concepts. *Monograph of the Society for Research in Child*

Development, *46*, 1-74.
Siegler, R.S. (1983). Information processing approaches to
    development. In: P.H. Mussen & W. Kessen (Eds.), *Handbook of*
    child psychology: History, theory and methods, *vol. 1*, pp.129-
    211. New York: Wiley.
Siegler, R.S. (1986). Unities across domains in children's strategy
    choices. In: M. Perlmutter (Ed.), *Minnesota symposium on child*
    psychology, *vol.19*, pp.1-48. Hillsdale, N.J.: Erlbaum.
Siegler, R.S., & Shrager, J. (1984). Strategy choices in addition
    and subtraction: How do children know what to do ? In:
    C. Sophian (Ed.), *Origins of cognitive skills*, pp.229-293.
    Hillsdale, N.J.: Erlbaum.
Smith, J.D., & Baron, J. (1981). Individual differences in the
    classification of stimuli by dimension. *Journal of Experimental*
    Child Psychology, *7*, 1132-1145.
Sternberg, R.J. (1984). Mechanisms of cognitive development: A
    componential approach. In: R.J. Sternberg (Ed.), *Mechanisms of*
    cognitive development, pp.163-186. New York: Freeman.
Strauss, S., & Ephron-Wertheim, T. (1986). Structure and process:
    Developmental psychology as looking in the mirror. In: I. Levin
    (Ed.), *Stage and structure*, pp.59-76. Norwood, N.J.: Ablex.
Trowbridge, D.E, & McDermott, L.C. (1980). Investigation of
    student understanding of the concept of velocity in one
    dimension. *American Journal of Physics*, *48*, 1020-1028.
Vergnaud, G. (1983). Multiplicative structures. In: R. Lesch & M.
    Landau (Eds.), *Acquisition of mathematics concepts and processes*.
    New York: Academic Press.
Wallace, I., Klahr, D., & Bluff, K. (1987). A self-modifying
    production system model of cognitive development. In: D. Klahr,
    P. Langley & R. Neches (Eds.), *Production system models of*
    learning and development, pp.359-435. Cambridge, Ma: The MIT
    Press.
Wilkening, F. (1981). Integrating velocity, time, and distance
    information: A developmental study. *Cognitive Psychology*, *13*,
    231-247.
Wilkening, F. (1988). A misrepresentation of knowledge
    representation. *Developmental Review*, *8*, 361-367.
Wilkening, F., & Anderson, N.H. (1982). Comparison of two rules
    assessment methodologies for studying cognitive development and
    knowledge structure. *Psychological Bulletin*, *92*, 215-237.
Wilkinson, A. (1976). Counting strategies and semantic analysis as
    applied to class inclusion. *Cognitive Psychology*, *8*, 64-85.
Winer, G.A. (1980). Class-inclusion reasoning in children: A
    review of the empirical literature. *Child Development*, *51*, 309-
    328.
Young, R.M. (1976). *Seriation by children: An artificial*
    intelligence analysis of a Piagetian task. Basel: Birkhauser.

DEVELOPMENTAL PSYCHOLOGY
Cognitive, Perceptuo-Motor, and Neuropsychological Perspectives
C-A. Hauert (Editor)
© Elsevier Science Publishers B.V. (North-Holland), 1990

CHILD PERCEPTUO-MOTOR DEVELOPMENT:
NORMAL AND ABNORMAL DEVELOPMENT OF SKILLED BEHAVIOUR

Judith I. LASZLO

Department of Psychology and Physiology
The University of Western Australia
Nedlands WA 6009, Australia

*Perceptual-motor skills are goal directed and flexible.
They can be classified as endogenous or exogenous.
Exogenous skills are considered here. Assessment of skilled behaviour is either task-orientated, recording motor
proficiency, or process-orientated, focusing on the processes which contribute to motor proficiency. The
process-orientated approach is based on a closed-loop
model. Emphasis is placed on the experimental studies
relating to kinaesthesis, spatial and temporal programming
and on the measurement of these processes. Finally,
application of the process-orientated diagnoses and consequent focal therapy in perceptuo-motor dysfunction is
described.*

1. INTRODUCTION

1.1. Definition and classification of skills

In this chapter normal and abnormal perceptual-motor development is
discussed from a process-orientated viewpoint. Firstly, I describe
some of the prevailing views, then turn to a selective review of the
work carried out in my laboratory, and finally I attempt to assess
the possible advances made in understanding normal and abnormal perceptual motor behaviour in children aged 5-12 years.

The definition of skills in the Encyclopedic Dictionary of Psychology is given by Legge (1983, p.575) and is representative of the
views of many researchers (Adams, 1987; Schmidt, 1982): "Capabilities to perform particular tasks or to achieve particular goals."
He elaborates by stating that the two major characteristics of
skills are: Effectiveness in achieving the goal and flexibility in
the way the goal is reached.

Legge proceeds to classify skills as falling into two categories:
Either acquired through practice, or the result of normal maturational processes which are not dependent on specific training. In
agreement with Legge, Bairstow, in the same volume, describing the
development of skilled behaviour suggests two types of skills:
Endogenous and exogenous. Endogenous skills, such as grasping an

object or walking, emerge as the child grows older. Endogenous
skills do not depend on tuition, though they are practised spontaneously by the child. There is marked stereotypy in both the age
and the order in which these skills emerge (Bairstow, 1983). While
stereotyping undoubtedly exists in both age and order of emergence
of endogenous skills, it is equally true that individual variations
occur frequently enough to deserve consideration. Both in psychological and paediatric texts developmental milestones or norms vary
from author to author, there is even some disagreement on the order
in which the various skills become manifest.

Individual differences are considered seriously by Holt (1981) who
argues that an unexpected order in emergence of the various skills,
dependent on maturation, cannot be taken as signs of abnormal development but are reflections of normal variations. Acceptance of
Holt's stand point --and I certainly agree with him-- would relieve
parents from unnecessary concern and would eliminate the early labelling of children as developmentally retarded if they do not conform to the specific developmental yardstick that the professional,
dealing with the child, has chosen.

Exogeneous skills are superimposed on the endogenous repertoire.
These skills are acquired through imitation and are aided by systematic training. For instance, once walking and running skills have
been consolidated (endogenous), the child can be taught to hop and
skip; or simple manipulative skills, such as grasping a rattle,
might lead through guided practice, to the use of tools. Bairstow
(1983) emphasizes pronounced individual differences in both the age
and the order in which exogenous skills are learned and the level of
proficiency the child will reach in different skills.

Bairstow points out that the development of endogenous skills depends, to a large extent, on maturational factors in the Central
Nervous System and body structure, which he refers to as 'hardware'.
Exogeneous skills, on the other hand, are based on 'software' changes, which are superimposed on maturation. However, exogenous
skills can bring about structural changes as when a child, by practising swimming a lot, develops strong shoulder and arm muscles.

In this chapter I intend to concentrate on exogenous skills, as
these are of major interest from age five onwards. Exogeneous skills
can be classified further in different ways.

Skills can be divided according to gross and fine skills --that is
skills one performs with the whole body and skills which involve
mainly the hands and fingers. Ball games are gross motor skill,
while handwriting would be an example of fine skills. Another way
of classifying skills is to look at the demand they place on the
performer. All 'motor skills' are, in effect, cognitive-perceptual-
motor skills. The difference between skills lies in the relative
importance of these factors for example, in swimming the motor demands are paramount; in copying a simple pattern perceptual and motor factors are important; while in car driving cognitive and perceptual demands are relatively greater than motor demands.

An often used dichotomy is closed versus open skills (Marteniuk,
1976). The theoretical argument is advanced (Desmedt and Godaux,

1979; Lashley, 1951; Schmidt, Zelaznik, Hawkins, Franks and Quinn,
1979; Smyth and Wing, 1984; Woodworth, 1889) according to which
closed skills or ballistic movements are performed without reliance
on feedback while in open skills feedback does play a part. Legge
(1983; p.756) maintains that high level skills are found in "open-
loop operations". However, taking ball throw as an example of a
closed skill, is it indeed independent of feedback ? Before throwing the ball both visual information and postural, kinaesthetic
feedback are received. Without this information the throw could not
be planned or initiated (Laszlo and Bairstow, 1985a). But it is
said (Anderson and Pitcairn, 1986) that the throwing movement is
over before it could be modified by feedback. The work on trans-
cortical reflexes (Evarts and Granit, 1976; Evarts and Tanji, 1976)
indicates that 100 ms are long enough for modification. It was
shown that response modification, following instructions, when
unpredictable perturbations are introduced during the course of a
ballistic movement (Tanji and Evarts, 1976) can and are responded
to. Finally, feedback received from the throw is stored in memory
and recalled before the next attempt (Laszlo and Bairstow, 1985a) in
order to improve the performance. The argument that in a series of
ballistic movements, such as in playing the piano, feedback cannot
influence each keystroke because there is no time to receive the
feedback is even less acceptable than in a discrete task like ball
throwing. Does a pianist play individual keystrokes, or does he
plan musically meaningful phrases ? Certainly the latter is the
case, and hence shortage of time cannot be given as a reason for
feedback free play. It seems to me that it is no more logical to
take key stroke as the unit of piano playing than to take ankle
flexion as a unit in running. I am suggesting that closed versus
open skills differ from each other only from the observer's or experimenter's point of view, but depend on similar processes as far
as the performer is concerned. If indeed closed and open skills
would differ in qualitative terms we would expect to find children
who can perform closed skills but fail open skills. This has not
been reported, nor have I found children with motor difficulties who
present this picture.

Consequently, for the purpose of this chapter I will make no distinction between classes of skills beyond focusing on exogenous
skills.

2. ASSESSMENT OF MOTOR BEHAVIOUR. MEASUREMENT PROBLEMS

There are two reasons for assessing motor behaviour: To record the
proficiency in motor performance or to obtain insight into the
underlying processes which determine motor proficiency i.e., task-
orientated approach and process-orientated approach. In the task-
orientated approach development and clinical assessment is focused
on the performance of individual tasks, or overt behaviour, while in
the process-orientated assessment the perceptual and motor processes
are evaluated and overt behaviour is considered as a consequence of
the level of development reached in the various processes. In this
section I am describing assessment of motor behaviour within the
task-orientated framework which is the framework used by most workers.

With age motor proficiency improves in two ways: The child's motor
repertoire widens and motor tasks are performed with gradually increasing efficiency. Developmental progression has been described
in detail, based on observation or measurement of performance.
Reading the literature on motor development one often encounters a
catalogue of age related 'can' and 'cannot' do list of skills. When
assessing the individual child the level of motor development is referred to this catalogue. Only occasionally is the question raised
of why a child fails to conform to age expected norms.

Observational techniques, though used frequently and with enthusiasm, have some serious weaknesses. Firstly, observers vary regarding the specific actions they choose to focus on i.e., what each
observer considers to be the best indicator of motor status. These
variations make it difficult to compare observational data across
observers. Secondly, the problem of observer bias lessens the
reliability of this technique. It has been well established that
the type of child the observer is most familiar with influences the
criterion used during observation. Let me give an example. I was
watching a demonstration of the revised Stott, Moyes and Henderson
(1984) Test of Motor Impairment often called TOMI. The child tested
was eight years of age, suspected of being clumsy. With me, behind
the one-way mirror were an eminent paediatrician, a psychologist
working with visually impaired children, a paediatric occupational
therapist, and a teacher from a main-stream primary school. After
the test was completed an argument ensued regarding the boy's ball
catching ability. According to the paediatrician, psychologist and
therapist the boy did very well. The teacher maintained that the
task was performed very poorly. The boy caught every ball by clut-
ching it against his chest rather than by grasping it in his hands
as would be expected from a normal eight year old. The tester acted
as referee: The boy was pronounced as performing this task at the
level for his age --he didn't drop the balls. A footnote to this
example: The boy had an easy job --the tester aimed each ball with
precision-- she is an accomplished player in a number of ball-games.

Observation has its rightful place as an aid to assessment, provided
the observer is aware of the shortcomings of this technique.

Objective measures should give a more reliable index of motor proficiency than observation. Timing, as a measure of performance is
certainly reliable, and is the only possible score in reaction time
tasks. But is it a valid measure in skills such as dressing or
drawing ? Does the time score favour the speed orientated performer
while penalising the accuracy orientated one ? Pew (1969) argues
that speed or accuracy bias is a personality trait in adults. There
is no reason to assume that children do not fall into these categories. Time scores should be used, if and only if, instructions
stress the need for speed in tasks with low accuracy demands.

Pass-fail is another often used scoring method. The effectiveness
of this score depends on how clearly the dividing line between pass
and fail can be defined. Even in such a seemingly clear-cut case as
ball catching, arguments can arise whether at age eight a ball
caught to the chest should be considered acceptable as 'pass' performance. Aiming at a target is, on the surface, a suitable skill
to score by pass or fail. Yet a fail score does not indicate how

much the target was missed, 1 mm or 100 mm; valuable information is lost. The same task can be scored by recording the point of nearest approach to the centre of the target (Bairstow, 1987). This scoring method eliminates the need to set an arbitrary cut-off point between pass and fail. The graded scores yield a continuous scale, useful in statistical treatment of the data, rather than the restrictive dichotomy of pass or fail.

In short, improvement in measurement and scoring techniques would lead to a better understanding of motor development.

There are two reasons for assessing motor behaviour: To record the proficiency in motor performance, task-orientated approach, or to obtain insight into the underlying processes which determine motor proficiency, process-orientated approach. Both reasons are valid, though confusion can arise when the purpose of the assessment is not identified and the test results are used inappropriately.

Most tests of motor function (Gubbay, 1975; Stott et al., 1984) aim at assessing the child's motor status or motor proficiency. Combining the scores from various test items, the tester can obtain a single, global index of motor performance. The index score should indicate the child's standing on the developmental scale, or the severity of motor impairment but these tests do not reveal the reason for the dysfunction. Yet this inherent limitation is often disregarded. Rather than using the score as an index of overt behaviour, the tester argues from the results about the abilities or developmental capabilities of the child. How unwarranted these inferences from response to underlying abilities are, can be demonstrated when assessing a child's drawing. Let us consider the task of drawing the human figure. Drawing of a figure depends on what we know about the human figure i.e., the cognitive aspect of the task; and to an equal degree on how well we can translate our knowledge into drawing movements, the perceptual-motor aspect. While I am fairly certain (having passed my anatomy examination) that I have a working knowledge of the visible characteristics of the human body, the best I can do in representing this knowledge on paper is to draw a "stick man" which bears scant ressemblance to the real figure and conspicuously lacks proportionality of the various body parts. To deduce from my "stick man" that I lack 'body awareness' would (I hope) underestimate my cognitive development, but would indicate my lack of drawing proficiency, though it could not pin-point which of the perceptual-motor processes failed to reach adequate level necessary for the drawing task. Even when the cognitive loading is reduced as in a copying task, children, or adults cannot produce a perfect replica of the model. The assumption that motor output can be taken as an index of any one single process, be it in the cognitive, perceptual or motor domain, is not acceptable.

Perhaps the complex interactions between the processes which underlie the overt motor act and which determine the success or failure of the performance of motor skills, have deterred test constructors from the process-orientated approach, preferring to stay within the task-orientated limits.

3. PROCESS-ORIENTATED ANALYSIS OF PERCEPTUAL-MOTOR BEHAVIOR

There are two schools of thought amongst research workers regarding
motor control: Action theory (Kelso, 1982; Kugler, Kelso and
Turvey, 1980; Turvey, Shaw and Mace, 1978) versus information processing theory (Laszlo and Bairstow, 1985a; Marteniuk, 1976; Pew,
1974a). Action theory takes a mechanistic view of motor behaviour,
and does not provide an explanatory framework for skill acquisition
or motor development.

Figure 1:   The Laszlo-Bairstow closed-loop model of motor
            control.

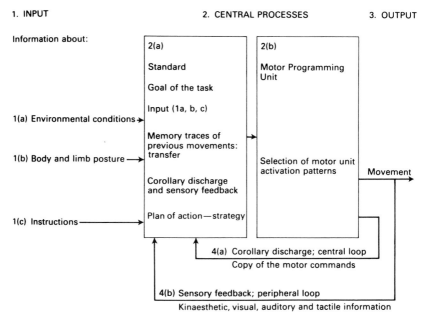

1. INPUT   2. CENTRAL PROCESSES   3. OUTPUT

Information about:

2(a)	2(b)
Standard	Motor Programming Unit
Goal of the task	

Input (1a, b, c)

1(a) Environmental conditions →

Memory traces of
previous movements:
1(b) Body and limb posture → transfer

Selection of motor unit
activation patterns   Movement

Corollary discharge
and sensory feedback

1(c) Instructions ────→ Plan of action—strategy

4(a) Corollary discharge; central loop
Copy of the motor commands

4(b) Sensory feedback; peripheral loop
Kinaesthetic, visual, auditory and tactile information

4. FEEDBACK LOOPS

I prefer the information processing models which can account for the
goal directed, flexible and adaptable nature of skilled behaviour.
Many authors working within this theory have proposed closed-loop
models of perceptual-motor behaviour (Keele and Summers, 1976;
Laszlo and Bairstow, 1985a; Pew, 1974a). The closed-loop model is
well suited to incorporate research data from the various disciplines which contribute to our present knowledge of perceptual-motor

function, such as neurophysiology, psychology, engineering, biophysics and medicine. Most closed-loop models have one common
characteristic: They stress the importance of feedback. Not surprisingly I intend to mount my argument using the Laszlo-Bairstow
model (Laszlo and Bairstow, 1985a).

The model incorporates cognitive, perceptual and motor components.
Within the closed-loop model behaviour is regarded as continuously
ongoing activity rather than a series of isolated acts. While the
beginning of a skilled act can be pin-pointed clearly by an observer, for the subject the new act is developed gradually from the
prevailing postural control; it is a gradual change rather than a
start from no action to action. Kinaesthetic input is continuously
generated and monitored, providing information about static posture
and the superimposed movements. There is no break in the inflow of
kinaesthetic input, nor can the monitoring of the information be
discontinued. Instructions, explicit or implicit, form part of the
input initiating a skilled act.

The Central Processing Unit or "Standard" generates the plan of
action. This is based on current sensory input and on instructions
received preceding the desired act or recalled from memory. Instructions and motivation define the goal of the action. Planning is
assisted by memory traces of previous attempts. Motor planning,
within the model, is not a conscious or cognitive process. The motor plan is restricted to the selection of the starting point of the
movement, to the determination of where directional changes should
be made, and the definition of timing. Thus motor planning can be
considered as the construction of a task related general programme.

The plan of action is conveyed to the Motor Programming Unit
(Freund, 1985; Roland, Skinhoj, Lassen and Larsen, 1980) where it is
translated into appropriate motor unit activation patterns or specific subprogrammes. To some extent spatial and temporal parameters
of movement are programmed independently of each other (Brooks,
1981; Desmedt and Godaux, 1981; Evarts, Fromm, Kroller and van
Jennings, 1983; Fetz and Cheney, 1980; Freund, 1983; Georgopoulos,
Kalaska and Massey, 1981).

Activation of the motor units results in motor output of the movement itself. The course of the movement is monitored continuously
through feedback by the Central Processing Unit resulting in error
detection and consequent ongoing error correction.

Sometimes students argue with me that error detection --feedback--
is over-emphasized in the model. They consider continuous error
monitoring an unnecessary complication. Unknown to them, they
reflect the viewpoint of action theorists and researchers who consider ballistic or closed skills as non-correctable acts, acts which
do not rely on feedback (Desmedt and Godaux, 1979; Lashley, 1951;
Schmidt et al., 1979; Smyth and Wing, 1984; Woodworth, 1889). However, rather than complicating the system, the concept of continuous
error monitoring streamlines and simplifies it if one considers why
errors occur. Errors can occur due to inefficient motor planning,
unpredicted or unexpected changes in the environment and changes in
the functional state of the muscles, e.g. fatigue. Information
about posture and about the course and outcome of the movement is

relayed to the Central Processing Unit without a break. This information is used to refine the plan of action for the subsequent
attempt leading to improvement. Unexpected environmental changes
can alter the course and outcome of the movement, however well it
has been planned. Through feedback the skilled act can be adapted
to environmental demands either at the stage of movement initiation
(tossing a ball which is heavier than anticipated) or en route
(avoiding a suddenly appearing opponent while running with a ball).
Lastly, a change in the physiological state of the musculature could
alter the output if feedback would not be monitored. For instance,
maintenance of steady posture induces fatigue in postural muscles.
With fatigue, changes in posture occur. Through feedback these
changes are perceived and errors are corrected by activating non
fatigued motor units. These are certainly sufficient reasons for
incorporating continuous monitoring of feedback into the model, especially as experimental data are available in support of this concept (Bairstow, 1986; Kirsch and Rhymer, 1987; Laszlo, Bairstow,
Ward and Bancroft, 1980; Paillard, 1987; Pew, 1974b).

The closed-loop model has the advantage of leading to taxonomy in
the motor skill field. All exogenous skills can be considered as a
single class of behaviour provided they are analysed in terms of the
processes included in the closed-loop model. Consider a closed and
an open skill: Baby hitting a rattle, a tennis player returning a
ball, respectively. The baby, at first, seems to wave both arms
randomly and by lucky chance hits the rattle and receives pleasant
visual and auditory signals. Arm waving has a purpose now and the
rattle is hit with increased frequency. Rattle hitting has the
hallmarks of skill acquisition and skilled performance. The behaviour is goal directed, the response is refined by practice and
environmental changes are responded to i.e., changes in relative
position of baby and rattle are taken into account. All these changes can be observed in the tennis player, the differences are quantitative, not qualitative. The response in tennis is more complex,
though both rattle hitting and tennis involve aiming and in both
skills the control of force, when hitting the target, changes the
outcome of the response. Without a doubt the environmental changes
are more complex in tennis than in the rattle hitting skill but in
both tasks, for success, environmental demands must be taken into
account.

Nor is there a need to postulate separate structures for performance
and acquisition of skills within the closed-loop system. Acquisition is characterised by improvement in performance. It has been
shown (Fitts and Posner, 1967) that even in highly skilled perfor-
mers asymptotic level is never reached, performance continues to
improve, albeit slowly. Certainly top level musicians and ballet
dancers keep practising throughout their career. Thus demarcation
between learning and performance must remain arbitrary. Learning
and performance curves, plotted along trials are never smooth,
though trial by trial variance is greater in the novice than in the
expert. However, even the experienced typist has 'bad patches' and
great ballet dancers might perform better on one night than on the
next. The intertrial variance might be due to overcorrection of
errors which occurred on the previous trial, to inadequate responses
to unexpected changes in the environment, or to changes in the
neuro-muscular apparatus. Thus both acquisition and performance de-

pend on identical processes, though the relative importance of motor planning, motor programming and feedback processing would vary between tasks and according to the stage of expertise of the performer.

4. IN SEARCH OF PROCESS-ORIENTATED MEASUREMENT

Motor development can be considered either from a task or a process-orientated viewpoint, as I have argued previously. In the main, the literature has adopted the task-orientated approach, emphasizing age related milestones and defining the age at which a child could be expected to master specific skills in the course of normal development. As our knowledge of motor function advanced, and the information processing theories gained experimental support (Bairstow and Laszlo, 1980; Bairstow and Laszlo, 1982; Laszlo and Bairstow, 1971; Laszlo, Bairstow and Baker, 1979; Laszlo and Baker, 1972; Laszlo and Ward, 1978) it became possible to turn to the process-orientated approach.

Could the process-orientated approach be an advance over task-orientated approach ? In the first place, process-orientated assessment could lead to a better understanding of perceptual-motor development than could be achieved by task-orientated methods. In the latter, assessment results in a list of tasks the child can perform at a certain age. However, confounding variables, such as motivation, opportunity and interest, will have a decisive influence on the types of skills the child has practised and can perform well. If, on the other hand, developmental progression in underlying processes, which contribute to learning and performance, can be established --process-orientated approach-- it should be possible to assess which tasks the child is ready to acquire and whether the child is functionning according to his ability level or below it.

Secondly, for a child presenting motor difficulties, task-orientated assessment can only reconfirm the list of tasks the child cannot perform adequately. The process-orientated diagnosis can establish the reason or reasons why the child cannot master some of the skills expected of him. That is, process dysfunction can be diagnosed and following causal diagnosis, focal therapy, aiming at improvement of the defective process, can be given.

4.1. Kinaesthesis: The Kinaesthetic Sensitivity Test

The first step in the search for a comprehensive process-orientated approach focused on kinaesthetic development.

The role of kinaesthesis in motor control was the central issue of my research from as far back as 1963 (Laszlo, 1966, 1967a, 1967b, 1968; Laszlo and Baguley, 1971; Laszlo and Bairstow, 1980). Kinaesthesis, or proprioception is served by four classes of receptors: Muscle spindles, tendon organs, joint and skin receptors (McCloskey, Macefield, Gandevia and Burke, 1987; Matthews, 1972). The input from these receptors is combined to convey information about the relative position of limbs and body parts, the direction and extent of movements, their speed and velocity and the force of contraction or tension generated in the muscles.

In 1970 Phillip Bairstow joined my research group and we continued
to delineate the importance of kinaesthesis in the acquisition and
performance of motor skills in finer detail (Bairstow and Laszlo,
1978a, 1978b, 1979a, 1979b, 1980, 1981, 1982; Laszlo and Bairstow,
1971). All our studies led to the one conclusion: Kinaesthesis is
the modality most intimately involved in the control of posture and
movement and it has a decisive role in motor behaviour.

Interestingly, at about the same time the mass-spring theory was
proposed and strongly supported in the U.S.A. Mass-spring theorists
focused on unidimensional forearm movements (Bizzi, Morasso and
Polit, 1978; Kelso, Holt, Kugler and Turvey, 1980; Polit and Bizzi,
1978)) and finger movements (Polit and Bizzi, 1979) and argued that
the control of movements is independent of sensory input, but is
determined by inherent characteristics of the muscles themselves.
It is outside the scope of this chapter to evaluate critically the
experimental methodology which led to this somewhat extreme theory.
Suffice it is to say that all our work, to be described, negate the
basic tenet of the mass-spring theory while supporting the information processing model, and pointing to the essential contribution
made by kinaesthesis to effective movement control.

*Figure 2:   Schematic illustration of the experimental set-up
in the 'nonsense' pattern experiment.*

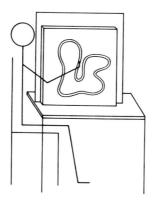

Coding and retention of kinaesthetic input was investigated by
Bairstow in a series of studies (Bairstow and Laszlo, 1978a;
Bairstow and Laszlo, 1979a, 1982). In these studies 'nonsense'
patterns were presented to the blindfolded subjects in the form of

grooved stencils. The subject, holding a stylus, traced around the
pattern either actively or passively i.e., the subject moved the
stylus around the groove, or the experimenter guided the subject's
arm, respectively. Three tasks were investigated: Tracking, recognition and reproduction. In tracking, the subject shadowed the
tracing hand with his other hand; in recognition, after the tracing
movement had been completed, the subject was shown a set of line
drawings where the traced pattern was displayed alongside slightly
distorted patterns; in reproduction the subject was required to draw
the pattern, after tracing it. Based on the findings Bairstow proposed a model in which the relative importance of kinaesthetic perception and memory and motor programming processes, in complex movements, was delineated.

Figure 3: Bairstow's model of tracking, recognition and recall.

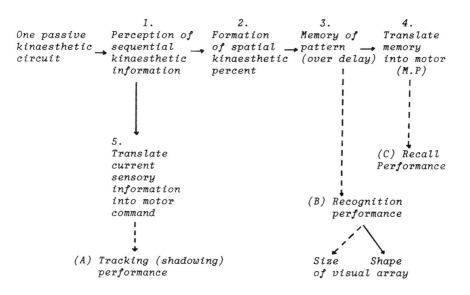

In all the studies where reproduction was the dependent variable,
subjects differed considerably in the accuracy with which the patterns were recalled. While the between subject variance was pronounced, within subject reproduction accuracy across patterns was
uniform. We argued that subjects might differ in the amount of
detail they can code per circuit. The able subject could extract
sufficient information during the set number of tracing circuits for
accurate coding of the pattern, allowing accurate reproduction,
while the less able subject would need additional circuits to build
a sufficiently detailed percept. In the study (Bairstow and Laszlo,
1982) designed to obtain evidence for this possible reason for individual differences, the subjects were encouraged to trace each pat-

tern in as many circuits as they thought necessary, until they were
confident that they 'felt' the pattern clearly and would be able to
reproduce it. Some subject chose to trace the patterns 2-4 times,
others used a great number of circuits. One subject went as far as
tracing a pattern 64 times. There was little variance in the number
of circuits within subjects, across patterns. The results were contrary to our expectations. Instead of finding a positive correlation between the number of circuits and the accuracy of recall, we
obtained significant negative correlation ! Our hypothesis, that
repeated exposure to the same input would eliminate the differences,
had to be abandoned. It became clear that subjects differed in
their basic ability to perceive and/or memorise kinaesthetic information.

Adults have reached, presumably, full development in kinaesthetic
ability, yet the level attained varies between individuals. It is
reasonable to assume that children differ from each other to an even
greater extent than adults considering that children develop abilities at very different rates.

We turned our attention to the measurement of normal kinaesthetic
development, realising that development of kinaesthetic processing
ability has not been investigated previously. While the need for an
adequate test of kinaesthesis has been recognised as early as 1955
(Scott, 1955), such a test was not available. All test procedures,
which had been claimed to assess children's kinaesthetic function
(Ayres, 1972a, 1972b) confounded perceptual and motor factors. The
validity of a perceptual test is extremely doubtful if the response
depends on both perception and motor control. A rather extreme
example will illustrate the point. If an athetoid, cerebral palsied
child is asked to touch his nose with his forefinger (usually with
eyes closed) he will predictably fail to do so. He might fail because he is unable to feel the direction in which his arm is moving
--kinaesthetic, perceptual disability-- or he might fail because the
motor programme generated is inappropriate and/or because the involuntary movements, that he can't control, interfere with the planned
voluntary movement --motor disability.

We set out to design a test of kinaesthesis free from confounding
factors. We searched for test items in which the stimuli were presented kinaesthetically, uncontaminated by other modalities or motor
demands and hence the scores obtained would depend solely on the
subject's kinaesthetic sensitivity; we looked for items in which the
subject could indicate the response without difficulty, even if his
level of motor control was low; and finally we wanted items which
could be scored quantitatively and objectively.

Two items of kinaesthetic processing are included in the final version of the Kinaesthetic Sensitivity Test, (KST; Laszlo and
Bairstow, 1985b) assessing two aspects of kinaesthesis: Kinaesthetic acuity and kinaesthetic perception and memory.

Kinaesthetic acuity is assessed by comparing the movement and position of the two arms. The apparatus consists of two ramps, mounted
parallel to each other onto a baseboard.

Figure 4:   K S T   Apparatus.

Kinesthetic acuity   Kinaesthetic perception and
                                                    memory

The ramps can be set, independently of each other, at different angles from the horizontal. Two pegs, mounted on blocks are held by
the subject. The apparatus and the subject's arms are covered by a
masking box. With the ramps set at different predetermined angles,
the tester guides the pegs up and down the runways moving the two
hands simultaneously. The task is to indicate which hand went up
higher. The response can be given by wriggling a finger on the chosen side, or by knocking the appropriate peg, by tilting the head or
by any means the child finds convenient. We do not accept verbal
'right' or 'left' responses --as children of this age are known to
have difficulties differentiating left from right ! Thirty-two
trials are given, with 40 or 60 separations at ages 5-6 years, 30 or
50 from seven years onwards. The score is the number of incorrect
responses out of 32.

For assessing kinaesthetic perception and memory we adapted the previously described pattern tracing task of the Bairstow studies.
Curved 'nonsense' patterns are cut into round discs. The discs fit,
centrally, onto a turntable. On the turntable, surrounding the
disc, 360° are marked in 1° steps. Again the test is given under

the masking box. The subject holds a stylus in the preferred hand,
the flange of the stylus fits into the pattern groove. The stylus
is guided by the tester around the pattern of two circuits, and the
child's hand is removed from the apparatus. The tester rotates the
disc and removes the masking box. The subject's task is to reorien-
tate the pattern of its original position. The error score is given
by the difference in degrees between the original setting and the
reorientation setting. In this task the subject is required to ro-
tate the disc, a relatively simple motor response. However, if the
child finds rotation difficult, the tester can help with the rotation and the child can indicate when the pattern is in the 'right'
position. None of the children in the normative sample needed help
with rotating the discs. Only twice did we have to assist children,
both suffered from cerebral palsy.

Normative data were collected in Western Australia, England and
Canada. 5-12 year old children and adults were tested. Test reliability and validity have been described previously (Laszlo and
Bairstow, 1985a, 1985b). Of interest here are the developmental
trends for the two aspects of kinaesthetic processing assessed by
the KST, which are graphically shown in Figure 5.

Figure 5: Kinaesthetic developmental trends.

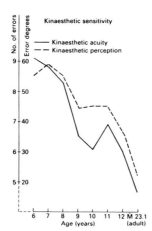

Developmental progression is similar for the two tasks. Both kinaesthetic acuity and kinaesthetic perception and memory develop
rapidly from 5-8 years, a plateau is evident from 8 to 11, with further improvement to adulthood. Thus kinaesthesis was shown to be a
late developing sense. When the range of scores for each age group

is considered, similarities between the tasks is apparent again.

TABLE 1

A: Kinaesthetic Acuity

Age(years)	5	6	7	8	9	10	11	12	M22 (adult)
Mean	19.0	13.4	7.8	4.7	3.6	6.1	5.2	3.5	3.0
Standard deviation	17.6	10.9	9.2	3.5	2.3	5.0	3.4	3.3	3.0
Range:Best	1.8	2.7	2.1	1.3	1.1	1.1	1.6	.9	1.0
Worst	52.0	35.5	42.2	16.5	8.6	20.6	15.0	12.6	13.5

B: Kinaesthetic perception and memory

Age(years)	5	6	7	8	9	10	11	12	M22 (adult)
Mean	78.1	75.7	75.5	64.1	60.9	58.9	62.9	58.3	36.0
Standard deviation	19.2	20.1	13.9	17.6	15.6	19.9	14.4	19.7	19.0
Range:Best	38.2	33.9	44.5	39.6	37.7	20.4	36.9	24.6	11.1
Worst	112.7	116.3	93.2	93.4	92.0	99.1	87.3	86.1	80.8

Some children in the youngest age group have developed kinaesthetic processing ability close to the adult mean, while at the lower end of the range the error scores reflect near random performance. Indeed, detailed examination of the results revealed that approximately 30 percent of the 6-7 year old groups performed one or both kinaesthetic tasks at this low level.

Both test items of the KST assess spatial aspects of kinaesthesis. In the acuity task concurrent input from the upper limbs must be discriminated, while in the perception and memory task the sequentially received information needs to be structured into a spatially coherent pattern which is stored in memory and retrieved when the pattern is reorientated.

The two test items correlate positively but the correlation is low, r=0.20. High positive correlation would indicate considerable commonality between the items and would render one of them superfluous. Some children can discriminate the 4° and 6° or 3° and 5° differences in arm movement and position; their kinaesthetic acuity is well developed, yet they cannot perform the kinaesthetic perception and memory task adequately. The reason would be that they

cannot form an image based on the sequentially received input generated during pattern tracing and/or they cannot store this information. On the other hand some children might be able to code and
memorize the kinaesthetic input only if the directional changes are
greater than 5° or 6°, as is the case in the patterns. Of course
there are children whose kinaesthetic development reaches the level
where both tasks are performed well, and there are those who have
not developed kinaesthetic sensitivity sufficiently for either
tasks.

The child who is below age expected level in one aspect of kinaesthetic processing might find particular motor skills more difficult
to perform than others depending on whether fine discrimination of
kinaesthetic stimuli or continuous processing and memorizing of
kinaesthetic input is of greater importance in the task.

Once we had established that the KST was a valid and reliable test,
we carried out some preliminary investigations on the relationship
between kinaesthetic function and motor performance. In Waterloo,
Canada, we compared two groups of University students (enrolled in
Kinesiology) on the KST. Ballet dancers and gymnasts were in one
group, students engaged in other sport activities were selected for
the second group. The groups did not differ in kinaesthetic acuity,
but the ballet dancers and gymnasts were significantly better at
kinaesthetic perception and memory than the other group (Bairstow
and Laszlo, 1981). We proposed that ballet and gymnastics are
skills which demand fine continuous kinaesthetic processing more so
than, ball skills. The results confirmed our hypothesis, but more
importantly, they indicated that, through practice, kinaesthetic
processing ability can be improved.

With children we confined our investigation to paper-pencil skills,
drawing and writing (Laszlo and Broderick, 1985). We decided to
investigate paper-pencil skills for a number of reasons: They are
practised by all children in primary school; large individual differences are apparent in rate of acquisition and level of performance; and kinaesthesis would be important in both performance and
acquisition. Error detection and consequent error correction would
be based kinaesthetically. In addition, kinaesthetic memory traces
would need to be stored at each practice trial in order to improve
the next attempt. It has been argued that vision is the most important source of information in paper-pencil skills. Certainly the
visually perceived lines give knowledge of results about the outcome. However, by the time the line appears on the paper, it is too
late to alter the course of the movement. For ongoing monitoring
kinaesthesis is necessary.

We calculated (Bairstow and Laszlo, 1981) correlations between kinaesthetic scores, drawing and writing, and obtained r=0.77 between
kinaesthetic acuity and drawing and r=0.68 between kinaesthetic perception and memory and writing. The correlation results supported
our prediction that kinaesthetic processing ability is important for
adequate performance in paper-pencil skills. Yet, on reflection, we
realised that to seek a simple relationship between one single process and a complex skill is not a theoretically valid procedure as
all motor skills rely on a combination of a number of perceptual and
motor processes. A strong validation procedure for establishing the

hypothesesed importance of kinaesthetic processing ability in paper-pencil skills is through the use of test-train-retest experimental paradigm. In 1983 (Laszlo and Bairstow, 1983) we carried out our first test-train-retest study in order to validate our theoretical standing i.e., adequate kinaesthetic sensitivity is necessary in acquisition and performance of motor skill. The children were tested on the KST, and in drawing, trained in kinaesthesis and retested on KST and drawings. I will describe a far more comprehensive test-train-retest study than the 1983 study, later in this chapter. I will not go into details here, except to say that following kinaesthetic training children improved in paper-pencil skills.

4.2 Motor programming: Perceptual-Motor Abilities Test

Kinaesthetic processing, however important in motor behaviour, is but one of the component processes in the closed-loop system. Evidence for the interrelationship between sensory and motor systems have been presented by both anatomists and neurophysiologists (Brooks, 1979; Fetz and Cheney, 1980; Fromm and Evarts, 1982; Macpherson, Marangoz, Miles and Wiesendanger, 1982; Godschalk, Aremon, Nijo and Kuypers, 1981). Thus for a comprehensive assessment of perceptual-motor development from a process-orientated viewpoint, it is necessary to assess, in addition to kinaesthetic development, age related progression in motor programming and motor planning. Successful construction of the KST encouraged us to extend the test to include assessment of motor processes.

Difficulties confronted us as soon as we started to look for suitable test items. Idealy we should choose items we would consider to be dependent on a single process: Spatial programming, temporal programming or motor planning. This proved to be an unrealistic aim. Firstly there is no motor task which does not involve perceptual processes. We could be fairly certain that in normal children visual and auditory perception reached a level adequate for performing most skills by age five. This is not the case with kinaesthetic processing, as we have seen from the developmental data. Thus scores for any test item will be influenced not only by the level of the motor process we are attempting to assess but by the level of kinaesthetic ability attained by the child as well.

A further difficulty emerged when we searched for tasks depending on temporal programming alone, without a spatial component. There are tasks in which the goal is defined spatially, without temporal restrictions, but whether one is supposed to move quickly or slowly, one is also moving 'somewhere'. Even in the most temporally defined task, reaction time, one must aim for the key or lever. Indeed, originally we did include a simple reaction time item, with a large response key and observed many misses especially in the younger age groups. As has been shown by Laszlo and Livesey (1977) varying accuracy demands changes response time.

Rather than trying to find tasks depending on single processes, we decided to use tasks in which the processes under examination were combined in predetermined combinations and to subject the data to factor analysis.

Once the decision regarding process combinations in test items had

been reached, we had to define some further principles we were to
follow in the construction of the Perceptual-Motor Abilities Test,
PMAT (Laszlo and Bairstow, 1985a).

In contrast to most existing motor tests in which 'everyday' tasks
are used (Bruininks, 1978; Gubbay, 1975; McCarthy, 1972; Stott et
al., 1984), we aimed at designing novel tasks. The argument that
everyday tasks have greater ecological validity than 'laboratory'
tasks is debatable, especially if one considers such 'everyday'
tasks as drawing lines and crosses simultaneously (Bruininks, 1978),
balancing a tennis ball on a small wooden board while walking (Stott
et al., 1984) or throwing an eight cm2 beanbag through a circular
hole of 12 cm diameter from a two meter distance (McCarthy, 1972).
Most motor tests (including the PMAT) are designed to test children
with possible motor problems. Expectation of failure in everyday
tasks would reduce the child's motivation when performing the item.
Children referred for assessment come to the diagnostician with a
list of skills they cannot perform satisfactorily. We saw little
use in including items such as tying shoelaces (Gubbay, 1975) when
this skill is already listed as one the child has difficulties with.
Lastly everyday tasks are practised to different degrees by children
and this practice effect would be difficult to account for when
attempting to assess abilities.

Thus we tried to design items to include in the PMAT which are novel
and in which different amounts of pretesting practice do not influence the test scores, and expectation of failure is lessened. Because our aim was to assess underlying processes rather than overt
behaviour, we needed items which could be given to all age groups,
from 5 years to adults. By changing tasks from age group to age
group, as done in existing tests, the relative weighting of the processes across age groups would vary in an ill-defined way. While it
is not easy to find tasks which are not too difficult for the younger age group or trivial for the adults --it is not impossible. We
avoided commercially available toys such as the 'posting-box'
(Gubbay, 1975) which are perceived as 'baby toys' even by five year
olds and tasks where the instructions are complex and would tax the
cognitive capabilities of the children. Wherever possible, we tried
to find items which could be perceived as games to increase motivation. Finally only items which could be scored quantitatively and
objectively were included in the PMAT.

The following is a list of the test items (for detailed description
see Laszlo and Bairstow, 1985a) grouped according to the process or
processes they were designed to assess:

a.   Planning and spatio-temporal programming:
        Ward-game - rolling balls at a moving target; ball-handling-
        transferring different sized balls from one bucket to another
        as fast as possible.

b.   Spatio-temporal programming:
        Catching balls rolled down a chute, with the chute at five
        settings of increasing steepness; aiming at stationary
        targets, dots on paper to be touched with a pen as fast as
        possible; video game, crossing targets presented on a
        television screen.

c.   Motor planning and spatial programming:
      Copying simple geometric shapes.

d.   Spatial programming:
      Pencil tracing between lines and over lines using the same
      geometric figures as in the previous task.

e.   Temporal programming:
      Simple reaction time task.

f.   Force programming:
      Maintenance of force over 10 sec.

g.   Kinaesthetic sensitivity:
      Kinaesthetic acuity; kinaesthetic perception and memory;
      imitation of static posture in the supine position.

h.   Velocity discrimination:
      Comparison of two stimuli moving at different velocities;
      stimulus presentations were either both visual, both
      kinaesthetic or cross-modal, one visual one kinaesthetic.

i.   Balance:
      Heel-to-toe and one legged stands, with and without vision.

Two tasks had to be excluded from the test. One was force programming, as even the six year olds could perform it practically without
error. The reaction time task was omitted because the spatial programming demand made it unsuitable as a measure of temporal programming only. As the spatial component could not be included into the
score, it could not be used as a spatio-temporal task either. In
the copying task three geometric shapes were presented to the child,
a square, the square turned by 45° i.e., 'diamond' and a horseshoe.
On analysis we found large individual differences in the copy of the
squares in the younger age groups but no significant age related improvement, possibly due to practice effects. Accordingly we used
the 'diamond' and horseshoe scores only in the main analysis. In
later studies the child was given two figures only. The square was
not scored in the tracing task either. In all remaining tasks significant improvement with age was found (Laszlo and Bairstow,
1985a). In all but two items, ball catch and balance, the developmental trend appeared to be step-wise rather than continuous.

The graphs indicate that development progresses at the fastest rate
in the youngest age groups, followed by apparent plateaux. From 11
years on improvement seems continuous. Statistically all developmental trends were significant within tasks. Detailed comparisons
established distinct age groupings across tasks. Six and seven year
olds formed two separate groups, and they differed from the eight
and nine year old group. The eight and nine year olds and the 10
and 11 year olds formed the next two groups. Thus development was
shown to progress in distinct steps up to 11 years from whereon it
is probably continuous.

The developmental analysis just described was based on task performance and hence could not reflect directly the development of the
processes we set out to assess. Only through factor analytical

Figure 6:   Developmental trends in PMAT Tasks.

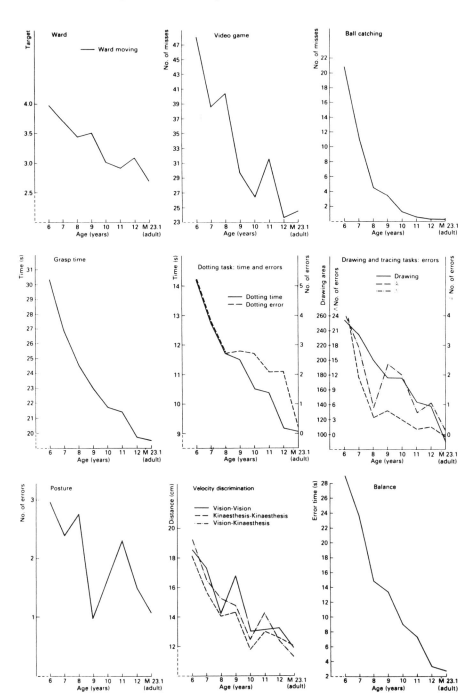

methods could we establish whether the tasks were indeed indicators
of underlying processes, and, if so, whether various processes would
emerge at different ages. Four analyses were carried out, using the
scores from six, seven, eight and 11 year old children. These four
ages represented the four steps in task development established by
the statistical procedure already described. The results were en-
couraging, though the factor structures were by no means as definitive as we had hoped for.

Velocity discrimination with kinaesthetic, visual and cross-modal
input emerged as Factor 1 in all four age groups, with all three
velocity tasks loading on this factor. Between tasks analysis
showed that kinaesthetic discrimination was no more difficult than
visual discrimination at any age. This is in marked contrast to our
findings on kinaesthetic development using the KST, where both test
items related to spatial aspects of kinaesthesis. The difference
between velocity and spatial information processing could be due to
the difference in neural signals generated in response to velocity
versus directional changes of movements (Matthews, 1972). It appears that the sharper neural signal generated by velocity change is
easier to code than the slowly graded signal denoting muscle length
or directional changes. Velocity information is processed with
equal efficiency, regardless of whether the presentation is intra-or
cross-modal when vision and kinaesthesis are compared at least from
six years of age.

Factors 2 and 3 were remarkably similar in the two youngest age
groups. The best description of item groupings would be steadiness
and ball handling hardly a process-orientated classification !

At eight years of age Factor 2 included only those items which were
hypothesized to rely on spatio-temporal programming, while Factor 3
loaded on all items which depended on spatial programming. These
results are interpreted to show that by age eight spatial and
spatio-temporal programming have developed sufficiently to emerge as
a decisive factor in perceptual-motor performance.

In the 11 year old group Factors 2 and 3 could not be interpreted.

Motor planning did not appear in the factor structure. However,
evidence for the importance of motor planning and of motor planning
as a process independent of motor programming has been obtained by
Broderick (Broderick and Laszlo, 1987, 1988). We found, on scoring
the original PMAT data, and from one of Broderick's studies that a
square is copied more accurately than a 'diamond' at all ages tested, from 6 years on and including adults. This was the case even
though the two figures were identical and differed only in orientation i.e., the diamond we refer to is a square rotated by 45°.
Broderick hypothesised that the diamond is more difficult to copy
than the square because the motor planning demands are more exacting
for the obliquely placed figure than for one with a horizontal-
vertical orientation; and that the differential motor planning demand would apply to figure components as well as to whole figures.
In order to test her hypothesis she presented figure components in
both horizontal-vertical and oblique orientations, comprising single
lines or two lines, systematically varying the planning demands,
while keeping programming demands unchanged i.e., the movements to

be made were identical. Horizontal-vertical figure components were
copied more accurately than obliques within the same planning conditions. As planning demands increased across tasks, so did the difference in copying accuracy increase between horizontal-vertical and
oblique lines. Her results showed that motor planning improves with
age, and that advanced levels of planning are reached by 10 years of
age.

I am aware that we appear to ignore cognitive factors and their contribution to perceptual-motor behaviour. This is however, not the
case. Rather than ignoring cognition, we are deliberately aiming at
minimizing cognitive demands. By doing so we feel justified in focusing on perceptual and motor processes --a difficult enough problem by itself. In any case cognitive deficits are outside the
boundaries of our diagnostic and therapeutic area.

In all PMAT tasks instructions are simple and performance is loaded
on perceptual and motor processes with cognitive demands held to a
minimum. For instance children are asked to copy figures, rather
than draw them from memory. In the KST items, the tasks are demonstrated first with full vision, then the child performs them with
vision before the masking box is applied; we are certain, before
testing is started, that the child fully understands what he is
expected to do.

5. PERCEPTUAL-MOTOR DYSFUNCTION: CAUSAL DIAGNOSIS AND FOCAL THERAPY

It has been shown by applying the PMAT to normal children that the
test is effective in assessing the following perceptual and motor
processes: Kinaesthetic acuity, kinaesthetic perception and memory,
spatio-temporal programming and spatial programming.

The next step in our investigation was to establish whether the PMAT
could be used as a diagnostic tool with children presenting motor
problems. That is, would the disabled sample differ from normal
children on the PMAT and if so, would the test results identify developmental delays in specific processes. If the PMAT scores do
indicate dysfunction in specific processes the diagnosis could be
followed by treatment designed to alleviate the dysfunction.

We decided to use children variously labelled clumsy children
(Gubbay, 1975) or children with "Minimal Brain Dysfunction" (Gordon
and McKinlay, 1980). There are a number of reasons for focusing on
this group. Firstly there is a general consensus that clumsy children are free of hard neurological signs, though Knuckey, Apsimon and
Gubbay (1983) did claim that with brain scan some abnormality in
some clumsy children could be discerned. The absence of neurological abnormalities points to developmental delays as a possible cause
for the clumsy child syndrome. If developmental delay is the cause,
process-orientated diagnosis and therapy should be effective.

Another reason for our choice was the high incidence rate of clumsiness --approximately 10 percent-- in the 7-12 year age group, and
the serious effects clumsiness has on the children who suffer from
this condition. The problems caused by the primary motor symptoms

are aggravated by the secondary emotional and social consequences.
The secondary symptoms are due to the frequent criticism from teachers and parents, and rejection and ridicule by peers. Furthermore, while the primary motor difficulties can be camouflaged, secondary symptoms often persist into adolescence (McKinlay, 1988).

Finally, there is no reliable evidence to support the efficacy of
the task-orientated diagnostic and treatment methods in use.

5.1. Causal diagnosis

We restricted our sample to 7.5-12 year old children. We found
(Laszlo and Bairstow, 1983, 1985a) that in the 5-7 year group 33
percent of the children performed one or both kinaesthetic items of
the KST at a level below that needed for adequate performance of
finely graded skills. Rather than diagnosing these children as
clumsy one should consider them within the normal, albeit slow end,
of the developmental range.

The study was conducted at the Department of Developmental Paedia-
trics (The Wolfson Centre, TWC) in London. The children were referred for participation in the study by teachers of six mainstream
Junior Schools. Teachers were asked to select children, who in
their opinion had difficulties with motor skills such as writing,
dressing, playing ball games or PE. It was stressed that we were
looking for children who performed all or some of the motor skills
less efficiently than their classmates, and whose motor development
appeared to lag behind their intellectual attainments.

Forty seven children were referred. On referral the class teachers
completed a questionnaire for each child. Three behavioural areas
were included in the questionnaire pertaining to academic attainment, motor and social behaviour.

Each child came to TWC with parent/s for the first testing session.
The testing protocol included:

a.   The child's medical and family history was obtained from the
       parent by a paediatric neurologist.

b.   A questionnaire was administered to the parent regarding the
       child's motor, social and emotional status.

c.   Each child was given an extensive medical and neurological
       examination.

d.   The child was encouraged to discuss his problems with me,
       without the parent being present.

e.   The PMAT was administered.

f.   The TOMI was administered.

We wanted to include a task-orientated test into our assessment protocol and compare the process and task orientated assessment methods
to see if the severity of motor impairment could be assessed by both
methods. The TOMI (Stott et al., 1984) being independent of the

PMAT, served as a control especially in retest. The TOMI was chosen
from the available task-orientated tests because test items are scored objectively and because the individual item scores are combined
to give a single score of the severity of motor impairment.

The video-game from the PMAT was omitted and instead a more extensive "video-game" was used. Bairstow tested the children on two
tasks: One was aiming for a moving target --an upgraded version of
the PMAT tasks (Bairstow, 1988)-- and the other involved tracking
and recall of a target moving along a circular path (Bairstow and
Laszlo, submitted).

The entire programme was completed within three hours. Favourites
with the children were the PMAT and video-games and the refreshments
we served.

Seven children were excluded from the original 47 as these children's scores were nearly on the mean for their age on both PMAT and
TOMI.

Of the remaining 40 children, 31 were boys, and four children were
left handed. Proportional representation of the various ethnic
groups in the sample approximated that the school population. The
full range of intellectual abilities was seen in the sample including the three brightest boys from one school (teacher's opinion) to
one boy who was to be placed into a school for slow learners.

On completion of the testing programme the PMAT raw scores were
transformed into Z scores. Using the normative means and standard
deviations, each PMAT item score was standardized.

We found that some tasks did not discriminate between normal and
clumsy children, namely the Ward game and the three velocity discrimination tasks. It seems that velocity discrimination, as I discussed earlier, relies on different kinaesthetic signals from the signals denoting spatial changes. The fact that the present sample
did not differ from the normative sample indicates that perception
of movement velocity develops independently from perception of the
spatial aspects of kinaesthesis and that developmental delay in
kinaesthetic perception of velocity occurs only rarely if at all.

What are the conclusions we can draw from the results of the testing
programme ? The results of the neurological examination confirmed
previous findings. Antecedents of clumsiness were not found, nor
were hard neurological signs. Soft signs occurred with no greater
frequency than would be expected in a normal sample. We are, therefore, justified in assuming that clumsiness is caused by developmental delay, the cause of which is unknown at present.

We compared the results of the PMAT and TOMI. In order to facilitate the comparison, the PMAT item Z scores were combined for each
child yielding a PMAT 'index' score. The correlation between PMAT
index score and TOMI global score was r=0.65, a significant, and
even respectable, correlation. Thus it is possible to assess the
severity of motor impairment by both process- and task-orientated
testing method.

The PMAT results were graphed for each child. The items were ordered to reflect the processes they were designed to assess. Thus for
each child a process profile was plotted. Examples of two profiles
are given in Figure 7.

Figure 7: Process profile of two children.

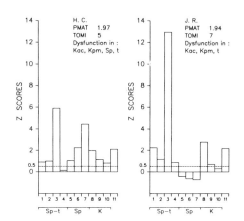

Tasks are plotted in the following order: 1. Ward game; 2. Ball
handling; 3. Ball catch; 4. Dotting; 5. Drawing; 6. Tracing between
double lines; 7. Tracing over single line; 8. Kinaesthetic acuity;
9. Kinaesthetic perception and memory; 10. Posture; 11. Balance.
Tasks 1-4 assess spatio-temporal programming; tasks 5-7 assess
spatial programming; tasks 8-10 assess kinaesthetic sensitivity.

The profiles and hence process disability configurations varied
markedly. Children with similar symptoms and similar PMAT index
scores and TOMI scores would present different process profiles.
For instance for one child the major dysfunction was located in
kinaesthetic acuity and kinaesthetic perception and memory and temporal programming, while the other child showed high error scores in
all kinaesthetic and programming items.

The most often diagnosed deficiency was in kinaesthetic sensitivity.
29 children (73 percent) processed kinaesthetic input at below one
standard deviation for their age in kinaesthetic acuity and/or kinaesthetic perception and memory. Kinaesthetic disability, in all 29
children was combined with spatial and/or temporal programming problems. Of the remaining 11 children three were found to have temporal programming difficulty, one had spatial programming and seven
had spatial and temporal programming difficulties.

The prevalence of kinaesthetic dysfunction supports our contention
-adequate kinaesthetic processing ability is an important factor in
motor proficiency. Indeed, we feel justified to suggest that
Perceptual-Motor Dysfunction (PMD) should be substituted for the
emotive label of clumsiness or the ill-defined term Minimal Brain
Dysfunction.

5.2. Validation of the process-orientated approach:
      The test-train-retest paradigm; focal therapy

A strong method to validate our theoretical standpoint is the application of the Test-Train-Retest design. If we intend to establish
that the diagnosed deficiencies are the cause of the overt symptoms,
we can attempt to alleviate, through training, the process deficiencies, and then measure the change in overt symptoms.

Accordingly, the forty children who had been tested were allocated
into four groups. Group allocation was achieved by stratified ran-
domization based on the PMAT index scores.

The four groups differed from each other in the type of training the
children received. Children in Group 1 were trained kinaesthetically in one or both, kinaesthetic acuity and kinaesthetic perception
and memory, depending on their PMAT scores, and were also given
training to correct any programming problems; Group 2 was trained
kinaesthetically only although the children had programming difficulties as well; in Group 3 spatial and/or temporal programming was
trained although the children needed kinaesthetic training also;
while Group 4, the control group, received task-orientated remedial
exercises in paper-pencil skills, body awareness and in some gross
motor skills i.e., the training was not based on diagnosed dysfunction but was similar to remedial training used by teachers and the-
rapists.

Training, in kinaesthetic and programming processes was designed on
the following principles: Training tasks were chosen which depended
on single processes; each task could be graded from easy to difficult in small steps so that the children seldom experienced failure
and could monitor improvement; as far as possible, tasks had "fun"
value. The last principle applied to the Group 4 training tasks as
well.

On average each child had nine training sessions of 20-30 minutes
duration spread over 2-2.5 weeks. Immediately following training
the PMAT and TOMI were readministered.

The test-retest results are summarized in Figure 8 (Laszlo,
Bairstow, Bartrip and Rolfe, 1988).

Groups 1 and 2 improved significantly on both PMAT and TOMI. Group
3 and 4 did not. Correlation between PMAT and TOMI on retest was
r=0.67.

Three months after retest the teachers filled in the follow-up questionnaire. Significant improvement was found in Motor Behaviour in
Groups 1 and 2 only.

Two major theoretical implications can be drawn from these results.
Firstly, the results validate the hypothesized process structure
underlying perceptual-motor behaviour.   Processes were identified
and diagnosed dysfunctions alleviated.   Process-orientated training
generalized to everyday skills, resulting in improved performance.
Secondly, it was shown conclusively that adequate kinaesthetic processing is a necessary prerequisite for efficient motor function
i.e., Group 2 improved, while Group 3 did not.

Figure 8:   Test-retest results.

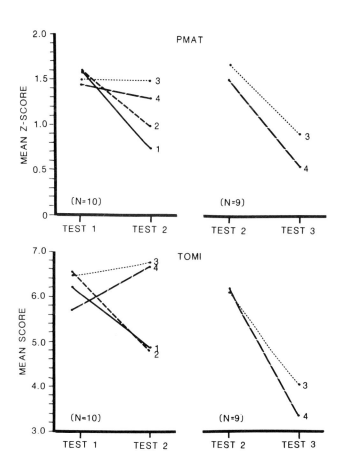

For ethical reasons and as a replication procedure, Groups 3 and 4
were then retrained. Group 3 received kinaesthetic training only,
Group 4 children were trained in all processes which were diagnosed
as deficient. In Figure 8 the results are presented graphically.
The previous findings were replicated. Both PMAT and TOMI results
(correlation r=0.65) showed significant improvement for both groups.
A replication study restricted to Groups 1 and 4 was conducted recently in England. Our results were confirmed.

One further point needs to be made. In simple tasks children did
improve as soon as process deficiencies were alleviated. This was
shown by improvement on the TOMI and observed during the training
period e.g., a number of children, from Groups 1 and 2, and during
retraining of Group 3 and 4, started to participate in ball games
with some success. However, complex skills, such as writing did not
improve overnight. Given the ability needed to perform the skill,
the child had to learn the skill, with practice. Figure 9 is an
example of improvement over three months in handwriting, shown by
Nicholas.

Figure 9:   Pre- and post training handwriting samples.

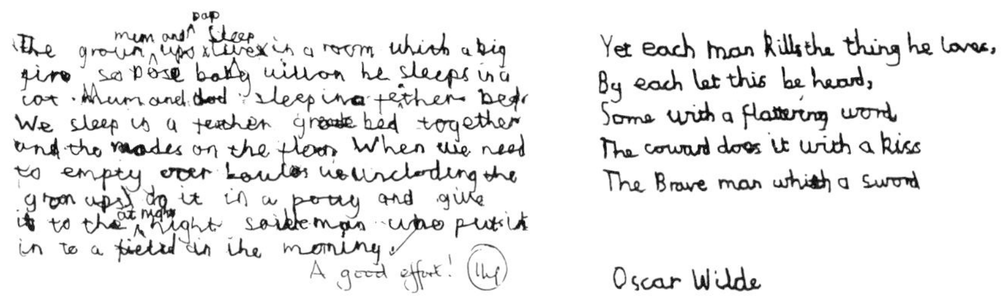

Lefthand side sample was written just prior to training; righthand
side sample was written two months after completion of training.
Nicholas, a bright 9 year old, was diagnosed as a sever PMD (PMAT
index score 2.34; TOMI score 7) with deficiencies in both kinaesthetic and both programming processes, and trained, in Group 1.

Finally, the results of Bairstow's 'Video-games' need to be considered. The 40 PMD children were tested on both the aiming and tracking tasks at the first testing session, on retest, and Group 3 and
4 again after retraining.

Normal developmental trends were established for both the interception task and the tracking and recall task in children 5-12 years
and adults (Bairstow, 1987, 1988; Laszlo et al., 1988). In the
interception task the aim was to cross over the target which moved
down the television screen. Each aiming response was analysed in
terms of temporal and spatial movement parameters. It was shown
that temporal control of the movement was planned, to a large extent, during movement initiation time, while the spatial aspects of

the response were under continuous control throughout the course of the movement --further evidence for the independence of temporal and spatial processes. In the tracking task the target moved on a circular path for two circuits. The subject was required to hold the stylus on the target. After the second circuit the target disappeared and the subject attempted to continue the movement as though the target would still be visible --recall circuit. Performance was again analysed in temporal and spatial terms.

Bairstow examined 11 variables for each of his tasks to arrive at the fine grained comparison between normal and PMD children (Bairstow and Laszlo, submitted). I can only give a brief resume of his findings here. His major conclusions were that PMD children are a heterogeneous group, with the children varying greatly in the way they cope with motor demands. Some cannot plan their movements, others have difficulties with ongoing control. Yet, despite their disabilities, some managed to compensate by using different strategies, and reach unexpected accuracy from time to time. He also showed that kinaesthetic dysfunction impairs performance on these tasks and that kinaesthetic training improves motor function especially in the tracking and recall tasks.

The results of the 'video-game' studies lend further strong support for our view: That the processes, which underlie motor performance can be experimentally defined and independently assessed and that kinaesthetic processing is necessary for adequate motor function. Equally important is the demonstration that similar performance level on a task reached by different children does not indicate similar abilities or disabilities. That is, task-orientated assessment cannot reveal the nature of the underlying perceptual-motor dysfunction.

6. OVERVIEW

Both practical and theoretical issues arise from the work I have been describing in this chapter.

In normal children, the process-orientated approach has led to an understanding of the development of the processes underlying perceptual-motor behaviour. We showed that the gradually increasing proficiency in motor performance with age is due to stepwise development of both perceptual and motor processes. I am not claiming that we were the only group who attempted to look at perceptual-motor processes. Ayres (1972a, 1972b) formulated a diagnostic-treatment system on a process-orientated approach. The theory she proposed, and on which she based her system, has been evaluated and criticized in detail (Laszlo and Bairstow, 1985a; Cratty, 1981). The major weakness in Ayres system lies in her theory, which lacks experimental support. The test and therapy of Sensory Integration is difficult to relate to existing knowledge, and her results are difficult to interpret.

The advances in neurophysiology enable us to anchor the closed-loop model to established findings, and in some instances strengthen the physiological results by behavioural data. The separation of spatial and temporal aspects of kinaesthesis is one example. We have

shown, as far as I know for the first time, that processing of kinaesthetic information on movement velocity develops earlier, and
independently from kinaesthetic information about the direction and
extent of movements.

With the aid of the KST we have established that normal kinaesthetic
development (spatial aspect) is slow and stepwise throughout childhood, that large individual differences in kinaesthetic development
occur and that kinaesthetic processing ability is necessary for the
acquisition and performance of motor skills. These findings need to
be considered in both the clinical and educational setting. Clini-
cally, the most frequent cause of motor dysfunction was found to be
inadequate kinaesthetic processing, and alleviation of kinaesthetic
disability was essential in the alleviation of the motor dysfunction.

In education, the developmental level of the children should be considered when setting curricular demands in early schooling. Writing
is a task relevant to my argument. Reading readiness is generally
taken into account, but it is tacitly accepted that children who are
ready to read, should also be ready to write. Certainly the cognitive demands are similar in the two skills. But writing includes
perceptual-motor abilities, especially kinaesthetic processing ability, which are additional to those needed in reading. We have
found that one in three children at the beginning of their schooling
have not reached kinaesthetic processing ability necessary for the
acquisition of finely graded motor skills, such as handwriting.
These children are disadvantaged from the outset of their schooling,
with resulting loss of self esteem and motivation. The concept of
kinaesthetic readiness should be incorporated into curricular considerations.

Physiological findings showing that temporal and spatial programming
are controlled independently were supported by our developmental
data. The results of the studies on motor development showed that
motor planning develops at a different rate from programming, high-
lighting the complexity of perceptual-motor process structure.

Once the development of perceptual-motor processes could be verified
experimentally and normal trends were established, we could consider
diagnostic and treatment methods for children with motor disabilities. We predicted that process-orientated diagnosis and therapy
would be superior to the task-orientated approach for two reasons:

1. Process-orientated method should be effective because skilled
performance of a task depends on the adequately developed processes
necessary for task performance. Practising a task, as done in task-
orientated treatment, cannot lead to improvement if process dysfunction persists.

2. Many and varied tasks rely on common processes. Alleviating process dysfunction should improve performance in all tasks reliant on
the same process, that is improvement in a process would generalize
to a wide variety of tasks. What we did not predict was the ease
with which process dysfunction can be alleviated if treatment is
focused sharply on the process or processes which were diagnosed to
be deficient. In practical terms process-orientated training can be

successful after 2-3 hours training spread over a two week period, which compares favourably with months or years of task training. Furthermore the success of task orientated training has not been evaluated under strict experimental conditions.

The finding that kinaesthetic dysfunction is the most frequent cause of perceptual-motor dysfunction and that improvement in kinaesthetic processing has a significant and beneficial effect on the performance of a large variety of skills is possibly the single, most important result of our work. Yet it would be a mistake to assume that kinaesthesis is the only factor which determines motor proficiency. In a highly complex system, such as the perceptual-motor system, components interact. Thus it is not valid to assess the importance of one isolated process by applying, somewhat naively, simple correlational techniques comparing a selected process with performance on a skill hypothesized to depend on the chosen process. This is what we did in 1981 (Bairstow and Laszlo, 1981) when we correlated kinaesthetic scores with writing and drawing. Some of the correlations were positive, even significant, but the picture was far from clear. In retrospect this is what we should have expected as some children we tested might have reached adequate level of kinaesthesis but lagged behind in motor planning and/or spatial programming. Yet some authors (Doyle, Elliot and Connolly, 1986; Elliot, Connolly and Doyle, 1988; Lord and Hulme, 1987) choose tasks apparently at random and correlated each task with each kinaesthetic test item. It is not surprising that they were confronted by a set of results they cannot explain, especially if some of the motor tasks have high loadings on such factors as visuo-spatial orientation or cognitive strategy formation (Elliott et al., 1988). From our study on PMD children, using not simple correlational measures, but the strong design of test-train-retest, we have irrefutable evidence that kinaesthetic processing is a necessary attribute in skilled behaviour, but that other factors contribute and can determine performance levels as well.

I will now return to some of the theoretical issues mentioned earlier. The results of our studies tend to negate both mass-spring and action theories. It is possible to argue, however, that the two approaches, the mechanistic school and the information processing framework differ from each other not through conflict in theory but through the choice of the behavioural acts they try to explain. In the former, theorist elect to examine strictly controlled acts, working with movements which allow the performer limited degrees of freedom only, while the latter research is focused on skills which demand flexibility and adaptability in responding.

Skill classification did not seem relevant to our work. The process structure we are working with seems to apply to skills regardless of their classification. We did not see PMD children whose motor disorders were confined to a specific class of skills. The overt difficulties the children presented were as varied as was the combination of dysfunctional processes. The two skills most often listed which a PMD child could not perform adequately were writing and ball games, rather different skills in any classification. In addition, alleviation of process dysfunction did improve performance on tasks across classes of skills. From a process-orientated viewpoint task classifications are not particularly useful.

Perhaps I should end this chapter on a positive note, yet I do not
want to sidestep the question that the research has opened up and to
which we as yet cannot find an answer: Why do some children fail to
develop perceptual-motor processes at a developmentally expected
rate ? A child suffering from dyskinaesthesia, for instance, can,
through kinaesthetic training become aware of kinaesthetic information. We were witnessing, repeatedly, the sudden "break through"
from inability to process the input to instant awareness. In the
kinaesthetic acuity training the "A-ha" phenomenon was particularly
clear to see. The children who failed to discriminate 22° differences between their arms in previous trials, exclaimed "I can feel
it". Invariably the children showed delight at their discovery.
Once they managed to feel a large runway separation, they mastered
the discrimination task quickly through graded increase in difficulty level of the task. It is clear that the reason for the pretrai-
ning dysfunction is not neurologically based. Neither receptor pathology nor neural pathway damage could be "cured" by a few trials,
even if these trials focus the child's attention on the kinaesthetic
signal alone, excluding all other sensory cues and motor control
demands. The question is: What is the cause of the developmental
delay ? An answer to this question would indicate possible preven-
tive measures and might have considerable theoretical implications.
I am hoping to approach this area of research in the near future.

REFERENCES

Adams, J.A. (1987). Historical review and appraisal of research on
    the learning retention, and transfer of human motor skills.
    Psychological Bulletin, 101, 41-74.
Anderson, W., & Pitcairn, T. (1986). Motor control in dart
    throwing. Human Movement Science, 5, 1-18.
Ayres, A.J. (1972a). Southern California Sensory Integration tests.
    Los Angeles: Western Psychological Services.
Ayres, A.J. (1972b). Southern California Sensory Integration tests.
    Los Angeles: Western Psychological Services.
Bairstow, P.J. (1983). Development of motor skills. In: R. Harre &
    R. Lamb (Eds.), The Encyclopedic Oxford Dictionary of Psychology.
    Oxford: Basil Blackwell Limited.
Bairstow, P.J. (1986). Postural control. In: H.T.A. Whiting &
    H.G. Wade (Eds.), Theories in motor development. NATO ASI
    Series. Dordrecht: Martinus, Nijhoff.
Bairstow, P.J. (1987). Analysis of hand movement to moving targets.
    Human Movement Science, 6, 205-231.
Bairstow, P.J. (1988). Development of planning and control of hand
    movement to moving targets. British Journal of Developmental
    Psychology. In press.
Bairstow, P.J., & Laszlo, J.I. (1978a). Perception of movement
    patterns. Recognition from visual arrays of distorted patterns.
    Quarterly Journal of Experimental Psychology, 30, 311-317.
Bairstow, P.J., & Laszlo, J.I. (1978b). Perception of movement
    patterns. Recall of movement. Perceptual and Motor Skills, 47,
    287-305.
Bairstow, P.J., & Laszlo, J.I. (1979a). Perception of movement
    patterns. Tracking of movement. Journal of Motor Behavior, 11,
    35-48.
Bairstow, P.J., & Laszlo, J.I. (1979b). Perception of size of

movement patterns. *Journal of Motor Behavior*, *11*, 167-178.
Bairstow, P.J., & Laszlo J.I. (1980). Motor commands and the perception of movement patterns. *Journal of Experimental Psychology: Human Perception and Performance*, *6*, 1-12.
Bairstow, P.J., & Laszlo, J.I. (1981). Kinaesthetic sensitivity to passive movements in children and in adults and its relationship to motor development and motor control. *Developmental Medicine and Child Neurology*, *23*, 606-616.
Bairstow, P.J., & Laszlo, J.I. (1982). Complex movement patterns: Learning, retention and sources of error in recall. *Quarterly Journal of Experimental Psychology*, *34*, 183-197.
Bairstow, P.J., & Laszlo, J.I. (Submitted for publication). *Deficits in the planning, control and memory of hand movements in children with perceptuo-motor dysfunction.*
Bizzi, E., Dev, P., Morasso, P., & Polit, A. (1978). Effect of load disturbance during centrally initiated movements. *Journal of Neurophysiology*, *41*, 542-556.
Broderick, P., & Laszlo, J.I. (1987). The drawing of squares and diamonds: A perceptual-motor task analysis. *Journal of Experimental Child Psychology*, *43*, 44-61.
Broderick, P., & Laszlo, J.I. (1988). The effects of varying planning demands on drawing components of squares and diamonds. *Journal of Experimental Child Psychology*, *45*, 18-27.
Brooks, V.B. (1979). Motor programs revisited. In: R.E. Talbot & D.R. Humphrey (Eds.), *Posture and movement: Perspective for integrating motor research on the mammalian nervous system*. New York: Raven Press.
Brooks, V.B. (1981). Task related cell assemblies. In: O. Pompeiano & C.A. Marsan (Eds.), *Brain mechanisms and perceptual awareness*. New York: Raven Press.
Bruininks, R.H. (1978). *Bruininks-Oseretsky test of motor proficiency*. Circle Pines, Minnesota: American Guidance Service.
Cratty, B.J. (1981). Sensory-motor and perceptual-motor theories and practices: An overview and evaluation. In: R.D. Walk & M.C. Pick (Eds.), *Intersensory perception and sensory integration*. New York: Plenum Press.
Desmedt, J.E., & Godaux, E. (1979). Voluntary motor commands in human ballistic movement. *Annals of Neurology*, *5*, 415-421.
Desmedt, J.E., & Godaux, E. (1981). Ballistic contractions in fast and slow human muscles discharge patterns of single motor units. *Journal of Physiology*, *285*, 185-196.
Doyle, A.J.R., Elliot, J.M., & Connolly, K.J. (1986). Measurement of kinaesthetic sensitivity. *Developmental Medicine and Child Neurology*, *28*, 188-193.
Elliot, J.M., Connolly, K.J., & Doyle, A.J.R. (1988). Development of kinaesthetic sensitivity and motor performance in children. *Developmental Medicine and Child Neurology*, *28*, 194-197.
Evarts, E.V., & Granit, R. (1976). Relations of reflex and intended movements. *Progress in Brain Research*, *44*, 1-14.
Evarts, E.V., & Tanji, J. (1976). Reflex and intended responses in motor cortex pyramidal tract neurons of the monkey. *Jounal of Neurophysiology*, *39*, 1069-1080.
Evarts, E.V., Fromm, C., Kroller, J., & van Jennings, A. (1983). Motor cortex control of finely graded forces. *Journal of Neurophysiology*, *49*, 1199-1215.
Fetz, G.E., & Cheney, P.D. (1980). Postspike facilitation of forelimb muscle activity by primate corticomotoneuronal cells.

Journal of Neurophysiology, 44, 751-772.
Fitts, P.M., & Posner, M.I. (1967). *Human performance*. California: Brooks/Cole Publishing.
Freund, H.J. (1983). Motor unit and muscle activity in voluntary motor control. *Physiological Review, 63*, 387-436.
Freund, H.J. (1985). Clinical aspects of premotor function. *Behavioral Brain Research, 18*, 187-191.
Fromm, C., & Evarts, E.V. (1982). Pyramidal tract neurons in somatosensory cortex: Central and peripheral inputs during voluntary movements. *Brain Research, 238*, 186-191.
Georgopoulos, A.P., Kalaska, J.F., & Massey, J.E. (1981). Spatial trajectories and reaction time of aimed movements: Effects of practice, uncertainty and change in target location. *Journal of Neurophysiology, 46*, 725-743.
Godschalk, M., Aremon, R.N., Nijo, H.G.T., & Kuypers, H.G.J.M. (1981). Behavior of neurones in monkey peri-arcuate and peri-central cortex before and during visually guided arm and hand movements. *Experimental Brain Research, 44*, 113-116.
Gordon, N., & McKinlay, I. (1980). *Helping clumsy children*. Edinburgh: Churchill Livingstone.
Gubbay, S.S. (1975). *The clumsy child. A study of development apraxia and agnosic ataxia*. London: W.B. Saunders.
Holt, K.S. (1981). Review: The assessment of walking in children with particular reference to cerebral palsy. *Journal of Child Care, Health and Development, 7*, 281-299.
Keele, S.W., & Summers, J.J. (1976). The structure of motor programs. In: G.E. Stelmach (Ed.), *Motor Control: Issues and Trends*. New York: Academic Press.
Kelso, J.A.S. (1982). *Human motor behavior: An introduction*. London: Erlbaum Associates.
Kelso, J.A.S., Holt, K.G., Kugler, P.N., & Turvey, M.T. (1980). On the concept of coordinative structures on dissipative structure, II. Empirical lines of convergence. In: G.E. Stelmach & J. Requin (Eds), *Tutorials in motor behavior*. Amsterdam: North Holland.
Kirsch, R.F., & Rynier, W.Z. (1987). Neural compensation for muscular fatigue: Evidence for significant force regulation in man. *Jounal of Neurophysiology, 57*, 1893-1909.
Knuckey, N.W., Apsimon, T.T., & Gubbay, S.S. (1983). Computerized axial tomography in clumsy children with development apraxia and agnosia. *Brain and Development, 5*, 14-19.
Kugler, P.N., Keslo, J.A.S., & Turvey, M.T. (1980). On the concept of coordinative structures as dissipative structures: 1. Theoretical line of convergence. In: G.E. Stelmach & J. Requin (Eds.), *Tutorials in motor behavior*. Amsterdam: North Holland.
Lashley, K.S. (1951). In: L.A. Jeffres (Ed.). *The problem of serial order in behaviour and cerebral mechanisms in behavior*. New York: J. Wiley.
Laszlo, J.I. (1966). The performance of a simple motor task with kinaesthetic sense loss. *Quarterly Journal of Experimental Psychology, 18*, 1-8.
Laszlo, J.I. (1967a). Training of fast tapping with reduction of kinaesthetic and tactile sensations and with combined reduction of kinaesthetic and tactile, visual and auditory sensation. *Quarterly Journal of Experimental Psychology, 19*, 344-349.
Laszlo, J.I. (1967b). Kinaesthetic and exteroceptive information

in the performance of motor skills. *Physiology and Behavior, 2*, 359-365.
Laszlo, J.I. (1968). The role of visual and kinaesthetic cues in learning a novel skill. *Quarterly Journal of Experimental Psychology, 20*, 191-196.
Laszlo, J.I., & Baguley, R.A. (1971). Motor memory and bilateral transfer. *Journal of Motor Behavior, 3*, 235-240.
Laszlo, J.I., & Bairstow, P.J. (1971). Accuracy of movement, peripheral feedback and efference copy. *Journal of Motor Behavior, 3*, 241-252.
Laszlo, J.I., & Baker, J.E. (1972). The role of visual cues in movement control and motor memory. *Journal of Motor Behavior, 4*, 71-77.
Laszlo, J.I., & Livesey, J.P. (1977). Task complexity, accuracy and reaction time. *Journal of Motor Behavior, 9*, 171-177.
Laszlo, J.I., & Ward, G.R. (1978). Vision, proprioception and corollary discharge in a movement recall task. *Acta Psychologica, 42*, 477-493.
Laszlo, J.I., & Bairstow, P.J. (1980). The measurement of kinaesthetic sensitivity in children and adults. *Developmental Medicine and Child Neurology, 22*, 454-464.
Laszlo, J.I., & Bairstow, P.J. (1983). Kinaesthesis: Its measurement, training and relationship to motor control. *Quarterly Journal of Experimental Psychology, 35*, 411-421.
Laszlo, J.I., & Bairstow, P.J. (1985a). *Perceptual-motor behavior: Developmental assessment and therapy.* London: Holt, Rinehart and Winston.
Laszlo, J.I., & Bairstow, P.J. (1985b). *Kinaesthetic sensitivity test.* Perth, WA: Senkit Pty Ltd., London: Holt, Rinehart and Winston.
Laszlo, J.I., & Broderick, P.A. (1985). The perceptual-motor skill of drawing. In: N.H. Freeman & M.V. Cox (Eds.), *Visual order. The nature and development of pictorial representation.* Cambridge: Cambridge University Press.
Laszlo, J.I., Bairstow, P.J., & Baker, J.E. (1979). Dependence on feedback following practice. *Perceptual and Motor Skills, 1*, 195-209.
Laszlo, J.I.., Bairstow, P.J., Ward, G., & Bancroft, H. (1980). Distracting information, motor-performance and sex differences. *Nature, 283*, 377-381.
Laszlo, J.I., Bairstow, P.J., Bartrip, J., & Rolfe, V.T. (1988). Clumsiness or perceptuo-motor dysfunction ? In: A. Colley & J. Beech (Eds.), *Cognition and action in skilled behavior.* Amsterdam: North Holland.
Legge, D. (1983). Skills. In: R. Harre & R. Lamb (Eds.), *The Encyclopedic Oxford Dictionary of Psychology.* Oxford: Basil Blackwell Limited, p.575-577.
Lord, R., & Hulme, C. (1987). Kinaesthetic sensitivity of normal and clumsy children. *Developmental Medicine and Child Neurology, 29*, 720-725.
McCarthy, D. (1972). *McCarthy scales of children's abilities.* New York: The Psychological Corporation.
McCloskey, D.I., Macefield, A., Gandevia, S.C., & Burke, D. (1987). Sensing position and movements of the fingers. *N.I.P.S., 2*, 226-230.
McKinlay, I. (1988). Clumsy children. *British Medical Journal, 296*, 717.

Macpherson, J.M., Marangoz, C., Miles, T.S., & Wiesendanger, M. (1982). Microstimulation of the supplementary motor area in the awake monkey. *Experimental Brain Research, 45*, 410-416.

Marteniuk, R.G. (1976). *Information processing in motor skills*. New York: Holt, Rinehart and Winston.

Matthews, P.B.C. (1972). *Mammalian muscle receptors and their central actions*. London: Edward Arnold.

Paillard, J. (1987). Cognitive versus sensorimotor encoding of spatial information. In: P. Ellen & C. Thinus-Blanc (Eds.), *Cognitive processes and spatial orientation in animal and man*. Amsterdam, The Netherlands: Martinus-Nijhoff.

Pew, R.W. (1969). The speed-accuracy operating characteristic. *Acta Psychologica: Attention and Performance, II, 30*, 16-26.

Pew, R.W. (1974a). Human perceptual-motor performance. In: B.H. Kantowitz (Ed.), *Human information processing: Tutorials in; performance and cognition*. Hillsdale, N.J.: Erlbaum.

Pew, R.W. (1974b). Levels of analysis in motor control. *Brain Research, 71*, 393-400.

Polit, A., & Bizzi, E. (1978). Processes controlling arm movements in monkeys. *Science, 201*, 1235-1237.

Polit, A., & Bizzi, E. (1979). Characteristics of motor programs underlying arm movements in monkey. *Journal of Neurophysiology, 42*, 183-194.

Roland, P.G., Skinhoj, E., Lassen, N.A., & Larsen, B. (1980). Different cortical areas in man in organisational of voluntary movements in extrapersonal space. *Journal of Neurophysiology, 43*, 137-150.

Schmidt, R.A. (1982). *Motor control and learning: A behavioral emphasis*. Champaign: Human Kinetics.

Schmidt, R.A., Zelaznik, H., Hawkins, B., Franks, J.S., & Quinn, J.T.Jr. (1979). Motor output variability: A theory for the accuracy of rapid motor acts. *Psychological Review, 86*, 415-451.

Scott, G.M. (1955). Measurement of kinaesthesis. *Research Quarterly, 26*, 324-341.

Smyth, M.M., & Wing, A.M. (1984). *The psychology of human movement*. London: Academic Press.

Stott, D.H., Moyes, F.A., & Henderson, S.E. (Henderson Revision). (1984). *Test of motor impairment*. Guelph: Brook Educational Publishing.

Tanji, J., & Evarts, E.V. (1976). Anticipatory activity of motor cortex neurons in relation to direction of an intended movement. *Journal of Neurophysiology, 39*, 1062-1068.

Turvey, M.T., Shaw, R.E., & Mace, W. (1978). Issues in the theory of action: Degrees of freedom, coordinative structures and coalitions. In: J. Requin (Ed.), *Attention and performance VII*. Hillsdale, N.J.: Erlbaum.

Woodworth, R.S. (1889). The accuracy of voluntary movement. *Psychological Review Monograph Supplements, 3*, No.3.

DEVELOPMENTAL PSYCHOLOGY
Cognitive, Perceptuo-Motor, and Neuropsychological Perspectives
C-A. Hauert (Editor)
© Elsevier Science Publishers B.V. (North-Holland), 1990

PERCEPTUO-MOTOR DEVELOPMENT IN THE CHILD AND THE
ADOLESCENT: PERCEPTUO-MOTOR COORDINATION

Pierre G. ZANONE

Center for Complex Systems
Florida Atlantic University
Boca Raton, U.S.A.

*Although, at first glance, perceptuo-motor development
during childhood seems to unfold more slowly and progressively than during infancy --this may explain in part the
relative lack of interest of developmental psychologists
in this topic--, a more thorough investigation shows that
a consistent enhancement of perceptuo-motor performance
takes place between two and fifteen years of age.
Furthermore, several experimental findings strongly suggest that the child improves her/his performance not only
quantitatively (i.e., speed, precision, force, etc.), but
also qualitatively. Indeed, dramatic changes occur in the
acquisition of perceptuo-motor skills between four and
seven years of age, entailing temporary "regressions" in
performance. These have been interpreted as functional or
strategical changes, which influence the way movement is
controlled. To understand these so-called "U-shaped"
trends, and to present a brief and partial state of the
art, this chapter reviews alternative interpretations of
these behavioral changes, based on the most prevailing
frameworks in the domain. Although this discussion provides no definite conclusion regarding the issue of
perceptuo-motor development, it points out the necessity
of a more rigorous approach at the methodological level,
and perhaps, a more open-minded attitude within the
theoretical realm.*

1. INTRODUCTION

It is probably daily-life experience and popular knowledge that have
led one to distinguish two main periods in human development, which
are articulated about the emergence of the most bewildering and fas-
cinating human capability, namely, the use of language, or, more
generally, of symbolic functions. It is then not surprising that
the word "infant" means etymologically "non-speaker", and characterizes the little human below 16 months. It is also not surprising
that the classical developmental theories consistently place a dividing line between two stages of development at this moment. Inci-
dentally, it should not be overlooked that this ultimately aids the
organization of developmental psychology textbooks.

As far as perceptuo-motor development is concerned, common sense
still continues to promote this distinction. On the one hand, from
birth, when the baby seems ill-prepared for adapted action, considerable and fairly rapid progress, both quantitative and qualitative, seems to provide the two year-old with a repertoire of basic
coordinated skills (e.g., eye-hand coordination, locomotion, stable
posture, etc...) that allow him/her to interact more autonomously
with the milieu. Afterwards, the child needs only to refine and
strengthen these existing skills, or adapt and combine them into new
ones. On the other hand, the development of perceptuo-motor behavior appears to unfold in a slower and more monotonous fashion than
the concurrent development of symbolic abilities.

Following the vivid debate during the 1930s between maturationist
and environmentalist theses about ontogenesis, research in developmental psychology has focused primarily on perceptuo-motor behavior
in infancy (e.g., Gesell, 1929; Halverson, 1931; McGraw, 1932;
Piaget, 1952; Shirley, 1931). Even if the existence of symbolic
activities during this early period in development had been accepted, the frequent and dramatic transformations in perceptuo-motor
behavior would have been thought to be independent thereof. Relatedly, interest has been diverted from perceptuo-motor aspects of
development during childhood in favor of more prominent cognitive,
social, moral, and affective aspects. However, the absence of symbolic abilities during infancy, or their independence from
perceptuo-motor processes is nowadays strongly challenged (e.g.,
Bower, 1974; Bruner, Olver and Greenfield, 1966; Mounoud and Vinter,
1981).

Probably more in response to educational than to epistemological
preoccupations, numerous studies of perceptuo-motor development have
been carried out from a task-oriented perspective, that is, motor
behavior is described and assessed in straightforward performance
measures. This approach can be compared with a process-oriented
perspective, which seeks to capture the covert mechanisms underlying
performance and its change with age. Within the first category,
many thorough and elegant accounts for the development of fundamental motor skills, such as catching, running, throwing, and so forth,
can be found in recent literature (e.g., Cratty, 1986; Gallahue,
1982; Wickstrom, 1983). Based on macroscopic criteria (e.g.,
smoothness of performance, the number of bodily segments mobilized
and their temporal sequence), several stages in the acquisition of
these complex skills were differentiated. It is by no means trivial
to arrive at such classifications. A main difficulty is to identify
pertinent descriptors of perceptuo-motor behavior. A series of
studies by Roberton (1978, 1982), and Roberton and Langendorfer
(1980) illustrate very nicely the quest for such descriptors in the
case of overarm throwing. This is also, to our knowledge, the only
longitudinal study in the area, covering an age span of almost 15
years. This task-oriented approach has given rise to a number of
insights (e.g., the decrease in trunk mobilization in arm movement)
pertaining to general features of perceptuo-motor development. On
the other hand, a second domain of the task-oriented approach has
developed following the attempt to provide reliable tests of
perceptuo-motor behavior (for a review and a critical discussion,
see Laszlo and Bairstow, 1985). However, a major flaw of this
approach is that it fails to provide a more functional account of

perceptuo-motor behavior and its development.

In this chapter, we will discuss perceptuo-motor development in the child from a process-oriented perspective. While this perspective holds promise for understanding the development of perceptuo-motor behavior, we would like to state at the outset that no definitive answer will be given. Instead, new questions will arise, exemplifying the unsatifactory state of the art at the moment. Therefore, one must think of this chapter as the logbook of an exploratory journey in a field, where each obstacle removed clears the path ... to a bigger obstacle.

We shall consider a developmental sequence during childhood that, in our opinion, is noteworthy in two respects. First, the observed performance across ages does not follow a monotonous improvement, but rather a discontinuous, so-called "U-shaped" trend (for a review and a theoretical account, see Bever, 1982; Strauss, 1984). Second, the sequence illustrates how results can be experimentally validated, and the specific hypothesis tested within the process-oriented perspective.

2. AN INTRIGUING DEVELOPMENTAL SEQUENCE

We will focus on a perceptuo-motor behavior one might call targeting, which encompasses hand and forearm movements like aiming, catching, pointing, positioning, reaching, and so on. Indeed, to understand the general processes of perceptuo-motor development, it is necessary to consider different tasks within this family of movements. However, the consequences of slight "sidesteps" across tasks have to be carefully evaluated at the methodological level. We will first review a series of experiments by Hay (1978, 1979, 1981), and then discuss them in light of the results of Brown, Sepher, Ettlinger and Skreczek (1986), and Brooks (1974), Brooks, Cooke and Thomas (1974).

To begin, let us consider a study by Hay (1978). Free pointing to a visual target is reported as very accurate, because visual feedback allows one to reduce the positional mismatch between the limb and the target. Nevertheless, it is well-documented that, without vision of the moving limb (open-loop pointing), adults slightly undershoot a target, an error that would be eliminated by feedback if vision were allowed. A classical explanation for such an accurate open-loop performance assumes that proprioceptive afferences arising from ongoing movement supply feedback for the final positioning (e.g., von Holst, 1954; Sperry, 1950). Therefore, proprioception must be matched, coordinated, or calibrated with vision to provide a common frame of reference (Hein and Held, 1967; Paillard and Brouchon, 1974; From the developmental perspective, Birch and Lefford, 1967; Connolly and Jones, 1970). However, at present, this view would be vehemently contested. The seminal works of Asatrian and Fel'dman (1965), Fel'dman (1966a, 1966b), Kelso (1977), or Polit and Bizzi (1978) clearly demonstrate that these movements are also possible in the absence of any sensory feedback, although active movements lead to a better match between vision and proprioception than passive ones (Held and Freeman, 1963). Thus, the coordination of proprioception and vision as it develops with age, and the diffe-

renciation of active and passive movements are two issues worthy of
investigation.

These issues motivated Hay's first experiment. Children aged 4 to
11 years and adults were asked to move their arm, which was placed
in a splint to restrict movement at the shoulder joint in a horizontal plane. They were instructed to point as precisely as possible
to a target without seeing the moving limb (active condition). In a
second condition (passive), the limb was moved by the experimenter
and stopped on the subject's request at the position thought to be
that of the target. The results were quite surprising. In the
active condition, subjects under the age of seven (especially the
five year-olds) performed the task very accurately, even better than
adults. In contrast, seven-year-olds showed a large undershoot,
which progressively decreased in older children until they attained
the level of adult proficiency. The accuracy of 4- to 6-year-olds,
as well as that of 11-year-olds and adults was comparable. In the
passive as compared to the active condition, children over five
years showed significantly less accuracy. However, for four- and
five-year-olds, performance was equally accurate in both conditions.
Furthermore, no improvement was observed in the passive condition
after the age of seven.

This age-related trend in the active condition suggests that the
lack of visual feedback impedes pointing in a differentiated manner
across age. Hay suggests that below seven years, children preprogram their movement, and have no need for additional visual information to improve accuracy. In contrast, seven year-olds rely on
such feedback, so their performance deteriorates dramatically if
vision is hindered. The improvement in older children's performance
was interpreted as a gradual coordination of proprioception with
vision, allowing for more precise pointing on the basis of proprioceptive cues alone, a process that Hay nicely calls "acquisition of
spatial significance" (ibid., p.1081). However, as Hay admits,
changes observed with age in the passive condition are difficult to
interpret in this framework. These changes are assumed to be either
artifacts or due to some vaguely defined "specific spatial encoding
of proprioceptive cues" (ibid., p.1082) at these ages.

To test this hypothesis, Hay (1979) replicated the previous experiment with 5-, 7-, 9-, and 11-year-olds. Her goal was to classify
the movements according to kinematic criteria. One class comprised
the so-called "ballistic" movements, that is, brief movements showing only one peak of velocity, and very sudden acceleration and de-
celeration. The second category contained movements characterized
by an abrupt acceleration followed by a prolonged braking phase,
several pairs of acceleration-deceleration ("steps movements"), or a
fairly constant low velocity ("ramp movements"). With this classification scheme, Hay suggested that the ballistic kinematic pattern
corresponds to totally preprogrammed movements independent of any
feedback, whereas other patterns imply feedback control. One has to
keep in mind that, in this case, feedback control can only rely on
proprioceptive afferences, since vision is prevented. The results
showed that the majority of five-year-olds' movements were ballistic
(about 65%), whereas seven year-olds executed about the same proportion of long-braking movements. Ramp and steps movements were in-
frequent for five-year olds (10%), and remained at a constant per-

centage of about 30% in older children. These results agree with Hay's first experiment and suggest that braking activity under feedback control is more often concentrated near the end of movement. This sequence consisting of a "transport", "distance-covering", or ballistic phase followed by a "homing", controlled one is the well-known pattern observed in adults for goal-directed hand movements (for recent work, see Pélisson, Prablanc, Goodale and Jeannerod, 1986; Prablanc, Pélisson and Goodale, 1986; Zelaznick, Hawkins and Kisselburgh, 1987).

To further test of hypothesis, Hay (1979) asked 5- to 11- year-old children to point at a target while wearing prismatic glasses which shifted the perceived position of the target from the actual one. The time when the hand path to the virtual target is corrected in the direction of the actual target provides a relevant clue as to the extent which ongoing movement is preprogrammed. The later this correction, the more preprogrammed and ballistic is the intended movement. The results strongly supported the developmental sequence postulated by Hay (1978). Indeed, five-year-olds corrected their pointing closest to the virtual target, sometimes even after over-passing it. By contrast, children aged seven modified the trajec-tory toward the actual target much sooner, and older subjects showed an intermediate moment of correction.

Finally, a third study by Hay (1981) provides more indirect support for this general developmental sequence. Children were asked to point alternately to two targets at maximal speed and precision (re-ciprocal tapping or "Fitts' paradigm"). The task becomes more dif-ficult as the distance between the targets increases, and/or as the target size decreases. Following the procedure proposed by Welford, Norris and Shock (1963), Hay removed the effect of each requirement on the dependent variable --movement time-- by a posteriori measu-ring its change as a function of one constraint, while the other constraint is constantly maintained. The results showed that five year-olds were more influenced by requirements for movement preci-sion than by those for amplitude, while for children between 7 and 11 years of age the opposite was true. Assuming that amplitude re-quirements affect mostly the transport phase, and precision require-ments influence the homing phase, Hay concluded that younger sub-jects were able to satisfy the former because of their fundamentally preprogrammed behavior. However, older children performed better under precision requirements because of their tendency to control movements.

To summarize, this series of experiments provides a coherent sequen-ce of perceptuo-motor behaviors within the same age interval. The different tasks are comparable in that they imply free movements di-rected towards a visual target. At a functional level, a basic re-sult is that children between four and six years essentially execute preprogrammed movements. More precisely, they need neither visual nor proprioceptive feedback to achieve a fairly precise final limb position. By contrast, older children more steadily control their movements and proprioceptive control improves in efficiency within this age range.

This picture, however, may not be quite so clear. Brown et al. (1986) had two- to eight-year-old children point to several visual

targets on a vertical board placed in front of them. Under experimental conditions similar to Hay's, vision of the limb was prevented, while the target was visible during movement. In this situation, the error in pointing decreased linearly with age. Five-
year-olds were less accurate than 8-year-olds, but this difference
did not reach statistical significance due to the large variability
in performance at five years. Such findings obviously contradict
Hay's results (1978) in open-loop positioning.

To explain this inconsistency, Brown et al. pointed out that their
method of measuring error differed from Hay's. This difference
(i.e., radial vs. linear error) is related to the type of targetting
task (i.e., pointing vs. positioning). In other words, pointing
involves planning the direction of movement, whereas positioning
involves controlling its extent. Indeed, Bard and Hay (1983) showed
that simple directional pointing (i.e., projection of the hand
towards the target without braking under the target) becomes more
accurate with increasing age between 6 and 11 years. Recent work by
Hay, Bard and Fleury (1986) also demonstrates this point. In an
open-loop condition, angular error was constant across ages (i.e.,
6, 8, and 10 years) when the task consisted of projecting the hand
toward a target (direction requirement). However, eight-year olds
were consistently less accurate if they had to point precisely under
the position of the target (distance requirement). Notwithstanding,
one might wonder whether the task studied by Brown and colleagues
was in fact constrained only with respect to direction, since subjects had to brake before attaining the screen and could not actually overpass it. Interestingly, Hay et al. (1986) showed that when
movement requires simultaneously specifying distance and direction,
a gradual improvement with age in the accuracy of positioning is
observed.

How are we to interpret such a fairly complex developmental picture ? Hay and colleagues claim that "two spatial coordinate systems,
variably distinct depending on age" (1986, p.336) exist. The first
system, dealing with direction specification, would be efficient
earlier in development than the second, which pertains to distance,
and whose maximal functional capacity is not attained within this
age range. The assumption, owing to Paillard (see 1986), is that
direction results from sensori-motor coding of spatial information,
but amplitude involves cognitive coding. The former involves predominantly peripheral vision, and the latter, central vision.
Paillard provides several arguments for relating these two functions
to subcortical and cortical information processing, respectively.
An analogous distinction is proposed by Jeannerod (see 1986) concerning the foundations of visuo-motor co-ordination. He identifies
two independent "visuo-manual channels". Functionally, one of them
is specifically related to the transport, the other, to the homing
phase of goal-directed hand movements. These two models are equivalent. Both express the same functional duality in targetting
(preprogramming/control), but because of the task studied (pointing
vs. prehension), each focuses on specific dimensions of movement
(direction/distance vs. amplitude/precision). The existence of such
a dichotomy in the visuo-motor system has been widely recognized
(e.g., Arbib, 1981; Schneider, 1969; Trevarthen, 1968). Nevertheless, invoking structural differences in the central nervous system (CNS) and asynchronous functional development only transforms

the problem into a biological one. Ultimately, the following questions posed to biology remain. How can the observed asynchrony be
explained ? What are the contents and the rules of the coordinations between proprioception and vision ? And regarding the development of targetting, how can one account for the decrease in performance around eight years ?

In the field of psychology, these questions are puzzling as well.
For the sake of interpretation, let us review the work of Brooks and
colleagues (1973, 1974), on the identification of movement patterns
in targetting. These authors studied self-paced open-loop positioning movements in monkeys. They distinguished continuous and discontinuous movements according to one simple criterion. In continuous movements, the acceleration curve crosses the zero axis only
once, so there is only one velocity peak. On the other hand, discontinuous movements exhibit several velocity peaks. Brooks et al.
demonstrated that the movements of the first type were centrally
preprogrammed and the others were influenced by feedback. Compared
to Hay's more ad-hoc classification (see above), the preprogrammed
character of five-year-olds behavior is confirmed, since ballistic
movements are unambiguously continuous. This is the most important
point. However, ramp movements are continuous, and therefore, would
not belong to the same class as steps movements. Moreover, the long
braking movement (Hay's type 2) may or may not be continuous, according to the criteria of Brooks and colleagues. This raises the
question of to what extent Hay's description of the development of
positioning beyond the age of seven years (see below) is valid.

Two points regarding the study by Brooks et al. can be made. First,
the subjects were highly trained animals. Second, movements of the
continuous kind were observed only in a completely predictable task
(i.e., after several trials in a given experimental condition),
whereas discontinuous movements occured in the case of uncertainty
(i.e., just after a change in the experimental condition). These
observations suggest that motor learning and predictability may play
a crucial role in the way that movement is executed. We will discuss these two issues below, in an attempt to understand the developmental trend observed in targetting. Obviously, the separation
into learning and predictability is somewhat artificial and is only
adopted for the sake of clarity. One could claim that the psychological state of predictability results from the very learning of the
perceptuo-motor task. Accordingly it can be shown (e.g., Wing,
Turton and Fraser, 1986) that mere knowledge about the usual outcome
of a skilled movement (i.e., prediction about its expected accuracy)
significantly affects its trajectory (for a more general discussion
of the "cognitive penetrability" of perceptuo-motor processes, see
Fodor, 1983; Haugeland, 1978; Pylyshyn, 1981).

3. MOTOR LEARNING

Several models of motor learning have been proposed to account for
the improvement in performance that results from the repetition of
discrete movements, a class to which targetting belongs. To discuss
these models, we must state explicitly a postulate that was tacitly
assumed until now. The unfolding of movement depends to some degree
upon the existence of a structural support, the motor program (MP).

In the case of ballistic movement, the entire course of the movement is determined by the specification of the MP "in absence of peripheral feedback", to cite the classical criterion (Keele, 1968). In other movements, control through feedback replaces preprogramming after a certain point in the course of movement.

Adams (1971, 1976) assumed that for each movement to be executed, a memory trace allows for its triggering. The memory trace can be thought of as a tiny MP responsible for the first impulse initiating the limb movement. Then, almost immediately, a perceptual trace yields a reference of correctness used through feedback control to achieve an accurate final limb position. The perceptual trace is in turn reinforced with an increasing number of repetitions of the same movement. The more the movement is practiced, the more precise the reference for the next movement. The main shortcoming of this framework is that one must assume that specific memory and perceptual traces are stored for each distinct executed movement, as well as for each potential movement. Consequently, the number of traces to be stored is almost infinite.

As a partial solution to this problem, these ideas were extended by Schmidt (1975, 1976). "Recall and recognition schemata" are rules pertaining to a class of movements that allow one to generate a specific motor response and the reference for its control in an anticipatory fashion. The recall schema would account for the ballistic phase of positioning, while the recognition shema would be responsible for the homing phase. In this framework, the MP is no longer movement-specific, but is the common structure for a class of movements. It possesses mutable parameters allowing its adaptation to the various conditions in which each movement is actually performed. Both schemata improve in strength, generality, and accuracy through repetition in various situations within the same class of movement. It must be stressed that the novelty of schema theory lies in the postulate that not only does drilling a given movement reinforce the related schemata, but also executing whatever movement belonging to the same class. This insures transfer of learning to other movements within this class.

From the developmental point of view, there is fairly consistent support for the hypothesis that motor learning in children can be explained by such model (for a review, see Shapiro and Schmidt, 1982). One might assume that memory traces endowed with schema-like properties exist during childhood. Thus, with development, the schemata will acquire increasing accuracy in specifying their output in a wider range of applications, so that improvement in performance within as well as across ages might rely in part on the extensive enhancement of the memory traces specific to each class of movement.

To return to the topic of the development of targetting during childhood, schema theory might account for the progressive increase in accuracy observed after the age of seven years. Perhaps children have ample opportunity in daily life to perform positioning or pointing movements similar to those studied experimentally, and therefore, they improve the schemata and perform more accurately. From a broader perspective, one might assume that the different tasks referred to as targetting belong to the same class of movement, and thus pertain to the same schemata.

However, such a general vision has two main shortcomings. The first problem resides in the extensional definition of a class of movement, and, relatedly, in the more specific interpretation of changes in the topology of movement, within the a priori same class. An enlightening example is found in Hay et al. (1986). When children aged 6 and 10 years perform the projecting task (directional requirement), the classical kinematic pattern "triggered-homing" (i.e., a rapid increase in velocity, followed by a more or less progressive decrease) seems inverted. Therefore, the velocity peak is markedly delayed and occurs after half the distance has already been covered. This inversion is not observed in eight year-olds. A reasonable explanation of this change may be that no braking was implied since no explicit positioning under the target was required. Nevertheless, the motor program is conceptualized as structurally invariant, with variable parameters (i.e., velocity, force, etc..), resulting in movements of different size, speed, etc.., but of identical temporal patterns, or "phasing" (Schmidt, 1982). Thus, questions arise whether these movements exhibiting different temporal patterns are truly part of the same class, and how to explain the transition between them. Ultimately, the same general issue is addressed when one considers the instantaneous and more dramatic changes in the topology of gait in centipedes after successive pairs of limbs are amputated (von Holst, 1973). This topic is highly relevant to perceptuo-motor development, where subtle as well as steep changes occur in the execution of an identical task. A second shortcoming of the schemata framework is that it provides no way to understand the U-shaped trend observed by Hay because the schemata are always assumed to improve with accumulating experience.

A more general question about schemata concerns the process(es) pertaining to their improvement with repetition. Let us briefly recall that schemata are rules abstracted from two common types of information: The initial conditions and the response outcome. One specific type of information about what happens in between is directed to each schema (i.e., the current parameters of the MP and the sensory consequences of movement). The two former types of information, which are vaguely defined and result from the integration of various afferences (extero- and proprioceptive), have been experimentally manipulated to test the principles leading to schema formation (i.e., variability of practice). But the very process of abstracting a rule from such sources of information has not been yet directly addressed, although such an endeavor is possible.

Nevertheless, some indications can be obtained from studies on the effect of knowledge of result (KR) on motor performance. Indeed, KR is one kind of information that can be used to determine movement outcome. Newell and Kennedy (1978) showed that in a positioning task, older children were able to handle more precise, abstract levels of KR (i.e., qualitative vs. various metric scales) to improve response accuracy. Anwar (1981) studied children according to their chronological and mental age. Results indicated that using either age scales, children were able to deal with more sophisticated information about movement outcome as a function of age. These findings suggest that cognitive activity involved in deciphering available information of varying complexity improves with age in perceptuo-motor tasks. However, Gallagher and Thomas (1980) asked children aged 7 and 11, and adults to point to a target under preci-

se timing requirements. Different post-KR intervals were adminis-
trated, before the onset of the following movement. While accuracy
in timing increased steeply with age for short post-KR intervals,
these differences vanished for longer intervals. The authors concluded that if sufficient time is given to process information
yielded by KR, age-related differences are considerably reduced.
Processing speed increases thus with age. Similarly, Barclay and
Newell (1980) provided more direct evidence that children require
less time for processing KR with increasing age.

Several developmental studies with tasks that provide a more or less
direct measure of CNS processing speed show an increase in speed
with age. For example, simple reaction time gradually decreases by
about 20 ms per year between 3 and 15 years of age (Southard, 1985;
Thomas, Gallagher and Purvis, 1981; Wickens, 1974). The same tendency is found in more sophisticated reaction time paradigms (Clark,
1982; Fairweather and Hutt, 1978; Goodenough, 1935). Moreover, the
studies using Fitts' reciprocal tapping task show a gradual decrease
in movement time between 5 and 15 years and suggest an enhancement
in processing speed (Connolly, Brown and Bassett, 1968; Hay, 1981;
Kerr, 1975; Salmoni, 1983; Sugden, 1980; Wallace, Newell and Wade,
1978).

Where then might the improvement in the "mental capacity" to process
information come from ? Some authors close to the Piagetian approach propose that structural changes in memory are related to an
increase in the number of available schemes and an improved capacity
to simultaneously cope with them (Pascual-Leone and Smith, 1969;
Todor, 1978). Most authors, however, invoke functional changes in
one or another mental operation along the information processing
stream in short term memory (e.g., as rehearsal, retrieval, search,
etc...). For example, Winther and Thomas (1981) showed that providing children aged 5 and 10 years with the coding-labelling strategy
that adults spontaneously utilize in such a situation, drastically
enhanced the recall and the accuracy of pointing movements, so that
10-year-olds attained an adult level of performance, and 5-years-old
that of 10-year-olds. Gallagher and Thomas (1984) demonstrated that
when children were given an appropriate strategy for rehearsing a
series of movements, accuracy in pointing clearly improved.

These findings are in accordance with studies of other categories of
memory, and suggest that strategies (grouping, semantic coding,
etc), previous knowledge (e.g., perceptual familiarity), and so
forth, dramatically affect performance (either recall or recognition) (e.g., Chi, 1976; Flavell, 1970; Paris, 1978). Although these
results indicate that memory processes can affect perceptuo-motor
coordination in a particular manner, it must be kept in mind that, a
priori, the tasks specifically involve a high demand for memory
activity. Therefore, one might be assessing the memory processes
per se, irrespective of their real involvement in pure perceptuo-
motor tasks. In other words, the latter are only utilized as a
indirect measurement of the former, without any interest in the
observed phenomenon. In this respect, this attitude is close to
that of the Piagetian approach, where the result of an action is
deemed to more or less directly express the underlying cognitive
activities, without any regard for the movement itself. This attitude is stigmatized by Gallahue (1982), who states that "Developmen-

tal psychologists tend to be only marginally interested in motor
development, and then only as a visual indicator of cognitive functioning" (p.4).

In our search for some functional explanation of schemata formation,
which we invoked to interpret the age-related trend observed in positioning, we have been led to the general topic of memory. This is
not surprising, inasmuch as, by definition, schemata are memories,
and then, may be expected to involve the same processes. Unfortunately, the processes specifically implied in schemata formation cannot be addressed directly. One is only inclined to assume the implication of common mechanisms to all categories of memory, which
are undoubtedly of a cognitive nature (e.g., abstraction, storage,
retrieval, etc...), and which are, seemingly, easier to assess experimentally. Consequently, no explanation for the remaining problem
of the U-shaped trend can be provided, except strategical changes in
one or some of the mental activities related to memory.

4. PREDICTABILITY

At first glance, targetting is a very simple and highly predictable
task, which basically involves specifying a motor response in terms
of distance and direction. For open-loop pointing, the coordination
of vision and proprioception becomes essential to achieve an accurate final limb position. To discuss predictive processes and their
relationship to perceptuo-motor behavior, we shall briefly review
the development of predictable visuo-manual tracking in children and
attempt to provide a tentative interpretation of the U-shaped problem by comparing tracking with targetting.

Visuo-manual tracking requires the subject to maintain the spatial
coincidence between the position of a moving target and a response
device through appropriate movements. With a minimal strategy,
successful performance can be achieved through a continuous attempt
to reduce the spatial mismatch between the positions of the response
and of the stimulus. Typically, these movements are controlled by
visual feedback (Craik, 1947; Elkind, 1956). The task becomes
easier as the target motion becomes more predictable (Krendel and
McRuer, 1960; Poulton, 1952). The possibility of prediction allows
the execution of a movement fundamentally based upon a motor pattern
that matches the general spatio-temporal features of target displacements. The pattern is then intermittently adjusted to the specific task requirements through several control mechanisms. Expressed
more specifically, the parameters of the motor program are largely
determined in an anticipatory manner according to predictions about
the target motion. These predictions allow for the construction of
an internal model of the target displacements, which is mapped into
a movement pattern by the motor system.

Developmental studies of rotatory tracking, where the target trajec-
tory is a circle, showed a gradual improvement in performance (measured as "time on target") between 5 and 16 years, as well as a
steady improvement as a function of pratice (Ammons, Alprin and
Ammons, 1955; Davoll, Hastings and Klein, 1965; Dunham, Allan and
Winter, 1985). A similar trend is reported by Pew and Rupp (1971)
for 9- and 15-year-olds, who were tracking a unidimensional unpre-

dictable target (i.e., with a pseudo-random horizontal motion). The temporal lag between the response and the target decreased as a function of age and pratice. Since the use of predictive strategies can be ruled out a priori, these findings suggest that part of the enhancement in tracking performance results from a reduction of the time delay introduced by the visuomanual loop. This would stem from a general increase in the processing speed of the CNS. However, the authors noted that the improvement in performance measured with respect to spatial mismatch did not follow such a monotonous trend with age, but rather suggested some strategical change between 12 and 15 years.

A series of experiments attempted to specifically investigate the role of prediction in visuomanual tracking. Subjects were asked to pursue a target whose displacement was periodic, constant in ampli- tude, but of varied frequency. Magdaleno, Jex and Johnson (1970) demonstrated that for adults, a response based uniquely on correc- tive mechanisms through visual feedback is no longer operant for tracking a target moving at a frequency above 0.5 Hz. Instead the generation of a proper motor pattern is required (cf. Poulton, 1981). This allows adult pursuit to remain accurate within a large range of target frequencies (e.g., Noble, Fitts and Warren, 1955).

In children, Mounoud, Hauert, Mayer, Gachoud, Guyon and Gottret (1983) showed that children under five years of age only partially master the task at 0.8 Hz. Three-year-olds usually reproduced the target amplitude but at incorrect frequency. However, the opposite was true for four-year-olds. Their responses matched target fre- quency, but not amplitude. The fact that every child reported a sa- tisfactory assessment of his own performance despite the gross and overt mismatch suggests that he performs according to his intended and predicted plan. An acceptable rate of success was only attained at five years, when 30% of the subjects were able to pursue a target at 0.8 Hz for about 40 seconds. 100% was reached only at nine years (Mounoud, Viviani, Hauert and Guyon, 1985). At a lower frequency (0.2 Hz) however, the majority of the subjects correctly performed the task. These results were interpreted in light of the findings of Magdaleno et al. (1970), as the consequence of an increased abi- lity to execute an appropriate motor pattern within this age range.

Further analyses provide some indication about the processes under- lying this age-related trend. First, Mounoud et al. (1985) obser- ved a dramatic and consistent decrease in response amplitude in six- year-olds (i.e., half that of their neighbors in age). Second, the strongest enhancement in synchronization with the target was noticed within the same age interval. Finally, on the basis of kinematic as well as spectral analysis of the movements, five-year-olds produced a response that consisted of successive ballistic pointing movements toward the current position of the target. This strategy, efficient at low frequencies, resulted in unsuccessful pursuit at a higher frequency because of the lack of time remaining after one pointing movement to plan and execute the following one. In contrast, older children used a response that reproduced the global characteristics of the target motion through the modulation of a proper motor pat- tern, even if simple corrective functioning through visual feedback would have sufficed to succeed in the task. This general picture suggest that between five and seven years of age, a fundamental

change in the perceptuo-motor strategy occurs that stems from the
ability to produce an adequate motor pattern of the age of six. The
sharp reduction in amplitude observed at six years might be a consequence of the supplementary processing load associated with the synchronization of the motor pattern, and/or with its adjustment in amplitude.

Such a framework can be supported by findings from a continuation
paradigm (Zanone, 1989). Boys between 6 and 15 years of age, who
were pursuing a periodic target, were asked to continue executing
the same movement after the target had actually been removed (a kind
of "open-loop tracking"). In this case, the response is assumed to
be based on the motor pattern used for tracking and stored in memory. The results showed a clear improvement with age in response
matching to the target motion in terms of frequency, suggesting that
the underlying motor pattern was more consistent with respect to the
target. Moreover, this open-loop response increased in stability
with age. Not only did the drift of the response frequency with
time progressively disappears, but its variability diminished as
well. One can thus assume that the ability to generate a more consistent and stable motor pattern with regard to the optimal response
may in part explain the improvement in tracking performance observed
by Mounoud and colleagues within this age range.

Following the initial postulate that periodic tracking depends on a
predictive model of target motion, a general interpretation can be
attempted. At three and four years of age, the child makes a partial prediction about only one dimension of target motion (i.e.,
amplitude or frequency, respectively), resulting in a failure to
simultaneously reproduce its temporal and spatial characteristics.
At five, a piecewise, short-term anticipation is possible, leading
to a ballistic type of behavior. From six years on, a coordinated
and complete model is available, allowing the generation of a motor
pattern. The enhancement in the consistency of the motor pattern
with respect to the actual pattern to be produced entails an improvement in tracking performance. Nevertheless, the precise matching
of the response with the target motion necessitates an intermittent
control through visual feedback to finely adjust the pattern to the
spatio-temporal requirements of the task. From this point of view,
there is an apparent paradox, in that a more predictive behavior,
such as that emerging since the age of six, entails a more controlled response. This is related to the inaccuracy of children's predictions, which ask for numerous adjustments of the motor pattern
through visual feedback. Adults do not exhibit any observable signs
of correction, suggesting that the anticipated pattern is fairly
accurate and does not need to be dramatically adjusted.

It is interesting to recall that in targetting, a similar developmental sequence --the change from a triggered to a controlled motor
behavior-- was also observed between five and seven years of age.
It is tempting to attribute these changes to the general ability to
plan movement in a more or less complete and adequate manner. Indeed, in positioning, which is a fairly simple movement, even a
short-term prediction, characteristic of children at five years,
would suffice to yield a correct performance. Later on, the inadequacy of proprioceptive cues in defining the final position of the
limb would lead children to visually control their movements. In an

open-loop task, two alternative hypotheses are suggested but, because of the shortcomings in Hay's classification of movements, they cannot be resolved. If movements are continuous but not ballistic, children would still preprogram movement, but would be misled by the inaccurate calibration between vision and proprioception. However, a remaining question concerns the reason for such a temporary change in the calibration. If movements are mostly discontinuous, one might assume that this inadequacy would render the actual outcome unpredictable, and therefore imply the use of a more cautious, controlled strategy. This postulate is supported by the kinematic analysis of positioning in 8 year-olds, which shows a very low velocity and a large undershoot in the response, and has been interpreted as "overcontrolled functioning" (Hay et al., 1986).

5. TOWARD GENERAL FRAMEWORKS

From this review of targetting and tracking in children, a global picture of perceptuo-motor development emerges which suggests predominantly ballistic behavior before seven years of age, and more controlled functioning afterwards. This change seems to be largely dependent upon the child's ability to predict various aspects of the movement to be produced.

Further support for this can be found in studies using the coincidence-anticipation paradigm. This task is more complex than simple pointing because it requires the synchronization of a targetting response with the occurence of an event at a time that must be predicted by the subject. At six years of age, preprogrammed functioning was reported by Ball and Glencross (1985), whereas older children produced more controlled movements. Also, Williams (1985) showed that six year-olds were unable to predict the exact moment of movement achievement, and resorted to stereotyped behavior, irrespective of the specific temporal contraints. To summarize, coincidence-anticipation, six-year-olds differ from older children by showing a deficiency in predicting all the characteristics of the movement (in particular, the correct duration of movement), as well as by exhibiting ballistic behavior.

Within the same age range, an analogous developmental trend has been shown for lifting objects (Mounoud and Hauert, 1982). Unlike older subjects, children aged four to five years performed mostly continuous movements. If one ignore the slight shift in the age of occurence of the triggered behavior (possibly due to the large difference between tasks), these findings suggest that this developmental sequence is fairly general in perceptuo-motor behavior.

The development of goal-directed movements in infancy reveals a similar pattern of alternating between triggered and controlled motor behavior (e.g., Bruner and Koslowsky, 1972; Bower, 1974; von Hofsten, 1980; McDonnel, 1975; White, Castle and Held, 1964). It would lead us too far afield to enter into the debate about the primacy of one functioning over other (e.g., Trevarthen, 1984; von Hofsten, 1983), or the debate about their order in the sequence (see Bushnel, 1985). In our opinion, this discussion continues because of the dissimilarities among these different experiments. Indeed, different criteria have been used to observe the babies' behavior in

various experimental situations, at different ages, and so on.
These technical difficulties aside, a striking outcome of these
studies is that the acquisition of perceptuo-motor skill involving
goal-directed movements seems to occur several times in ontogeny.
For instance, catching during infancy, which has been thoroughly
studied by von Hofsten and colleagues (e.g., von Hofsten, 1983; von
Hofsten and Lindhagen, 1979), is basically a coincidence-
anticipation task whose complete mastery is achieved in late childhood (Dorfman, 1977; Dunham, 1977). Now, from the standpoint that
changes in the control of movement are related to changes in its
predictability, it follows that identical movements vary in the
degree of predictability during two periods in ontogeny, once in
infancy and once in childhood. This is somewhat bewildering and
deserves a specific discussion.

A two-step evolution over infancy and childhood evokes the Piagetian
framework (Piaget, 1952, 1954). The former period pertaining to
sensori-motor development is contrasted with the latter pertaining
to (pre)operational development thanks to the availability of the
semiotic function from the age of about 18 months on. Nevertheless,
the U-shaped sequence previously described does not fit into the
Piagetian model in two respects. First, according to Piaget,
perceptuo-motor behavior implies practical knowledge and characterizes only infancy. During childhood conceptual knowledge is acquired
and is considered to be totally independent of perceptuo-motor
development. Second, both developments are monotonic processes.

These contradictions may be reconciled in the cognitivist framework
promoted by Mounoud, whose basic postulate is to refute the independence of action and knowledge at whatever stage (Mounoud, 1986;
Zanone and Hauert, 1987; Hauert, Zanone and Mounoud, 1989). Briefly, from birth on, the individual's memory contents, or representations, are submitted to four successive elaborations during
ontogenesis, the first of which occurs at about two years of age.
Each of these (re)elaborations unfolds according to a similar
sequence and stems from the availability of specific codes. This
repeated process allows for more and more abstracted representations
as a function of the number of (re)elaborations. The representations involved in perceptuo-motor performance (internal models,
schemata, etc...) also go through these processes. Thus, during
each (re)elaboration, a similar sequence of perceptuo-motor functioning develops, pertaining to the fixed order in the elaboration
of representations. Moreover, a temporary decrease in performance
may be observed, resulting from more or less specified and complete
representations as a function of their level of elaboration.

However, such a global view, which promotes a cognitive interpretation of perceptuo-motor development based upon the child's predictive abilities, needs clarification because it relates to several contradictory experimental results, and is subject to a more theoretical discussion.

In a less constrained task than visuomanual tracking, where subjects
were free to choose either the amplitude or the frequency of movements, five- to seven-year-old children all showed very similar behaviors, without any specific change at six year (Viviani and
Zanone, 1988). Furthermore, all subjects could execute periodic

movements of the same amplitude as that required in tracking experiments, but at a lower frequency. Moreover, they rarely produced the
frequencies used in these studies (i.e., 0.2 and 0.8 Hz) in a spontaneous fashion. Thus, five-year-old children are able to predict
and plan back-and-forth movements to the same extent as older subjects. Therefore, an explanation based exclusively on changes in
the predictive ability must be challenged. Instead, it could be
argued that the problem lies in the spatio-temporal constraints
imposed by the tracking task as compared to a more "natural" situation. Indeed, when six-year-olds were asked to track a target
whose displacements have a smaller amplitude than that of the studies by Mounoud and colleagues, they pursued the stimulus quite
accurately (Hauert and Zanone, 1984). In other words, when confronted with experimental contraints that are more compatible with natural behavior --recall that they largely undershot target amplitude
in the standard condition--, six-year-olds show behavior similar to
both younger and older children. Along this same line, Sugden
(1980) showed that children performing Fitts' reciprocal tapping
task no longer produced the usual alternating pattern of pointing
movements at the two targets if the requirement on movement precision was very strong. Instead, they executed a series of ballistic
movements from one target to the other. Thus, a change in the manner to perform periodic movements analogous to that observed in
tracking between five and six years was induced by changing the
experimental constraints. With this in mind, the developmental
trend observed by Mounoud et al. (1985) may be specific only to
certain spatio-temporal constraints on the movement.

Besides the fact that many developmental findings in similar tasks
as those envisaged here do not show any U-shaped trend with age, a
more basic criticism can be addressed to the previous approach. To
understand the fairly complicated development of positioning, a cas-
cade of entities was postulated post hoc (e.g., motor program, schemata, frames of reference, memories, representations, etc...), forming a large organization that allows one to plan and control the
movement. This framework stems from information theory and cybernetics and conceives of movement as anticipatedly and/or more or less
continuously prescribed by a central processor (i.e., the CNS). The
CNS is endowed with the properties of "sensing, attending to, transforming, retaining, and transmitting information" (Stelmach, 1982,
p.64). Then, once this construct is accepted, it is a matter of
taste to attribute changes in the observed perceptuo-motor behavior
to the one or the other of the functions of the CNS, or, relatedly,
to one or several of its structural entities. But, ultimately, such
a regress through the levels of explanation results in asking the
question at a biological level. In the case of the U-shaped trends
envisaged here, the aforementioned hypothesis promoted by Hay bears
directly on the biological maturation of CNS, invoking two separate
neural substructures. In the more cognitivist framework proposed by
Mounoud and colleagues, although the elaboration of representations
is clearly a psychological process, the occurence of new coding capacities pertains to a biological level.

One must also keep in mind that the control mechanisms involved in
this organization are basically metaphorical. In particular, feedback, which has been presented here as the principal means of controlling movement, is a functional metaphor. A given system can be

observed that exhibits the formal features of feedback regulation, but, in reality, its functioning is only determined by its actual physical properties. A marble placed on the bottom of a incurved cup is formally equivalent to a feedback mechanism, insofar as any displacement from the equilibrium point is compensated for by a force that pulls it toward its original position. However, on the one hand, the feedback property cannot be ascribed to either the marble or the cup, but emerges through their interaction in a gravitational field. On the other hand, the system does not contain a reference signal, comparator or other such entities. In this case, the metaphorical character of the theoretical description is obvious. But more generally, one may also question the value of these conceptions borrowed from control theory for understanding both physical systems that spontaneously recover a stable state and biological systems that are endowed with this property, such as perceptuomotor system. Instead, one may view understanding the physical laws that govern a system as a first crucial step, before postulating a control process. The control theory framework is tempting because by using its formal tools, one can construct self-regulated machines that exhibit behavior similar to those of biological systems. Nevertheless, this is neither the only possible view, nor the approach that other sciences, such as physics have adopted.

This contention is a cornerstone of the so-called "natural/dynamic" approach (e.g., Kelso, Holt, Kugler and Turvey, 1980; Kugler, Kelso and Turvey, 1980, 1982; Kugler, 1986; Kugler and Turvey, 1987). Its basic insight owes to Bernstein (1967; see Whiting, 1984). Given the tremendous complexity of the neuro-muscular and skeletal systems, his concern was to explain how the CNS is capable of simultaneously governing all the degrees of freedom implied in executing a coordinated movement. As a solution to the problem of reduction of the degrees of freedom, he put forth the concept of synergy, which is an ensemble of neuromuscular components grouped into a task-specific functional unit (thus, implying only one degree of freedom). Synergy allows for the emergence of spatio-temporally ordered behavior in a complex system such as the motor system. The notion of coordinative structure, an analogical avatar of the dissipative structures of physics, first introduced by Turvey (1977), stems directly from the idea of synergy.

A different, though compatible, approach comes from a field that originated in physics, and is concerned with the formation of ordered patterns in non-equilibrium systems. This pattern formation is common to many physical, biological, and chemical systems (see Haken, 1983). Although they may differ completely in their material substrate, the same principles govern their (self-)organization. These have been described in "synergetics", a theory of spontaneous formation of structure in open systems (for an introduction, Haken, 1983, 1985). This self-organization results from the cooperative interplay of a large number of subsystems and pertains to the dissipative properties of the system dynamics. Therefore, the system, regardless of its initial state, will eventually attain a stable and stationary state. This state constitutes an attractor for the system's behavior. If perturbed, the system will spontaneously recover its stable state after a given duration called relaxation time (RT). The RT is an assessment of the strength of the underlying attractor: The smaller RT, the stronger the attractor (for an introduction,

Schoner and Kelso, 1988a). Dissipative systems may also have multiple stable states under the same external conditions. The system
would then occasionally switch from one stable state to another, but
this occurs in a much slower time scale (i.e., equilibration time,
ET). These spontaneous switches are due to various types of noise
acting on the system. In more intuitive words, the long ET yields
the structural stability of the system, while the short RT allows
for functional flexibility. An important insight ground from synergetics is the recognition of so-called phase transitions (Haken,
1983). These occur when parameters influencing the system cause the
stationary state to become unstable. The system does not return to
the stable state after a small perturbation but instead abruptly
switches to a different state. At these points the system reveals
its basic organizational principle: A pattern exists as long as it
is stable.

As with many other physical systems, and this is our point of interest, a phase transition was also found in motor behavior, specifically in interlimb coordination (Kelso, 1981, 1984). When asked to
rhythmically move two homologous fingers, adults showed two possible
stable patterns, described by the phase between the two periodic movements. These patterns were in-phase and anti-phase movements.
However, the anti-phase pattern inevitably shifted to in-phase (phase transition) as soon as the movement frequency was scaled up to a
critical value. Above this point, only one pattern remained (in-
phase). However, the converse change did not occur when the frequency was decreased below the critical value. The in-phase pattern
is always performed, since the underlying attractor is still present
and more stable. The point is that, given the existence of the phase transition, the intrinsic coordination between homologous fingers
in unidimensional movements is entirely accounted for by the dynamics of the collective variable (Haken, Kelso and Bunz, 1985). A
theoretical model led to several predictions about the nature of the
pattern switch (Schoner, Haken and Kelso, 1986). The main idea is
that one can observe the loss of stability through several new measures (e.g., RT, variability of the collective variable). These
predictions have been tested and verified experimentally (for a
review, Kelso and Schoner, 1988; Schoner and Kelso, 1988a).

These results illustrate the relevance of a dynamic approach to
understand stability, flexibility, and changes in motor behavior.
Several aspects must be emphasized concerning this viewpoint.
First, the existence of intrinsic patterns does not imply that motor
behavior is independent of intention, or completely stereotypic.
Instead, behavior is constrained by the dynamics of the system.
Below a critical frequency value which leads to phase transition,
one can voluntarily switch between both intrinsic patterns. However, the temporal characteristics of switching are contingent upon
system dynamics (e.g., faster change from anti- to in-phase pattern,
than the reverse) (Kelso, Scholz and Schoner, 1988). Along this
same line, it is possible to execute finger movements with other
phase relationships by synchronizing them with an external model
(Tuller and Kelso, in press). But such patterns increase in variability because they are further removed from the intrinsic ones. In
this respect, variability is an assessment of how much performance
is distorted with respect to the intrinsic patterns in order to produce the required pattern (for a theoretical account, see Schoner

and Kelso, 1988b). Finally, let us recall that these perceptuo-motor patterns are definitely impossible above the critical value of frequency, where the only possible intrinsic pattern (in-phase) governs the system.

The second remark focusses upon the fact that, up until now, behavior has been accounted for by temporal ordering because of the choice of the collective variable. Spatial aspects of behavior, such as movement amplitude, are not described by relative phase. Nevertheless, at a lower level of description, which considers the two fingers as weakly coupled oscillators, movement kinematics (i.e., the relationships between spatial and temporal dimensions) are also covered (Haken et al., 1985). Moreover, from these dynamics result those of relative phase through a mere mathematical derivation. There is thus coherence between the different levels of dynamical descriptions of the same behavior.

The last point is critical for the topic of development. The results of Kelso and colleagues demonstrate that abrupt, discontinuous changes in behavior may occur as a function of the progressive scaling in the value of a parameter. By analogy, topological changes in movement along several time scales --thus, through ontogeny-- may be viewed as resulting from the gradual modification of the value of a specific parameter, which moves the system into an altogether different collective state.

The most convincing --and may be the only-- developmental example of such changes in motor behavior is found in a series of studies by Thelen and colleagues on infant legs movements. At about two months of age, stepping movements which were present at birth, suddenly disappear from the infant's spontaneous repertoire (McGraw, 1932). However, with intensive training, this type of walking is not suppressed (Zelazo, Zelazo and Kolb, 1972). Furthermore, a similar pattern, described in terms of the phase relationship between the excursions of the involved joints, emerges in the form of coordinated kicking movements, once the infant lies supine (Thelen and Fisher, 1983). These authors suggested that the apparent loss of this pattern results from an increase in limb weight which is not compensated for by an increase in muscular strength. This impedes lifting the limb in the upright position. They argued that fat mass increases considerably while musculature remains fairly constant. Confirmation of this interpretation is provided by Thelen, Fisher, and Ridley-Johnson (1984). Infants who exhibited normal stepping considerably reduced the number of stepping movements when the limbs were loaded by supplementary weights. However, the normal stepping pattern reappeared in children who spontaneously had shown little stepping, when their legs were submerged in water, which reduces the effect of gravity, and thus, limb weight.

From these results emerges the idea that the ability to generate stepping movements does not vanish at two months of age, but rather is hindered by changes in a particular physical characteristic of the limb at this time (i.e., the relative weight of the limb). Accordingly, the developmental sequence observed during this period is viewed by Thelen and colleagues as the effect of a specific parameter that drives the system into specific collective states (attractors). A definite stable behavior among several potential ones

emerges as a function of this parameter. Therefore, their is no
need to assume that the ability of the CNS to generate locomotor-
like patterns goes through dramatic changes from birth. This ability always exists in an unspecific form, which is realized in different spatiotemporal coordinations (or even not at all) as a function
of the parameter. In support of this assumption, Thelen, Uhlrich
and Nils (1987) showed that at one month babies already exhibit
coordinated stepping when supported on a moving treadmill.

If one concedes that the limb patterns observed in the different
conditions (i.e., spontaneous, supine, weighted, treadmill, etc...)
are similar with respect to the chosen collective variable, it might
be assumed that the change in the system dynamics is also the same,
and may be related to modifications in the relative weight of the
limb. Nevertheless, several questions arise which are highly relevant to the developmental perspective.

First, the theoretical picture is quite different from the example
with hand movements in adults. In fact, the parameter suggested by
Thelen and colleagues (i.e., weight/force relation) changes very
slowly when compared to the time scale where an infant spontaneously
switches between different behaviors.

Second, one can argue about the similarity of the observed limb
movements. A basic assumption of this approach is that the ordered
pattern is task-specific. At first glance, spontaneous and treadmill stepping are fundamentally different tasks. Thus, to compare
them and to establish their expected similarity, identifying the
stable patterns is important. Therefore, pertinent collective descriptors must be found that allow one to determine whether response
stability is attained. Moreover, one must observe the system on the
correct time scale (between RT and ET), where stable behavior
exists. The fulfillment of these requirements is particularly important --and also particularly tough-- with children, whose performance is likely to be very noisy and unstable. In the terms
already used above, such a strategy is instrumental in defining
whether movements belong to the same class. As a consequence, it
could allow one to establish a behavioral repertoire of spontaneous
movement patterns at different ages. This would be a valuable
breakthrough in developmental psychology.

Third, what moves the system from one stepping pattern into the
other through ontogeny is developmental time. Relative limb weight
is only a reasonable and inferred candidate for parametrizing the
change. But other factors might also make either of these patterns
more or less likely to be observed. For example, Thelen et al.
(1987) observed that the treadmill pattern persisted until the age
of four months. Moreover, this behavior is also observed in seven-
months-olds (Thelen, 1986). This contradicts the observation that
spontaneous stepping in the upright position has vanished between
two and eight months. Thus, it is possible to elicit stepping movements when the limb weight should actually inhibit such a behavior.
This suggests that at least another parameter might be identified to
account for the apparition of the treadmill stepping pattern during
this period. Furthermore, about six months later, spontaneous stepping reappears. Even if a comparable transition has been obtained
through the experimental modification of the limb weight, it is

unlikely that it still constitutes a reasonable parameter along developmental time at this age, where the effects of growth on the physical characteristics of the limb are entirely different. Therefore, given the intricateness of various parameters influencing the system at different times, the only evidence of the implication of one specific parameter (e.g., limb weight) in the spontaneous disparition or apparition of stepping would be provided by a longitudinal study assessing this parameter along these transition periods.

Finally, to our knowledge, the actual dynamics of this developmental sequence have not been proposed. This may be due to the difficulty in unambiguously describing infant motor behavior following the appropriate method, as mentionned in the previous paragraphs. Such an endeavour is feasible and is a necessary step to establish the value of a dynamic account of developmental change.

6. TOWARD ONE METHOD

In this chapter, three sets of experiments have been reviewed that present discontinuous trends in perceptuo-motor development, and their various interpretations have been discussed. Studies on targetting and tracking relied on a kinematic description of performance to infer changes with age in the manner that movement is controlled. In targetting, these changes are often interpreted in terms of asynchronous maturation of distinct neural structures. In tracking, a cognitivist interpretation of change in the representational contents involved in movement planning and control is favored. Finally, studies on infant stepping suggest that the disappearance and the subsequent recovery of this behavior can be accounted for by a dynamic approach.

It is not surprising that the different interpretations of these experimental findings in perceptuo-motor development stem from three of the main theoretical streams in current psychology. A somewhat caricatural way to characterize each of them is to sketch how they conceive the nature of perceptuo-motor coordination. For the neuro-biological approach, coordination results from the activity of successively organized structures in the CNS, from sense organs to motor effectors, which specifically process and transmit bioelectrical pulses so that relevant information emerges for adapted motor behavior. A typical example of this approach is the distributed motor control model of Pitts and McCullock (1947). A cognitivist framework would attribute these functions to abstract memory contents or rules (either built-in or constructed), which provide meaning through the mediation of sensory afferences. In particular, they give rise to the type of information needed for motor planning and control. A good example is the (neo)Piagetian framework, especially from the developmental point of view. Finally, in the dynamic approach, perceptual information is fundamentally what moves the system away from its intrinsic patterns, or what entails observable changes in behavior. In this respect, the behavioral character of information is very similar to the (neo)Gibsonian, ecological concept of direct perception. To quote Beek (1986), "Action is the realization of an affordance" (p.191).

It is beyond the scope of the present paper --and the competence of

its author-- to enter into the debate, sometimes bordering on pole-
mics, about the relevance and drawbacks of each approach at the
epistemological level. We prefer instead to limit our ambitions to
a more conciliative, and perhaps constructive attitude at a methodological level. On the one hand, the studies on targetting and tracking converge in showing that the period between four and seven
years is crucial in the development of perceptuo-motor coordination.
More specifically, children tend to utilize incoming information
about movement outcome in different ways at different ages. This
point merits more thorough investigation. On the other hand, the
dynamic approach provides a powerful method to lawfully describe
motor behavior. Its application to the topic of development and
its practical range clearly deserve more discussion.

The choice of an adequate collective variable as well as the internal coherence amongst the different levels of description have repeatedly been underscored as mandatory in describing behavior. In
Hay's experiments, performance accuracy (thus its amplitude) and its
kinematics are in tight agreement with regard to proposed interpretation. In light of the results of Kelso and colleagues and those
of Thelen, one may wonder whether a temporal descriptor, such as a
phase relationship between joint angular displacements for instance,
could not be found that includes both descriptions, and constitutes
therefore a more pertinent and unidimensional order parameter. In
the same way, hand-trajectory formation in tridimensional space has
been shown to be accounted for by phase relationships between the
different joints involved (Soechting and Terzuolo, 1986).

Longitudinal studies over four or five years of age are costly in
time, effort, and, last but not least, money. Thus, a wise strategy might be to investigate a large number of subjects using a
cross-sectional design, and to sample along this time scale with
fine stepping. This might allow one to define a repertoire of the
most frequently adopted stable behaviors. Age-related changes might
then consist of variations in the relative frequency of the observed
patterns. This strategy is reminiscent of the work of Roberton and
colleagues cited in the introduction. However, tracking the age-
related transitions requires sampling in a consistent manner with
respect to the rate of change in the supposed parameter. By contrast, one may reasonably expect little insight from coarse investigations along developmental time. Unfortunately, these are frequent and usually lead to the trivial conclusion that perceptuo-
motor performance improves with age. Therefore, they provide little
insight regarding the underlying process.

Once such a hypothesis has been put forth, considerable care should
be devoted to its operational assessment. Even if this point is a
basic to the experimental method, it is not so trivial in psychology, where the level of interpretation rapidly become distant from
the observable behavior. For instance, the somewhat tricky use of
prismatic glasses in Hay's experiment is a particularly sensible
manner to test the role of the postulated visual feedback. From our
point of view, and in accordance with the dynamic framework, pertur-
bing the system constitutes a priveleged method to test the existence of a process.

Finally, we would like to emphasized that the value of a dynamic

approach does not only reside in the determination of the actual
parameter that accounts for behavioral change, even though this is
important at the epistemological level. Instead, establishing a
dynamic theory of the change amongst the observed patterns is important. One must keep in mind that the parameters of the model (i.e.,
non-linear equations) are both contentless and dimensionless.
Mapping real physical variables is less enlightening than providing
the theoretical bases for stability and change in perceptuo-motor
behavior. This pragmatic attitude that favours finding lawful
relationships among several observables seems promising. Such a
theory might be paradigmatic of stability and change in other behavioral domains where a similar repertoire (state space) is observed.
The potential generality of this framework contributes to its
attractiveness.

Nevertheless, in spite of this appeal in the domain of perceptuo-
motor coordination, a simple semantic trade in the use of concepts
is likely to be vain and void. Ultimately, the motor program and
the coordinative structure are the putative means that CNS utilizes
for coping with the problem of degrees of freedom. Saying that the
child is provided with numerous coordinative structures allowing
stability, besides the obvious misuse of the term, or that change
appears functionally contingent on the emergence of such a structure, does not entail per se any real advance in the concern. Well
before, and toward a new theory, one should first adopt a method
that favors the operational assessment of each interpretative concept used. Undoubtedly, this is the only certain statement among
all the postulates, assumptions, hypotheses, and interpretations
contained in the present chapter (for a grand total of 60 occuren-
ces).

AKNOWLEDGMENTS

The author is indebted to J.J. Jeka, G. Schoner, and C.A. Hauert for
their help along the process of writing this chapter. This article
was prepared while the author was supported by the Swiss National
Science Foundation, Grant 83.459.0.87, and the Center for Complex
Systems.

REFERENCES

Adams, J.A. (1971). A closed-loop theory of motor learning. *Journal
of Motor Behavior, 3*, 111-150.
Adams, J.A. (1976). Issues for a closed-loop theory of motor
learning. In: G.E. Stelmach (Ed.), *Motor control: Issues and
trends*. New York: Academic Press.
Ammons, R.B., Alprin, J.I., & Ammons, C.H. (1955). Rotatory pursuit
performance as related to sex and age of preadult subjects.
Journal of Experimental Psychology, 49, 127-133.
Anwar, F. (1981). Visual-motor localization in normal and subnormal
development. *British Journal of Psychology, 72*, 43-57.
Arbib, M.A. (1981). Perceptual structures and distributed motor
control. In: V.B. Brooks (Ed.), *Handbook of Physiology*.
Bethesda: American Physiological Society.
Asatryan, D.G., & Fel'dman, A.G. (1965). Functional tuning of the

nervous system with control of movement or maintenance of steady
posture I. Mechanographic analysis on the work of the joint on
execution of a postural task. *Biophysics, 10*, 925-935.
Ball, C.T., & Glencross, D. (1985). Developmental differences in a
coincident timing task under speed and time constraints. *Human
Movement Science, 4*, 1-15.
Barclay, C.R., & Newell, K.M. (1980). Children's processing of
information in motor skill acquisition. *Journal of Experimental
Psychology, 30*, 98-108.
Bard, C., & Hay, L. (1983). Etude ontogénétique de la coordination
visuo-manuelle. *Journal Canadien de Psychologie, 37*, 390-412.
Beek, P.J. (1986). Perception-action coupling in the young infant.
In: M.G. Wade & H.T.A. Whiting (Eds.), *Motor development in
children*. Dordrecht: Nijhoff.
Bernstein, N. (1967). *The coordination and regulation of movement*.
London: Pergamon Press.
Bever, T.G. (1982). *Regression in mental development: Basic
phenomena and theories*. Hillsdale, NJ: Erlbaum.
Birch, H.G., & Lefford, A. (1967). Visual differentiation,
intersensory integration and voluntary movement. *Monograph of the
Society for Research in Child Development, 32*, (Whole £ 10).
Bower, T.G.R. (1974). *Human development*. San Francisco: Freeman.
Brooks, V.B. (1974). Some examples of programmed limb movements.
Brain Research, 71, 299-308.
Brooks, V.B., Cooke, J.D., & Thomas, T.F. (1973). The continuity
of movement. In: R.B. Stein, K.G. Pearson, R.S. Smith & J.B.
Redford (Eds.), *Control of posture and locomotion*. New York:
Plenum Press.
Brown, J.V., Sepher, M.M., Ettlinger, G., & Skreczek, W. (1986).
The accuracy of aimed movements to visual targets during
development: The role of visual information. *Journal of
Experimental Child Psychology, 41*, 443-460.
Bruner, J.S., & Kozlowsky, B. (1972). Visually pre-adapted
constituents of manipulatory action. *Perception, 1*, 3-12.
Bruner, J.S., Olver, R.R., & Greenfield, P.M. (1966). *Studies in
cognitive growth*. London: Wiley.
Bushnell, E.W. (1985). The decline of visually guided reaching
during infancy. *Infant Behavior & Development, 8(2)*, 139-155.
Chi, M.T.H. (1976). Short term memory limitations in children.
Capacity or processing deficits ? *Memory & Cognition, 4(5)*, 559-
572.
Clark, J.E. (1982). The role of response mechanisms in motor skill
development. In: J.A.S. Kelso & J.E. Clark (Eds.), *The
development of movement control and coordination*. Chichester:
Wiley.
Connolly, K., & Jones, B. (1970). A developmental study of
afferent-reafferent integration. *British Journal of Psychology,
61*, 259-266.
Connolly, K., Brown, K., & Bassett, E. (1968). Developmental
changes in some components of a motor skill. *British Journal of
Psychology, 59(3)*, 305-314.
Craik, K.J. (1947). Theory of the human operator in control system.
British Journal of Psychology, 38, 56-61.
Cratty, B.J. (1986). *Perceptual and motor development in infant and
children*. Englewood Cliffs: Prentice Hall.
Davoll, S.H., Hastings, M.L., & Klein, D.A. (1965). Effect of age,
sex and speed of rotation on rotatory pursuit performance by

young children. *Perceptual & Motor Skills, 21, 351-357.*
Dorfman, P.W. (1977). Timing and anticipation: A developmental perspective. *Journal of Motor Behavior, 9,* 67-79.
Dunham, P. (1977). Age, sex, speed and practice in coincidence-anticipation performance of children. *Perceptual & Motor Skills, 45,* 187-193.
Dunham, P., Allan R., & Winter, B. (1985). Tracking ability of elementary school-age children. *Perceptual & Motor Skills, 60,* 771-774.
Elkind, J.I. (1956). Characteristics of simple manual control system. M.I.T. Lincoln Laboratory Technical Report 111. Lexington, Massachussets.
Fairweather, H., & Hutt, S.J. (1978). On the rate of gain of information in children. *Journal of Experimental Child Psychology, 26,* 216-229.
Fel'dman, A.G. (1966a). Functional tuning of the nervous system with control of movement or maintenance of steady posture II. Controlable parameters of the muscles. *Biophysics, 11,* 565-578.
Fel'dman, A.G. (1966b). Functional tuning of the nervous system with control of movement or maintenance of steady posture III. Mechanographic analysis of execution of the simplest motor task. *Biophysics, 11,* 766-775.
Flavell, J.H. (1970). Developmental studies of mediated memory. In: H.W. Reese & L.P. Lipsitt (Eds.), *Advances in child development and behavior,* 5. New York: Academic Press.
Fodor, J.A. (1983). *The modularity of mind.* Cambridge, Mass.: M.I.T. Press.
Gallagher, J.D., & Thomas, J.R. (1980). Effects of varying post-KR intervals upon children's motor performance. *Journal of Motor Behavior, 12,* 41-46.
Gallagher, J.D., & Thomas, J.R. (1984). Developmental effects of grouping and recoding on learning a movement series. *Research Quarterly for Exercise and Sport, 57(2),* 117-127.
Gallahue, D.L. (1982). *Understanding motor development in children.* New York: Wiley.
Gesell, A. (1929). Maturation and infant behavior. *Psychological Review, 36,* 307-319.
Goodenough, F.L. (1935). The development of reactive process from early childhood to maturity. *Journal of Experimental Psychology, 18,* 431-450.
Halverson, H.M. (1931). An experimental study of prehension in infants by means of systematic cinema records. *Genetic Psychology Monographs, 10,* 107-283.
Haken, H. (1983). *Synergetics: An introduction.* Berlin: Springer.
Haken, H. (Ed.) (1985). *Complex systems: Operational approches in neurobiology, physical systems, and computers.* Berlin: Springer.
Haken, H., Kelso, J.A.S., & Bunz, H. (1985). A theoretical model of phase transitions in human hand movements. *Biological Cybernetics, 51,* 347-356.
Hauert, C.A., & Zanone, P.G. (1984). Etude d'une tâche cognitive chez l'enfant: La poursuite visuo-manuelle. *Comportements, 1,* 123-126.
Hauert, C.A., Zanone, P.G., & Mounoud, P. (1989). Development of motor control in the child: Theoretical and experimental approaches. In: W. Prinz & O. Neuman (Eds.), *Issues on perception and action.* Berlin: Springer.

Haugeland, J. (1978). The nature and plausibility of cognitivism. *Behavioral and Brain Sciences, 2*, 215-260.

Hay, L. (1978). Accuracy of children in an open-loop pointing task. *Perceptual and Motor Skills, 47*, 1079-1082.

Hay, L. (1979). Spatial-temporal analysis of movement in children: Motor program versus feedback in the development of reaching. *Journal of Motor Behavior, 11*, 189-200.

Hay, L. (1981). The effect of amplitude and accuracy requirements on movement time in children. *Journal of Motor Behavior, 13*, 177-186.

Hay, L., Bard, C., & Fleury, M. (1986). Visuo-manual coordination from 6 to 10: Specification, control and evaluation of direction and amplitude parameters of movement. In: M.G. Wade & H.T.A. Whiting (Eds.), *Motor development in children*. Dordrecht: Nijhoff.

Hein, A., & Held, R. (1967). Dissociation of the visual placing response into elicited and guided components. *Science, 158*, 390-392.

Held, R., & Freedman, S.J. (1963). Plasticity of human sensory-motor control. *Science, 142*, 455-461.

Hofsten, C. von (1980). Predictive reaching for moving objects by human infants. *Journal of Experimental Child Psychology, 30*, 369-382.

Hofsten, C. von (1983). Catching skills in infancy. *Journal of Experimental Psychology: Human Perception & Performance, 9*, 75-85.

Hofsten, C. von, & Lindhagen, K. (1979). Observations on the development of reaching for moving objects. *Journal of Experimental Child Psychology, 28*, 158-173.

Holst, E. von (1954). Relation between the central nervous system and the peripheral organs. *British Journal of Animal Behavior, 2*, 89-94.

Holst, E. von (1973). *The behavioral physiology of animal and man*. Coral Gables: University of Miami Press.

Jeannerod, M. (1986). Mechanisms of visuomotor coordination: A study in normal and brain-damaged subjects. *Neuropsychologia, 24(1)*, 41-78.

Keele, S.W. (1968). Movement control in skilled motor performance. *Psychological Bulletin, 70*, 387-403.

Kelso, J.A.S. (1977). Motor control mechanisms underlying human movements. *Journal of Neurophysiology, 3*, 529-543.

Kelso, J.A.S. (1981). On the oscillatory basis of movement. *Bulletin of the Psychonomic Society, 18*, 63.

Kelso, J.A.S. (1984). Phase transition and critical behavior in human bimanual coordination. *American Journal of Physiology, 240*, 1000-1004.

Kelso, J.A.S., & Schoner, G. (1988). Self-organization of coordinative movement patterns. *Human Movement Science, 7*, 27-46.

Kelso, J.A.S., Scholz, J.P., & Schoner, G. (1988). Dynamics govern switching among patterns of coordination in biological movement. *Physics Letters A, 134(1)*, 8-12.

Kelso, J.A.S., Holt, K.G., Kugler, P.N., & Turvey, M.T. (1980). On the concept of coordinative structures as dissipative structures: II. Empirical lines of convergence. In: G.E. Stelmach & J. Requin (Eds.), *Tutorials in motor behavior*. Amsterdam: North Holland.

Kerr, R. (1975). Movement control and maturation in elementary

grade children. *Perceptual and Motor Skills*, 41, 151-154.
Krendel, E.S., & McRuer, D.T. (1960). A servomechanisms approach to skill development. *Journal of Franklin Institute*, 269(1), 24-42.
Kugler, P.N. (1986). A morphological perspective on the origin and evolution of movement patterns. In: M.G. Wade & H.T.A. Whiting (Eds.), *Motor development in children*. Dordrecht: Nijhoff.
Kugler, P.N., & Turvey, M.T. (1987). *Information, natural law, and the self-assembly of rhythmic movement*. Hillsdale, NJ: Erlbaum.
Kugler, P.N., Kelso, J.A.S., & Turvey, M.T. (1980). On the concept of coordinative structures as dissipative structures: I. Theoretical lines of convergence. In: G.E. Stelmach and J. Requin (Eds.), *Tutorials in motor behavior*. Amsterdam: North Holland.
Kugler, P.N., Kelso, J.A.S., & Turvey, M.T. (1982). On the control and co-ordination of naturally developing systems. In: J.A.S. Kelso & J.E. Clark (Eds.), *The development of movement control and coordination*. Chichester: Wiley.
Laszlo, J.I., & Bairstow, P.J. (1985). *Perceptuo-motor behavior. Developmental assessment and therapy*. New York: Preager.
McDonnel, P.M. (1975). The development of visually-guided reaching. *Perception & Psychophysics*, 18, 181-185.
McGraw, M.B. (1932). From reflex to muscular control in the assumption of an erect posture and ambulation in the human infant. *Child Development*, 3, 291-297.
Magdaleno, R.E., Jex, H.R., & Johnson, W.A. (1970). Tracking quasi-predictable displays. Subjective predictability gradations, pilot models for periodic and narrowband inputs. Proceedings of the 5th Annual NASA-University Conference on Manual Control, 391-428.
Mounoud, P. (1986). Action and cognition. In: M.G. Wade & H.T.A. Whiting (Eds.), *Motor development in children*. Dordrecht: Nijhoff.
Mounoud, P., & Vinter, A. (1981). Representation and sensory-motor development. In: G. Butterworth (Ed.), *Infancy and epistemology*. Brighton: Harvester Press.
Mounoud, P., & Hauert, C.A. (1982). Development of sensori-motor organization in young children. In: G.E. Forman (Ed.), *Action and thought: From sensori-motor schemes to symbolic operations*. New-York: Academic Press.
Mounoud, P., Viviani, P., Hauert, C.A., & Guyon, J. (1985). Development of visuo-manual tracking in the 5 to 9 years-old boys. *Journal of Experimental Child Psychology*, 40, 115-132.
Mounoud, P., Hauert, C.A., Mayer, E., Gachoud, J.P., Guyon, J., & Gottret, G. (1983). Visuo-manual tracking strategies in the three- to five-year-old child. *Archives de Psychologie*, 51, 23-33.
Newell, K.M., & Kennedy, J.A. (1978). Knowledge of results and children's motor learning. *Developmental Psychology*, 14, 531-536.
Noble, M., Fitts, P.M., & Warren, C.E. (1955). The frequency of response of skilled subjects in a pursuit tracking task. *Journal of Experimental Psychology*, 49, 249-256.
Paillard, J. (1986). Cognitive versus sensorimotor encoding of spatial information. In: P. Ellen & C. Thinus-Blanc (Eds.), *Cognitive processes and spatial orientation in animal and man. (vol. 2)*. Dordrecht: Nijhoff.
Paillard, J., & Brouchon, M. (1974). A proprioceptive contribution to the spatial encoding of position cues for ballistic movements. *Brain Research*, 71, 273-284.

Paris, S.G. (1978). Memory organization during children's repeated recall. *Developmental Psychology, 14*, 99-108.

Pascual-Leone, J., & Smith, J. (1969). The encoding and decoding of symbols by children: A new paradigm and neo-Piagetian model. *Journal of Experimental Child Psychology, 8*, 328-353.

Pélisson, D., Prablanc, C., Goodale, M.A., & Jeannerod, M. (1986). Visual control of reaching movements without vision of the limb, II. *Experimental Brain Research, 62*, 303-311.

Pew, R.W., & Rupp, G.L. (1971). Two quantitative measures of skill development. *Journal of Experimental Psychology, 90(1)*, 1-7.

Piaget, J. (1952). *The origin of intelligence in children*. New York: Norton.

Piaget, J. (1954). *The construction of reality in the child*. New York: Basic Books.

Pitts, W.H., & McCullock, W.S. (1947). How we know universals, the perception of auditory and visual forms. *Bulletin of Mathematical Biophysics, 9*, 127-149.

Polit, A., & Bizzi, E. (1978). Processes controlling arm movement in monkeys. *Science, 201*, 1235-1237.

Poulton, E.C. (1952). The basis of perceptual anticipation in tracking. *British Journal of Psychology, 43*, 295-302.

Poulton, E.C. (1981). Human manual control. In: V.B. Brooks (Ed.), *Handbook of physiology*. Bethesda: American Physiological Society.

Prablanc, C., Pélisson, D., & Goodale, M.A. (1986). Visual control of reaching movements without vision of the limb, I. *Experimental Brain Research, 62*, 293-302.

Pylyshyn, Z.W. (1981). The imagery debate: Analogue media versus tacit knowledge. *Psychological Review, 88*, 16-45.

Roberton, M.A. (1978). Longitudinal evidence for developmental stages in forceful overarm throw. *Journal of Human Movement Studies, 4*, 167-175.

Roberton, M.A. (1982). Describing 'stages' within and across motor tasks. In: J.A.S. Kelso & J.E. Clark (Eds.), *The development of movement control and coordination*. Chichester: Wiley.

Roberton, M.A., & Langendorfer, S. (1980). Testing motor developmental sequences across 9-14 years. In: C.H. Nadeau, W.R. Halliwell, K.M. Newell & G.C. Roberts (Eds.), *Psychology and Sport - 1979*. Champaign: Human Kinetics.

Salmoni, A.W. (1983). A descriptive analysis of children performing Fitts' reciprocal tapping task. *Journal of Human Movement Studies, 9(2)*, 81-95.

Schmidt, R.A. (1975). A schema theory of discrete motor skill learning. *Psychological Review, 82*, 225-260.

Schmidt, R.A. (1976). The schema as a solution of some persistent problems in motor learning theory. In: G.E. Stelmach (Ed.), *Motor control: Issues and trends*. New-York: Academic Press.

Schmidt, R.A. (1982). *Motor control and learning*. Champaign: Human Kinetics.

Schneider, G.E. (1969). Two visual systems: Brain mechanisms for localization and discrimination area dissociated by tectal and cortical lesions. *Science, 163*, 895-902.

Schoner, G., & Kelso, J.A.S. (1988a). Dynamic pattern generation in behavioral and neural sytems. *Science, 239*, 1513-1520.

Schoner, G., & Kelso, J.A.S. (1988b). Dynamic patterns of biological coordination: Theoretical strategy and new results. In: J.A.S. Kelso, A.J. Mandel & M.F. Schlesinger (Eds.), *Dynamic*

patterns in complex systems. Singapore: World Scientific.
Schoner, G., Haken, H., & Kelso, J.A.S. (1986). A stochastic theory
of phase transitions in human hand movement. *Biological
Cybernetics, 53*, 247-257.
Shapiro, D.C., & Schmidt, R.A. (1982). The schema theory: Recent
evidence and developmental implications. In: J.A.S. Kelso & J.E.
Clark (Eds.), *The development of movement control and
coordination*. Chichester: Wiley.
Shirley, M.M. (1931). *The first two years. A study of twenty-five
babies*. Minneapolis: Minnesota University Press.
Soechting, J.F., & Terzuolo, C. (1986). An algorithm for the
generation of curvilinear wrist motion in an arbitrary plane in
three-dimensional space. *Neuroscience, 19(4)*, 1393-1406.
Southard, D. (1985). Interlimb movement control and coordination in
children. In: J.E. Clark & J.H. Humphrey (Eds.), *Motor
development*. Princeton: Princeton Book.
Sperry, R.W. (1950). Neural basis of the optokinetic response
produced by visual inversion. *Journal of Comparative and
Physiological Psychology, 43*, 482-489.
Stelmach, G.E. (1982). Information processing framework for
understanding human motor behavior. In: J.A.S. Kelso (Ed.),
Human motor behavior: An introduction. Hillsdale, NJ: Erlbaum.
Strauss, S. (1984). *U-shaped behavior and growth*. New York:
Academic Press.
Sugden, D.A. (1980). Movement speed in children. *Journal of Motor
Behavior, 12(2)*, 125-132.
Thelen, E. (1986). Development of coordinated movement:
Implication for early human development. In: M.G. Wade & H.T.A.
Whiting (Eds.), *Motor development in children*. Dordrecht:
Nijhoff.
Thelen, E., & Fisher, D.M. (1983). The organization of spontaneous
leg movements in newborn infants. *Journal of Motor Behavior,
15(4)*, 353-377.
Thelen, E., & Fisher, D.M., & Ridley-Johnson, R. (1984). The
relation between physical growth and a reflex. *Infant Behavior &
Development, 7*, 479-493.
Thelen, E., Ulrich, B.D., & Niles, D. (1987). Bilateral
coordination in human infant: Stepping on a split-belt
treadmill. *Journal of Experimental Psychology: Human Perception
& Performance, 13*, 405-410.
Thomas, J.R., Gallagher, J.D., & Purvis, G.J. (1981). Reaction time
and anticipation time: Effect of development. *Research
Quarterly, 52*, 359-367.
Todor, J.I. (1978). A neo-Piagetian theory of constructive
operators: Applications to perceptual-motor development and
learning. In: D.M. Landers & R.W. Christina (Eds.), *Psychology
and Sport - 1977*. Champaign: Human Kinetics.
Trevarthen, C. (1968). Two mechanisms of vision in primates.
Psychologische Forschung, 31, 299-337.
Trevarthen, C. (1984). How control of movements develops. In:
H.T.A. Whiting (Ed.), *Human motor action - Bernstein reassessed*.
Amsterdam: North Holland.
Tuller, B., & Kelso, J.A.S. (in press). Environmentally-specified
patterns of movement coordination in normal and split-brain
subjects. *Experimental Brain Research*.
Turvey, M.T. (1977). Preliminaries to a theory of action with
reference to vision. In: R. Shaw & J. Bransford (Eds.),

Perceiving, acting and knowing: Towards an ecological psychology;. Hillsdale, NJ: Erlbaum.

Viviani, P., & Zanone P.G. (1988). Spontaneous covariations of movement parameters in children. *Journal of Motor Behavior, 20(1)*, 5-16.

Wallace, S.A., Newell, K.M., & Wade, M.G. (1978). Decision time and movement time as a function of movement difficulty in preschool children. *Child Development, 49*, 509-512.

Welford, A.T., Norris, A.H., & Shock, N.W. (1963). Speed and accuracy of movement and their changes with age. *Acta Psychologica, 30*, 3-15.

White, B.L., Castle, P., & Held, R. (1964). Observations on the development of visually-directed reaching. *Child Development, 35*, 349-364.

Whiting, H.T.A. (Ed.) (1984). *Human motor action - Bernstein reassessed*. Amsterdam: North Holland.

Wickens, C.D. (1974). Temporal limits of human information processing: A developmental study. *Psychological Bulletin, 81*, 739-755.

Wickstrom, R.L. (1983). *Fundamental motor patterns*. Philadelphia: Lea & Febiger.

Williams, K. (1985). Age differences on a coincidence-anticipation task: Influence of stereotypic or "preferred" movement speed. *Journal of Motor Behavior, 17(4)*, 389-410.

Wing, A.M., Turton, A., & Fraser, C. (1986). Grasp size and accuracy of approach in reaching. *Journal of Motor Behavior, 18(3)*, 245-260.

Winther, K.T., & Thomas, J.R. (1981). Developmental differences in children's labeling of movement. *Journal of Motor Behavior, 13(2)*, 77-90.

Zanone, P.G. (1989). Tracking with and without target in 6- to 15-year-old boys. Manuscript submitted for publication.

Zanone, P.G., & Hauert, C.A. (1987). For a cognitive conception of motor processes: A provocative standpoint. *European Bulletin of Cognitive Psychology, 7(2)*, 109-129.

Zelaznick, H.N., Hawkins, B., & Kisselburgh, L. (1987). The effects of movement distance and movement time on visual processing in aimed hand movements. *Acta Psychologica, 65*, 181-191.

Zelazo, P.R., Zelazo, N.A., & Kolb, S. (1972). "Walking" in the newborn. *Science, 177*, 1058-1059.

DEVELOPMENTAL PSYCHOLOGY
Cognitive, Perceptuo-Motor, and Neuropsychological Perspectives
C-A. Hauert (Editor)
© Elsevier Science Publishers B.V. (North-Holland), 1990

NEUROPSYCHOLOGICAL DEVELOPMENT IN THE CHILD
AND THE ADOLESCENT:
FUNCTIONAL MATURATION OF THE CENTRAL NERVOUS SYSTEM

Daniel S. O'LEARY

Psychology Department
University of Health Sciences/
The Chicago Medical School
Chicago, U.S.A.

*Anatomical measures of fiber tract myelination and corti-
cal thickness indicate that brain maturation is hierarchical both within and across functional systems. Electro-
encephalographic (EEG) measures support this view and
indicate that functional maturation is most rapid in the
first six years of life with slower development thereafter. Recent EEG data indicates that there are spurts in
development that occur at different ages in the two hemispheres, the left shows a spurt at age four to six years
and the right hemisphere at ages four to six, and again at
eight to ten years. Maturation is bilateral and primarily
frontal from age 11 to maturity. There is at present no
good evidence that major changes in brain development are
associated with the achievement of new cognitive abilities
in the child. While the hypothesis of correlated brain
and cognitive development is attractive, both brain maturation and cognitive development are highly complex and
both present difficult measurement problems.*

1. INTRODUCTION

It is clear that the dramatic changes in cognitive function occuring
during childhood must be related to development of the nervous system. Detailed study of the relationship between bahavioral and
brain development is, however, complicated by a number of factors.

One such factor is that until recently developmental changes in the
anatomy of the brain could be measured only through post-mortem
examination. Such examinations have demonstrated that the nervous
system undergoes characteristic maturational changes during normal
development. There are, for example, changes in cortical thickness
(Conel, 1939-1963), in synaptic density (Huttenlocher, 1979) and in
myelination of fiber pathways (Yakovlev and Lecours, 1967). As is
discussed below these neural changes occur in a consistent sequence
in differing parts of the brain and are presumably related to the
cognitive behaviors which change during childhood.

Correlations between such indices of brain maturation and behavioral
change may give little detailed information, however, because both
neural and behavioral measures are often too global. Riesen (1971)
noted that many relatively independent changes may be occuring during the same time period in the developing child. Any two variables which change within the same time span will necessarily be
correlated with one another whether or not their relationship is
causal. To be meaningful, developmental correlations must be established between changes in specific brain structure and clearly
defined cognitive abilities (Fischer, 1987).

There are also difficulties involved in developmental studies that
utilize the classical approach of studying the effects of brain
damage on cognitive behavior. While such studies have provided
important data concerning the neural substrate of cognitive functions in adults, there are complications involved in utilizing these
techniques with children (see discussion below).

These considerations greatly complicate basic methodological tasks
such as achieving a reasonable sample size of subjects with similar
neural impairment, establishing control groups to deal with factors
that may co-vary with the factors of interest, and selection of
valid and reliable tests. Such methodological issues are of critical importance for the establishment of a valid data base concerning
the relationship between cognitive development and the brain. The
methodological issues are complex and important but are beyond the
scope of the present chapter. For discussion of methodological
concerns specific to developmental neuropsychology see Parsons and
Prigatano (1978), Spreen, Tupper, Risser, Tuokko and Edgell (1984),
and Witelson (1987).

While study of the relationship between neuropsychological development and brain maturation involves a number of complex issues, there
is reason for optimism concerning the possibility of finding meaningful relationships. Great progress has been made in recent years
in both the neurosciences and in developmental psychology and neuropsychology. There is increasing awareness of the benefits of interaction between researchers in different disciplines. A recent special section of the journal Child Development (1987, 58(3)), devoted
to a dialogue between developmental psychologists and neuroscien-
tists is a reflection of the new spirit of interdisciplinary integration.

The remainder of this chapter will discuss data and concepts relevant to maturation of the brain and neuropsychological development
in children from two years of age to adolescence. Data concerning
nervous system maturation will be reviewed and the major cognitive
achievements occuring in this age span will be discussed. Information concerning the effects of brain damage upon cognitive function will then be noted.

As will become obvious, available data do not yet permit firm conclusions concerning the relationship between brain maturation and
neuropsychological development. It is also not yet possible to draw
conclusions from this data concerning major developmental themes
such as the nature of representation at differing ages and the stage
notion of development. Data concerning brain maturation can, how-

ever, offer a perspective on cognitive development that is different
from that available from the study of behavior alone. The major
developmental issues which are the theme of the present volume will
be briefly discussed from this perspective.

2. BRAIN MATURATION

2.1. Anatomical data

Brain maturation occurs in an organized pattern which may be studied
by both anatomical and physiological measures. A gross anatomical
measure of maturation can be obtained by comparison of overall brain
size and weight at differing ages with the average adult value. For
example, at age two years the brain weighs an average of 1064 grams,
or 76% of the average adult weight of 1400 grams (Dekaban, 1970).
This compares to an average weight at birth of 350 grams or 25% of
the adult weight. More precise anatomical measures include the
extent of myelination of fiber pathways, measures of cortical thickness, and measures of synaptic density. All but the last measure
(i.e., synaptic density) may now be obtained from magnetic resonance
imaging (MRI) in living subjects.

Physiological maturation may be studied through measurement of the
electrical activity of the brain which can be recorded at the skull
surface (Woodruff, 1978; Thatcher, Walker and Guidice, 1987). Spontaneous electrical activity may be recorded as well as activity
time-locked to the presentation of sensory stimuli. Direct assessment of the metabolic activity of the brain is also possible through
regional cerebral blood flow (rCBF) and positron emission tomography
(PET) measures (Chuagini and Phelps, 1986).

The most frequently cited data concerning brain maturation is the
Yakovlev and Lecours (1967) study of the myelination of fiber systems in the human brain. Yakovlev and Lecours examined a large number of fetal, child, and adult brains obtained post-mortem. They
unfortunately had relatively few brain specimens in the childhood
years that are the topic of the present chapter. Other autopsy studies of myelination (Dobbing and Sands, 1973; Davison and Peters,
1970) had a similar paucity of pediatric brains.

Yakovlev and Lecours used a preparation that stained fiber pathways
from light gray to blue-black depending upon their degree of myelination. The beginning of myelination was defined by the first appearance of light gray stain in fibers in the fetal brain. Maturation of a fiber system was arbitrarily defined as achievement of the
intensity of staining seen in the brain of a 28 year old male.

Yakovlev and Lecours emphasized the importance of the *cycle* of myelination defined not only in terms of the beginning of myelination
but also by how rapidly it occurs. They assumed that completion of
myelination indicated functional maturation of a fiber system and
that the myelogenetic cycle of the system defined its position in a
hierarchy of functional organization of the developing system.

A great deal of maturation has already occured in the central nervous system (CNS) by age two years. Yakovlev and Lecours' data

indicate that all of the spinal and cranial nerve roots, primary
motor and sensory systems (except for the acoustic radiations) and
most limbic structures have completed their myelogenetic cycles by
age two.

Fiber systems which continue to myelinate past age two but which
complete their cycle by age four include parts of the striatum, the
acoustic radiation, the middle cerebellar peduncle and the fornix.
The corpus callosum and the non-specific thalamic radiation continue
to myelinate until age seven years or later.

An MRI study of brain maturation in 59 normal children (Holland,
Haas, Norman, Brant-Zawadski and Newton, 1986) largely corroborated
the autopsy data of Yakovlev and Lecours. Myelination was found to
be most rapid in the first two years of life with subtle changes
through the first decade. The adult appearance of the brain was
reached by puberty. However, in contrast to the autopsy studies,
Holland at al. (1986) found that the corpus callosum had an adult-
like appearance by one year of age (see also Barkovich and Bent,
1988). They speculate that the increasing myelination seen histo-
logically by Yakovlev and Lecours was beyond the resolution of the
MRI.

Yakovlev and Lecours found that two fibers systems continue to myelinate into at least the second decade of life, and are thus at the
highest level of their functional hierarchy of development. These
are the intracortical fibers of frontal, parietal and temporal association areas and fibers of the reticular formation. In Luria's
(1973) influential neuropsychological model these fiber systems take
part in different components of the three functional units of the
brain which work in concert during complex behavior.

Reticular fibers in Luria's model are part of an arousal and attention unit which also includes other brainstem structures as well as
parts of the limbic system and hippocampus. The intracortical fibers of the frontal, parietal and temporal association areas take
part in the other two units. Temporal and parietal cortical areas,
along with occipital cortex and thalamic projections are involved in
information reception, analysis and storage. The frontal lobes are
part of a unit involved in the programming, regulation and verification of activity. The myelination data suggest that all three functional systems continue to develop into adulthood.

Changes in cortical thickness give information concerning maturation
in addition to that available from myelination studies. Rabinowicz
(1979) found that most cortical areas show alternative periods of
thickening and thinning. A major decrease in thickness 15 months
after birth was followed by an increase at age 2 years. The primary
and secondary visual areas were unique in that they achieved a stable thickness by 6 and 15 months respectively. Huttenlocher, de
Corten, Garey and van der Loos (1982) also found that human visual
cortex achieved adult volume at a much earlier age (4 months) than
did other cortical areas. Rabinowicz found that other cortical a-
reas showed changes in thickness over a longer age range.

Conel (1939-1963) measured cortical thickness at different sites
across a number of ages. Greenough, Black and Wallace (1987) re-

plotted Conel's data and note that there are differences in the pattern of growth across brain regions. While most areas of cortex
sampled showed a peak in thickness between 10 and 20 months of age
and again at 50 months, prefrontal cortex showed steadily increasing
thickness throughout the first six years of life.

Since neural cell division ceases after birth, changes in cortical
thickness reflect factors such as growth of cell bodies and dendritic processes, the addition or deletion of synapses, increases in
glial cells and blood vessels, and/or selective neural death. It is
not yet clear which of these factors are operative at specific ages.

Rakic, Bourgeois, Eckenhoff, Zecevic and Goldman-Rakic (1986) found
that there is a stricking increase in synaptic density in primate
cortex in the first four post-natal months. Surprisingly, the increase occured synchronously over all cortical areas. Each area
passed through a period of synapse "overproduction" at roughly the
same age, with densities well above adult values. The changes in
density occured concurrently in all six layers of cortex. The period of overproduction was followed by a longer period during which
densities declined to adult levels. Goldman-Rakic (1987) notes that
it is not yet known whether the phase of synaptic elimination occurs
at the same pace in all areas of primate cortex.

Huttenlocher (1979) and Huttenlocher et al. (1982) presented data
indicating that the human cortex undergoes a similar early period of
synaptic overproduction followed by a longer period of selective
elimination. Huttenlocher (1979) found that the density of synapses
in frontal cortex was 50% above that of the adult value at 2 years
of age. This gradually declined to a density 36% above the adult
mean by age 7 years. Data presented by Huttenlocher et al. (1982)
indicated that occipital cortex matures at a more rapid pace than
does frontal cortex.

Huttenlocher proposes that cortical maturation has two phases in
humans. The first phase lasts from birth to one year and involves
dendritic growth, with large increases in both the number of synapses per neuron and in synaptic density. Because overall cortical
volume increases greatly in this phase the density of neurons per
unit volume decreases. The second phase lasts from one year through
adolescence and involves a slower continuation of dendritic growth,
with a decrease in the density of synapses per dendrite. Selective
cell death also occurs during this phase and may explain the maturational decrease in neural "plasticity" following brain damage.

Goldman-Rakic (1987) suggests that there may be a level of synaptic
density that is optimal for information processing since at maturity
the same densities are found throughout all regions of the cortex as
well as in subcortical area (e.g., caudate nucleus).

Greenough et al. (1987) similarly note that while environmental enrichment increases the number of synapses per neuron by as much as
20% in rats, there is no change in the density of synapses per unit
volume. The cortex as a whole simply increases to maintain a constant density.

Greenough et al. (ibid) review data concerning the effects of expe-

rience upon cortical morphology in animals. Considerable data now
indicate that animals raised in an "enriched" environment, with
opportunities for exploration and social interaction, have heavier
and thicker cortices than animals raised in more "deprived" environments. The additional thickness results from an increase of 20-25%
in the number of synapses per neuron as well as from increased cell
body size and increased number of glia.

Greenough et al. (ibid) suggest that two different neural mechanisms
may underlie changes in the brain resulting from experience.
Experience-expectant processes underlie species-typical behaviors.
These are mediated by a genetically-programmed overproduction of
synapses early in development. The experience-expectant process
relies on the probability that all members of the species will have
environmental experiences similar to those ubiquitous throughout the
evolutionary history of the species. These experiences will result
in activity in certain pathways and a lack of activity in others.
The activity, in turn, determines which synapses survive. Greenough
et al. speculate that experience-expectant processes occur early in
development and mediate "critical" or "sensitive" period phenomenon.

A second type of behavioral plasticity relies on *experience-
dependent* processes. This is involved in the storage of information
that is unique to the individual and requires the formation of new
synapses. Experience-dependent processes occur later in development
as the organism encounters unique experiences. Experience-expectant
and dependent processes are not completely independent. Experience-
dependent processes may also involve an initial over-production of
synapses, with learning resulting in a pruning of non-functional
connections.

The anatomical data suggest that brain maturation occurs in a hierarchical fashion both within and across functional systems. Functional systems in the brain are organized vertically, with spinal,
brainstem, diencephalic (thalamus and hypothalamus), and subcortical telenchephalic components interacting with cortical mechanisms.

Within functional systems, maturation occurs largely in a caudal to
rostral pattern, with spinal and brainstem components maturing before higher mechanisms. This pattern is supported by both myelination studies and by studies that have found that adult values of
synaptic density are reached in subcortical structures such as the
caudate nucleus (Brand and Rakic, 1984) and superior colliculus
(Cooper and Rakic, 1983), well before these levels are reached in
the cortex.

Maturation also appears to be hierarchical across functional systems. The traditional view was articulated by Yakovlev and Lecours.
Their concept of myelogenetic cycles held that primary sensory and
motor systems mature prior to higher-level systems which utilize
association cortex. This view must be reconsidered in light of
Rakic et al.'s (1986) finding that an early period of synaptic overproduction takes place simultaneously in all areas of cortex.

The traditional hierarchical view may still be defended if maturation is defined as achievement of adult levels of synaptic density

and fiber tract myelination. The early period of synaptic overproduction appears to be followed by a slower phase of decreasing
synaptic density and myelination. While there is relatively little
data as yet, this later phase appears to differ in time course
across regions (Huttenlocher, 1979; Huttenlocher et al., 1982). The
slower phase of cortical maturation may be reflected in electro-
encephalographic (EEG) changes that occur during normal development.

2.2. EEG maturation

EEG recorded from the scalp primarily reflects activity in apical
dendrites in the superficial cortical layers (Nunez, 1981).
Rhythmic EEG activity is thought to represent the synchronous activity of large numbers of cortical units, with the synchrony perhaps
driven by thalamic pacemakers. The predominant rhythm in adults is
alpha, an 8 to 13 cycles per second (cps) waveform with an amplitude
of about 50 microvolts which is most prominent over occipital lobes.
While there is individual variability in the frequency of alpha,
activity slower than 8 cps is rarely seen in awake adults. EEG in
adults frequently shows 13-30 cps beta activity which is lower in
amplitude (2-20 microvolts), and which has a more anterior distribution than does alpha.

Alpha frequency changes in a characteristic fashion across the
lifespan, and may be an index of brain maturation and functional
integration (Nunez, 1981). There is little synchronous EEG activity
at birth. Alpha first emerges at approximately three months of age
at a frequency of 3-4 Hz. While this is well below the 8-13 Hz frequency range found in adults, there is general agreement that similar neural generators underlie the posterior rhythm in infants and
in adults (Woodruff, 1978).

The emergence of alpha at three post-natal months corresponds to a
period of cellular maturation in occipital cortex at this age
(Conel, 1939-1963; Huttenlocher et al., 1982). Following the onset
of the posterior alpha rhythm at three months there is a rapid increase in frequency to 6-7 Hz by the end of the first year. There
is then a slower increase in frequency until the adult average of
between 10 and 11 Hz is reached by age 12.

The years between age two and puberty are characterized by a decrease in the amount of slow wave activity that appears in the waking
record as well as the increase in frequency of the posterior alpha
rhythm (Niedermeyer, 1982). Between 3 and 5 years the posterior
rhythm is about 8 cps but is higher in amplitude than in the adult.
Very little beta is seen anteriorly until approximately 6 years.
There is then a slow increase in the amount of beta until 12 years
of age. Rhythmic activity in the alpha range increases in anterior
leads throughout these years also.

Thatcher et al. (1987) have recently reported data from a large
cross-sectional EEG study of 577 normal children ranging in age from
two months to early adulthood. Mean EEG coherence and phase measures were computed between all pairwise combinations of 16 electro-
des. Coherence and phase are indices of cortical connectivity
rather than measures of frequency or amplitude. Coherence and phase
give estimates of the extent to which different cortical generators

show correlated activity.

Thatcher et al. found that development was relatively continuous, with rapid growth in the first six years and slower growth thereafter. There was, however, evidence of growth spurts, or sudden increases in the progression of the phase and coherence measures toward adult values. The growth spurts occured at different ages in the left and right hemispheres.

The left and right hemispheres both showed a slow developmental course from birth to about age three with phase and coherence relatively disorganized. The left hemisphere showed a marked increase in coupling in frontal-occipital and frontal-temporal regions from age four to six while the right hemisphere showed a localized frontal pole increase in this age range. The right hemisphere showed a spurt in frontal-temporal coupling between eight and ten years. Growth in the ages from 11 to 15 and from 15 to adulthood was bilateral and predominantly involved the frontal lobes.

Thatcher et al.'s data support the concept that brain maturation is hierarchical across functional systems. Thatcher et al. conclude that "relatively specific anatomic connections within the left and right human cerebral hemispheres develop at different rates and at different post-natal onset times." (1987, p.1113). They also argue that their data support an ontogenetic hypothesis of cortical development in which specific connections mature at genetically programmed ages.

2.3. Conclusions

The human brain undergoes a very prolonged period of post-natal maturation. The anatomical and electrophysiological data reviewed above indicate that the maturation takes place in a characteristic and predetermined pattern. A great deal of maturation has already occured by two years of age. The brain has achieved approximately 75% of its adult volume by this age and myelination is well developed in all fiber systems. The data reported by Rakic et al. (1986) and by Huttenlocher (1979) and Huttenlocher et al. (1982) indicate that all cortical areas have already passed through a period of synaptic overproduction and that some areas (i.e. occipital cortex) have achieved adult characteristics.

Maturation past the age of two appears to involve changes in cellular attributes which result in decreasing synaptic density in cortical areas and increasing myelination in fiber pathways. The decrease in synaptic density per unit volume of cortex may result from several mechanisms. The growth of dendrites may space synapses farther apart in the same cell, non-functional synapses may be eliminated as many neurons (Huttenlocher et al., 1982), and glial cells may push synapses farther apart (Greenough et al., 1987). Cortical thickness may increase or decrease at differing ages as a result of these processes (Conel, 1939-1963; Rabinowicz, 1979). These cellular maturational process may underlie the EEG changes that are seen in childhood.

3. DEVELOPMENT OF BRAIN AND BEHAVIOR

A number of investigators have suggested that major changes in brain development are associated with the achievement of new cognitive stages in the child (Fischer, 1987; Epstein, 1978; White, 1970). Epstein (1978) coined the term "phrenoblysis" to refer to correlated growth spurts in brain and mind. He presented data supporting the concept that spurts in brain growth occur at ages in which major cognitive changes occur corresponding to developmental stages of the Piagetian model.

Epstein's suggestion has important implications and has been widely discussed. However, the methodology upon which he formulated his concept is flawed (Marsh, 1985), and a longitudinal study which directly tested the concept found no evidence to support it (McCall, Meyers, Hartman and Roche, 1983). Epstein based his argument concerning brain growth spurts upon measurements of head circumference, which appear to correlate fairly well with brain size (Epstein and Epstein, 1978). However, Marsh (1985) re-analyzed the data cited in Epstein (1978) using several different procedures and found no evidence for Epstein's hypothesis that brain circumference shows growth spurts in the ages suggested by Epstein.

McCall et al. (1983) analyzed longitudinal data on head circumference and intelligence (Binet IQ test) gathered yearly on 80 normal subjects from 2 to 17 years of age. No relationship was found between changes in head circumference and mental age growth-rate patterns. Additionally, half of the subjects showed no spurts in head circumference, and for the other subjects spurts were observed outside of the predicted age periods.

It is not surprising that developmental changes in head circumference, a measure which correlates only with gross brain size, shows little correlation with psychometrically defined mental abilities. The maturational changes occuring in the brain between two years of age and puberty are regional and seem unlikely to cause changes in overall brain volume that would be reflected in growth spurts in head circumference. Additionally, it is unclear what impact the maturation of specific brain regions would have on measures of general cognitive function.

With few exceptions, the relationship between brain regions and specific human abilities is not well established. Primary sensory and motor functions are mediated by localized systems whose integrity may be assessed by neuropsychological tests in both children and adults (Spreen et al., 1984). However, the more complex abilities which show the greatest increases between the ages of two and puberty are much more difficult to localize to specific brain regions.

There have been a number of attempts to measure developmental change in behaviors which rely upon brain systems which mature relatively late. The corpus callosum and the frontal lobes have been the primary systems investigated. Yakovlev and Lecours' data indicate that the corpus callosum does not complete its myelogenetic cycle until age six or later, while intracortical fibers connecting frontal lobes to other cortical region show evidence of increasing myelination into the second decade of life.

Damage to the corpus callosum in adults produces characteristic
disconnection phenomenon (e.g. Gazzaniga, Bogen and Sperry, 1962)
and crossed sensory and motor systems allow relatively straightforward behavioral assessment of callosal function. While damage to
the frontal lobes produces less definitive behavioral effects in
adults, there are tasks that show specific reliance upon prefrontal
cortex in primates (Goldman-Rakic, 1987), and there have been
demonstrations of developmental changes in highly similar behaviors
in human infants (Diamond, 1985; Diamond and Goldman-Rakic, 1983).

A number of behavioral studies have now shown that there is a developmental increase in children's ability to transfer information
from one side of the body to the other (Galin, Diamond, Nakel and
Herron, 1979; O'Leary, 1980; Quinn and Geffen, 1986). The increase
in interhemispheric transfer has been shown to occur over a wide age
range in various studies (from three to nine years) and presumably
reflects maturation of the corpus callosum.

The paradigms utilized allow each child to serve as his or her own
control for factors which also change in the studied age range (e.g.,
attention or memory), and thus provide a relatively clean measure of
interhemispheric transfer. But the efficiency of interhemispheric
transfer at specific ages has been shown to depend upon task complexity and to interact with other cognitive parameters of the task
(Hauert and Koenig, 1987). It seems likely that tasks assessing the
development of the corpus callosum also relies on other brain areas
which may mature at different rates (Hatta, 1987).

There is controversy concerning the age at which the frontal lobes
achieve functional maturation in normal children. Diamond (1985),
and Diamond and Goldman-Rakic (1983) have shown that performance on
a task which relies on prefrontal cortex in primates (delayed alteration) is mature by age 12 months in human infants. Luria (1980)
on the other hand believed that prefrontal cortex was not mature
until ages 4 to 7, and Golden (1981) asserts that the prefrontal
cortex does not begin to mature until adolescence. Frontal lobe
damage in adults frequently results in perseveration and desinhi-
bition (Luria, 1980). There is evidence that children show perseverative errors and have difficulty with response inhibition until at
least age 12 (Passler, Isaac and Hynd, 1985; Becker, Isaac and Hynd,
1987) which has suggested to some researchers that the frontal
lobes do not mature until this age.

A major problem with the assessment of frontal lobe function in both
children and adults is that tasks which show deficits following
frontal lobe damage are typically complex and require the integration of activity from a number of brain regions. Damage to any one
of the areas required for task performance will cause deficits similar to that caused by frontal damage. Similarly, tasks designed to
measure frontal lobe maturation in children require complex skills
and integration of activity in many neural systems. Tasks purpor-
ting to measure frontal lobe maturation may in fact be measuring the
development of the brain as integrated system.

4. THEORIES OF NEUROPSYCHOLOGICAL DEVELOPMENT

Two major theoretical formulations of the development of cerebral organization have been discussed (Spreen et al., 1984). Both assume that cognitive abilities developing during the childhood years rely upon multiple brain systems.

MacLean (1970) proposed the concept that the human brain is *triune*, composed of three hierarchically interrelated levels. The earliest level to mature developmentally is the phylogenetically old proto-reptilian brain, consisting anatomically of the upper spinal cord, midbrain, diencephalon and parts of the basal ganglia. This level of the brain is proposed to mediate "instinctive" actions. The next level to mature is the paleomammalian brain, which consists largely of the limbic system. The paleomammalian brain mediates emotions and self-awareness. The highest level, which has the capacity to modulate the activity of the two lower levels, is the neomammalian brain. This level has evolved most recently in phylogenetic terms and is the last level to develop ontogenetically.

Van der Vlugt (1979) discusses the implications of the triune brain concept for developmental neuropsychology. He notes that a basic error in neuropsychology has been to assume that cognition is exclusively neocortical, overlooking the importance of subcortical mechanisms. MacLean's concept is that each successive level interacts with the lower levels, refining their abilities and allowing more differentiated behavior. Van der Vlugt notes that this concept is in line with stage theories of cognitive development. As each brain level matures there is reintegration of the processes of the preceding stage into a more complex and hierarchically integrated form of adaptation.

Luria's (1973, 1980) model of brain organization emphasizes the interaction between three functional brain systems. An arousal unit consisting of the reticular formation and related structures modulates input and controls cortical activation. A sensory input unit is composed of the posterior parts of the cerebral hemispheres. An output/planning unit consists primarily of the frontal lobes and is responsible for planning and carrying out actions.

Each of the functional systems is hierarchically-organized. The sensory input unit, for example, consists of primary, secondary, and tertiary cortex. The development of higher levels of the hierarchy in each system depends upon the functional integrity of the lower levels. Development proceeds from the modality-specific primary cortical areas to the supra-modal tertiary areas which mediate behavior in adults. Psychological abilities which depend upon tertiary zones do not develop until late childhood.

MacLean's model of neuropsychological development was based upon comparative anatomy, neurochemistry, and evolutionary theory. Luria's model was an extension of his general theory of brain function which was based upon the effects of brain damage in adults. Testing of the models is potentially possible through study of the effects of brain damage upon cognitive function in children of different ages. As will be noted, however, such studies are complicated by a number of factors.

5. BRAIN DAMAGE IN CHILDREN

Much of what is known about the relationship between specific brain
regions and behavior has resulted from study of the effects of localized lesions in adults. It is, however, difficult to draw firm
conclusions concerning brain-behavior relationships from study of
the effects of brain damage in children. Fletcher and Taylor (1984)
provide a detailed discussion of the problems involved in attempts
to generalize from adult to developmental neuropsychology.

The types of brain injury suffered by children differ from that
typical in adults, with children more frequently experiencing generalized damage (Kinsbourne, 1974). In adults, cerebral vascular
accident, intracerebral tumor, and traumatic head injury often causes localized damage to a neural structure. Brain-damage in children more frequently involves congenital disorders, anoxia, infec-
tion, and toxins (e.g., lead intoxication) that cause diffuse brain
impairment (Spreen et al., 1984; Barkley, 1983). It is, therefore,
much more difficult to establish links between specific structures
and cognitive function in children than in adults.

Brain-damage in children perturbs a developing system rather than
damaging brain tissue that has already assumed its mature function.
The cognitive deficits that are seen therefore depend upon a number
of factors. These include the age of the child at the time of injury, the nature, size, and location of the injury, and the type and
complexity of the cognitive ability that is measured (Boll and
Barth, 1981; Chelune and Edwards, 1981).

The cognitive sequelae of brain injury which occurs at differing
ages remains one of the most controversial topics in child neuropsychology. The "Kennard principle" states that recovery from brain
damage is more complete when it occurs early in development
(Schneider, 1979). This principle was based upon research in which
motor cortex was lesioned in infant and adult monkeys.

The concept that the young brain is more plastic than the adult
brain resulted in part from Kennard's (1936) description of relatively minor post-operative deficiencies in the infant monkeys. Her
observation of increased spasticity and motor incoordination as the
young monkeys matured has been relatively ignored (Fletcher, Levin
and Landry, 1984). The importance of the post-operative interval
before follow-up testing is emphasized by Goldman's (1974) finding
that the deficits caused by frontal lobe lesions in young monkeys
were not apparent until the age at which the frontal lobes mature in
normal monkeys.

The effects of brain injury upon cognitive function in children are
complex and cannot be easily summarized. However, a few general
statements are possible. Recovery of function following localized
damage in children is sometimes, but not always, better when the
injury occurs early (Spreen et al., 1984). Early damage to localized sensory areas may result in nearly complete recovery of simple
functions (e.g., localization, simple pattern discrimination), but
permanent impairment may remain for more complex visual-spatial
tasks (Rudel, Teuber and Twitchell, 1974; Hécaen, Perenin and
Jeannerod, 1984). Recovery is sometimes dramatic following early

unilateral damage to areas which mediate language (Witelson, 1987),
although complex syntactic functions may show impairment. It remains unclear whether sparing, when it occurs, involves a reorganization of undamaged tissue, or a release of preexisting potentials
(Bulloch, Liederman and Todovric, 1987).

The long-term effects of generalized or diffuse damage seem to be
greater than the deficits caused by localized damage (Almli and
Finger, 1984). Early generalized damage is likely to cause greater
impairment than does later damage (O'Leary and Boll, 1984). The
cognitive deficits associated with early damage more typically involve a lowering of overall psychometric IQ rather than a loss of
specific cognitive abilities. There is some evidence that verbal IQ
may be less impaired than performance IQ, but there is no consistent
pattern that is exhibited by all children with diffuse damage.

6. CONCLUSIONS

Despite great advances in both the neural and behavioral sciences,
relatively little is known about the overall relationship between
brain maturation and the cognitive functions which emerge in the
years from 2 to puberty. Abilities such as language and reasoning
are highly complex and uniquely human. This makes it impossible to
utilize the animal models and lesion techniques that have provided
valuable information about the neural basis of more elementary sensory and motor functions. Study of the cognitive effects of brain
damage in children is much more complex than in adults, and to date
permits few conclusions concerning the development of brain-behavior
relations.

This pessimistic assessment must be modulated by the possibilities
emerging from new technologies that allow measurement of brain
variables in intact subjects. Longitudinal as well as cross-
sectional studies of the relation between cognitive performance and
brain variables such as cortical thickness are possible with the
MRI. Metabolic imaging techniques offer the possibility of measuring regional brain activation during the performance of cognitive
tasks. Advances in signal processing techniques are also opening up
new possibilities for EEG studies. Thus the futur of developmental
brain-behavior studies appears bright.

At present neuropsychological data can offer a unique perspective on
developmental issues such as the stage notion and the nature of representation. Studies of myelination and cortical structure suggest
that differing functional brain systems mature at characteristic
ages. This lends support to stage notions of development as the
maturation of a functional system may mediate the reorganization of
earlier maturing systems. EEG measures of the onset of coherent
activity in spatially distant generators may offer a means of assessing the age range in which such changes occur, particularly if the
EEG measures are obtained during the performance of cognitive tasks
which show developmental change.

Fischer (1987) has noted that the concept of representation has
different meanings for researchers from a Piagetian tradition and
those from a neuropsychological or information processing perspec-

tive. Those from a Piagetian tradition refer to a representation as
a complex evoked memory, something used when evoking an object, person, or event that is not present. When used in this fashion representation implies intention on the part of the child and the representation is a conscious phenomenon.

Researchers from a neuropsychological perspective use the term representation to refer to any encoding of a stimulus situation. For
example, a representation may be an encoding of the shape of an
object, or its last seen location in a delayed alteration task. The
encoding is assumed to be synonymous with the activation of neural
units. In the recent parallel distributed processing models
(Rumelhart and McClelland, 1986) the representation is a pattern of
activation distributed across a network of neurons. Used in this
fashion representation does not imply consciousness or intention.

Study of the brain systems involved in the performance of any task
makes it clear that multiple sensory and motor encodings of the same
event must occur in parallel (Kolb and Whishaw, 1980). The size,
color, shape, and spatial location of a perceived object are all encoded in separate and parallel sensory pathways. Information concerning the "meaning" of the object, i.e., its function, association
with other objects, emotional valence etc., also involve multiple
brain locations. All of these neural systems may be viewed as
simultaneous representations of an object.

There is no coherent theory of how activity in the multiple neural
systems which encode an object could result in the unitary conscious
phenomenon that is a representation according to the Piagetian perspective. It seems unlikely, in fact, that conscious phenomenon will
be understandable in terms of neural processes in the foreseeable
future. The Piagetian notion of representation and other concepts
that imply consciousness appear to have explanatory power for developmental processes. To the extent that this is true, theories at
the purely psychological level of explanation must continue to play
a guiding role in developmental research.

REFERENCES

Almli, C.R., & Finger, S. (Eds.) (1984). *Early brain damage. Vol.
    1: Research orientations and clinical observations.* New York:
    Academic Press.
Barkley, R.A. (1983). Neuropsychology: Introduction. *Journal of;
    Child Clinical Psychology, 12,* 3-5.
Barkovich, J.A., & Bent, O.K. (1988). Normal postnatal development
    of the corpus callosum as demonstrated by MR imaging. *American
    Journal of Neuroradiology, 9,* 487-491.
Becker, M.G., Isaac, W., & Hynd, G.W. (1985). Neuropsychological
    development of nonverbal behaviors attributed to "frontal lobe"
    functioning. *Developmental Neuropsychology, 3,* 275-298.
Boll, T.J., & Barth, J.T. (1981). Neuropsychology of brain damage
    in children. In: S.B. Filskov & T.J. Boll (Eds.), *Handbook of
    Clinical Neuropsychology.* New York: Wiley.
Brand, S., & Rakic, P. (1984). Cytodifferentiation and
    synaptogenesis in the neostriatum of fetal and neonatal rhesus
    monkies. *Anatomy and Embryology, 169,* 21-34.

Bulloch, D., Liederman, J., & Todovric, D. (1987). Reconciling stable asymmetry with recovery of function; An adaptative systems perspective on functional plasticity. *Child Development, 58,* 689-697.

Chelune, G.T., & Edwards, P. (1981). Early brain damage: Ontogenetic-environmental considerations. *Journal of Consulting and Clinical Psychology, 49,* 777.

Chuagini, H.T., & Phelps, M.E. (1986). Maturational changes in cerebral function in infants determined by [18]FDG positron emission tomography. *Science, 231,* 840-843.

Conel, J.L. (1939-1963). *The postnatal development of the human cerebral cortex* (7 vols.). Cambridge, Ma: Harvard University Press.

Cooper, M.L., & Rakic, P. (1983). Gradients of cellular maturation and synaptogenesis in the superior colliculus of the fetal rhesus monkey. *Journal of Comparative Neurology, 215,* 165-186.

Davidson, A.N., & Peters, A. (1970). *Myelination.* Springfield, Ill: Thomas.

Dekaban, A. (1970). *Neurology of early childhood.* Baltimore: Williams and Wilkins.

Diamond, A. (1985). Development of the ability to use recall to guide action as indicated by infants' performance on AB. *Child Development, 56,* 868-883.

Diamond, A., & Goldman-Rakic, P.S. (1983). Comparison of performance on a Piagetian object performance task in human infants and rhesus monkeys: Evidence for involvement of prefrontal cortex. *Society for Neuroscience Abstracts, 9,* 641.

Dobbing, J., & Sands, J. (1973). Quantitative growth and development of human brain. *Archives of Disabled Child, 48,* 757-767.

Epstein, H.T. (1978). Growth spurts during brain development. In: J. Chall & F. Mirsky (Eds.), *Education and the brain* (NSSE Yearbook pt.2, pp.343-371). Chicago: University of Chicago Press.

Epstein, H.T., & Epstein, E.B. (1978). The relationship between brain weight and head circumference from birth to age 18 years. *Journal of Physical Anthropology, 48,* 471-474.

Fischer, K.W. (1987). Relations between brain and cognitive development. *Child Development, 58,* 623-632.

Fletcher, J.M., & Taylor, H.G. (1964). Neuropsychological approaches to children: Towards a developmental neuropsychology. *Journal of Clinical Neuropsychology, 6,* 39-56.

Fletcher, J.M., Levin, H.S., & Landry, S.H. (1984). Behavioral consequences of cerebral insult in infancy. In: C.R. Almli & S. Finger (Eds.), *Early brain damage. Vol. 1: Research orientations and clinical observations.* New York: Academic Press.

Galin, D., Diamond, R., Nakel, L., & Herron, J. (1979). Development of the capacity for tactile information transfer between hemispheres of normal children. *Science, 204,* 1330-1332.

Gazzaniga, M.S., Bogen, J.E., & Sperry, R.W. (1962). Some functional effects of lesioning the cerebral commissures in man. *Proceedings of the National Academy of Sciences, 48,* 1765.

Golden, C.J. (1981). The Luria-Nebraska children's battery: Theory and formulation. In: G.W. Hynd & J.E. Obrzut (Eds.), *Neuropsychological assessment and the school aged child,* pp.277- 302. New York: Grune & Stratton.

Goldman, P.S. (1974). Plasticity of function in the CNS. In: D.G. Stein, J.J. Rosen & N. Butters (Eds.), *Plasticity and recovery of function in the central nervous system.* London: Academic Press.

Goldman-Rakic, P.S. (1987). Development of cortical circuitery and cognitive function. *Child Development, 58,* 601-622

Greenough, W.T., Black, J.E., & Wallace, C.S. (1987). Experience and brain development. *Child Development, 58,* 539-556.

Hatta, T. (1987). Developmental changes of hemispheric collaboration for tactile sequential information. Presented at the IXth Biennial ISSBD Meetings, July 12-16, Tokyon, Japan.

Hauert, C.A., & Koenig, O. (1987). Tactile perception in a developmental perspective: Role of successive versus simultaneous matching procedures. Presented at the IXth Biennial ISSBD Meetings, July 12-16, Tokyo, Japan.

Hécaen, H., Perenin, M.T., & Jeannerod, M. (1984). The effect of cortical lesions in children: Language and visual functions. In: C.R. Almli & S. Finger (Eds.), *Early brain damage. Vol.1: Research orientations and clinical observations.* New York: Academic Press.

Holland, B.A., Haas, D.K., Norman, D., Brant-Zawadski, & Newton, T.H. (1986). MRI of normal brain maturation. *American Journal of Neuroradiology, 7,* 201-208.

Huttenlocher, P.R. (1979). Synaptic density in human frontal cortex. Developmental changes and effects of aging. *Brain Research, 163,* 195-205.

Huttenlocher, P.R., de Corten, C., Garey, L.J., & van der Loos, H. (1982). Synaptogenesis in human visual cortex. Evidence for synapse elimination during normal development. *Neuroscience Letters, 33,* 247-252.

Kennard, M.A. (1936). Age and other factors in motor recovery from precentral lesions in monkeys. *American Journal of Physiology, 115,* 138-146.

Kinsbourne, M. (1974). Mechanisms of hemispheric interaction in man. In: M. Kinsbourne & W.L. Smith (Eds.), *Hemispheric disconnection and cerebral function.* Springfield, Ill: Charles C. Thomas.

Kolb, B., & Whishaw, I.Q. (1980). *Fundamentals of human neuropsychology.* (2nd Edition). New York: W.H. Freeman.

Luria, A.R. (1973). *The working brain.* New York: Basic Books.

Luria, A.R. (1980). *Higher cortical function in man.* New York: Basic Books.

MacLean, P.D. (1970). The triune brain, emotion and scientific bias. In: F.O. Schmitt (Ed.), *The Neurosciences: Second study program.* New York: Rockfeller University Press.

Marsh, R.W. (1985). Phrenoblysis: Real or chimera ? *Child Development, 56,* 1059-1061.

McCall, R.B., Meyers, E.D., Hartman, J., & Roche, A.F. (1983). Developmental changes in head circumference and mental performance growth rates: A test of Epstein's hypothesis. *Developmental Psychobiology, 166,* 457-468.

Niedermeyer, E. (1982). Development of waking and sleep patterns. In: E. Niedermeyer & F.L. da Silva (Eds.), *Electroencephalography. Basic principles, clinical applications and related fields.* Baltimore: Urban & Schwarzenberg.

Nunez, P.L. (1981). *Electrical fields of the brain.* New York: Oxford University Press.

O'Leary, D.S. (1980). A developmental study of interhemispheric transfer in children aged five to ten. *Child Development, 51,* 743-750.

O'Leary, D.S., & Boll, T.J. (1984). Neuropsychological correlates of generalized brain dysfunction in children. In: C.R. Almli & S. Finger (Eds.), *Early brain damage. Vol. 1: Research orientations and clinical observations*. New York: Academic Press.

Parsons, O.A., & Prigatano, G.P. (1978). Methodological considerations in clinical neuropsychological research. *Journal of Consulting and Clinical Psychology, 46*, 608.

Passler, M.A., Isaac, W., & Hynd, G.W. (1985). Neuropsychological development of behavior attributed to frontal lobe functioning in normal children. *Developmental Neuropsychology, 1*, 349-370.

Quinn, K., & Geffen, G. (1986). The development of tactile transfer of information. *Neuropsychologia, 24*, 793-804.

Rabinowicz, T. (1979). The differentiate maturation of the human cerebral cortex. In: F. Flakner & J.M. Tanner (Eds.), *Human growth. Vol 3: Neurobiology and nutrition*. New York: Plenum Press.

Rakic, P., Bourgeois, J.P., Eckenhoff, M.F., Zecevic, N., & Goldman-Rakic, P.S. (1986). Concurrent overproduction of synapses in diverses regions of the primate cerebral cortex. *Science, 232*, 232-235.

Riesen, A.H. (1971). Problems in correlating behavioral and physiological development. In: M.B. Sterman, D.J. McGinty & A.M. Adinolfi (Eds.), *Brain development and behavior*. New York: Academic Press.

Rudel, R.G., Teuber, H.L., & Twitchell, T.E. (1974). Levels of impairment of sensorimotor functions in children with early brain damage. *Neuropsychologia, 12*, 95-109.

Rumelhart, D.E., & McClelland, J.L. (1986). *Parallel distributed processing*. Cambridge, Ma: The MIT Press.

Schneider, G.E. (1979). Is it really better to have your brain lesion early ? A revision of the "Kennard principle". *Neuropsychologia, 17*, 557-584.

Spreen, O., Tupper, D., Risser, A., Tuokko, H., & Edgell, D. (1984). *Human developmental psychology*. New York: Oxford University Press.

Thatcher, R.W., Walker, R.A., & Guidice, S. (1987). Human cerebral hemispheres develop at different rates and ages. *Science, 236*, 1110-1113.

van der Vlugt, H. (1979). Aspects of normal and abnormal neuropsychological development. In: M.S. Gazzaniga (Ed.), *Handbook of behavioral neurobiology: Vol. 2. Neuropsychology*. New York: Plenum Press.

White, S.H. (1970). Some general outlines of matrix of developmental changes between five and seven years. *Bulletin of the Orton Society, 20*, 41-57.

Witelson, S. (1987). Neurobiological aspects of language in children. *Child Development, 58*, 653-688.

Woodruff, D.S. (1978). Brain electrical activity and behavior relationships over the life span. In: P.B. Baltes (Ed.), *Life-span development and behavior* (pp.112-179). New York: Academic Press.

Yakovlev, P.I., & Lecours, A.R. (1967). The myelogenetic cycles of regional maturation of the brain. In: A. Minkowsky (Ed.), *Regional development of the brain in early life* (pp.3-70). Oxford: Blackwell.

DEVELOPMENTAL PSYCHOLOGY
Cognitive, Perceptuo-Motor, and Neuropsychological Perspectives
C-A. Hauert (Editor)
© Elsevier Science Publishers B.V. (North-Holland), 1990

CHILD NEUROPSYCHOLOGICAL DEVELOPMENT:
LATERALIZATION OF FUNCTION - HEMISPHERIC
SPECIALIZATION

Olivier KOENIG

Department of Psychology
Harvard University, Cambridge, U.S.A. and
Faculty of Psychology and Educational Sciences
University of Geneva, Switzerland

*The first part of this chapter presents a brief review of
the evidence that has been used to support different theories of lateralization of cerebral functions in children.
Then some weak points in these theories are highlighted.
In the second part, a new approach to cerebral hemispheric
asymmetry is presented. This approach focuses on high-
level visual processing, with special emphasis on a computational view of cerebral function and on recent neuroanatomical and neurophysiological data.*

1. INTRODUCTION

For over 100 years, researchers have focused on single dimensions to
describe the differences in processing between each cerebral hemisphere. For example, the left cerebral hemisphere is described as
important for processing details, while the right hemisphere is
thought to be specialized for global processing. As a consequence,
cognition has tended to be divided into dichotomous and opposite
processing systems (for reviews, see Bradshaw and Nettleton, 1981;
Bertelson, 1982).

Research has often been conducted using brain-damaged patients in
clinical studies but numerous experiments have also been carried out
with normal populations. In the visual modality, for example, researchers have tried to relate perceptual asymmetries (i.e., differences in speed of processing or in accuracy depending on the visual
field in which the stimulus is presented) to the way each cerebral
hemisphere processes information. Although this area has been tremendously productive during the past 25 years --after the first studies carried out by Bryden and Rainey (1963)-- a precise and detailed characterization of cerebral hemispheric asymmetry has not yet
been proposed. In addition, many findings have been shown to be
unstable and are difficult to replicate (see Beaumont, 1982; White,
1969). Focussing on the developmental aspects of cerebral hemispheric asymmetry only adds complexity to the problem. In the past
20 years, many have argued about whether cerebral hemispheric asym-

metry develops with age or is stable from birth to adulthood. For
Lenneberg (1967), there is an equipotentiality of each cerebral
hemisphere at birth, followed by a progressive lateralization of
cerebral functions. Kinsbourne (1975, 1976), in contrast, proposes
an early, invariant asymmetry in the organization of cerebral functions, and Witelson (1977) takes a position intermediate between
the two extreme views.

It is important to note that the conceptual framework used in developmental studies is the same as the one used in adult studies.
That is, authors have studied cerebral functions in the same dichotomous terms as those used for adults. The critical issue has been
to find out when in development a given "adult" asymmetry can already be observed. Much of the researchers has concentrated on the
visual modality, where differences with age in performance between
left- and right-visual field presentations (visual lateral differences) have been assessed (for a review, see Beaumont, 1982; Koenig,
1986; Witelson, 1977).

The growing interest and recent developments in cognitive neuroscience may substantially modify earlier conceptions of laterality.
In the past few years, much information has accumulated regarding
the neuroanatomy and neurophysiology of vision (Arbib and Hanson,
1987; Mishkin, Ungerleider and Macko, 1983; Van Essen, 1985). Some
have referred to these data to construct theories of visual cognition (see Kosslyn, 1987, for an example). Indeed, theories have
been developed in which psychological processes are described in
terms of the operation of functional brain components, and brain
function is conceptualized in terms of computations. This approach
offers precise descriptions of how information is processed in the
brain and provides substantial benefits for understanding high level
cognitive mechanisms. It may also represent a dramatic improvement
over traditional theoretical frameworks in that more precise hypotheses can be generated regarding perceptual asymmetries in a variety of tasks, in children as well as in adults. In return, divided
visual field studies may provide dramatic evidence of dissociations
between different functional systems which can be used to support
theories of psychological processing (Hellige, 1983; Kosslyn, 1988;
Zaidel, 1983).

In the next section, the evidence for different theories of hemispheric asymmetries in children is briefly summarized. A number of
articles, monographs and books providing interesting reviews have
been published in the last few years (Beaton, 1985; Beaumont, 1982;
Best, 1985; Bryden, 1982; Code, 1987; Dailly and Moscato, 1984; Hynd
and Obrzut, 1981; Kinsbourne, 1978; Kinsbourne and Hiscock, 1977,
1983; Moscovitch, 1977; Springer and Deutsch, 1985; Van Hout and
Seron, 1983; Witelson, 1977; Young, 1982) and it would take too long
to present thoroughly this large and growing literature. After this
brief review, I will focus on the relationships between cerebral
hemispheric asymmetry and cognitive strategies. Finally, some suggestions will be offered about how a precise analysis of a task --in
terms of the different cognitive components needed to perform it--
motivated by a theory of processing can lead to more precise hypotheses in the domain of cerebral hemispheric asymmetry in the developing child.

2. CEREBRAL HEMISPHERIC ASYMMETRY IN CHILDREN: SOME CLASSICAL
SOURCES OF EVIDENCE

2.1. Anatomical evidence

Some research has focussed on anatomical differences between the two
cerebral hemispheres in the human brain and it has been proposed
that cerebral dominance is based on structural asymmetries.
Geschwind and Levitsky (1968) reported that the planum temporale
--the upper surface of the posterior portion of the temporal lobes--
is larger in the left cerebral hemisphere in the adult brain. Because this area is part of the temporal speech region of Wernicke,
it has been proposed that this asymmetry may be responsible for the
localization of speech in the left cerebral hemisphere. The same
kind of evidence has been found by Teszner, Tzavaras, Gruner and
Hécaen (1972), Wada, Clark and Hamm (1975) and Witelson and Pallie
(1973). This asymmetry of the planum temporale has also been observed in newborn infants (Teszner et al., 1972; Wada et al., 1975;
Witelson and Pallie 1973) and in human fetuses (Teszner et al.,
1972; Wada et al., 1975). These data have been interpreted as evidence for a very early basis for the localization of speech in the
left cerebral hemisphere.

Although the asymmetry of the planum temporale is perhaps the easi-
est one to observe in the human brain, many other asymmetries have
also been found (for reviews, see Eidelberg and Galaburda, 1984;
Geschwind and Galaburda, 1985, 1987; Habib and Galaburda, 1986;
Witelson, 1977, 1980, 1983). The general observation that emerges
from anatomical studies is that asymmetries already exist at birth,
if not before, and this supports the hypothesis of a very early
asymmetry in the organization of cerebral functions. However, the
presence of an early anatomical asymmetry is obviously not proof of
the presence of a functional asymmetry. For Habib and Galaburda
(1986), the nature of the relationship between morphological and
functional asymmetries remains hypothetical.

2.2. Electrophysiological evidence

Electrophysiological studies measuring auditory evoked responses in
newborns and infants have provided interesting data. Molfese and
Molfese (1979) presented auditory linguistic stimuli (nonsense
syllables formed by consonant-vowel pairs or words such as consonant-
vowel-consonant) and nonlinguistic stimuli such as piano chords or
noises to newborns and infants. Preterm infants only 36-weeks-old
had higher response rates in the left cerebral hemisphere for linguistic stimuli and higher response rates in the right cerebral
hemisphere for nonlinguistic stimuli. Further evidence of a dissociation between speech- and nonspeech material has been reported in
preterms and newborns by Molfese (1977), and Molfese and Molfese
(1980). Similar data have been obtained by Davis and Wada (1977)
and Gardiner and Walter (1977), using measures of EEG power distributions in infants as young as 2 weeks. Therefore, electrophysiological studies also tend to support the hypothesis of an
early asymmetry in the organization of cerebral functions and contradict a theory of a total equipotentiality of each cerebral
hemisphere at birth. It is worth noting that these asymmetries
exist before any linguistic influence from the environment.

2.3. Motoric asymmetries

Observations of asymmetrical motor preferences or asymmetrical
skills in infants and children are numerous. Usually, consistent
evidence for right-hand biases is obtained. The well-known tonic-
neck reflex described by Gesell (1938) is a good example of this
asymmetrical behavior and is observed in both newborns and preterms.
Siqueland and Lipsitt (1966) reported that in newborns, spontaneous
head movements toward the right side were more frequent than movements toward the left side. Similar observations have been reported
by Turkewitz (1977, 1980) and Harris and Fitzgerald (1983). Infants
as young as 3 months keep an object in the right hand longer than in
the left hand (Caplan and Kinsbourne, 1976). In addition, a stronger grasp by the right hand has been observed in 2-week-olds (Petrie
and Peters, 1980). Ramsay (1979) reported a right-hand advantage in
a tapping task in 10-month-olds. The same author also reported that
7-month-olds catch an object more often using the right hand
(Ramsay, 1980). A preference for right-hand reaching has been observed even earlier, in infants as young as 4-months-old (Michel,
1981). Similar asymmetrical biases toward the right side have been
reported for feet. When infants or neonates are suspended and
lowered towards a flat surface, consecutive leg movements --which
are referred to as the stepping reflex-- show a bias toward the
right leg for the first step (Peter and Petrie, 1979).

For Kinsbourne and Hiscock (1983), these asymmetries reflect an
early dominance of the left cerebral hemisphere. However it is unknown whether these asymmetries relate to subsequent handedness or
whether they are a consequence of any aspect of asymmetry in the organization of cerebral functions. As suggested by Witelson (1985),
some of the early motoric behaviors may depend on subcortical mechanisms independent of neocortical functional asymmetry. Unfortunately, the relationship between early left hemispheric dominance,
right-sided motoric asymmetries and cerebral lateralization for
language functions appears to be quite complex. If a simple correlation did exist between these different phenomena, the proportion
of individuals with left-hemisphere language should be identical to
the proportion of right-handed individuals. However, the facts are
different; the functions that subserve the language mechanisms appear to be lateralized to the left cerebral hemisphere in almost all
right-handed adults and also in many left-handers (Branch, Milner
and Rasmussen, 1964). Consequently, this proportion is higher than
the proportion of righthandedness in the population (67 percent,
according to Oldfield, 1971).

To summarize, on the one hand, early motoric asymmetries are compatible with the notion of early asymmetry in the organization of cerebral functions. However, on the other hand, such observations do
not seem able to provide clear evidence in favor of this position.

2.4. Concurrent tasks

Kinsbourne and Cook (1971) suggested that if two different tasks
that depend on cerebral areas localized in the same hemisphere were
carried out simultaneously, then a decrease in performance would be
observed in at least one of these tasks. Several experiments using
concurrent interfering tasks were then carried out. Among right-

handed adults, speaking decreases the performance of the right hand more than the left (Briggs, 1975; Hicks, 1975; Lomas and Kimura, 1976). These results are interpreted as evidence that the left cerebral hemisphere controls both speech output and right-hand movements. Furthermore, the low interference rate observed for the left hand gives some support to the hypothesis that the control of speech and left-hand movements is divided between the two cerebral hemispheres.

Several experiments have been carried out in children, using unimanual tapping tasks in conjunction with speech. As Hiscock and Kinsbourne (1978) and Kinsbourne and Hiscock (1977) pointed out, the choice of the tapping rate as the dependent variable seems specially appropriate for developmental studies, because it avoids the problem of floor and ceiling effects that could appear in perceptual laterality studies (see Section 2.6). It has been reported that speaking disrupts right-hand performance more than left-hand performance, even in children as young as three years of age (Hiscock, 1982; Hiscock and Kinsbourne, 1978, 1980; Hiscock, Kinsbourne, Samuels and Krause, 1985; Marcotte and LaBarba, 1985; Piazza, 1977). Because this interference is observed in both young children and adults, it has been considered support for the hypothesis of an early lateralization of speech control in the left hemisphere, which is consistent with Kinsbourne's (1975, 1978) hypothesis of an early asymmetry in the organization of cerebral functions that does not change with age.

2.5. Evidence from clinical studies

Perhaps the most important source of information about functional hemisphere asymmetry comes from studies of brain-damaged patients. But as far as developmental aspects of this question are concerned, two critical issues must be considered.

First, it is well known that compared to an adult brain, a child's brain shows much greater functional plasticity. For example, very early lesions affecting the left or the right cerebral hemisphere do not prevent the development of language abilities, although these abilities may be retarded (Basser, 1962; Van Hout and Seron, 1983). Lenneberg (1967) considered these data critical for his theory of equipotentiality of cerebral functions at birth. According to Lenneberg, if both hemispheres participate in the process of language acquisition very early in life, damage affecting either the right or the left cerebral hemisphere should not impair the development of language. However, if these data fully support the concept of functional plasticity in the immature brain, they do not necessarily imply an early equipotentiality of the cerebral hemispheres for language functions. One should not equate plasticity with equipotentiality. As noted by Young (1982, p.190): "There is no reason to connect loss of plasticity with an increase in lateralization."

Second, Lenneberg (1967), using data from Basser (1967), pointed out that the frequency of aphasia following a lesion sustained by the right cerebral hemisphere was higher in children than in adults. Basser showed that unilateral damage to either hemisphere between the ages of 2 and 5 years will impair language abilities, at least temporarily. This observation was interpreted as support for the

hypothesis of an early equipotentiality of cerebral functions (i.e.,
if language functions are initially represented in both cerebral
hemispheres, language impairments should result from right-
hemispheric as well as from left-hemispheric lesions). However,
more recent studies have provided different results: Both early
unilateral lesions and early hemispherectomies often lead to important cognitive deficits that are indeed related to the side of the
lesion (Annett, 1973; Day and Ulatowska, 1980; Dennis and Whitaker,
1976; Kershner and King, 1974; Kohn and Dennis, 1974; Rudel, Teuber
and Twitchell, 1974; St. James-Robert, 1981). Furthermore,
Kinsbourne and Hiscock (1977) reported that the frequency of aphasia
following right-hemispheric lesions is not higher in children than
in adults. Among a group of 58 aphasic children who had sustained
early unilateral cerebral lesions, 50 cases of a left-hemisphere
damage were reported, compared to 8 cases of right-hemisphere damage. These more recent data have led certain authors to critically
re-examine Basser's (1962) study (St. James-Roberts, 1981; Satz and
Bullard-Bates, 1981; Woods and Teuber, 1978). Woods and Teuber
(1978), for example, suggested that the proportion of left-handers
was higher in Basser's study than in a normal population. In addition, these authors suggested that, although the patients described
by Basser (1962) were thought to have sustained unilateral lesions
only, both hemispheres may have been damaged. For a detailed discussion of this question, see Van Hout and Seron (1983).

To summarize, the evidence from clinical studies does not support
the hypothesis of an early equipotentiality in the organization of
cerebral functions. Rather, it supports a model of early asymmetry
in this organization.

2.6. Perceptual studies

Perceptual studies are generally divided according to the sensory
channel they refer to: Visual, auditory or tactile. They are non-
invasive studies comparing performance that depends on the side of
the stimulation (i.e., left or right visual hemifield, left or right
ear and left or right hand). Specific experimental paradigms are
used that are usually referred to as divided visual field, dichotic,
or dichhaptic paradigms. These different paradigms are easy to use
and hundreds of experiments have been published in the past 25
years. Developmental studies, however, pose some difficulties
usually not encountered in adult studies. Usually, a substantial
number of trials is required in order to obtain stable measures of
response time, for example. Anybody who has ever worked with children has probably experienced the difficulty of ensuring that subjects maintain their concentration after a delay. Furthermore,
these paradigms require the subjects to follow instructions carefully (e.g., to focus on the fixation point in divided visual field
studies).

2.6.1. Divided visual field studies

The key to this method (referred to as tachistoscopic lateralized presentation) is to present a visual stimulus for a very short
time (usually less than 180 msec) in one hemifield only, while the
subject is asked to focus on a central fixation point. This short
presentation time prevents the subject from moving his/her eyes in

order to focus on the stimulus and thus ensures that only one half
of the retina is stimulated. Because the left part of each retina
only projects into the left cerebral hemisphere (and the right part
of each retina only projects into the right cerebral hemisphere),
this method allows one to send information to each hemisphere
separately. Several reviews of the developmental studies in this
specific area have already been published (Beaumont, 1982; Bryden,
1982; Koenig, 1986; Witelson, 1977; Young, 1982).

It is important to note that the tachistoscopic procedure is not
recommended for children under 5 or 6 years of age. It is especially difficult to ensure that young children follow the instructions
and focus on the fixation point. In addition, if the relevant dependent variable is response time, further problems can be encountered with younger children.

In a recent review of 41 different experiments (Koenig, 1986), it
appeared that the same types of asymmetries found in adults are
usually observed in children (the studies reviewed included children
from five years of age and older). Those experiments (n=7) that
dealt with the processing of human faces led to a left-visual-field
(right-hemisphere) advantage, whereas the ones (n=16) that used
words showed a right-visual-field (left-hemisphere) advantage. When
letters were used as stimuli (n=8), the results were less consistent. Indeed, the expected left-hemisphere advantage for processing
of verbal material was reported only in 6 experiments. It is usually assumed that letters can be processed in a variety of ways
(Beaumont, 1982). The other studies reviewed (n=10) used digits or
nonverbal stimuli such as lines for which orientation was the critical feature, dot collections in an enumeration task, shapes or colored squares. For digits, a left-hemisphere advantage was observed,
but a right-hemisphere advantage appeared or tended to appear in the
other studies. A general conclusion from this review is that the
most consistent data were observed when words were used as stimuli.

As far as age differences in the observed asymmetries are concerned,
only 3 of the studies reviewed showed significant variations.
Turner and Miller (1975) reported an increasing left-hemisphere advantage in girls and boys from 6 to 9 years of age (4 groups) in a
word-identification task. This advantage did not appear in a word-
discrimination task. The stimuli consisted of three-letter words
written vertically as well as horizontally. These data suggest that
the type of task (i.e., identification versus discrimination) is a
critical factor. A discrimination task can be performed on the
basis of spatial cues, even, as the limiting case, by subjects who
have not yet developed good reading abilities. Such a strategy
seems less likely to be used for a word-identification task.
Gibson, Dimond and Gazzaniga (1972) observed such a dissociation in
adult subjects. A left-hemisphere advantage was obtained in a word
nominal comparison task (identification needed), whereas a right-
hemisphere advantage appeared in a physical comparison task. It
could be hypothesized that, in the Turner and Miller (1975) experiment, 6-year-olds --or some of them-- tended to use a physical-based
judgement in the word-identification task, given their relatively
poor reading abilities. This could have reduced the left-hemisphere
advantage at this age, compared to older subjects. Two other studies report significant variations with age in the patterns of asym-

metries. In the first study (Grant, 1980), subjects from 5 to 10
years of age were asked to identify the color of colored squares
flashed in each visual field. Subjects made fewer errors in their
verbal responses when the stimuli were presented to the right hemisphere. However, this effect was consistent only in 5- and 10-year-
olds. Seven-year-olds showed a reduced effect. These results were
later replicated in a longitudinal study (Grant, 1981). The author
interpreted these data in terms of possible changes with age in
cognitive strategies, without further specification.

In brief, perceptual studies in the visual modality do not provide
any evidence in favor of a model of progressive lateralization of
cognitive functions. Only 3 studies among the 41 reviewed clearly exhibited developmental changes in the patterns of asymmetry.
Indeed, adult patterns of asymmetry can usually be observed among
the youngest children studied.

2.6.2. Dichotic studies

Perhaps the best known procedure for assessing cerebral laterality
effects is the dichotic listening task. The first studies were done
by Kimura and appeared in the literature in the early sixties (e.g.,
Kimura, 1961). These studies exploit the following characteristics
of the auditory system. Auditory information is transmitted from
each ear to both contralateral and ipsilateral cortical areas.
However, contralateral pathways are stronger (they have a greater
number of fibers and higher transmission speed). The key to this
procedure is to present information to both ears simultaneously, so
that the stronger pathway will occlude the weaker one. In this way,
information can be presented to each hemisphere separately, just as
in the tachistoscopic procedure. (For a detailed review of the
dichotic methodology, see Bryden, 1982.)

The same results as those obtained in adults are usually found in
children (i.e., a right-ear (left-hemisphere) advantage for the processing of verbal material and a left-ear (right-hemisphere) advantage for the processing of music or emotional stimuli and environmental sounds). Dichotic studies in children present quite consistent results. Witelson (1977) reviewed 36 studies using verbal
material; 30 reported a right-ear superiority (left-hemisphere
advantage) even in the youngest groups (3 years of age in some
studies). In a longitudinal study, Bakker, Hoefkens and Van der
Vlugt (1979) presented pairs of digits to children (girls and boys)
tested 4 times between 6 and 11 years of age. They reported a
right-ear (left-hemisphere) advantage, without any sex- or age-
related differences. Saxby and Bryden (1984) presented spoken sentences that differed in the emotional content of the voice to girls
and boys divided in three groups (5-6, 9-10, and 13-14 years of
age). A left-hemisphere advantage was observed for the processing
of the verbal content of the sentences, whereas a right-hemisphere
advantage was reported for the analysis of the emotional content of
the voice. Fennell, Satz, and Morris (1983) also used pairs of digits to test left- and right-handed children (girls and boys) divided into three age groups (5-6, 7-8 and 10-11 years of age). They
observed a left-hemisphere advantage in right-handers only, and this
effect interacted with age. The left-hemisphere advantage was weak
for the youngest group, substantial for the middle group and inter-

mediate for the oldest group. This interaction might have been due to an unequal proportion of girls and boys in each age group. Unfortunately the number of subjects of each sex was not reported by the authors.

It has been shown that attentional strategies can play a critical role in ear asymmetries (Geffen, 1976, 1978; Geffen and Sexton, 1978; Geffen and Wale, 1979; Obrzut, Boliek and Obrzut, 1986). If such strategies are controlled, no variation with age in the pattern of asymmetries should be observed.

Best, Hoffman, and Glanville (1982) have used a variant of the dichotic procedure in order to test very young subjects. They used the cardiac-habituation response recovery method in order to test discrimination ability for phonetic and music timbres in 2- to 4-month-olds. A greater response to right-ear stimulation (left-hemisphere advantage) was observed for speech stimuli in 3- and 4-month-olds, but not in 2-month-olds. It was suggested that the failure to observe an asymmetry in the youngest subjects was because an appropriate cognitive skill had not yet developed. On the other hand, a right-hemisphere advantage following musical stimulation was observed in all subjects, even those as young as 2-month-olds.

To summarize, dichotic studies tend to report the same asymmetries as those observed in adults, in children as young as can be tested. In addition, no evidence of variation with age in asymmetries appears.

2.6.3. Dichhaptic studies

The dichhaptic procedure was proposed and used for the first time by Witelson (1974) in an experiment with children. This procedure is a tactile analogue to the dichotic listening procedure. In the original study, Witelson asked her subjects to palpate two unseen stimuli --one with each hand-- with the index and middle finger, for a limited period of time (10 seconds). The subjects were then asked to select the two stimuli just palpated among those presented in a visual display. This procedure is supposed to generate a competition between the two perceptive fields --and between the two cerebral hemispheres-- that should yield the best performance for the perceptive field sending information to the specialized hemisphere.

Most of the dichhaptic studies have been carried out with children. The dichhaptic task usually yields an advantage for the left hand (right hemisphere) if nonsense shapes are used as stimuli (Cioffi and Kandel, 1979; Dawson, 1981; Denes and Spinaci, 1981; Etaugh and Levy, 1981; Gibson and Bryden, 1983; Van Blerkom, 1985; Walch and Blanc-Garin, 1987; Witelson, 1974, 1976). However, a few experiments have failed to replicate Witelson's data (Cranney and Ashton, 1980; Labreche, Manning, Golbe and Markman, 1977). When letters are used as stimuli, results appear even less consistent. Performance exhibits either no significant lateral difference (Gibson and Bryden, 1983; Witelson, 1974) or a left-hemisphere advantage (Cioffi and Kandel, 1979). It is usually assumed that the processing of letters through the tactile channel requires an important spatial (right-hemisphere) component that may decrease --or even eliminate-- the asymmetry due to the linguistic part of the processing

(Witelson, 1977).

As suggested elsewhere (Koenig, 1986), one difficulty with the
dichhaptic procedure is that it can lead to a variety of strategies
used to perform the task. This problem becomes critical in those
studies that have used an especially long palpation time (e.g., 10
seconds as in Witelson's (1974) original experiment). In addition,
because each research project uses a procedure that differs in some
respect from the one used in another project, the results are difficult to compare. I have shown (Koenig, 1987) in a study with adult
subjects that the dichhaptic procedure yields robust data when substantial constraints are introduced into the palpation procedure (in
particular, when subjects are only allowed to make brief unidirec-
tional movements with both hands simultaneously).

As far as the topic of variation with age in tactual asymmetries is
concerned, no significant trend appeared in the studies reviewed
here, except for one of the two experiments reported by Van Blerkom
(1985). A right-hemisphere advantage was observed in 11-year-olds,
but a left-hemisphere advantage was obtained in 7- and 15-year-olds.
In the second study, however, the same author observed an invariant
right-hemisphere advantage from 8 to 16 years of age using the same
stimuli (nonsense shapes). Koenig and Hauert (1986) deliberately
chose complex stimuli for a dichhaptic experiment designed to reveal
age-related changes in the cognitive processes underlying the performance of 5- to 10-years-old children. The procedure was inspired
by Witelson's (1974) study, with the exception that the subjects had
to palpate the stimuli (nonsense shapes), placed in the palm of each
hand, with all their fingers. The trick of the experiment was that
although the pertinent dimension of the stimuli was shape, the
square shape also differed in texture (with a texture gradient from
one side of the object to the other). Furthermore, the squares differed in the center of gravity. Some were filled with lead in one
half, with the other half lightened to provide the same overall
weight as the other stimuli. The analysis of the visual choices
after each trial showed that, at certain ages only, the complex
stimuli (the squares with the texture gradient or with the deplace-
ment of the center of gravity) seemed to lead to distortions in the
reported shapes of the objects. These complex stimuli were more
often perceived as trapezoids, compared to control square stimuli.
The appearance of these distortions was interpreted as evidence of
changes with age in the underlying cognitive processes. In addition, changes with age were also observed in the lateral differences, and these changes were interpreted as reflecting the changes in
cognitive strategy.

Briefly, dichhaptic studies --just like the other perceptual stu-
dies-- do not provide any evidence of an age-related trend in the
observed asymmetries that could account for a modification with age
in the organization of cerebral functions.

2.6.4. Studies dealing with special populations

Some perceptual studies of lateralization of cerebral functions have
also been carried out with special populations such as deaf children. The logic behind this approach is as follows: If the organization of cerebral functions is genetically pre-programmed, it is

assumed that a sensory deprivation should not have important effects
on this organization and that lateral differences should not differ
from those observed in normal control subjects. On the other hand,
if there is a progressive lateralization of functions that develops
with experience, lateral differences might differ in children with
sensory deprivation when compared to normal controls.

The dichhaptic procedure has often been used in this area. Cranney
and Ashton (1980) tried to replicate Witelson's (1974) task in 10-
year-old deaf children. They did not observe any significant lateral difference either in deaf children or in normal controls.
Vargha-Khadem (1982) used nonsense shapes and letters. An overall
advantage for the right-hand (left-hemisphere) was reported only for
the processing of letters, both in deaf children and normal controls. Finally, Gibson and Bryden (1984) also presented letters and
nonsense shapes to deaf and normal children. The task revealed
significant asymmetries only when letters were used as stimuli.
Indeed, a right-hemisphere advantage was observed in deaf children,
whereas a left-hemisphere advantage appeared in normal controls.

This approach, however, raises important problems and it seems difficult to draw any clear conclusions. Several criticisms can be
addressed to the logic that supports the above hypotheses. On one
hand, it is rather difficult to interpret a null finding. If the
observed lateral differences do not differ between children with and
without sensory deprivation, it does not necessarily means that the
organization of functions is pre-programmed. Indeed, both groups
may have their own (however different) language experiences that
lead to the development of the same pattern of perceptual asymmetry.
On the other hand, one could hypothesize that deaf children have a
representation of verbal stimuli that in some relevant respect differs from that of normal controls. Both groups may consequently
perform the task in a different way, using different strategies.
What sense then should be attributed to the observation of different
patterns of lateral differences in each group ? As I will show
later, changes or differences in cognitive strategies play a critical role in the domain of cerebral hemispheric asymmetry and may
account for part of the variations and inconsistencies that appear
in different studies.

2.7. Some concluding comments

Although the general issue presented here pertains to many different
research areas in the domain of cerebral hemispheric asymmetry, I
will mainly focus on laterality studies in the visual modality.

The previous section was devoted to an overview of the principal
sources of evidence used to support different conceptions of lateralization of cerebral functions in the developing child brain. The
general finding that emerged from the review is that an asymmetry in
the organization of cerebral functions already exists very early,
perhaps at birth, or even before. No evidence of development with
age in this asymmetry appears. These observations support
Kinsbourne's (1975, 1976) hypothesis of an early asymmetry in the
organization of cerebral functions and disagree with Lenneberg's
(1967) conception of a progressive lateralization of functions after
an initial period of equipotentiality of both cerebral hemispheres.

However, two critical issues can be addressed at this point. First, although divided visual field studies classically show an increase in performance with age, without any evidence of age-related change in the pattern of asymmetry, there are reports of deviant results (change with age in the perceptual asymmetry, no asymmetry, opposite asymmetry). As mentioned earlier, Turner and Miller (1975), for example, reported an increase with age in the observed left-hemisphere advantage in a word identification task. Second, the way the developmental question is usually addressed in most of the studies reported here (i.e., by a simple assessment of change with age in the pattern of asymmetry, without any further consideration) may be too simple and may not be really helpful for our understanding of cognitive development in general or, more specifically, for our understanding of the way children process a given task. In other words, this domain seems to suffer from the lack of a theoretical framework.

Several factors could account for the observation of deviant results. First, as far as changes with age in lateral differences are concerned, they could be nothing but type 1 error (false rejection of the hypothesis of no difference). Second, deviant data could result from poor methodology or from differences in methodology. It is well known (see Beaumont, 1982, for example) that lateral differences are highly sensitive to small methodological variations. Third, deviant data may result from grouping factor (i.e., chronological age or grade, for instance) or age selection. In the hypothetical example of inversion in lateral differences occuring each successive year between 5 and 9 years of age, testing 5-, 7- and 9-year-olds only could lead to the conclusion that no variation with age occurs in the pattern of asymmetry. On the other hand, testing 5-, 6-, and 7-year-olds, for instance, could lead to the conclusion that the pattern of asymmetry varies with age. This example shows how important age selection might be and how critical it is that this choice be motivated by a theory of development. Indeed, without such a theory, it seems impossible to know which age groups should be selected. Fourth, deviant data could result from a sampling bias or from individual differences. Indeed, children of the same age may not be at identical maturational level and if they are, there may be some individual differences in how their brains are lateralized.

However, the point I will now discuss is very different. Changes in cognitive strategies are thought to be --at least partially-- responsible for most of the deviant results. If subjects of different ages were to perform the same task using different cognitive strategies, then the observed pattern of asymmetry might be confounded with the change in cognitive functioning. The exact nature of the relationship between lateral differences and cognitive strategies is usually not studied. However, it is generally accepted that the tasks used to assess laterality effects in children should be "easy enough" in order to be carried out "the same way" throughout a large age span.

In a recent experiment (Koenig, in press) I contrasted different tasks --one "easy" right-hemispheric task (color naming), one "easy" left-hemispheric task (word reading) and one "complex" interference task (the Stroop color-word task)-- to study the relationship between cognitive strategies and visual lateral differences. Right-handed boys from 7 to 15 years of age (9 age groups) were tested. No variation with age in lateral differences was observed in the two "easy" tasks from 7 to 15 years of age: An invariant right-hemisphere advantage was observed in the color naming task and an invariant left-hemisphere advantage was obtained in the word reading task. Consequently, it was proposed that each of these two tasks were carried out the same way (i.e., by using the same cognitive strategy). However, a complex pattern of lateral differences was observed in the Stroop task, where inversions with age in lateral differences occurred. This observation provides some support --with other independent sources of evidence-- for the hypothesis of changes with age in cognitive strategies for the processing of the complex Stroop stimuli.

Consequently, it appears that the precise way a task is processed may have dramatic effects on the observed pattern of asymmetry. However, to further investigate the relation between lateral differences and cognitive strategies, one needs a very clear description of how a given task is processed at a given age. Of course, every subject of the same age may not perform the task the same way, because of possible differences in the rate of development and possible individual differences (see above). In the weakest case, one must assume that there is a prototypical way of functioning that characterizes a given age, and that most of the subjects are following the rule. In the strongest case, we may have some evidence about how each subject performs the task --evidence which is independent of lateral differences-- and we may consider regrouping subjects according to manner of processing at each age.

Unfortunately, laterality studies where special emphasis is given to the way the task is processed are rare. The typical strategy consists in attributing to each cerebral hemisphere one single dimension that can capture the way a given hemisphere processes information. This can be misleading. Cerebral functions are often described in vague terms (e.g., analytical, holistic, sequential, parallel, verbal, spatial) that are not grounded on a precise theory of processing. This kind of categorization leads to descriptions of psychological processes in equally vague terms. Improving this traditional approach is not easy. However, in the last few years, our knowledge about how the brain functions has improved tremendously, and as I will show in the next section, it now seems possible to constrain models of psychological processes using neuroanatomical and neurophysiological data and to use these models as theoretical frameworks for laterality studies.

3. A THEORY BASED APPROACH

3.1. A componential analysis of laterality studies

In this section, I will try to present an improved approach to visual laterality studies. Because the general issues that will be discussed here are applicable to any population, I will not initially focus on children.

The critical point is that it does not seem reasonable to study

brain-behavior relationships using perceptual studies without having
i) a clear description of the necessary steps or operations that
must be accomplished to process a given task, and ii) precise hypotheses regarding the demands of these operations on the cognitive
system.

Labelling a task --or a hemispheric way of processing-- as global
(analytical) or verbal (visuo-spatial), for example, reveals little
about the cognitive components that are engaged in the processing.
It seems oversimplified to assume that a complex task, like high-
level visual shape processing, will be better handled by the right
cerebral hemisphere simply because this hemisphere may be specialized to deal with visuo-spatial information. Similarly, it also
seems too simple to assume that complex tasks such as spelling,
reading or writing, for example, will be better carried out by the
left cerebral hemisphere just because this hemisphere is specialized
to process verbal material. Of course, no one would argue against a
critical involvement of the left cerebral hemisphere in language
processing. However, one also needs to know what, in terms of
information processing, accounts for this advantage. Let me consider this case in greater detail. On the one hand, it is now well
known that what are usually called the language functions are not
localized solely in the left cerebral hemisphere. In the past ten
years, data have accumulated showing specific abilities of the right
cerebral hemisphere in dealing with certain types of verbal material
or verbal processings (see Code, 1987, for a review). On the other
hand, clinical data provide dramatic evidence of many possible language impairments, so varied that some even claim it is impossible
to use categories of language disorders (e.g., Caramazza, 1986).
Indeed, each patient can be considered a specific case to be individually studied. The variety of language impairments makes difficult
to consider language as a whole; on the contrary, this gives support
to the existence of many different functional systems involving
hordes of cognitive components (or subsystems), organized in complex
networks. It seems reasonable to hypothesize that at least some of
these components are more effective in the right than in the left
cerebral hemisphere. The hypothesis of a general advantage of the
left cerebral hemisphere for language processing is not helpful for
a complete understanding of both normal language processes and the
nature of a given deficit.

A better way to understand the nature of a deficit is by constructing a theory or a model of what could be called the "functional
architecture" of a cognitive system such as reading and spelling
(Caramazza, 1986). Such a model can be described in terms of an
organized network of different processing subsystems that are motivated by a theory. Psychological processes are conceptualized in
terms of the operation of functional components and brain functions
are seen in terms of computations. This approach can offer precise
descriptions of how information is processed in the brain and provides substantial benefits for the understanding of high-level cognitive mechanisms. Even if the theory is only partially true, it will
be constrained and upgraded by new experimental and clinical data.
It is worth noting that the different components of a cognitive system could probably be divided into several other ones at a deeper
level of analysis. However, any subsequent division should respect
the borders of the upper level of hierarchy.

When one focuses on the developmental aspects of language, the problem appears even more complex. Language acquisition requires the
development of such a large variety of different skills, such as
phonetic parsing of the speech stream, recognizing similar speech
productions as perceptually equivalent, organizing phonetic segments
into contrasting categories, and so on, that it again seems inadequate to assume that all these skills are implemented in one (or a
few) small area(s) of the left cerebral hemisphere. With this in
mind, the assessment of perceptual asymmetries for "language"
--considered as a unitary ability-- appears erroneous.

In the case of a computational approach, a precise analysis of the
task to be processed is required. Indeed, the ensemble of components that are used may differ depending upon the task requirements.
A change in cognitive strategy for the processing of a given task
will be seen in terms of a change in the organization of the cognitive components. I will define a "cognitive strategy" in terms of a
set of cognitive components (or subsystems), each of them being implemented in a given area of the brain. Some components will be
hypothesized as being more efficient --or perhaps exclusively loca-
lized-- in one cerebral hemisphere. Such an approach can yield more
precise hypotheses regarding perceptual asymmetries in children as
well as adults. The definition of a perceptual asymmetry becomes
quite different: It no longer reflects a vague, general capacity of
a given hemisphere to perform a task, but rather it depends on the
cerebral hemispheric asymmetry of each of the specific components
used to perform the task. In other words, the perceptual asymmetry
is the result of all the partial (componential) asymmetries. Allen
(1983) suggested a similar approach, where a horde of "subprocessors" was hypothesized, that could be implemented in one hemisphere
only or in both hemispheres, with different patterns of lateralization. The model, however, was not motivated by a theory of processing, and no specific role was attributed to each subprocessor.

3.2. A model of high level visual cognition

Theories of visual cognition can be formalized today in part because
of the substantial amount of information acquired in the past few
years about the neurophysiology and neuroanatomy of the visual system. Kosslyn (1987, 1988) showed how this knowledge can be used to
construct models or theories of visual cognition.

For example, one main concern of the visual system is the problem of
position variability. The same object may appear at different locations in the visual field and its image is likely to stimulate different parts of the retina. However, this object is recognized
wherever it may fall on the retina. On the one hand, as proposed by
McClelland and Rumelhart (1981), a separate representation may be
associated with each possible location of the image. On the other
hand, one could hypothesize that only a single representation is
needed to encode an object, provided that the system uses representations that are associated with an ensemble of positions in the
visual field. Kosslyn (1987) suggested looking at the way the primate visual system deals with position variability. Ungerleider
and Mishkin (1982) provided evidence for the existence of two cortical visual systems in the monkey. The first system (the ventral
system) runs from the primary visual cortex (OC) down to the infe-

rior temporal lobe (area TE) and is hypothesized to deal with the
processing of the shape (the "what") of the object. The second
system (the dorsal system) runs from area OC to the parietal lobe
(area PG) and is thought to be concerned with the analysis of the
location (the "where") of an object. Various experiments with monkeys (see also Mishkin and Appenzeller, 1987) have shown that a
selective lesion to one of these systems elicits a clear dissociation. If only the temporal lobes are removed, the monkeys are severely impaired in tasks that require a discrimination between visual
patterns. However, selective removal of the parietal lobes causes
the animal to show a dramatic impairment in discriminating on the
basis of location.

Kosslyn (1987) pointed out that converging evidence can be found in
humans. Patients suffering from bilateral temporal lobe damage have
difficulties in shape identification but do not have localization
problems (often observed in the Kluver-Bucy syndrome). On the other
hand, patients suffering from bilateral damage to the parieto-
occipital regions show difficulties in localizing stimuli, but not
in recognition (often observed in Balint's syndrome; see De Renzi,
1982).

Neurophysiological studies also provide supporting evidence. The
visual areas in the parietal lobe rarely include the fovea and do
not strongly respond to shape, size and color but respond to direction of motion. In contrast, visual areas in the temporal lobe
appear to be sensitive to shape, texture and color (Desimone,
Albright, Gross and Bruce, 1984). Taken together, these different
observations led Kosslyn (1987) to hypothesize a set of subsystems
in the ventral system that encode shape and a set of subsystems in
the dorsal system that encode location.

Furthermore, Kosslyn claims that the dorsal system does more than
simply represent the locations of objects in a scene. This system
can also be used to represent spatial relations between different
parts of a single object. There is indeed good evidence (see
Kosslyn, 1987, 1988) that a given object is not encoded as a whole;
rather, it may be parsed into different parts that are encoded separately. If so, it seems necessary in some circumstances for the
visual system to take into account the relative locations of different parts. This may be very important when an object is processed
with multiple eye fixations, where different parts stimulate the
fovea over time. The ability to represent the location of parts
relative to other ones may be very useful for any system designed to
recognize shapes. Indeed, a single object can appear in many different shapes (for example, imagine all the various shapes animate objects can have). If a separate representation were associated with
each previously seen shape, the appearance of a new (unfamiliar to
the system) shape of this object might not correspond to a representation already stored in memory and the object might not be recognized. The brain seems to accomplish this task in a more economi-
cal way. It seems to focus on invariant properties of the object,
such as the relations between parts of the object that will not
change no matter what the configuration of the object might be
(e.g., the relations "above", "below", "connected to", "to the left
of", and so on).

Therefore, Kosslyn postulates a subsystem that processes categorical spatial relations among objects or parts of an object. However, there are objects that differ only by subtle variations from instance to instance, such as human faces. In these cases, computing only categorical relations may not be enough. Another kind of representation that computes metric spatial relations is hypothesized. Hence, the precise coordinates of objects --or of parts of an object-- are specified relative to a single origin. Therefore, both a categorical and a coordinate subsystem are postulated in the dorsal system by the theory.

Finally, outputs from the ventral and dorsal systems are hypothesized to be put together in associative memory, probably implemented in the posterior, superior temporal lobe.

I have just described a few subsystems of Kosslyn's (1987) model of high-level visual processing (for a complete version of the model, please refer to the original article). I have chosen to focus below on two components that are hypothesized to be clearly lateralized, and to give an example of how neuroanatomical and neurophysiological data may constrain a model of information processing.

Kosslyn, Feldman, Maljkovic and Hamilton (1988) claimed that categorical spatial relations are "language-like", because they usually correspond to word-concepts. Thus, the left cerebral hemisphere is hypothesized to be better at processing categorical spatial relations than the right hemisphere. In contrast, the coordinate subsystem is hypothesized to be more efficient in the right cerebral hemisphere. This hypothesis is supported by evidence that the right hemisphere is more efficient at processing metric spatial relations (see for instance De Renzi, 1982). It is important to note, however, that each component of the model is represented in both hemispheres. Nevertheless, certain components may be more trained or more efficient in one given hemisphere.

A question arises at this point. One could argue that the categorical/coordinate distinction is nothing more than an additional dichotomy in the field of cerebral hemispheric asymmetry (see Section 2 of this Chapter). The difference, compared to traditional dichotomies, is that the actual distinction is clearly motivated by a theory of information processing and is intended to reflect how the brain computes only a single sort of visual information. Indeed, it is worth noting that the actual distinction only applies to one part of the whole process. In addition, traditional dichotomies are usually not objectively definable, whereas the questions raised by the categorical/coordinate distinction are very explicit and tasks can be set up that are tied directly to theory, as will be shown in the next section. I claim that this distinction goes beyond traditional ones. For instance, a right-visual-field (left-hemisphere) advantage for language processing could arise because many of the language skills require the use of some kind of categorical subsystem. In other domains, such as face perception, for example, the traditional left-visual-field (right-hemisphere) advantage could appear not because there is a specific system specialized for face encoding and processing in the right hemisphere, but because a metric (coordinate) subsystem is often needed to process this type of stimuli. As a matter of fact, recent evidence seems to confirm that face perception is not an independent mechanism (see Bruyer, 1988, for a review).

3.3. Some experimental evidence

In four experiments inspired by Kosslyn's (1987) model, we recently tested the hypothesis that categorical relations are better computed in the left cerebral hemisphere while coordinate relations are better computed in the right cerebral hemisphere (Kosslyn, Koenig, Barrett, Cave, Tang and Gabrieli, in press). I will present only one of these experiments here. Subjects (an equal number of female and male Harvard undergraduates) were shown a pattern formed by one horizontal line and a dot (shown on a computer screen). This pattern appeared during each trial for 150 milliseconds either in the left visual field, in the right visual field or in the center of the screen, after a central fixation point. The pattern could undergo 12 different variations. In 6 cases, the dot was above the horizontal line, in 6 others, the dot was below the line. Within each group of 6 patterns, 3 used a dot location that was within 3 millimeters of the line, whereas in the other 3 the dot was more than 3 millimeters away. In one condition (Categorical condition), subjects were asked to report whether the dot was presented above or below the line. In another condition (Coordinate condition), subjects were asked to decide whether the dot was within 3 millimeters of the line or more than 3 millimeters away. Different subjects participated in each condition and the two conditions were similar in all respects, except for the instructions given to the subjects. A task analysis (in terms of the different cognitive components that were required to process these tasks) suggested that the asymmetry due to the categorical and the coordinate subsystems was sufficient to provide an overall left- and right-hemisphere advantage, respectively, for the two tasks.

The response time analysis showed a clear dissociation between the two types of processing. A right-visual-field (left-hemisphere) advantage appeared when categorical relations were processed and a left-visual-field (right-hemisphere) advantage was observed when metric or coordinate relations were to be computed. In addition we hypothesized that with practice, the metric subsystem would be required less and less for the processing of the coordinate task (indeed, the subjects may progressively introduce some degree of categorization within the whole set of stimuli). Consequently, we hypothesized a decrease with practice in the observed right-hemisphere advantage for the coordinate task, but no change with practice was expected in the categorical task. Insofar as the categories are known and can be used to process the stimuli from the beginning of the experiment, there is no need for a change of strategy over time. The results confirmed the expectations: The left-hemisphere advantage in the categorical task did not vary over trials, whereas the right-hemisphere advantage in the coordinate task rapidly decreased, than disappeared with practice. The disappearance of the right-hemisphere advantage with practice was due to a decrease in left-hemisphere response time, which supports the hypothesis of increasing computation of categorical spatial relations. Another experiment reported in Koenig, Gabrieli and Kosslyn (1988) showed that the disappearance of the right-hemisphere advantage with practice when subjects are asked to process metric rela-

tions is sensitive to the complexity of the spatial judgment. For
example, when the metric task was more difficult (by increasing the
number of dots and by increasing the critical distance between the
line and the in/out limit), the right-hemisphere advantage lasted
longer. It was suggested that the increased complexity of the metric judgment made it more difficult for subjects to develop categories. In addition, it appears that the practice effect on lateral
differences extends to other classes of material. The disappearance
of the right-hemisphere advantage with practice has also been observed in a letter naming task where the stimuli were drawn in a very
difficult font, so that the initial identification of letters would
first require the computation of precise metric relations (Koenig et
al., 1988).

A task-by-hemisphere interaction provides support for the existence
of two distinct functional systems (see Hellige, 1983; Zaidel,
1983). In the previously described experiments, we provided evidence for the psychological and neurological reality of a distinction
between two different ways to process visual information, one using
categorical spatial relation representations, the other one using
coordinate spatial relation representations.

3.4. Accounting for practice effects and individual differences

Changes with practice in the observed patterns of lateral difference
have often been reported in visual laterality studies (see Beaumont,
1982, for example). These effects are not well understood and their
origin is usually attributed to unspecified kinds of noise. For
Young (1982, pp.24-25), "Effects of practice reported in the literature are complex and inconsistent, and studies have not been successful in disentangling effects attributable to practice at given
tasks from those that may have arisen from increased familiarity of
stimuli and from covert and overt changes in subject strategies."
The problem is difficult, because several factors might partially
and simultaneously account for these practice effects. An effect
may be sensitive to the number of trials in the experiment and also
to characteristics of the practice session (which is almost always
used at the beginning of any laterality study). Practice effects
also may depend upon a wide range of factors such as the nature of
the stimuli, the nature and the difficulty of the task, the familiarity of the material and procedure, the number and duration of the
rest pauses, and so on. In addition, because performance usually
improves with practice (i.e., there is a decrease in mean response
time or in error rate), one has to avoid a progressive extinction of
lateral differences due to a floor or ceiling effect.

Beaumont (1982, p.82) proposed an even more subtle explanation:
"...an increasing adaptation to the unnatural process of attending
to strongly lateralized presentation... may reflect a more fundamental adaptation and rearrangement by which the relatively lateralized nature of the processing systems is modified to compensate
for the asymmetry in performance in the two visual fields".

In terms of a dynamic model of cerebral functioning (for a definition, see Cohen, 1982) practice effects could be explained by differences in activation or in the balance of attention between the two
cerebral hemispheres (see Kinsbourne, 1975). However, while this

model seems able to account for any type of results, it may be difficult to predict new ones.

An important factor to consider is the direction of the eventual
shift in lateral differences. As already noted by Beaumont (1982)
and Goldberg and Costa (1981), when a shift in lateral differences
occurs with practice, it does not seem to appear randomly. Beaumont
(1982, p.81) reported: "...other studies have found an effect of
practice, which has most commonly been seen as a shift from an initial left-visual-field advantage to a later right-visual-field
advantage." The same finding was reported by Goldberg and Costa
(1981, p.165) "...transfer of initial right-hemispheral to left-
hemispheral superiority has been demonstrated by more than one author for both nonverbal (visual forms, patterns of dots) and verbal
(same-letter judgments) visual input tasks." The different factors
that have been hypothesized above as being the origin of changes
with practice in lateral differences could hardly provide an explanation for the direction of the shift. Without excluding the possible influence of other factors, I suggest again, that variations in
cognitive strategies may be primarily responsible for these practice
effects. Thus, different strategies may reflect the operation of
different sets of cognitive components that together produce a different pattern of asymmetry. With this in mind, a specific change
in component operations may be responsible for the shift from a
initial left-visual-field advantage to a later right-visual-field
advantage. I suggest that the kinds of visual spatial relations
that need to be computed might be a critical factor. One could
hypothesize that some visual tasks must be processed by first computing coordinate relations, but with practice, they become progressively more likely to be performed using categorical relations.
Indeed, the repeated-measures design often used in laterality studies may contribute to this processing shift.

Individual differences are well known in the domain of cerebral
hemispheric asymmetry and many aspects of the problem have been discussed elsewhere (for differences in lateral preference and handedness, see Annett, 1982; Porac and Coren, 1981; for sex differences,
see Bryden, 1982; Fairweather, 1982; Harris, 1978). I would like to
emphasize a few points directly related to a strategy-centered approach that describes a cognitive system in terms of an ensemble of
components.

The first point refers to the task analysis. One should first determine whether there are different ways to perform a given task.
If different subjects process the task using different strategies
(i.e., different ensembles of components), the overall asymmetry
(i.e., the result of all the componential asymmetries) may vary from
individual to individual. The second point could be a potential
problem. One has no guarantee that the same subsystem is implemented in the same brain area from individual to individual or even
that it is implemented in the same hemisphere. Although one has
reason to assume that at least some regularity appears from person
to person, this factor could also account for some variability in
the group studies. Third, differences may occur in the degree to
which certain subsystems are lateralized in the brain. Kosslyn,
Sokolov and Chen (1988) reported simulation data which showed that
different degrees of lateralization may be obtained for each compo-

nent, depending upon the simultaneous interaction of certain developmental rules.

Let me briefly summarize the main issues that have been addressed in
this third section. I have claimed that (i) the traditional dichotomies that refer to different abilities of each cerebral hemisphere
are often vague; (ii) one needs a clear description of a task, in
terms of the different cognitive components required for its processing; (iii) hypotheses about the asymmetry of the hemispheric imple-
mentation of each component must be formulated; and (iv) the observed visual lateral difference reflects the sum of all the individual
(componential) asymmetries. I have briefly summarized a model of
high-level visual processing based on recent neurophysiological and
neuroanatomical data and I have also presented some examples of
experiments motivated by this theory. I then raised the question of
variability in lateral differences (intra- as well as inter-subject
variability) by referring to an approach based on a task analysis in
terms of component processes. I will now try to delineate what such
an approach may contribute to the developmental issue of cerebral
hemispheric asymmetry.

3.5. Componential approach, development and lateral differences

When examining the developmental approach from a componential point
of view, at least three different sources of variation with age in
visual asymmetries may be hypothesized (see Figure 1).

Figure 1: *Possible sources of variation with age on the basis of
asymmetric performance on laterally presented stimuli.
The bottom line represents the observed lateral
differences.*

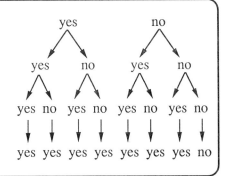

First, as mentioned earlier, changes in cognitive strategy may involve some modification in the set of components used to perform a
task. If the components are differently lateralized in the brain,
then some change may occur in the overall pattern of asymmetry
(again given the hypothesis that the perceptual asymmetry reflects
the sum of all the partial --componential-- asymmetries). However,
a change in cognitive strategy may not be covered by the assessment
of the perceptual asymmetry. Indeed, even if the set of components
is different, the final asymmetry may be identical. Furthermore,
the set of components used might be different not only because of a
change in cognitive strategy, but also because of the possible emergence of new components. Indeed, new components are expected during
the course of development as a result of the maturation process of
the central nervous system. This process becomes critical in development, for it allows the child to use more and more powerful ways
of processing. Second, changes with age may occur in the respective
localization in the brain of different cognitive components. This
seems more likely to occur during the first months or years of the
life, when the functional plasticity of the brain is known to be
substantial (see Section 2.5 of the present Chapter). Third, changes with age in the relative capacity or potential of the components
may occur. Different mechanisms could be the origin of these changes. The first one could be explained in terms of a dynamic model
of functioning (for a definition, see Cohen, 1982). An augmentation
in the activation of one cerebral hemisphere --which may result from
modifications in internal states, as well as from external sources
of variation-- may increase the activation of the subsystems localized in this hemisphere. In return, this increase in activation
might lead to a perceptual orientation toward the contralateral perceptual field (Kinsbourne, 1975). A second mechanism can be proposed in terms of the weighting of each component. The relative importance or weight of a given component might be different from age
to age and might depend on slight modifications in the task requirements. For example, a difference in the weight of certain components might be expected according to whether speed or accuracy is
emphasized in the instructions for the task. It can also be hypothesized that this effect interacts with age in a complex way. A
third mechanism could perhaps account for age-related changes in the
relative capacity of the different subsystems. As suggested by the
Kosslyn, Sokolov, and Chen (1988) simulation model, the strength of
each subsystem on the left and right sides of the brain may differ
throughout the course of development.

The bottom line of Figure 1 reveals that changes with age in lateral
differences may occur in seven of the eight possible cases. The
brief review of divided visual field studies presented above (see
Section 2.6.1) does not allow us to conclude that changes with age
in perceptual asymmetries appear as often as predicted here. On the
contrary, a conclusion of no variation is most common. Four explanations might be considered at this point. First, each of the different cognitive subsystems may be represented bilaterally and only
a few of them might be significantly more efficient in one side of
the brain than in the other. Second, the numerous methodological
problems that have been pointed out earlier might make it difficult
to precisely address the question of development with age in lateral
differences. Third, studies are difficult to compare with each
other. Slight methodological variations could have dramatic conse-

quences on task requirements and hence, on the set of components used. This point appears to be critical when researchers fail to replicate previous results. Finally, the problem of change(s) with practice in lateral differences may also yield misinterpretations. As shown earlier in this chapter, a significant hemisphere advantage might disappear after practice. Consequently, some studies may have failed to show lateral differences, because the critical effects might have occurred during the course of the practice session only. However, studies showing changes with age in lateral differences are the most interesting ones for developmental psychologists, for they may reveal some age-related changes in cognitive strategies. Of course, as I suggested above, there are many possible sources of variation in lateral differences. Some of them may be difficult to study. However, I suggest that a componential approach can help one to study the source of variation that is possibly the most interesting for developmental psychology, that is, the one that calls upon differences in cognitive strategy.

I have shown that the coordinate and categorical components are two critical subsystems in high-level vision. They seem to be strongly lateralized and they may account for part of the intra-individual variability in perceptual studies. A number of developmental studies (see Carey, 1985; Piaget and Inhelder, 1948) show that the representation of certain classes of objects (e.g., living things) in children does not conform to the same principles of categorization as in adults. In a review of the literature, Younger and Cohen (1985) present some evidence that perceptual categories (e.g., stuffed animals) can be constructed in infants as young as 7 months of age. It has also been reported that 7-month-old babies have surprisingly powerful face encoding and face recognition skills (see Fagan, 1979). However, it remains unknown what features are used as the basis for the categorization, and what features are used in face encoding and face processing. Is the visual system already able to compute the same kinds of visual spatial relations as in adults ? Probably not. The kind of categorical spatial relations that are computed in adults (such as "inside," "outside," "connected to," "above," "below," etc...) are highly explicit for adult subjects and there is good reason to think that they are not so for 7-month-old babies. However, if babies construct perceptual categories, they must have the ability to treat as equivalent objects that can be perceived as different. In other words, they should have an internal "prototypical" representation of an object or a class of objects. Whether this representation consists of a template, a feature or a set of features, or a primitive kind of categorical spatial relations and whether it corresponds to the most frequent exemplar ever seen, remains still unknown. Goldberg and Costa (1981) suggested that structural features of the left hemisphere may be more suitable for mediating this kind of prototypical representation. Therefore, certain visual and language processes are lateralized in the left hemisphere because the neural organization of that hemisphere is conducive to categorical computations.

A similar kind of analysis can be applied to face encoding and face processing mechanisms. The fact that newborns are attentive to face-like stimuli (see Goren, Sarty and Wu, 1975, for example) also implies the existence of an early form of categorical representation. Again, the content of this representation remains unclear.

However, the increasing ability to differentiate faces may result
from an increasing ability to use coordinate spatial relations.
Indeed, such relations seem critical in differentiating stimuli that
only vary by subtle spatial distinctions. As it has been shown in
Section 3.2, the right cerebral hemisphere is critical for this
kind of processing.

4. CONCLUSION

Cognitive and neuropsychological development have often been perceived as two independent facets of child development. However, more
recently, some have come to believe that our understanding of cognitive development may benefit from recent neuropsychological findings. Consequently, many neuropsychological experiments have been
carried out with normal subjects, using relatively simple paradigms
such as dichhaptic palpation, dichotic listening or tachistoscopic
presentation. The accessibility of these techniques --they require
less expertise and are much cheaper than some other ones such as
positron emission tomography (PET) scans or cerebral blood flow
(CBF), for example-- probably explain their popularity. Although
this approach is popular today, it may not be as helpful as expected
for understanding cognitive development, unless the questions raised
are motivated by an appropriate theoretical framework.

In the first sections of this present chapter, I briefly reviewed
different sources of evidence usually used to assess the question of
lateralization of cerebral functions in the developing child brain.
Most of the studies reviewed found a very early asymmetry. In addition, the pattern of asymmetry does not seem to differ from the
adult one. I have tried to show that the traditional theoretical
framework used in laterality studies, which is based on coarse dichotomies that differentiate the functioning of both hemisphere, is
in some respects, misleading and not helpful for our understanding
of cognitive development. Some examples of laterality studies have
been discussed to demonstrate that the way a task is processed (in
terms of different cognitive strategies) might be a critical factor
affecting the measure of lateral differences. I have proposed that
to interpret the relationship between cognitive strategy and perceptual asymmetry from a developmental perspective, a precise description of the cognitive system (i.e., in terms of different functional
subsystems) motivated by a theory of processing is needed. Some
examples in high-level visual perception have been provided, where
the necessary steps of information processing needed to perform a
task were made explicit. Such an approach has been shown to provide
important information regarding the types of representations used in
high level vision. In this case, different patterns of lateral differences may provide evidence of dissociation between different processing systems. Although the example presented here concerned
adult subjects, the same logic was suggested for developmental studies.

In this chapter, I have chosen to focus on a particular perceptual
channel, the visual one. However, I believe that the points raised
here are also relevant to other modalities.

Interest in the relationship between cognitive development and some

index of brain functioning is perhaps motivated by a more basic concern, that is, what is the force driving cognitive development ? In
other words, what is the origin of changes in cognitive development
or in cognitive strategies ? The answer remains a mystery and the
precise role of biological mechanisms is in many respects still unspecified. It seems clear that competent performance on a task reflects the adequate organization of a system. By adequate organization, I mean a minimal set of components required to perform the
task --even if it is not yet the most elegant or powerful way to
perform it. At the weakest level, a preformed structure of some
primitive subsystem(s) (that is(are) already lateralized and can
yield the observation of perceptual or electro-physiological asymmetries) may control the precise way other subsystems are progressively integrated and lateralized into the system, with possible
individual variations in the mechanism.

ACKNOWLEDGMENTS

This work was supported by fellowship 88.357.0.86 from the Swiss
Science Foundation. The author thanks John Gabrieli, Stephen
Kosslyn and Michael Van Kleeck for critical readings.

REFERENCES

Allen, M. (1983). Models of hemispheric specialization.
    Psychological Bulletin, 93, 73-104.
Annett, M. (1973). Laterality of childhood hemiplegia and the
    growth of speech and intelligence. Cortex, 9, 4-33.
Annett, M. (1982). Handedness. In: J.G. Beaumont (Ed.), Divided
    visual field studies of cerebral organization. London: Academic
    Press.
Arbib, M.A., & Hanson, A.R. (1987). Vision, brain, and cooperative
    computation. Cambridge: MIT Press.
Bakker, D.J., Hoefkens, M., & Van der Vlugt, H. (1979). Hemispheric
    specialization in children as reflected in the longitudinal
    development of ear asymmetry. Cortex, 15, 619-625.
Basser, L.S. (1962). Hemiplegia of early onset and the faculty of
    speech with special reference to the effects of hemispherectomy.
    Brain, 85, 427-460.
Beaton, A. (1985). Left side, right side. New Haven: Yale
    University Press.
Beaumont, J.G. (1982). Developmental aspects. In: J.G. Beaumont
    (Ed.), Divided visual field studies of cerebral organization.
    London: Academic Press.
Bertelson, P. (1982). Lateral differences in normal man and
    lateralization of brain function. International Journal of
    Psychology, 17, 173-210.
Best, C.T. (1985). Hemispheric function and collaboration in the
    child. New York: Academic Press.
Best, C.T., Hoffman, H., & Glanville, B.B. (1982). Development of
    infant ear asymmetries for speech and music. Perception and
    Psychophysics, 31, 75-85.
Bradshaw, J.L., & Nettleton, N.C. (1981). The nature of hemispheric
    specialization in man. The Behavioral and Brain Sciences, 4,
    51-91.

Branch, C., Milner, B., & Rasmussen, T. (1964). Intracarotid sodium amytal for the lateralisation of cerebral dominance. *Journal of Neurosurgery, 21,* 399-405.

Briggs, G.G. (1975). A comparison of attentional and control shift models of the performance of concurrent tasks. *Acta Psychologica, 39,* 183-191.

Bruyer, R. (1988). La reconnaissance des visages. *La Recherche, 200,* 774-783.

Bryden, M.P. (1982). *Laterality: Functional asymmetry in the intact brain.* London: Academic Press.

Bryden, M.P., & Rainey, C.A. (1963). Left-right differences in tachistoscopic recognition. *Journal of Experimental Psychology, 66,* 568-571.

Caplan, P.J., & Kinsbourne, M. (1976). Baby drops the rattle: Asymmetry of duration of grasp by infant. *Child Development, 47,* 532-534.

Caramazza, A. (1986). On drawing inferences about the structure of normal cognitive systems from the analysis of patterns of impaired performance: The case for single-patient studies. *Brain and Cognition, 5,* 41-66.

Carey, S. (1985). *Conceptual change in childhood.* Cambridge, Ma: MIT Press.

Cioffi, J., & Kandel, G.L. (1979). Laterality of stereognostic accuracy of children for words, shapes and bigrams: A sex difference for bigrams. *Science, 204,* 1432-1434.

Code, C. (1987). *Language, aphasia, and the right hemisphere.* New York: John Wiley & Sons.

Cohen, G. (1982). Theoretical interpretations of lateral asymmetries. In: J.G. Beaumont (Ed.), *Divided visual field studies of cerebral organization.* London: Academic Press.

Cranney, J., & Ashton, R. (1980). Witelson's dichhaptic task as a mesure of hemispheric asymmetry in deaf and hearing populations. *Neuropsychologia, 18,* 95-98.

Dailly, R., & Moscato, M. (1984). *Latéralisation et latéralité chez l'enfant.* Bruxelles: Pierre Mardaga.

Davis, A.E., & Wada, J.A. (1977). Hemispheric asymmetries in human infants: Spectral analysis of flash and clicked evoked potentials. *Brain and Language, 4,* 23-31.

Dawson, G.L. (1981). Sex differences in dichhaptic processing. *Perceptual and Motor Skills, 53,* 935-944.

Day, P.S., & Ulatowska, A.K. (1980). Perceptual, cognitive and linguistic development after early hemispherectomy: Two case studies. *Brain and Language, 7,* 17-33.

De Renzi, E. (1982). *Disorders of space exploration and cognition.* New York: John Wiley & Sons.

Denes, G., & Spinaci, M.P. (1981). Influence of association value in recognition of random shapes under dichhaptic presentation. *Cortex, 17,* 597-602.

Dennis, M., & Whitaker, H.A. (1976). Language acquisition following hemidecortication: Linguistic superiority of the left over the right hemisphere. *Brain and Language, 3,* 404-433.

Desimone, R., Albright, T.D., Gross, C.G., & Bruce, C.J. (1984). Stimulus selective properties of inferior temporal neurons in the macaque. *Journal of Neuroscience, 4,* 2051-2062.

Eidelberg, D., & Galaburda, A.M. (1984). Inferior parietal lobule: Divergent architectonic asymmetries in the human brain. *Archives of Neurology, 41,* 843-852.

Etaugh, C., & Levy, R.B. (1981). Hemispheric specialization for tactile-spatial processing in preschool children. *Perceptual and Motor Skills, 53,* 621-622.

Fagan, J.F. (1979). The origins of facial pattern recognition. In: M.H. Bornstein & W. Kessen (Eds.), *Psychological development from infancy.* Hillsdale, NJ: Erlbaum.

Fairweather, H. (1982). Sex differences. In: J.G. Beaumont (Ed.), *Divided visual field studies of cerebral organization.* London: Academic Press.

Fennell, E.B., Satz, P., & Morris, R. (1983). The development of handedness and dichotic ear listening asymmetries in relation to school achievement: A longitudinal study. *Journal of Experimental Child Psychology, 35,* 248-262.

Gardiner, M.F., & Walter, D.O. (1977). Evidence of hemispheric specialization from infant EEG. In: S. Harnad, R.W. Doty, L. Goldstein, J. Jaynes & G. Krauthamer (Eds.), *Lateralization in the nervous system.* New York: Academic Press.

Geffen, G. (1976). Development of hemispheric specialization for speech perception. *Cortex, 12,* 337-346.

Geffen, G. (1978). The development of the right ear advantage in dichotic listening with focused attention. *Cortex, 14,* 169-177.

Geffen, G., & Sexton, M.A. (1978). The development of auditory strategies of attention. *Developmental Psychology, 14,* 11-17.

Geffen, G., & Wale, J. (1979). The development of selective listening and hemispheric asymmetry. *Developmental Psychology, 15,* 138-146.

Geschwind, N., & Levitsky, W. (1968). Human brain: Left-right asymmetries in temporal speech region. *Science, 161,* 186-187.

Geschwind, N., & Galaburda, A.M. (1985). Cerebral lateralization: Biological mechanisms, associations, and pathology: I. A hypothesis and a program for research. *Archives of Neurology, 42,* 428-459.

Geschwind, N., & Galaburda, A.M. (1987). *Cerebral lateralization.* Cambridge, Ma: MIT Press.

Gesell, A. (1938). The tonic neck reflex in the human infant. *Journal of Pediatrics, 13,* 455-464.

Gibson, C., & Bryden, M.P. (1983). Dichhaptic recognition of shapes and letters in children. *Canadian Journal of Psychology, 37,* 132-143.

Gibson, C., & Bryden, M.P. (1984). Cerebral laterality in deaf and hearing children. *Brain and Language, 23,* 1-12.

Gibson, A.R., Dimond, S.J., & Gazzaniga, M.S. (1972). Left field superiority for word matching. *Neuropsychologia, 10,* 463-466.

Goldberg, E., & Costa, L.D. (1981). Hemispheric differences in the acquisition and use of descriptive systems. *Brain and Language, 14,* 144-173.

Goren, C.G., Sarty, M., & Wu, P.Y.K. (1975). Visual following and pattern discrimination of face-like stimuli by newborn infants. *Pediatrics, 56,* 544-549.

Grant, D.W. (1980). Visual asymmetry on a color-naming task: A developmental perspective. *Perceptual and Motor Skills, 50,* 475-480.

Grant, D.W. (1981). Visual asymmetry on a color naming task: A longitudinal study with primary school children. *Child Development, 52,* 370-372.

Habib, M., & Galaburda, A.M. (1986). Déterminants biologiques de la dominance cérébrale. *Revue Neurologique, 142,* 869-894.

Harris, L.J. (1978). Sex differences in spatial ability: Possible environmental, genetic and neurological factors. In: M. Kinsbourne (Ed.), *Asymmetrical function of the brain*. Cambridge: Cambridge University Press.

Harris, L.J., & Fitzgerald, H.E. (1983). Postural orientation in human infants: Changes from birth to three months. In: G. Young, C. Corter, S.J. Segalowitz, & S. Trehub (Eds.), *Manual specialization and the developing brain*. New York: Academic Press.

Hellige, J.B. (1983). *Cerebral hemisphere asymmetry*. New York: Praeger Publishers.

Hicks, R.E. (1975). Intrahemispheric response competition between vocal and unimanual performance in normal adult human males. *Journal of Comparative and Physiological Psychology, 89*, 50-60.

Hiscock, M. (1982). Verbal-manual timesharing in children as a function of task priority. *Brain and Cognition, 1*, 119-130.

Hiscock, M., & Kinsbourne, M. (1978). Ontogeny of cerebral dominance: Evidence from time-sharing asymmetry in children. *Developmental Psychology, 14*, 321-329.

Hiscock, M., & Kinsbourne, M. (1980). Asymmetry of verbal-manual time sharing in children: A follow-up study. *Neuropsychologia, 18*, 151-162.

Hiscock, M., Kinsbourne, M., Samuels, M., & Krause, A.E. (1985). Effects of speaking upon the rate and variability of concurrent finger tapping in children. *Journal of Experimental Psychology, 40*, 486-500.

Hynd, G.W., & Obrzut, J.E. (1981). *Neuropsychological assessment and the school-age child*. New York: Grune & Stratton.

Kershner, J.R., & King, A.J. (1974). Laterality of cognitive functions in achieving hemiplegic children. *Perceptual and Motor Skills, 39*, 1283-1289.

Kimura, D. (1961). Cerebral dominance and the perception of verbal stimuli. *Canadian Journal of Psychology, 15*, 166-171.

Kinsbourne, M. (1975). The mechanism of hemispheric control of the lateral gradient of attention. In: P.M.A. Rabbit & S. Dornic (Eds.), *Attention and performance V*. London: Academic Press.

Kinsbourne, M. (1976). The ontogeny of cerebral dominance. In: R.W. Rieber (Ed.), *The neuropsychology of language*. New York: Plenum Press.

Kinsbourne, M. (1978). *Asymmetrical function of the brain*. Cambridge: Cambridge University Press.

Kinsbourne, M., & Cook, J. (1971). Generalized and lateralized effects of concurrent verbalization on a unimanual skill. *Quarterly Journal of Experimental Psychology, 23*, 341-345.

Kinsbourne, M., & Hiscock, M. (1977). Does cerebral dominance develop ? In: S. Segalowitz & F. Gruber (Eds.), *Language development and neurological theory*. London: Academic Press.

Kinsbourne, M., & Hiscock, M. (1983). The normal and deviant development of functional lateralization of the brain. In: P. Mussen (Ed.), *Handbook of child psychology, infancy and developmental psychobiology*. New York: John Wiley & Sons.

Koenig, O. (1986). Approche neuropsychologique du développement cognitif. Unpublished doctoral dissertation, University of Geneva.

Koenig, O. (1987). Dichhaptic recognition of textures in normal adults. *Neuropsychologia, 25*, 295-298.

Koenig, O. (in press). Hemispheric asymmetry in the analysis of

Stroop stimuli: A developmental approach. *Developmental Neuropsychology*.

Koenig, O., & Hauert, C.A. (1986). Construction de l'objet chez l'enfant de 5 à 9 ans: Approche dichhaptique. *Cahiers de Psychologie Cognitive, 6*, 21-39.

Koenig, O., Gabrieli, J.D.E., & Kosslyn, S.M. (1988). Hemispheric specialization for the processing of metric relations: The effect of practice. Harvard University manuscript.

Kohn, B., & Dennis, M. (1974). Selective impairments of visuo-spatial abilities in infantile hemiplegics after right cerebral hemidecortication. *Neuropsychologia, 12*, 505-512.

Kosslyn, S.M. (1987). Seeing and imagining in the cerebral hemispheres. *Psychological Review, 94*, 148-175.

Kosslyn, S.M. (1988). Aspects of a cognitive neuroscience of mental imagery. *Science, 240*, 1621-1626.

Kosslyn, S.M., Sokolov, M.A., & Chen, J.C. (in press). The lateralization of Brian: A computational theory and model of visual hemispheric specialization. In: D. Klahr & K. Kotovsky (Eds.), *Complex information processing comes of age*. Hillsdale, NJ: Erlbaum.

Kosslyn, S.M., Feldman, J.R., Maljkovic, V., & Hamilton, S. (1988). Image generation in the left and right cerebral hemispheres: Evidence for two types of visual mental images. Harvard University manuscript.

Kosslyn, S.M., Koenig, O., Barrett, A., Backer Cave, C., Tang, J., & Gabrieli, J.D.E. (in press). Evidence for two types of spatial representations: Hemispheric specialization for categorical and coordinate relations. *Journal of Experimental Psychology: Human Perception and Performance*.

Labreche, T.M., Manning, A.A., Goble, W., & Markman, R. (1977). Hemispheric specialization for linguistic and nonlinguistic tactual perception in a congenitally deaf population. *Cortex, 13*, 184-194.

Lenneberg, E.H. (1967). *Biological foundations of language*. New York: Wiley.

Lomas, J., & Kimura, D. (1976). Intrahemispheric interaction between speaking and sequential manual activity. *Neuropsychologia, 14*, 23-33.

Marcotte, A.C., & LaBarba, R.C. (1985). Cerebral lateralization for speech in deaf and normal children. *Brain and Language, 26*, 244-258.

McClelland, J.L., & Rumelhart, D.E. (1981). An interactive activation model of context effects in letter perception: Part 1. An account of basic findings. *Psychological Review, 88*, 375-407.

Michel, G. (1981). Right-handedness: A consequence of infant supine head-orientation preference ? *Science, 212*, 685-697.

Mishkin, M., & Appenzeller, T. (1987). The anatomy of memory. *Scientific American, 256*, 80-89.

Mishkin, M., Ungerleider, L.G., & Macko, K.A. (1983). Object vision and spatial vision: Two cortical pathways. *Trends in Neurosciences, 6*, 414-417.

Molfese, D.L. (1977). Infant cerebral asymmetry. In: S. Segalowitz & F. Gruber (Eds.), *Language development and neurological theory*. London: Academic Press.

Molfese, D.L., & Molfese, V.J. (1979). Hemisphere and stimulus differences as reflected in the cortical response of newborn

infants to speech stimuli. *Developmental Psychology*, *15*, 505-511.
Molfese, D.L., & Molfese, V.J. (1980). Cortical response of preterm
infants to phonetic and nonphonetic speech stimuli. *Developmental
Psychology*, *16*, 574-581.
Moscovitch, M. (1977). The development of lateralization of
language functions and its relations to cognitive and linguistic
development. A review and some theoretical speculations. In:
S. Segalowitz & F. Gruber, (Eds.), *Language development and
neurological theory*. London: Academic Press.
Obrzut, J.E., Boliek, C.A., & Obrzut, A. (1986). The effect of
stimulus type and directed attention on dichotic listening with
children. *Journal of Experimental Child Psychology*, *41*, 198-209.
Oldfield, R.C. (1971). The assessment and analysis of handedness:
The Edinburgh inventory. *Neuropsychologia*, *9*, 97-113.
Peters, M., & Petrie, B.F. (1979). Functional asymmetries in the
stepping reflex of human neonates. *Canadian Journal of
Psychology*, *33*, 198-200.
Petrie, B.F., & Peters, M. (1980). Handedness: Left-right
differences in intensity of grasp response and duration of rattle
holding in infants. *Infant Behavior and Development*, *3*, 215-223.
Piaget, J., & Inhelder, B. (1948). *La représentation de l'espace
chez l'enfant*. Paris: Les Presses Universitaires de France.
Piazza, D.M. (1977). Cerebral lateralization in young children as
measured by dichotic listening and finger tapping tasks.
Neuropsychologia, *15*, 417-425.
Porac, C., & Coren, S. (1981). *Lateral preferences and human
behavior*. New York: Springer-Verlag.
Ramsay, D.S. (1979). Manual preference for tapping in infants.
Developmental Psychology, *15*, 437-442.
Ramsay, D.S. (1980). Onset of unimanual handedness in infants.
Infant Behavior and Development, *3*, 377-385.
Rudel, R.G., Teuber, H.L., & Twitchell, T.E. (1974). Levels of
impairment of sensori-motor functions in children with early
brain damage. *Neuropsychologia*, *12*, 95-108.
Satz, P., & Bullard-Bates, C. (1981). Acquired aphasia in children.
In: M. Sarno (Ed.), *Acquired aphasia*. New York: Academic Press.
Saxby, L., & Bryden, M.P. (1984). Left-ear superiority in children
for processing auditory emotional material. *Developmental
Psychology*, *20*, 72-80.
Siqueland, E.R., & Lipsitt, L.P. (1966). Conditioned head turning
in human newborns. *Journal of Experimental Child Psychology*, *4*,
356-357.
Springer, S.P., & Deutsch, G. (1985). *Left brain, right brain*. New
York: Freeman & Company.
St. James-Robert, I. (1981). A re-interpretation of hemispherectomy
data without functional plasticity of the brain. *Brain and
Language*, *13*, 31- 53.
Teszner, D., Tzavaras, A., Gruner, J., & Hécaen, H. (1972).
L'asymétrie droite-gauche du planum temporal, à propos de
l'étude anatomique de 100 cerveaux. *Revue Neurologique*, *126*,
444-449.
Turkewitz, G. (1977). The development of lateral differences in the
human infant. In: S. Harnad, R.W. Doty, L. Goldstein, J. Jaynes
& G. Krauthamer (Eds.), *Lateralization in the nervous system*. New
York: Academic Press.
Turkewitz, G. (1980). Mechanisms of a neonatal rightward turning
bias: A reply to Liederman and Kinsbourne. *Infant Behavior and*

Development, 3, 239-244.
Turner, S., & Miller, L.K. (1975). Some boundary conditions for laterality effects in children. *Developmental Psychology, 11,* 342-252.
Ungerleider, L.G., & Mishkin, M. (1982). Two cortical visual systems. In: D.J. Ingle, M.A. Goodale & R.J.W. Mansfield (Eds.), *Analysis of visual behavior.* Cambridge, Ma: MIT Press.
Van Blerkom, M.L. (1985). Developmental trends in dichhaptic lateralization. *Perceptual and Motor Skills, 60,* 951-959.
Van Essen, D. (1985). Functional organization of primate visual cortex. In: A. Peters & E.G. Jones (Eds.), *Cerebral cortex (Vol. 3).* New York: Plenum Press.
Van Hout, A., & Seron, X. (1983). *L'aphasie de l'enfant.* Bruxelles: Pierre Mardaga.
Vargha-Khadem, F. (1982). Hemispheric specialization for the processing of tactual stimuli in congenitally deaf and hearing children. *Cortex, 18,* 277-286.
Wada, J., Clark, R., & Hamm, A. (1975). Cerebral hemisphere asymmetry in humans. *Archives of Neurology, 32,* 239-246.
Walch, J.-P., & Blanc-Garin, J. (1987). Tactual laterality effects and the processing of spatial characteristics: Dichhaptic exploration of forms by first and second grade children. *Cortex,* 23, 189-205.
White, M.J. (1969). Laterality differences in perception: A review. *Psychological Bulletin, 72,* 387-405.
Witelson, S. (1974). Hemispheric specialization for linguistic and nonlinguistic tactual perception using a dichotomous stimulation technique. *Cortex, 10,* 3-17.
Witelson, S. (1976). Sex and the single hemisphere: Specialization of the right hemisphere for spatial processing. *Science, 193,* 425-426.
Witelson, S. (1977). Early hemispheric specialization and interhemispheric plasticity: An empirical and theorical review. In: S. Segalowitz & F. Gruber (Eds.), *Language development and neurological theory.* London: Academic Press.
Witelson, S. (1980). Neuroanatomical asymmetry in left handers: A review and implications for functional asymmetry. In: J. Herron (Ed.), *The neuropsychology of left handers.* London: Academic Press.
Witelson, S. (1983). Bumps on the brain: Right-left anatomic asymmetry as a key to functional lateralization. In: S.J. Segalowitz (Ed.), *Language functions and brain organization.* London: Academic Press.
Witelson, S. (1985). On hemisphere specialization and cerebral plasticity from birth: Mark II. In: C.T. Best (Ed.), *Hemisphere function and collaboration in the child.* New York: Academic Press.
Witelson, S., & Pallie, W. (1973). Left hemisphere specialization for language in the newborn: Neuroanatomical evidence of asymmetry. *Brain, 96,* 641-646.
Woods, B.T., & Teuber, H.L. (1978). Changing patterns of childhood aphasia. *Annals of Neurology, 3,* 273-280.
Young, A.W. (1982). Asymmetry of cerebral hemispheric function during development. In: J.W.T. Dickerson & H. McGurk (Eds.), *Brain and behavioural development.* London: Surrey University Press.
Younger, B.A., & Cohen, L.B. (1985). How infants form categories.

In: G. Bower (Ed)., *The psychology of learning and motivation: Advances in research and theory*. New York: Academic Press.

Zaidel, E. (1983). Disconnection syndrome as a model for laterality effects in the normal brain. In: J.B. Hellige (Ed.), *Cerebral hemisphere asymmetry*. New York: Prager Publishers.

DEVELOPMENTAL PSYCHOLOGY
Cognitive, Perceptuo-Motor, and Neuropsychological Perspectives
C-A. Hauert (Editor)
Elsevier Science Publishers B.V. (North-Holland) 1990

389

COGNITIVE DEVELOPMENT: ENRICHMENT OR IMPOVERISHMENT ?
HOW TO CONCILIATE PSYCHOLOGICAL AND NEUROBIOLOGICAL
MODELS OF DEVELOPMENT

Pierre MOUNOUD
Faculty of Psychology and Educational Sciences
University of Geneva, Switzerland

*This chapter compares two conceptions of cognitive
development. The psychological model called "enrichment"
considers development as a shift from elementary to complex behaviors by means of mechanisms of coordination.
The neurobiological model called "impoverishment" describes the opposite shift by means of selective mechanisms
for adaptation. An interpretation based on a combination
of these two models is suggested. From Edelman's neurobiological theory and Harnad's psychological one, the
development of categorization skills is presented as the
"groundwork of cognition." Finally, it is argued that the
development of categories is accompanied by qualitative
shifts usually ignored in contemporary research.*

1. INTRODUCTION

The topic of this book is *cognitive development* but the chapters
refer not so much to different "domains" but to different approaches
or methods. However, this point of view will not be unanimously
accepted by all the authors of this book nor by all the readers.

Perhaps it would be more judicious to speak of the development of
'cognitive functions' rather than to speak of 'cognitive development'. Cognitive functions are often described in terms of "components," "modules," "subsystems," "subprocessors," etc. These different terms imply the existance of one complex cognitive system,
with a hierarchical functional organization (cf. O'Leary). Recent
theories often suggest that the various components function separately, but this does not appear to be the case.

2. REFLEXIONS ON COGNITIVE DEVELOPMENT AND ITS STUDY

Concerning frames of reference

From this general starting point, I received the overall impression
that most of the authors of the six chapters in this part of the
book have been working in some conceptual and theoretical isolation.
Except for a few references to Atkinson and Shiffrin (1968) and
Anderson (1983), it is difficult to understand the lack of reference

to the work of Tulving (1972) on episodic and semantic memory,
Baddeley (1976) on working memory, Craik and Lockhart (1972) and
Snodgrass (1980) on levels of information processing, Fodor (1983)
on modularity, and McClelland and Rumelhart (1986) on parallel/
distributed processing. These different theories enable one to distinguish types of analysis and integration (e.g. physical and semantic aspects), simple vs complex levels of representation (for example of semantic attributes or chunks), and different coding systems
(simple, double, triple), and processing levels (stock of prototypic
images and propositional or semantic stock). These notions or
others seem necessary for understanding the complex and often para-
doxical problems of development.

The same applies to Piaget's theory which is often presented in an
overly simplified manner. Often the distinction between figurative
and operative systems is not made, nor are the roles attributed to
them by Piaget discussed. Furthermore, no reference is made to the
logical "functions" which define preoperative reasoning, according
to Piaget. How can one speak of initial classifications without
considering the difficulties 4- to 5-year-old children have disso-
ciating infralogical and logico-mathematical aspects, or without
considering current hypotheses on the elaboration of representations ?

Also, regarding classifications or categorizations, it is difficult
to understand a lack of reference to the work of Kemler (1983) on
problems small children have isolating pertinent dimensions of a
situation, Rosch and Mervis (1975) on prototype structure, Smith,
Shoben and Rips (1974) on semantic memory in categorization activities, and Smith and Medin (1981) on categories and concepts.

Concerning "domains" and cognitive processes

A brief review of the problem of "domains" may be helpful at this
point. The existence of fields of knowledge cannot be doubted.
Following the tradition of Kant, Piaget analysed children's behaviours according to "categories" of knowledge. The fact that a
child's knowledge does not develop at the same rate in the different
domains, in my opinion, does not present any major theoretical problem, although others may disagree (see e.g. Brainerd, 1978, and
compare Levin, 1985). The fundamental problem is to know whether
general mechanisms determine the process of development in the different domains, or whether specific mechanims should be postulated
for each domain and temporal sequence.

For example, in each domain, the objects that define it require an
identification or categorization by the subject. Must we imagine
processes of categorization specific to each domain --a hypothesis
which has long been proposed for speech ("the speech-is-special
hypothesis")-- or is it possible that general processes of categorization (perceptive, conceptual) apply to all domains ? My hypotheses clearly favor general processes.

A particular case illustrates this well. In her chapter on
perceptuo-motor development in children, Laszlo said she tried to
define specific experimental tasks that avoid, as much as possible,
other "domains" like cognitive capacities. However, her tasks are

described as calling for motor planning activities and spatial and
temporal motor programming. It would be difficult to consider these
activities something other than cognitive, with planning usually
regarded as a high level cognitive mechanism.

Let us examine in more detail one of these tasks involving kinaesthetic perception and memory. Blindfolded subjects are asked to
trace curved nonsense patterns engraved in a support. Then they
must either recognize the pattern among drawings, or reproduce it.
They are described by Laszlo as having to "structure the sequentially received information into a spatially coherent pattern," to
"extract sufficient information for accurate coding of the pattern,"
to "build a percept," to "form an image based on the sequentially
received input," and to "store the kinaesthetic information." By
all means, these processes seems to be cognitive. Why should this
situation, which consists of identifying or categorizing a pattern,
be different from other experimental situations of discrimination or
categorization ? While the task does involve specific receptors and
effectors, I do not think that in psychology the difference in domains can be based on perceptual modalities. Psychology seems more
concerned with the functional aspects of behavior than with particular sensori-motor modalities. Therefore, I suggest the chapters
of this book differ more with respect to methods than domains.

Concerning identification and categorization

The fundamental problem of cognitive development is to understand
how and under what circumstances children are able to identify,
categorize, and conceptualize the objects or situations they confront. This supposes, of course, the capacity to detect invariance.
However, most research examines cognitive development as if subjects
have no problems identifying or categorizing objects and situations.
It looks as if a subject's environment is composed of defined objects which can be characterized by a certain number of variables.
However, the experimenter generally does part of the work himself by
organizing the components of the situation for the subject when he
selects the pertinent "objects," "dimensions," and "variables."

However, the subject's point of view is not always that of the expe-
rimentalist ! If it is now clearly established that babies are born
with identification and categorization capacities (the result of
phylogenesis and embryogenesis), it must also be acknowledged that
in the course of development, children build new capacities or new
procedures to identify and categorize situations. In fact, the same
applies to adults.

Concerning the perspective of information processing

If the categories by which we perceive the world are constantly modified, it may be impossible to study development from the perspective of information processing. But this was what most developmental psychologists did during the last twenty years.

What it means to place oneself in this perspective should be specified. Crépault and Nguyen-Xuan, in their chapter, write that from
the perspective of information processing, the human subject is considered as "a system manipulating symbols." However, they do not

specify what the symbols are, and do not discuss symbols again in
the rest of their text. Instead, they discuss "criteria," "modalities," logical and empirical "inference rules," "objects," "variables," "relations" and "inference schemes." Case and Griffin speak
of "components" and "variables," "concepts" and "relations between
concepts." Laszlo uses the terms "sensorial information," "perceptions," "images" and "coding." Koenig focused on the cerebral functions he calls "components," and speaks of "categorical or metric
properties and relations," of "invariant properties," and of "cognitive strategies." Finally, Zanone deals with "information," "co-
dings" of different nature and levels, and "rules" and their "ab-
stractions."

Without trying to be exhaustive or systematic, this enumeration is
interesting because it raises the following question. Is it possible to speak of information, objects, components, variables or properties as if they were realities having an equivalent status for
all children at different ages, and without distinguishing levels of
representation or abstraction ? Also, is it possible to specify how
children are able to identify these "realities" ?

Let us examine the problem more closely with an example: The famous
balance experiment (the "informational" version of the Piagetian
situation) called the "balance beam task." This has been studied in
particular by Case and also by other researchers. Case and Griffin
analyze the situation in terms of variables (weight, length, number), these variables being described as either "polar" for 5-year-
old children (relational stage), or "quantifiable" for 7-year-olds
(dimensional stage). Whatever the age of the children (from 4 to 10
years), these authors always consider the same reality, the same
dimensions, the same splitting or segmentation. However, in other
studies together with Hayward, Case (1987) showed how a baby in the
sensori-motor stage becomes progressively able to identify the different dimensions of the balance situation. But it looks as if this
problem of object identification was specific to the sensori-motor
stage, and that no similar problems arise later on. This is similar
to Spelke's (1988) assertation that after the emergence of what she
calls the "concept of object" in 2- to 3-month-old babies, there is
no further development of object concepts at different levels of
representation.

In fact, these "variables" or "objects" which they describe do not
have the same status for a child of 5 or 7 years, and although they
produce apparently equivalent judgements (concerning weight or
length), these statements do not have the same status or the same
significance, and do not correspond to the same "concept" of objects
(cf. particularly Carey, 1978; Keil and Carroll, 1980; Mounoud,
1986b). The opposition between "polar" and "quantifiable" variables, introduced by Case and Griffin, also raises problems. It can
be shown that before the age of 7, a child is able to analyze objects by means of quantifiable dimensions or variables.

A newborn, for example, manifests behaviors that show his/her capacity to process certain variables quantitatively, because of an organization I call "sensorial." Thus, the frequency of sucking in
newborns is modulated in accordance with the different variables
that characterize liquids (taste, viscosity, etc.) (Kobre and

Lipsitt, 1972). Furthermore, because of an organization described as "perceptual" (Mounoud, 1986b), 3 1/2 to 4 year-old children are able to fit objects into others taking into account size as a quantified variable (Greenfield, Nelson and Saltzman, 1972). This quantification might be described as intensive and not extensive, thus using a distinction introduced by Inhelder and Piaget (1959). Between 7 and 9 years, children will again succeed in quantifying certain variables because of an organization called "conceptual."

In this discussion, I hope to have shown the necessity of studying how, at different stages of development, children are able to isolate the "objects" which define a given situation and abstract the pertinent variables (characteristics, dimensions, properties). A child, like an adult, does not operate directly on the objects or variables, but on representations. These latter remarks lead to the introduction of another problem I call "levels of maturity."

Concerning the concept of "maturity"

It clearly results from the actual level of knowledge on development and, in particular, from the chapters of this book, that a satisfactory discussion of the problem of "maturity," of both neural structures and behaviors, is not yet possible. The preceeding chapters contain many examples of this problem, either regarding the maturity of callosal or frontal neural structures, where variations of several years exist relative to the ages when these structures are supposed to become mature (cf. O'Leary; and Young), or regarding the maturity of a given behavior such as the apparition of the capacity to quantify variables which we have just mentioned.

One way to resolve this problem is to say that it stems from insufficiently defining the structures involved or the situations or tasks confronting the subjects. This is often true. Therefore, almost all the chapters give special attention to defining experimental situations. However, the problem remains. The main focus of developmental research has been determining the ages at which given behaviors appear or given structures begin functioning. This led to polar or global reasoning such as "a structure or a behavior is or is not mature," instead of considering levels of maturity as a relative concept. There are only relative states of maturity (Mounoud, 1971). A developing system attains only relative equilibrium and is always confronted with new changes or new problems. This results from either new capacities of the organism, or from changes in the external world. Thus, the organism (or the species) is faced with changes for which it cannot entirely compensate by means of its available structures and therefore must create new ones. There is no single solution or definitive comprehension of a given phenomena and consequently, every theory is relative to the issue raised or to the disturbance experienced. This meets Harnad's formulation (1987): "All categories and the features on which they are based will always remain provisional and approximate."

An example of the confusion caused by polar reasoning is the problem of "manual lateralization" in children from birth to 10 years. Gottfried and Bathurst (1983) concluded that a clear manual preference was present by 18 months, if not sooner. Bates, O'Connel, Vaid, Sledge and Oakes (1986) reported that a right preference was

clearly present by 13 months. However, McManus, Sik, Cole, Mellon,
Wong and Kloss (1988) concluded that handedness was poorly defined
before 2 years, and Archer, Campbell and Segalowitz (1988) reported
that at 24 months, 41% of the boys in their study did not have a
clear hand preference. However, it may be necessary to distinguish
degrees of lateralization (cf. McManus et al., 1988), or different
forms or types of manual lateralization. Furthermore, these may
appear and disappear during the course of development due to both
relative levels of maturity of certain neural structures, and the
types of situations children confront. The problem of manual lateralization might best be considered in a wider frame which includes
various forms of bimanual cooperation, and of which lateralization
is just one particular case (cf. Corbetta, 1989; Corbetta and
Mounoud, in press; Fagard, in press).

The same can be said of hemispheric specialization where two divergent positions are found. Koenig, in this volume, suggests that
cognitive functions are localized and lateralized from birth, with
further development resulting from cognitive strategies which lead
to the hierarchic and temporal organization of these functions. On
the other hand, Molfese and Betz (V. Molfese and Betz, 1987; D.
Molfese and Betz, in press), suggest that hemispheric specialization
is progressive.

Concerning the concept of development

The problem of maturity is related to general theories of development, where two models coexist. One will be called *development-
enrichment* and the other *development-impoverishment*.

The concept of *impoverishment* is predominant in developmental neurobiology. Several authors in this volume refer to it (O'Leary and
Young, in particular), and, when discussing the development of the
nervous system, refer to the elimination, reduction, or suppression
of cells or connections. In other words, they are referring to
decline and regression, if not decrease.

The concept of *enrichment*, which is predominant in psychology,
describes development in terms of increase, adjunction, addition,
and the appearance of new capacities and structures. In other
words, they discuss progression and growth.

Psychologists resist defining development as an impoverishment.
However, some do discuss developmental data which reveals regressions. For example, Zanone's chapter describes some examples of
momentary declines in performance. Developmental regressions are
also discussed by Bever (1982) and Strauss (1982).

It is interesting to note that the discovery of "regressive" phenomena in development was made independently by psychologists and
biologists in the early 1970s. However, among psychologists, the
coexistence of these two very divergent concepts of development is
surprising. Biological models might enable psychologists to take
the phenomena of impoverishment into more general consideration.

Therefore, an important part of this chapter will be the presentation of a biological model of development which deals particularly

with an explanation of categorization procedures.

Let us again briefly consider cognitive development in terms of categorization. The existance of perceptual or conceptual categories
implies the *elimination* of irrelevant variability in the structure
or configuration of representations. Similarly, the existence of a
category of movement would mean eliminating or uncoupling irrelevant
variability in a coordinated structure. What is invariant or relevant in relation to a given problem is retained, to sort, filter or
decrease the structure of inputs or outputs. This way of thinking,
where certain characteristics are discarded in favour of others, has
also been called idealization or abstraction (Keil, 1987). This
analysis of the categorization process should help us to conceptualize development as requiring selective mechanisms.

It now seems possible to reconcile the apparent antagonism between
the terms "enrichment" and "impoverishment." Both should be thought
of as relative. Therefore, the selective impoverishment, of which
biologists speak, is only a relative impoverishment if it leads to a
better adaptation to the environment. The same applies to "regressions" shown by psychologists which should be described as apparent
regressions.

It is also possible to view development in a context I call "loss
and gain" (Mounoud, 1988). The gains that are acquired with the
ability to categorize, plan, and control time and space, but are
relative to limited aspects of the environment, compensate for losses in other aspects such as elimination, discard, selection, and
sorting certain dimensions of the environment or certain forms of
behavior. An example is the loss at one year of the ability to
discriminate between contrasting phonemes that do not exist in the
baby's native language (Werker and Tees, 1983).

But there seems to be another way to reconcile these two antagonis-
tic concepts. Could we not imagine development as alternating stages or periods which could even overlap ?
Some stages could be mainly characterized by the selection of behaviors most likely to achieve the best adaptation to situations and
problems confronting the subject. This corresponds to what Paillard
(1988) calls "the idea of a simple selection" and is related to "the
debates which, at present, still agitate the psychology of development." But let me add that Paillard seems still concerned with
theories creating order out of disorder.
Other stages could be characterized by the appearance of variation
or richness of behavior resulting either from internal transformations, confronting new problem-situations, or both, with a "proliferation" of new behaviors.

In this book, we were asked to take a position regarding to the
Piagetian heritage. The concepts and interpretations of cognitive
development proposed by Piaget focused on explaning novelty (new
schemes, new structures). His concept of development is the enrichment type, although it was inspired by the theories of evolution.

Concerning some interpretations

One of the dominant themes in developmental psychology belongs to
the "enrichment" orientation and is based on the mechanisms of *coordination* and the *establisment of relationships*, such as motor and
sensori-motor coordinations, and the establishment of sensory or
perceptual relations, or more generally, coordination or composition
of elementary structures. Thus, the construction of new behaviors
has often been explained exclusively by the coordination of elementary actions or intramodal or unimodal perceptions. Case and
Griffin (this volume) often describe development in terms of coordination. This is supposed to help us understand how children
establish or build intermodal (or crossmodal) correspondances from
elementary actions or structures. For twenty years, I have strongly
opposed this explanation, particularly in the context of Piagetian
theory. Not only is it insufficient and incomplete, it neglects
another fundamental mechanism: *Dissociation* or *decomposition*.
Development does not proceed from simple to complex, from elementary to composed. If there were no initial motor, perceptual, and
intersensori-motor coordinations (Mounoud and Vinter, 1981), the
organism would never accomplish these general coordinations because
of the extreme complexity of the system (Mounoud, 1971, 1976, 1979).
I hypothesized that there must be initial coordinations or complex
behavior, and that the first fundamental mechanism of successive
(re)construction (development) was the dissociation or decomposition
of these coordinated structures, not the coordination of isolated
and disjointed structures (Mounoud, 1971).

This dissociation or decomposition into elements or components is a
necessary condition before the re-elaboration at another level of
representation by abstraction or transposition. This hypothesis was
later supported by experimental results, including the phenomenon of
precocious infant imitation (Maratos, 1973; Meltzoff, 1976;
Fontaine, 1987; Vinter, 1983. For a review, cf. Vinter, 1989).

A similar change in interpretation has taken place in theories of
motor control. Influenced by information processing theories and
classical neuro-physiological concepts, the development of movement
was thought to consist of coordinated or sequentially ordered elementary units such as muscle groups or articulations controlled by a
sensory system or subsystem. In fact, 15 years passed before
Bernstein's ideas (1967) radically changed this interpretation by
demonstrating that the basic units of movements are very complex.
These units were called synergies or coordinative structures by
Kugler, Kelso and Turvey (1982). However, the identification of
coordinative structures does not explain their development or the
learning of new behaviors. In this context also, the main mechanisms seem to be dissociation, decomposition, elimination, uncoupling and selection. While these dissociations can be momentary and
partial, they help explain the development of more complex coordinative structures.

Those accepting the existence of complex initial coordinations have
often been suspected of preformist thinking. However, even with a
rich, complex initial organization, important transformations still
characterize development. Initial intersensori-motor coordination
does not imply the absence of subsequent reconstruction. In fact,

it suggests a basis for rich exchanges with the environment.

The notion that development is exclusively a coordination of elementary units is partly due to traditional conceptions of the nervous system as having a serial functioning where neurons act as feature detectors and transmitters of information. However, in the last ten years, an important discovery was made in neurobiology: The parallel functioning of the nervous system (Edelman and Mountcastle, 1978). Here, the fundamental unit changes to neuronal groups or populations. Thus, according to Feldman and Ballard (1982, p.208 quoted by Reeke, Sporns and Edelman, 1988), "Neurons do not transmit large amounts of symbolic information. Instead, they compute by being appropriately connected." For some, these discoveries led to a rejection of information processing theories (Edelman, 1987). Convinced that these theories are important for developmental psychology, I shall present Edelman's (1987) in detail. His main objective was to explain the development of perceptual categorization and generalization, an important issue in cognitive development. It is also interesting to discuss a psychological theory of categorical development and so I will present Harnad's (1987) recent model.

3. DEVELOPMENT OF CATEGORIES

Development of categories from the neurobiological point of view

Edelman and colleagues (Edelman, 1978, 1981, 1987; Reeke et al., 1988; Edelman and Finkel, 1984; Edelman and Reeke, 1982; Reeke and Edelman, 1984) attempt to explain the ontogenesis of categorization and generalization from a neurobiological point of view. They do not accept that objects of the physical world are divided into categories or classes prior to development and learning. Their rejection of information processing theories was suggested by the nature of the organization of the nervous system itself. No longer are neuronal models based on the functioning of conventional computers. In particular, neurons are not seen as binary threshold units, whose interconnections result in symbolic logical operations. "Conclusive evidence that computation on a symbolic or subsymbolic level actually occurs inside the brain is lacking" (Reeke et al., 1988, p.21).

This view clearly differs from present models of connectionism and parallel/distributed processing (PDP), where neurons are usually binary threshold devices without internal dynamic. The wiring of the connections is supposed to be exact, the connectivities are often complete and learning algorithms can only succeed if the exact desired ouput vector of the system is known in advance and purposeful microscopic synaptic changes are made. These features do not correlate well with known neurobiological facts (Reeke et al., 1988, p.17-22). However, it is important to note that authors of PDP models do not focus on neural modelling, but rather on neurally inspired modelling of cognitive processing.

For Reeke et al., the brain has highly *variable* units and connections where "not only are neuronal connections geometrically imprecise, but their strength can vary with experience" (op.cit. p.15). There is no precise point to point wiring, but immense dendritic and axonal overlap. Although precise neural map boundaries can be defined,

there is immense variability in cortical mapping. Neural areas
dedicated to single sensory modalities are multiple, parallel, and
widely dispersed (Edelman, 1987, p.39). The units are defined as
collections of strongly interconnected neurons, called *neuronal
groups* (or populations). These neuronal groups are themselves
assembled in *primary* anatomical *repertoires* (higher order population) and *secondary* functional *repertoires*. The stimuli an organism receives from its environment or echoniche are described as *polymorphous sets* and are sampled by independent parallel channels.
Finally, the world of potential stimuli and the collections of neuronal groups are two initially *independant domains* of variation.

The theory of neuronal group selection (Edelman, 1987) defines principally two periods of selection. (1) A first period of *developmentaℓ*
selection leads to the construction of primary repertoires and (2) a
second period of *experimental* selection leads to the construction of
the secondary repertoires. Let us examine these two periods in more
detail.

(1) The *primary repertoires* are anatomically variable neuronal
groups of a given brain region serving a specific function. Anatomical connections composing the primary repertoires are the result
of a variety of selective mechano-chemical events regulated by cell
and substrate adhesion molecules (CAMs and SAMs). This selective
process is called the *regulator hypothesis*. This regulator process
produces a significant number of non-identical groups of cells
within a primary repertoire. Each of these cell groups can respond
more or less well to a particular input. The presence in each
repertoire (brain area) of different neural structures (groups) that
are functionally equivalent but non-isomorphic, is the consequence
of a process called *degeneracy*. Thus, the existence of various
degenerate networks of neuronal groups is the obligatory result of
epigenetic events that occur in developmental selection (mainly
embryogenetic). Although structures in a particular area of the
brain are similar among members of the same species, there is a
large degree of *individual* variation in shape, extent, and connectivity at the level of axonal and dentritic ramification. This
perhaps is one of the origins of interindividual differences.

(2) *Secondary repertoires* are functioning groups of cells which
develop during the period of experimental selection. This selection invokes independent pre- and post-synaptic rules (dual rules)
altering synaptic efficacy (variation in the strength of synaptic
connections) at short-term or long-term and produces a continuous
source of new variation in the system. Thus, the sampling of
stimuli by independent sensori-motor channels progressively selects
certain degenerate sets of cell groups that will form the secondary
repertoires. These temporally relate stimuli (according to
frequency and situation) with receptor sheet space so that specific
responses of certain groups of neurons are favored. In this way,
local maps are formed. These subserve different modalities, each
with the possibility of independent disjointed sampling in one
stimulus domain. When different stimuli simultaneously affect
different reciprocally connected local maps after motor activity,
because of the temporal correlation, *global maps* are created.

These temporal correlations are possible because of the presence of
phasic reentrant signals which are moved by the reciprocal (reentrant) connections between different local maps. These reciprocal
connections are realized, for example, by thalamo-cortical and
cortico-thalamic pathways, callosal connections, and various connections between primary and secondary sensory and motor areas.
This dynamic linkage among different systems of neuronal groups
belonging to separate repertoires but forming global maps, is a
mechanism for perceptual categorization and generalization.

Edelman specifies that reentrant connections within sensory systems
are not sufficient to insure the spatial and temporal continuity
required for perceptive categorization. It is also necessary to
include output to the motor system for two tasks. The first task is
to select appropriate inputs by altering the relationship between
sensory systems and the environment by spontaneous or learned movements. The second task is to verify by action the instantaneous and
dynamic responses and the enhanced connectivities that result from
the action of neuronal groups in both primary and secondary repertoires.

To illustrate this complex process, Edelman (1987) describes the
"classification couple." A classification couple is composed of
the following.

1) One set of sensory *feature detectors*, such as neurons in the
visual system that act as feature detectors. These features are
represented as local maps in a higher level brain structure which
contains repertoires (cf. under 3).

2) Another set of *feature correlators* which work simultaneously
with the detectors, either in a different modality or in a sensorimotor system that correlates connected features of stimulus category
or object by means of motion. Thus, other neurons, for example
those related to the tactile exploration of an object, act as feature correlators. These features are represented in local maps in
another area of the brain (cf. under 3).

3) *Independent repertoires* of degenerate groups to which these two
sets of detectors and correlators are separately connected (neuronal network and structures of the CNS connected with receptor structures) and which realize representations in the form of local maps.

4) *Reciprocal connections* which exist at the anatomic level and
connect the repertoires with a means of controlling or correlating
the direction and reentrant flow of signal traffic. These reentrant
connections insure that the patterns of neuronal groups responding
to unique features in one map can be associated with another map to
yield new invariant patterns.

If certain groups in a mapped network show simultaneous activity
with certain groups in another mapped network, *then* the possibility
of linking these independently activated groups arises by strengthe-
ning their mutual connectivity via synaptic alterations in reentrant
fibers. If these synaptic alterations are maintained, a *global map*,
is formed and will function to correlate or categorize simultaneously occurring features of an object. Generalization can occur by

combining local features or feature correlations that result from disjunctive sampling of signals from novel objects.

Edelman's model of neuronal group selection resembles Changeux's model of "selective stability" (Changeux, 1983; Changeux and Dauchin, 1976; Changeux, Heidmann and Patte, 1984). This latter model has been discussed elsewhere (Mounoud, 1986b). However, as Edelman points out, both Changeux and Young's model on memory (J.Z. Young, 1973, 1978) do not provide "a detailed consideration of relationships necessary and sufficient to yield categorization." (Edelman, 1987, p.321).

These neurobiological models have an important feature for developmental psychology. They discard what Edelman calls the paradigm of *instruction* and (re)introduce the paradigm of *selection*. These theories place the organism in an *adaptation* perspective. Developmental psychologists have tended to ignore this essential aspect of Piaget's theory, the notion that thought is the most specialized "organ" for *adaptation* to the environment. To appreciate the originality of Piaget's genetic psychology, "one has to refer to the great problems of evolution and the theories of transformism reevaluated at the beginning of the century in the light of new discoveries in heredity. Since then, interest in these problems has readily increased as a result of new concepts in population genetics and in cellular biology. The problem of evolution is to determine the basis of variation, whether at the level of the individual (ontogenetic) or at the level of the species (phylogenetic). It is necessary to define the roles of the organism and of the environment, that is, the roles of the subject and the object, when we consider phenomena such as *selection* and *adaptation*" (Mounoud, 1971).

As a result of neurobiological discoveries, this new concept of development is in opposition to prevailing ideas in developmental psychology. Edelman's and Changeux's work reveals an extraordinary richness and variety in the NS. They try to explain development mainly by selective mechanisms. Here again we find the concept of "impoverishment" towards a better adaptation.

Criticism of Edelman's theory

However, Edelman's ontogenetic theory does not take into account initial capacities for categorization and generalization. This is similar to Piaget not acknowledging the existence of initial general coordinations which determine the behavior of the newborn. Piaget described ontogenesis as beginning with heterogenous, disjunctive spaces corresponding to isolated elementary schemes. He also failed to acknowledge primitive forms of representations in newborns, as if the existence of these initial competencies would have simplified too much the explanation of behavioral ontogenesis. Why should a complex organism like the human being not be provided with categorization and generalization capacities at birth, resulting from evolutionary adaptation ? Such reasoning is in opposition to Edelman's theory. He writes in particular that, "It would be a mistake to indulge glib analogies between the theory of neural group selection and evolution" (Edelman, 1987, p.321). Nevertheless, as a result of research by Eimas (1982), Jusczyk (1981), and Kellman and

Spelke (1983), Edelman seems to acknowledge categorical perception in newborns. He concludes that the world may not be amorphous, but it does not come in fixed or predesignated categories. Referring to Marler (1982), he states that certain "natural categories" can be fixed during the evolution of a species in a relatively stable eco-niche. "It does not preclude the possibility that morphogenetic variants arising in ontogeny can be selected during evolution to yield certain built-in patterns and species-specific categoriza-tions" (Edelman, 1987, p.320).

This careful formulation seems rather ambiguous. Why should feature detectors and correlators be the only inherited structures in evolu-tion ? Why are global maps not inherited ? Either the model of neuronal group selection explains the development of categories from an initial state of no capacity for categorization, or else the organism is provided with this initial capacity. In the second case, the problem is different. It becomes necessary to explain new categorizations or re-categorizations while taking into account existing ones. Edelman chose extreme conditions which do not cor-respond well with the ontogenesis of human behavior. His theory is an interesting hypothesis from a phylogenetic point of view. How-ever, from the ontogenetic point of view, acknowledging initial categories may simplify, although not eliminate, the role of gestu-res and movement in his model.

As soon as the organism possesses the capacity for categorization, it is possible to say that sets of stimuli represent "information," as recognized by Edelman (op.cit. p.317). If we study the functio-ning of an organism already adapted to a given environment without considering the development of that adaptation, information proces-sing models seem adequate. A great deal of research on children and adults has been conducted with this perspective. Thus, there are many studies with babies between 2- and 3- months-old that do not deal with development and try exclusively to define a state of adap-tation. However, information processing models are inadequate to account for the processes of development and learning, for reasons mentioned in the first part of this chapter.

Thus, development is not a question of the presence or absence of categorization capacities. Instead, it can be defined as passing from one level of categorization to another. Consequently, we suggest considering the construction of categories as a reoccuring process. Edelman's theory, in fact, explains the continuous appea-rance of variation within the system.

Because Edelman does not recognize initial categorization capaci-ties, he treats stimuli from the environment as polymorphous sets. However, in my opinion, stimuli from the environment are only poly-morphous sets in relation to developing categorization capacities. With regard to existing categorization capacities, certain stimuli form organized information patterns. The initial categories are not necessarily fixed and they are only predesignated for somatic but not evolutionary time.

For Edelman, there are initially two independent domains of varia-tion: The world of potential stimuli and the collections of neuro-nal groups. Again, I partially disagree with this affirmation.

There is a relative independence concerning the categorization procedures in construction, but there is, of course, no independence as
to the initial categorization procedures, which --let us repeat--
change considerably the explanation of development.

To conclude, I will use Edelman's terminology to describe the features that I think characterize any developmental and learning process.

(1) Both stable repertoires of neuronal groups causally linked with
events, and variable repertoires of neuronal groups not linked causally with events. Later, these variable repertoires will be the
basis of the selection process.

(2) Opportunities for contact with the environment. Properties of
the environment will change because of both internal and external
variation and this allows the selection of favorable alternatives.
In development and learning, exchanges between the organism and its
surroundings should be considered as both strictly determined with
regard to certain subsystems (repertoires) and events, and as
partially determined with regard to others. These are the phases of
lability in the system (Mounoud, 1984, 1987b). Edelman adds a third
essential category (1987, p.9 and 17), "A means of differential reproduction or amplification with heredity of the selected variants
in a population." This seems to correspond to one of Piaget's
(1967) main biological theses, the neolamarkian notion of heredity
of aquired features, something for which he was strongly critized.

As you could realize before, I do not share Edelman's strict view
when he rejects any form of reasoning by analogy. From my point of
view, reasoning by analogy is one type of scientific reasoning, weak
but necessary and at the origin of all our theories at stages where
a certain maturity has not yet been achieved.

As a developmental psychologist, despite of a partial disagreement
with Edelman's theory, what interests me about it are the following
features.

1. The noninstructionist explanation of the development of percep-
    tual categories.
2. Through selection processes, the progressive construction of
    local maps (linked with sensorial modalities), and then global
    maps (plurimodal or supramodal and motoric) to account for the
    appearance of perceptual categorization and generalization
    capacities.
3. The fact that the constructed categories or categorization
    procedures are always relative and not absolute.
4. The capacity of the model to explain not only the features
    characterizing the species but also individual features.
5. The fact that it is a motor theory of the development of
    categories. Global maps cannot be established without activity.

The development of categories from a psychological point of view

Edelman's neurobiological theory can be compared to Harnad's (1987)
psychological theory of the development of perceptual categorization capacities. Both attempt to show that models for simple featu-

re detection or those based on the existence of prototypes fail to produce a general explanation of the development of categorization. Also, both adopt an inductive "bottom up" approach.

Harnad describes two types of internal representation to explain the learning of perceptual categorization by sensory experience or "acquaintance," rather than by verbal description.

(1) *Iconic representations* (IR). An iconic representation is an analog of the sensory input (more specifically, the proximal projection of the distal stimulus on the device's transducer surface). The physical transformation is called analog because the process is invertible (reversable). Iconic representations make stimulus discrimination possible (same-different judgements, stimulus matching, copying). These discriminations are modality-dependent. The iconic representations (like Edelman's local maps) preserve the spatio-temporal structure (i.e., the physical "structure") of the input. They blend into one another and share some overall similarity because the configurations they represent share physical similarities (in the same way that Edelman's cortical maps have important overlaps). They are strengthened by repeated exposure to a class of input. Their principal characteristic is that they are "unbound" in the sense that nothing links them to a shared category.

(2) *Categorical representations* (CR) are the result of an analog/digital filter of the unbound feature configurations (IR). The transformation is called digital because it is not physically invertible (reversable), but a formal one which depends on conventional rules. The filter sorts invariant features, *eliminating* most of the raw configurational structure of IRs and retaining only what is invariant. The conjunction of the CR with the IR preserves the spatio-temporal structure of the input (as reentrant connections maintain spatio-temporal continuity in Edelman's model). In this case, it is also a selective process, in a manner similar to the way global maps are constructed from local maps in Edelman's model. However, Edelman's more complex and detailed model better specifies this detection of invariance, principally by the temporal correlations between local maps and reentrant circuits. Categorical representations, like Edelman's global maps, are plurimodal or supramodal. They allow identification and categorization of objects. CRs are considered to be "bound" representations. They have the limits or boundaries of categories.

To these two types of internal representation Harnad adds a third type called *symbolic representation*. He considers that categorical representations are associated with the names of the categories used as atomic symbols of the symbolic representations. The symbolic representations sustain speech and make learning by description possible. Moreover, Edelman considers that his theory provides the initial basis to take into consideration the superior brain functions related to the formation of concepts and language and to the beginning of learning by social transmission (Edelman, 1987).

For both Harnad and Edelman, categories are provisional and approximate in the sense that they are relative to experience. There are no absolute features but only certain invariant features in a particular context of alternatives.

Harnad's theory does not give the role of action as much importance as Edelman's. Harnad thinks the motor theory of categorical perception produces more questions than answers. Nevertheless, he states that "temporal processes seem by their nature to require active "realtime" filtering and integration" (Harnad, 1987, p.553). This is precisely one of the reasons Edelman considers action so important.

It is not surprising that both Edelman and Harnad do not accept Gibson's theory. Although Harnad recognizes the important contribution of this theory to the concept of invariance in perception, he thinks that "direct perception has not so far proven useful in modeling invariance extraction in category formation, particularly in the *important cases in which learning is involved.*" However, he admits that external invariance must certainly underlie all successful categorization (Harnad, 1987). Edelman also states that while laws of physics provide major constraints, they are insufficient for explaining the ontogeny of categorization (Edelman, 1987). According to Edelman, "the ecological viewpoint of Gibson has served an important function in directing attention to those adequate combinations of stimuli that simultaneously excite different receptor sheets. But it surpasses the problem of categorization and ignores the nature of the neural systems and the continual motor sampling ..." (Edelman, op.cit., p.234-235).

This criticism seems justified in the context of development and learning. However, if one studies the *adapted* functioning of an organism in his ecological niche, as Gibson did (1966), it is possible to discuss direct perception because, in this case, there is an optimal coupling between the organism and its environment. We thus uncover the Gestaltist point of view that inspired Gibson. It should be remembered that the Gestaltists went so far as to postulate the existence of an isomorphism between the structure of the environment and the nervous system.

On the other hand, in the Gibsonian view, it is not possible to analyze the process of development. The concept of "affordance" does not resolve the difficulties raised by the concept of direct perception. An "affordance" is the result of an adaptation process, which is still to be explained. The problem of its transformation during development remains.

Criticism of Harnad's theory

I shall make the same general remarks regarding Harnad's theory as I did for Edelman. Why insist on explaining the development of perceptual categories without taking into account the initial capacities of the newborn ? In his/her interactions with the environment, the newborn does not confront a confusing, completely variable universe. Only certain aspects and events in the environment are initially confusing and unintelligible. The environment is "intelligible" for the baby in that it calls for adapted behaviors which are determined by already acquired capacities and by certain particularities of the niche. It is also probable that this initial organization serves important adaptive functions such as guaranteeing the unity of the subject and that of his environment and constituting a sort of anchorage for future constructions.

Consequently, in spite of my admiration for Harnad's attempt, I do not favor the purely inductive explanation ("bottom up"). The development of categories should be explained as both inductive and deductive. We should acknowledge that a newborn begins his/her life with some initial deductive capacities.

4. QUALITATIVE SHIFTS IN THE GENESIS OF CATEGORIZATION PROCESS

The major reproach addressed to several authors in the first part of this chapter relates to the fact that they consider the environment as consisting of definite objects, characterized by a number of variants. This perspective is the result of adopting theories of information processing. I hope to have shown the problems associated with regarding the physical world as a composition of categories or classes of well defined, non-ambiguous objects. For this reason, the last part of this chapter will focus on qualitative shifts in the way a child categorizes the world throughout development. I shall concentrate on one essential class of shifts, with the risk of drawing too simple a picture of development.

The existence of general qualitative shifts in cognitive development has been recognized for a long time, particularly regarding the development of categorization and classification capacities (Inhelder and Piaget, 1959; Piaget and Inhelder, 1941; Piaget and Szeminska, 1941; Vygotsky, 1962; Wallon, 1945; Werner et Kaplan, 1968). During the last years, renewed attention has been given to these qualitative shifts (e.g. Carey, 1978; Karmiloff-Smith, 1979, 1986; Keil, 1987; Mounoud, 1976, 1986b). The strategic changes discussed in the chapters of Koenig and Zanone seem related to these qualitative shifts, especially the passage from metric to categorical judgements discussed by Koenig. On the other hand, the chapters by Case and Griffin, Crépault and Nguyen-Xuan, and Laszlo do not sufficiently account for the changes in the way children perceive and segment reality at the various stages of development.

Reporting on the construction of tools by children (Mounoud, 1970), I emphasized a substantial qualitative shift around the age of 6 in the construction of tools and their categorization and classification. At a symposium in Tel Aviv in 1983 on "Stage and Structure," I described a general shift in the manner children define and understand objects. A child goes from conceptions based on *elementary juxtaposed* (or amalgameted) *properties* to conceptions based on *whole defining property(ies) by means of relationships between parts of object* (or on relationships between objects related to one or various properties or features) (Mounoud, 1986b). This shift was compared to the shift from the pragmatic or semantic to the morphological or formal segmentation of sentences (Bronckart, 1977), to the shift from syllabic ("concrete") to phonemic ("abstract") segmentation of words (Liberman, Shankweiler, Fisher and Carter, 1974) and to the shift from surface markers to deep structure markers in the acquisition of language (Karmiloff-Smith, 1979). More generally, this shift was defined as a shift from a principally *pragmatic or semantic* to a *morphological or abstract* organization.

Table I: Qualitative shifts in conceptual representations.

          MOUNOUD (1986b)   KEIL AND KELLY (1987)

- Object Conceptions   - Perceptual and conceptual
                                          development

  elementary juxtaposed   *all salient dimensions*
  (or amalgamated) properties
            ↓   ↓
  whole defining property(ies)   *a few meaningfully*
  by means of relationship   *related dimensions*
  between parts

- Motor development   - Perceptual categorization
  (Mounoud et al., 1985)   *(Garner, 1974)*

  local control and planification   *integral dimensions*
            ↓   ↓
  global control and planification   *separable dimensions*
                                          ("integral-to-separable shift")

- Language acquisition   - Word meaning
  (Karmiloff-Smith, 1979)   *(Smith et al., 1974)*

  surface makers   *characteristic features*
            ↓   ↓
  deep structures   *defining features*
                                          ("characteristic-to-defining
                                          shift")

- Words segmentation   - Syllabes similarity
  (Liberman et al., 1974)   *(Trieman et Baron, 1981)*

  syllabic segmentation   *overall similarity*
            ↓   ↓
  phonemic segmentation   *phonemic constituents*

- Sentences segmentation   - Lexical categories
  (Bronckart, 1977)   *(Maratsos, 1983)*

  pragmatic or semantic indices   *semantic heterogeneity*
                                          (prototype)
            ↓   ↓
  formal or morphosyntaxic   *structural homogeneity*
  indices   *(structural rules)*

- Representations   - Representations

  analogic   *prototype-based*
            ↓   ↓
  abstract   *theory-based*

The shift was explained as a construction of representations ranging from *analogical* to *abstract* representation (today I would say from disjunctive analogical and abstract to conjunctive analogical and abstract representations). The peculiarity of the model was its recurrent character. This general developmental sequence reoccurs several times in the course of development. These general qualitative shifts take place around the age of 6 years (between 5 and 7 years) for "conceptual" organization, and around 9 months (between 6 and 12 months) for "perceptual" organization. In my opinion, these general shifts concern the functioning of cognitive structures, which might result from shifts in inter- and intrahemispheric collaboration determined by maturation processes (Mounoud, 1988). The qualitative shifts of representation can take place only when the neural structures involved achieve certain levels of maturation. But the maturation of these structures does not imply that shifts will appear simultaneously in different domains. They depend, of course, on the subject's experience. The capacity to segment words phonetically is a good example. In fact, it appears only with learning to read and write in our alphabetic system. It consequently *does not exist with illiterates*. The temporal decalages between domaines do not allow one to reject the hypothesis of a general shift in the functioning of cognitive structures.

I was happy to discover that Keil also specifies a general qualitative shift (Keil and Kelly, 1987) comparable to one I proposed. A comparison of the two approaches appears in Table I. For Keil and Kelly, this shift applies to conceptual as well as perceptual development. Because of this shift, a child passes from a level where he/she uses *all salient dimensions* in a given domain to define and categorize objects according to their maximum resemblance, to a level where he/she uses only *a few meaningfully related dimensions*. This shift is comparable to the shift from using "characteristic features" to using "defining features" in the development of comprehension of word significance ("characteristic-to-defining" shift; Smith, Shoben and Rips, 1974) and to the shift from the use of "integral dimensions" to "separable dimensions" in the development of perceptual categories ("integral-to-separable" shift; Garner, 1974). Keil and Kelly also bring together other experimental data related to the development of the perception of similarity among syllabes (Trieman and Baron, 1981) and to the development of lexical categories (Maratsos, 1983).

More generally speaking, the qualitative shifts are defined by the shift from *prototype based representations* to *theory based representations*. Keil and Kelly (1987) suggest various mechanisms to explain these qualitative shifts. First, of course, they describe the importance of *experience* and the *degree of expertise*. Then, they discuss "an *internal tendency* toward principled organization of conceptual domains" (p.505). Thus, since the conceptual domains organized around prototypes are atheoretical by nature, the internal tendency to construct theory-based representations produces the principal motivation for the shift. They also mention an adaptative explanatory mechanism borrowed from social psychology: That qualitative shifts are linked to requirements related to *communication efficiency*. Finally, they discuss a mechanism linked with the word itself, which according to Vygotsky (1979), is a tool

rather than a sign. As young children often sort objects in terms
of thematic rather than taxonomic relations, the *power of the word*
seems to direct their attention to taxonomic relations (Markman and
Hutchinson, 1984). I confess, however, that I am not entirely convinced of the utility of these mechanisms related to "internal tendency," "communication efficiency" and "the power of the word."

However, in conclusion, Keil and Kelly also affirm that these qualitative shifts "are determined by a priori domain-specific and
domain-general constraints and predispositions" (p.508). Furthermore, they suggest that "*broad structural constraints* on conceptual
structure may be at work throughout the period during which knowledge differentiates and shifts away...."

My views on the construction of new capacities in children for conceptualizing or categorizing the world appear elsewhere (cf. in
particular Mounoud, 1986a and b, 1987a, 1988; also Vinter, 1989).
Many examples show the shift from prototype based representations of
"iconic" or "analogic" or "presymbolic" objects or events where objects are represented as sets or amalgams of unbound features (cf.
local maps by Edelman) to theory-based, "categorical" or "abstract"
or "symbolic" representations, in the form of delimitated, bound,
invariant sets of features (cf. global maps by Edelman). In this
case, the levels of representations are distinct and correspond to
two of the five stages, which I defined in the recurrent process of
construction of representations.

As described by Keil and Kelly, these qualitative shifts reduce a
complex domain of knowledge to a few criterial dimensions and to a
few values along these dimensions.

To conclude, categorization can be defined as a process of sorting,
filtering, elimination, reduction, and discard, which corresponds to
the concept of development-impoverishment. Thus, we realize again
the importance of the selection and impoverishment phenomena, which
plays a fundamental role in the process of cognitive development. I
hope to have expressed clearly that selection phenomena can only
exist as a result of preliminary enrichment phenomena. Cognitive
development, therefore, results both from enrichment and impoverishment. The internal and external surroundings of an organism are
thus the source of enrichment and selection.

The opposition between two stages of the complex process of representation that I have tried to emphasize in the last part of this
chapter corresponds partly to the opposition introduced by Piaget
(1968b) between the so-called qualitative *identities* and quantitative *conservations*. In his opinion, the first results from dissociations and syntheses of properties of objects and explains the preoperative reasoning of a child. The second results from quantitative compositions possibly due to logico-mathematical operations,
which themselves spring from the general coordinations of action and
which demonstrate the presence of operative reasoning. Without
agreeing to Piaget's interpretation, this final reference is to pay
homage to the notion of categorization, introduced so brilliantly by
Piaget in the domain of cognitive development in children.

ACKNOWLEDGEMENTS

I would like to thank Nelly Braure and Karen Olson for translating
the text, Françoise Schmitt for her valuable secretariat assistance,
and P. Bovet, C.A. Hauert, A. de Ribaupierre, L. Rieben and D.
Stern for their very helpful comments.

REFERENCES

Anderson, J.A. (1983). *The architecture of cognition*. Cambridge,
    Ma: Harvard University Press.
Archer, L.A., Campbell, D., & Segalowitz, S.J. (1988). A prospec-
    tive study of hand preference and language development in 18- to
    30-months-olds: I. Hand preference. *Developmental Neuro-
    psychology, 4(2)*, 85-92.
Atkinson, R.C., & Shiffrin, R.M. (1968). Human memory: A proposed
    system and its control processes. In: K.W. Spence & J.T. Spence
    (Eds.), *The psychology of learning and motivation, Vol. 2*. New
    York: Academic Press.
Baddeley, A. (1976). *The psychology of memory*. New York: Harper
    and Row Publishers.
Bates, E., O'Connel, B., Vaid, J., Sledge, P., & Oakes, L. (1986).
    Language and hand preference in early development. *Developmental
    Neuropsychology, 2(1)*, 1-15.
Bever, T.G. (Ed.). (1982). *Regressions in mental development: Basic
    phenomena and theories*. New York: Erlbaum.
Bernstein, N. (1867). *The coordination and regulation of movements*.
    Oxford: Pergamon.
Brainerd, C.J. (1978). The stage question in cognitive-developmen-
    tal theory. *The Behavioral and Brain Sciences, 2*, 173-213.
Bronckart, J.P. (1977). *Théories du langage, une introduction
    critique*. Bruxelles: Mardaga.
Carey, S. (1978). *Conceptual change in childhood*. Cambridge, Ma:
    MIT/Bradford Press.
Case, R. (1987). The structure and process of intellectual
    development. *International Journal of Psychology, 22(5/6)*,
    571-607.
Case, R., & Griffin, S. (1989). Child cognitive development: The
    role of central conceptual structures in the development of
    scientific and social thought. In: C.A. Hauert (Ed.), *Develop-
    mental psychology: Cognitive, perceptuo-motor and neuro-
    psychological perspectives*. Amsterdam: North Holland.
Changeux, J.P. (1983). *L'homme neuronal*. Paris: Fayard.
Changeux, J.P., & Danchin, A. (1976). Selective stabilization of
    developing synapses as a mechanism for the specification of
    neuronal networks. *Nature, 264*, 705-711.
Changeux, J.P., Heidmann, T., & Patte, P. (1984). Learning selec-
    tion. In: P. Marler & H.S. Terrace (Eds.), *The biology of
    learning*. New York: Springer-Verlag, pp.115-137.
Corbetta, D. (1989). La bimanualité chez l'enfant de 5 à 9 ans.
    Ph.D. Thesis, University of Geneva.
Corbetta, D., & Mounoud, P. (in press). Early development of
    grasping and manipulation. In: C. Bard, M. Fleury & L. Hay
    (Eds.), *Development of eye-hand coordination across lifespan*.
    University of South Carolina Press.
Craik, F.I.M., & Lockhart, R.S. (1972). Levels of processing: A

framework for memory research. *Journal of Verbal Learning and Verbal Behavior, 11,* 671-684.

Crépault, J., & Nguyen-Xuan, A. (1989). Child cognitive development: Objects, space, time, logico-mathematical concepts. In: C.A. Hauert (Ed.), *Developmental psychology: Cognitive, perceptuo-motor and neuropsychological perspectives.* Amsterdam: North Holland.

Edelman, G.M. (1978). Group selection and phasic reentrant signaling: A theory of higher brain function. In: G.M. Edelman & V.B. Mountcastle (Eds.), *The mindful brain: Cortical organization and the group-selective theory of higher brain function.* Cambridge, MA: MIT Press, pp.51-100

Edelman, G.M. (1981). Group selection as the basis for higher brain function. In: F.O. Schmitt, F.G. Worden, A. Adelman & S.G. Dennis (Eds.), *Organization of the cerebral cortex.* Cambridge, Ma: MIT Press, pp.535-563.

Edelman, G.M. (1987). *Neural Darwinism. The theory of neural group selection.* New York: Basic Books.

Edelman, G.M., & Finkel, L.H. (1984). Neuronal group selection in the cerebral cortex. In: G.M. Edelman, W.E. Gall & W.M. Cowan (Eds.), *Dynamic aspects of neocortical function.* New York: Wiley.

Edelman, G.M., & Reeke, G.N. Jr. (1982). Selective networks capable of representative transformation, limited generalization, and associative memory. *Proc. Natl. Acad. Sci. USA, 79,* 2091-2095.

Eimas, P.D. (1982). Speech perception: A view of the initial state and perceptual mechanisms. In: J. Metzler, E.C.T. Walker & M. Garrett (Eds.), *Perspectives on mental representation.* Hillsdale, N.J.: Lawrence Erlbaum Associates, pp.339-360.

Fagard, J. (in press). The development of bimanual coordination. In: C. Bard, M. Fleury & L. Hay (Eds.), *Development of eye-hand coordination across lifespan.* University of South Carolina Press.

Feldman, J.A., & Ballard, D.H. (1982). Connectionist models and their properties. *Cognitive Science, 6,* 205-254.

Fodor, I.E. (1983). *The modularity of mind.* Cambridge, Ma: MIT Press.

Fontaine, R. (1987). Conditions d'évocation des conduites imitatives chez l'enfant de 0 à 6 mois. Ph.D. Thesis, Ecole des Hautes Etudes en Sciences Sociales, Paris.

Garner, W.R. (1974). *The processing of information and structure.* Potomac, MD: Erlbaum.

Gibson, J.J. (1966). *The senses considered as perceptual systems.* Boston: Houghton Mifflin.

Gottfried, A., & Bathurst, K. (1983). Hand preference across time is related to intelligence in young girls, not boys. *Science, 222,* 1974-1976.

Greenfield, P.M., Nelson, K., & Saltzman, E. (1972). The development of rulebound strategies for manipulating seriated cups: A parallel between action and grammar. *Cognitive Psychology, 3,* 291-310.

Harnad, S. (1987). Category induction and representation. In: S. Harnad (Ed.), *Categorial perception. The groundwork of cognition.* Cambridge: Cambridge University Press. 535-565.

Inhelder, B., & Piaget, J. (1959). *La genèse des structures logiques élémentaires.* Neuchâtel et Paris: Delachaux et Niestlé. (English translation, *The early growth of logic in the child.* London: Routledge & Kagan, 1964).

Jeeves, M.A., Silver, P.H., & Milne, A.B. (1988). Role of the

corpus callosum in the development of a bimanual motor skill.
Developmental Neurosychology, 4(4), 305-323.
Jusczyk, P.W. (1981). The processing of speech and non-speech
sounds by infants: Some implications. In: R.N. Aslin, J.R.
Albers & M.R. Petersen (Eds.), *Development of perception,
vol I*. New York: Academic Press. pp.192-215.
Karmiloff-Smith, A. (1979). *A functional approach to child langua-.
ge. Linguistic theories*. Cambridge: Cambridge University Press.
Karmiloff-Smith, A. (1986). Stage/structure versus phase/process in
modelling linguistic and cognitive development. In: I. Levin (Ed.),
Stage and structure. New York: Ablex, 164-190.
Keil, F.C. (1986). On the structure dependent nature of stages of
cognitive development. In: I. Levin (Ed.), *Stage and structure:
Reopening the debate*. Norwood, NJ: Ablex.
Keil, F.C., & Carroll, J.J. (1980). The child's conception of "tall":
Implications for an alternative view of semantic development.
Papers and Reports on Child Language Development, 19, 21-28.
Keil, F.C., & Kelly, M.H. (1987). Developmental changes in category
structure. In: S. Harnad (Ed.), *Categorial perception. The
groundwork of cognition*. Cambridge: Cambridge University Press,
491-510.
Kellman, P.J., & Spelke, E.S. (1983). Perception of partly occluded
objects in infancy. *Cognitive Psychology, 15*, 483-524.
Kemler, D.G. (1983). Exploring and reexploring issues of integrali-,
ty perceptual sensitivity, and dimensional salience. *Journal of
Experimental Child Psychology, 36*, 365-379.
Kobre, K.R., & Lipsitt, L.P. (1972). A negative contrast effect in
newborn. *Journal of Experimental Child Psychology, 14(1)*, 81-91.
Koenig, O. (1989). Child neuropsychological development:
Lateralization of function - hemispheric specialization. In:
C.A. Hauert (Ed.), *Developmental psychology: Cognitive,
perceptuo-motor and neuropsychological perspectives*. Amsterdam:
North Holland.
Kugler, P.N., Kelso, J.A.S., & Turvey, M.T. (1982). On the control
and coordination of naturally developing systems. In: J.A.S.
Kelso & J.E. Clarke (Eds.), *The development of movement control
and coordination*. Chichester: Wiley.
Laszlo, J.I. (1989). Child perceptuo-motor development: Normal and
abnormal development of skilled behaviour. In: C.A. Hauert (Ed.),
*Developmental psychology: Cognitive, perceptuo-motor and
neuropsychological perspectives*. Amsterdam: North Holland.
Levin, I. (Ed.). (1985). *Stage and structure*. Norwood: Ablex.
Liberman, I.Y., Shankweiler, D., Fisher, F.W., & Carter, B. (1974).
Reading and the awareness of linguistic segments. *Journal of
Experimental Psychology, 18*, 201-212.
Maratos, O. (1973). The origin and the development of imitation
during the first six months of life. Ph.D. Thesis, University
of Geneva.
Maratsos, M. (1983). Some current issues in the study of the
acquisition of grammar. In: P. Mussen (Ed.), *Handbook of child
psychology (vol. 3)*. New York: Wiley.
Markman, E.M., & Hutchinson, J.E. (1984). Children's sensitivity
to constraints on word meaning: Taxanomic versus thematic
relations. *Cognitive Psychology, 16*, 1-27.
Marler, P. (1982). Avian and primate communication: The problem
of natural categories. *Neurosciences Biobehav. Rev., 6*, 87-94.
McClelland, J., Rumelhart, D., & the PDP Research Group. (1986).

Parallel distributed processing, vol. 2: Psychological and
biological models. Cambridge, Ma: MIT Press, Broadford Books.
McManus, I.C., Sik, G., Cole, D.R., Mellon, A.F., Wong, J., & Kloss,
J. (1988). The development of handedness in children. British
Journal of Developmental Psychology, 6(3), 257-273.
Meltzoff, A. (1976). Imitation in early infancy. Ph.D. Thesis,
University of Oxford.
Molfese, V., & Betz, J. (1987). Language and motor development in
infancy: Three views with neuropsychological implications.
Developmental Neuropsychology, 3, 255-274.
Molfese, D., & Betz, J. (in press). Electrophysiological indices of
the early development of lateralization for language and cogni-
tion and their implications for predicting later development. In:
D. Molfese & S. Segalowitz (Eds.), Developmental implications of
brain lateralization. New York: Guilford.
Mounoud, P. (1970). Structuration de l'instrument chez l'enfant.
Neuchâtel et Paris: Delachaux et Niestlé.
Mounoud, P. (1971). Développement des systèmes de représentation et
de traitement chez l'enfant. Bulletin de Psychologie, 296, 5-7,
261-272. Translation in B. Inhelder & H. Chipman (Eds.), Piaget
Reader. New York: Springer Verlag, 1976, 166-185.
Mounoud, P. (1976). Les révolutions psychologiques de l'enfant.
Archives de Psychologie, 44, 171, 103-114. Translation in T.G.
Bever (Ed.), Regressions in development: Basic phenomena and
theoretical alternatives. New York: Lawrence Erlbaum, 1982.
Mounoud, P. (1979). Développement cognitif: Construction de
structures nouvelles ou construction d'organisations internes.
Bulletin de Psychologie, 33, 343, 107-118. Translation in I.E.
Sigel, D.M. Brodzinsky & R.M. Golinkoff (Eds.), New directions
in piagetian theory and practice. Hillsdale, N.J.: Erlbaum,
1981, 99-114.
Mounoud, P. (1984). A point of view on ontogeny. Human Development, 27, 329-334.
Mounoud, P. (1986a). Action and cognition. Cognitive and motor
skills in a developmental perspective. In: M.G. Wade & H.T.A.
Whiting (Eds.), Motor development in children. Dordrecht:
Nijhoff, 373-390.
Mounoud, P. (1986b). Similarities between developmental sequences
at different age periods. In: I. Levin (Ed.), Stage and
structure. Norwood: Ablex, 40-58.
Mounoud, P. (1987a). L'utilisation du milieu et du corps propre par
le bébé. In: J. Piaget, P. Mounoud & J.P. Bronckart (Eds.), La
psychologie. Encyclopédie de la Pléiade. Paris: Gallimard, 563-
601.
Mounoud, P. (1987b). Les bases neurophysiologiques des conduites.
In: J. Piaget, P. Mounoud & J.P. Bronckart (Eds.), La psycholo-.
gie. Encyclopédie de la Pléiade. Paris: Gallimard, 1359-1377.
Mounoud, P. (1988). The ontogenesis of different types of thought.
In: L. Weiskrantz (Ed.), Thought without language. Oxford:
Oxford University Press, 25-45.
Mounoud, P., & Vinter, A. (1981). Representation and sensorimotor
development. In: G. Butterworth (Ed.), Infancy and epistemology:
An evaluation of Piaget's Theory. Brighton, Sussex: Harvester
Press.
Mounoud, P., Viviani, P., Hauert, C.A., & Guyon, J. (1985).
Development of visuo-manual tracking in 5 to 9 years-old boys.
Journal of Experimental Child Psychology, 40, 115-132.

O'Leary, D.S. (1989). Neuropsychological development in the child and the adolescent: Functional maturation of the central nervous system. In: C.A. Hauert (Ed.), *Developmental psychology: Cognitive, perceptuo-motor and neuropsychological perspectives.* Amsterdam: North Holland.

Paillard, J. (1988). Dialogues sensori-moteurs et représentation mentale: Un problème d'interface. In: X. Seron (Ed.), *Psychologie et cerveau.* Paris: Les Presses Universitaires de France.

Piaget, J. (1967). *Biologie et connaissance.* Paris: Gallimard.

Piaget, J. (1968a). *Epistémologie et psychologie de la fonction.* Etudes d'Epistémologie Génétique (vol. 23). Paris: Les Presses Universitaires de France.

Piaget, J. (1968b). *Epistémologie et psychologie de l'identité.* Etudes d'Epistémologie Génétique (vol. 24). Paris: Les Presses Universitaires de France.

Piaget, J., & Inhelder, B. (1941). *Le dévelopment des quantités physiques chez l'enfant.* Neuchâtel et Paris: Delachaux et Niestlé.

Piaget, J., & Szeminska, A. (1941). *La genèse du nombre chez l'enfant.* Neuchâtel et Paris: Delachaux et Niestlé.

Reeke, G.N. Jr., & Edelman, G.M. (1984). Selective networks and recognition automata. *Ann. N.Y. Acad. Sci., 486,* 181-201.

Reeke, G.N., Sporns, O., & Edelman, G.M. (1988). Synthetic neural modeling: A darwinian approach to brain theory. Paper presented at the International Conference "Connectivism in Perspective," SGAICO Science Project 88, University of Zurich, Switzerland, 10-13 October 1988.

Rosch, E., & Mervis, C. (1975). Family resemblances: Studies in the internal structure of categories. *Cognitive Psychology, 7,* 573-605.

Smith, E.E., & Medlin, D.L. (1981). *Categories and concepts.* Cambridge, Ma: Harvard University Press.

Smith, E.E., Shoben, E.J., & Rips, L.J. (1974). Structure and process in semantic memory: A featural model for semantic dimensions. *Psychological Review, 81,* 214-241.

Snodgrass, J.G. (1980). Towards a model for picture and word processing. In: P.A. Kolers, M.E. Wrolstad & H. Bouwa (Eds.), *Processing of visible language 2.* New York: Plenum Press.

Spelke, E.S. (1988). The origins of physical knowledge. In: L. Weiskrantz (Ed.), *Thought without language.* Oxford: Oxford University Press, 168-184.

Strauss, S. (Ed.). (1982). *U-shaped behavioral growth.* New York: Academic Press.

Trieman, R., & Baron, J. (1981). Segmental analysis ability: Development and relation to reading ability. In: T.G. Waller & G.E. MacKinnon (Eds.), *Reading research: Advances in theory and practice (vol. 3).* New York: Academic Press.

Tulving, E. (1972). Episodic and semantic memory. In: E. Tulving & W. Donaldson (Eds.), *The organization of memory.* New York: Academic Press.

Vinter, A. (1983). Imitation et représentation durant les premiers mois de le vie. Ph.D. Thesis, University of Geneva (published by Delachaux et Niestlé, 1985).

Vinter, A. (1989). Sensory and perceptual control of action in early human development. In: O. Neuman & W. Prinz (Eds.), *Relationships between perception and action: Current approaches.* Berlin: Springer.

Vygotsky, L.S. (1962). *Thought and language.* Cambridge, Ma: MIT Press.

Vygotsky, L.S. (1979). The development of higher forms of attention in children. *Soviet Psychology, 18,* 67-115.

Wallon, H.B. (1945). *Les origines de la pensée chez l'enfant.* Paris: Les Presses Universitaires de France.

Werker, J.F., & Tees, R.C. (1983). Developmental changes across childhood in the perception of non-native speech sounds. *Canadian Journal of Psychology, 37,* 278-286.

Werner, H., & Kaplan, B. (1968). *Symbol formation.* New York: International Universities Press.

Young, J.Z. (1973). Memory as a selective process. In: Australian Symposium on Biological Memory, pp.22-45. Camberra: Australian Academy of Science.

Young, J.Z. (1978). *Programs of the brain.* Oxford: Oxford University Press.

Young, G. (1989). Early neuropsychological development: Lateralization of functions - hemispheric specialization. In: C.A. Hauert (Ed.), *Developmental psychology: Cognitive, perceptuo-motor and neuropsychological perspectives.* Amsterdam: North Holland.

Zanone, P.G. (1989). Perceptuo-motor development of the child and the adolescent: Perceptuo-motor coordination. In: C.A. Hauert (Ed.), *Developmental psychology: Cognitive, perceptuo-motor and neuropsychological perspectives.* Amsterdam: North Holland.

Castagnola (TI)
February 1989

PART IV

CONCLUSION

DEVELOPMENTAL PSYCHOLOGY
Cognitive, Perceptuo-Motor, and Neuropsychological Perspectives
C.-A. Hauert (Editor)
© Elsevier Science Publishers B.V. (North-Holland), 1990

417

DEVELOPMENTAL PSYCHOLOGY: A BRIEF INVENTORY OF FIXTURES

Claude-A. HAUERT

Faculty of Psychology and Educational Sciences
University of Geneva, Switzerland

*Data on the development of perceptual and motor capacities
are discussed first. A symbolic-representational hypothesis is proposed to explain age-related modifications in
these capacities. Next, so-called cognitive development
is envisaged. Finally, the question of perceptual-
cognitive-motor interfaces in the developmental perspective is addressed. Some links are proposed between these
perceptual-cognitive-motor interfaces and the theoretical
concepts of schemes, schemas, executive functions, control
structures, cognitive strategies and representations.*

1. PRELUDE

As discussed in the introduction to this volume, a central problem
in psychology today is understanding the organization and articulation of ideational and executive levels of behavior. From a developmental perspective, the main goal is to try to understand the
development of these levels and their articulation *from birth to
adult age*. This precision is important given the many works that
focus only on one transition between two periods, or on transitions
that occur only within one period. It is unlikely these studies
will lead to the establishment of a comprehensive theory of development.

As also discussed in the introduction, following an epistemological
tradition deeply rooted in Piagetian theory, developmental psychology --and more generally behavioral sciences-- suffers from a deba-
teable apriori full of theoretical consequences. Ideation, which is
considered a cognitive mechanism, involving some kind of internal
representation is implicitely or explicitely assumed to be strictly
a conscious mechanism. Accordingly, the execution of action is
considered a function mainly ensured by unconscious non-cognitive
automatisms.

This dichotomy provides a basis for a clear work division.
Psychologists are supposed to be interested in the soft-ideational
aspects of behavior while neurophysiologists are considered specia-
lists of the hard-executive pole. When both present their views on
action, its determinants, and the modalities of its control, they
naturally overestimate the importance of their own field (Zanone and

Hauert, 1987).

In general, cognitive psychologists have been quite satisfied with
this work division and avoid dealing with the sensory and motor
components of behavior. Recent texts reviewing the main tendencies
of developmental cognitive psychology (e.g. Sternberg, 1987; Case,
1987) are clear testimonies of this situation. But other disciplines, particularly neuropsychology, emphasize the artificial character of this conception and resist this 'horizontal splitting' of the
individal. Recall, for example, Luria's neuropsychological model
that O'Leary presents in his chapter (this volume). According to
Luria, behavior always implies the joint action of three great
anatomo-functional systems which are responsible for attentional
processes (brain stem), receiving and processing information
(parietal, occipital and temporal cortices), and programming and
controlling action (frontal lobes). Recall also Bruner or
Zaporojets, previously mentioned in the introduction. One of the
interesting aspects of their work is the study of the way by which
so-called cognitive mechanisms can actually control behaviors.

Consequently, in our opinion, a *multiple* approach seems necessary
today more than ever, to avoid a distorted and biased understanding
of behavior and its development. Therefore, this volume presents
three perspectives on development that we hope to bring closer
--cognitive, perceptuo-motor and neuropsychological-- because they
all, in fact, deal simply with different aspects of the same reality. This volume calls thus for an attitude which focusses on more
than just the development of perceptual and/or motor capacities on
one hand, and the so-called cognitive capacities on the other.
Rather, a new approach should also focus on the development of the
interrelationships and interactions of all the capacities. Therefore, we shall speak of the "interface" or "interfaces" between
these capacities.

For certain authors this integrated approach seems possible and has
been more or less clearly proposed. For example, Young (this
volume) presents a very ambitious model of development which inte-
grates data related to cognitive and affective functions as classically described in psychology, and related to perceptuo-motor links
as described in both the psychology and neuropsychology of development. This integration stems from a hypothesis inspired by neuropsychology which suggests that the left hemisphere holds an advantage over the right for sophisticated inhibitory functions. Other
authors, perhaps more cautious (e.g. O'Leary, this volume), find
such an endeavour premature --although desirable-- for both methodological and theoretical reasons.

The scheme chosen for our conclusion is the following. First, we
discuss data on the development of perceptual and motor capacities.
We try to show that even at this level, and even if only early
development is considered, the possible intervention of cognitive
mechanisms must be addressed. We next focus on these mechanisms.
Finally, we address the question of perceptual-cognitive-motor
interfaces in the developmental perspective. Particular attention
will be given in this discussion to recent work studying the relationship between neuro-psychological and cognitive aspects of development.

2. THE DEVELOPMENT OF PERCEPTUAL AND MOTOR CAPACITIES

In her chapter, McKenzie (this volume) reviewes the precocity of certain acquisitions and the necessity of a "radical revision of our description of the starting points for later development." Developmental psychology has been interested in these early perceptual-motor performances during the past fifteen years or so and has demonstrated both their extreme diversity and their sophisticated organization in terms of early sensori-motor coordination and intersensori-motor coordination. Regarding this point, the princeps publication is the book edited by Stone, Smith and Murphy in 1973, dedicated to a 'competent infant'. Since then, the prevailing picture of newborn and infant behavior as an unorganized set of rigid reflexes has been replaced by an infinitely richer and more diversified description (to be convinced, see the part II of this volume).

Today, this early diversity is generally accepted and we agree with McKenzie's suggestion that it is now more important to examine the *significance of these behaviors* rather than continue to catalogue them. We address this first topic using the example of imitation in neonates. This will allow us to discuss several hypotheses regarding the development of early behavior. One of them will finally be retained to discuss later development.

The meaning of early behavior and initial developmental transitions: The example of early imitation

The description of the richness and diversity of early sensori-motor connections is a relatively recent contribution from psychology to our knowledge of the postnatal period. As just mentioned, the traditional and rigid catalogues of infant neurological reflexes have been replaced by infinitely more differentiated and surprising observations. Regarding sensory capacities, for example, McKenzie (this volume) demonstrates that size perceptual constancy stems from an innate mechanism. As an example on the motor side, both Young and Lockman (this volume) review recent observations on early manual reaching and its modulation in relation to characteristics of the "surroundings".

Early imitation is an excellent topic for discussing the status of the initial organization of newborn behavior and the nature of the relationship between sensory afferences and motor efferences. By definition, producing an imitative response implies a close relationship between the sensory pattern of the model and the performed motor pattern.

What is early imitation ? Like "early prehension" or "early manual reaching", early imitation covers a number of behaviors --imitative in this case-- present since the first days of post-natal life. Its developmental progression leads to a 'disappearance'. Therefore, the so-called early imitation behaviors can only be elicited and observed in the very first months of life. Thus, vocal imitations or imitative behaviors as described by Piaget during stages 2 and 3 of sensori-motor development are not included in this definition.

There are many observations and experimental studies of early imitation (Preyer, 1887; Valentine, 1930; Zazzo, 1957; Brazelton and
Young, 1964). However, this relative richness of empirical data has
aroused a major controversy over the very existence of early imitative behavior (Maratos, 1973; Meltzoff and Moore, 1979; Hayes and
Watson, 1981; McKenzie and Over, 1983; representing the earliest
works; for a review, see Vinter, 1988).

Early imitation challenges developmental psychologists if its existence is clearly demonstrated, as we believe it is (1). The scepti-
cal reader may consult Kleiner and Fagan III (1984), Abravanel and
Sigafoos (1984), Kaitz, Meschulach-Sarfaty, Auerbach and Eidelman
(1988) for a series of negative views.

On the positive side, early imitative behavior is thought to be present since the first hours of life. Research has focused on newborns reproductions of facial movement, especially tongue protrusion
and mouth opening and closing (Meltzoff and Moore, 1979; Jacobson,
1979; Fontaine, 1984; Vinter, 1985, 1986). Imitation of facial
expressions (Field, Woodson, Greenberg and Cohen, 1982; Field,
Goldstein, Vega-Lahr and Porter, 1986), and manual movements
(Meltzoff and Moore, 1979; Vinter, 1985) also seems possible, but
evidence is less clear for these two categories. Finally, it must
also be emphasized that developmental research in this field has
shown that these behaviors disappear --like other nonimitative
behaviors-- during the first months of life (Maratos, 1973;
Fontaine, 1984; Vinter, 1985; Ikegami, 1987).

Having reviewed these observations, we may approach the question of
what is the relationship between sensory afferences and motor efferences in this kind of behavior. Therefore, we will discuss the
eliciting dimensions of the model and describe the properties of the
responses that are produced.

The first study that addressed the issue of how to identify the
eliciting properties of the model was conducted by Jacobson
(Jacobson, 1979; Jacobson and Kagan, 1979). She selected five
models, three of which were inanimate objects. At 6 weeks, tongue
protrusion was elicited by both a person's protruding tongue and a
pen moving towards and away from the infant's mouth. A moving ball
was less effective in triggering this response. Similarly, a dang-
ling ring moving up and down above the infant's hand was as effective as the adult model in eliciting hand opening and closing at 14
weeks. These results suggest that movement, and to some extent, the
shape of the model, are meaningful dimensions for eliciting imitation. The importance of model movement in eliciting imitation was
confirmed when Vinter (1986) demonstrated that infants do not imitate static models but do imitate dynamic ones.

Ikegami (1984, 1987) has confirmed this result. One-month-olds were
faced with different types of dynamic stimuli which produced either

----

(1) Many thanks to Annie Vinter who definitively convinced us of the
existence of early imitative behaviors and who amically provided us
with the relevant information we used in this part of the chapter.

tongue protrusion or maintaining the tongue completely extended.
These stimuli included a schematic face, an eye-mouth pattern in a
shapeless face, a "scrambled face", and the pattern of a face without eyes. Only dynamic models elicited imitation responses. Moreover, Ikegami has demonstrated the following phenomena related to
the roles played by different facial features in early imitation.
One-month-olds imitate tongue protrusion in response to the human
face, but also in response to its mirrored image, to a schematic
face, and to a stimulus in the form of a mouth pattern. After two
months of age, a rectangular figure with an emerging "tongue" mimi-
cing protrusion also produces imitative reponses.

Generally considered, these studies show that an essential dimension
for eliciting imitative responses is movement. Furthermore, a per-
ceptible, although extremely schematic, configuration of the mouth-
tongue complex seems necessary.

Regarding these eliciting stimuli, two theoretical questions can
be asked. First, can these behaviors be considered fixed-action
pattern (FAP) i.e., stemming from innate releasing mechanisms, as
suggested by Jacobson (1979) or Eibl-Eibesfeldt (1979) ? Or, second, are these imitation responses related to the oral reflex
observed in the development of certain senile dementiae ? These
questions will be discussed later.

Before that, a detailed examination of the morphology of early imitations is needed, because it may lead to an objective differentiation between these behaviors and the imitative responses that appear
later in development. Vinter (1985) has demonstrated that some dimension of differentiation could be seen in the global imitative
movements of a newborn. Indeed, only older infants are able to
reproduce individually certain components of these movements. For
newborns, a large majority of tongue protrusions were correlated
with lateral head movements, and a large proportion of hand openings
and closings were observed contingently with arm or forearm movements. In other words, a newborn does not produce an isolated imitative movement, but instead a movement clearly integrated into a
more global pattern. Interestingly, these global patterns of action
characterize only the postnatal period, then they dissociate during
the first months of life.

These results suggest that the distinction between early and later
imitations can be expressed by the following hypothesis: Imitation
of tongue protrusion by newborns is apparently not of the same nature and cannot be compared with imitation at 10-12 months. It is
noteworthy that most of the authors who studied early imitation and
who are convinced of its existence do not come to the same conclusion, with the exception of Maratos (1973). Their position, that
these behaviors demonstrate early imitation capacities, gave rise to
the controversy over Piaget's theory of imitation and the theoretical concept of representation (see Meltzoff and Moore, 1977, for
example). However, Vinter's study (1985) showed that these early
imitations are of a different nature than later ones. Consequently,
criticism of Piagetian theory should not be based on the assumption
that the kind of imitation present since birth requires the same
capacity for representation that later imitation requires. Piaget
focused on the development of this later form of imitation during

the first 18 months of life.

Possible hypotheses about early imitation

To explain these behaviors, four hypotheses can be proposed: The
neurological, ethological, ecological and symbolic hypotheses.

Recently, Bjorklund (1987) suggested using a relatively new concept
in neurosciences --"transient ontogenetic adaptation" (Oppenheim,
1981)-- to understand neonatal imitation.

According to this *neurological hypothesis*, any behavior
dependent upon transient ontogenetic adaptation can be identified by
three criteria: First, it disappears or its frequency decreases in
the course of development.   Second, it must assume a function or a
specific role in the adaptative process of an individual to his/her
immediate environment.   Finally, a transient behavior is not functionally or structurally related to later adapted behaviors.   The
stepping reflex (see Jouen and Lepecq in this volume) is now the
classical illustration of this concept.   This behavior is already
present in the fetus and disappears during the first months after
birth.   In the neurological perspective, its function is thought to
be positioning the fetus vertically before birth.   Thus, it would
not be related to intentional walking in one-year-olds.   Regarding
this point, some data showed that exercising the automatic walking
reflex would facilitate the early appearance of intentional walking
(Zelazo, Zelazo and Kolb, 1972; Jouen and Lepecq, this volume).   In
opposition to the neurological hypothesis we have just presented,
this empirical observation suggests a clear functional continuity
between reflex behavior (stepping) and voluntary behavior (walking).
Moreover, Thelen (1986; see also Jouen and Lepecq, this volume;
Zanone, this volume) presents data indicating that the disappearance
of reflex behavior as well as the appearance of intentional walking
could be explained by physical variables (see later).   However,
regarding this question Forssberg (1985) expressed a point of view
rather opposite to Thelen's and which is more compatible with the
neurological hypothesis.

According to Bjorklund (1987), early imitation might be a transient
adaptation and thus depend on mechanisms of biological determination.   The ability to imitate adult facial movements may function to
maintain adult-newborn interaction at an age when babies have no
other means of control.   This capacity disappears when the infant
can intentionally direct his/her communicative movements towards the
adult (at least as far as eye and head movements are concerned).

The assimilation of newborn mouth and tongue facial imitations to
the oral reflex observed in senile dementia could lead to a neurological understanding of this phenomenon.   If such an analogy made
sense, this would mean that neonatal imitation might be a reflex
similar to the grasping reflex or to the cardinal points, reflexes
which disappear in the first six months of life and, in some cases,
reappear in senile dementiae.

The main criticism of this hypothesis is related to the functional
aspects of early imitation.   It must be emphasized that imitation by
a newborn in the natural social context is very rare.   Its "social"

function, according to the neurological hypothesis, should certainly be built on more frequently sollicitated capacities (the attraction of the human voice, for instance). Moreover, the newborn also seems to be able to imitate an adult's hand movements without seeing his/ her face, which makes it clear that Bjorklund's hypothesis cannot be generally applied to all cases of early imitation.

Eibl-Eibesfeldt (1979) and Jacobson (1979) have discussed early imitation from an *ethological perspective* and have studied characteristics of the model's behavior and the newborn's responses. Early imitation responses are considered fixed action patterns (FAP) which depend on innate releasing mechanisms. Support for this hypothesis comes from the "innate" character of early imitations (Eibl-Eibesfeldt, 1979) and from the fact that they are not associated with a specific human model, but can be elicited by animate or inanimate models with certain characteristics (Jacobson, 1979). Kaitz et al. (1988), in particular, suggest that imitation of tongue protrusion is not a "real" imitation, but rather, an automatic response elicited by a "protruding nipple-like stimulus".

There are a number of similarities between early imitations and FAP. They are immediate, global, and integrated reactions. Thus, the imitated movement is not isolated, but is part of a more complex motor sequence. Immediacy and integration are also important characteristics of FAP. The relevant features of the eliciting stimuli include, of course, the shape --not yet sufficiently studied. But also, movement is essential.

In our opinion, this kind of hypothesis implies but one limitation concerning development. Actually, the developmental course of early imitation as described by Vinter (1985) is hardly compatible with the ethological hypothesis.

Third, one can invoke an *ecological hypothesis*. Today, ecological theories are very popular in psychology. However, as far as we know, only Prinz (1987) has addressed the topic of early imitation in this theoretical context.

Comparing the nature of the links between sensory afferences and motor efferences, Prinz distinguishes two kinds of models. "Single-hyphen" models describe the links between inflow (visual for imitation) and outflow (the produced movement) as direct. "Double-hyphen" models assume the existence of internal mediation structures between inflow and outflow. In imitation, visuo-motor coordination is probably mediated by a kinetic image of movement. Two mechanisms can establish these direct or indirect links: 'Mapping' and 'matching'. Matching requires the presence of common properties in the units to be linked, whereas mapping needs less specific connections.

From these premises, Prinz interprets general imitation as a "direct similarity-based match between inflow and outflow" i.e., a direct link between perceptual input and motor efferences (single-hyphen model). The connection is established by extracting features common to the two events. Thus, according to Prinz, early imitation can be explained by a complementary hypothesis that is limited to facial movements: "... When a baby perceives an event with a certain spatiotemporal structure (say, a model opening his mouth), he re-

peats the structure of this event with the only reliable event generator at his command."

If this interpretation is correct, we should be able to observe
mouth opening and closing in response to a model opening and closing
his/her hand. The spatio-temporal parameters of the stimulus are
similar for both movements and the newborn should respond to this
configuration by producing an identical movement with the only reliable motor generator. However, newborns do not respond to hand
opening and closing by opening and closing the mouth, nor vice
versa.

Thus, this criticism remains valid even though the controlling capacities of a newborn's motor system are not limited. In fact, ignoring the hypothesis that representation of the body mediates between
afferences and efferences (some kind of double-hyphen model), makes
it difficult to understand why 12-month-olds do not confuse mouth
opening and closing with hand opening and closing. In our view, it
is difficult to not acknowledge the possibility of early representation of the body. This leads to the fourth hypothesis which we
could call *symbolic*.

Meltzoff and Moore (1977, 1983a and b) interpret early imitation by
suggesting that this behavior: "... is mediated by a representational system that allows the infant to unite within one common
framework his own body-transformations and those of others"
(Meltzoff and Moore, 1983a). This representation capacity is
furthermore described as supramodal or amodal, since it would necessarily be based on the processing of abstract and invariant information by means of sensory modalities.

In our opinion, a newborn's capacity to selectively reproduce facial
movements and one or more manual movements cannot be explained without hypothesizing the existence of body representation. Facial imitations at birth seem richer and more varied than manual imitations
and it is unclear whether body representation is more precise and
detailed for the face than other parts of the body, or whether this
is caused by different levels of "maturity" of the proximal and
distal motor systems.

In both cases, however, these representations act as an interface,
that is they mediate between sensory afferences and motor efferences
at birth. They have been described as sensory representations
(Mounoud, 1986) to be distinguished from perceptual representations,
which appear later in development. Exchanges between a neonate and
his/her environment most likely take place by means of a close connection between internal coding of sensory inflow and motor efferences. Thus, a newborn should automatically respond to a particular
sensory configuration with a specific sequence of movements. In a
strict sense, perception does not actually exist at birth because
sensory information cannot be referred to specific properties of
objects in the external world. Therefore, this analysis and the
hypothesis of fixed action patterns (FAP) are compatible provided
that sensori-motor organization --strictly speaking-- is being
studied.

It thus appears that early imitation can be seen as the result of this sensori-motor organization of behavior. In the same line, the 'disappearance' of early imitation is due to a new coding capacity, the perceptual code, available from the first weeks of life. The development of this new code probably involves a progressive re-construction of the interface controlling initial intersensori-motor coordination. This reconstruction is likely responsible for drama-tic qualitative transformations of newborn behavior (Mounoud, 1981, 1982; Mounoud and Vinter, 1981).

In other words, it seems that at birth low-level sensori-motor connections automatically carry out a sequence of movement in res-ponse to a particular sensory configuration. The appearance of the perceptual code should not trigger the disappearance of this loop, but rather, at this higher level, it should lead to the progressive control of the elicitation and achievement of this loop. The appea-rance of new coding capacities causes thus a functional change in the way behavior can be controlled. As a matter of fact, we will adopt further this general "symbolic" hypothesis to consider the entire course of development.

The above discussion can be applied to the topic of newborn postural and locomotor development as presented by Jouen and Lepecq (this volume), as well as to the topic of perceptual-motor coordinations as presented by Lockman (this volume). Jouen and Lepecq abandon classical maturation hypotheses in favour of a conceptualization that proposes a "postural system" to process information by means of intersensory and sensory-motor connections subject to the bio-mechanical constraints of the body. Their argument is convincing, but one question remains in light of our symbolic hypothesis. Is information to the postural system always the same from the sub-jects's point of view, with no regard to the experience, learning, age, coding capacities, inferences and anticipations of the sub-ject ? This clearly is not the case. As far as coordinated per-ceptual-motor activity is concerned, Lockman claims in his chapter that active experience plays a role in its development. How to describe in detail this role remains an open question.

Some elements of a response can be found in the chapters by Laszlo (see for example the crucial role that can be attributed to kines-thetic experience in the efficiency of perceptual-motor behavior) and by Zanone (see his presentation of the constraints that physical variables prescribe on perceptual-motor behavior) in this volume which are very clever, complete and up-to-date presentations of the field of perceptuo-motor development in children.

Particularly, these authors note that one encounters today an 'emer-ging' conceptualization which postulates that the initial cause of the development of material action is the modifications of the phy-sical features of the body in the course of ontogenesis. These modifications, interacting with the impact of the physical environ-ment, seem to give rise to new possibilities for action without it being necessary to postulate the intervention of "symbolic" control mechanisms. Although very recent, this emerging position encounters a rather favourable echo of which Butterworth's rallying is just a recent and striking testimony (Butterworth, 1989; and this volume).

The most interesting, if not the only example of this position from

a developmental perspective can be found in Thelen's recent work
with newborns (see also Jouen and Lepecq, and Zanone, this volume).
Thelen was interested in "kicking" i.e., the rhythmical cycling
activity of the lower limbs which exists at the beginning of postnatal life (Thelen and Fisher, 1983). This capacity for action,
like many others, disappears quite rapidly from a newborn's repertoire of behavior and reappears later in a similar form. This
disappearance is traditionally interpreted (McGraw, 1963; see also
Jouen and Lepecq, this volume) as a result of the initial functioning of inhibitory mechanisms on reflex behavior. This functioning presumably becomes possible with the maturation of the central
nervous system. Nevertheless, Thelen, Skala and Kelso (1987)
demonstrate experimentally that once the kicking has apparently
disappeared, it is possible to make it reappear by dipping the newborn's legs into water i.e., by modifying the force of gravity on
the limbs. The authors explain this observation as follows. When a
newborn grows, fat mass develops more rapidly than muscular mass.
Kicking disappears because it is a simple physical problem and it
will reappear if the physical constraint is lessened by immersing
the body into water. Hence the basic capacity has actually not
disappeared. It is momentarily masked until the newborn develops
sufficient muscle strength to again displace the mass of the body.
It is thus not true that a central control mechanism is involved in
this process. In the course of natural development, kicking will
reappear later --helping to walk-- when an infant again has the
physical possibility of moving his limbs with regard for all the
biomechanical constraints that characterize the upright position and
walking. Hence, walking appears to be a behavior emerging from this
set of circumstances.

Opposed to this, there is another conceptualization which suggests
that the development of perception and action depends on central
identification, categorization and inference mechanisms to carry out
the processing of input to the system, as well as the programming
and control of output.

Let us discuss the 'knowledge of results' paradigm an example of
this concept. The perceptual-motor system is potentially always fed
by proprioceptive and exteroceptive reafferences. In this latter
category, we can distinguish between visual, tactile and auditory
reafferences generated either by movement or information concerning
performance received from a third person or an ad hoc device. This
information has the generic name 'knowledge of results' and is thus
a score given to a subject according to his/her performance.

Many experiments have demonstrated that knowledge of results is a
determining factor in learning actions under certain conditions, and
that the nature of this score is important. In general, the more
precise the score, the more marked is its effect (Hatze, 1976;
Barclay and Newell, 1980; Newell et Walter, 1982; Ramella, 1982;
Singer, Hagenbeck and Gerson, 1981; Winther and Thomas, 1981; for a
review, see Salmoni, Schmidt and Walter, 1984).

This discovery is interesting because it shows that a subject
--child or adult-- can profit from a determining effect while learning perceptual-motor behaviors, the cognitive nature of which
cannot be doubted. Learning and development of the capacities for

action is, in this sense, not strictly determined only by a number
of physical factors linked with the internal or external world, as
postulated in an emerging model. The intervention of a cognitive
mechanism can also be postulated at the outset of action. The 'true
professionals' of development (parents and educators) know this
well. Indeed, a fundamental aspect in practice consists of showing
a model. This representation most likely allows the subject optimal
control over his/her actions when it is elaborated cognitively.

In this context, we would like to point out van Wieringen's (1988)
recent observation. In opposition to the particular kind of training given to actors in the Grotowski theater in Warsaw, and as a
strong affirmation of emerging dynamic theory on the nature of
principles underlying the organization of motricity, this author
concludes that: "Actors and dancers may be better described as
cultural systems performing cultural activities than as natural
systems performing natural activities." (p.250). We continue this
idea by saying that a child or an adult always produces --or tries
to produce-- a motricity adapted to the various physical as well as
not physical aspects of his/her surroundings (except in artificial
experimental situations). At the very least, they are adapted to
the internal representations they have of these aspects. However,
it must be emphasized that these adaptations can only occur within
the physical limits or constraints that the dynamic approach cleverly describes (see, for example, Zanone, this volume).

3. THE DEVELOPMENT OF COGNITIVE CAPACITIES

In his chapter on the early development of cognitive functions,
Langer refers to the basic components of Piagetian theory: "The
functions of gnostic acting comprise assimilating, accommodating,
and organizing knowledge. These adaptive biopsychological functions
are continuous in the phylogeny, ontogeny, and history of ideas."
However, he also makes clear that the structures of gnostic acting
are discontinuous through both phylogenetic evolution and ontogenetic development.

In opposition to the traditional Piagetian view, Langer suggests
that, in addition to physical cognition, logico-mathematical cognition also originates *directly* from infant action. As a theoretical
consequence, his originalist hypothesis rules out the necessity of
language for the development of logico-mathematical, as well as
physical, cognition.

Evidence for this position comes from the observation that an infant
can perform actions on objects or a series of objects, such as the
pragmatic operations of composing/decomposing, adding, substracting,
multiplying and dividing, and correspondence and exchange. Because
infants have only limited motor abilities for manipulation, most of
the reported empirical observations begin with 6-month-olds. Langer
shows how these pragmatic operations develop between 6 months and 2
years. From "elementary and weak", they become "complex and powerful". To differentiate these operations from those that appear
later, they are called first-order operations. Second-order operations are operations on operations, e.g. compositions of compositions, and these begin to appear in the second year.

Langer's observations on the development of object classification
are particularly interesting. At 6 months infants group objects
that are different. At 8 months, groupings are random. At 12
months, however, objects are put together according to their resemblance. This sequence illustrate how first-order operations require
an identification and analysis of the objects' properties, otherwise
there would be no criterion for grouping. Therefore, in terms of
structure, it is impossible to differentiate 6-month-olds from 12-
month-olds in these observations. Langer describes infants who are
at least 6 months old as already having a rich history and who cannot be compared with, for instance, a 1-month-old. At 6 months,
infants are doubtlessly capable of relatively rich and diversified
perceptual representation. We agree with Langer that perceptual
categorization most likely preceeds pragmatic classification.
Therefore, the modifications that characterize the development of
early pragmatic classification can be seen as more closely linked to
the dynamics of perceptual representation than to structural constraints.

This is obviously not Langer's viewpoint. He identifies certain
structural constraints --such as the number of manipulated objects--
which disappear in the course of development. He also proposes that
second-order operations develop from transformations of the first-
order operations. He does acknowledge that the most important engine of development lies in an alternation of imbalances and re-
equilibrations occuring within an organized system. The origin of
this lack of equilibrium seems to be structural, resulting from
"disparities between sensorimotor operations" (for example, between
commuting, substituting, and classifying) (Langer, this volume).
Langer suggests that disparities also exist for monkeys, even more
markedly than for infants. It is obvious that as a consequence
there is no apparent advantage for the development of a monkey's
cognitive system. According to Langer, the organization of a monkey's cognitive system is less elaborated than an infant's and does
not allow reequilibration.

Nevertheless, it is getting interesting and necessary, in this context, to look at data on the cognitive development of infants less
than 6 months of age. In her chapter, McKenzie reviews research on
the mechanism of perceptual constancy in newborns and recent studies
on object permanence. Experimental evidence today suggests that
there is an early version of the mechanism of perceptual size constancy present since birth. The expression 'early version of this
mechanism' is ours. Consistant with our analysis of early imitation, we consider it important to repeat that early behaviors must
not a priori be assimilated to the behaviors of an older infant. In
Spelke's view (1988) for example, before reaching Piaget's substage
IV, an infant possesses a early version of the concept of object.
As an empirical exemplary observation, a partially hidden object
with two extremities in view is perceived as a single object by a
4-month-old if both parts move together.

Spelke's theory can be labelled "centralist". The mechanism by
which objects are perceived is thought to be central. It operates
on representations and not directly on the sensations themselves. It
also is amodal. "Objects do not appear to be apprehended by separa-

te visual and haptic mechanisms but by a single mechanism that operates on representations arising either through vision or through
touch" (p.175). Nevertheless, the "object" perceived by 4-5 month-
olds, for certain aspects, differs from an adult's "object". In
particular, an infant's "object" violates laws of gravity (Macomber,
Spelke and Keil, in prep., quoted by Spelke). Spelke proposes that
an infant disposes of an initial theory of object which is based on
four principles (cohesion, boundednesss, substance, spatio-temporal
continuity). To summarize, "... the spontaneous development of
physical knowledge is a process of theory enrichment, in which an
unchanging, core conception of the physical world comes to be sur-
rounded by a periphery of further notions." (Spelke, 1988, p.181)

Spelke's position appears incompatible with the information processing approach. Actually, --in the same volume as Spelke mentioned
above-- Cohen (1988) describes research on the visual perceptual
capacities of infants. Some of these studies demonstrate that with
development, an infant not only enriches his/her basic theory, in
Spelke's terms, but also reformulates and reorganizes it: "... A
recurring developmental trend keeps appearing, from an ability to
process independent parts [of what the adult calls an object] to an
ability to process some higher order integration of those parts.
This constructivist trend appears at different ages, and items that
serve as a perceptual 'whole' at one age may serve as only a 'part'
of some more elaborated 'whole' at a subsequent age." (Cohen, 1988,
p.218).

Furthermore, Cohen examines the infants's capacity to construct
perceptual categories. These capacities are present very early in
development and are also found in animals (e.g. birds). In infants,
it appears they undergo a complex transformation with age. Younger
and Cohen (1986), using a habituation paradigm, studied whether an
infant works on independent perceptual features or the relationships
between them. They demonstrated a "'habituation to no habituation
again' development shift" between 4, 7 and 10 months. Regarding
these early capacities for perceptual categorizing, let us recall
Mounoud's criticism (this volume) of Edelman's theory.

Because perceptual categorization exists even in animals, Cohen sees
the complex development in infants as an indication of the manner in
which they are able to use and organize information: "Thus, what
may vary over age is not the ability to categorize in general, but
the ability to use certain types of information in the formation of
categories." (Cohen, 1988, p.225)

Without really participating in the debate over connectionism and
the relationship between neurogenesis and the development of perceptual categorization capacities (c.f. Mounoud, and Butterworth,
this volume), the following remark should be kept in mind. Both
positions --on the one hand Spelke's theory attributing very strong
structural capacities to newborns and on the other hand Cohen, who
suggests that the formation of categories in infants is mainly a
problem of information processing-- are not compatible with a theory
like Edelman's.

On the contrary, Butterworth (this volume; and 1989) suggests
rejecting both Spelke's conceptualization and the information

processing approach for a dynamic "presentationalist" hypothesis
more in line with Edelman's theory. Explicit reference is made to
Gibson's theory which "... emphasises the information available to
perceptual systems inherent in the dynamic relation between the
infant and a structured environment." (Butterworth, this volume).

In this perspective, perception is considered immediate. Therefore,
perceptual systems process information without first interpreting
it. Their function is reduced to the simple transmission of pre-
existing information to the internal memories of the system. "However, a necessary evolutionary assumption of the position advocated
here is that perceptual systems are pre-adapted for certain kinds of
information and from this, knowledge about specific objects may
flow. Knowledge may be acquired not only as a consequence of action
but also by attending to the information generally available in the
environment (...). None of this *requires* prior knowledge or the
mediation of perception, or inferences (...)." (Butterworth, 1989).

Although this general hypothesis is easy to apply the beginning of
ontogenesis we find it difficult to account for repeated experiences. Butterworth emphasizes that: "The hypothesis that information
available to perceptual systems, through repeated encounters, may
give rise to knowledge is one approach to the problem of the causes
of development. Registration and storage of information in memory,
may give rise to qualitatively new forms of "anticipatory", "feed-
forward" perception that may accurately be characterised as dependent upon particular knowledge." (Butterworth, this volume).

As we understand this perspective, the relationship between perception (meaning *sensation*, see above) and cognition is 'one way'
during the postnatal period. However, as soon as a newborn disposes
of a minimal amount of knowledge, it intervenes in the organization
of the sensations. If this formulation seemed legitimate to
Butterworth, we would share his point of view. In the terminology
we have adopted, the newborn works on sensory representations at
birth. Therefore, after the first contact with his/her new environment, representations of another nature (perceptual) progressively
replace the previous ones and allow him/her to control his/her behavior in a new way.

Possible contributions of neuropsychology to an
understanding of early cognitive development

Diamond (1988) summarizes work in which she tries to relate classically described modifications in 6- 12-month-olds with maturation of
the frontal regions. Her approach is based on the observed similarity between the behaviors of an infant and those of adult monkeys
suffering from bilateral lesions of dorso-lateral prefontal cortex
as demonstrated in several experimental paradigms: The "A-notB
error", the "delayed response" (DR), and the object retrieval (OR)
paradigms.

In the A-notB paradigm, a typical experiment involving object permanence, the infant sees an object put before him/her in place A and
then it is covered (see also McKenzie, this volume). He/she "is
asked" to find the hidden object. Before 7 1/2 months, the infant
does not try. From 7 1/2 to 11 months, he/she looks for the object

at the place where it was covered. During this age range, if an object that was hidden at A and found at A is moved to B in front of the subject, he/she continues to search for it at A. This behavior, largely studied in the literature on early development, is traditionally referred to as A-notB error.

The classical DR paradigm used to test prefrontal functioning is identical except that a temporal delay is imposed between the time the object is hidden (for the monkey: food) and the time the subject is allowed to search for it. The experimental data reviewed by Diamond show that: "The performance of infants from 7 1/2-9 months on A-notB matches, in considerable detail, that of monkeys with prefrontal cortex lesions on DR" (p.338) i.e., the experiment succeeds if the delay preceeding the response is zero. It fails if the delay is not zero. However, in the latter case, success is possible if the subjects --infants or monkeys-- "are allowed to keep looking at, or orienting their body toward, the correct well during the delay." (p.338). Also, for both subjects, spatially marking the correct well facilitates success whatever the delay. Controls, by the way, have included intact monkeys and monkeys suffering from bilateral parietal or hippocampic lesions. In this case, the A-notB error pattern does not apply. Finally, intact baby-monkeys between 1 1/2-4 months show a developmental pattern comparable to that of infants between 7 1/2 and 12 months for A-notB error.

The object retrieval paradigm (OR) "is a detour task with the goal object inside a rectangular box open on one side" (p.349). This box is transparent and the subject is simply asked to grasp the object placed in the box by the experimenter. To succeed, the subject must not advance his/her hand straight forward towards the object to be grasped (food), but turn it around the obstacle, which the box's walls represent. Moll and Kuypers (1977, quoted by Diamond, 1988) have demonstrated that adult monkeys with frontal lesions fail at this task. The role of the frontal lobe has been demonstrated in a very convincing manner by the following observation from Diamond: "When a unilateral frontal lobe lesion was combined [in Moll and Kuypers's experiments] with a commissurotomy, the hand contralateral to the lesion persisted in reaching at the plate's centre, while the hand connected to the intact hemisphere *of the same monkey* reached through the hole to the food !" (p.350). Diamond has demonstrated that infants between 6 and 8 months behave in this task like monkeys with cerebral lesions and they master this problem-situation only at around 12 months. Moreover, "although OR and A-notB are quite different tasks, improvement on each occured over the same age range [suggesting] that these improvements are, at least in part, maturationally based." (p.355).

From these observations, Diamond hypothesized that maturation of the frontal lobes underlies at least some cognitive improvements from 6 to 12 months after birth.

What sort of improvements ? Diamond suggests two kinds. The first is the ability to "relate" and "integrate" several pieces of information "over space and time". One characteristic of the OR paradigm is that the experimenter can manipulate whether the opening of the box and the object to be grapsed are spatially united. If they are not, younger subjects do not succeed at this task, demonstrating the

role of spatial differences. In the A-notB paradigm, the object to
be grapsed and the indication of its place can be temporarily disjointed, thereby requiring the help of mnemonic resources. This
task is more difficult for young infants. Diamond recognized a
similarity between infant responses to this type of problem and certain aspects of frontal symptomatology in adults.

A second mechanism is the ability to inhibit a fundamental tendency
to respond "directly", or to respond according to a previously
reinforced answer. "In OR, the tendency to reach straight to a visible target must be inhibited. (...) In A-notB, a conditioned tendency or 'habit' to reach to 'A' (where the subject was rewarded)
must be inhibited when the bait is hidden at 'B'". Again, Diamond
emphasizes the analogy between this early difficulty to inhibit direct responses and classical frontal symptoms in adults.

In short, the utility of an approach which tries to relate neurobiological maturation with the development of cognitive functions is
quite evident. The developmental processes which underlie performance in traditional studies of cognitive development can be inferred from such an analysis: These include an increase in spatial and
temporal coordination abilities and an increased capacity to control
action.

An approach such as Diamond's is certainly promising for an *integrated* understanding of development. Another interesting example
of the attempt to bring together neuropsychology and developmental
psychology is Welsh and Pennington's review (1988): "Assessing frontal lobe functioning in children: Views from developmental psychology".

This article focuses on the key-concept of 'executive function' "as
the ability to maintain an appropriate problem-solving set for attainment of a future goal". Welsh and Pennington, referring to
Luria (1966) state that: "This set can involve one or more of the
following: (a) An intention to inhibit a response or to defer it to
a later more appropriate time, (b) a strategic plan of action sequences, and (c) a mental representation of the task, including the
relevant stimulus information encoded in memory and the desired
goal-state" (pp.201-202). This functional concept is used in both
cognitive psychology (e.g. Posner, 1978; Neisser, 1967) and neuropsychology in relation to frontal lobes (e.g. Fuster, 1985).

Welsh et Pennington have a developmental perspective similar to
Diamond (1988). They examine data with infants and monkeys in the
A-notB and OR paradigms as well as certain data related to 'self-
control behaviors' (memory-for-location, metacognition, problem-
solving paradigms) in infants and school children. Nevertheless, as
pointed out by Welsh and Pennington, much remains to be done from
this perspective.

In the present volume, the possible contributions of neuropsychology
to an understanding of psychological development are presented in
chapters by Young, O'Leary, and Koenig. While Young and Koenig
clearly appear convinced that multiple connections can be drawn between the data of developmental neuropsychology and classical cognitive and/or perceptual-motor approach to development, O'Leary is

more reserved, or in other words, less speculative.

On the basis of a large amount of empirical and theoretical data, Young formulates an original conceptualization of psychological development in children. It is built on the hypothesis of a close interdependence between cognition and hemispheric specialization. The different stages and substages of both cognitive and motor development are thought to be determined by the different levels of functional hemispheric specialization which characterize neuro-psychological development. A particularly important inhibitory role is attributed to the left hemisphere, whose effects throughout the course of development may explain these levels of specialization. However, Young clearly demonstrates that this biological factor is not completely responsible for these levels. The origin can be found in the complex interactions between this and other factors of the environment.

In line with other authors, Young and Koenig propose concepts of control units (Young) or cognitive strategies (Koenig) as mechanisms involved in the realization and control of behavior.

The originality of Young's position stems from his proposition that while the control units change at each sub-stage of development, functional hemispheric specializations do not change qualitatively throughout development. His model contains 20 sub-stages (4 stages of 5 sub-stages each). Thus, 20 control units appear in the course of development: Reflex pairs, reflexive hierarchies, primitive schemas, schema, independent schema, schema coordination, schema coordination hierarchies, primitive representations, plans, symbolic plans, symbolic plan coordination, symbolic plan hierarchization, symbol plan systems, concrete operations, logic in imagination, abstract thought, abstract hierarchization, abstract systematization, relativist abstraction, and abstract universality. The functional relations between these different control units, however, are not systematically discussed by Young. Within one stage, the relationships are explicitly hierarchical. But, from one stage to another, we find Young's position similar to Piaget's (1974a, 1974b) concerning the relationship between action and cognition (see Introduction).

Koenig also suggests that hemispheric specializations do not change with age. His basic hypothesis assumes that the cognitive strategies follow age-related transformations strongly linked to modifications in interhemispheric collaboration. His examples show complex age-related trends --i.e., changes in hemispheric dominance-- for the processing of letters or words and colors in the Stroop paradigm. For letters, it is generally accepted that these stimuli can be processed in two different ways i.e., linguistically or spatially. According to the experimental context, the question asked to the subject, his/her age, etc., hemispheric resources can thus be involved differently. For interferences between words and colors in the Stroop paradigm, Koenig's data (1986) show complex trends from the age of 7. However, this is not the case for the control conditions of simple word reading and color designation.

Koenig's resolutely computational approach to the relationship between cognitive development and hemispheric specialization seems

promising: "A change in cognitive strategy for the processing of a
given task will be seen in term of a change in the organization of
the (involved) cognitive components. I will define a "cognitive
strategy" in terms of a set of cognitive components (or subsystems),
each of them being implemented in a given area of the brain."
(Koenig, this volume).

But apart from this discussion, we are astonished at the correspondance between the concept of 'executive function', control units, or
cognitive strategies, and the conceptualization we proposed for the
relationship --the interface-- between perception, cognition and
motricity in either the synchronic or the developmental perspective
(Zanone and Hauert, 1987; Hauert, 1988; Hauert, Zanone and Mounoud,
1989). This analogy deserves some explanation which the reader will
find in the section on the development of the perceptual-cognitive-
motor interface.

First, however, let us recall that, in studies of cognitive development, Case and Griffin (this volume) present a conceptualization
similar to the classical Piagetian one. The subject disposes of a
central conceptual structure i.e., "an internal network of concepts
and conceptual relations, which plays a central role in permitting
children to think about a wide range of (but not all) situations at
a new epistemic level, and to develop a new set of control structures for dealing with them" (ibid.). In this chapter, Case's theoretical model is thus enriched, at each stage of development, by a
'super-structure' --a central conceptual structure-- ensuring the
interrelationship of control structures. The concept of a central
conceptual structure is somewhat analogous with but also somewhat
different from the 'structure of the whole' in Piagetian theory.
For us, one important analogy is that these structures are acquired
through progressive coordinations depending on autoregulative processes such as equilibration and reflexive abstraction. However,
Case and Griffin suggest that they are acquired via "socially facilitated processes" and that they "are potentially teachable". The
control structures are defined as "tripartite problem-solving structure[s]" which include: "(a) A representation of the problem situation, (b) a representation of the goal which the situation entails,
and (c) a representation of the procedures that will take the child
from the current situation to the goal state." (ibid, footnote 1).
Thus the logical and procedural aspects of actions are involved in
these memories.

We suggest that control structures, in the sense used by Case and
Griffin, could also be considered as necessary for perceptual-
cognitive-motor links. The similarities and differences between
this notion of the connecting function and those proposed by other
authors will be presented in section 4.

Still regarding so-called cognitive development, Crépault and
Nguyen-Xuan (this volume) acknowledge the existence of two fundamental types of knowledge. They distinguish between 'general knowledge', which is related to various domains of knowledge (space, time),
and 'inferred knowledge', which is inferred from general knowledge
and allows the specification of each situation (a given spatial
disposition, a certain temporal sequence, etc...). These types of
knowledge concern logico-mathematical and infra-logical, as well as

physical aspects of any situation. Inferred knowledge may not be
compatible with general knowledge, and this incompatibility is thus
responsible for an unstable system. Stability will return after the
child either rejects presently inferred knowledge or reorganizes
general knowledge. Thus, cognitive development is characterized by
a perspective with "some analogy to the equilibration process".
Inferred knowledge is conceived of as a kind of intermediary between
the actual requirements of a situation and the logical formalism of
general knowledge. Whith this point of view, the Piagetian hypothesis of a structure of the whole guiding all the behaviors of one
developmental level has not been accepted by Crépault and Nguyen.

Finally, the analyses of the processes of perceptual categorization
presented by Mounoud (this volume) can also contribute to our reflections. In his comments on the chapters focusing on children and
adolescents, Mounoud expresses his astonishment that the authors
attach little or no importance to the mechanisms of identification
and categorization through which the subject perceives his environment. Today these mechanisms are thought to be very precocious (see
e.g. Cohen, above). But we must also recall, in this context, the
chapter by Butterworth. His position on early behavior is not compatible with the hypothesis that categorization capacities exist
early in development.

4. THE DEVELOPMENT OF THE PERCEPTUAL-COGNITIVE-MOTOR INTERFACE

The general thesis we have approached in the preceding pages is that
development is the history of the appearance and setting of several
control systems. These functional systems allow the subject to progressively manage a basic and preformed repertoire of highly organized and diversified actions. From our analysis of early behavior,
we propose that these control systems are of a representational nature at birth and can be justifiably designated as perceptual-
cognitive-motor interfaces.

In Vergnaud's terms, the main function of representation is "conceptualizing the real to act efficiently." From this perspective, "the
interaction between the subject and the real is essential, since the
subject creates and experiences his/her representations and conceptions due to this interaction. At the same time, they are responsible for the way he/she acts and controls action to the real."
(Vergnaud, 1985, p.246). The logical consequence of this assertion
is that "adaptation cannot be measured by other criteria than that
of conformity between the subject's expectations and the real facts
occuring, and that of efficient action. Representation cannot be
functional if it does not intervene in the regulation of action and
the subject's expectations. (...) Actions aim at transforming or
questioning the real (difference between effect and prediction) and
consequently lead to the adaptation evolution of the system of invariants constituting representation. (...) The importance granted
to signification again conferes a central role to the concept of
scheme in the functionning of representation." (ibid, p.249-250).
According to Vergnaud, a scheme is defined as an organized set of
four types of representational elements: Operative invariants,
inferences, action rules and predictions. Operative invariants
i.e., objects, intra- and inter-objects relations, as well as pro-

cesses that thought identifies and categorizes in reality, are seen
by Vergnaud as the "hard core of the representation."

Consequently --and we agree with Vergnaud-- schemes can be thought
of as representative instances guaranteeing the connection between
significance and behavior. This concept of a scheme is close to
that of 'schemas' proposed by Schmidt, 'executive functions' suggested by Welsh and Pennington, or Case and Griffin's 'control
structures'. Regarding the same topic, let us also mention work
from Geneva on procedures and strategies and Cellérier's (1979a and
b) notion of pragmatic transformation, generally ignored by anglo-
saxon authors to the justified astonishment of Brown (1988).

We can establish the following table as a short recapitulation:

Welsh & Pennington	Case & Griffin	Schmidt	Vergnaud
Executive function	Control struct.	Schemata (see below)	Schemes
-intention to inhibition			
-strategic plan of action sequences	-representation of procedures		-action rules -operative
-mental representation of the task and its goal	-representation of the task and its goal	-desired outcome,	invariants
		state of system	-predictions
		-response specification	-inferences

In brief, the mechanisms ensuring the links between ideational and
executive levels of behaviors --i.e. the unity of the subject-- is
seen as a set of representations and memories which enable him/her
to organize his/her present actions in terms of past actions and the
present situation. Although this may appear trivial, we should not
forget that for Piaget, cognitive structures do not perform this
function.

We have recently tried to depict in a detailed manner the mechanisms
ensuring the production, control and development of motor behaviors
in this theoretical frame (Hauert, Zanone and Mounoud, 1989; Zanone
and Hauert, 1987). From Schmidt's well known Schema Theory (1975,
1976, 1982), we borrowed the concepts of generalized motor program
and recall and recognition schemata --respectively, a motor and a
sensory memory-- to coordinate them with Mounoud's model of representational development. In Schmidt's theory, motor behaviors are
possible because the subject has at his/her disposal two kinds of
schemata. First, a recall schema which is some kind of motor memory
of the transfer function progressively built through various individual experiences between the initial conditions of actions, their
possible goals and past motor commands. The recall schema allows
the subject to interpolate a specific motor command for the current
action. In addition, the subject is thought to possess another
schema related to the reafferential aspects of his/her actions. It
is the recognition schema, the sensory memory of the transfer function between the initial conditions of actions, their possible

goals, and past sensory consequences of actions. From this memory trace, the recognition schema allows the subject to generate the expected sensory consequences of the intended action which furnish a clear internal reference for the control of action. Therefore, for us, these schemata do not work directly on sensory events but on their internal coding i.e., representations. From this postulate, the coordination of the schema conceptualization and Mounoud's model becomes particularly relevant.

The main characteristics of Mounoud's model are as follows (for a detailed presentation, see Mounoud, 1982, 1986; for an indirect relation, see Young, this volume). First, given the extent of new-born competence, one might conclude that a general organization of action exists at birth. It is likely that many developmentalists will agree with this point (as an example, see the concept of a 'pattern generator' in Thelen, 1986). However, it is also likely that many others will disagree because it clearly allows us to postulate that the structures underlying behavior are preformed and do not develop with age. Second, capacities of representation are present at birth. Mounoud calls them sensorial representations. Early imitations provide clear evidence in favour of this view (see above, and Vinter, 1985). Third, later development consists of the construction and re-construction of new representations of object properties, of self and of others. New coding capacities, presumably appearing because of maturational processes, make these recursive constructions possible according to the following schedule: An initial period from birth to approximately 2 years of age (perceptual representations), a second period from 2 to 11 years (conceptual representations, corresponding to the Piaget's symbolic functions), and a third period from the age of 11 (semiotic representations).

In Mounoud's model, the (re)construction of representations at a given developmental period always consists of a five step process. During the first step, the representations are global, syncretic and undifferentiated. At the second step, they become isolated in the sense that the child constructs representations corresponding to dissociated and juxtaposed properties of objects as the result of a subjective segmentation of reality. In the third step, the child puts these representations together and realizes new internal representations of reality. However these new representations remain global since the child has not yet constructed the relationship between them. This construction takes place during step 4. Finally, at the last step, objects are conceived of as a set of coordinated properties and their interrelationships are fully mastered. Apparent regressions in development can appear during steps 2 and 4 when the perceptual-cognitive-motor interface poocesses isolated or incomplete representations of objects.

This five step process is recursive at each representational level of development. Furthermore, this model applies to the entire course of development and treats the subject strictly in the same way regardless of his/her actual age. Therefore, it allows us to avoid some of the dramatic weaknesses of Piagetian-like models which arbitrarily resort to structural or functional explanations of behavior, either post-hoc (as in horizontal decalages) or depending on whether the subjects is an infant or a child or an adult.

To conclude, it seems to us that developmental psychology today is at the beginning of a step 2 (pessimistic conclusion) or of a step 4 period (optimistic conclusion), step 1 or 3 corresponding to the acme of Piagetian theory. Let us the reader choose his/her own conclusion and the consequences which ensue.

REFERENCES

Abravanel, E., & Sigafoos, A.D. (1984). Exploring the presence of imitation during early infancy. *Child Development, 55,* 381-392.
Bjorklund, D.F. (1987). A note on neonatal imitation. *Developmental Review, 7,* 86-92.
Brown, T. (1988). Ships in the night: Piaget and American cognitive science. *Human Development, 31,* 60-64.
Butterworth, G. (1989). Knowledge and representation: The acquisition of knowledge in infancy. In: P. Van Geert (Ed.), *Annals of theoretical psychology, vol. VI: Developmental Psychology.* New York: Plenum Press.
Barclay, C.R., & Newell, K.M. (1980). Children's processing of information in motor skill acquisition. *Journal of Experimental Child Psychology 30,* 98-108.
Brazelton, T.B., & Young, G.C. (1974). An example of imitative behavior in a nine-week-old infant. *Journal of the American Academy of Child Psychiatry, 4,* 53-67.
Case, R. (1987). Neo-piagetian theory: Retrospect and prospect. *International Journal of Psychology, 22,* 773-791.
Cellérier, G. (1979a). Structures cognitives et schèmes d'action. I. *Archives de Psychologie, 47,* 87-106.
Cellérier, G. (1979a). Structures cognitives et schèmes d'action. II. *Archives de Psychologie, 47,* 107-122.
Cohen, L.B. (1988). An information-processing approach to infant cognitive development. In: L. Weiskrantz (Ed.), *Thought without language.* Oxford: Clarendon Press.
Diamond, A. (1988). Differences between adult and infant cognition: Is the crucial variable presence or absence of language ? In: L. Weiskrantz (Ed.), *Thought without language.* Oxford: Clarendon Press.
Eibl-Eibesfeldt, I. (1979). Human ethology. *The Behavioral and Brain Sciences, 1,* 9-10.
Field, T.M., Woodson, R., Greenberg, R., & Cohen, D. (1982). Discrimination and imitation of facial expressions by neonates. *Sciences, 218,* 179-182.
Field, T.M., Goldstein, S., Vega-Lahr, N., & Porter, K. (1986). Changes in imitation behavior during early infancy. *Infant Behavior and Development, 7,* 415-421.
Fontaine, R. (1984). Fixation manuelle de la nuque et organisation du geste d'atteinte chez le nouveau-né. *Comportements, 1,* 119-121.
Forssberg, H. (1985). Ontogeny of human locomotor control. I. Infant stepping, supported locomotion and transition to independent locomotion. *Experimental Brain Research, 57,* 480-493.
Fuster, J.M. (1985). The prefrontal cortex, mediator of cross-temporal contingencies. *Human Neurobiology, 4,* 169-179.
Hauert, C.A., (1986). The relationship between motor function and

cognition in the developmental perspective. *The Italian Journal of Neurological Sciences, Suppl.* 5, 101-107.

Hauert, C.-A., Zanone, P.G., & Mounoud, P. (1989). Development of motor control in the child: Theoretical and experimental approaches. In: O. Neuman & W. Prinz (Eds.), *Relations between perception and action: Current approaches*. Berlin: Springer.

Hatze, H. (1976). Biomechanical aspects of a successful motion optimization. In: P.V. Komi (Ed.), *Biomechanics V-B*. Baltimore: University Park Press.

Hayes, L.A., & Watson, J.S. (1981). Neonatal imitation: Fact or artifact ? *Developmental Psychology, 17,* 655-660.

Ikegami, K. (1984). Experimental analysis of stimulus factors in tongue protruding imitation in early infancy. *The Japanese Journal of Educational Psychology, 2,* 117-127.

Ikegami, K. (1987). Imitation and visual fixation of 1-month-old infants to protruding tongue face stimuli. Poster presented at the ISSBD Conference, Tokyo, July.

Jacobson, S.W. (1979). Matching behavior in the young infant. *Child Development, 50,* 425-430.

Jacobson, S.W., & Kagan, J. (1979). Interpreting "imitative" responses in early infancy. *Sciences, 205,* 215-217.

Kaitz, M., Meschulach-Sarfaty, O., Auerbach, J., & Eidelman, A. (1988). A reexamination of newborns' ability to imitate facial expressions. *Developmental Psychology, 24,* 3-7.

Kleiner, K.A., & Fagan III, J.F. (1984). Neonatal discrimination and imitation of facial expressions: A failure to replicate. *Infant Behavior and Development, 7,* 184.

Koenig, O. (1986). Approche neuropsychologique du développement cognitif: Effet Stroop et asymétrie hémisphérique fonctionnelle chez l'enfant de 7 à 15 ans. Unpublished doctoral dissertation of the University of Geneva.

Koenig, O., & Hauert, C.-A. (1986). Construction de l'objet chez l'enfant de 5 à 9 ans: Approche dichhaptique. *Cahiers de Psychologie Cognitive, 6(1),* 21-29.

Luria, A.R. (1966). *Higher cortical functions in man*. New York: Basic Books.

McKenzie, B., & Over, B. (1983). Young infants fail to imitate facial and manual gestures. *Infant Behavior and Development, 6,* 85-89.

Maratos, O. (1973). The origin and the development of imitation during the first six months of life. Unpublished doctoral dissertation of the University of Geneva.

Maratos, O. (1982). Trends in the development of imitation in early infancy. In: T.G. Bever (Ed.), *Regressions in mental development: Basic phenomena and theories*. Hillsdale, N.J.: Lawrence Erlbaum.

Meltzoff, A.N., & Moore, K.M. (1977). Imitation of facial and manual gestures by human neonates. *Science, 198,* 75-78.

Meltzoff, A.N., & Moore, K.M. (1983a). The origins of imitation in infancy: Paradigm, phenomena and theories. In: L.P. Lipsitt & C. Rovee-Collier (Eds.), *Advances in infancy research*. Norwood: Ablex.

Meltzoff, A.N., & Moore, K.M. (1983b). Newborn infants imitate adult facial gestures. *Child Development, 31,* 78-84.

Moll, L., & Kuypers, H.G.J.M. (1977). Premotor cortical ablations in monkeys: Contralateral changes in visually guided reaching behavior. *Science, 198,* 317-319.

Mounoud, P. (1981). Cognitive development: Construction of new
    structures or construction of internal organizations. In: I.E.
    Sigel, D. Brodzinsky & R.M. Golinkoff (Eds.), *New directions in
    Piagetian theory and practice*. Hillsdale, N.J.: Lawrence Erlbaum.
Mounoud, P. (1982). L'évolution des conduites de préhension comme
    illustration d'un modèle de développement. In: S. de Schonen
    (Ed.), *Les débuts du développement*. Paris: Les Presses
    Universitaires de France.
Mounoud, P. (1986). Similarities between developmental sequences at
    different age periods. In: I. Levin (Ed.), *Stage and structure*.
    Norwood: Ablex.
Mounoud, P., & Vinter, A. (1981). Representation and sensorimotor
    development. In: G. Butterworth (Ed.), *Infancy and epistemology*.
    Brighton: The Harvester Press.
Neisser, U. (1967). *Cognitive Psychology*. New York: Appleton-
    Century-Crofts.
Newell, K., & Walter, C.B. (1982). Kinematic and kinetic parameters
    as information feed-back in motor skill acquisition. *Journal of
    Human Movement Studies, 7(4)*, 235-254.
Oppenheim, R.W. (1981). Ontogenetic adaptations and retrogressive
    processes in the development of the nervous system and behavior.
    In: H.F.R. Prechtl & K. Connolly (Eds.), *Maturation and
    development*. London: SIMP.
Piaget, J. (1974a). *La prise de conscience*. Paris: Les Presses
    Universitaires de France. (Translation: Piaget, J. (1976). *The
    grasp of consciousness: Action and concept in the young child*.
    Cambridge, Ma: Harvard University Press.)
Piaget, J. (1974b). *Réussir et comprendre*. Paris: Les Presses
    Universitaires de France. (Translation: Piaget, J. (1978).
    Success and understanding. Cambridge, Ma: Harvard University
    Press.)
Posner, M.I. (1978). *Chronometric explorations of mind*. Hillsdale,
    NJ: Lawrence Erlbaum.
Prechtl, H.F.R. (1981). The study of neural development as a
    perspective of clinical problems. In: K.J. Connolly & H.F.R.
    Prechtl (Eds.), *Maturation and development*. Londres: SIMP.
Prechtl, H.F.R., & O'Brien, M.J. (1982). Behavioral states of the
    full-term newborn. The emergence of a concept. In: P. Stratton
    (Ed.), *Psychobiology of the human newborn*. New York: Wiley.
Preyer, W. (1887). *L'âme de l'enfant, observations sur le
    développement psychique des premières années*. Paris: Alcan.
Prinz, W. (1987). Ideo-motor action. In: H. Heuer & A.F. Sanders
    (Eds.), *Perspectives on perception and action*. Hillsdale, NJ:
    Lawrence Erlbaum.
Ramella, R.J. (1982). Acquisition of a simple motor skill by low
    and high academic achievers. *Perceptual and Motor Skills, 54*,
    377-378.
Salmoni, A.W., Schmidt, R.A., & Walter, C.B. (1984). Knowledge of
    results and motor learning: A review and critical appraisal.
    Psychological Bulletin, 95(3), 355-386.
Schmidt, R.A. (1975). A schema theory of discrete motor skill learnin
    Psychologial Review, 82, 225-260.
Schmidt, R.A. (1976). The schema as a solution of some persistent
    problems in motor learning theory. In: G.E. Stelmach (Ed), *Motor
    control: Issues and trends*. New-York: Academic Press.
Schmidt, R.A. (1982). *Motor control and learning*. Champaign: Human
    Kinetics.

Singer, R.N., Hagenbeck, F., & Gerson, R.F. (1981). Strategy enhancement of serial motor skill acquisition. *Bulletin of the Psychonomic Society, 18,* 148-150.

Stone, L.J., Smith, H.T., & Murphy, L.B. (1973). *The competent infant. Research and commentary.* New York: Basic Books.

Spelke, E.S. (1988). The origins of physical knowledge. In: L. Weiskrantz (Ed.), *Thought without language.* Oxford: Clarendon Press.

Spelke, E.S. (1979). Perceiving bimodally specified events in infancy. *Developmental Psychology, 15,* 626-636.

Sternberg, R.J. (1987). A day at developmental Downs: Sportscast for race #2 - Neo-piagetian theories of cognitive development. *International Journal of Psychology, 22,* 507-529.

Thelen, E. (1986). Development of coordinated movement: Implications for early human development. In: M.G. Wade & H.T.A. Whiting (Eds.), *Motor development in children: Aspects of coodination and control.* Dordrecht: Martinus Nijhoff Publishers.

Thelen, E., & Fisher, D.M. (1983). The organization of spontaneous leg movements in newborn infants. *Journal of Motor Behavior, 15(4),* 353-377.

Thelen, E., Skala, K.D., & Kelso, J.A.S. (1987). The dynamic nature of early coordination: Evidence from bilateral leg movements in young infants. *Developmental Psychology* (in press).

Valentine, C.W. (1930). The psychology of imitation with special reference to early childhood. *Journal of Psychology, 2,* 105-132.

Vergnaud, G. (1985). Concepts et schèmes dans une théorie opératoire de la représentation. *Psychologie Française, 30,* 245-251.

Vinter, A. (1985). *L'imitation chez le nouveau-né.* Paris et Neuchatel: Delachaux & Niestlé.

Vinter, A. (1986). The role of movement in eliciting early imitations. *Child Development, 57,* 66-71.

Welsh, M.C., & Pennington, B.F. (1988). Assessing frontal lobe functioning in children: Views from developmental psychology. *Developmental Neuropsychology, 4(3),* 199-230.

Wieringen, van, P.C.W. (1988). Discussion: Self-organization or representation ? Let's have both ! In: A.M. Colley and J.R. Beech (Eds.), *Cognition and action in skilled behaviour.* Amsterdam: Elsevier Science Publishers B.V.

Winther, K.T., & Thomas, J.R. (1981). Developmental differences in children's labeling of movement. *Journal of Motor Behavior, 13,* 77-90.

Zanone, P-G., & Hauert, C-A. (1987). For a cognitive conception of motor processes: A provocative standpoint. *Cahiers de Psychologie Cognitive/European Bulletin of Cognitive Psychology, 7(2),* 109-129.

Zazzo, R. (1957). Le problème de l'imitation précoce chez le nouveau-né. *Enfance, 10,* 135-142.

Zelazo, P.R., Zelazo, N.A., & Kolb, S. (1972). Walking in the newborn. *Science, 176(4032),* 314-315.

INDEXES

SUBJECT INDEX
(english terms)

AUTHORS INDEX